HURRICANES OVER MALTA

JUNE 1940 – APRIL 1942

BRIAN CULL
AND FREDERICK GALEA

GRUB STREET · LONDON

Published by
Grub Street
The Basement
10 Chivalry Road
London SW11 1HT

British Library Cataloguing in Publication Data
Cull, Brian
  Hurricanes over Malta, June 1940 – April 1942 – Rev. ed.
  1. Hurricane (Fighter planes) 2. World War, 1939-1945 – Campaigns – Malta
  3. World War, 1939-1945 – Aerial operations, British
  I. Title II. Galea, Frederick III. Malta
  940.5′421585

ISBN 1 902304 91 8

Typeset by Pearl Graphics, Hemel Hempstead

Printed and bound in Great Britain by
Biddles Ltd, Guildford and King's Lynn

BRIAN CULL is the author of the following Grub Street titles:

AIR WAR FOR YUGOSLAVIA, GREECE and CRETE 1940-41 with
  Christopher Shores and Nicola Malizia
MALTA: THE HURRICANE YEARS 1940-41 with Christopher Shores and
  Nicola Malizia
MALTA: THE SPITFIRE YEAR 1942 with Christopher Shores and Nicola Malizia
BLOODY SHAMBLES Volume 1 with Christopher Shores and Yasuho Izawa
BLOODY SHAMBLES Volume 2 with Christopher Shores and Yasuho Izawa
SPITFIRES OVER ISRAEL with Shlomo Aloni and David Nicolle
TWELVE DAYS IN MAY with Bruce Lander and Heinrich Weiss
WINGS OVER SUEZ with David Nicolle and Shlomo Aloni
249 AT WAR
THE DESERT HAWKS with Leo Nomis
HURRICANES OVER TOBRUK with Don Minterne
SPITFIRES OVER SICILY with Nicola Malizia and Frederick Galea
WITH THE YANKS IN KOREA Volume 1 with Dennis Newton

CONTENTS

ACKNOWLEDGEMENTS

In 1987, Grub Street published *Malta: The Hurricane Years 1940-1941* compiled by Christopher Shores and myself, with contributions from Nicola Malizia. Since that publication, much 'new' information has come to light, including diaries of a number of Hurricane pilots. It was therefore decided that a revised and updated account of the gallant Hurricane pilots who helped defend Malta during those dark years was warranted – hence *Hurricanes over Malta* – the third volume in Grub Street's mini series. Sadly, many of those who contributed to *Malta: The Hurricane Years* are no longer with us, but a number of their original accounts are used within.

Jim Pickering, a former member of 418 Flight and 261 Squadron, is the main contributing Malta veteran to this volume. His many, mainly amusing, anecdotes enhance the early chapters, for which we thank him wholeheartedly. Jim has also kindly provided the Foreword and many of the photographs, the majority of which emanated from the late Harry Ayre, also a veteran of 418 Flight and 261 Squadron.

Our dear friend Lorraine Balmforth, widow of Grp Capt Tommy Balmforth DSO DFC, has been most generous and interested, and has provided copies of her late husband's logbook and photographs. For making a copy of Bob Matthews' diary available to us we thank Mrs Gill Newberry and her late husband Andrew who was in fact Bob's nephew. Similar gratitude is extended to Bob Needham, who kindly provided a copy of his uncle Ted Wood's diary. We also thank the Strickland Foundation for allowing us (or rather Frederick) to photocopy Oliver Ormrod's 500-plus page journal, a copy of which they hold in their archives. Extracts from the journal of James MacLachlan were used with the permission of Roland Symons; he and I are writing a biography of MacLachlan, based on his journals in the possession of his sister Mrs Elisabeth Scratton, whom we also thank.

Our good friend and fellow author Tony Rogers has been extremely helpful, as has his partner Sonja Stammwitz. Tony read and corrected the draft while Sonja translated a number of German documents for us. Andy Thomas, as usual, has been of great assistance, while Joe Caruana provided updated information on the Gladiators used at Malta. Richard Caruana kindly let us use quotes from his book *Victory in the Air* and spent time endeavouring to enhance a poor quality picture. Once again, Paul Sortehaug kindly opened his files and supplied details on several New Zealand pilots, including the late Reg Hyde, another of the 418 Flight/ 261 Squadron veterans. We acknowledge both the National War Museum Association and the Malta Aviation Museum Foundation for use of archive material and photographs. Thanks are due to Alex, Louie and Issy Meyers-Bickel for help with the computer; Chris Shores for photographs, Chris Thomas for his latest creation – the jacket illustration - and John Davies of Grub Street for his continuing support.

Last but certainly not least, my continuing thanks go to my wife Val whose practical assistance with research at the Public Record Office and in Malta has been invaluable; her patience, encouragement, tolerance and understanding have been priceless. Her reward? Another visit to Malta, where we have spent many happy hours in the company of Frederick and his charming wife Val during our frequent visits to the island. Long may they continue.

Brian Cull, Bury St Edmunds 2001

FOREWORD

Flt Lt James Pickering AFC 418 Flight/261 Squadron 1940-41

Probably more has been written about the siege of Malta in 1940-1942 than any campaign other than the Battle of Britain. Much that has been written had to rely more on imagination than written evidence, and very many of the protagonists of the air war died in action in Malta, or elsewhere later. History can be defined as a continuous methodical record of events. By itself, the record does not create the spirit of an earlier age. We misinterpret the past by trying to understand it through contemporary eyes. Myths are created and perpetuated by historians repeating each other. I think now, 60 years after the siege of Malta began, will be the last time it is possible to compile a definitive version of the air air in which the recollections of the few who still survive could be joined to the official record of events. In my opinion, Brian Cull's writings on Malta – which began many years ago – are based on facts, and Brian is best fitted to provide a version of events that will survive the test of time. He pays tribute to the young men of both sides who fought in Malta's skies, many of whom paid in full.

I was one of a small draft of RAFVR Sergeant Pilots who had earned RAF wings before the war through weekend and evening training. On mobilisation we had been sent on attachment to the Fleet Air Arm, but preferred to remain in the RAF. We remained together as a unit on several adventures during which two were killed in flying accidents. Eventually nine of us were posted to 418 Flight, formed to fly the first Hurricane reinforcement to Malta from the deck of HMS *Argus*. After almost a year as colleagues, we were also personal friends. We – the NCO pilots of 418 Flight – had (or were being trained for) responsible positions in our civilian occupations. We had no career ambitions in the RAF. We had enlisted in the Reserve to serve in a national emergency and this had arisen. At the beginning of the war the standing of Sergeant Pilots was very high. They were RAF tradesmen who had been selected as suitable material for pilots. The Flying Training Schools where the VRs were trained, also trained applicants for Short Service Commissions. They only had bicycles. We all had cars. Some of them failed the course. This was very rare for VRs – VRs had been selected. We therefore had no sense of inferiority to junior officers when we were mobilised. By the time we arrived in Malta we had made a number of moves so it was necessary for our documents to follow after us. In the normal course of events we would have been interviewed for commissions after completing our training, and this occurred when we were on HMS *Argus* off Toulon. We turned it down. The documents for Harry Ayre and myself did not catch up with us until we were in Cairo in the spring of 1942 – our promotion was meteoric: Flight Sergeant for one day, Warrant Officer for two weeks, Acting Pilot Officer for a few days, Pilot Officer for a few days, Flying Officer for a few days, and Flight Lieutenant for a few days. Then an Air Ministry order surfaced that promotion to Flight Lieutenant could not be made without six months service as Pilot Officer and Flying Officer, so back to Flying Officer! We discovered that our original recommendation for commissioning dated back to 1939, before we were mobilised. We lost seniority from the delay, but escaped being made instructors! My nine months in Malta was only a small part (about one per cent) of my aviation. Between my first solo (1937) and last flight (1998) was 61 years. I let my Pilots' Licence lapse last year (2000). Malta is therefore, as far as I am concerned, a part of a much wider experience. *Hurricanes over Malta* is a fine tribute to the many pilots lost in action over the island, but for me, as the last surviving RAFVR pilot of 418 Flight, it is special for the memory of Roy O'Donnell, Dennis Ashton, Bill Timms and Eric Kelsey – all lost in defence of the island. When memory fades they will still be there, a part of Malta's history.

Jim Pickering

PREAMBLE

THE FRIEND OF YESTERDAY, THE FOE OF TODAY

The place of Malta in the general strategy of Britain's interests determined whether it would be abandoned or defended. A dilemma arose in the 1930s from Mussolini's development of Italian colonies in North Africa and his annexation of Ethiopia. His claim that the Mediterranean Sea was *Mare Nostrum* ("Our sea"), just as the Romans had done many hundreds of years earlier, threatened Britain's access to Egypt and the Near East, the Suez Canal, India and the Far East. Whilst Britain and France were allies there was some security of passage, but even in the early 1930s there were doubts in Britain about the political stability of France. An air route from Britain to Portugal, and round to the south of French North Africa and on to Khartoum was designed, and construction commenced, although there were no aircraft in production with the necessary performance. The route was initially intended for the four-engined de Havilland Dragon and various flying boats using rivers and lakes.

Malta was also somewhat politically unstable in the mid 1930s. There was an influential minority who had Italian sympathies and another minority who wanted independence from Britain. After the declaration of war in September 1939, the first priority for reinforcement from Britain was the British forces in France, which ended in Dunkirk. The second priority was Norway, which was equally disastrous in its loss of men and equipment. By June 1940, when Italy joined Germany against Britain and France, its allies in the Great War, Gibraltar and Egypt also became priorities for reinforcement, while the Royal Navy was tasked to hold the Italian Fleet in the Mediterranean. Retention of Malta was initially seen to be more of a liability than an asset, but with the surrender of France, and a hostile Germany and Italy astride the direct air route from Britain to Egypt and the trans-African route still under construction, the air link between Britain and the East had been severed, so Malta had become the only possible place to refuel aircraft between Britain and Egypt. To secure Malta, it was necessary to build up its defences including fighter aircraft. But no fighter had sufficient range to fly from any British base to Malta. The decision to defend the island was a radical change of policy, requiring immediate actions. It was not a simple redeployment of existing resources.

In mid-April 1939, 24 crated Sea Gladiators were despatched from Britain on board the freighter *Nailsea Court*, on charter to the Sea Transport Department, arriving at Malta on 30 April. Six of the fighters (N5512-5517) were then transferred to Alexandria for deployment in the Middle East, whilst the other 18 (N5518-5535) were to be assembled at Malta for use by 802 Squadron on board HMS *Glorious*; at this time the aircraft carrier was based at Alexandria as part of the Mediterranean Fleet. The 18 Sea Gladiators were immediately assembled at Hal Far. On 14 May, *Glorious* brought three Sea Gladiators (N5512, 5513 and 5517) from Alexandria and these were also assembled at Hal Far. 802 Squadron participated in an anti-invasion exercise on 19 May, during which N5534 crashed into the sea near Filfla. The remaining 20 Sea Gladiators were flown aboard *Glorious* on 6 June, but one of them (N5512) was transferred to HMS *Eagle* during August. *Glorious* set sail for the Indian Ocean on 9 October, to search for the German battleship *Graf Spee*, leaving her fighter complement behind at Alexandria, where N5528 crashed two days later. The 18 Sea Gladiators were disassembled, re-crated and taken to the French Naval base at Hyeres, where they flew training sorties during October and November 1939. Following the German blitzkrieg against Poland and the worsening situation in Northern Europe generally, the Sea Gladiators were again disassembled, re-crated and taken to Malta on board the freighter *Maritima*, arriving on 23 December; there, they were laid-up in storage at Kalafrana.

Glorious arrived at Malta on 17 January 1940 for a refit. In late February, while the carrier was still under overhaul, eight of the Sea Gladiators (N5518, 5521, 5525-5527, 5530, 5532 and 5533) were again assembled and were air-tested at Hal Far by pilots of 802 Squadron. Her refit completed, *Glorious* sailed for Alexandria on 30 March, minus her fighters, but was almost immediately recalled for service in the North Sea. On reaching the vicinity of Malta on 11 April, the eight Sea Gladiators of 802 Squadron were flown from Hal Far to the carrier, leaving the remaining ten in storage at Kalafrana.

With war clouds looming menacingly on the Mediterranean horizon, measures were now taken to provide Hal Far with a Fighter Flight by utilising a number of the Sea Gladiators currently stored in crates at Kalafrana. Permission was forthcoming and four machines were assembled (N5519, 5520, 5524 and 5531) to form the Hal Far Fighter Flight on 19 April, together with a number of volunteer pilots under the command of Sqn Ldr A.C. 'Jock' Martin, who was the CO of RAF Luqa. Martin, who walked with a limp as a result of a bad aircraft crash some years earlier, "was getting on in years for fighter work but he insisted on flying as much as anyone else."[1] The other pilots were Flt Lt Peter Keeble and Flg Off William Woods – the latter an Irishman inevitably known as 'Timber' – from the Hal Far Station Flight, Flg Off John Waters[2] and Flg Off Peter Hartley, both of whom had been flying Swordfish floatplanes from Kalafrana with 3 AACU. They were soon joined by Flt Lt George Burges – a former flying boat pilot who had been based at Kalafrana but who was now ADC to the AOC, Air Vice-Marshal F.H.M. Maynard AFC – and Flg Off Peter Alexander, a Canadian in the RAF who had been operating radio-controlled Queen Bee target drones.

At the beginning of May 1940, three of the stored fighters (N5513, 5517 and 5535) were taken to Egypt in their crates for employment on board *Eagle*. There now remained three Sea Gladiators (N5522, 5523 and 5529) in storage at Kalafrana. Meanwhile, the Fighter Flight at Hal Far inevitably suffered the occasional accident during its training period including a wayward landing involving Sqn Ldr Jock Martin, who hit a large wooden packing case on the side of the runway, flipping the Gladiator (N5524) onto its side; Martin was unhurt. The assembled fighters were subsequently fitted with armour plate behind the pilot's seat and with variable pitch, three-bladed propellers. At the same time the arrester hook and its fitting were removed, since it was not required, and to compensate for the increase in the aircraft's overall weight by the fitting of the armour plating. Thus, it can be seen that the Fighter Flight was no last minute panic organisation, but had been in existence and equipped for nearly two months prior to the outbreak of hostilities.

Across the Sicilian Channel, some 60 miles to the north, was ranged the might of the Regia Aeronautica's 2^Squadra Aerea with almost 140 SM79bis tri-motor bombers based at Comiso, Catania, Gela, Sciacca and Castelvetrano, plus over 40 CR42 biplane fighters and 26 of the newly introduced MC200 monoplane fighters dispersed at Trapani, Palermo and Catania. In addition, there were about 50 Z501 and Z506B seaplanes for maritime reconnaissance and air-sea rescue duties based at Augusta, Syracuse, Melenas and Marsala. With such a large force available, the Italians felt more than confident that an aerial assault against Malta would pose little threat. They were abundantly aware of Malta's unprepardness and lack of fighter defence. As recently as the evening of 9 June, the regular Sicily to Malta air service *Ala Littoria* seaplane had taken off from Marsaxlokk Bay, overflying Hal Far and undoubtedly noting the availability of British aircraft on the RNAS airfield. Other frequent Italian visitors had also been using the civil aerodrome at Takali and the flying boat and seaplane bases at St Paul's Bay.

CHAPTER I

HURRICANES ARRIVE –
BUT FIRST THE GLADIATORS . . .

June-July 1940

Shortly before 0700 on the morning of 11 June 1940, the operator of Malta's lone mobile radar unit – 242 AMES sited in isolation on Dingli Cliffs – picked up blips of unidentified aircraft approaching the island from the north. Meanwhile at Hal Far, three Gladiators (N5519, N5520 and N5531) of the Fighter Flight stood by in anticipation of the expected arrival from Sicily of bombers of the Regia Aeronautica. Nearby, relaxing in deckchairs but ready to spring into action, were Sqn Ldr Martin, Flt Lt Burges and Flg Off Woods. Within minutes of the blips being observed on the radar screen, a horn blared from Hal Far's control tower signalling the three pilots to scramble. Engines roared into life simultaneously, and within minutes the Gladiators were racing down the runway. As the pilots gunned their engines in order to gain altitude, bombs were already falling on Valetta and on Hal Far itself.

There was no shortage of targets. The first wave of bombers comprised 30 SM79bis of 34°Stormo BT from Catania, their crews briefed to bomb Hal Far. These were followed 15 minutes later by 15 more SM79bis from 11°Stormo BT from Comiso, with orders to bomb the Dockyard. A few minutes later ten more from 41°Stormo BT took off from Gela to attack Kalafrana seaplane base – making a total of 55 bombers escorted by 18 MC200s from 6°Gruppo CT. Flt Lt Burges (N5531), who had the faster of the three Gladiators, saw nine bombers turning in a wide circle south of the island in prepartion for their return to Sicily. Cutting across the circle, he and Sqn Ldr Martin gave chase. Burges fired most of his ammunition at one bomber, an aircraft of 52°Gruppo BT piloted by Cap Rosario Di Blasi, hitting it in the fuselage but without obvious result. Returning crews reported that the Gladiators fired from long range. So ended Malta's first air raid[1]. As soon as he landed, Burges was sent for by the AOC, who was keen to learn the outcome of the combat; Burges reported:

> "As soon as I opened up, the Italians poured on the coal and the Gladiator just couldn't catch up with them. I think our only chance is to scramble and climb as fast as we can and hope that we are four or five thousand feet above them when they arrive over the island. It's no good trying to overhaul them. We shall just have to get into the air quicker and climb faster – somehow."[2]

The AOC agreed that more speed was required and promised he would have a word with the Command Engineer Officer. Meanwhile, small-scale incursions by the Italian bombers continued throughout the day. These were mainly unchallenged, although Flg Off Waters (N5520) intercepted a lone reconnaissance SM79bis of the 11°Stormo BT shortly before midday, which he believed he had shot down. In fact it was merely driven away, making for Sicily without being able to complete its mission. Waters was airborne four times during the day. The eighth and final raid came in at 1925 that evening, the Gladiators being scrambled to intercept. Flg Off Woods (N5519) was again involved, and on this occasion dog fought a MC200, which he similarly believed he had shot down but, in fact, the Macchi had not even been seriously damaged. Evasive action, and the black exhaust smoke from a hastily-opened throttle, had apparently misled him into thinking he had inflicted damage to the Macchi's engine. However, the mere fact that RAF fighters could be seen opposing the Italian raiders proved to be a wonderful morale-boosting experience for an understandably fearful Maltese civil population. Although they could not strike back, nor escape the bombing, they could certainly cheer the sight of the three Gladiators challenging the might of Mussolini's Regia Aeronautica. Flt Lt Burges later commented:

"There is no doubt that the Gladiators did not wreak death and destruction to many of the enemy, but equally they had a very profound effect on the morale of everybody on the island, and most likely stopped the Italians just using the island as a practice bombing range whenever they felt like it."

With the day's fighting over, pilots and staff had time to reflect. Sqn Ldr A.E. Louks, the Command Engineer Officer, was called to see the AOC to discuss the Gladiators' lack of performance, and later wrote:

"The Gladiator story began with their inability to intercept the Italian bombers, which came and went unescorted, so I suggested to the AOC that I should modify them to improve matters. We had a variety of crashed Blenheims – from being a staging post to the Middle East – and he gave me a free hand. The Blenheims had two-pitch propellers and I calculated a revised pitch angle setting would suffice to 12,000-14,000 feet for climb, and using a blend of 87 and 100 octane (the latter in very short supply) raised the boost by 2-lb/inch. I later tested the first one – N5529 – to 10,000 feet in under five minutes. I also took a template to the dockyard for an armour plating shield behind the pilot, which they made from their lightest gauge material."

Such modifications would take time and the Fighter Flight pilots were initially instructed to use emergency boost in order to catch the bombers, but in order to produce the extra speed it was still necessary to make adjustments to the engines and controls. All were aware that running the engines at maximum boost for long periods would eventually ruin them, but the need was urgent and immediate.

The bombing on this first day had not caused a great deal of damage to military property, although six soldiers of the Royal Malta Artillery were killed at Fort St Elmo, and six Maltese naval personnel were killed when two launches were sunk at Xghajra. Many civilian buildings around the Dockyard were hit and 11 civilians were killed and 130 injured, the first fatalities – Mrs Nina Farrugia and her two young sons, Joe aged four and Ninu aged five – occurring at Pieta at 0650. But the most severe raid of this first day was the last one, at sunset, when the localities of Gzira, Zabbar and Cospicua suffered heavily. The bombing prompted the civilian population living near the Dockyard to seek safety elsewhere:

"The road leading from Cospicua to Zabbar Gate presented a pitiful sight. Women with bundles on their heads or with bundles hanging from their arms, carrying babies, with one or two children holding to their skirts, with a boy or a girl pushing a pram loaded with the most essential belongings, crowded the road, walking without destination in view, but leaving their beloved homes, abandoning the city, going anywhere as far away as possible from the target area. Buses, touring cars, cabs and other horse-drawn vehicles carrying the more fortunate families who either owned a vehicle or could afford to hire one, moved in this crowd of walking and less fortunate humanity also proceeding in the direction of Zabbar."[3]

People fled to outlying areas of the small island, to Dingli, Siggiewi, Lija, Birkirkara, Attard, Balzan, Zebbug, in fact anywhere away from the bombing. It was estimated that about 100,000 people left their homes in the first few days. The authorities did what they could, but until some form of discipline was imposed there was chaos everywhere. Churches were opened to house the refugees, as were schools, clubs and other suitable buildings.

Following the onslaught of the first day of hostilities, cloudy weather on 12 June brought a respite. Next day individual bomber and reconnaissance SM79bis returned, the former causing only minimal damage. One SM79 of 60^Squadriglia was engaged by two Gladiators, but escaped. This would appear to have been the aircraft attacked by Flg Off Waters in N5520, who again believed that he had shot down his quarry. Flt Lt Burges

(N5520) twice attacked SM79bis during the day, albeit without success. Of these early operations, Burges recalled:

> "As we were six pilots, three of us took the first and third watches, and the other three did the second watch and the fourth. The day was split into four watches; dawn to 0800, 0800 to noon, noon to 1600, 1600 to 2000. After the first day we realised that, if instead of sitting in a deckchair until the bell went, we sat in the aircraft, all strapped up and ready to go, it meant a gain of 2,000 feet; that is what we did the following day. Besides being very hot, it got extremely uncomfortable sitting for long periods in the cockpit, and we started to get piles! The Station Medical Officer was against this practice and recommended that we had two days on duty and a day off."

At about midday on 13 June, onlookers were excited to see three Hurricanes, accompanied by a Hudson, touch down at Luqa. These were the first modern fighters to be seen at Malta. Reinforcements at last, but the euphoria was short lived, however, when it was learned that the Hurricanes, which had flown in from El Aouina via Medjiz-el-Bab on the Tunisian coast, were only staging through Malta and were destined for Egypt. Despite Malta's urgent need for modern fighters, Egypt's plight was deemed to be even greater. After lunch and a brief rest, the three pilots – Sqn Ldr C. Ryley, Flt Lt T.M. Lockyer and Plt Off D.T. Saville took off for the last leg of their journey to Mersa Matruh on the Egyptian coast, a distance of about 100 miles.

The Hurricanes were part of a group of six which – notwithstanding the dire need for modern fighters to defend the United Kingdom following the disastrous losses in France – had been authorised by the Air Ministry as reinforcement for the RAF in Egypt, where the only fighters available were Gladiators and Gauntlets. The Hurricanes were drawn from stocks held at 10 Maintenance Unit based at RAF Hullavington. An appropriate number of ferry pilots were assembled, including a relief pilot who was to travel aboard one of two Hudsons of 233 Squadron assigned to accompany the Hurricanes on their epic journey to the Middle East. The other four Hurricane pilots were Sqn Ldr C.W.M. Ling, Flg Off F.F. Taylor, and Plt Off H.A.R. Prowse. Plt Off T. Balmforth, as the reserve, alternated with Sqn Ldr Ling in flying one of the Hurricanes during the long journey, his logbook showing that he flew P2641 on 8, 10 and 12 June. The two Hudsons and six Hurricanes had set out for their destination on the morning of 8 June, calling at Tangmere to refuel before heading for Rennes in southern France, then Toulouse and Marseilles/Marignane for a final refuelling stop before crossing the Mediterranean and making for El Aouina/Tunis airfield. While landing at Marignane, Plt Off Prowse's aircraft (P2644) ran into a filled-in bomb crater and its port oleo snapped off, causing the Hurricane to swing to starboard before tipping onto its nose. Pilot and aircraft had to be left behind.

The five remaining Hurricanes and two Hudsons finally reached El Aouina airfield on 10 June, but more problems were encountered. Sqn Ldr Ryley signalled the Air Ministry with the news that due to defective auxiliary fuel pumps two Hurricanes were unable to fly non-stop from Tunis to Mersa Matruh, as intended. He requested permission from both the Air Ministry and Malta AHQ to take the two aircraft to Malta, where he assumed the problems could be rectified, but the request was refused by Malta AHQ:

> "In view [of] today's raids on Hal Far and the absence of Merlin or Hurricane spares at Malta, also your specific instructions regarding alternative route in the event of hostilities with Italy, I have refused permission [to] land Malta and have advised every effort to obtain local repairs in Tunisia."

In the light of this, the Air Ministry signalled Sqn Ldr Ryley accordingly:

> "If confident that auxiliary fuel pumps of the three serviceable Hurricanes are functioning satisfactorily, these Hurricanes with one escorting Hudson should proceed on first

following wind. If in doubt, all Hurricanes should wait arrival of fitter from Hawkers who is leaving UK by air today, with twelve new auxiliary pumps, which will provide for all eventualities. The second escorting Hudson and remaining two Hurricanes are to proceed as soon as serviceable on first following wind. The fitter from Hawkers on return journey will land Marignane and make serviceable the auxiliary pump on the Hurricane which is now awaiting repair at this place."

Events were now moving fast as signals were transmitted to and from the Air Ministry. On 12 June, Governor Sir William Dobbie informed the War Office:

"Raids here yesterday [11 June] show importance of fighter aircraft. The four Gladiators here, though successful in bringing one plane down, are too slow. There are five Hurricanes in Tunis en route to Egypt. AOC has asked Air Ministry to let them be directed here. Wish strongly to support this request. Believe a few effective fighters would have far reaching deterrent effect and produce very encouraging results."

It seems that War Office agreement was forthcoming, for RAF Middle East signalled AHQ Malta:

". . . I agree to proposal that five Hurricanes now at Tunis en route to Egypt be allotted Malta for the time being. Presume you will arrange with Admiralty for movement of stores understood to be now at Gibraltar."

However, the confusion continued when the first three Hurricanes to arrive at Malta on 13 June did not remain on the island but continued on to Egypt as originally intended, where they were handed over to 80 Squadron at Amiriya.

In the meantime, the Italians continued to carry out daily small-scale bombing and reconniassance sorties over Malta, while the Gladiators attempted interceptions whenever possible, the Fighter Flight having taken delivery of two more Gladiators, N5522 and 5529. However, the first loss sustained by the Italians was due to the weather. At dawn on 14 June, five SM79bis from 214^Squadriglia which had set out to bomb the Dockyard and Grand Harbour ran into bad weather. One of two returning to base prematurely crashed near Catania while attempting to land and blew up with the loss of the crew. The Gladiators were up again next day (15 June) when ten SM79bis of 11°Stormo with nine escorting MC200s appeared, but were unable to intercept until the bombing was over. One of the bombers was claimed possibly damaged by Flg Off Hartley who recalled, ". . . several times I shot pieces off enemy bombers . . ." One SM79bis did in fact return to base showing signs of battle damage although its crew attributed this to AA fire, adding that the Gladiator assault was ineffective. Next day however, an SM79bis from 41°Stormo BT was damaged by fighter attack, possibly another of Hartley's victims. On returning from one such interception sortie, Sqn Ldr Martin was heard to exclaim: "Lord, what a party, I damn nearly bought it this time. The boost's gone, can't get near them. A bloody big Macchi came up and wiped my tail for me . . ."[4]

Landing from another sortie on 17 June with a slightly damaged aircraft (N5519), Flg Off Waters related that as he came in astern of a formation of five SM79s above Grand Harbour, one of the bombers detached itself from the rest of the formation and started to straggle some way behind the others. Taking advantage of the situation, Waters attacked. The straggler lost height and then flew beneath the other four bombers. Waters stuck to its tail and followed him down, whereupon the bombers above opened fire with their downward-firing, movable guns. The Gladiator was fortunate to escape with only superficial damage.

The island enjoyed a brief respite as the Italian bombers turned their attention to targets in the French protectorate of Tunisia. The reprieve did not last for long, however, and on the night of 20/21 June, the Italians carried out their first nocturnal raid against Malta, when six SM79bis of 34°Stormo BT and one from the Reparto Volo (Flying Detachment) of 3°Divisione took off singly and at intervals. A total of 42 100kg bombs were dropped on the island during a four-hour period; among the casualties was the floating dock – a 40,000-ton structure – which was sunk in Grand Harbour. Although these attacks were little more than nuisance raids and generally did negligible damage, the events of 21 June were of more immediate concern. During the morning Sqn Ldr Martin crashed one of the precious Gladiators (N5522) while taking off, but survived unhurt, and in the afternoon, as Flg Offs Hartley and Alexander took off from Hal Far, Hartley's aircraft (N5524) struck a packing case and lost a wheel, causing the Gladiator to overturn on landing. Hartley, though shaken was only slightly injured. Both of the aircraft involved in these accidents were deemed non-repairable. The Command Engineering Officer, Sqn Ldr Louks, assessed the damage and considered one good aircraft could be constructed out of the two wrecks; to quote Louks, ". . . so it was out with the hacksaws (metaphorically speaking) and a hybrid was born out of two corpses." Flt Lt Burges commented:

> "An enormous amount of improvisation had to go into keeping aircraft operational and a 'new' fuselage would have 'second-hand' wings or engine. As the 'rudder number' [serial number] was on the fuselage this would seem to be yet another new aircraft."

The growing frustration of the Gladiator pilots was alleviated somewhat by the arrival, at last, of reinforcements in the form of the two Hurricanes from El Aouina. P2645 piloted by Flg Off Eric Taylor and P2614 flown by Plt Off Tommy Balmforth landed at Luqa with the second Hudson during a lull between air raids, presumably following remedial work on their faulty fuel pumps. Once at Malta, Taylor and Balmforth learned they were to remain with the two Hurricanes on attachment to the Fighter Flight, while Sqn Ldr Ling, who had arrived aboard the Hudson, soon departed by Sunderland for a training post at RAF Habbaniya in Iraq.

Shortly after lunch on 22 June, two more Hurricanes arrived at Luqa following the long flight from Bizerta. After the aircraft had landed and taxied to a halt, Plt Off R.W.H. Carter emerged from P2544 and Plt Off C.R. Glen from P2651. Both were pilots attached to 4 Ferry Pilots Pool based at Kemble, and were mightily relieved to have reached friendly territory after a long and tortuous journey across southern France and along the North African coast. At 1700 there arrived from the same group two more Hurricanes flown by Plt Off W.P. Collins (P2623) and Plt Off A.G. McAdam (P2641). Another pair arrived with the onset of darkness. Without radio they were unable to announce their arrival and feared being fired upon by the defences. Plt Off W.R.C. Sugden, who was flying P2629, recalled:

> "As per instructions we circled a rock – Filfla – just off the coast and then, very, very thankfully, we landed at Luqa after four days of the most exciting, or frightening, flying I had ever had. As an anti-climax, the aerodrome at Luqa was obstructed with old motor buses, cable drums, and the like, and after I landed I hit my wing on a bus. I was too tired to worry much, but it infuriated me, nevertheless."

His companion, Plt Off R.H. Barber in P2653, landed safely despite having lost his tailwheel earlier. Out of a dozen Hurricanes and a similar number of Blenheims that left England on 18 June, only six Hurricanes and two Blenheims had reached Malta (see Appendix III). Plt Off Sugden added:

> "We were told by the AOC that we would have to give up all hope of going on to our destination as he wanted the Hurricanes and us in Malta. I was a bomber pilot not a fighter pilot. All spare pilots had been drafted into an aircraft ferry pool in England – I was awaiting an instructors course – when I volunteered to fly a Hurricane to the Middle East. I had ferried a new Hurricane to France in about March or April and, as soon as I had got there, I had to fly fighter patrols but had no experience of fighting."

The first confirmed success also came the way of the Fighter Flight on this date, when, during the afternoon, a lone SM79bis from 216^Squadriglia flown by Ten Francesco Solimena approached the island on reconnaissance. Two Gladiators were scrambled, as recalled by Flt Lt Burges (N5519):

> "Timber Woods and I were on the 1600 to dusk watch when the alarm went off. We took off and climbed as hard as we could go, as was the custom. We did not attempt to maintain close formation because if one aircraft could climb faster than the other then the additional height gained might be an advantage. Ground Control, as usual, gave us the position and course of the enemy. The enemy turned out to be a single SM79, presumably on a photographic sortie. It came right down the centre of the island from Gozo, and on this occasion we were 2,000-3,000 feet above it. Timber went in first but did not see any results. I managed to get right behind it and shot off the port engine. I was told this happened right over Sliema and Valetta and caused quite a stir in the population. The aircraft caught fire and crashed in the sea off Kalafrana."

The pilot and the observer (Sottoten Alfredo Balsamo) of the Savoia (MM22068) were rescued from the sea off St Thomas Bay to become prisoners, but the other crew members were lost. Some distance away, the crew of a patrolling Z506B floatplane intercepted a distress call from the stricken bomber, and subsequently but inaccurately reported that it had been shot down by the AA defences.

Flt Lt Burges was to achieve a success of similar importance next day (23 June) when he and Flg Off Woods again scrambled after an incoming raid. This time the raiders were from 11°Stormo accompanied by an escort of MC200s. The two Gladiators engaged the bombers without obvious result. Burges (N5519) was then attacked by a Macchi flown by Serg Magg Lamberto Molinelli of 71^Squadriglia. Burges whirled his Gladiator round and a "real old World War I dogfight" began over the sea off Sliema. The faster Macchi had the advantage but overshot the nimble Gladiator, allowing Burges to "belt him up the backside as he went past". After four of five such passes the Macchi suddenly caught fire and Molinelli baled out into the sea. Swiftly recovered from the water, the Italian pilot was taken to M'tarfa Hospital where Burges later visited him, reporting that he did not find his victim very friendly! Twenty-four-year-old Molinelli later told his interrogators:

> "I am under the impression that I was hit by more than one fighter. When I was first hit one of my controls must have gone. I tried to control the aircraft but could not succeed. I jumped out when, at the second attack, the engine was wrecked and oil burst all over me. Flames started to pour out and I took to the parachute. It is my first parachute jump. Our parachutes have two gadgets, one is a delayed opening gadget and the other is a hand arrangement which opens the parachute immediately. At the moment of jumping down I was at about 400 metres. The parachute opened at once through my using both gadgets."

While landing from this action, Flg Off Woods had collided with a Queen Bee target drone, causing damage to yet another Gladiator (N5531). The Hurricanes had indeed arrived in the nick of time.

There were now eight Hurricanes at Malta, of which two (P2629 and P2653) were damaged and temporarily unavailable while one other (P2623) had a hole in its petrol tank, although all three were repairable locally. Since Malta now had more Hurricanes than Egypt, instructions were issued for three to fly on to Alexandria after they had been serviced. Thus, on 24 June, P2544 (Plt Off Carter), P2651 (Plt Off Glen) and P2641 (Plt Off Collins) accompanied by three transit Blenheims departed for Mersa Matruh. The remaining three pilots, Plt Off Barber – known as Jock although born in South Africa – Plt Offs Allan McAdam and Sugden also found themselves attached to the Fighter Flight, together with their Hurricanes. Neither Barber nor Sugden had any fighter training, while McAdam had not distinguished himself during his brief service with a fighter squadron[5].

By 26 June France had capitulated, allowing the bombers of 2^Squadra to be unleashed again upon Malta, 25 SM79bis raiding Hal Far and Valetta during the morning. There were five alerts during the day and the last raid involved five SM79bis, the Fighter Flight making an interception but made no claims. The bombers jettisoned their bombs over the Marsa area, one incendiary hitting a crowded bus at Marsa crossroad. People rushed to help but the bus was rapidly engulfed in flames. All told, 21 passengers were killed outright in the tragedy, and seven others succumbed to their burns and injuries. In addition, two Marsa residents were killed nearby. Further raids followed, and next day (27 June) two SM79s of 11°Stormo BT were intercepted by Flg Off Woods, who inflicted damage on an aircraft of 33°Gruppo BT flown by Ten Remo Maccagni. The pilot and two other members of the crew were wounded, while 1°Av/Mot Angelo Alvisi, apparently affected by fumes from a punctured fuel tank, baled out into the sea and was lost. Woods was credited with the destruction of the bomber which, in fact, managed to return to base. Plt Off Barber flew his first operational sortie from Hal Far on the last day of the month, in Hurricane P2614, but failed to make an interception.

At this time the Italians suffered a small but serious setback to their activities when, following two fatal crashes, the MC200 fighters were grounded throughout the Regia Aeronautica; for a while, therefore, the bombers were forced to operate without escort.

July 1940

July saw the entry of the Hurricanes into the defence of Malta, while in Sicily there arrived replacement fighters to escort the bombers. From 4°Stormo CT came three squadriglie of CR42s of 9°Gruppo as escort for the SM79bis on 2 July. No British fighters were scrambled, but two of the 34°Stormo BT bombers were slightly damaged by anti-aircraft fire. First blood was drawn for both of the new fighter types next day (3 July), when, at 1010, two SM79bis approached the island on reconnaissance, covered by nine CR42s led by the Gruppo commander, a Spanish Civil War veteran with an artificial leg, the legendary Magg Ernesto Botto. One of the Hurricanes scrambled to intercept was flown by Flg Off Waters (P2614), who attacked the pair of 259^Squadriglia bombers. The fire from the Hurricane's eight guns proved devastating and Ten Mario Sguario's aircraft crashed into the sea five miles from Kalafrana, breaking up as it fell, the crew being seen to bale out. As Waters returned to land, he was set upon by the CR42s. His aircraft was badly shot up and he crashed on landing and although he was not hurt, the Hurricane had to be written off. Credit for shooting him down went to Magg Botto, who believed his victim to have been a Spitfire. Although a search was mounted for the downed Italian airmen, none was found. Plt Off Tommy Balmforth had also scrambled, in P2623, for his first operational flight, but failed to contact the enemy during this or a second sortie flown shortly afterwards.

Following this encounter, the Italians attempted to surprise the RAF fighters on the ground on 4 July. Early in the morning, two dozen CR42s took off from Comiso and headed for Malta. As they neared the island they divided into three sections: six fighters swept in to strafe Hal Far, nine provided close cover at 1,000 feet, while the rest remained overhead as high cover. The Italian pilots returned having claimed seven fighters and one bomber destroyed on the ground. Actual losses were two Swordfish of 830 Squadron damaged, both of which were repairable. Plt Off Dick Sugden, having had time to access the situation, wrote:

"With the limited means at Malta's disposal, I think it was a pretty well organised defence. One of the main weapons was radar, giving us early warning approach of enemy aircraft. Sometimes it didn't give you quite enough time, though, with the Italians only 60 miles away. By the time they had appeared on the radar and we got our aircraft into the air, they were waiting above, and by the time you got up to their height they were there watching and could time their attacks accordingly."

Raids by the Regia Aeronautica were now becoming much more frequent. During the afternoon of 6 July, 30 SM79bis attacked Valetta, Hal Far and Takali, gunners at the Dockyard claiming one shot down, which was reported to have fallen in flames north-east of Kirkop. Two Hurricanes which had been scrambled failed to make contact. Shortly before dusk Flg Off Woods (P2653) and Plt Off Sugden (P2645) were scrambled just after a plot in the vicinity of Filfla, and spotted a floatplane about 100 feet above the sea between the islet and the mainland, as Sugden recalled: "We intercepted it near Filfla very low down. It was getting misty. We both made one quick firing pass and saw no result at all." As Sugden broke away the floatplane waggled its wings. Both pilots drew back, fearing they had misidentified their quarry – the previous day a French Latécoère 298B floatplane had arrived at Malta, having defected from Vichy-controlled Tunisia – but it was probably a similarly-configurated, but larger Italian Z506B floatplane on a clandestine operation. A number of enemy aircraft came over during the hours of darkness. The guns opened fire and observers excitedly reported an aircraft down in flames over Benghaisa at 2117, followed by two more near Mosta a few minutes later, but all proved to be red flares apparently fired by the bombers.

Flg Off Woods had better success shortly after 0900 the next day (7 July), when he and others were scrambled to intercept two formations each of five SM79bis escorted by nine CR42s. On this occasion the Dockyard was targeted. Nine civilians and two Royal Navy personnel were killed, and six were wounded. Woods (P2653) succeeded in shooting down one SM79bis from 233^Squadriglia, flown by Ten Pellegrino Zagnoli. Again there were no survivors. Plt Off Balmforth undertook two interception sorties during the day, flying P2645 on both occasions, but had no luck. Ground observers thought they saw a Hurricane in trouble as it was seen to dive rapidly and then disappear from sight, but it was obviously simply flattening out after an attack on one of the bombers.

On 9 July Malta had one alert, during the morning, and two Hurricanes flown by Flt Lt Burges (P2645) and Plt Off Jock Barber (P2653) were scrambled to intercept. The latter recalled:

> "This was my first combat. George Burges and I took off in two Hurricanes at about 10 o'clock in the morning [official sources suggest the Hurricanes scrambled at precisely 0802]. Beautiful, clear day and very hot. We were going up to intercept an SM79 and escorting CR42s. Banjo (our Controller) vectored us beautifully onto the enemy, George leading, and the plan was for George to take out the bomber, which I think was on a reconnaissance mission, whilst I had to try and keep the CR42s off him. We approached the Italians from the perfect quarter-attack position, the fighters flying in formation just behind the SM79. George went for the bomber and I attacked the leading CR42 from dead astern at a range of about 100 yards and closing very rapidly. He did what appeared to be a flick-roll and went spinning down, and the next minute I found myself engaged in dogfighting with the remaining CR42s. This went down to about 10,000 feet; by then I had used up all my ammunition without much success, although I'm convinced I got quite a few strikes on the leader in the initial contact. I realised pretty quickly that dogfighting with biplanes was just not on. They were so manoeuvrable that it was very difficult to get in a shot, and I had to keep diving and turning to keep myself from being shot down. George had by this time disappeared – but it turned out that he had in fact shot down the SM79 – so I stuck my nose down and, with full throttle, was very thankful to get out of the way."

Although Burges believed his victim had crashed into the sea, the badly damaged SM79bis of 192^Squadriglia was in fact able to reach Sicily where the second pilot carried out an emergency landing at Comiso. The aircraft's commander and first pilot, Cap Valerio Scarabellotto, had been killed at the controls and the gunner fatally wounded. On landing, Burges' aircraft was found to have suffered minor damage, but that evening Rome Radio reported that one of the two intercepting 'Spitfires' had been shot down in flames.

Malta again came under heavy attack next day (10 July), when at least four formations totalling some 20 SM79bis appeared over the island at 0750, bombs falling on Zabbar, Tarxien, the Dockyard and submarine base at Manoel Island. On this occasion casualties were somewhat lighter, being listed as two military personnel slightly injured, one civilian killed, and three injured. For the Italians it was to prove a costly raid. The main formation of 15 SM79bis were drawn from 87° and 90° Gruppi BT from Sciacca. They were almost an hour behind schedule and subsequently their fighter escort, which had been circling the rendezvous point waiting for them to appear, was forced to return to base low on fuel, leaving the bombers to proceed to Malta unescorted. Three Hurricanes of the Fighter Flight had scrambled from Hal Far at 0749 and were waiting over the target area. Flg Off Eric Taylor (P2645) attacked and shot down Sottoten Felice Filipi's 195^Squadriglia aircraft (195-6), which fell in flames over Grand Harbour, crashing onto a beach post near Fort Leonardo. The occupants of the fort dashed out of the post before the aircraft exploded but three soldiers of 1/Dorsets suffered burns, two of whom later died. Meanwhile, Flg Off Woods (P2653) attacked a second SM79bis flown by Sottoten Luigi Illica Magnani of 192^Squadriglia, which he claimed probably destroyed. This was later upgraded to confirmed when it was established that it had also crashed into the sea in flames. A third SM79bis, an aircraft of 194^Squadriglia, was badly damaged by Flg Off Peter Hartley (P2623). It carried out a forced-landing at Comiso with one gunner mortally wounded. Ten more of the bombers suffered shrapnel damage from the AA barrage, and several crewmen were wounded. Gunners aboard the hard-hit bombers reported shooting down four Hurricanes but losses were in fact nil. The action was witnessed by many on the ground, one of whom wrote:

> ". . . at 8 o'clock in the morning . . . the air raid alarm was given . . . Everyone had ample time to get into shelters . . . but soon the word went around all over the island from the less discreet people that some very spectacular fights were taking place high up in the sky. This was followed shortly after by the excited shouts, 'Qed in-nizzluhom' (we are shooting them down); and then, long before the 'Raiders Passed' signal was given, people ignoring the police and Special Constables, rushed to the terraces, to the streets, and other vantage points . . . All over the country there were cheers and excited cries, as the people saw the enemy meet their just fate at the hands of our gallant pilots, and our English [sic] and Maltese anti-aircraft gunners. In one fishing village there was a demonstration, boys and girls carrying trophies from the destroyed plane . . ."[6]

Hurricanes were again scrambled on 12 July. In one raid, Ten Gino Battagion of newly arrived 70^Squadriglia claimed to have shot down what he tentatively identified as a Spitfire, while two pilots of 72^Squadriglia, M.llo Magli and Serg Abramo Lanzarini, jointly claimed another. The Hurricane pilots involved have not been identified, but no losses whatsoever were inflicted upon the Fighter Flight. The CR42s returned next day, 11 fighters from 74^ and 75^Squadriglie led by TenCol Tito Falconi of 23°Gruppo CT claiming two more Hurricanes shot down while on a reconnaissance mission over the island. One victory was claimed by Cap Guido Bobba of 74^Squadriglia, and the other jointly by Cap Ottorino Fargnoli and Cap Antonio Chiodi, assisted by Serg Magg Celso Zemella and Serg Magg Renzo Bocconi of 75^Squadriglia. Their opponents were in fact a single Hurricane (P2653) flown by Plt Off Dick Sugden and a Gladiator (N5524) with Flt Lt Burges at the controls, the former providing an account of the action:

> "There were two of us standing by – George Burges in the Gladiator and myself in the Hurricane. It was one of those cloudless Mediterranean days, the horizon shimmering with heat and the edge of the cockpit burning hot if one's elbow touched it. We were about half way through our readiness period – midday till 4pm – and had been sitting cramped in our straps for two hours, reading and dozing. An instant and everything springs to life. The ground crews leap towards the starter batteries as the blare of the horn comes from the

control tower. I hear the R/T crackle into 'Scramble – Scramble – Scramble!' A touch of the button and the engine roars into life. Within ten seconds, George and I are tearing down the runway – pressure on the stick and I'm airborne, snapping up the undercart and trying to tighten up my helmet and straps as we start a steep climbing turn. It hardly seems possible that in so short a time my brain has been roused from a gentle doze into a thing of concentration – concentrating on listening for the Controller's orders and concentrating on trying to look at the whole of the sky at once. The engine is beating away perfectly, the aircraft is fine. The Controller's voice comes through with terrific volume – 'Hello Visor, Banjo calling. Bandits 15-plus, ten miles north of Zambuk [codename for St Paul's Bay], Angels 15.' That means there are more than 15 enemy aircraft coming in from the north at 15,000 feet. If only I could climb quicker. It's a nasty feeling knowing they are above you, probably watching you stagger up to meet them. George's Gladiator had gone now, it climbs much more steeply than the Hurricane.

At last I'm at 15,000 feet and I obey the Controller and circle round Grand Harbour. I should be able to see them now, they are very close to me. Where the hell are they? Hello, there's the flak – now, where are they – there! A mile away I see two biplanes, diving slightly, going towards St Paul's Bay, in line astern. The rear one's a CR42 – is that George he's chasing? I just remember to scream out 'Tally-ho!' over the radio as I start to overhaul the little brute chasing George. Guns on 'Fire', reflector sight on, coming in fast from dead astern. Just before I fire I see they are both CR42s, no Gladiator there. The whole aircraft shakes as the eight guns rattle. I see the nose drop and hurriedly correct, but the Fiats turn steeply, right and left, then dive. I shove the nose down, the engine cuts and picks up again and I am just going to fire again when – what is this? Red sparks shooting past me, over each wing, coming from the sea. I hear a hiss and a crack and do a steep turn to the left. Oh, my God! There are about six little CR42s dancing up and down behind me. They follow me easily on the turn, much more manoeuvrable than the Hurricane. There's only one thing to do and I half-roll onto my back and go down vertically, leaving them standing. I curse myself bitterly for being such a fool as to (a) miss the bloke I was shooting at and (b) to be trapped so beautifully by his pals.

At 4,000 feet I pull out, smack over Tigne, where the other chaps are probably bathing (they were, as it happens). Engine going OK, everything seems all right. I start to climb again. Obviously they are up there watching me and I cannot see them, but what else can I do? I climb in a south-westerly direction, towards the sun and suddenly catch a glimpse of three of them circling about 5,000 feet above. I climb steadily, watching them hard and trying to watch my tail as well. As I do a climbing turn away from the sun, they gently start to dive towards me and then I see tracer going past again – there are their blasted friends again! This time I really dive, the controls almost solid but the engine has been hit; coolant starts to stream past, the cockpit fills with fumes and the windscreen smears with glycol. The engine merely splutters when I pull out of my dive at about 1,000 feet. Thank Heaven! There's no one shooting at me now as I call up Banjo and tell them I may have to bale out. The air speed indicator is not working but I have tons of speed to make the aerodrome.

I stagger on at about the same height and, with a terrific feeling of relief, I see the aerodrome getting closer and closer – at last I see I can make it. I turn straight in, downwind along the long runway, down undercart and flaps, and come sailing in to make one of the best landings I've ever made, with the airspeed indicator still jammed at 280mph. The brakes are working and I leap thankfully out. The ground crews come running out of their shelter (the raid is still on) and I can remember shouting a warning to them that the engine might go up in smoke. It didn't, however, but continued to make a noise like a steam engine. It felt good to be on solid ground again, after seeing all the holes in my machine."

Sugden was immediately called to the telephone in the control tower. The AOC was on the other end and the conversation went something like, "Sugden, I told you before – I have told all the fighter boys – don't get mixed up with the fighters!" Within a week Sugden was posted. He made only three more sorties with the Fighter Flight – all on Gladiators – and then joined what remained of 3AACU to fly Swordfish.

No further activity was noted for the Fighter Flight until the morning of 16 July, when a dozen CR42s from 23°Gruppo CT again appeared over Malta on a reconnaissance. Flt Lt Keeble in Hurricane P2623 and Flt Lt Burges in a Gladiator had been scrambled at 0910, and dived on this formation. Keeble attacked one CR42 – probably the aircraft flown by Sottoten Mario Benedetti of 74^Squadriglia – but then came under attack himself by two more flown by Ten Mario Pinna and Ten Oscar Abello. After a long chase Keeble was hit and his aircraft dived into the ground at Wied il-Ghajn and blew up[7]. It was immediately followed by Benedetti's CR42 (MM4368), which crashed within 100 yards of the Hurricane. Keeble was killed outright, and Benedetti died soon afterwards. Burges made no claim on this occasion, and it can only be assumed that Benedetti's aircraft had been hit by Keeble before he was shot down, although a machine-gun manned by men of 1/Dorsets also submitted a claim. The Italians claimed a second Hurricane – by Serg Magg Bocconi – but this was not allowed. Many people on the ground witnessed the action including Plt Off Jock Barber:

> "I actually witnessed this from the ground. He [Keeble] tried dogfighting in a Hurricane with some CR42s. His engine was obviously hit and smoking pretty badly, but it was quite amazing because the CR42 was on his tail and followed him right down and crashed very close to where he did. One thought was that the CR42 had been shot down by ground fire, but I don't know that he wasn't concentrating so much on shooting Peter down that he went straight in. It was quite a fantastic spectacle, including the dogfighting I had witnessed earlier – the Hurricane trying to turn with the CR42 – and this reinforced my previous view of the folly of trying to dogfight with these biplanes."

Another who witnessed Flt Lt Keeble's fate was Wg Cdr Carter Jonas, the new CO at RAF Luqa:

> "The sounds of firing and diving aircraft had almost ceased when Peter Keeble was killed, his Hurricane rocketting down out of a patch of blue sky, flattening out for a moment as if to attempt some sort of landing, and then diving into the ground to the right of the wireless masts at Rinella . . . a day or two later we buried him in a quiet little cemetery up at Bighi, with the wind sighing in the fir trees overhead."

Incredibly, 24-year-old Benedetti was still alive when rescuers reached him but died shortly thereafter. His body was taken to the civilian hospital at Vincenzo Bugeja where officers from the Intelligence Office examined his clothing in an attempt to establish his identity. Their subsequent report revealed:

> "The airman was unconscious when brought to the hospital and he succumbed to his injuries shortly after admission. According to the brass badge on the right arm of the wind jacket worn by the deceased, he held the rank of Sottotenente. The deceased's clothing consisted of: White shorts; blue knitted sweater with zip-fastener neck; canvas flying suit; life jacket (cork-filled). In the pocket of the shorts were: cigarette packet with one cigarette; box of matches; small comb in case; handkerchief with initials MQ or MB or vice-versa. There was no maker's name on any of the clothing worn by the deceased. On the life jacket there was merely the figure 1."

Sottoten Benedetti, son of the Commissioner of Police at Genoa, and a graduate of the Air Academy at Caserta, was accorded a military funeral. Within days his identity had been established following a telephone enquiry by RAF Intelligence to their counterparts in Sicily. At this stage, the war was being conducted in a gentlemanly and civilised manner.

As a result of Keeble's loss, a meeting was called to discuss the best ways of countering the agile CR42s, as Jock Barber recalled:

"It was shortly after this we had a big meeting of all the pilots and senior staff officers when tactics were discussed on how to cope with the CR42s. I remember someone suggesting that the Hurricane should put down a bit of flap as this might enable it to turn with the CR42. This was of course absolute nonsense – there just wasn't any answer but to climb above these chaps to get the upper hand."

Sporadic raids continued until the end of the month and AA gunners continued to greet each attack. Hardly any Hurricanes were now serviceable and the main air defence was left to the guns and the Gladiators, Flg Off Waters and Plt Off Balmforth being scrambled in two Gladiators on 17 July but to no avail. Plt Offs Barber and Sugden experienced a similar lack of success against 13 CR42s two days later. The guns seriously damaged one SM79bis on 21 July, the bomber being forced to ditch about 20 miles off Cape Passero as it desperately tried to reach its base. Two Gladiators flown by Barber and Balmforth were up again on 24 July to intercept ten CR42s but there were no casualties on either side. Gladiators took to the air on each of the last five days of the month, albeit without any tangible success; Flt Lt Burges recording three sorties, as did Barber and Balmforth while Flg Off Waters participated in two scrambles. On the last day of the month all three available Gladiators were scrambled when, at 0945, a single reconnaissance SM79bis approached the island with an escort of nine CR42s from 75^Squadriglia. As Flg Off Hartley (N5519) led Flg Off Woods (N5520) and Flg Off Taylor (N5529) in an attack on the enemy formation, the SM79 turned away, but a dogfight at once began between the opposing fighters. After much manoeuvring, Woods succeeded in shooting down the leader of the CR42s, Cap Antonio Chiodi's aircraft falling into the sea five miles east of Grand Harbour, but Serg Manlio Tarantino also managed to attack Hartley's aircraft. Hit in the fuel tank, the Gladiator burst into flames. Hartley baled out, suffering severe burns, and his aircraft crashed near the coast not far from Marsaxlokk. He was soon plucked from the sea by a motor launch from Kalafrana. Plt Off Barber was a witness:

"Peter's Gladiator must have been hit in its centre tank because his aircraft burnt just like a magnesium flare, an absolutely brilliant light in the sky – and it was a clear blue sky, with no clouds. He baled out into the sea, very badly burnt about the knees, arms and face. We flew in khaki shirts, shorts and stockings, and it was the exposed portion of his body which got damaged."

Flg Off Hartley, suffering multiple third degree burns, was rushed to M'tarfa Military Hospital. Wg Cdr Carter Jonas remembered:

"For many months afterwards, Peter lay in M'tarfa Hospital, suffering from severe burns, and I used to visit him at least once a week. For the first few weeks the doctors considered it to be extremely doubtful whether Peter would recover at all, after the long immersion in salt water following the shock of the burns. And I remember my first few visits to the hospital, with Peter lying rigid and motionless, speechless with pain; only his half-closed eyes moved, restless and frightened, beseeching relief. Youth, and a strong constitution, however, combined with devoted nursing, eventually won through, and many weeks later a somewhat scarred Peter was flown back to England by flyingboat, to complete his convalescence in a more suitable climate."

While the pilots of the Fighter Flight were understandably distressed about the plight of Hartley, the gloom was somewhat lifted when it was announced that Flt Lt Burges had been awarded an immediate DFC – the island's first decoration. At the close of the month the defences were considered to have accounted for at least a dozen Italian raiders, but without spares for the Hurricanes, and with the Gladiators kept airworthy only by cannibalisation, the strength of the Fighter Flight had diminished to one serviceable Hurricane and two Gladiators, with only half a dozen relatively combat-inexperienced pilots available. Reinforcements were desperately needed. Malta's plea for help did not go unheeded, for she had a champion in high position. Despite Britain's own precariousness, with imminent invasion a distinct possibility, Prime Minister Churchill had taken a personal interest in Malta's plight. On 12 July he wrote to the First Lord and First Sea Lord:

> "I thought that *Illustrious* [the new 23,000-ton armour-decked aircraft carrier] might well go to the Mediterranean and exchange with *Ark Royal*. In this case *Illustrious* could take perhaps a good lot of Hurricanes to Malta. As we have a number of Hurricanes surplus at the moment, could not the Malta Gladiator pilots fly the Hurricanes themselves? This would not diminish our flying strength in this country."[8]

Three days later he followed this up with another reminder for urgent action:

> "It becomes of high and immediate importance to build up a very strong anti-aircraft defence at Malta, and to base several squadrons of our best fighter aircraft there. This will have to be done under the fire of the enemy . . . I understand that a small consignment of AA guns and Hurricanes is now being procured, and that the main equipment is to follow later . . . The urgent first consignment should reach Malta at the earliest moment . . ."[9]

Help was immediately to hand.

CHAPTER II

MORE HURRICANES ARRIVE:
261 SQUADRON IS FORMED

August – October 1940

As soon as Italy became embroiled in the war it had become abundantly clear to the British authorities that if Malta was to be held, additional reinforcements organised on a more formal basis than a handful of Hurricanes flown across France, would be necessary. With the fall of France the direct route was, in any event, closed. Two possibilities remained: either to deliver crated aircraft direct to Egypt aboard ship via the Suez Canal, or to West Africa by ship or aircraft carrier, before flying them across Central Africa along the long and arduous Saharan route to Egypt – or alternatively to fly them off a carrier from maximum range, about 350-400 miles west of Malta so as to avoid Italian naval and air forces located along the Libyan coast and at Sardinia, Pantelleria and Sicily. The latter course was undoubtedly quicker, and offered a much better chance of the aircraft reaching their destination. The orders to send a squadron of Hurricanes by aircraft carrier came direct from Prime Minister Churchill.

Although this would seem to have been a natural mission for the Fleet Air Arm, they had no combat-experienced pilots trained to fly modern fighters. Consequently, during mid-July, nine Sergeant Pilots currently with Fighter Command were ordered to report in great secrecy to RAF Uxbridge where they were labelled 418 Flight. The nine had enjoyed a roughly similar past service history: they had been seconded to the Fleet Air Arm and had experience of flying from the deck of an aircraft carrier. They were flown to RAF Hullavington from where they collected their Hurricanes, which they then ferried to Abbotsinch near Glasgow. There, they learned that they were to fly their Hurricanes from the deck of the small training carrier HMS *Argus* to an unknown destination, in company with five RAF officers who were also posted to 418 Flight (see Appendix IV). The pilots selected to fly the Hurricanes[1] were Flt Lts D.W. Balden, R.N. Lambert, A.J. Trumble and J. Greenhalgh, Sgts D.K. Ashton, O.R. Bowerman, R.J. Hyde, E.N. Kelsey, R. O'Donnell, J. Pickering, F.N. Robertson and W.J. Timms.

Argus sailed from Greenock on 23 July with fourteen pilots (including two spares), twelve Hurricanes and two FAA Skuas stowed between the decks. The two spare Hurricane pilots (Flg Off H.F.R. Bradbury and Sgt H.W. Ayre) were to be conveyed in the Skuas. *Argus* arrived at Gibraltar a few days later following an uneventful journey from Scotland. While the Hurricanes were being re-assembled and ranged on deck, a quantity of spares for the Hurricanes were loaded into one of the two Sunderland flyingboats which were to accompany the flight in the rôle of flying 'lifeboats', in the event of any of the Hurricane pilots being obliged to ditch en route; the second Sunderland carried 23 airmen who were to service the Hurricanes on Malta. It had originally been proposed that two Blenheims should be carried aboard *Argus* to act as navigational aircraft following the fly-off, but this was considered impracticable, and the Skuas has been included for this duty instead. On 31 July, *Argus* finally entered the Mediterranean, escorted by the Royal Navy's Force H including the carrier *Ark Royal*, the battleships *Hood*, *Valiant* and *Resolution*, two cruisers and ten destroyers. At this stage the pilots were briefed by the Captain of *Argus* that they were to fly off to Malta, but were incredulous of the proposed launch point, which they immediately realised was well beyond the Hurricane's flying range. Flt Lt Duncan Balden, in charge of 418 Flight, was adamant:

"This meant we would have to fly 400 nautical miles, when 330 nautical miles with a 20 per cent safety margin was considered to be the Hurricane's accepted endurance. I was not satisfied and spoke to Commander (Flying), who agreed to carry out tests. We finally compromised at 360 nautical miles."

Deadlock ensued until radio silence was broken to contact London, whereupon the pilots' assessment was confirmed. By evening the Italians had discovered the fleet, but a subsequent bombing attack from Sardinia caused no damage. Skuas of 803 Squadron from *Ark Royal* succeeded in shooting down one of the SM79bis, carrying the Generale commanding the Italian bomber force based in Sardinia. There were no survivors. The fleet was now greatly at risk, and *Argus*' Captain decided that the Hurricanes were to depart as quickly as possible at dawn next morning, 2 August.

Each flight of six Hurricanes was to be led by a Skua. In the event, both Skuas were also flown by Hurricane pilots when it was realised that neither of the FAA pilots originally allocated had sufficient experience on Skuas to take off from the carrier, so Flg Off Bradbury agreed to pilot one (L2969) and Sgt Harry Ayre the other (L2611), with Sub Lt W.R. Nowell and Capt K.L. Ford RM as navigators. With 14 aircraft ranged on deck, the area for take-off looked very small to the waiting pilots, as Sgt Jim Pickering recalled:

"The leading Skua therefore had the shortest take-off run. The ramp on the *Argus* bumped it into the air at too low an airspeed for comfort, and at an obviously too steep an angle of attack. It sank slowly below the level of the *Argus*' bows and out of my sight. I was next off and scores of permutations of circumstances cascaded through my mind. We had no plan of action if the lead Skua pranged on take-off. If a Hurricane had trouble on take-off, the pilot would bale out and hope to be picked up by one of the escort ships. Survival from ditched monoplanes was less likely. If this happened en route to Malta, the lead Skua would send a morse signal of the position to the Sunderland. However, the lead Skua did not hit the sea. Harry Ayre carried out a balancing act that kept it just above the water whilst it built up enough flying speed to climb, and Bats waved me off before either he or I could see the Skua, but all was well. The Hurricane [N2715] leapt from the deck even without full throttle. We formed up into vic formation of seven aircraft in one wide circuit of the *Argus* and headed eastward into the sun on a fine, clear day, with the north coast of Africa just discernible in the distance on our starboard beam. The second flight then had space to open out and start their engines and set course later without problem."

With their greater power/weight ratio the Hurricanes got off without any trouble, and the historic flight was soon under way, avoiding a direct overflight of Pantelleria. Malta was reached two hours and 20 minutes and some 380 miles later. Thus, as the Hurricanes came in to land at Luqa, Operation 'Hurry' had been almost a complete success – almost, until Sgt Jock Robertson in N2700 crashed on landing. According to Robertson's logbook entry, this was due to a faulty petrol gauge, but it was only part of the reason, as Plt Off Jock Barber recalled:

"Sgt Robertson and two other Sergeant Pilots arrived in a vic formation over Luqa – they came in very, very low and carried out a fast beat up of the airfield, followed by a roll by Robertson off the top while his No2 and No3 did upwards charlies. Robertson made a typical carrier-type, split-arse approach – very low and very steep turn and, as he made the final turn to line-up with the runway, his motor cut. Very audible to us on the ground. The aircraft flicked over to the right onto its back and ploughed into the ground upside down. I think it went through at least three stone walls. We were shattered to say the least – this was our first reinforcement of pilots and aircraft and we had really been looking forward to this. We wrote him off but, fantastic as it may seem, he only sustained minor concussion and was flying again within a few days."

Obviously the offending gauge had led Robertson to believe that he had more fuel left than was in fact the case. Wg Cdr Carter Jonas, OC Luqa, dashed to the scene, helped Robertson into his car and drove him to the Station medical centre. Flg Off Bradbury's Skua also crashed when he stalled on landing, but while his aircraft was badly damaged when it skidded into an air raid shelter near the control tower, no one was hurt. Flt Lt Trumble, who had flown N2673, noted:

> "On arrival we were met by the Station Commander, Wg Cdr R.C. Jonas, and the AOC Malta, Air Commodore Maynard. After the welcome came the bombshell that we were to stay on as Malta was short of fighter pilots."[2]

The 418 Flight pilots had been under the impression that their carrier experience was being utilised only to ferry the Hurricanes to the island, and had expected to be flown to Gibraltar by Sunderland immediately afterwards. Indeed, Trumble had made an appointment to meet his wife in England a few hours after his expected return from Malta. As it turned out, he would not see her for five years[3]. Others were equally as shocked and dismayed. Sgt Pickering remembered:

> "Uproar broke out. We were only on attachment to 418 Flight we said. Our squadrons in the UK were expecting us back. We had no tropical kit. There was a Sunderland at Kalafrana Bay waiting to fly us back to Gib. The AOC sat patiently until protests started to subside. He seized the initiative. 'If you will kindly be quiet,' he said, 'I will be able to telephone Kalafrana to tell it [the Sunderland] to leave without you'. And he did just that."

It was to be a few days before the Hurricanes were fully ready for operations, the remainder of the spares and other equipment for them being delivered a couple of days later by the submarines *Pandora* and *Proteus*. However, as Flt Lt Greenhalgh recalled:

> "The serviceable Hurricanes were instantly placed at readiness and day by day, throughout daylight hours, we sat in our cockpits ready to scramble. There was no fuel for practice flights and there was no ammunition for practice firing. I would not claim that for any of us our first flight from the island resulted in combat, but I do aver that the first time I fired the guns of a Hurricane it was in combat. I recall also my first sight of tracer passing either side of me which, briefly I mused one early morning, was a strange thing for the exhaust sparks to be doing!"

The first three days of August had been fairly quiet for Malta's defenders. Only single reconnaissance aircraft ventured over the island but these still resulted in Fighter Flight's readiness section having to be scrambled. Plt Off Tommy Balmforth was airborne in Gladiator N5529 on 2 August, as was Flt Lt Burges later in the day, when he broke a wheel on landing, although he was able to fly the repaired aircraft next day, accompanied by Balmforth flying N5524. No contact was made with enemy patrols during these sorties. At 1530 on 4 August the air raid alarm was sounded when unidentified aircraft were plotted approaching from the north, but these turned out to be fighters flying at great height and again no contact was made. Obviously aware of the presence of the Hurricane reinforcements, the Italians launched a heavy raid next day (5 August), damaging Hurricanes P2614 and P3733 on the ground. Plt Off Balmforth, on this occasion flying one of the new Hurricanes (N2484), claimed an SM79 probably destroyed, while Flt Lt Burges (N2716) reported being attacked by eight CR42s. Next day (6 August) Sgt Harry Ayre, accompanied by Capt Ford, flew the Skua on a reconnaissance sortie to Catania, Augusta and Syracuse to observe activity in the harbours, the potentially hazardous flight taking two hours 20 minutes. Neither fighters nor flak were encountered, as noted by Ayre:

> "Did recce in Skua with Capt Ford RM over Sicily, looking for enemy convoy forming up. No sign of convoy but much shipping in Catania, Augusta and Syracuse harbours. Few naval ships. Flew right over one Italian cruiser. No AA fire. Was sorry we had no bombs."

On this date, Sgt Jim Pickering also experienced his first, albeit uneventful, flight from Malta. He recalled a typical airfield scene:

> "When we arrived at Malta, Luqa was covered with many dispersed derelict vehicles and other obstacles to discourage an attack by airborne troops. The runways were clear, but during the day they had some buses with drivers on them. When aircraft landed or took off, the buses were driven clear of the runway. At least this is what was intended to happen. Air raid alarms were sounded for more than one reason and not all scrambles of aircraft – particularly those for single reconnaissance aircraft – justified an air raid alarm for the whole island. Radar's information was not always accurate, so the timing of warnings before a raid could be erratic. The aircraft at readiness were at the end of the long runway, and the warning to scramble was transmitted by phone through the airfield control tower, which also had to signal to the buses to clear the runway.
>
> Whilst at Luqa we were at readiness strapped in our aircraft, flying helmet on, with the starter trolley plugged in. With the order to scramble, it was only necessary to prime the engine and press the starter button. The trolley was quickly pulled away with the wheel chocks, one turned on the oxygen and radio and when all engines were running we were ready to roll in unison. It was however boring and uncomfortable sitting strapped in an aircraft four hours at a time. It was cold at dawn and very hot at midday. It was necessary to have some overhead cover for which some of us chose umbrellas. These were cast away with the books we were reading when the scramble order was given. Not all the buses always moved with the same alacrity. They received their instructions by a combined visual and sound signal from the control tower. Flags or Very cartridges, bells or sirens."

It was also necessary to clear the runways not only for take-off but also for aircraft arriving, so when the alarm was given at the control tower, the reaction at the aircraft dispersal was to check the telephone to make sure it still worked:

> "The flight hut was a motor bus sited near the aircraft. It was necessary to start up each of the aircraft at first light to warm up the engines and check the magnetos and carry out the daily inspection. If it was necessary to air test an aircraft, the runway had to be cleared and the signal to the buses from the control tower was the same as for an air raid. If the radar failed to pick out a lone reconnaissance aircraft, the first warning was the anti-aircraft guns firing at it. It was not unknown for a bus driver to take cover without first moving his bus! Eventually this procedure of blocking the runway ceased and was never introduced into Takali when we moved there. A parachute or glider landing was a new military strategy to guard against, and Malta could have been as vulnerable as the Dutch fortress that had been captured in the Spring Blitzkrieg."

The remaining aircraft of Fighter Flight were incorporated into 418 Flight on 6 August, and an initial squadron composition was put together under Sqn Ldr Jock Martin on a three Flight basis:

A Flight	B Flight	C Flight
Flt Lt D.W. Balden	Flt Lt A.J. Trumble	Flt Lt J. Greenhalgh
Flt Lt G. Burges	Flt Lt R.N. Lambert	Flg Off F.F. Taylor
Flg Off R.H. Barber	Plt Off T. Balmforth	Plt Off A.G. McAdam
Sgt R.J. Hyde	Sgt J. Pickering	Sgt O.R. Bowerman
Sgt E.N. Kelsey	Sgt D.K. Ashton	Sgt H.W. Ayre
Sgt R. O'Donnell	Sgt F.N. Robertson	Sgt W.J. Timms

Flg Off H.F.R. Bradbury, Flg Off J.L. Waters and Flg Off W.J. Woods were held as reserves, while Flg Off P.B. Alexander was posted away to other duties. A rota system was introduced, allowing the pilots of each Flight to have one day off in four:

Readiness	0430-0830	0830-1230	1230-1630	1630-2030
6 August	A Flight	B Flight	A Flight	B Flight
7 August	B Flight	C Flight	B Flight	C Flight
8 August	C Flight	A Flight	C Flight	A Flight
9 August	A Flight	B Flight	A Flight	B Flight
10 August	B Flight	C Flight	B Flight	C Flight
11 August	C Flight	A Flight	C Flight	A Flight
12 August	A Flight	B Flight	A Flight	B Flight

In theory, this was for all-day manning of six aircraft, two of which were to be Gladiators. The rota was quickly amended to include one or two Hurricanes on stand-by against night attacks. In fact, the first recorded engagement following the arrival of the new Hurricanes did not occur until the night of 13 August. An impromptu night fighter section had been formed, with Flg Off Eric Taylor and Plt Off Jock Barber being initially selected for this duty. Between 2110 and 2301 a number of bombers came over singly and in pairs, and Barber was ordered off in N2715:

> "The Savoias were in the habit of coming over on moonlit nights – for some reason they didn't come over on dark nights – and would drop the odd bomb and generally create a nuisance. So it was decided we should do some night fighting in Hurricanes. Eric Taylor and myself were selected, and on 9 August I did one hour, 20 minutes night-flying with searchlight co-operation. The two of us took it in turns to be coned by the searchlights whilst the other did dummy attacks. In fact our guns were loaded and I remember each time the one was attacking the other, the one being attacked would call out over the radio, 'Make bloody sure you've got the tit on safe, for God's sake.'
>
> On this particular evening I was scrambled and was told a single SM79 was on its way. Unfortunately, my Hurricane was overheating – it was a very hot night – and I was obliged to climb in coarse pitch to keep my glycol temperature within limits. The SM was beautifully coned in the searchlights and had a clear bombing run with no ack-ack as I was in the air, of course. Eventually it passed to the south of the island out of the searchlights before I could reach his height. I managed to keep my eyes glued to him until I eventually reached his height. I pulled up underneath him and just kept on firing into his belly until I stalled and fell out of the sky, and I then lost sight of him. I was most disappointed because I'd hoped for a flamer. I flew around to the south of the island, losing height and hoping to find him, but no joy. I could only claim him as damaged."

His fire had indeed done its job better than he had realised; the SM79, an aircraft of 259^Squadriglia, was badly hit and failed to make it home, coming down in the sea five miles from the Sicilian coast. Two members of the crew were drowned; the other three swam ashore near Marina di Ragusa. This was the first aircraft shot down during the war by a night fighter outside Western Europe.

Two days later, during the early afternoon of 15 August, ten SM79s of 60°Gruppo BT in two equal formations approached Hal Far, escorted by 18 CR42s of 17°Gruppo CT with one from 23°Gruppo CT. At 1340 four Hurricanes of A Flight led by Flt Lt Balden attempted to intercept, but were engaged by the escort. Ten Sartirana of 72^Squadriglia succeeded in shooting down into the sea Sgt Roy O'Donnell's aircraft (N2716); he was not seen to bale out. Meanwhile, Flt Lt Balden (N2672), with Sgt Eric Kelsey as his No2, chased one straggling CR42 which they spotted north of the island. Balden fired one long burst whereupon the biplane looped and was lost from sight; it was claimed as damaged. On the ground at Hal Far bombs destroyed a FAA Swordfish and damaged a second, while two personnel were wounded by splinters.

Next day (16 August), 418 Flight and Fighter Flight officially amalgamated to become 261 Squadron, and a complete reorganisation of the previous three-Flight arrangement took place. Sqn Ldr Martin[4] now stood down and was posted to AHQ, Flt Lt Balden being promoted to take command of the new unit which was now reorganised into two Flights:

A Flight Flt Lt J. Greenhalgh, Flt Lt G. Burges, Flg Off H.F.R. Bradbury, Flg Off W.J. Woods, Plt Off A.G. McAdam, Plt Off T. Balmforth, Sgt J. Pickering, Sgt R.J. Hyde, Sgt D.K. Ashton.

B Flight Flt Lt A.J. Trumble, Flt Lt R.N. Lambert, Flg Off J.L. Waters, Flg Off F.F. Taylor, Flg Off R.H. Barber, Sgt F.R. Robertson, Sgt E.N. Kelsey, Sgt O.R. Bowerman, Sgt H.W. Ayre.

Thus, in time-honoured RAF peacetime tradition, command of 261 Squadron and of both Flights went to the senior officers in preference to both longer-serving Malta personnel and the combat-experienced NCO pilots. This would have been acceptable if the more experienced pilots were allowed to lead in the air, as would occur throughout the RAF later in the war. At this stage however, not only did the AOC insist on established procedure, but it was natural for officers to take such responsibilities for granted. Sgt Jim Pickering later wrote:

> "Both as Reservists and NCOs, we respected service traditions of officer leadership, but in the air it proved to be less than ideal when the Squadron was formed, though to say so is not a criticism of the officers concerned. They themselves were pawns in a hierarchy and had not been trained for their posts."

In the event the system did not work well, and in due course pressure for changes in command were to come, initially from the original Fighter Flight pilots. Sgt Pickering continues:

> "There were a number of rapid changes of CO and flight commanders. Appointments were made in order of seniority and when each proved unsatisfactory in the air, he was removed to a ground appointment. One had so much difficulty starting Hurricane engines that shortly after we arrived in Malta it was thought advisable to be sure of his services at HQ Malta than be unsure of him getting airborne. The pressure for these changes could only come from the officers. The changes were made without recriminations. The removal of each pilot meant additional watches for each remaining pilot, because there was not then the acceptance that if a pilot most senior in rank was not the most experienced pilot, he could fly as a squadron pilot. Both officer and NCO pilots used the same crew room when on watch. This practice started in RAF fighter squadrons and was by no means general on all RAF units then, even in England. Nevertheless, most aspects of service protocol were retained. Even after the more senior officers had been discarded, leadership in the air was still by the senior officer airborne.
>
> We – the NCOs – were accommodated at Luqa in the Sergeants' Mess. Catering was provided by a Maltese café owner. The Mess was well run and the food reasonable. In addition to the Station staff and the NCOs of 261 Squadron and 431 Reconnaissance Flight, there was a small flow of Wellington crews en route from England to Egypt. There was a large single-storey barrack block of single rooms and communal ablutions near to the Sergeants' Mess, and a deep air raid shelter cut down into solid rock within 50 yards."

Out of tragic and frightening times would emerge the odd humorous incident to help calm nerves; Pickering continues:

> "One of the Station NCOs was under the shower one day, and did not hear the air raid alarm. The first warning to him was a string of bombs exploding ever nearer. He first took cover under his bed. When a bomb exploded far too close for further comfort, he grabbed his tin hat and ran through the dust and smoke to the air raid shelter and straight down the steps. The shelter was occupied mainly by some of the Maltese female civilian staff. It was only then he realised that his only cover was his tin hat. Some of the women feigned the shock required of their strict religious upbringing. Others made no attempt to hide their

mirth. The air raid seemed less important. It took some time, whilst waiting for the all clear, to negotiate surrender of a few surplus articles of clothing to provide minimal cover for his return to his room."

The remainder of the month was not unduly hectic for the pilots of the new Squadron, even though the Hurricanes were invariably scrambled at least twice a day, Plt Off Balmforth alone completing four interception sorties in two days. Early on 20 August, shortly after 0900, six SM79s from the newly arrived 105°Gruppo BT escorted by 16 CR42s from 23°Gruppo CT, raided the airfields, four Hurricanes being despatched to intercept. The formation was broken up and Sgt Jock Robertson, on his first Malta sortie in N2715, was credited with a CR42 damaged. In return, the Italian fighter pilots claimed a Hurricane probably shot down. In fact, there were no losses on either side. However, on the ground at Hal Far two FAA Swordfish were slightly damaged, while three Blenheims in transit to Egypt were also hit, one being burnt out.

Shortly after midday four days later (24 August), 17 CR42s of 23°Gruppo CT escorted six SM79bis of 192^ and 193^Squadriglie in raids on Hal Far and Kalafrana. Four Hurricanes were again scrambled, led by Flt Lt Burges in P3731, who attacked three of the bombers. He observed pieces fall from one, which headed for Sicily losing height rapidly. He was then set upon by CR42s of 75^Squadriglia and Ten Mario Rigatti scored a number of strikes on his aircraft. Visibility was poor and Burges managed to escape, but on landing the undercarriage of his aircraft collapsed. Meanwhile, Rigatti's aircraft was attacked by another Hurricane – probably that flown by Sgt Reg Hyde (N2715). The Italian pilot was seriously wounded although he was able to reach Comiso and land safely in his badly damaged aircraft. Hyde reported:

> "Separated from remainder of section, I attacked large enemy formation of bombers and fighters from astern, coming from slightly above. I attacked centre bandit of six or seven covering and saw my bullets entering fuselage and burst of bullets in cockpit. The other CR42s peeled off up and sideways, as they always do, but enemy fired on turned over and dived straight down, but I could observe nothing further as I was attacked by remaining fighters but evaded them by diving straight down. However, one CR42 followed me down 8,000 feet but did not hit the aircraft. This action took place about 15 miles south of Malta with enemy heading for Sicily after bombing raid."

There was a handwritten note on the Combat Report which stated that "this once confirmed but due to loss of Report given as probable". A second CR42 from 75^Squadriglia was shot down by Flg Off Taylor, Serg Magg Renzo Bocconi baling out over the island only to drift out to sea, from where he was rescued by a British craft. At Hal Far another Swordfish was badly damaged during the bombing. Sgt Jim Pickering provides an insight into the tactics employed at this stage of the air war:

> "Air tactics were based on pre-war ideas. These required close formation during the climb and in combat – this was essential anyway to retain visual contact in bright sunlight. In a section of three or five aircraft (the last was a rare luxury), the senior officer led. Other officers would fly as No2 (or No2 and No3 in a section of five) and NCO pilots as No3 (or No4 and No5). In theory the section would try to obtain height advantage over incoming bandits and given this would change to line astern to carry out an attack. If not, the aircraft remained in formation for another attack. The following aircraft were not there only to back up the leader's attack, but to protect his tail. One idea was that if attacked by hostile fighters we would fly in a circle to protect each other's tail, but these ideas never worked and in any case we couldn't practice them adequately. Where aircraft retained formation – as they were supposed to do – the leader had the first shots and he would be the only one to file a report. If, for example, No3 fired and he had no one behind him to confirm damage, a positive claim could not be made. No3 was invariably an NCO pilot. In flying

No2 or No3 in a section operating in formation, there was no need for individual reports. If, after making a formation attack, the aircraft became separated they had already lost height advantage and probably lost sight of the bandits and there would be nothing additional to report.

I am sure that all pilots fired many times without being able to make positive individual claims of victories. I have always been confident that claims by 261 were understated, but the importance of individual claims has been overstressed. Basic to consideration of claims is that discussion of them – except immediately on landing – was bad form. The personality cult was inflicted on individual pilots by the press, mainly to boost civilian morale. It had little part in squadron life, where all pilots had similar experiences. Shooting a line with non-pilots was disparaged and such gaffes as leaving one's logbook lying around for others to read would generate ridicule, albeit initially good natured. Combat was a life and death matter that was partly a lottery for both opponents and oneself, and although one could take professional pride in carrying out each successive task to the best of one's ability, this was far removed from gloating over the losers or ostentatiously exhibiting one's prowess."

The only other raid of note during this period occurred shortly before 0900 on 29 August, when ten newly arrived Z1007bis bombers of 106°Gruppo BT raided Luqa from high level. Escort was provided by 18 CR42s of 23°Gruppo CT and seven from 157°Gruppo CT. Plt Off Jock Barber (P2653) led off four Hurricanes to intercept but they were too late to catch the bombers, being bounced by half a dozen CR42s without result. However, one of the bombers and one of the escort were each slightly damaged by AA splinters, and another bomber collided with a small building on landing at Trapani, the whole crew suffering injuries. About 50 bombs fell in the Marsa area; there were no military casualties although the civilian population again suffered.

On the last day of the month, the new armoured aircraft carrier HMS *Illustrious* arrived to take her place in the Mediterranean Fleet based at Alexandria. She set course for her new home with an escorted Force H from Gibraltar which was to escort her as far as the Sicilian Narrows, where she would be met by the Mediterranean Fleet and escorted to Egypt. As a precaution against the anticipated Italian response, she had embarked Fulmars of 806 Squadron. The accompanying *Ark Royal* also had on board Skuas of 803 Squadron.

September 1940

By the time the force was within range of Malta on 2 September, there had been several skirmishes between Fulmars, Skuas and Italian raiders and shadowers. In the morning, two Fulmars landed at Hal Far, one with a damaged engine and the other low on fuel. The former was left to be repaired and its crew picked up by one of *Illustrious*' Swordfish and flown back to the carrier. On this date also, Sgt Harry Ayre (N2715) reported probably shooting down a CR42 after he had been scrambled with three other Hurricanes led by Flg Off Waters to intercept a raid. Sgt Jock Robertson, who flew three interception sorties during the day in P2653 claimed a MC200 probably destroyed during the second scramble. Plt Off Balmforth flew four interception sorties, although he was unable to make any claims. Flt Lt Trumble noted there were seven scrambles on this date, one section reaching 28,000 feet in an endeavour to gain height on the raiders – a record for Malta's fighters.

On 4 September, Malta suffered its first visit – the first of many – by the much-dreaded Stukas, on this occasion Italian-flown Ju87Bs of 96°Gruppo Ba'T operating out of Comiso. The unit had only recently taken delivery of its dive-bombers from Germany, where the crews had trained, and currently 15 of the aircraft under the command of Magg Ercolano Ercolani were available for operations against Malta and British naval forces operating in the central Mediterranean. In fact, the Italian Ju87s had made the début against elements of the large naval force south of Malta two days earlier, arriving to attack a cruiser at a moment when no carrier fighters were aloft. The cruiser was claimed damaged, and one of the attacking aircraft was damaged by AA fire. It was now the turn of Malta to be on the receiving end of their attacks. The first raid was by five aircraft only, their crews briefed to attack shipping in Grand Harbour but, in the event, suitable targets were not found and Fort Delimara was bombed instead. CR42s and MC200s provided escort. There were no reported interceptions by 261 Squadron.

Between 1015 and 1045 next day (5 September), eight SM79bis of 34°Stormo BT appeared over the island at 16,000 feet and targeted Grand Harbour, Luqa and Hal Far, while the escort of 17 CR42s circled above Grand Harbour. Six Hurricanes led by Flg Off John Waters (P2653) were up, including N2673 flown by Sgt Jim Pickering, but there were no interceptions. Later, during the early evening, six Ju87s carried out a dive-bombing attack on Grand Harbour with little effect. Army observers reported seeing black crosses on the wings of some of the Stukas, and the number '109' on one machine which swept by at low level. At 1815 a pilot was seen to bale out. Three minutes later it was reported that two aircraft were down after being intercepted by four Hurricanes of A Flight led by Flt Lt Greenhalgh, the pilots claiming three CR42s shot down or damaged. One of these was seen to crash into the sea five miles off Grand Harbour, while the *Times of Malta* reported that one Italian pilot landed in a ditch and was taken prisoner, as a result of "some of the most thrilling air battles of the war over Malta. There were thousands of eye-witnesses, all thrilled to the core." Flt Lt Greenhalgh was credited with one victory. Plt Off Barber in N2673 made no claim, while Sgt Ayre (N2717) was obliged to carry out an emergency forced-landing: "Was attacked by 17 CR42s!! Fired one burst then dived out of the combat. Engine blew up in the dive! Landed at Luqa covered in oil."

The bombers were back on 7 September, ten SM79bis from 36°Stormo BT raiding Valetta shortly after midday, while 17 CR42s flew top cover. Three Hurricanes and three Gladiators were up on this occasion, Flt Lt Greenhalgh, Flt Lt Lambert and Plt Off Barber (in the Hurricanes, Barber flying N2622) jointly shooting down an aircraft of 258^Squadriglia, while a second was claimed probably destroyed by the AA guns. The SM79 came down in the sea a mile off Marsa Scirocco. Four of the crew were seen to bale out and the MV *Trout* was despatched to rescue them from the sea off Wied Zurrieq. The CR42 leader TenCol Tito Falconi and Ten Oscar Abello of 23°Gruppo CT reported engaging two of the Hurricanes, each claiming one shot down. There were no British losses but two Hurricanes were slightly damaged. Meanwhile the Gladiators, one of which was flown by Flg Off Waters (N5524), failed to make contact. About 30 bombs fell in the dockyard area causing minor damage to naval property, but the Admiralty tug *Hellespont* was sunk and five civilians were slightly injured.

With the raids worsening, seven SM79bis of 34°Stormo BT bombed Valetta and Kalafrana on 14 September, Sgts Robertson and Pickering being scrambled in Gladiators N5529 and N5524 to assist the Hurricanes led by Flg Off Waters, one of which (N2673) was flown by Plt Off Balmforth, although no contact was made. A single raider appeared over the island shortly before midnight. It was held by searchlights and observed to make a long left-hand orbit of Grand Harbour before departing, followed by a stream of Bofors fire. At 0800 next morning (on 15 September), the dive-bombers returned to attack Hal Far. This raid included a dozen Ju87s and a single twin-engined SM86W[5] dive-bomber, the latter the prototype, flown by test pilot M.llo Elio Scarpini. Escort was provided by 18 CR42s and six MC200s. Both Hurricanes and Gladiators intercepted. One fighter was claimed shot down by the gunner in Ten Fernando Malvezzi's Ju87, but no losses were suffered by 261 Squadron although one Hurricane was seen limping back to base, with its engine and undercarriage apparently damaged. This may have been the occasion when Sgt Bill Timms carried out a forced landing at Luqa after his engine had blown up as he boosted it while still in fine pitch, as recalled by his friend Sgt Jim Pickering:

". . . having shaken off the bandits, he glided back towards the island and decided he could reach Luqa for a force-landing instead of baling out. As Malta terrain is impossible for force-landings this decision was wrong but he was, in fact, undershooting the airfield, and although the engine had a conrod through the crankshaft and other internal damage, he got a trickle of power out of it that just carried him in."

HQ (South) Infantry Brigade later submitted a report of the action, as witnessed by ground observers:

"At about 0759 enemy aircraft were heard approaching from the east but owing to sun could not be seen. Continuous machine-gun fire heard and occasionally a Hurricane was seen at the bottom of its dive. This battle continued for some minutes. At about 0805 one Hurricane observed limping back to Luqa at a height of about 100-200 feet. 0812 enemy aircraft heard. Six bombers appeared out of the sun at about 15,000 feet and dived on Hal Far, releasing a number of bombs. Within one minute a second formation of six repeated the attack, chased by one Hurricane. Giacomo Battery saw the second formation begin to dive, swung their guns and fired four rounds almost horizontally, which burst right in amongst the six machines as they began to flatten out of their dive. Although difficult to judge, it appeared extraordinary good shooting. Approximately 50-60 bombs appear to have been dropped in Hal Far area. Guard Room, Ration Store and M/T Garage were hit. No casualties to military personnel."

In fact, two Maltese soldiers and a civilian were injured during the attacks on Hal Far, although on this occasion no aircraft were damaged on the ground.

There were no engagements the following day when three Hurricanes pursued three enemy aircraft in the morning. A few minutes after the Hurricane section had landed, however, six more enemy aircraft approached the island. The heavy guns opened fire but without effect. The Stukas returned again mid-morning on 17 September, when seven from 236^Squadriglia and five from 237^Squadriglia from Pantelleria approached, while 21 CR42s and six MC200s provided escort. Luqa was the target, where a transit Wellington was totally destroyed by fire, and a Hurricane, minus its engine, was burnt out inside the hangar. When the bombing was over, Ten Malvezzi strafed the airfield, firing on a twin-engined aircraft, but a reported eight Hurricanes and five Gladiators[6] – a gross overestimate of available strength – then attacked. Two Gladiators were claimed shot down by the Stukas including one by Ten Brezzi but his own Ju87 came under attack from two Hurricanes and was badly damaged. On return to Sicily he counted eleven bullet strikes in his aircraft and found the gunner, 1°Av/Arm Gianpiero Vio, dead in his cockpit. This was probably the aircraft claimed shot down by Sgt Harry Ayre (P3731), who was credited with its destruction. Another Ju87 from 237^Squadriglia, flown by Serg Magg Luigi Catani, failed to return, shot down by Plt Off Barber in N2484:

"The Ju87s had put on a very good show of dive-bombing Luqa. There were about three or four of us up at the time and, as we approached the Ju87s with their escort of CR42s, they started their dive. I followed one and had a quick squirt at him as I went down. He had his dive brakes out and was going down vertically. I was going like the clappers. I pulled out to the south of the island and, near Filfla, saw a lone Ju87 and made a bee-line for him. As I approached, his rear-gunner obviously saw me and he turned to meet me. We did head-on attacks – I was firing and he was firing, I don't know how many guns he had but not nearly as many as I had. We made in fact three head-on attacks and during the last attack my guns ran out of ammo and I thought, 'Oh, damn! Another one and I haven't got him.' I whipped round in a turn as we passed and, to my amazement, I saw him losing height rapidly with glycol pouring from his engine – he wasn't on fire – and he landed with a very big splash in the sea. It floated actually."

A launch from the Marine Craft Section at Kalafrana picked up the pilot and his dead gunner, 1°Av/Arm Francesco di Giorgi, eight miles north-west of Filfla. Barber continued:

"The pilot was later picked up. They told me the air gunner had been killed, I had apparently put a bullet through this poor fellow's head. I went to see the pilot who had been taken to the hospital at M'tarfa. I took him several beers which he seemed to enjoy. He didn't speak English but we had an interpreter, one of the Maltese nurses. We compared notes and so on. He was a very brave and skilful pilot and he put up a very good show. This was a red letter day for me, my first aircraft shot down. I don't think there is anything to describe the exhilaration that a pilot feels when he shoots down another aircraft. A most fantastic feeling."

Meanwhile, Flg Off Timber Woods had latched onto Sottoten Francesco Cavalli's 70^Squadriglia CR42, which crashed near Mgarr after the pilot had baled out. An eye-witness reported:

"The end for the machine came quickly. It suddenly looped the loop and the pilot was seen struggling to free himself from the cockpit. Just as the machine started to nose-dive at a sharp angle, the pilot baled out, and his parachute opened not a second too soon, for no sooner was he clear than flames burst out. The aircraft crashed into a field and buried its nose some five feet deep into the red earth. A big explosion followed and flames leapt up two storeys high; it continued smouldering right into the night. Meanwhile, its pilot was floating in the air, swinging dangerously. It took him six minutes to land . . . everyone was still undecided whether he was a British or enemy pilot and, as he landed, there was a rush to the spot. There were some angry cries when some of the villagers discovered that he was an enemy, but the man was lying helpless on his back. He asked for a glass of water, which was quickly brought to him; he asked whether his mother would be informed he was alive. He was placed on a stretcher and carried to the village, where he was taken charge of by military personnel."[7]

Both Serg Magg Catani and Sottoten Cavalli were taken in captivity and were later interrogated. Catani, the Ju87 pilot, revealed:

"This was my first trip to Malta. It is only a week since I became a dive-bomber pilot. Before that I was a fighter pilot at Trapani and Comiso with CR42s. I was not expecting to be on this trip at all but one of the pilots who was supposed to come over fell ill. I was roped in without warning. I have not yet completed my training nor have I yet done the dive-bombing exercises, so my first lesson was this morning's raid. My companion on this trip was the machine-gunner whose name is Francesco di Giorgi. I am quite certain that your fighters brought me down, Hurricanes. The anti-aircraft [fire] did not worry us much and they were nowhere near me. I was done in because, having been a fighter [pilot] I tried to engage another fighter and that was my undoing. I do not understand how my companion was killed. Before jumping [out] I told him to bale out and he answered normally. I gave him some time before I jumped out and when I got to the sea I noticed that his safety belt was inflated and his parachute open. I can only suggest that his parachute may have opened after he had hit the water or, at least, before it had time to take effect, as my parachute only opened a few seconds before I touched the water. Of course, it is quite possible that he might have been hit by a part of the aircraft. Our life jackets are German as also are our parachutes."

Meanwhile, during interrogation, the CR42 pilot Sottoten Cavalli, a Sicilian from Catania, claimed:

"I was not hit by AA fire or by a fighter, but my oil-feed burst and, as I expected a fire at any moment, I baled out. We know you have Hurricanes, Spitfires and Glosters, because I have seen them myself. I would go anywhere if I had a Spitfire. Your AA is excellent, two bursts came so close I thought the end had come. Sometime back, your AA followed us from Marsa Scirroco to Gozo. We are not afraid of a fight but your AA puts the wind up us. It is very precise. We all say that."

During the afternoon three escorted reconnaissance aircraft approached the island, undoubtedly to report on the damage inflicted by the Stuka attack, and possibly to search for the missing aircraft. Three Gladiators were airborne, led by Sgt Robertson in N5529, but no engagement occurred. Next day (18 September) three Hurricanes and two Gladiators were scrambled to meet a mid-morning fighter sweep, at least seven CR42s being sighted and engaged, one of which Plt Off Balmforth (N2715) claimed shot down. During the combat a bullet entered his cockpit and another caused an oil leak, burning oil inflicting painful burns to both hands, although he was able to land safely. Despite his injuries, Balmforth was back in the air four days later. Although Hurricanes or Gladiators, and sometimes both, were frequently scrambled, it was not until 25 September that the next contact occurred, when just before midday three Hurricanes and two Gladiators were scrambled, one of the latter (N5529) being flown by Plt Off Jock Barber. On this occasion the Hurricanes encountered six MC200s of 79^Squadriglia, which were over Malta on reconnaissance. The aircraft flown by M.llo Gino Lagi was shot down by Flg Off Eric Taylor, the aircraft crashing at 1208 between Bidni and St Thomas Bay. Lagi was only just alive when dragged from the wreck, one arm having been completely severed, and he died shortly afterwards; wreckage was scattered over six fields near Delimara Camp. Meanwhile, Sgt Jock Robertson (N2484) attacked two more Macchis and claimed one probably destroyed which he believed fell into the sea:

> "Not being able to keep formation with Blue 1 owing to high engine temperature, I was climbing alone off southern side of the island when I saw a formation of machines proceeding towards Hal Far from the northern end of the island. I had to get close but lost them in haze and then saw two machines flying out to sea from the Grand Harbour. Thinking they were Hurricanes, I was about 50 yards astern [and] about to go into formation when I realised they were enemy aircraft. I immediately fired a burst of 50 rounds per gun into the leader, after which he turned over and dived down. The other aircraft did a climbing turn to the right and came down on my tail in company with two others who must have been above."

His victim was probably the aircraft flown by the formation leader, Cap Giuliano Giacomelli, which returned to base with its right wing severely damaged. The third Hurricane pilot, Sgt Pickering flying P3731, did not make any claims. During late afternoon two days later (27 September), SM79bis of 34°Stormo BT targeted Hal Far, their bombs narrowly missing the airfield. They also attacked Luqa, where a hangar received a direct hit and a Hurricane was slightly damaged by blast and debris. On this occasion the Hurricanes were not scrambled in time to intercept, but AA guns put up a spirited barrage. One bomber was shot down at 1706, four of its crew baling out over Kalafrana and another two over Zeitun.

The appearance of Stukas over Malta prompted Governor Dobbie to signal the Chiefs-of-Staff, emphasising Malta's vulnerability to invasion since it lacked the means and the men to repel either a seaborne or airborne assault. Consequently, Prime Minister Churchill wrote to the CIGS:

> "The telegram confirms my apprehensions about Malta. Beaches defended on an average battalion front of 15 miles, and no reserves for counter-attack worth speaking of, leave the island at the mercy of a landing force. You must remember that we do not possess the command of the sea around Malta. The danger therefore appears to be extreme. I should have thought four battalions were needed . . ."[8]

In a note to the Secretary of State for War he added:

"Do you realise there is no command of the sea at Malta, and it might be attacked at any time by an expeditionary force of twenty or thirty thousand men from Italy, supported by the Italian Fleet?"[9]

October 1940

Following a further relatively quiet spell, six Hurricanes – and at least one Gladiator (N5529) flown by Sgt Jim Pickering – were scrambled to meet a further incursion of Malta's skies at 1000 on 4 October. They met a reported nine MC200s of 6°Gruppo CT including a photo-reconnaissance Macchi, MM4585 flown by Ten Mario Nasoni, which was shot down by Sgt Reg Hyde (N2715); a second Macchi was damaged by Sgt Jock Robertson (P2653). Of his combat, Hyde reported:

"Attacked right hand aircraft of formation of five from astern and followed same right down in spiral dive. Enemy seen to strike water off Ghain Tuffieha."

Ten Nasoni was killed when his aircraft crashed near Ghain Tuffieha Bay at 1020. Next day, Sgt Pickering was scrambled in Hurricane N2484, while Sgt Robertson followed him in Gladiator N5524, but there were no engagements.

The bombers were back after dark on 8 October, when Kalafrana was raided by five SM79bis of 36°Stormo BT, two of these aircraft held by the searchlights. On this occasion Flg Off Taylor was manning the night fighter Hurricane and, with the aid of the searchlights, succeeded in shooting down an aircraft of 257^Squadriglia, which fell in flames into the sea between Benghaisa and Octopus Creek. There were no survivors from Ten Adolfo Ferrari's machine. Taylor then spotted a second bomber illuminated by the searchlights and was able to carry out an attack before it evaded and disappeared into the darkness; he was credited with one destroyed and one damaged. On reaching Sicily, the SM79bis headed for Comiso rather than their own base at Castelvetrano. The damaged aircraft landed with some difficulty and carrying three wounded crew members. Gunners aboard the returning bombers believed they had shot down one of their attackers, but as Taylor's was the only Hurricane airborne, it seems probable that they had misidentified Ferrari's burning aircraft.

At dusk on 10 October, a balance was drawn. In four months of war the island's fighter defences had recorded 72 interceptions by day and two by night, while flying hours for the Gladiators and Hurricanes totalled precisely 343.50. During this period the fighters were credited with 22 confirmed (nine SM79bis, seven CR42, four MC200, two Ju87), nine probables (five SM79bis, two CR42, one MC200, one Ju87) and eight damaged. Anti-aircraft defences also claimed three SM79s shot down, three probables and two damaged, plus a CR42 probable and an MC200 damaged. Losses in the air totalled two Hurricanes and one Gladiator destroyed, while on the ground two Hurricanes had been written off, and a Gladiator badly damaged.

The approach of a Malta-bound convoy attracted the attention of the Italian air and naval forces on 12 October. The carriers *Illustrious* and *Eagle* provided fighter protection until the convoy safely reached Malta three days later, by which time the Navy's Fulmars and Sea Gladiators had shot down for certain two SM79bis and a Z506B, and damaged several other bombers, all without loss to themselves. In addition, two Italian destroyers were sunk by an escorting cruiser.

October was to prove a fairly quiet month for 261 Squadron, with only the occasional raid or reconnaissance to deal with or investigate. Two Gladiators were scrambled on 11 October and again three days later. There occurred some excitement next day (15 October) when a patrol of Hurricanes, including P2653 piloted by Sgt Robertson, were vectored onto an unidentified plot approaching from the south-west. This turned out to be a French

Loire 130 floatplane flown by Deuxième-Maitre Georges Blaize[10], who had defected from Vichy-French Tunisia. The aircraft was one of two based aboard the French battleship *Richelieu* for catapult launching. During a proposed ferry flight from Bizerta to Dakar in French West Africa, both crews decided to make a bid for freedom. One aircraft ditched in Bizerta Lake where it was destroyed and the crew captured. They were subsequently court-martialled. That flown by Blaize was escorted by the Hurricanes to Kalafrana where it made a safe landing, there to join another French floatplane, a Latécoère 298B which had escaped from Bizerta at the beginning of July. The two aircraft became the vanguard of the clandestine Z Flight which would later include other seaplanes, namely ex-Norwegian Naval Air Force He115s. The Latécoère, crewed by Première-Maitre René Duvauchelle and Quartier-Maitre Jacques Mehouas, had, since its arrival, flown a number of clandestine sorties to North Africa. Sgt Jim Pickering recalled:

> ". . . they first of all joined us in the Sergeants' Mess at Luqa. Bill Timms spoke fluent French and others had some French, so they were not isolated. They were operating the Latécoère from the flying boat base at Kalafrana and so moved to the Sergeants' Mess there, after which we arranged to meet them at one of the bars in Valetta. René and Jacques had different characters. Jacques was happy-go-lucky but René was of thoughtful, nervous disposition. He was pessimistic about the usefulness of the Latécoère, and its performance and serviceability without spares. I think he converted to Marylands with relief."

With the constant wear and tear on the Hurricanes, it would appear that all three serviceable Gladiators (N5520, N5524 and N5529) were now being used with increasing regularity. However, it was a Hurricane which claimed the next success when, on 16 October, Flg Off John Waters (P2645) reported shooting down an SM79bis after being scrambled with two or three other Hurricanes, and Gladiator N5524 flown by Flt Lt Burges. No further action was reported until 27 October, when six Hurricanes and two Gladiators (N5524 and N5520 flown by Flt Lt Burges and Sgt Ayre respectively) were scrambled at 1055. Nine MC200s of 6°Gruppo CT led by Magg Vezio Mezzetti were encountered and one was claimed probably destroyed by Flg Off Eric Taylor. This was probably the aircraft flown by M.llo Marasco which returned to Sicily badly damaged, the pilot baling out over his own airfield rather than risk a landing. A second Macchi was also damaged in this action, while Cap Carlo Ruspoli claimed two Hurricanes shot down although none were, in fact, lost.

With a reduction in the bombing raids, morale amongst the population improved. Mgr Emmanuel Brincat, Archpriest of Senglea, wrote of this period:

> ". . . the fierceness of the raiders abated. There were more air fights but less bombing. Our air defences had, by now, increased sufficiently to keep the raiders back. These air fights became, in time, a cause of excitement and to an extent, of amusement. Men and lads left the security of their refuge and came out into the open to watch and even enjoy these aerial combats. In less dangerous areas one could even see people on roof-tops enjoying the better the spectacle of these air combats. When an enemy plane was hit and damaged, and bends its nose down in its dive earthwards to its death, sheer shouts of exultation rent the air."[11]

Sgt Jim Pickering, who had by now acquired considerable combat experience, later commented on the Squadron's opponents:

> "The quality of the Italian pilots was very good. The CR42s came between the Gladiators and the Hurricanes in performance, and their pilots were aggressive and skilled. A stern attack by a Hurricane on a CR42 could result in the CR42 pulling upwards sharply and, at the top of the loop, opening fire head-on at the Hurricane whilst still inverted. It was necessary for the Hurricanes to use air tactics for attacking CR42s similar to those used by

Messerschmitt 109s against Hurricanes. The Macchis were faster than the CR42s but less manoeuvrable. Their tactical handling was not good and one suspects they were brought into service with insufficient practice-combat experience. The SM79 bombers were operationally obsolete.

SM79 raids were made at between 15,000 feet and 18,000 feet. There was insufficient warning for Hurricanes to climb to 20,000 feet before the raiders were over the target. A low climb in low airscrew pitch created heating problems in the engine. Changes were made to the airscrew stops to coarsen the fine pitch and this permitted a long climb in fine pitch. However, if one climbed below a raid, the fighter escort of the raiders could pounce on the climbing Hurricanes when they were most vulnerable and unmanoeuvrable. If the Hurricanes climbed towards Sicily to intercept raiders on their return flight, they would be bounced by the second fighter escort. The main tactic became for the Hurricanes to gain height in a climb to the south of the island, and then turn north to try to get to 20,000 feet over the raiders after they had turned for home. This would have been more effective with better radar, but vectoring and height information was not very accurate. On their homeward run, in a shallow dive towards Sicily, SM79s were almost as fast as maximum cruising speed of the Hurricanes, and interceptions occurred more from luck than calculation."

Off-duty pilots took advantage of what little entertainment existed. The more adventurous made use of the Squadron's own car, an old American vehicle which had once been the property of the Archbishop of Gozo. With the car suitably camouflage-painted:

". . . the [officer] pilots of 261 would roar down the stone-walled roads of the island, pleasure-bent. Very often it took them to Dragonara Palace, the beautiful home of the Marquis Scicluna built out on a lovely promontory overlooking the sea, where they had a standing invitation and were always welcome. To leave the dust, the dirt and danger of Luqa and drive to Dragonara was to escape into a brilliant, exotic world, where they were entertained like mythical heroes from a land of noble adventure, where the Marquis even kept a camel for the amusement of the children who ran laughing through the corridors of the Palace."[12]

Not to be outdone, the NCO pilots had acquired their own personal transport and had selected a suitable hostelry, as Sgt Pickering recalled:

"We – the NCO pilots – had selected a very small bar in Valetta as our focal point in town. Also, we had commandeered one of the cars used as an airfield obstruction. It was a Lagonda of Rolls-Royce dimensions and presence. Its blemish was a chipped cog wheel on one of the intermediate gears but could be driven without using this gear. When not in use it was looked after by some of the M/T staff. We never queried why the petrol in the tank never went down! There was only one place in Malta that had a good bathing beach. It was at the western end of the island near to the Gozo ferry. We used the Lagonda to go there. We had an alternative of taking the ferry from Valetta to Sliema and swimming from the rocks at St George's Bay at the army barracks in St Julian's. This had the advantage of the hospitality of the army's Sergeants' Mess."

While still based at Luqa, 261 Squadron had begun to operate from the civil airfield at Takali, the pilots flying their aircraft over each morning. Takali was now organised as a fully operational if somewhat sparsely equipped RAF station under the command of Wg Cdr G.R. O'Sullivan, and 261 Squadron was soon able to move in permanently, leaving Luqa clear for multi-engined aircraft. Jim Pickering again takes up the story:

". . . the Squadron moved to Takali. It had no station buildings and was merely an empty airfield. The Officers' Mess was a large private house in Mosta on the north side of the airfield, and the Sergeants' Mess and accommodation on the south-west side. It was an extraordinary building known as the Mad House. It was built with expensive masonry, with stables on the roof and attics in the basement. Living quarters and bedrooms were reversed in between. It was decided that the Squadron was so split that it was necessary to have a venue at which members of the Squadron – officers, NCOs and ORs – could meet at leisure in off-duty time. A reconnaissance was made of bars and night clubs in Valetta and *Auntie's* seemed the best choice. Auntie was almost venerable in years. She had a staff of about six Hungarian girls as waitresses, and to perform a dancing act in return for free drink. In the words of a well-known barrack-room ballard:

> 'They drink coloured water, whilst you paid for champagne,
> But they say, "not tonight, dear", we'll see you again.'

The second time Bill Timms and myself were there, a military policeman had been sent to enforce a notice of 'Officers Only'. In high dudgeon, we went to the Provost Marshal's office to discover the reason. We were informed that it was by order of General Dobbie. We explained to the Provost Marshal – an army officer – that it was intended to be used as a Squadron meeting place. 'If I was a Maltese waiter' said Bill, 'I could go there, but I'm barred because I'm wearing the King's uniform'. 'That is so', said the PM. 'Is there anything else you wish to know. If not, Good Evening.' When we got as far as the door, he said, 'Just a minute. If you obtain a permit from your Squadron and wear civilian clothes when off duty, my military police do not have authority to question you or stop you going anywhere. If you make a nuisance of yourselves, the Maltese police will take care of it. Make sure your Squadron knows that.'

This information put ideas into our heads. Why not apply for both permission to wear civvies and local leave? Subsequently, I applied to stay at the Osborne Hotel in Valetta for a few days. With a little time on my hands and the aid of telegrams, I became engaged to the girl I left behind. Also, I found a large furnished flat in Valetta that I rented for the Sergeant Pilots of 261 Squadron on monthly terms. We purchased such clothes as we wanted and changed into them at the flat. When off duty next day, we slept at the flat. We were able to repay a little of the hospitality given to us, but I suffered some criticism for renting a fourth-story flat without a lift. It was a long climb with crates of ale – and they didn't last long!"

CHAPTER III

THE TRAGEDY OF OPERATION 'WHITE'

November – December 1940

Generally, the first days of November saw a resurgence of aerial activity, initially centred over the Sicilian Channel and brought about by the arrival at Malta of a small force of Wellingtons for night raids against targets in Sicily, the Italian mainland and along the Libyan coastline, and for attacking enemy convoys in an effort to prevent supplies from reaching North Africa. While searching for a missing Wellington on 1 November, a Sunderland from Kalafrana was intercepted and shot down by two MC200s. That afternoon, a second flying boat was intercepted by a CR42 and two more Macchis (one of which was flown by Ten Giuseppe Pesola, who had survived the encounter with Flg Off Woods at the end of June), but this time the damaged Sunderland was able to escape and return to Malta with two wounded crew members on board. Both actions were too far out to sea for 261 Squadron to be able to provide protection.

Next day (2 November), a force of 20 SM79bis of 34°Stormo BT attacked Valetta and Takali shortly before midday, while 11 MC200s led by Magg Bruno Brambilla and five CR42s led by Cap Luigi Corsini of 17°Gruppo CT flew top cover and close escort. The Italians reported being engaged by five Hurricanes, M.llo Leonida Carozzo claiming one shot down, but Serg Abramo Lanzarini of 72^Squadriglia was killed when his Macchi crashed near Zeitun, possibly the victim of Plt Off Allan McAdam. 261 Squadron had in fact scrambled six Hurricanes of B Flight led by Flg Off John Waters (P3730) and two Gladiators including N5520 in the capable hands of Flt Lt Burges who reported an engagement with the CR42s, claiming one possibly shot down although he did not see it crash, and a second as damaged. A second Macchi was claimed probably destroyed by another pilot, while AA gunners believed they had shot down a bomber. Bombs fell on Luqa, where an empty hangar received a direct hit, and on Zabbar where four houses were demolished, fortunately without inflicting any casualties.

There was little or no enemy aerial activity next day and only a minor intrusion on the 4th, when a lone CR42 followed returning Wellingtons home from a night raid and therefore escaped radar detection on approaching the island. The Italian pilot fired a few ineffective bursts into Marsaxlokk Bay before returning to base. That night, at 2205, the sirens heralded the arrival of a lone bomber which approached at 3,000 feet from the south-westerly direction. A Hurricane was airborne and an engagement followed in which the bomber was claimed damaged before it escaped into the darkness, having dropped several bombs which fell harmlessly into the Grand Harbour. At 0615 on the morning of 6 November, another lone CR42 made a surprise strafing attack, damaging one of the Sunderlands riding at anchor in Marsaxlokk Bay.

There again followed a relatively quiet spell for 261 Squadron, though there was much activity out to sea as Italian air units attacked convoys en route to Malta. From Gibraltar sailed the *Ark Royal*, her squadrons of Skuas and Fulmars providing protection for two cruisers and three destroyers conveying troops, their equipment, and supplies for the Malta garrison, while five cargo vessels steamed from Alexandria, with aircraft from the carriers *Illustrious* and *Eagle* as air cover. Italian shadowers soon located the convoys. During the ensuing six days while the carriers were in range, many furious actions were fought resulting in *Ark Royal*'s fighters claiming three SM79bis and two Z506Bs, while *Illustrious*' Fulmars claimed a further three SM79bis, four Z501s, and three Z506Bs – all without loss. In between these daylight actions, *Illustrious* launched her Swordfish during the night of 11/12 November for a devastating attack on the Italian Naval Base at Taranto.

Meanwhile, the convoy from Alexandria had reached Malta safely on 9 November, and was followed into Grand Harbour the next day by warships from Gibraltar.

The early morning raids were repeated by CR42s which attacked Hal Far after approaching behind returning Wellingtons. Sweeping in at low level just after 0600 on 10 November, they machine-gunned Har Far and inflicted damage on a parked Swordfish. When the siren sounded at 0809 the following morning, three Hurricanes including N2484 flown by Flg Off Waters were quickly airborne in an attempt to catch the sneak raiders but, on this occasion, an attack failed to materialise. With the British fleets now out of range, 2^Squadra Aerea rejoined the offensive on Malta, a dozen MC200s of 6°Gruppo CT flying a reconnaissance over the island during the morning of 12 November. AA fire split up the formation, enabling Hurricanes to press home an attack. The aircraft of Ten Giuseppe Volpe was shot down in flames just off St Thomas Bay at 0954, and the pilot's body recovered by a trawler after the Hurricane pilot had indicated the position of the crash. Two days later (14 November), five Hurricanes were scrambled to meet two SM79bis and eight escorting CR42s. Plt Off Jock Barber's Hurricane (N2622) suffered an overheated engine and he became separated from the others:

> "The score when the engine got overheated was to climb in coarse pitch and then level out. I believe a bit of a scrap went on above me. By the time I had managed to get a few angles, I was above the formation of CR42s. I finally caught up with them north of Gozo and made a series of diving attacks using my superior speed and then climbing up again until my ammunition was finished. I don't think I shot anything down but I may have got the odd strike here or there. The one thing I did learn from this engagement was the advantage one had if above the enemy, and of course with superior speed even if the engine was a bit duff."

Barber was credited with the probable destruction of one of the CR42s.

Following the successful delivery of 418 Flight with its Hurricanes in August, a repeat performance was now being readied under the codename Operation 'White'. In mid-November the old carrier *Argus* again sailed for Gibraltar with a dozen Hurricanes and two Skuas embarked, plus 13 RAF pilots and two naval crews. Escort was provided by *Ark Royal*, the battleship *Renown*, three cruisers and seven destroyers. When it was learned that the Italian Fleet was at sea, the captain of the *Argus* was determined that the launch would take place at the earliest opportunity. At dawn on 17 November, the first six Hurricanes were ranged on the deck:

V7474 Flt Lt J.A.F. MacLachlan DFC	V7346 Sgt J.K. Norwell
V7370 Plt Off C.E. Hamilton	V7413 Sgt R.A. Spyer
V7548 Plt Off H.W. Eliot	V7374 Sgt W.G. Cunnington

The navigating Skua (L2882) was crewed by Sub Lt(A) Nowell, who had participated in Operation 'Hurry', and Sub Lt(O) P. Gordon-Smith. The first engine gunned into life at 0615. It took 15 minutes to get all seven aircraft airborne and formed up into two sections, by which time they had already used one-third of their safety margin. It was some 400 miles to Malta. If flown at optimum speed, revs and altitude, the Hurricanes were expected to have reached the island with 45 minutes' fuel to spare. This was now reduced to 30 minutes. At last they set off, as recorded by the Hurricane Flight leader Flt Lt James MacLachlan:

> "Captain Rushbrook came up and said goodbye, and we got into our kites. Mine started straight away and ran beautifully smoothly. It seemed very strange sitting up there in the moonlight waiting for the signal to take off. I could see Chubby [Eliot] and Hamilton out of the corner of my eye, and was watching Chubby's spinner when I suddenly realised they were waving me to take off. I opened her up to 6-lbs boost and, in spite of a fuselage full of junk, she was off before I reached the accelerating fairing. I turned on my navigation lights while the others took off, and formed up. At last we were all together and I signalled

the Skua who set course for Galite Island where we were to meet a Sunderland. By this time it was nearly 0630 and just beginning to get light. We had a 20mph tailwind and I felt quite happy about petrol.

It was quite light when we got to Galite and we spotted the Sunderland without any difficulty. I exchanged the usual recognition signals with the Skua, and we all set off in the direction of Pantelleria Island. We had been flying for about an hour and a half when I checked up on my petrol, and was horrified to find that I had already used about 45 gallons (leaving me about 50). The wind, too, had backed slightly and was now almost full abeam, blowing at about 30 mph. The Sunderland led us south to Pantelleria, this adding about 15 miles to our trip, and completely foxing me. After flying about two and a half hours, I began to get extremely worried about my petrol. I formated on the Sunderland and asked for our estimated time of arrival (ETA) with my identification lights. They said 20 minutes more, and as I then had about 15 gallons, I thought I could just make it.

The second section of Hurricanes were about half a mile behind, and about 1,000 feet above us. I could only see two of them but did not worry as I thought the third was probably dead behind me. Five minutes later the Sunderland turned back, and I realised that there was only one of the rear section still flying. There was still no sign of Malta and my fuel gauge was showing only eight gallons. I don't think I've ever prayed so hard as I did then. The thought of drowning never occurred to me, but I imagined having to bale out and lose my logbooks, camera and binoculars (a fate far worse than death!). The visibility had deteriorated but I did not realise it was as poor as it proved to be. Suddenly the Skua turned to port and started waggling its wings. I turned to follow it, and through the mist was just able to make out the brown cliffs of Gozo about a mile away. I wish I could describe the marvellous feeling of relief that came over me. I could have slow-rolled and looped till I was dizzy if I'd enough gas, but I had only six gallons. I got my section to close in as we crossed the coast, and watched the Skua firing its recognition cartridge.

We circled the first aerodrome we came to (Takali) and, having chosen a runway that was more or less into the wind, I landed. I then had four gallons left. Just as I was taxying off the runway, I saw Hamilton doing an exceptionally split-arse approach from which he carried out a very spectacular crosswind landing. He had apparently run out of petrol while circling the aerodrome, and landed with a dead motor. The Sergeant Pilot, Norwell, had three gallons, and Chubby had 14. It was 0920. We went off to a sort of mess and had eggs and bacon. We had actually landed at Takali, so after refuelling we went on to Luqa – our original destination. There was no news of the second flight, but we heard that the Sunderland had picked up Sgt Spyer, the second of my flight to bale out. Sgt Cunnington was drowned."

The second flight of Hurricanes[1] followed an hour later, and comprised: Flg Offs R.W. Clarke, E.G. Bidgood, P.W. Horton (New Zealand), J.R. Walker (Canada), and Plt Offs F.J. Boret and J.M. Horrex. Their navigating Skua (L2987) was flown by PO(A) W.E.J. Stockwell and Sub Lt(O) R.C. Neil. This part of the operation was to prove disastrous. First, the Sunderland which was to escort the aircraft failed to take off from Gibraltar. Then the flight missed their landfall at Galite Island, failed to rendezvous with a bomber sent from Malta, and became hopelessly lost. The Skua navigator radioed for help, but his receiver was found to be faulty. As the crew searched desperately for somewhere to land, one Hurricane after another fell from the formation until none was left. Finally, just before the Skua itself ran out of fuel, the crew observed through a curtain of mist the coastline of south-western Sicily. Before Stockwell could land, however, anti-aircraft fire opened up, and the Skua crash-landed in a damaged condition on the beach at Punta Palo on the Isola delle Correnti, near Syracuse. Both Stockwell and Neil were taken prisoner. A Maryland sent out from Malta to search for survivors found nothing; it seems that all six Hurricane pilots had perished in the sea. Flt Lt MacLachlan wrote in his diary: "Today has been one of the most tragic in my life. Nine [*sic*] chaps who were alive and well twelve hours ago are dead, and I might easily have been one of them."

MacLachlan was of course unaware of the fate of the missing Skua and its crew. A few days later, he and Sub Lt(O) Gordon-Smith were summoned to attend a Court of Enquiry at Gibraltar, which found that the loss of the aircraft was "mainly due to a lack of knowledge on the part of the Hurricane pilots as to how to fly their aircraft when fitted with constant speed airscrews" and "bad navigation on the part of the observer of the second Skua." Nonetheless, Vice-Admiral Sir James Somerville, C-in-C Force H, privately accepted some of the blame. He wrote on the day after the loss of the aircraft: "I feel now that in spite of the risk of meeting superior Italian surface forces, it would have been better if I had proceeded 40 miles further east . . ."

It was subsequently tacitly agreed that (a) inadequate weather forecasting – the latest meteorological report received was 19 hours out of date; (b) a lack of liaison between Navy and Air Force as to the Hurricane's true range, with the pilots instructed to fly at 2,000 feet where the air is "heavier" than at the height prescribed in the handling notes available to the Air Operations Officer aboard *Argus*, which stated the range of a Hurricane Mk II (tropicalised) in still air, at 130 knots, was 521 miles – but only when flying at 10,000 feet; and (c) over-cautious handling of the fleet had, in fact, played a much greater part in the tragedy than had aircrew error. The loss of so many pilots was particularly damaging, since all had enjoyed the benefit of operational experience with fighter squadrons in England[2]. Much was learned from this tragic experience which resulted in proper planning and preparation for future ferry flights. Prime Minister Churchill later wrote of the incident: "Never again were the margins cut so fine, and though many similar operations took place in the future never did such a catastrophe recur."[3]

In the meantime, the spare Hurricane pilot on *Argus*, Sgt C.S. Bamberger, returned to Gibraltar with the carrier, from where he was transported to Malta aboard the destroyer *Hotspur* and duly arrived at Malta on 28 November. Of the tragic operation, Bamberger commented:

"Flt Lt MacLachlan, whom I got to know well in Malta, would not have taken off from the *Argus* if he had anticipated a flight lasting three hours. On any long-distance flight, particularly if it were over the sea, it would be against the very nature of any fighter pilot not to economise on petrol. To my mind the Navy did not take them close enough."[4]

Of the new arrivals, Sgt Pickering recalled:

"When the reinforcement arrived – partially – the pilots brought in ideas that had evolved in the Battle of Britain. Apart from air tactics, these included the selection of air leaders other than by seniority in rank."

The new Hurricanes did allow for a stronger reception during the next attack on Malta. This occurred shortly after midnight on the morning of 22 November, when a single raider emerged from heavy cloud to drop three HE bombs and four incendiaries, which caused little damage and no casualties, before escaping just as a Hurricane was manoeuvring to intercept. As the bomber swept low over the island a lone Lewis gunner opened fire and belts of machine-gun ammunition fell from the aircraft, these being recovered by soldiers in the area. Presumably, in his anxiety to return fire, the Italian air gunner accidentally lost the ammunition belts overboard. With the arrival of daylight, an Italian fighter sweep comprising a dozen CR42s in two flights of six, approached the island at 22,000 feet. AA opened fire and one of the biplanes was reported to have been hit and to crash into the sea about eight miles south-east of Delimara.

Another raid came in during the morning of 23 November, when ten SM79s targeted Takali while 16 CR42s provided top cover. Eight Hurricanes, including Sgt Jock Norwell in N2701, scrambled to intercept the raid as it came over Filfla at 16,000 feet. At 1115 the

Hurricanes engaged and shortly afterwards an aircraft was reported falling in flames over Luqa. The raiders returned at 1516, four bombers and 16 fighters being sighted east of Grand Harbour, six Hurricanes scrambling four minutes later. In company with two others, Flt Lt Burges in V7548 attacked the bombers, one of which he thought he hit "pretty hard", and saw it going down although he did not see it crash. He then shot pieces off another. Army observers reported "one bailer-out" over Benghaisa at 1532 and, eight minutes later, one aircraft crashed five miles off Benghaisa and another apparently five miles further out, adding that a speed boat had gone out to the "bailer" who had drifted out to sea. Meanwhile, Sgt Jock Robertson (V7474) also tried to attack the bombers:

> "I was Green 3 when a large formation of bombers and fighters crossed the island. Green 1 turned towards them and I was following when we were attacked by about six CR42s and had to take avoiding action. I fired at four different machines during the engagement, my fire tearing fabric off the top mainplane of one which I chased into cloud. He is very unlikely to have reached his base but I did not see him crash."

The third Hurricane of Green Section was badly damaged when it was also engaged by several CR42s, Its pilot, Flg Off Bradbury, carrying out an emergency forced-landing at Luqa. Sgt Reg Hyde (N2672) reported:

> "I was Blue 3 and when over Luqa sighted large formation of enemy bombers and fighters proceeding to Takali. The section turned to engage them when I was attacked by two CR42s from directly ahead, but they turned before I could fire my guns. In taking avoiding action my engine stopped so I was forced to descend vertically, the engine re-starting at 10,000 feet. When about five miles south of Filfla, I sighted two enemy fighters trying to engage one of our Hurricanes at 7,000 feet. I engaged one CR42 getting in two good bursts of fire from above and behind at close range. The CR42 appeared to be in difficulties and dived into a large cloud. As there were other enemy aircraft in vicinity it was not advisable to follow, so I proceeded to carry out search for further enemy."

Hyde wrote on the bottom of the Combat Report: "This e/a once confirmed but due to loss of report only granted as a probable". It was the second such report which he had so annotated, obviously believing that he had achieved more victories than those for which he was officially credited[5].

One Hurricane was claimed by Cap Guido Bobba of 74^Squadriglia, two more by Ten Claudio Solaro and Serg Pardino Pardini of 70^Squadriglia, while a fourth was credited to 75^Squadriglia as a whole. All the CR42s returned safely to their airfield at Comiso. A delivery Blenheim was shot down near Pantelleria during the day by a MC200 scrambled from the island. Next day (24 November) two CR42s from Comiso shot down a Wellington. At sunset, six more CR42s led by TenCol Tito Falconi carried out a surprise attack on Luqa and claimed three aircraft destroyed on the ground; a Wellington was reported to have been destroyed as a result of this attack, and a second sustained damage. On returning to base, one of the CR42s ran short of fuel and its pilot baled out into the sea just off Marsala, from where he was rescued.

Two days later, at 0930 on 26 November, CR42s of 23°Gruppo CT were again in action with three aircraft of 74^Squadriglia undertaking a reconnaissance of Malta. They were intercepted by two of six patrolling Hurricanes, Sgt Dennis Ashton (N2701) shooting down Ten Giuseppe Beccaria, whose aircraft fell in flames six miles off Delimara. Almost immediately Ashton's own aircraft came under attack from Cap Bobba and was also shot down into the sea south of the island. Neither Beccaria nor Ashton, who had learned only the day before that he had recently become a father, survived; the Italian pilot's body was later recovered from the sea by HSL107 and buried in St Andrew's Cemetery. Apparently a second CR42 was claimed shot down during this action, as noted in a diary maintained by an unidentified airman of 261 Squadron, hereafter referred to as Airman X[6]:

"Air raid at 0300 this morning. Got out of bed but the Italians didn't drop anything so returned to bed. Awoke at 0730; breakfast awful. Air raid this morning at 0935. Six of our aircraft took off and engaged the enemy and brought down two. Five of ours returned and one was shot down in the sea. His name is Sgt Hashley [*sic*]; his first nipper was born two months ago."

Following the recent highly successful attack on Taranto, a further convoy into the Mediterranean was swiftly organised by the British, and by late November three large cargo vessels loaded with armoured vehicles and other munitions urgently required for Wavell's forces in Egypt had gathered at Gibraltar.

With Force H providing protection, they set sail on 25 November; simultaneously, a strong naval force departed from Alexandria to take over escort duties at a point south of Malta. *Ark Royal*'s Fulmars and Skuas were first into action, shooting down two or three SM79bis, two seaplanes (a Z506B and an Ro43), and a Vichy Farman 223.4 civil transport which had strayed into the battle zone; one Fulmar and its crew was lost. Meanwhile, the Mediterranean Fleet carrier *Illustrious* made a diversionary attack on the Italian-occupied island bases in the Aegean.

On 28 November, with the convoy safely out of harm's way, *Illustrious* was off Malta when six of her patrolling Fulmars were directed to intercept six CR42s heading for Malta on reconnaissance. The Fulmars found the highly manoeuvrable biplanes difficult to fight, but succeeded in shooting one down 30 miles off the Sicilian coast, its pilot being killed; one Fulmar was also damaged in the action. At Takali, 261 Squadron was not called upon to provide assistance. However, six Hurricanes were scrambled at 0910 when two plots appeared on the radar and, 20 minutes later, a group of CR42s was sighted heading northwards ten miles east of Delimara. The Hurricanes intercepted and one CR42 flown by Serg Magg Arnaldo Sala was shot down, the pilot being killed. His victor was, it is believed, Flt Lt Greenhalgh. Two more CR42s were claimed possibly damaged by other pilots. In return, Serg Magg Raffaele Marzocca of 74^Squadriglia claimed a Hurricane. The second plot turned out to be a bomber raid and five more Hurricanes were scrambled to join the two still airborne, but no interception occurred. The Hurricanes were also required to assist a returning Maryland reconnaissance machine and a flight of three Blenheims arriving from Gibraltar. Although engaged by the Italian fighters, all aircraft landed safely. The raiders were back at 1330 when ten SM79bis of 30°Stormo BT approached the island, escorted by a dozen CR42s of 23°Gruppo CT and six MC200s from 6°Gruppo CT. The Macchis flew ahead of the main formation to "lure and distract" the four Hurricanes which had been scrambled – a ruse which did not succeed for, after a brief skirmish, the Hurricanes managed to engage the bombers at 1408. For once the defending fighters had been ordered off in good time and found themselves above the bombers. Sgt Jock Robertson (V7346) fired at the CR42s on his way through their formation:

". . . and delivered a quarter attack, finishing up as a stern attack, on the SM79s. I sprayed the whole formation at first and then concentrated my fire on the left-hand rear machine, firing all my ammunition into him. I finished my attack at about 25 yards range, and had to break away upward, not stopping to see the result as the CR42s were peeling off onto my tail."

He evaded these and returned to Takali, whereupon he submitted a claim for a bomber probably destroyed. This was upgraded to confirmed when two crew members were picked up from the sea, including the pilot Sottoten Gaio Del Cerro. A Hurricane was claimed shot down by one of the 30°Stormo BT gunners though none were, in fact, lost. Airman X again recorded some of the action in his diary, suggesting greater success for the Hurricanes:

"Ten scrambles, one big raid. Mediterranean Fleet came in, Italian bombers came over and bombed the bay in which the fleet was but failed to score. Dropped four bombs on Valetta. Saw everything as I was only five miles from the bay and had a pretty good view. Our fighters brought down one in the morning and two in the afternoon. All the damage caused to our fighters was two bullet holes in the port wing of a Hurricane. Didn't affect the flying but was put up and sent to Luqa for repairs. Very successful day for 261 Squadron."

Sgt Jock Norwell flew two sorties in N2672 but failed to claim. Air HQ summarised the month's successes by Malta air defence against the raiders as nine aircraft shot down, five probables and eight damaged during the course of 26 raids, eight of which had not crossed the coast. One Hurricane had been shot down and one Wellington destroyed on the ground, while five other aircraft were damaged.

In an effort to increase the performance of both the remaining Gladiators and Hurricanes, the Command Engineering Officer, Sqn Ldr Louks, and his team of technicians continued to look for ways to improve the efficiency of the aero engines:

"On 28 November I flew another variable pitch Gladiator [N5520]. Also, I was testing Hurricanes to improve their performance because, as delivered, they could not keep up with the revised Gladiators! Eventually, by utilising the same principle with their two-pitch propellers, brewing 92-94 octane fuel, and raising the boost by 4lb/inch, they became very lively. I reckoned it was better to risk engines rather than scramble a few impotent fighters. Unfortunately, my AOC [Air Commodore Maynard] being a trifle euphoric from the successes we achieved, suggested I should tell [RAF] Middle East, to improve their potency. This I reluctantly did, and back came a signal from AOA (an Air-Vice Marshal) which said: 'Restore aircraft to normal forthwith. Cease use of unauthorised modifications. No spare engines will be forwarded until they are restored to normal' – or words to that effect.

Maynard did not tell me to obey the order, he asked me what we should do. I suggested he should leave matters in my hands until after I had had words with the Air Ministry. I signalled them, giving details of the modifications, finishing with a statement that, reverting to standard would leave us without any fighter defences. After another blasting from [RAF] Middle East – asking why they hadn't been told when we complied with their previous request – I wrote a mind-boggling letter, with more differentials and multiple integrals than any fair minded person should pen-plagiarise from the Royal Aeronautical Society Journal on the cooling effect of multi-bladed propellers including contra-rotational effects, researched by an Italian Professore, no less, and sat back. After six weeks I asked for a reply from the Air Ministry and by return received 'concur all your modifications'. I sent this on to [RAF] Middle East (for the attention of the AOA) and subsequently learned that the day following he fell sick of the palsey – a heart attack – and I had unknowingly removed a minor stumbling block to the business of warmongering."

December 1940

With the beginning of December there were a number of changes in command; Flt Lt John Trumble was promoted to lead 261 Squadron in place of Sqn Ldr Balden, who was now posted to HQ Luqa as Sqn Ldr (Admin). Plt Off Tommy Balmforth was now back with the Squadron having been discharged from hospital care following treatment for his burnt hands, which had developed a skin infection that necessitated the removal of his finger nails. While convalescing, he had been taken under the wing of Mrs Michie, wife of Wg Cdr W.D.J. 'Pop' Michie, OC Kalafrana, Within a few days of being passed fit for flying duties he had participated in three interception patrols although his burned hands still had to be protected by cotton gloves.

The increase in aerial activity witnessed during November trailed off during December, with only the occasional small fighter sweep and sporadic night raids, the latter mainly by single aircraft. Late on 18 December, Sgt Jock Robertson took off in P3731 for a defensive patrol. At 2350, while at 15,000 feet, he saw below an aircraft illuminated by searchlights between Grand Harbour and Kalafrana:

"I dived from 15,000 feet over Filfla towards the intersection of the beam, and did a quarter attack on the enemy machine. I then closed to 200 yards and put three bursts of fire into it from dead astern, the first from slightly above and the last two from slightly below. The enemy aircraft burst into flames, first the fuselage and then the wing-roots, and dived straight into the sea. Having a high oil temperature, I then asked for permission to land and pancaked at Luqa."

The SM79bis of 193^Squadriglia piloted by Ten Guilio Molteni dived into the sea two miles east of Kalafrana Bay; there were no survivors. On landing, Robertson received a message of congratulation from the AOC, who had witnessed the action. Three days later, on 21 December, 30°Stormo BT undertook another minor raid over Malta. Hurricanes intercepted as the bombers were on their way home, one returning to base with battle damage although the pilot was able to land safely, Flt Lt Greenhalgh the probable victor.

For 261 Squadron, this turned out to be the last success of the year, taking the official total of fighter victories to 30 destroyed (13 SM79s, nine CR42s, six MC200s, and two Ju87s), plus 11 probables and 14 damaged. For the same period the Aeronautica della Sicilia acknowledged 18 bombers and 9 fighters shot down by RAF fighters, and five bombers and three fighters lost to AA fire, although several of the aircraft believed by the Italian authorities to have been lost to anti-aircraft fire had, in fact, fallen to fighter attack including at least one bomber and two fighters.

With his score standing at five confirmed and one probable, Flg Off Timber Woods was now awarded a DFC, while Flg Off Eric Taylor received a Mention in Despatches. Woods left the Squadron at this time under somewhat of a cloud, being posted to Egypt and on to Greece where he joined 80 Squadron[7]. The reason for the sudden departure of such a successful and experienced pilot is revealed by Sgt Pickering:

"The Governor, General Dobbie, was very straight-laced. One of the officer pilots on the Squadron [Woods] became too friendly with the grass widow of a Naval officer away on duty. This was reported to General Dobbie and the pilot was immediately despatched from the island. Amongst ourselves we debated (with levity) whether the wife of a hospitable station NCO we knew might have provided our own escape! Later [in April 1941], when four of us were told we had to fly to Greece next day, we complained that we hadn't had the benefit of Woods' experience, but the humour was lost on the briefing officer! It was of course hushed-up in Malta and never mentioned in front of NCOs and Other Ranks."

Plt Off Tommy Balmforth was another who would soon leave 261 Squadron, albeit in different circumstances. Having made what turned out to be his final flight at Malta on 22 December in V7548, he was readmitted to hospital for further treatment to his burns, and was then posted back to the UK shortly thereafter[8]. Flt Lt John Greenhalgh also left the Squadron for duties at Air HQ, newly promoted John Waters taking his place as A Flight commander, while Flt Lt Lambert took over B Flight.

At the end of 1940 the defenders could look back on the previous six months with some satisfaction. Malta remained a striking base, with destroyers, submarines, flying boats, FAA torpedo aircraft, and a number of medium bombers and reconnaissance aircraft. There had been 211 air raid alerts, with 85 civilians killed – 66 of them during the first month; many more had been injured, and damage to private property had been considerable, while the giant floating dock and an Admiralty tug had been sunk in the harbour. However, despite repeated attacks, the Dockyard remained operational, although steps had been taken to remove much machinery into tunnels beneath the rocky terrain. Nothwithstanding these setbacks, the recent convoys had maintained supplies, although the numbers of Hurricanes and Gladiators available for defence were dwindling.

On a lighter note, a lone CR42 appeared over Malta on Christmas Day, its pilot[9] dropping a small metal cylinder. It contained a Christmas Greeting addressed to "the boys of Hal Far and Kalafrana", and was a cartoon of a brawny Italian pilot reaching from the cockpit of his CR42 to knock down several Hurricanes with his fists, one giant hand clutching the throat of one of the pilots. In the background a crowd of sad-looking RAF pilots queued at the Pearly Gates waiting for St Peter to let them in! Flt Lt John Greenhalgh, who had by now departed 261 Squadron and was deskbound at AHQ, remembered the unofficial code of chivalry that then existed between the RAF at Malta and the Regia Aeronautica in Sicily:

> "During the summer of 1940 there was an evening telephone call between our Intelligence staff and the Italians in Sicily, to enquire about casualties and survivors. This would cease with the arrival of the Germans – the whole tempo then changed."

Across the sea in Sicily, 261 Squadron's major adversaries – the CR42s of 23°Gruppo CT – were transferred to Libya, leaving 6°Gruppo CT with its MC200s, and 17°Gruppo CT with CR42s, to do battle with Malta's Hurricanes.

CHAPTER IV

THE GERMANS ARRIVE IN SICILY

January – February 1941

On 28 October 1940 the Italians had invaded Greece as part of Mussolini's ambitious plan to subjugate and control all around him, and in keeping with the successes achieved by Hitler's forces in Northern Europe. Hitler, although not entirely in agreement with Mussolini's aims at this time, nevertheless proposed aid to Italy as early as 20 November, before the tide had started to turn against the Italians in both Greece and North Africa. By early December the German offer was looking very attractive and, on 10 December, airfields in southern Italy and Sicily were allocated to the Luftwaffe, the first priority for the Germans being to neutralise Malta and the British Mediterranean Fleet, thereby safeguarding the sea lanes to Libya. Consequently, elements of the Luftwaffe with anti-shipping experience were chosen for service in the new theatre, and the staff of Fliegerkorps X from Norway under General Hans Giesler were ordered to Sicily, where they were to set up headquarters at Taormina. On 11 January 1941, Hitler issued Directive No22 entitled 'German Support for the Battles in the Mediterranean Area':

> The situation in the Mediterranean area, where England is employing superior forces against our allies, requires that Germany should assist for reasons of strategy, politics and psychology.
>
> Tripolitania must be held and the danger of further collapse on the Albanian front must be eliminated. Furthermore, the Cavallero Army Group must be enabled, in co-operation with the operations of the 12th Army, to go over to the offensive from Albania.
>
> I therefore order as follows:
>
> (1) Commander-in-Chief Army will provide covering forces sufficient to render valuable service to our allies in the defence of Tripolitania, particularly against British armoured divisions. Special orders for the composition of this force will follow.
>
> (2) X Air Corps will continue to operate from Sicily. Its chief task will be to attack British Naval forces and British sea communications between the Western and Eastern Mediterranean.
>
> The Italian Government will be requested to declare the area between Sicily and the North African coast a closed area in order to facilitate the task of X Air Corps and to avoid incidents with neutral shipping.
>
> German transports available in the Mediterranean and suitable for the purpose will be used, in so far as they are not already on convoy duties to Tripoli, for the passage of forces to Albania. The group of Ju52 transport aircraft will also be employed in moving troops.
>
> Every effort will be made to complete this movement of the main body of German forces to Albania before the movement of the covering force to Libya which will require the bulk of German shipping.

The new year started quietly for the defenders of Malta, and for the first week nothing was to be seen by the patrolling Hurricanes. Rumour was rife, however. One disconcerting story had a German Air Fleet on its way from Northern Europe. This proved to be more than just a rumour and, by 8 January, there was already in Sicily the advanced element of Fliegerkorps X, the first of almost 200 bombers and dive-bombers – 29 He111Hs of II/KG26, 80 Ju88As of Stab, II and III/LG1 and 80 Ju87Rs of I/StG1, II/StG2 and Stab StG3 – due to arrive within the next few weeks. More aircraft would soon follow including 34 Bf110Cs of III/ZG26, a force of Ju52/3ms of KGzbV.9 for air transport duties, and later still a dozen reconnaissance Ju88Ds of 1(F)/121, while He59s and Do24s of

Seenotkommando X provided an air-sea rescue service. By the end of the month the number of Luftwaffe aircraft available in Sicily had reached 141 and, following the arrival of reinforcement units including a Staffel of He111H torpedo-bombers (2/KG4), a Staffel of Bf110D night fighters (1/NJG3), and a Staffel of Bf109Es (7/JG26), Fliegerkorps X's strength would peak at 243 aircraft. By way of contrast, 261 Squadron comprised just 16 Hurricanes[1] and four Gladiators, not all of which were currently serviceable.

Malta's main preoccupation, therefore, was reinforcement and supply, with a new convoy – codenamed Operation 'Excess' – due shortly from Gibraltar. There were five large cargo ships, four of which were destined for Greece and one, the MV *Essex*, bound for Malta. Among the supplies aboard *Essex* were 4,000 tons of ammunition and a deck cargo of a dozen crated Hurricanes[2], which would go far to making good the failure of the November reinforcement flight. The convoy, which was to be escorted by Force H including *Ark Royal*, set sail on 6 January, although one of the Greek-bound freighters had to pull out due to storm damage. From the other end of the Mediterranean two cruisers, with 500 more soldiers and airmen on board, had departed Alexandria bound for Malta and these arrived safely at Grand Harbour on 8 January. Having offloaded their human cargo, the two cruisers set out to meet Force H and the convoy. Meanwhile, a major portion of the Mediterranean Fleet including the carrier *Illustrious* and two battleships, plus cruisers and destroyers left Alexandria to meet the convoy and assist Force H. Included in this force was an auxiliary vessel and a freighter which were also destined for Malta. As the British warships and merchant vessels all headed for the centre of the Mediterranean, much was afoot in the Axis camp. A number of Ju87s of 96°Gruppo Aut Ba'T had been despatched to Comiso on 8 January, where it was soon joined by the advance elements of Fliegerkorps X in preparation for attacks on British shipping. On the morning of 9 January, *Ark Royal* launched a reinforcement flight of six Swordfish for Malta, these arriving safely at Hal Far, but shortly after midday the 'Excess' convoy encountered its first opposition when Sardinian-based SM79bis attacked. Two of the bombers were shot down by one of the carrier's Fulmars, and no damage was suffered by any of the ships. Later, a trio of Skuas were engaged by a similar number of CR42s in an inconclusive encounter.

Meanwhile, the arrival of the Luftwaffe 60 miles across the sea had no immediate effect on the situation in Malta, where the daily trials and tribulations of the hard-working groundcrews continued, as noted by Airman X of 261 Squadron:

> "Changing accumulators most of the afternoon. Accumulator in kite 4845 [?] dud, 1.4 volts across the whole six cells. Later, P/O Bellamy pancakes in kite 4845 and leaves undercarriage lights and reflector sight on. So that's twice in two hours we changed the accumulator for him. The dim twerp!"

In his defence, Plt Off Gerald Bellamy, who had only just joined 261 Squadron from 3AACU to help fill the gaps, recalled:

> "I was posted off to Takali and given cockpit drill in a Hurricane. The only monoplane I had flown was for a few hours in the 3AACU Magister. This was supposed to make me fit to fly a Hurricane!"

Malta saw its first action of the year on 9 January when, during the late morning, 16 MC200s of 6°Gruppo Aut CT were led to the island by Magg Vezio Mezzetti to attack Luqa, while nine Ju87s of 96°Gruppo Aut Ba'T bombed Kalafrana, as their escort of CR42s circled overhead. Six of the Macchis swooped on Luqa at 1100, claiming damage to five aircraft on the ground (in fact, three Wellingtons were damaged); Airman X wrote:

> "My first taste of real war. Four machines dived on Luqa drome where we were operating, and machine-gunned across the drome ... Have one of the small .5-inch cannon bullets. Sprained my ankle and twisted my knee getting out of the way of bullets."

The Macchis were then attacked by five Hurricanes, four of which had been led into the air by Flg Off Taylor; the other three were piloted by Plt Off Eliot (V7548), Plt Off McAdam and Flt Lt MacLachlan (V7474), who had only just returned to the island from Gibraltar; the latter recorded:

"Eric [Taylor] was leading and we climbed steeply to 22,000 feet well up-sun of the island. Suddenly Eric started to dive steeply towards Grand Harbour and, on following him, I saw a formation of enemy aircraft about 10,000 feet below us and five miles to port. I went straight for them and saw Eric turn to follow me. Ack-ack shells were bursting all around them and, as I closed in, some of these burst unpleasantly close to me! At first I could not make out what type of aeroplane they were and tried to overtake them so that I could do a head-on attack. As I drew closer, however, I realised they were Macchi 200 fighters, so did a normal astern attack on the right-hand man of the second section of three (there were six kites altogether). I opened fire at about 200 yards and saw most of the burst go into the Macchi. He did a steep diving turn to the right, but I managed to follow and gave him two more full deflection squirts while in the turn. The first of these just missed his tail, but I think most of the second squirt got him. Suddenly, to my amazement, the pilot baled out and I nearly hit his half-opened parachute as it disappeared under my nose. Somehow I had expected the kite to catch fire and, as it had not done so, I instinctively followed it and fired again. I was very close to the Macchi and could see the incendiary bullets pouring into the empty cockpit as it plunged earthwards in a spiral dive. For a few seconds I did not realise that I had shot down my first kite – it all happened so quickly and was so simple. I must have wasted a lot of precious ammo and even more precious altitude before I abandoned the chase and looked around to get my bearing . . ."

MacLachlan then pursued a lone Macchi for about 25 miles as it tried to catch up with the others returning to Sicily. Gradually closing in, he opened fire, only to see the Macchi pull into a tight, climbing turn before it went "into a terrifyingly steep dive". MacLachlan followed and continued firing until his ammunition was expended. He began to pull out of his dive when he saw a large splash which he took to be the Macchi crashing. On turning for home, he observed a vivid sheet of flame on the surface of the sea. He circled the small patch of burning oil but could see no sign of life, so flew back towards the island:

"About three miles off St Paul's Bay I found the pilot of the first machine I had shot down, still attached to his parachute. I flew low past him and having made sure that a boat was going out to rescue him, returned to Luqa where I landed. I was first down . . . next down was Eric Taylor, who had also got two, one of which was the one I saw crash in flames. The rest of our pilots came in, none of them however had been able to catch the Itis . . ."

Although MacLachlan records only four Hurricanes being involved in this action, Flt Lt Waters had also taken off in V7474 and claimed to have badly damaged a Macchi in a "good fight". Two Macchis of 88^Squadriglia were in fact lost: MM5787 flown by M.llo Ettori Zanandrea who was killed, was clearly one of Taylor's victims, and MM4586 flown by Cap Luigi Armanino who baled out wounded in the arm and thigh, obviously MacLachlan's victim; the wounded pilot, a veteran of the Spanish Civil War, was plucked from the sea and taken to M'tarfa Hospital. There were further scrambles during the day, Plt Off Barber flying two sorties in N2622 although he failed to sight any enemy aircraft.

Sections of Hurricanes were sent off at intervals on the morning of 10 January as the convoy and its escort came within range of Malta's fighters, Flt Lt MacLachlan alone flying four sorties. On his second flight he sighted five CR42s:

"Hoping they had not seen me I made for the tail of the starboard man. Before I could close to effective range, two or three of them whizzed back over my head and were coming down on my tail. Knowing that I should stand no chance against five kites that could out-manoeuvre and out-climb me, I half-rolled and screeched back towards the convoy . . ."

At about 1700 MacLachlan was again airborne with a number of others to patrol the convoy, now some ten miles south of Gozo. When at around 17,000 feet the Hurricanes were fired upon by *Illustrious*' pom-poms and 4.5s, some of which burst close by. MacLachlan later wrote:

"If the Navy weren't so easy on the trigger we might give them some sort of protection, but they fire on us as soon as we fly within their range . . ."

Fulmars of 806 Squadron from *Illustrious* had been warding off attacks all day long. Newly arrived Ju87s from both I/StG1 and II/StG2, joined by three Italian dive-bombers of 236^Squadriglia, had singled out the carrier, while torpedo-carrying SM79bis of 279^Squadriglia concentrated on the merchant vessels. Two of the torpedo-bombers were shot down by the Fulmars, and five of the dive-bombers were later claimed by the Naval fighters, and three more by the guns, but this did not prevent *Illustrious* being severely damaged during this and a second attack by Stukas a few hours later. During the first attack, the Fulmar crewed by Lt(A) Bill Barnes and Lt(O) Desmond Vincent-Jones had just taken off as the dive-bombers swept in; Vincent-Jones, in the back seat, recalled:

"When we had reached a few hundred feet we found ourselves surrounded by Ju87s as they were pulling out of their dives, and some of them were pretty close, one hundred yards or so, and I could clearly see their gunners firing at us. Two bullets went through my plotting board, and others lodged in my seat. I looked down and saw the poor *Illustrious* passing through huge columns of water, her guns blazing and a fire and smoke coming from the aft end of the flight deck. The first 500kg bomb had scored a direct hit on the Fulmar which had failed to start – no sign of it or its crew was ever seen again . . ."

Close to the action was a *Reuters* correspondent aboard *Illustrious*:

"Three Ju87s approached out of the clouds. Simultaneously the guns of all the British ships opened up a terrific barrage. More planes swooped down. The sky was filled with a confused mass of bursting shells and twisting planes. The noise was appalling. As the leading plane dived through the inferno I watched a single 1,000-lb bomb hurtle towards us. It fell in the sea slightly astern. Then a wave of 15 bombers dived on the Fleet. My attention was divided between watching these and watching our own fighters taking off from the flight deck. A few seconds after our last machine [*sic*] had flown off, a tremendous explosion shook the ship. A 1,000-lb bomb released by one of the Junkers diving very low had scored a direct hit. The next moment the wing of a German plane fell across the after lift.

The hit was apparently immediately below the bridge. I have a vivid impression of a sudden sheet of flame and choking smoke. I felt a severe blow on my shoulder from the blast, and then I was pulled into the wireless cabin and thrown on the floor. We lay coughing and listening to the sudden roar of aeroplane engines close overhead. The diving planes swooped so low that they sounded as though they were landing on the flight deck. Near misses sent shudder after shudder through the ship. The German bombers converged from all sides and then dived one after another in the face of blazing gunfire. They held their bombs until the last minute, then swerved quickly off.

After what seemed an eternity, gunfire ceased. We opened the door. Splintered and riddled steel pipes and wires lay where we had been standing a few minutes before. The deck was covered with foam from the fire extinguishers. The flight deck was covered from end to end with debris from the bomb explosion. Further forward was a twisted crane, a heap of bomb splinters and empty shell cases. Through all the action the gun crews never ceased for a moment. Every man moved with precision. Spaces below decks, including the church, were cleared for casualty stations. Wounded were tended as fast as possible . . ."

On Malta, the first most knew of the attack was when four Fulmars arrived at Hal Far, followed soon after by two more. One was flown by Barnes and Vincent-Jones:

"Refuelling and re-arming, in particular, took much longer than usual as the ground crews at Hal Far were not familiar with Fulmars, neither did they have the right loading equipment. We waited with growing impatience as the fumbling went on and we heard reports of another big wave of enemy aircraft passing near Malta on its way to the fleet. After an hour or so the six Fulmars were ready and Barnes and I got airborne with five others in company. We soon sighted *Illustrious* on her way towards Grand Harbour with smoke pouring out of her, but still making a good 20 knots. She had parted company with the rest of the fleet. We were not in time to intercept before the attack developed, but we caught up with the enemy on their way back to Sicily . . ."

The attacks continued even as the damaged carrier reached Malta's coastline. Torpedo-carrying SM79bis attempted to sneak in at sunset, but were beaten off by gunfire. *Illustrious* had been hit by a total of six 1,000-lb bombs; her steering gear was crippled, her lifts were out of action, half her guns were silenced, and her flight deck was wrecked. She finally docked at 2100, with 126 dead and 91 wounded on board. Among the dead were ten air crew, including several who had taken part in the successful strike against Taranto the previous November.

On the morning of 11 January, the pilots of 261 Squadron and the gunners of the anti-aircraft batteries prepared for the inevitable attacks on the carrier in Grand Harbour. At 0845 a single reconnaissance SM79bis appeared at 23,000 feet. Led by Flt Lt MacLachlan, six Hurricanes were scrambled to intercept but failed to catch the intruder. However, following the return of the Hurricanes, it would seem that the SM79bis returned as, shortly thereafter, Sgt Bill Timms scrambled in N2622, as recalled by Sgt Pickering:

"Bill Timms was scrambled solo from Takali with instructions to climb above the island with all haste. I would assume that radar had picked up a lone reconnaissance and the only hope of interception was to have height advantage. I was dozing in the sun on the Sergeants' Mess balcony, and watched part of the climb until I lost sight of the aircraft, and I would have expected it to be over 20,000 feet when the engine noise rose quickly to a scream and suddenly stopped . . . once you have heard a Merlin engine over-rev and blow up, you cannot mistake the sound . . . lack of oxygen was suspected. He may have forgotten to turn his oxygen on during the climb, and have passed out, or there may have been a failure in the oxygen supply. We had the old rubber tubes connecting the oxygen bottle to the face mask, and there was a suspicion that moisture could collect in a bend and freeze. Bill had control of the aircraft when he passed over Takali at 2,000 feet, and was heading for Luqa with the obvious intention of force-landing there. He should have made a normal forced landing at Takali but Luqa was bigger. We could see that Luqa was too far to glide to and we were all shouting for him to use his parachute. When he did so, he was already too low. I saw him leave the aircraft and knew there was no hope."

A young Maltese civilian, John Galea, was on the roof of his house at Zebbug as the Hurricane approached:

". . . I heard the sound of an engine coming at speed right over my village. As soon as it passed over, heading to Luqa, it just turned over and dived headlong. The pilot baled out at too low an altitude and his parachute never opened. His body was only a short distance from the aircraft. On his jacket was the name 'Timms'. The place of the crash was a field in a nearby valley known as Wied Qirda . . ."[3]

Bill Timms and Jim Pickering had been close friends, as the latter recalled:

"I was most affected by the loss of Bill. We had been to the same school, been opponents in rugby matches and, by coincidence, enlisted in the RAFVR on the same day. I knew his parents [Bill's father owned a timber importing business] and wife Kay, and obviously had to write to them. I also had to deal with such personal effects as there were by listing them and sending them to stores, with instructions to send them to his next of kin. As we had left the UK without embarkation leave and with little more that what we were wearing, our possessions in Malta were few. I cut the RAF wings from his tunic and with a few documents and his flying logbook, that was all. I burnt the rest. Bill's wrist watch was returned to me. It had stopped at the moment of impact. Drac [Bowerman] offered to try and mend it, but I destroyed it with his other effects. In prewar days, if a Sergeant Pilot had financial responsibilities such as a wife and family, some items of his would be auctioned in the Mess. It was an alternative method of making a gift to his dependants. Fellow sergeants would bid as much as they could afford to give for a worthless knife, fork or spoon as a souvenir of a friend. This was a less embarrassing procedure than passing round a hat, or starting a subscription list. No such methods were necessary for the casualties in Malta. Few had dependants."

That evening, the *Essex* and her valuable cargo which, in addition to the crated Hurricanes and ammunition, included 3,000 tons of seed potato, arrived safely in Grand Harbour. Unloading began immediately. Surprisingly, all remained quiet at Malta next day (12 January) with only the odd reconnaissance aircraft putting in an appearance. Having ascertained the whereabouts of the damaged carrier, an operation was planned by Fliegerkorps X for the following morning. But, in a pre-empted strike, ten Wellingtons from Malta raided Catania after dark. Whereas the crews believed they had probably destroyed nine Ju87s on the ground, they had in fact destroyed a Ju88 of II/LG1, two Ju52/3ms of KGzbV.9, an SM79bis and a Ca133; in addition six He111s of II/KG26 and 11 MC200s were damaged by blast and debris.

With daylight on the morning of 13 January came the anticipated initial raid by German aircraft. This comprised a small formation of Ju87s of I/StG1, each aircraft carrying a 1,000kg bomb. The target was obviously *Illustrious* in Grand Harbour's French Creek, but on this occasion none of the bombs found their mark. Although Hurricanes were scrambled, no interceptions were made. Flt Lt MacLachlan was among those scrambled twice during the day. By now, the carrier's Fulmars were stationed at Hal Far for servicing and repair; they were also fitted with local frequency R/T to enable them to be controlled by Malta Ops when airborne. Since Fulmars normally carried a TAG or observer, rear-view mirrors were not included as standard, but while operating from Malta as part of the fighter defence there would be no need for a crewman, and so mirrors from some of Hal Far's Transport Section's older vehicles were commandeered and fitted to the Fulmars' cockpits.

With so few fighters available it was clear that the guns would have to play a major part in defending the carrier. An immediate conference was held, drawing on the experience acquired in the earlier Italian dive-bomber raids. Valetta's Fort St Elmo was equipped mainly for coastal defence, although it did have some Bofors guns, others being located on the bastions and around Valetta itself. However, heavy batteries were situated on the other side of the city from Rinella to Marsa, and these provided the mainstay of Grand Harbour's defences. A box barrage of great intensity was planned over the harbour, so that every attacking aircraft would have to fly through it to reach its target. The plan also provided for the defending fighters to engage the Stukas as they approached, and when they were coming out of their dives and at their most vulnerable. Throughout the daylight hours of 14 and 15 January the pilots waited for the attack to start in earnest. Apart from the odd reconnaissance aircraft, all remained eerily quiet, although on the night of 15/16 January bombers roamed over the island, as an extremely frustrated Flt Lt MacLachlan noted in his diary:

". . . I sat in my kite with the engine running for a quarter of an hour, while a formation of Jerries flew up and down the island in full moonlight, but would they let me go up? Would they fuck!"

At about 1400 on 16 January, two large formations approached Malta from the north and the east comprising 17 Ju88s escorted by Bf110s, and a total of 44 Ju87s in five waves escorted by ten MC200s and ten CR42s. From the ground the sight of the approaching raid was awesome:

> "Thursday was a bright, sunny January day . . . It was 1.55pm when the alarm sounded. The Stukas came in waves. More and more flew into sight. And as they drew into range the Malta barrage was heard in all its strength for the first time in history. The heavies from the forts opened up with a reverberating roar. The guns round the Harbour area joined in with tremendous emphasis. The Navy's guns transformed the uproar into a stunning crescendo of sound. Through the symphony of gunfire could be heard the menacing drone of the Junkers as they raced towards their objective. The crash and clamour of the barrage was sharpened by a new note as the leading Stukas dipped their noses towards Parlatorio Wharf and dived into the maelstrom of steel, flame and smoke. With the whine of the dive . . . came the accompanying rush of the bombs as the Germans released them from their racks in the direction of the *Illustrious*, now hardly visible behind a pall of smoke and spouting columns of water.
>
> The entire island rocked to the shock of the battle. The thud of the heavy stuff which the Junkers were dropping, the roar of the bombs as they exploded, and the rumbling crash of falling masonry as Senglea and Vittoriosa caught the weight of the enemy's attack, completed an unforgettable sound-picture. The Stukas followed their squadron leaders in the screaming plunge into the inferno that was raging over the Creek. Some of them did not emerge. Hardly one came out unscathed. the defenders were just as tough as the attackers. It required nerve to stick to your guns with those thousand-pounders thudding and bursting around you, with those screaming furies diving over you. In spite of this danger, people looked on fascinated, watching the suicide tactics of the Germans. Others, in their shelters, rocked and swayed and wondered if this was the end of it all."[4]

Four Hurricanes and three Fulmars were scrambled as the bombers approached, but only the latter led by Lt(A) Barnes made a successful interception. They vectored on to the formation of II/LG1 Ju88s, of which they were credited with shooting down four and damaging three more: Sub Lt(A) Angus Hogg claimed two, Barnes one and at least one probable, and Sub Lt(A) Stan Orr (N1884) one. The Ju88 (L1+CT) flown by Oblt Kurt Pichler failed to return, six others crash-landed at Catania due to battle damage, and a seventh bomber force-landed at Pozzallo as a result of damage caused by AA fire. One of the Ju88s returned with two crew dead or dying and two wounded; another with three dead and one wounded, and a third with one dead and one wounded. Four of the aircraft were damaged beyond repair. The Hurricanes, meantime, had been directed to the wrong area. MacLachlan was still fuming when he later updated his diary:

> "No sooner had the Ju87s gone than the radar picked up four more formations coming in at 10,000 feet. Diving almost vertically to 2,000 feet they released their bombs and slowly turned for home in ones and twos. There was the chance that every fighter pilot prays for – and still not a fighter to be seen. Chubby [Eliot] and I could stand it no longer . . . we rushed off to dispersals where we got into two reserve machines and asked permission to take off. Imagine our consternation when we were told not to leave the ground. I've never come across such a panic-stricken, disorganised collection of incompetent lunatics as Fighter Control . . ."

The four Hurricanes returned with only two having actually encountered the enemy, causing MacLachlan to comment: ". . . out of 60 Ju88s and Ju87s we did not shoot down a kite. Honestly, I quit!" However, *Illustrious* had been missed by all but one bomb. Although the carrier had escaped major damage, the MV *Essex* received a direct hit causing an explosion in which 15 members of her crew and seven Maltese stevedores were killed, and others injured.

The fires were extinguished and work was resumed until all salvagable cargo had been unloaded; as far as can be determined, all the crated Hurricanes survived:

"A short interval. Then came the second assault by the Stukas. Again the titanic duel. Again the heavens seemed to split. Again the Three Cities shuddered with the impact of bombs which had either overshot or undershot their mark. Again the Stukas appeared to flirt with death. And again they were beaten with heavy losses. A dive-bomber, badly hit, released its load of high explosives at random, before crashing into the sea. The bombs landed on a block of flats in Old Mint Street, Valetta, which collapsed with an ominous, rumbling noise [five killed, although over a dozen more were rescued including a baby and two children]. Another bomb crashed perilously near the *Illustrious*, hitting the flight-deck in its seaward dive. Part of the ancient bastions of the Knights of Senglea crumbled with a roar on the rocks below after a direct hit. The British fighters joined in the battle and put up a magnificent show against tremendous odds. In the heat of the fight they seemed to chase the planes right into our murderous barrage, bent on destroying their prey. After what seemed an eternity, but was in reality some fifteen minutes, the noise stopped and a strange silence reigned as the smoke of battle wafted out to sea, and the clouds of dust gradually settled thickly on the ground."[5]

During the attacks, dock installations and nearby houses suffered severe damage. Philip Vella[6], then aged 13, later recalled:

"During the raid I was at home in Valetta. When it became clear that this was no ordinary attack, my mother told me and my sister Doris to run for it and take cover in the crypt of a nearby church; there were no rock shelters in the vicinity. It is difficult to describe the din; it sounded as if hell had been let loose. The noise of exploding bombs, flak of all calibres, and the screeching wail of the diving Stukas was so scaring that people just stood where they were and froze. Suddenly we heard a terrific explosion; a row of houses two blocks away was flattened, some said by an aerial torpedo and others mentioned two bombs chained together. At that stage people panicked as they realised that the only shelter we had above our heads was a big empty dome. I do not remember low long the attack lasted, but it certainly seemed a long time. Our experience was insignificant compared to what people at Senglea went through – Willi Mizzi and 11 others were trapped for 48 hours under 40 feet of rubble."

When the debris was removed and bodies recovered, the final toll for the day's raids amounted to 53 killed and 36 injured, four of whom later died. There followed an anti-climactic day (17 January) when the anticipated follow-up onslaught failed to materialise, allowing both sides a brief respite. The dive-bombers returned in force on the afternoon of 18 January when the airfields at Hal Far and Luqa were targeted by more than 50 Ju87s from I/StG1 and II/StG2 in an obvious attempt to cripple the fighter defences before further efforts were made to finish off *Illustrious*. As a result of these attacks, Luqa was for a time put out of action, the Luqa detachment of 2/West Kents reporting:

"1415, Air Raid Alarm sounded: a large number of dive-bombers appeared from the south-east and dive-bombed Hal Far; these planes flattened out over Luqa and were engaged by the ground defences. Several hits were claimed. Three Swordfish were destroyed at Hal Far and hangars were hit. The enemy planes left the island flying very low. A few minutes after these planes had left, a much larger number appeared and dive-bombed Luqa aerodrome. Four direct hits were made on hangars and one Wellington was destroyed by fire. Numerous hits were made on the main runway. Several enemy planes were seen to crash at different parts of the island. A report later received confirmed five enemy planes shot down and a probable ten damaged."

In addition to the Wellington destroyed, a Hurricane was also severely damaged. Flt Lt

MacLachlan, who was off duty, witnessed some of the action:

". . . the guns opened fire and I had quite a good view of the proceedings. Down through a gap in the clouds came a horde of Ju87s. The AA barrage was terrific, but they never wavered. These Jerries have guts, and I couldn't help but admire them. As far as I could make out they were attacking Luqa . . . we heard that the hangars as Luqa had been flattened and that two Maltese had been killed by a direct hit on their shelter. Two Wellingtons were burnt out and all the rest were temporarily u/s. We shot down six Jerries, the AA got five, and we lost two Fulmars. One pilot, however, was picked up OK."

Wg Cdr Carter Jonas, OC Luqa, with an eye for the ridiculous, recalled seeing a Maltese sentry on duty at Luqa:

". . . sticks of bombs straddled the lonely little soldier, while shrapnel, stones and debris must have been falling around him like rain. He had, however, a rifle and twelve rounds of ammunition, and standing there in the open and entirely unprotected, he solemnly proceeded to fire at twelve separate dive-bombers as they roared over his head. One can only hope that his impulsive bravery was rewarded by some good deflection shooting. Pressing the trigger the last time, instead of the customary kick on his shoulder, all that happened was a sharp metallic click. Now his rifle was merely a useless contraption of metal and wood. Here he found himself, unarmed and unprotected, in the centre of the target area, while enemy aircraft thundered above his head and bombs exploded around him. Suddenly, and without power to prevent it, blind panicky fear seized the soldier and, flinging his useless weapon across the tarmac, he ran as fast as his little legs would carry him to the nearest shelter, 25 yards away. Once safely below ground, breathless and incredulous of his escape, he flopped quietly down in a dead faint!"

Five Hurricanes and four Fulmars had been scrambled as the raid came in, and in a series of swirling actions claimed seven Ju87s shot down and two damaged. Flt Lt Burges (P3731), who was on his fourth scramble of the day, claimed one Stuka "almost certainly shot down" and two damaged. Flg Off Taylor claimed two more, and Plt Off Hamish Hamilton and Sgt Cyril Bamberger (P2629) one apiece. It seems that Fulmar pilots Lt(A) Robert Henley and Sub Lt(A) Jackie Sewell of 806 Squadron also claimed against the Stukas. However, despite all these claims, only one Ju87 was recorded by the Luftwaffe as being lost, A5+JK which crashed near Hal Far taking Fw Richard Zehetmair and his gunner Gfr Heinrich Müller to their deaths. A second Stuka returned to Sicily with a wounded gunner (Gfr Helmut Horn) on board. A Ju88 of 7/LG1 also failed to return, L1+ER flown by Lt Horst Dünkel coming down in the sea, while a MC200 of 6°Gruppo Aut CT flown by M.llo Persani, which was part of the escort, was also shot down into the sea. The Italian pilot may have been the victim of Sub Lt(A) Arthur Griffith, whose Fulmar however failed to return. Another Fulmar, Henley's aircraft, was forced to ditch in Marsaxlokk Bay:

". . . all available fighters scrambled – some four Fulmars – and we just [flew] around, uncontrolled, shooting at anything which took our fancy/came within range. The poor old Fulmar had problems gaining height and in gaining speed against the Ju88s. My aircraft was hit – I think, of all degrading things, by a Ju87 – which stopped the engine some miles east-south-east of Hal Far, and I decided to glide as close to Malta as possible because (a) my TAG, N/Air Rush[7], told me, at this point, that he couldn't swim and (b) there seemed to be so many aircraft about and such chaos reigning that I doubted that two little parachutes five to ten miles out to sea would be noticed, much less noted as British, by the ASR boys who were already having to face something of a racket. We ditched one mile off Kalafrana. A very brave Maltese AA gunner, who saw us go in, jumped into the sea and swam off to help us, and arrived even before the ASR launch [a motor boat from Kalafrana] . . ."

The Maltese soldier was Sapper Spiro Zammit of the Royal Engineers, who was awarded the British Empire Medal for this action, the citation stating:

> ". . . Sapper Spiro Zammit . . . immediately dived into the water and, reaching one of the pilots [sic], held him up until rescued by a speedboat. There can be no doubt that Zammit was largely instrumental in saving the life of the pilot [sic], who was in an extemely exhausted condition."

The rescued airman was N/Air Rush. A contemporary report of the action stated that one of the Fulmars – probably that flown by Sewell – followed a Ju87 through the AA barrage as the aircraft dropped its bomb and tried to escape at very low level through the harbour entrance. It was so low that it had to rise to clear the breakwater, wobbling badly as it did so; this gave the Fulmar a chance to catch up and shoot it down into the sea. At this stage, however, the Fulmar became the target of AA gunners and the pilot was lucky to reach Hal Far and land safely. The report added that the disgruntled Fulmar pilot later sent a message to AA Command stating that he did not think much of the accuracy of the guns' fire, which had missed the bomber and hit his own aircraft!

The first assault on the morning of 19 January came in at about 0830 and comprised about 40 Ju87s and Ju88s, against which six Hurricanes led by Flt Lt Lambert were scrambled. Amongst those intercepting was Sgt Jim Pickering (V7548) who claimed one of each type "probably destroyed but unconfirmed". As soon as the Hurricanes had been refuelled, A Flight took over but not before Pickering had been ordered off to investigate a suspicious plot:

> "It turned out to be a Z506B with a single CR42 as escort, which were circling to the north-east of the island. I chased the floatplane half-way to Sicily, finally making a long diving attack past the CR42 towards the stern of the Cant. I saw some hits but did not stay to watch the results as the fighter was now between me and Malta, and I returned to base at low level and high speed. Air-Sea Rescue aircraft and boats of the Luftwaffe and Regia Aeronautica were legitimate targets. Red Cross aircraft and shipping should have been free from attack when on non-combatant duties, but the Geneva Convention would not apply if they duplicated the services of Air-Sea Rescue units, nor if, in the course of legitimate operation, they collected intelligence information. There was a strong suspicion that this was why some Red Cross aircraft had flown across Malta."

More Ju87s approached the island at about 0945, Flt Lt MacLachlan (V7546) leading the Hurricanes into the air:

> ". . . we were ordered to scramble and had reached 12,000 feet when AA shells started bursting over Grand Harbour. I saw hordes of Ju87s starting to dive down through the barrage, so led my section round to the west of Valetta and came in behind one of the first machines to leave the harbour. I gave it a short burst, but I overshot it and had to break away in a climbing turn. I fully expected bullets pouring into my unprotected belly, but either the rear-gunner was dead or a rotten shot, for nothing hit me. Having lost the necessary speed gained in my dive, I selected another Ju87 and closed in from the rear and slightly below. The gunner started firing long before I was in range but after I fired one well-aimed burst, he packed up and I could see his gun pointing harmlessly into the air. The rest was fairly plain sailing. I closed in to about 100 yards and gave him five or six short squirts. Clouds of smoke came from his engine and, as he rolled into his last dive, I could see vivid tongues of flame streaking back from his port wing root. I watched him go in, and turned for home."

MacLachlan then came across a lone Ju87 "and after two or three squirts he started to smoke and dived into the sea." As he watched the Stuka crash MacLachlan was attacked by a CR42, but managed to evade with his aircraft having been hit in both wings, tailplane and rudder. Flt Lt Burges (P3730) also claimed two Ju87s shot down, both of which he saw crash into the sea off Grand Harbour, and knocked pieces off another. Others were credited to Plt Off McAdam, Sgts Bamberger (V7370) and Ayre (V7474), making a total of seven. Bamberger reported being chased by two or three fighters which he took to be Messerschmitt 109s but evaded these by diving to low level and flying alongside Dingli Cliffs. While so engaged he discovered a Ju87 doing the same and "blasted it". One Hurricane failed to return; 20-year-old Sgt Eric Kelsey (P2629), from Coventry, was last seen chasing a Stuka into the barrage; it was feared that he had been shot down by AA fire. Five Bf110s of III/ZG26 formed part of the escort and Maj Karl Kaschka, the Gruppen-kommandeur, claimed a Hurricane shot down at 1050; Kelsey may have been his victim, although returning Italian fighter pilots also claimed two destroyed and four damaged.

Sgt Jock Robertson (V7474) took off with five others at 1005, intercepting about 20 Ju87s and 24 CR42s north of Grand Harbour at 9,000 feet:

> "I was Green 2, and climbing up into the sun when I saw the anti-aircraft fire over Grand Harbour and then the enemy machines beginning to dive for their attack. I went round the firing zone and attacked a Ju87 as it was going away north. I put one burst into it from astern and below, causing it to turn over and dive straight into the sea from about 2,000 feet. Turning away I saw a CR42 coming straight for me and put a good head-on burst into him. He also turned over and dived straight for the sea but, being attacked by several other CR42s, I did not watch him to see what happened."

Robertson's Hurricane received one bullet hole through its starboard wing. With his latest victories he had raised his score to five confirmed and two probables. One of the artillery officers later related his impressions of the latest raid:

> "They came over at about 18,000 feet till they were over the harbour, and then went into what was practically a vertical dive . . . there were so many that some of our chaps thought the whole Luftwaffe were on the way. They dived in strings of about ten each, one string from one direction, the next from another, and so on, and all focused apparently on the *Illustrious*. Those Germans must have been brave pilots to come through that barrage. For a few seconds you couldn't see any of them while they were coming through. Then some of them did come through, still diving, down to about 100 feet. By this time we'd stopped firing the barrage and each gun took on the planes that came into its own area, over open sights . . . I saw one of our shells burst on the tail of a Junkers. He seemed to go out of control, recover for a moment, and then dive down, on fire. We were firing pretty solidly for half an hour. The attack finished and the last of the Germans trailed off."

At 1100, an aircraft was seen circling offshore and two Hurricanes flown by Flt Lt MacLachlan (V7545) and Sgt Bamberger were sent to investigate; the former recalled:

> "I saw a tiny speck in the distance and called 'Tally-ho!' I lost sight of it but saw another aircraft circling over the sea about five miles away. I closed in on it, carefully keeping between it and the sun. At about 100 yards I opened fire. It was a huge three-engined job, and I could hardly have missed it if I had tried. A sheet of flame burst from its starboard wing-root, so I ceased firing and flew very close to it. It did not seem to be losing height, but flew calmly on for about three miles, with flames and smoke pouring from it. I gave it another short squirt, but it was already doomed."

His victim was a red-cross marked Z506B rescue aircraft of 612^Squadriglia flown by Sottoten Ignazio Rossi. MacLachlan had only just landed when there was another alarm. The ground crews quickly refuelled and re-armed his aircraft, and within five minutes he was in the air. He was joined by Flt Lt Burges who had just returned in V7548, which he quickly changed for V7546 when the former was damaged on landing. MacLachlan continued:

"Again we saw the now familiar sight of AA shells bursting over the harbour. Down came the bombers, Ju88s this time. Burges went screaming down into the middle of them, but, hoping that Ju87s would follow, I hung around at 10,000 feet. I saw a Ju88 pull out of its dive and instead of turning out to sea, it kept flying south in the direction of Kalafrana . . . I got in a well-aimed full deflection shot, the port engine began to smoke badly and I thought for a moment that I had got it . . . I closed to 50 yards and gave it a five or six-second squirt . . . At about 3,000 feet one of the crew baled out and the bomber steepened its dive. Finally it crashed into a little bay near Zonqor Point."

On his return, Flt Lt Burges reported that he sat behind a Ju88 on which he used nearly all his ammunition. He last saw the bomber heading for Sicily with its port engine on fire. The rear-gunner kept up return fire during the pursuit, a bullet hitting one of Burges' parachute harness buckles and leaving a large bruise on his left shoulder. B Flight took over the Hurricanes at midday. When the next raid came in at 1255, Plt Off Jock Barber (P3733) led the fighters into the air:

"I led what aircraft we had, six Hurricanes, one Fulmar and one Gladiator. This was quite amazing. We intercepted the bombers, which were Ju88s and Ju87s escorted by various fighters, right over Grand Harbour. They started the dives, with the 87s going down vertically and the 88s pretty steeply, and we did the same thing – right through the barrage. Why none of us were not hit by ack-ack I'll never know. It was a pretty ding-dong battle that developed right down to sea level, and various individual fights broke out . . ."

Sgt Jock Robertson (P3731), on his fourth sortie of the day, met six Ju87s and about a dozen CR42s:

"I was Green 1 and was circling over St Paul's Bay when the enemy machines began their attack. I chased a Ju87 as it went away north, but was attacked by CR42s and had to take evasive action. Later I chased two CR42s [and] shot one down in flames – pilot baled out – and put a good burst into the second. It dived towards the sea, smoking, but as there were other enemy machines in the locality I did not see it hit the water. Several bullets in [own] machine [and] one in parachute pack."

Robertson's first victim was probably Serg Magg Ezio Iacone of 70^Squadriglia, who was reported to have baled out north of Valetta, and was presumed to have drowned. Sgt Harry Ayre (V7474), on his second sortie of the day, claimed a Ju87 probably destroyed, and it seems that one more Stuka was claimed by Plt Off Hamish Hamilton, taking the day's tally for the Hurricanes to nine Ju87s, two Ju88s, one CR42 and one Z506B; the guns claimed a further six Ju88s. In addition to the Hurricane lost, four more returned bearing the scars of battle.

Luftwaffe losses during the day included two Ju87Rs of 2/StG1 – A5+EK crewed by Uffz Rudolf Vater and Gfr Franz Walburg, and A5+BK crewed by Obfw Kurt Zube and Uffz Franz Buczek, and T6+LP of 6/StG2 flown by Obgfr Hans Küsters and Gfr Fritz Strubel. Another Ju87 of I/StG1 returned badly damaged. Two Ju88s of 8/LG1 were also lost, L1+AS flown by the Staffelkapitän Hptm Wilhelm Dürbeck, and L1+ES captained by Obfw Hans Schneider. Another Ju88, an aircraft of Stab III/LG1, force-landed at Pozzallo and was totally destroyed, although the crew survived, while a Bf110 of III/ZG26 crash-landed at Catania and was severely damaged; this crew also survived.

Despite the ferocity and intensity of the latest attacks, the *Illustrious* escaped further serious damage although the Dockyard and surrounding area again bore the brunt of the bombing. During one attack, what was described as a 'glider bomb' landed within the Three Cities at Vittoriosa, demolishing a nunnery, although it failed to explode. It was later rendered harmless. During the three days of attacks on *Illustrious* and the airfields – 16th, 18th and 19th – it was assessed that the defenders had accounted for 40 enemy aircraft destroyed, five probables and at least a dozen damaged, with AA being credited with 16 of those destroyed, plus a share of the probables and damaged. Actual Axis losses were considerably less, but nonetheless severe. While most pilots displayed the utmost courage in engaging the enemy, there were also those who were less keen. One pilot admitted that, as far as he was concerned, he had done enough in the Battle of Britain and was determined not to lose his life over Malta. When the Hurricanes scrambled he generally headed south to ensure sufficient height – as everybody else did – but usually found that by the time he entered the fray the battle had receded.

During a lull in the assault, a PRU Spitfire landed at Takali. Flown by Flt Lt P. Corbishley DFC, it had left England for a reconnaissance of Turin but owing to an unexpected westerly wind, the pilot found that he did not have sufficient fuel to return to England, so diverted to Malta[8]. Sgt Jim Pickering takes up the story:

> "[Sgt] Angus Norwell was manning the phone at dispersal and immediately contacted Ops, where Grp Capt Sanderson, the SASO, answered, and Norwell simply said 'There's a Spitfire in the circuit.' The SASO said words to the effect that there was no Spitfire at Malta, and didn't he [Norwell] know the difference between a Spitfire and a Hurricane, and, in any case, there were no aircraft airborne. Norwell, not knowing he was speaking to the SASO, passed some suitable comment. The SASO turned to the Duty Officer at Ops and said there was a bloody fool on the phone, this being overheard by Norwell, who said he entirely agreed but the bloody fool was not at his end of the line! We gathered to our amusement that this exchange was not shared by the SASO!"

Next day (20 January) Grp Capt Sanderson flew by Sunderland to Egypt to attend a conference, during which he pleaded for reinforcements. Immediate aid was forthcoming, and when he returned to Malta that evening he brought four fighter pilots (Plt Offs P.A. Worrall, P. Wyatt-Smith, J.J. Walsh, a Canadian, and I.R. Currie[9]), and an assurance that others would, with their Hurricanes, within days. Three days later, RAF Middle East signalled Malta:

> "Am despatching you six Hurricanes and seven Fulmars as soon as possible, and about ten Brewsters (probably in cases) by next convoy."

Owing to lack of spares and maintenance problems, the offer of the Fulmars and Brewster Buffaloes was declined, these aircraft being diverted to Alexandria, but the offer of six Hurricanes was accepted with alacrity. The situation was again becoming serious. However, despite the presence of almost 200 German aircraft in Sicily by this time, the assault now tailed off. On the night of 20/21 January, Malta struck back when seven Wellingtons again bombed Catania airfield, the crews claiming seven aircraft destroyed on the ground; two MC200s and a Ca133 were in fact destroyed and three other transport aircraft damaged. Further attacks continued on subsequent nights as Comiso, Catania and Naples were all targeted. Meanwhile, on 23 January, *Illustrious* had been sufficiently patched up to allow her to sail quietly out of harbour (minus her Fulmars) and on towards Alexandria and safety[10]. As soon as Fliegerkorps X realised she had escaped, six Ju88s of 8/LG1 were despatched from Catania on a search. Three of the aircraft subsequently ran out of fuel and crashed into the sea after their crews had baled out; only one man survived. During the morning, Plt Off Jock Barber (V7072) and Sgt Jock Robertson were scrambled on the approach of an unidentified aircraft, and sighted a single SM79bis, obviously on a reconnaissance sortie, with an escort of four CR42s, as Barber noted:

> "This was very similar to my very first interception way back in August, except on this occasion I attacked the bomber and Sgt Robertson went after the fighters. I pressed home the attack very close and very nearly collided with it, but I think I made the mistake of concentrating on its fuselage and not one of the engines. Anyway, I don't know what

happened to it. I claimed a probable."

Next day (24 January), Ju88 L1+HM of 4/LG1 flown by Uffz Gustav Ulrich failed to return from a reconnaissance sortie to Malta. It may have fallen victim to one of the Gladiators which were now temporarily serving with 806 Squadron, as about this time Sub Lt(A) Jackie Sewell was on a meteorological flight when he noticed tracer passing his starboard wings, followed a moment later by a Ju88 diving towards Hal Far. Sewell pursued the intruder and reportedly shot it down into the sea. Lt(O) Vincent-Jones, who witnessed the action, added: "From the ground it gave the impression of a terrier yapping at the heels of a mastiff!" Earlier that morning, at 0900, a Z506B from 170^Squadriglia RST – MM45307 flown by Sottoten Danilo Lucchesi – which had left its base at Stagnone for a patrol over the Central Mediterranean – also failed to return. It was reportedly intercepted and shot down by Malta-based fighters, but whether this was a pair of Hurricanes or Fulmars is not clear.

Two Fulmars and three Gladiators were scrambled from Hal Far on the morning of 25 January, without result. That night, however, a Z501 alighted on the sea north of Comino, the islet between Malta and Gozo, where its crew was captured. The pilot had become lost and a signal requesting a searchlight to guide him home was intercepted by the Y Service at Malta. The captured aircraft was moored pending being towed in but it was wrecked by high seas. Yet another Ju88 was reported missing over Malta on 26 January, a reconnaissance machine from 1(F)/121. The aircraft, 7A+DH flown by Lt Helmut Fund, was intercepted by two Hurricanes at 1630 when flying at 10,000 feet, and was chased all the way back to the coast of Sicily. When last seen by the Hurricane pilots, smoke was issuing from its port engine and the rear-gunner had been silenced. Shortage of fuel then forced the Hurricanes to turn away; obviously their attack had been more successful than they realised.

Little was seen of Axis aircraft during the closing days of the month. In fact, the Stukas of I/StG1 had already departed Sicily for Libya and were shortly to be followed by those of II/StG2, although more Stukagruppen were on their way from France. The only raid of note at this time was made during the early morning of 28 January when a single aircraft bombed Luqa, where four airmen were killed and nine wounded. Next day, the six reinforcement Hurricanes arrived from Egypt together with a navigating Wellington, the latter carrying three additional fighter pilots, the kits of all nine pilots and ammunition for the Hurricanes which had been removed to reduce weight. Flg Off C.D. Whittingham led the flight, and with him were Plt Offs J.F. Pain (V7564), P.J. Kearsey, D.J. Thacker, D.J. Hammond, C.E. Langdon, a New Zealander, and Sgts A.H. Deacon, C.W. McDougal and C.G. Hodson[11]. All bar one had ferried Hurricanes to Egypt across Central Africa from Takoradi (see Appendix V). Of the flight to Malta, Plt Off John Pain, a Scottish-born Australian in the RAF, wrote:

"In order to lighten the aircraft we were instructed to take out our wireless and all ammo, so what could we have done if the damned Wimpy was attacked? In return for our protection, it was to drop a dinghy if we dropped into the drink. What a help! With serious misgivings about our survival of this trip, we took off and formed a vic on either side of the Wimpy. One of the types turned windy at the last moment, so we had to clobber one of the 33 Squadron pilots for the trip. Unfortunately, the bloke that turned windy came on as a passenger in the Wimpy, a thing that we were to regret later on.

We flew along the coast as long as possible. Then we altered course slightly out to sea, and the coast of Cyrenaica faded away. There was nothing to be seen but the water, the Wimpy and the cloud. About half way across we sighted a destroyer. A welcome sight. Our course would have taken us right over the top of him but we did a wide circle round him as the navy blokes are notoriously trigger-happy. Not that I blame them. Anything with wings is enemy, to hell with markings and silhouettes. The next moment this speck erupted and the barrage burst about 2,000 feet below us. The Wimpy made a dignified concession and altered course to starboard by at least five degrees. The next burst was about 500 feet below us and slightly behind. It was quite astonishing how much muck came out of that little ship. We never did find out if it was Royal Navy or Italian. The weather started to get a bit thick soon after we passed the ship, and the closer we came to Malta the worse it got, until we were at sea level. Very damaging to our fuel consumption. Heavy rain started. We were close to the Wimpy by this time. It was very bumpy and the aircraft were approaching dangerously close to each other. Almost as suddenly as we ran into it, we came out of the rain into low, broken cloud with an occasional rain squall."

As the formation approached Malta a number of Ju87s and MC200s were observed. Pain mistook the fighters as Messerschmitts:

"We climbed a little, zig-zagging through cloud until we came about 50 miles south of Malta, where we went right down to the sea. This was the area any attack was expected. Pantelleria was 70 miles to our left, and Sicily 60 miles beyond Malta. Low down and far ahead appeared the smudge that indicated the cliffs of [Malta]. Rapidly they rose up so that we could see the houses at Hal Far. Almost immediately white puffs appeared above, and through gaps in the clouds we saw the Stukas come down in line astern. Through another gap dropped another flight of them. We counted 40, but where was the fighter escort? We saw them soon enough. We were circling south of Filfla at sea level when they appeared through a gap in the clouds above us. Thirty of the bastards, six of us with no ammo. There was only one thing to do – and that was to go for them. I waggled the others into a vic and one in the box. The Wimpy stayed below.

As the fighters swung down at us, we turned up at them in a head-on attack and straight through the middle of them. We steep-turned to the left onto where they should have been, but instead of going for the Wimpy they had turned and were going south away from the island. I thought we had got the biggest fright, but apparently they had. Turning once more for Hal Far, the drome at which we were to land, the recipient of quite a lot of recent hate, we circled above the battered white houses with their broken walls, the runway with its white craters, and aircraft burning on the boundary. Only two, as they were well dispersed. We saw the Wimpy land at Luqa and then we came in between the craters to the surprising sight of a Wing Commander in full blue, waving us into our various dispersal points. Having landed safely, we were met by AVM Maynard – the first and only time I saw the man – who was intrigued by our un-RAF appearance. This included some six days' growth of beard and six days' accumulation of sand where the grit would be most irritating. Water in the desert was reserved for tea, not washing! Subsequently, Whittingham suggested to the AOC that we merited a Mention in Despatches for our flight, but he knocked that back."

The next day, a further batch of six pilots was brought in by Sunderland: Flt Lt S.R. Peacock-Edwards, a Rhodesian, who, like MacLachlan, had flown Battles in France before transferring to fighters; having subsequently fought in the Battle of Britain, he had two victories to his credit. The others were Plt Offs A.J. Rippon and C.F. Counter, and Sgts L. Davies, A.G. Todd and L.J. Dexter. The new arrivals had also been conveyed to West Africa by the carrier *Furious* and had flown their Hurricanes to Takoradi, and from there across Africa to Egypt. At about this time Flt Lt Gerald Watson also joined 261 Squadron. A bomber pilot, he had crashed his Wellington and volunteered to fly Hurricanes while awaiting a replacement aircraft. Flt Lt Burges meanwhile joined 69 Squadron in exchange for Maryland pilot, Flg Off Terry Foxton. Before the month was out two further awards were announced for 261 Squadron, the DFC for Taylor, who now had seven and one probable victories, and MacLachlan, with six victories, receiving a Bar to his DFC.

By the end of January, AHQ Malta was able to report a quite satisfactory fighter strength as follows:

261 Squadron 28 Hurricanes (of which five were currently unserviceable)
806 Squadron 3 Fulmars (one unserviceable) and four Gladiators (one unserviceable)

For which there were currently 43 fighter pilots available. In addition, the island could boast 19 Wellingtons, four Marylands, one PR Spitfire, five Sunderlands, and a handful of Swordfish. Having had the opportunity to survey his surroundings, Plt Off John Pain wrote in his diary:

"From Hal Far we moved to Takali where we joined the remnants of 261 Squadron. The Officers' Mess was in Turri Kumbo, a large, stone two-storied house on the west side of the aerodrome opposite the old *Ala Littoria* buildings that were now the Station and Squadron Administration block. The Sergeants' Mess was in a building known as the Mad House, a few hundred yards further east. Turri Kumbo had been built in the year 0 or soon after, with a story about a princess who committed suicide because of unrequited love. The main entrance was by way of a divided stone staircase with a small circular balcony in between. On each balustrade was a .5-inch machine-gun. The ante-room was an old lounge – chairs, sofa, fireplace – and on either side of the fireplace was the insignia of the Italian Air Force cut from the wings of a CR42. Above them was a message streamer, and above that the pride of the mess – the Christmas card that had been dropped on the drome on Christmas Day by the Regia Aeronautica [see Chapter III]. Rather a last war gesture in keeping with the dropping of the boots of the dead airman on his home drome. We, unfortunately, were forbidden to return the gesture."

The arrival of reinforcements eased the pressure on the Malta veterans, and brought further profound comment from Sgt Pickering:

"When there was an increase in reinforcements of both aircraft and pilots, we, the longer survivors, started to see an escape route from what had seemed inevitable. From early flying instruction, we had accepted that you did not learn to fly to die for your country, but to ensure that some other pilot died for his. Ensure was the operative word. Once you were in combat, you were on your own with a duty to perform without instructions of any kind. We did not rate our chances of survival very high. We had enlisted to fly aircraft and assumed that this would be our occupation until either demise or the end of the war. It was only to be expected that when reinforcements arrived they wanted to do things their way. They had come to save their predecessors. Taking the reinforcement of Malta as a whole with both Hurricanes and, later, Spitfires, there was a pattern that each reinforcement was immediately followed by casualties amongst the newcomers. They had to learn the lessons that had made their arrival necessary."

February 1941

February began with a renewal of activity over Malta, during which some of the new arrivals were involved in their first operational sorties. At 1140 on the first day of the new month, two sections of Hurricanes took off to investigate approaching aircraft. Pink Section sighted an SM79bis of 193^Squadriglia closely escorted by four CR42s of 156°Gruppo CT. Sgt Robertson (V7116) reported:

"I was Pink 2 on patrol with Pink 1 when we sighted the enemy formation coming in over Gozo at 19,000. Pink 1 peeled off and attacked the SM79 which was leading the formation – I followed him down about 15 seconds later but was attacked by the CR42s which were above and behind the SM79. I gave one a good deflection burst as he was turning and caused him to spin. I watched him partially recover but he continued to lose height in a spiral dive until I finally lost sight of him just before he crashed."

The CR42 went down near St Andrew's Barracks and its pilot, Serg Magg Andrea Baudone, was killed. The SM79bis managed to struggle back to Sciacca on two engines and with two wounded crew members on board; on examination it was found to have about 100 bullet holes through its wings and fuselage. Meanwhile, Red Section – Flg Off Whittingham and Sgt Len Davies (N2715) – gave chase to the fighters. Davies attacked first, but the biplane evaded his approach; Whittingham then engaged and reported that he shot him down about 15 miles out to sea. Since only Serg Magg Baudone was confirmed lost during this action, it seems likely that Whittingham's victim survived. About ten minutes before dusk four sections of Ju88s with fighter escort appeared over the island, passing through the Grand Harbour barrage to attack Takali. Hurricanes were scrambled and Plt Off Pain (P3731) attacked one of the raiders:

> "1 February saw my first blooding over Malta in a fight with Ju88s and Me109s [*sic*], which started over the main island and finished off over Gozo, where I clobbered an 88. The last I saw of him was disappearing into cloud on fire in the starboard engine. I claimed a damaged, and had also observed strikes on two 109s earlier."

A Ju88 from 6/LG1 was damaged during this attack and subsequently crash-landed at Trapani, where it was totally destroyed; both the pilot, Obfw Fritz Wohlgemuth, and the observer were injured, while the gunner was killed.

The bombers returned two days later, destroying a Wellington on the ground at Luqa. On this occasion they escaped interception. They were not so fortunate next day (4 February) when, at dusk, three formations of Ju88s raided Hal Far, Luqa and Kalafrana. Eight Hurricanes and two Fulmars were scrambled including Hurricane P3730 flown by Flt Lt MacLachlan:

> "Just as B Flight were packing up watch, they were ordered to scramble. I was on my way over to do some night flying, so I jumped into an aeroplane and had just started the engine when the AA guns opened fire. I screeched off into the twilight and climbed as quickly as I could . . . It was now too dark for me to have any hope of finding a Jerry without the aid of searchlights, so I decided to land. There was no flare path at Takali, and I could only just make out the runway. There I met Sgt Robertson who had shot down a Ju88. We heard there was another formation coming in, so, without waiting for permission, we screamed off again. This time I got to 12,000 feet but could see nothing, so came down to land . . . finally went over to Hal Far and landed there."

Sgt Robertson (V7116), who now had eight confirmed victories, reported:

> "I was Blue 2 and in formation with Blue 1 when we saw two Ju88s coming in over Grand Harbour. I attacked one with a short burst from astern then, following him into a cloud, emerged in the same position on his tail. I fired at him again but he started to dive and I overshot and broke away upwards. I then dived and saw another Ju88 going away east at 8,000 feet. I carried out a stern attack on it, setting both engines on fire. He eventually dived into the sea about five miles east of Zonqor Point."

Robertson was credited with one destroyed and one damaged. Plt Off Pain in N2715 also claimed a Ju88 damaged off Gozo, before losing his victim in cloud; Sgt Len Davies (V7072) damaged another, which he left with one engine smoking, while Flg Off Barber (V7671) made three interceptions, claiming one probable and two damaged. One returning Hurricane crashed at Takali in the dark, obliging others to land at Hal Far. Jock Barber recalled:

> "We had continuous relays of attacks by the Germans that started at about 5pm and went on right through up to darkness. If the airfield switched on the landing lights, then they could only switch them on for a very short time, just as you were about to touch down. I was running short of fuel and, as I was landing at Takali, I was shot at by a Ju88. Fortunately, he did not damage me."

Meanwhile, two Fulmar pilots, Sub Lts(A) Stan Orr (N1884) and John Roberts, jointly claimed another bomber shot down, as recalled by Lt(O) Vincent-Jones:

"A raid of more than 100 [*sic*] aircraft was detected shortly before dusk, crossing the 60 mile channel separating Malta from Sicily. Orders came through to get all serviceable Fulmars into the air. I was in my bath at the time when Stan Orr gave me the news. Telling him to get down to dispersal and get the remaining Fulmars started up, I dried myself and pulled on my jacket and trousers faster than ever previously. I rushed after him and leapt into the rear seat as the chocks were pulled away. I had no time to collect a parachute or Mae West and, apart from my uniform and a towel, had nothing on except my flying helmet.

Looking upwards, the whole sky seemed covered with enemy aircraft, mostly Ju88s but also a fair number of He111s and Dorniers. Cursing the slow rate of climb of the Fulmar, we proceeded out to sea to gain altitude to get on terms with the bombers which were coming in at about 5,000 feet. By this time it was beginning to get darkish but we could clearly distinguish the bombs pouring down on Luqa. As we turned back towards the island, Orr sighted a Dornier silhouetted against the sunset to the westward and gave chase. We made our approach from the port quarter, and another Fulmar came up opposite us (I believe Roberts was the pilot) and concentrated on his starboard engine. The enemy rear-gunner did not seem able to see us and was firing directly behind him. What looked like a stream of pink golf balls passed between the two Fulmars without doing any damage. It was not long before the Dornier went down in a shallow dive with a fire breaking out in its cabin. The crew were clearly visible against the flames as by this time it was fairly dark. Moments later the Dornier hit the water which soon put the fire out. Orr was so intent on his gunnery that he only remembered to pull out in time, otherwise we might have dived in beside the Dornier, which I wouldn't have fancied, being Mae West-less. At least there was no doubt about this one."[12]

Despite these eyewitness reports of crashes, available German records note that while three Ju88s, all from II/LG1, were badly damaged during this action, all limped back to Catania with a total of five wounded crewmen on board. At Hal Far, a Swordfish and a Gladiator had been destroyed, and a second Swordfish damaged. The Gladiator was N5531, about which Plt Off Pain noted:

"All the hangars [at Hal Far] had been hit, but there were few aircraft in them. In one was *Hope* of the famous Malta trio. She was in the throes of becoming a six-gun Glad, the only one in the RAF, but she received a bomb smack through the centre section and that was the finish of her. *Charity* [N5519] had gone a little while before in a dogfight. *Faith* [N5520] was left."[13]

N5531 was one of the Gladiators being modified by Sqn Ldr Louks, the Command Engineering Officer, who was continually experimenting with parts salvaged from other wrecks:

"Louks took this machine and had it patched up. He took a more efficient propeller from another unserviceable machine and fitted it to the Gladiator. Then he improved the armament. The four machine-guns of the Gladiator had never really supplied enough fire power. If this machine was to shoot down Stukas he would have to increase its gun power. He did this by mounting two additional guns on the top wing, Great War fashion. When these modifications were finally complete, the old Gladiator really looked like something from the old Western Front, as if Mannock, or Ball, or Bishop had flown in to help the Hurricanes of Malta. [Observing] it in the half light of evening, out on the grass in front of the hangar, it looked a bit like a cross between a Nieuport Scout and an SE5A."[14]

Wg Cdr Carter Jonas, who referred to the modified Gladiator as the 'Bleariator', wrote:

"A bomb-blasted Blenheim and a damaged Swordfish provided the missing components, and the Bleariator was tested by the designer himself; powered with a Blenheim engine and Swordfish wingtips. The flight test was certainly encouraging as the performance as a whole, and particularly the climb, was considerably in advance of the more orthodox Gladiator."

Malta's daytime fighter activity had prompted Fliegerkorps X to undertake more night operations and, on 8 February, 261 Squadron prepared to intercept. Just after dusk radar plotted an incoming raid, and Flt Lt MacLachlan (V7671) led off six Hurricanes:

"We screeched up to 16,000 feet, but as it was almost dark by then, we split up and each stayed at a separate height, mine being at 16,000 feet. I saw a Ju88 [it was actually a He111] beautifully illuminated at about 10,000 feet over Rabat .. the rear-gunner must have seen me coming for he opened fire at the same moment as I did . . . I closed in to 50 yards and again ceased fire to take stock of the situation. I realised the fight was as good as won, so taking careful aim at very close range, I fired a fairly long burst. A long trail of smoke streamed out behind the bomber, but it did not catch fire. A few moments before I had been certain of a spectacular victory, but now it seemed I was to be cheated. When I took my head out of the cockpit the bomber had vanished . . . HQ later confirmed that this aircraft crashed into the sea. How they confirmed it is still a mystery."

In fact, Malta's Y Service had been listening to the crew's final, desperate radio calls before their aircraft, a He111 of 5/KG26, actually ditched. The crew survived although one was wounded. No sooner had MacLachlan landed than Plt Off Eliot took off, and patrolled for an hour but without result. On his return, MacLachlan again took off and climbed to 16,000 feet:

"I had been on patrol for about a quarter of an hour, when the searchlights came on and formed a fairly concentrated intersection over Luqa. I immediately turned towards it and, to my delight, saw a Ju88 beautifully illuminated at about 10,000 feet, slowly turning north . . . I watched its wings slowly growing in my sights. At last, its wings completely filled my sights and aiming at the top of the fuselage I let fly. Clouds of smoke came back and my cockpit was filled with the smell of burning aeroplane. I turned to one side to avoid hitting the Jerry and was immediately picked up by our searchlights. By the time I had extricated myself from these, my target had vanished."

MacLachlan asked if Control could confirm its destruction and was advised that Army personnel had seen the aircraft crash into the sea. However, German records suggest that the bomber, an aircraft of II/LG1, did manage to reach Catania, albeit severely damaged. After a further 30 minutes on patrol, MacLachlan landed, and Eliot went up again. This time he, too, spotted a bomber in the searchlights but was unable to get within range before it disappeared from view. Each pilot was to complete a third sortie before being stood down at 0300. Sgt Robertson (V7102) had also been airborne during the night:

"I was on patrol over Filfla at a height of 4,000 feet, the height at which I was ordered to fly, when I saw the enemy aircraft illuminated by the searchlights far above me. I climbed as fast as possible but was unable to close range before the searchlights lost the aircraft. I gave him two bursts of fire, however, one from astern and the other head-on, but at extreme range – about 500 yards."

Although he did not make a claim, a Ju88 of III/LG1 returned to Catania having been badly damaged. Both Takali and Hal Far had received visits from the night bombers, as Airman X recorded:

"Came out of shelter about 0430. German bombers had dropped bombs on hangars and crew room, also several just off the camp. Crossing tennis court on the way to billet and discover a big hole. A thousand-pounder fell there but had not gone off. As it was only fifteen yards from the billet we had to evacuate. Returned to Takali to find that Italians [*sic*] had machine-gunned our flare path while the crew were seeing Hurricane off. No one hurt but shook them up . . . Glad to be back at Takali. Big explosion about noon. Heard later that seven men and one officer were attempting to remove the unexploded bomb when it went off. All killed; they won't find much of them left."

At this stage AHQ Malta again drew up a balance sheet listing fighter successes for the past four months to 10 February: 41 confirmed (13 Ju87, 12 Ju88, six CR42, six MC200, two Z506B) plus ten probables and 19 damaged, to raise the overall claims to 63 confirmed, 19 probables and 27 damaged.

During the day the first Bf109Es reached Sicily when 7/JG26 landed at Gela. The unit was composed of battle-hardened veterans who had seen much action over England during the previous summer, and was commanded by Oblt Joachim Müncheberg, one of the Luftwaffe's outstanding fighter pilots at this time. A recipient of the Ritterkreuz, he had 23 victories to his credit. 7 Staffel – never more than nine aircraft strong – was to play a part quite disproportionate to its size during the next four months. Meanwhile, the Bf110s of III/ZG26, the Ju87s of II/StG2, the Ju88s of II and III/LG1, and the reconnaissance unit 1(F)/121, all began to transfer from Sicily to Libya in support of the new Deutsches Afrika Korps.

Malta's Wellingtons were despatched on the night of 10/11 February to raid Comiso airfield where five of KG26's Heinkels were damaged by blast and debris. Simultaneously, a small number of Ju88s headed in the opposite direction, resulting in Plt Off Eliot and Sgt Bamberger (P3731) being ordered off to engage, as the latter recalled:

"I orbited over Filfla for some time and was beginning to worry about the fuel situation when I was called into the searchlight area, only to be fired upon by the ack-ack. I advised control that I was coming in to land and requested that the flare-path be lit, but was told that there was still an alert in force and therefore no flare-path could be employed. A second request brought a blank refusal, but fortunately it was a bright, moonlit night, and I was able to make a perfect landing on a grass slope near Rabat."

Daylight on 12 February brought with it an even greater threat – the first appearance over Malta of the Messerschmitts of 7/JG26. During the afternoon, six Hurricanes of B Flight led by Flt Lt Watson were ordered off after three Ju88s were reported approaching at 20,000 feet. As they climbed after the quarry the Hurricanes were suddenly bounced by the Bf109Es, Oblt Müncheberg (White 1) claiming one at 1641, and Fw Leibing two more, the first at 1645 and the second two minutes later. They were his first victories. Flt Lt Gerald Watson in N2715 and Plt Off David Thacker in P3733 were both shot down into the sea, while Flt Lt Bradbury in V7768 forced landed at Luqa with a seized engine unaware that he had been attacked, as Sgt Jim Pickering (V7103) his No2, explained:

"We climbed towards the south of the island into broken cloud, that rose to 15,000 or 16,000 feet, and became separated. When I broke out of cloud into a gap, I could see Bradbury on the same course and at the same height about 500 yards on my port side. He had left his radio on 'transmit' instead of bringing back the control to 'receive'. This happened all too often and was not popular. When switched to transmit, the pilot could not receive information from either the ground control or any other pilot in the air. I veered left to join him again in formation (we were still climbing and therefore only at about 150mph) when a Me109 dived down towards his tail, fired a burst and was overtaking so quickly that it had to break immediately away in a steep climb over the Hurricane.

I had yelled like a pantomime audience, 'Behind you, behind you!' but, of course, Bradbury couldn't hear. Me109s would never be wandering about alone. If there were a pair, the immediate question was whether the one I'd seen was No1 or No2, but whichever it was, both had height advantage over us that required instant action. With his transmitter on, Bradbury started talking to himself. 'What's going on?', he said. 'Something's gone wrong with the engine. Where's the airfield?' Whilst he was making a slow, unhurried turn towards Luqa I expected to see two, or even a horde of Me109s, descending on us. He continued his glide and commentary. He hummed a snatch from a tune – 'First thing I'll have when I get down will be a 'Farsons' light ale.' Wheels and flaps came down and he made a forced landing on Luqa still without knowing he'd provided some target practice. We were not privy to what was said to him about those who left their radios on transmit!"

Meanwhile, Thacker, who had also been wounded, managed to bale out into St Paul's Bay, but Watson was killed, as noted in his diary by Flg Off Whittingham:

". . . poor old W [Watson] caught it. Some Ju88s came over, escorted by 109s. The 109s got into a good position and attacked two of our sections out of the sun, as we were positioning to attack the 88s. W was probably killed instantly for he went on his back and dived straight into the sea. B [Bradbury] was hit badly. His machine was ripped to hell by cannon. Amazing enough, however, he got it down and force-landed with his engine u/s. M [he obviously meant Thacker] jumped and landed seven miles out to sea. J.B. [Jock Barber], although being chased by a 109, saw M's falling parachute. He kept around until he could plot his position in the sea. This he did and informed the base by R/T. M was picked up by a speedboat after being in the sea for about an hour."

Only Plt Off Pain (P3731) was able to hit back with any success:

"Once again the loss of a pilot could be laid at the door of the AOC. He was still insisting that the most senior officer led the flight. Watson was a Wimpy pilot who had been press-ganged onto fighters while awaiting a replacement aircraft. He had little knowledge of Hurricanes and none of air fighting. He led us out to sea after four [sic] Ju88s in a long stern chase – always deadly, particularly over Malta – and when I saw we were actually overtaking the 88s, I realised they were acting as decoys. I pulled out to starboard and went through the gate [boosted the engine to maximum]. Watson, Thacker and Bradbury maintained their position and speed. As I banked to port to make a full beam attack on the nearest 88, I sighted the 109s coming down on the other three. I shouted a warning over the R/T and raked my 88 from nose to tail. One 109 closed with Watson who made no effort to evade, despite further calls from me. Thacker and Bradbury broke away and into the attackers. Watson rolled straight over on his back and went straight in [evidently the victim of Oblt Müncheberg]. I got the 109 which got Watson and he crashed into the drink about 200 yards from Watty. I got two more bursts into two other 109s before running out of ammunition and, thank God, targets. I have no idea what happened to the 88.

Thacker, who was the sort of swimmer who needed a Mae West to stay afloat in his bath, battled his burning Hurricane back over the Maltese coast at about 6,000 feet; he then pulled his hood back, rolled her and baled out. I was in company, but not formation. I followed him down. Unfortunately for Thacker the wind was offshore and instead of drifting over the island he went the opposite direction, out to sea. By now I was low on petrol and flew back to Takali after Thacker hit the water. I refuelled and re-armed and went back to keep an eye on Thacker, who was about three miles out in the channel. To my surprise, this man who could not swim a stroke, had covered a quarter of a mile towards Malta, judging by the fluorescine trail."

Flg Off Barber recalled:

"I'd seen Thacker shot down well to the north-east of the island, and was covering his parachute descent. Banjo told me all was clear. However, I continued weaving, force of habit, when I saw this big red spinner in my mirror. I went into a tight turn very quickly and, after a couple of turns, was beginning to get inside the 109 when he pulled up and climbed away from me, going very fast. Although out of range I gave him a long squirt, using plenty of deflection but no visible result, however. I stayed with Thacker until he was picked up by a rescue launch."

According to the rescued pilot, Plt Off Thacker:

"When I was shot down it was my first encounter with the enemy. I don't recall any organised attack. At about 15,000 feet presumably someone called 'Tally-ho!' because I suddenly saw three Ju88s, which were at the same height, slightly to my left, range about 1,000 yards, and heading away from Malta. I pulled the boost over-ride, but to my surprise was unable to close the range. The only other Hurricane of which I was aware at this time was flown by Hamish Hamilton, which was ahead and to my left. This aircraft was firing at the Ju88s from astern. I did not hear any calls warning of the presence of 109s, and very soon after first sighting the Ju88s, I became aware that my aircraft was being hit. I executed a hard right turn, but could not see any other aircraft in my vicinity. The instruments were shattered but the controls and engine were functioning, except the latter was spewing coolant vapour. I head back to Malta, well throttled back and losing height. At about 5,000 feet, when over St Paul's Bay, the engine cut; the vapour and smoke had now increased, so I baled out. Soon after hitting the water I saw a Hurricane above me, which I discovered later was Barber. I made violent splashes to attract his attention; he circled until a rescue launch picked me up some 30 to 45 minutes later.

Contrary to John Pain's statement, I have always been a reasonable swimmer and was convinced I would be able to reach the coast, which I could see. I suffered shrapnel wounds in the buttocks and one arm. I was in hospital and convalescent for about one month. In retrospect, the Luftwaffe's planning and execution of this combat is hard to fault, whereas the least said about our own efforts the better!"

One Ju88, an aircraft from 3(F)/121, returned to Sicily damaged and with a mortally wounded gunner on board, presumably as a result of being attacked by both Plt Offs Pain and Hamilton. Pain was also awarded a probable for the Bf109 he had claimed, but in fact 7/JG26 suffered no loss or serious damage to any aircraft. It would seem that he had seen another of the Hurricanes crash into the sea. Flt Lt MacLachlan noted:

"Poor old Watson was never found. The appearance of the 109s has greatly shaken the morale of the Squadron (and mine in particular). I think the sooner we hack some down the better . . ."

The Messerschmitts were back next day (13 February), MacLachlan leading the Hurricanes of A Flight, which he now commanded, up to 22,000 feet to the south of Comino where four of 7/JG26 were seen approaching:

"This afternoon I saw 109s for myself and am just as scared of them as I always was. I was up-sun of them and they did not see me until we were only about 1,000 yards apart . . . as soon as Jerry saw us, he broke formation and, turning steeply to starboard, they climbed away from us in a shambles. Our poor old Hurrybirds were no match for the 109s . . . for the rest of the patrol, I suffered from acute twitch . . . If someone doesn't shoot one down soon, the Squadron morale will be non-existent."

During a patrol on 14 February, Bf109s were again encountered, Sgt Len Davies' Hurricane (V7771) being slightly damaged before he managed to evade and return to Takali; he was not hurt. A second damaged Hurricane landed with "its port wing looking like a sieve." This was probably Sgt Gus Davies' aircraft, as Sgt Arthur Todd recalled:

"The Italians were using CR42s when I first arrived, until Gus Davies suddenly came down one day with a big hole in his Hurricane and said 'That was no CR42, that was a 109!'. Then Adrian Warburton, the PR boy, flew over and had a look at Catania, and sure enough, they were there. The Germans had arrived. So the trouble then was that every time we were scrambled – and the radar wasn't bad – by the time we got up to any height they were above us and we lost a lot of people that way." [15]

The Ju88s were back on the 15th, 7/LG1 reporting the loss of L1+JR over Malta, presumably shot down by AA fire. Another, from 4/LG1, returned to Sicily badly damaged. Next day brought an early morning low-level attack by a single He111 on Hal Far, where one or two Swordfish sustained damage. This was followed at 0900 by a single Ju88 escorted by an estimated dozen Bf109Fs. A Flight scrambled at 0915, Flt Lt MacLachlan leading in V7731:

> "As A Flight were on the 9 o'clock watch, John [Trumble] decided to have all the bloodthirsty pilots on in the hopes of getting a 109. We arranged that if we were attacked we would break away and form a defensive circle . . ."

About half an hour later, when the Hurricanes were patrolling over Luqa at 20,000 feet, they were suddenly attacked from above and astern by six Bf109s. The flight at once did as planned, the Messerschmitts overshooting them and climbing back to higher altitude. Sgt Bamberger then spotted four more coming down out of the sun – probably four of the original six making their second swoop. He warned MacLachlan, who later recorded:

> "Just as I took my place in the circle I saw four more Messerschmitts coming down out of the sun. I turned back under them, and they all overshot me. I looked round very carefully but could see nothing, so I turned on the tail of the nearest Hun, who was chasing some Hurricanes in front of him. We were all turning gently to port as I cut the corner. I was determined to get him, and must have been concentrating so intently on his movements that, like a fool, I forgot to look in the mirror until it was too late. Suddenly there was a crash in my cockpit – bits and pieces seemed to fly everywhere. Instinctively I went into a steep spiral dive, furiously angry that I had been beaten at my own game.
>
> My left arm was dripping with blood and, when I tried to raise it, only the top part moved, the rest hung limply by my side. Everything happened so quickly that I have no clear recollection of what actually took place. I remember opening my hood, disconnecting my oxygen and R/T connections, and standing up in the cockpit. The next thing I saw was my kite diving away from me, the roar of the engine gradually fading as it plunged earthwards. It was a marvellous feeling to be safely out of it, everything seemed so quiet and peaceful. I could clearly hear the roar of engines above me, and distinctly heard one long burst of cannon fire. I could not see what was happening as I was falling upside down and my legs obscured all view of the aircraft above me. My arm was beginning to hurt pretty badly, so I decided to pull my chute straight away in case I fainted from loss of blood. I reached round for my ripcord but could not find it. For some unknown reason I thought my chute must have been torn off me while I was getting out of my kite, and almost gave up making any further efforts to save myself.
>
> I remember thinking that the whole process of being shot down and being killed seemed very much simpler and less horrible than I had always imagined. There was just going to be one big thud when I hit the deck, and then all would be over. My arm would stop hurting and no more 109s could make dirty passes at me behind my back. I think I must have been gradually going off into a faint when I suddenly thought of mother reading the telegram saying that I had been killed in action. I made one last effort to see if my parachute was still there, and to my amazement and relief found it had not been torn off after all. With another supreme effort I reached round and pulled the ripcord. There was a sickening lurch as my chute opened and my harness tightened round me so that I could hardly breathe. I felt horribly ill and faint. Blood from my arm came streaming back into my face in spite of the fact that I was holding the stump as tightly as I could.
>
> I was able to breathe with the utmost difficulty, and my arm hurt like hell. I could see Malta spread out like a map 15,000 feet below me, and I longed to be down there – just to lie still and die peacefully. I was woken from this stupor by the roar of an engine, and

naturally thought some bloodthirsty Jerry had come to finish me off. I don't think I really minded what happened, though certainly the thought of a few more cannon shells flying past me didn't exactly cheer me up. To my joy, however, I saw that my escort was a Hurricane, piloted, as I later learned, by Eric Taylor. He had quite rightly decided that he could do no good by playing with the Huns at 20,000 feet, so came down to see that none of them got me."

MacLachlan eventually came down in a small field, where he was immediately surrounded by a number of Maltese. Shortly thereafter a doctor arrived and MacLachlan was taken by ambulance to a local advanced dressing station. From there he was conveyed to the Military Hospital at M'tarfa[16]. Meanwhile, the other Hurricanes had all returned to Takali, although Plt Off McAdam's aircraft had been virtually shot to pieces during the combat, and Flg Off Peacock-Edwards landed V7072 with numerous shell and bullet holes, and with the starboard aileron shot away. Neither pilot was hurt. It seems fairly certain that MacLachlan had been shot down by Oblt Müncheberg (White 1), who, at 0945, claimed a Hurricane from which the pilot baled out. In the first pass some seven minutes earlier, Müncheberg had also claimed a Hurricane, as did Uffz Georg Mondry. It seems likely these were the aircraft piloted by McAdam and Peacock-Edwards.

261 Squadron now underwent a number of changes. Sqn Ldr Trumble departed for Crete, where he was to assume command of the RAF aerodrome at Heraklion, his place being taken by newly promoted Sqn Ldr Lambert, while B Flight passed to Flg Off Peacock-Edwards following the death of Flt Lt Watson, and A Flight to Flg Off Whittingham in succession to Flt Lt MacLachlan. Meanwhile, Flt Lt Bradbury was despatched to Cairo for a rest. On 16 February, AHQ Malta recorded that 261 Squadron had 30 pilots available from 43 on its strength. There were 19 Hurricanes to hand, and nine more under repair.

A Bf110D night fighter of the newly arrived 1/NJG3 failed to return from a sortie to Malta on 17 February, a victim of the AA guns; its crew baled out off Cape Passero and were rescued. Few engagements were noted for the Hurricanes for several days, although Sgt Robertson saw three Bf109s overhead on 20 February, but was unable to reach their altitude. Next day a formation of aircraft identified as Do215s (probably Bf110s) were engaged by the Hurricanes, Plt Off Hamish Hamilton claiming one and "the rest of the boys sharing another. One or two of them collected the odd rear-gun bullet, but no one was seriously damaged", noted MacLachlan in his journal. Three days later, however, on 23 February, the Stukas of StG1 returned, the guns putting up a heavy barrage and claiming three destroyed. The Messerschmitts were back on the 24th, four attacking a flight of patrolling Hurricanes over M'tarfa. As they opened fire the Hurricanes broke away, Sgt Bamberger going into a spin as the 109s climbed towards the sun. Sgt Len Davies (V7102) had a lucky escape; having become separated from the others he was shocked to see a Messerschmitt closing on his tail. It fired from about 50 yards range – and missed, allowing Davies to turn out of harm's way.

Sgt Davies was in action again next day. Eight Hurricanes of A Flight led by Flt Lt Whittingham were scrambled after three aircraft reported as Do215s (in fact Bf110s) at 6,000 feet over the St Paul's Bay area. Whittingham noted in his diary:

"Everyone went off hell for leather at them. I saw one straggling about half a mile behind the rest, so left the squadron and attacked it from the stern. I had given him a three-seconds burst when he opened up on me. He was a good shot. His tracers were coming all round me. I broke away sharply to the right after about one and a half seconds of his fire. I did not see what happened to him, but the AA people reported having seen him burst into flames and go into the sea, so that is my second since coming here. H [Hamilton] got another, so did B [Barber]. All the flight fired their guns. We celebrated with a bottle of beer."

In addition to those claimed destroyed by Plt Offs Hamilton and Barber (V7102), another was claimed damaged by the joint efforts of Plt Off Walsh (V7346) and Sgt Davies (V7771), as the latter noted:

"With P/O Walsh I attacked a Do215 from quarter. Gave it a good grilling but did not see the outcome. Was hit in oil sump."

Sgt Robertson (V7116) also claimed one damaged, having chased it to a point ten miles west of Filfla:

"I was Blue 2 and when Blue 1 attacked the rear bandit of the enemy formation, I chased the other two, making a stern attack on one, followed by several deflection bursts. The e/a took violent evasive action and started to climb steeply, and I was unable to hold. I must have put the rear-gunner out of action as all return fire ceased after my third burst. Also, the starboard engine appeared to be on fire, with a thin continuous stream of black smoke coming from it, with occasional big black puffs."

Plt Off Pain (V7670) made a similar claim but correctly identified his victim as a Bf110. The guns also claimed one damaged. The returning pilots reported that nine Bf109s accompanied the raiders but made no attempt to come down "to play". It seems probable that the intruders were two Bf110s of III/ZG26 accompanying a reconnaissance Bf110 of 2(F)/123, since an aircraft flown by Fw Karl Bernhard of the latter unit failed to return from a sortie to Malta; the pilot and his gunner were posted as missing. That afternoon 7/JG26 was again over Malta, Oblt Müncheberg (White 1) claiming a Hurricane shot down over St Paul's Bay at 1545. It seems likely that his victim was Plt Off John Walsh (V7346), who was on patrol with Sgt Davies, as witnessed by a letter Plt Off Pain wrote to his mother:

". . . a Canadian [Walsh] sprang a glycol leak at 27,000 feet and he was forced to bale out. He landed about 300 yards from a destroyer and was picked up with a leg broken in four places, and a broken arm. Presumably he had hit the tailplane. He died in hospital from pneumonia."

Müncheberg had apparently attacked Walsh's Hurricane. Presumably his fatal illness was brought on by severe shock. Airman X's diary provides an account of the aftermath of the action:

"Big raids this morning. We got three bombers down. One of the Hurricanes landed in the sea due to engine trouble not enemy action. Hurricane 7771 comes in with a bullet hole in the sump, needs a new engine. Just had another raid, four 109s flew round the island for 45 minutes. None of our kites fired but one returned with cannon shell holes in the starboard wing."

On the following day (26 February), the Germans and Italians launched one of the biggest attacks on Malta to date – certainly the heaviest raid since that on *Illustrious* on 19 January. It came around 1300, with Luqa as the main target, the attacking force comprising 38 Ju87s of newly arrived II and II/StG1, a dozen Ju88s, ten Dorniers, ten He111s, with 20 to 30 escorting fighters. The latter included Bf109s of 7/JG26 led by Oblt Müncheberg, MC200s of 6°Gruppo CT and a dozen CR42s of 156°Gruppo CT led by Magg Vezio Mezzetti and Cap Luigi Filippi, respectively. Flg Off Taylor led off eight Hurricanes, climbing to 28,000 feet, whereupon many Ju87s were seen below at about 10,000 feet just as the AA barrage opened up. The Hurricanes dived on the Stukas, but the escorting fighters were quickly on their tails; at least two convoys of Ju87, Hurricane, and Bf109, all firing in line astern, were observed.

Plt Off Chubby Eliot made his first claims whilst flying from Malta, a Ju87 shot down in flames and a second of these as probably destroyed. Flg Off Terry Foxton also claimed two, one of which was credited as a probable. Foxton's Hurricane was then attacked by a Messerschmitt and, with its radiator and engine damaged, he carried out an emergency landing. Others were not so fortunate, both Plt Off Philip Kearsey (V7121) and Plt Off Charles Langdon (V7474) being shot down into the sea; neither survived. Flg Off Eric Taylor (V7671) also failed to return, and was last seen chasing a Stuka with a Bf109 on his own tail; his Mae West was later washed ashore with a cannon shell hole in the centre of the chest. It seems probable that Taylor had fallen victim to Oblt Müncheberg (White 1), who claimed a Hurricane at 1306 south of Krendi, and reported:

> ". . . the fighting spirit of the British pilot was fantastic; he tried, although very badly hit, to still attack a Ju88 [*sic*]".

Müncheberg claimed a second Hurricane four minutes later south of the island, Uffz Georg Mondry also claiming one at this time, while Lt Klaus Mietusch (White 2) reported shooting down another at 1317. It seems almost certain that Taylor had been attacking the Ju87 flown by Hptm Helmut Mahlke, Gruppenkommandeur of I/StG3, who later graphically recalled the experience:

> "A tremendous jolt, an ear-splitting crash, and my right wing burst open. My [Stuka] immediately fell away steeply to the right. I had automatically yanked the stick back into my stomach and now punched it hard left. It wasn't enough. The middle of my right wing had been blown completely open by a direct flak hit. The wind resistance was so fierce that I could scarcely hold her, even with full left flap and aileron. To make matters worse, I found myself crabbing towards a large hangar! Desperately, I trimmed her tail-heavy and applied full throttle. By now I was only four or five metres above the surface of the field and still heading for that hangar. The doors were wide open, and as it grew bigger I could see every detail inside, including three aircraft which, until a few moments ago, had presumably been undergoing repair. 'If I go, those three will be going with me', I thought, as I sat helpless, clutching the stick hard into my left side. Slowly the [Stuka] began to respond. Her nose rose above the horizontal and – almost as if she herself was putting her all into one final leap – we just cleared the hangar roof. But our difficulties were not yet over. In front of us was a hill topped by a line of telegraph poles. Not a very large hill, but in our state it might as well have been Mount Everest. Would we be lucky a second time? We scraped between two poles, our undercarriage taking a length of the wire in passing, and descended into a shallow valley leading southwards towards the coast and open water.
>
> Suddenly the voice of my gunner, Fritz Baudisch, sounded in my earphones: 'Hurricane coming up into firing position astern!' I had my hands full just keeping us in the air, and could do nothing except answer as calmly as possible, 'Well, shoot it down then, Fritzchen'. It was a tall order, one machine-gun against eight, even if Fritz's weapon had chosen that moment to jam after just one short burst. 'This is it', I thought, as I hunched down in my seat and watched tiny holes appearing in both wings. The Hurricane overshot on his first pass and curved round for a second. Fritz still hadn't cleared the stoppage. But now, quite out of character, he suddenly launched into an excited running commentary from the rear cockpit: 'Me109!! – a long way astern – turning in behind the Hurricane – still miles away – diving at a hell of a rate! The Hurricane's almost within firing distance – the 109's behind him. Still too far away, though. The 109's opened fire – still full pelt and at extreme range – but he's got him!! Still firing. The Hurricane's definitely been hit. He's on fire! He's going in!!'"[17]

Hptm Mahlke skilfully guided his crippled Stuka back to Comiso, where a creditable landing was achieved. Subsequent inspection of J9+AH revealed no fewer than 184 bullet strikes in its wings in addition to the flak damage. Two more Hurricanes were claimed by CR42 pilots. Plt Off Pain (V7114) returned safely, claiming a Dornier probably destroyed and a Bf109 damaged, while other pilots claimed another Dornier probably destroyed in addition to a Ju87 probably destroyed (the latter apparently awarded to the missing Taylor). AA gunners optimistically reported shooting down five Ju87s with four probables and one damaged. Afterwards, Plt Offs Barber and Pain were among those who went out to look for survivors, the latter flying a Magister, and two German airmen were found clinging onto a lifebuoy off Ghain Tuffieha. They were soon picked up by HSL107 from Kalafrana and proved to be Obfhr Roman Heil and Gfr Heinrich Stamm, the crew of Ju87 J9+JH of 7/StG1. Two Ju87s of 4/StG1 were also shot down, 6G+PR crewed by Fw Johann Braun and Fw Justin Kästl, and 6G+ER piloted by Uffz Heinz Langreder and Gfr Erwin Suckow, while 6 Staffel lost its Kapitän, Oblt Kurt Reumann, and his gunner Uffz August-Wilhelm Schulz, in 6G+GT which was seen to fall to a Hurricane. An aircraft of 5 Staffel returned badly damaged following combat, during which the gunner Uffz Robert Kolland was wounded. Two of the downed Stukas apparently fell on land, one being reported down at Ras Hanzir, and the other crashing near St Bartholomew's Leprosy Hospital. Flt Lt Whittingham, who was not involved in the action, later wrote in his diary:

> "A blitz started shortly before one a.m. About 30 fighters and 90 bombers came over. They consisted of Ju88s, Do215s and Ju87s. The dive-bombers attacked low. The others dropped their bombs from higher up. AA barrage was colossal. We lost three of our fellows. The strain under the uneven odds we are facing is colossal and one has a feeling now of just living from day to day. Now that the risk of death is so much more increased I've been doing a spot of philosophising. My attitude is that somebody has to do the job and if I get bumped off, I have experienced much more than the average bloke."

Many of the bombs intended for Luqa aerodrome missed their target and exploded in Luqa village:

> "The bombs just rained down all over and about the place. The village square hardly has a house standing . . . The Church of St Andrew escaped a direct hit, but bears the scars of battle all over. Some people who remained in their homes had miraculous escapes . . . . There were several soldiers in the square who just managed to reach the cover of an ordinary cellar shelter propped up with wood support. The house they were in a moment before crashed on top of the cellar, but it did not give way to the weight of the masonry. The behaviour of the people . . . was wonderful. One woman ignored her destroyed house but was keen to save her hens. A man displayed the greatest interest in rescuing his daughter's doll, because she would not sleep without it . . ."[18]

Few interceptions took place over the next few days as 261 Squadron licked its wounds. Hurricanes of A Flight encountered four Bf110s over the island on the last day of the month, but no claims resulted since heavy cloud prevented any serious contact. In just four brief engagements with 7/JG26 during the month 261 Squadron had lost five pilots killed (Watson, Walsh, Taylor, Langdon and Kearsey) and three wounded, but despite the increased intensity of operations since the arrival of the Messerschmitts, combat was not continuous and the survivors among the Hurricane pilots did have time to relax, as revealed by Flt Lt Whittingham:

> "I have been given a dog – a mongrel pup called 'Lady', and I have bought a wizard little pony and trap for £70 – a trim grey called 'Lucky'. He is one of the best ponies on the island. It's an excellent thing to have a hobby here. It's such a dangerous sort of life that one can't help thinking about it a bit. So it's a good thing to get one's mind off in one's spare time. P [Pain] and I drove 'Lucky' to Valetta in the morning. An air raid took place when we got there. The people rushing to the shelters upset 'Lucky' a bit. We stopped with him. The AA guns did not worry him much, nor did a bit of shrapnel that whistled down near him. What with continual air raids (seven times a day) and the presence of 109s about the place, it is a logical conclusion that our chances of survival are not very high. But one simply must not think about this; at any rate, I am enjoying myself while it lasts."

Another who had a pet dog was the now departed Flg Off Bradbury, as recalled by Sgt Jim Pickering:

"Bradbury had earlier purchased a dog. Described as a Maltese bulldog, its brindle colouring suggested a Staffordshire bull terrier amongst its ancestors. It remained close to Bradbury and when he was at relaxed readiness in the stand-by bus, it reclined contentedly at his feet. But occasionally it produced a most formidable smell. Words could not adequately describe it, and it aroused deep antagonism amongst others in the bus. Bradbury felt uncomfortable about the matter, and would light his pipe to ameliorate the smell, but there were those who said that his pipe was just as evil smelling. There were snide suggestions about the origin of his tobacco.

On one watch, when all was quiet and peaceful, the dog transgressed and someone shouted 'Gas attack!'. We all rushed to the door of the bus to get into the open air and this sudden burst of activity had a domino effect. The groundcrews thought it was a scramble and went into action stations by their aircraft. The pilots assumed, when the ground staff ran, that a 'scramble' signal had been received and also ran to their aircraft. Bradbury, who had remained in the bus, saw everyone else rushing about and ran to his aircraft. When he started the engine, the dog became excited and jumped into the revolving propeller. Radio instructions halted a take-off. Bradbury was most distressed at the death, and manner of death, of his dog. As so often happens, comedy is followed by tragedy. He didn't replace his loss."

CHAPTER V

MESSERSCHMITTS SUPREME

March – May 1941

Despite the rapidly deteriorating availability of Hurricanes, the few remaining Fulmars were considered too vulnerable to fighter attack and unsuitable as interceptors, and the policy was for them to remain around the fringes of a raid and try to pick off stragglers. On 2 March however, they were called upon to play a more central part in the defence, as Lt(O) Vincent-Jones relates:

> "The day started auspiciously when a He111 suddenly appeared out of the dawn mist with undercarriage down and started to make an approach to the main runway, presumably mistaking Hal Far for its own base in Sicily. The aircraft was about to touch down when the pilot found himself in unfamiliar surroundings and opened his throttle in time for his wheels to clear the cliff edge at the end of the runway. He had achieved total surprise and there was complete silence until the first Bofors opened up when he was out to sea and on his way back to the mainland.
>
> At about 1100 a smallish raid was detected leaving Sicily, on course for Malta. For some good reason no Hurricanes were available and orders were telephoned through for the Fulmars to get airborne and gain altitude over Hal Far. Bill Barnes took off with two others, one I believe was Orr, and had climbed to about 2,000 feet after making contact with the Malta tower who told them the raid was coming in low and very fast. Most of us were standing by the control tower when the fortress guns opened up to the northward, and coming through the flak we saw a series of black dots approaching directly towards us and, as they closed, we recognised them as yellow-nose Me109s. The Fulmars above us continued to circle totally oblivious, and we on the ground were powerless to warn them. We watched in horror as the enemy opened fire and chunks of metal could be seen falling off the luckless victim's wings and fuselage. The Me109s swept away out to sea and made no attempt to turn for a further attack. When we looked upwards again we were amazed to see all three Fulmars still flying but firing emergency landing signals. By some miracle all three aircraft landed safely and by an even greater miracle none of the three pilots was wounded. It had seemed like certain death from the beginning of this hideous drama we had just witnessed.
>
> It was the end of daylight flying over Malta for the Fulmars. Barnes[1] was laughing as he climbed out of the cockpit and pointed to a huge hole in one wingroot made by a cannon shell and another through the opposite wing. The other two aircraft had been damaged but got off with bullet holes only."[2]

At least one Hurricane got into the air, Sgt Jock Norwell (P2653) noting that he was also attacked by a Messerschmitt and his aircraft damaged. Oblt Müncheberg and Lt Hans Johannsen each claimed a Hurricane shot down at 1045, both in the same location – apparently the Fulmars, although one may have been responsible for the damage to Norwell's Hurricane.

The next sizeable raid occurred on 5 March, and on this occasion 7/JG26 was reinforced with a number of Bf109Es from I/JG27, which had arrived in Sicily en route to Libya. While on the island, the Gruppe undertook one or two flights over Malta in company with the resident Messerschmitt unit. During the afternoon an estimated 60 bombers approached the island, ten Hurricanes led by Flt Lt Whittingham being scrambled to intercept, as he later recorded:

"A flap on about 5 o'clock. I was up and saw them being bombed below. I positioned myself to run down in a right-hand dive in case of being chased by 109s. In doing so, I blacked out for a bit, but came out at about 1,200 feet. I soon recovered and attacked one of the many enemy aircraft in front of and below me. My first shot was at a Ju87 and next at a Ju88. They both fired back at me. I then spiralled to ground level for safety and to get away from any 109s that might by this time have been positioning themselves against me. Making for base, I saw about five Ju88s going out to sea. I hadn't much ammunition but decided to climb in their direction. This I did and pointed my nose at one and gave him a burst. I may have hit him but he fairly let me have it from his underneath guns. I twisted and was making for land when I saw a machine burst into gigantic flames about 100 yards from me. It was a Messerschmitt 110 which had been hit by ack-ack. It was a stroke of luck for myself, as I learned afterwards that he was firing at me just previous to being hit. I hadn't seen him. In the engagement the Squadron got seven confirmed. Poor old M [Sgt Charles McDougal] was killed. A 109 got him just after he had bagged an 87.''

Two Hurricanes were claimed by the Messerschmitt pilots of 7/JG26, the first by Oblt Müncheberg and the second two minutes later by Uffz Melchoir Kestler, although the latter's was not confirmed. It would seem that they both fired at Sgt McDougal's aircraft (V7102). Whilst the Hurricanes were thus engaged, a pair of Messerschmitts made a strafing attack on St Paul's Bay where a Sunderland and the Loire 130 were slightly damaged at their moorings. The Hurricane pilots achieved a number of successes, two victories being claimed by Sgt Jock Robertson (V7116):

"I was Pink 1 and dived with Squadron to attack first batch of dive-bombers over Hal Far. I chased a Ju88 and put three bursts into it from astern, setting its starboard engine on fire. I followed it until it finally ditched into the sea off Filfla. There appeared to be three persons in the water afterwards. I was then attacked by about 12 109s but took evasive action and got a good burst into one as he overshot. I last saw him diving in the direction of Filfla with clouds of white and black smoke coming from him, but could not see if he crashed as I was being attacked by another of the bandit fighter formation."

The Ju88 was L1+CM of 4/LG1 flown by Lt Reinhard Krause; he and his crew were posted missing. Sgt Robertson[3] was given credit for shooting down the Bf109 when AA personnel reported seeing a Messerschmitt (probably Sgt McDougal's Hurricane) crashing into the sea. It would seem that Robertson's action was also witnessed by Flt Lt MacLachlan, who was on a hospital outing to Valetta:

"As we emerged at the top of Merchant Street we heard the roar of engines and saw a 109 dive down and attack a Hurricane at about 15,000 feet over Grand Harbour. Just as the attacking Messerschmitt opened fire, the Hurricane pulled up into a vertical climb and I saw, for the first time, another 109 flying just above the Hurricane. The attacking Messerschmitt was going far too fast to follow the Hurricane, and apparently missed it altogether. Our kite however opened fire on the second 109 while still in a vertical climb, then keeping its sights on, it half-rolled out onto the tail of the Messerschmitt, firing all the time. The whole manoeuvre was marvellous to watch – certainly some of the best flying I have seen in this squadron. Unfortunately, Jerry was too well armoured to fall victim to what must have been a rather inaccurate attack."

Meanwhile, Sgt Harry Ayre's Hurricane (V7670) had been hit within ten minutes of becoming airborne – probably by Lt Willi Kothmann of I/JG27 – and he force-landed at Takali, but was soon up again in a different aircraft (P3731), meeting a Ju88 which he claimed shot down, probably the same 4/LG1 aircraft as that attacked by Sgt Robertson since only one Ju88 was lost. One report suggested that three Hurricanes had "shot the bomber to pieces" and that it had crashed in the direction of Marsa Scirocco Bay. Bf110Es from Stab/StG1 accompanied the Gruppe's Stukas, and two of these were engaged by Plt Off John Pain (P2645), although he misidentified them as Do215s:

> "I saw a Do215 at about 1,500 feet over 'Zambuk' [the codename for St Paul's Bay]. I climbed to attack below the beam and fired two two-second bursts which appeared to hit about halfway down the fuselage. I broke away and was patrolling when I attacked a Do215, which was already being attacked by P/O Rippon. I fired two three-second bursts from below and astern quarter. These did not have much effect. I broke away as a third Hurricane [Sgt Ayre] attacked, and blacked out completely."

The first Bf110 attacked by Pain was then hit by Bofors fire and was seen to explode in mid-air. Pain was also awarded a share of the second together with Plt Off Tony Rippon and Sgt Ayre; their victim was believed to have been DB+ND flown by the Geschwader Adjutant, Hptm Erich Müller, and Lt Hans Hörschgen, both of whom were posted missing. Rippon also reported shooting down a Ju87, while another was credited to the missing Sgt McDougal. Other pilots returned with claims for three more Ju87s damaged, while the AA gunners had a field day and reported shooting down nine aircraft including the Bf110 and damaging further more. Two Ju87s failed to return, J9+CH of 7/StG1 crewed by Uffz Wilhelm Singer and Obgfr Paul Stapf, crashing into the sea off Hal Far, reportedly the victim of fighter attack, while 6G+KR of 4 Staffel flown by Fw Georg Latzelberger and Uffz Hasslinger also crashed, killing the crew. A third Ju87, from II Gruppe, returned with a wounded gunner, Uffz Georg Dein. One of the Messerschmitts (KB+NC) crashed just north of Takali, and the crew, Oblt Rudolf Günther (the Staffelkapitän) and Uffz Hans Dittmayer, were both killed. Flt Lt MacLachlan was one of those who rushed to the scene of the crash:

> "We found the remains still burning in a field just across the road from the NW corner of the aerodrome. The Jerries had come down to machine-gun Takali, and had been attacked by a Hurricane and Bofors fire at the same time. It caught fire at 500 feet and went in at about 45°. The majority of the machine, including three [sic] horribly burnt and mutilated bodies, were smouldering in the middle of a small clover field. Both engines, and some of the heavier debris however, had been flung over the road into a field on the other side. As usual on such occasions, the air was sickly with the stink of burning flesh, and that peculiar smell that all German aircraft seem to have. I took off the number plate of one of the engines as a souvenir."

Flg Off Gerald Bellamy added:

> "The 110 was scattered over a wide area – we all went out to view the wreck. At luncheon, Bradbury's alsation dog was found to have retrieved a boot of a German airman and was chewing it under the table. Unfortunately, it still contained the foot!"

Hal Far had been on the receiving end of the attack, where two Swordfish, a Seal and a Gladiator were destroyed, and a hangar damaged. 261 Squadron received some welcome reinforcements next day when five Hurricanes flew in from Egypt, led by two Wellingtons, which carried two additional fighter pilots as passengers[4]. Most of these new arrivals had reached the area having ferried the Hurricanes across Central Africa from Takoradi on the west coast, to where they had been delivered by the carrier HMS *Furious* earlier in the year. Since then the pilots had been languishing in the Pilots' Pool at Ismailia. For some the stay was to be very brief. Next morning (7 March), several Hurricanes were up to cover the return of a reconnaissance Maryland and one of these – P2645 flown by Sgt Jessop on his first local flight – was shot down by Obfw Karl Kühdorf of 7/JG26, the wounded pilot baling out into the sea from where he was later rescued. At the same time the Maryland was attacked by Lt Hans Johannsen, mistaking it for a Blenheim. Wg Cdr Carter Jonas was watching the action:

". . . just as the Maryland crossed the coast preparatory to landing at Luqa, it was set upon by six Messerschmitts. In spite of the fact that one brave Hurricane came to the rescue [Sgt Jessop], the Maryland was soon on fire in one engine, and the rear-gunner killed by a cannon shell in the chest. The navigator, in spite of being wedged within the narrow confines of the glass nose, managed to scramble out and descended safely by parachute. And at barely 250 feet (after holding the aircraft steady for the navigator to get out), the pilot himself went head first over the side. But to bale out at 250 feet was tempting fate too much – and although the parachute had just time to spring out of its canvas cover before the pilot hit the ground, no time remained for the canopy to open and check his fall."

The pilot was found alive, but dying from multiple injuries, while the flaming Maryland crashed a mile or so north of Dingli. Another outstandingly gallant pilot achieved a remarkable feat at this time. Just 15 days after having his arm amputated, Flt Lt MacLachlan was at the controls of Takali's Magister:

"Chubby [Eliot] did a circuit and bump first, then I did one during which I shot up M'tarfa Hospital, flying past M3 [Ward M3] with my wingtip not more than ten feet from the windows. It shook the sisters, but not nearly as much as it shook me! After I had done two or three satisfactory landings Chubby got out, and I did about 20 minutes solo flying, during which I went and had a look at the field where I had landed by parachute. I can't describe the marvellous feeling of satisfaction that I got from flying again. During my first few days in hospital I went through untold mental agony, fearing that I should never be able to go back to the old game. Now I can cope I'll fight heaven and earth to get back on fighters again. My one ambition now is to get a 109 and, God willing, I'll do it."

Within a few days he had logged five hours solo on the Magister and had begun pestering Sqn Ldr Lambert to let him fly a Hurricane, but when Wg Cdr O'Sullivan, the Station CO, got to hear he forbade him to do so, although he did allow MacLachlan to continue flying the Magister.

With few Luftwaffe bombers remaining in Sicily, raids were desultory and mainly only of nuisance value during most of the remainder of March, the main torment for the defenders being the omnipresent Bf109Es of 7/JG26, of which Sgt Len Davies noted:

"Plots of large formations appearing then fading. Me109 fighters on patrol ready for the bloke who wasn't looking! Few interceptions these days but lots of twitch. No major engagements, but an occasional flash of courage on the part of the Hun. Dive and zoom tactics."

During 9 March numerous single aircraft appeared to strafe Takali where a Hurricane was burnt out and two others slightly damaged when attacked by a single Ju88 escorted by four Bf110s. One of the Messerschmitts flew into a 450 feet high ridge west of Nadur on Gozo, the pilot possibly having misjudged his height, and both crewmen were killed. Airman X of 261 Squadron at Takali wrote:

". . . four Me110s came across our drome and machine-gunned the Hurricanes and runway crews. They set one kite on fire and it burnt out, bullets flying in all directions. None of our personnel was hurt but as the siren hadn't sounded it rather shook everybody up."

This was possibly the occasion recalled by Cpl John Alton, when he wrote:

". . . the groundcrew used an old bus as a shelter whilst awaiting a fighter scramble. One airman, who was entering the bus, remarked that a couple of Hampdens were coming in from St Paul's Bay. Within seconds the roar of aircraft coupled with cannon-fire demonstrated that the Hampdens were in fact Me110s. They departed as rapidly as they arrived, leaving one Hurricane completely burnt out. The groundcrew bus was only about ten yards from the aircraft, and just a slight deflection of aim by the Luftwaffe pilot would have wiped out half the groundcrew at Takali. The few refuelling vehicles were soon damaged or burnt out, and a locally developed refueller was introduced. This was an old double-decker bus. A series of 50-gallon steel drums, suitably interconnected, were mounted on the upper deck. This allowed fuel to pass under gravity to the aircraft. Unfortunately, the experiment was short lived – and must have been a nightmare for the drivers."

During the afternoon a single reconnaissance Ju88 was intercepted by a pair of patrolling Hurricanes flown by Plt Off Tony Rippon and Sgt Jim Pickering (V7297) the latter noting:

"Rear-gunner killed by P/O Rippon . . . I pulled up underneath the enemy aircraft and gave him two bursts . . . the e/a was last seen at sea level, eight miles away, heading towards Sicily with some speed but apparently little concern."

Pickering's own aircraft was hit twice in the starboard wing by return fire, but he was able to return to Takali and make a safe landing. The Bf109Es were back next day, again strafing the flying boat anchorage at St Paul's Bay, where two Sunderlands were hit. One, which had been damaged during a previous attack, ultimately sank after efforts were made to tow it ashore. With the onset of darkness at least one Hurricane was scrambled when raiders approached, Plt Off Rippon reported shooting down a Do215 into the sea. This was possibly a Bf110C night fighter of 1/NJG3 (L1+BH) which failed to return from an intruder flight to Malta, Oblt Horst von Weegmann and his gunner, Uffz Wilhelm Banser, being posted missing. This was a rare night success, Airman X of 261 Squadron recording: "One of our Hurricanes went up at 2200 and shot down a Hun which was in the searchlights. We could see his tracers going right into the Jerry kite."

Malta was spared from any major attacks over the next few days, and few engagements were recorded. Messerschmitts from 7/JG26 caught a transit Wellington on the morning of the 15th as it approached Malta, Oblt Müncheberg shooting it down into the sea. The next day Obfw Ernst Laube and Uffz Leibing jointly claimed a Hurricane shot down, although this was not confirmed. No Hurricanes were actually lost on this occasion, and the only recorded action being when four Hurricanes led by Plt Off Jock Barber (V7797) encountered four Bf110s head-on, presumably from III/ZG26:

"We were flying in line-astern, dodging in and out of the clouds when we came head-on with four Messerschmitt 110s also flying in line-astern. I did two head-on attacks but nothing conclusive. I felt a hit from probably the rear-gunner after the second attack and the control column developed a six-inch play in the elevator control. This happened south of the island at about 1,000 feet. However, I managed to get back and land all right. A bullet had entered the radiator flap and had very nearly severed both elevator cables."

In this brief action the ever-aggressive Sgt Jock Roberston (V7370) claimed one of the Messerschmitts damaged.

On 18 March, a further reinforcement flight of six Hurricanes of 274 Squadron arrived from Benina in Libya, led by Flg Off Imshi Mason DFC, at the time the leading ace of the Middle East theatre with at least 14 victories to his credit. A seventh Hurricane crashed en route at El Abqar, the slightly burned pilot (Plt Off Tom Garland) and another pilot travelling aboard an accompanying Wellington[5]. One of the new arrivals, Flg Off Charles Laubscher, a South African from the Transvaal, recalled:

"My feelings were mixed at this news [of the move to Malta]. On the one hand there was at last the opportunity of some concentrated action and, with Imshi leading us, one could feel reasonably confident. On the other hand there was the undoubted fact we would be on the receiving end. The *Illustrious* had been subjected to vicious bombing only a short time previously, and the defending fighters had been battered by swarms of Me109s and Macchis. There was one compensating factor, however. We were to fly across, which suited me, as I had a morbid fear of being torpedoed at sea. Long-range tanks were fitted and tested, guns were checked and the Hurricanes generally prepared for the flight from Benina (near Benghazi) to Malta. We set off from Amriyah on 13 March and spent the night with 73 Squadron, as El Adem was unsafe due to the unfriendly attention it was receiving from enemy dive-bombers. Our escorting Wellington was delayed due to phenomenal sandstorms in the Delta area, and it was only on 18 March that it arrived and we set off for Benina to refuel before the sea leg to Malta. Garland crashed on landing, and journeyed to Hal Far as a passenger aboard the Wimpey. It was a pity that he was not left with his aircraft, as he was put on standby as soon as we arrived at Takali, and killed on his first operation from Malta . . ."

Shortly before their arrival, Malta's Hurricanes had been scrambled when enemy activity was reported to the north of the island, where a gaggle of CR42s was sighted, probably aircraft of 23°Gruppo CT which had just returned to Sicily from Libya. Plt Off John Pain (P3731) gained two successes in the clash:

"This was a brawl with some 15 CR42s in which the entire flight got mixed up some miles out to sea at about 18,000 feet between St Paul's Bay and Sliema. This was the usual madhouse performance the Italians always seemed to put on – a real World War I-style dogfight. I got my first in the sea close off Sliema and the second was on the way out, some miles further out, and he went in without a top wing. The last one was not confirmed but Whittingham, I think, confirmed the first."

No other claims by the Hurricanes are known, but all returned safely. Pain, with experience of the Battle of Britain, added, somewhat sarcastically:

"It was quite early in the piece that we became disgusted with the manner in which our claims were treated and, more often than not, many of us would not put in combat reports. Spy – F/Lt Anderson – had one hell of a job getting something together to pass to HQ. Even confirmation by other pilots was not enough for HQ and we felt we had to lob the bastards into Dobbie's or Maynard's front garden before we could get a confirmation.

The majority of combats – about 95 per cent – were against superior odds ranging as high as 20-30 to one. There was not time to do much but squirt, break, and squirt again at something else. The main objective being to break through the fighter escort and disperse the bombers. If you buggered about trying to see what happened to your target you bought it very quickly. This is what happened to most of the sprogs from England. Often one took off with a new No2, returned without him and didn't even know his name. It became very depressing."

There followed a brief lull before the Hurricanes were again called into action, an action which proved to be disastrous for 261 Squadron – and for three of the new arrivals in particular. The first engagement of 22 March was more or less routine, four Hurricanes being scrambled at 0830 on the approach of a reconnaissance aircraft, which was spotted flying at 21,000 feet. Sgt Jock Robertson (V7430) recalled:

"Jim Pickering was Red 1 and I was Red 2 . . . in company with Red 1 and Green Section when I saw a Ju88 engaged by AA about 1,000 feet above us. He saw me at this height and turned in a circle onto my tail. I pulled round inside his tail and he dived away towards Sicily. I gave one deflection burst from port beam at about 350 yards and one careful stern burst from the same distance, but could not keep pace with his shallow dive."

It is unclear whether this aircraft was in fact a He111 of 5/KG26, which returned to its base having been damaged while flying over Valetta; nonetheless, the pilot of the Heinkel, Hptm Teske (the Staffelkapitän), was wounded, as was a member of his crew, Obfw Hans Hoffmann. Ten more Ju88s with an escort of a dozen Bf109Es were reported approaching Grand Harbour during the afternoon, eight Hurricanes being scrambled in two flights of four led by Flg Offs Chubby Eliot and Johnny Southwell. Plt Off Doug Whitney (V7797), in the first flight, claimed a Messerschmitt which had just shot down a Hurricane:

"Chubby Eliot and self had a bit of a dogfight for a while, trying to get on each other's tail as we were not certain the other was not a 109 until we saw the roundels. It was in this fight that they [the 109s] bagged five of our eight. I certainly recall Garland being shot down with Southwell."

Five Hurricanes had indeed gone down, one of which was last seen being chased out to sea by a Messerschmitt. In addition to Plt Off Tom Garland (V7493) and Flg Off Johnny Southwell (V7799), Plt Off Dennis Knight (V7358) of the 274 Squadron detachment was also lost, as were Flg Off Foxton (P2653) and Sgt Dick Spyer (V7672). Plt Off Jock Barber was not flying on this occasion and saw what happened to Foxton:

"I was swimming when a battle started overhead. Suddenly a Hurricane came down in a screaming dive and splashed into the sea. This turned out to be P2653, the aircraft I had ferried to Malta in June of the previous year. Terry Foxton was killed."

It was a sad and disillusioning blow for 261 Squadron, as Plt Off John Pain noted:

"This was the one day when we thought we had the edge. It was the first time we had managed to get eight aircraft into the air in one formation in the two months I had been on the island. Of the eight pilots only three returned. Hamish Hamilton and I went on search for survivors but found nothing except marks of crashed aircraft."

None of the Messerchmitts were lost in this one-sided action in which claims for seven Hurricanes were submitted, three by Uffz Karl-Heinz Ehlen alone (his first three victories); two more were claimed by Oblt Klaus Mietusch (his 4th and 5th), another by Uffz Melchior Kestler while Obfw Karl Kühdorf was awarded a probable.

261 Squadron was somewhat vindicated the next day (23 March) when Ju87s were reintroduced to the battle. Possibly anticipating that the fighter defences had been crippled by the previous day's attrition, the Axis air forces appeared in force as a convoy reached the island. Just before 1500 a formation of Ju87s of III/StG1 departed their base in Sicily escorted by 15 MC200s of 6°Gruppo CT led by Magg Vezio Mezzetti. As they approached the island some 30 minutes later, 14 Hurricanes were scrambled and a savage mêlée developed as the Stukas targeted the ships. Watching the battle from the window of his house at Spinola, Maj Francis Gerard recorded:

"The convoy was still coming in. Even as I watched, a battered old tanker – her bow plates twisted, part of her superstructure missing, to show the punishment she had already taken – was rounding Ricasoli Point into the harbour. She'd been hit and hit hard, but somehow, through the grace of God and sheer guts of her crew, she had made it. A sudden, snarling roar in the sky and nine Hurricanes swept overhead in the direction of Pawla. Suddenly the heavy battery at Spinola, near where I live, opened up. Weaving about like mosquitoes above the bombers we could see the enemy fighter escort. More and more guns were joining in the ever-growing chorus. One of the Ju87s suddenly lurched out of formation and dropped, appeared to recover for a moment and hover for an instant. The next moment a vivid orange glow appeared in the fuselage. The Stuka raced towards the ground, writing a terrible sign in the sky. Two small white objects appeared suddenly in the smoke in its wake. The crew had baled out. Yet more Stukas came on, bent upon the destruction of the gallant ships whose precious cargoes spelt life and continued resistance to Malta.

The four of us stared at the bomber in the lead. The dive-bomber was coming straight in our direction. His target, as the bomb falls, was only 200 yards away. A Ju87 coming down almost to roof level, and not 50 yards from where we stood bunched in my window, screamed past. We saw the bombs release and started on their downward plunge. There was no doubting their objective. It was the battered old tanker still steaming into Grand Harbour. We watched, scarcely breathing. Came the thunder of the explosions and the tanker disappeared from sight in a solid sheet of water – it seemed an age before she re-appeared beyond the bomb splashes, untouched, unbeaten, her every gun spitting a vicious defiance at her attackers. The Stuka which had attacked the tanker was pulling out of its dive over Rinella. It seemed as though it must strike one of the great wireless masts which stabbed the sky. It was going out low, banking towards the north where lay Sicily and the safety which it was never to know. Out of the sun, perfectly positioned by the Controller, came a small black speck. It was a Hurricane. It was followed by others. We could hear the first squirt from the machine-guns. The Stuka's right wing fell away from it. The machine turned and dropped. We roared our approval. The bomber went into the sea somewhere off Ricasoli. Other Ju87s were pulling away from their dives, their bombs going harmlessly into the water or crashing onto the tortured rocks. As they turned the Hurricanes pounced on them. One caught fire and went down like a flaming torch."[6]

Sqn Ldr Lambert, who was leading the Hurricanes, ordered a line-astern attack on the Stukas and personally shot down the first aircraft he encountered. Flt Lt Peacock-Edwards (V7115) also claimed one destroyed and another damaged, and later commented: "Very good sport. The Ju87s were picked off like flies."

Single victories were also claimed by Sgt Harry Ayre (V7430) and Plt Off Doug Whitney (N2673). Another was claimed by Sgt Reg Hyde (V7370):

"Attacked Ju87 from astern just off the coast. No fire from rear-gun after first burst of fire and aircraft lost speed. Long burst at 50 yards range. Aircraft started shedding bits and pieces and started to rock very violently from side to side, apparently stalling and dropping. I was then attacked from beam by another Ju87 which I turned on and gave very short burst from beam. This one not claimed, result not observed."

Two more were credited to Plt Off Tony Rippon, and another brace was claimed by Sgt Jock Roberston (V7495) to bring his total to ten:

"Slipped into line astern about fifth and followed into the attack, which owed its success to the excellent leadership of Blue 1 [the CO]. I saw S/Ldr Lambert attack a Ju87 from astern and break away – as he broke off, the tail of the e/a fell away and it crashed into the sea. I then attacked another Ju87 from astern, setting it on fire under the starboard wingroot and saw it crash into the sea (Blue 1 also fired at this machine after I broke away). I was then attacked by another Ju87 from ahead and got a bullet in my port main petrol tank. I followed the e/a around in a very steep turn and finally shot it down into the sea. Next, I found that my aircraft was burning fiercely so I climbed to 700 feet over the sea to a position about a mile south of Rabat and baled out, landing in a field midway between Zebbug and Luqa aerodrome with a bruised knee. Smoked three-quarters of a Flag [cigarette] whilst coming down by parachute."

Robertson's two victories brought total Hurricane claims to nine. The guns claimed a further four and one damaged. During the raid bombs had fallen on Takali as Flg Off Bellamy recalled:

"Charles [Laubscher] and I were on standby and for some reason did not hear the scramble. Ju87s were dive-bombing the aerodrome. Charles dashed past my aircraft – I followed in haste but was too far from the slit trench to make it. I heard/saw a large bomb leave a Ju87 and was certain that it was coming straight at me. I threw myself flat and heard a 'whompf' and felt a mild warm blast of air. I was completely unharmed! Apparently I was on the edge of the crater and the main blast had gone over me. Had I been a few feet nearer the bomb I should have been blown to pieces – had I been a few feet further away I should have been cut to pieces by shrapnel. The only effect on me however, was a slight deafness for a few hours!"

Wg Cdr Carter Jonas, who had witnessed the attack from the ground at Luqa, provided a graphic description of the dramatic series of events:

> ". . . and then we saw them: vic following vic of small grey forms, 15,000 feet, 16,000 feet, perhaps even higher. The guns were firing now . . . little grey puffs miraculously appearing around the bombers, above, below, behind, before, rapidly increasing in size as the wind caught them. Still they came on . . . the leaders were beginning to dive now. Sticks against the dashboards, diving brakes on, down, down, down . . . the more reckless pilots dived down through the barrage, but those with more vivid imaginations pulled out of their dives several hundred feet above the shellbursts. But the ground defences were already hitting . . . a Ju87 disintegrated in front of us from a direct hit, while two others failed to pull out of their dives, disappearing vertically into the sea off the harbour entrance."

As Carter Jonas and his colleagues watched, fascinated by the spectacle, the Stukas began releasing their bombs:

> "Two eyes were not enough. There was so much to see. Quite clearly the bombs could be seen leaving the aircraft; sometimes one, sometimes two, sometimes even a salvo of four – small grey forms. Almost immediately, as they disappeared behind the buildings of Valetta, we saw the flash followed by the crump of bursting, and the black clouds of smoke rising vertically into the still air. Clustered in the doorway of the stone hut, we had forgotten our own fighters. Now was the time to attack the bombers, as they pulled out of their dives, snaking low over the water, slow and cumbersome. Then they came, diving out of the sun to our right, each picking up a Ju87. Now they were firing; short, rattling bursts. The rear-gunner in the Ju87 just in front of us was also firing. One watched the tracer and wondered if bullets ever struck each other in the air.
>
> All our fighters were coming in now – the noise was tremendous – bombs, guns and engines mingled in discordant sound. Out to sea a Ju87 zig-zagged at 500 feet, followed by a relentless Hurricane. Suddenly, the Junkers belched a long tongue of red flame, straightened out for a moment and then spun down into the water. At the same time a second Junkers glided past us, its airscrew slowly turning. It disappeared behind the rocky spur way to our left, to crash out of sight in some tiny stone-walled field. For a few minutes we slipped into the hut. The shrapnel and spent machine-gun bullets splattered down among the cactus like rain. The strange medley of sounds continued outside – inviting and too exciting to miss. We clustered in the narrow doorway, resting our useless hands upon our heads as substitutes for steel helmets. There we watched the rout of the dive-bombers, but the shrapnel pattered down again, and we drew back into the doorway. But we soon emerged again, for curiosity overcame caution. A black pall of smoke hung over Valetta. The raid was over. How many bombers had been brought down? How many fighters had we lost? What damage had been done? We did not know the answers."

Actual German losses appear to have been much lighter than those claimed, with four Ju87s failing to return: J9+JK (Oblt Walter Preis/Uffz Paul Hostmann) and J9+BH (Lt Leopold Jarosch/Gfr Josef Jarnucak) of Gruppenstab were both reported shot down by fighters, while J9+YL (Stfw Hans Ries/Uffz Walter Philipp) of 9 Staffel allegedly fell to AA fire, and an aircraft of 8 Staffel flown by Uffz Erich Kaubitzch ditched within ten kilometres of the Sicilian coast. The escorting Macchi pilots claimed four Hurricanes, one apiece being credited to Magg Mezzetti, M.llo Vittorino Daffara and Serg Magg Stabile, with the fourth being awarded to all the pilots jointly; however Robertson's Hurricane was the only casualty on this occasion, and that evidently the victim of a Ju87.

Macchis of 6°Gruppo CT were back over the island on the 24th, with seven aircraft escorting He111s of II/KG26. Because the attack was a high level raid the British identified all the raiders as Italian, causing Flt Lt Whittingham to note in his journal:

"Another high-level bombing attack took place just before dusk. We had 17 Hurricanes operating but did not make contact. Little damage was done. The bombers are believed to have been Italian. Let it be hoped they were. They are easier meat . . . Squadron Leader Lambert should go down in history for the calm courage and complete lack of side that he displays. He is a complete inspiration to every member of the Squadron. This, despite the fact that he has neither the liking nor the inclination to be a fighter pilot."

Again, no fighter interceptions could be made on the 25th, but AA was able to claim a Ju88 probable and two damaged during the main raid of the day. The next two days were relatively quiet for the defenders, Messerschmitts again appearing over Malta on the afternoon of the 28th, Oblt Müncheberg shooting down the Hurricane (V7430) flown by Sgt Reg Goode of the 274 Squadron detachment, who was severely wounded with shrapnel in his back and neck but nonetheless managed to crash-land his aircraft near Ghain Tuffieha. Meanwhile, Sgt Jock Livingston forced-landed his damaged aircraft (V7297) near Luqa, having been attacked by Oblt Klaus Mietusch. The Messerschmitts departed as quickly as they had appeared and no interceptions by the remaining Hurricanes were made. Two days later (30 March), Bf110s of III/ZG26 carried out a surprise raid on Takali, as noted in Plt Off John Pain's journal:

"First 110s bombed dispersal and lobbed three unexploded bombs between parked aircraft. Stones from one bomb damaged one Hurricane. Flg Off Bellamy, Flt Lt Peacock-Edwards and myself, all on tiptoe, moved the three Hurricanes to safety. Later, the bomb disposal squad found that all three bombs were duds!"

Despite such raids, AHQ was still able to record next day that 261 Squadron had 34 Hurricane on strength.

April 1941

Early in April *Ark Royal* again headed towards Malta with a dozen new Hurricane IIAs which had been delivered to Gibraltar by *Argus*. The Hurricanes were launched on the morning of 3 April, led by two Skuas for navigation purposes. One flight was led by Flt Lt P.W.O. Mould DFC, who had eight victories to his credit; the other by Flg Off I.B. Westmacott (in Z3032) with four victories including two shared[7]. When they reached the area of Kerkenah Island the Hurricanes were met by two Sunderlands and a Maryland and led to Malta. The latter almost fell victim to two Hurricanes flown by Sgts Len Davies and Tom Quinn, who mistook it for a Ju88 but spotted the markings just in time. Flg Off Innes Westmacott recorded in his diary:

"Was called at 0400 and got out of bed with great effort . . . We eventually took off at 0620 and everything went according to plan. The only snag was that [Plt Off] Auger made a bad take-off and punctured one of his auxiliary tanks and broke off his tailwheel. He was naturally scared stiff of using up all his remaining petrol and making a bad landing. However, all was well. He landed at the first aerodrome he saw . . . Most unfortunately, one of our sergeant pilots crashed on landing. He came in too fast and had to swing to avoid something at the end of his run – the undercarriage collapsed. It really is sickening to have an aeroplane, which is worth its weight in gold out here, broken through damned bad handling."

Operation 'Winch' – as this delivery was codenamed – was a most welcome reinforcement, arriving at a time when Axis operations had fallen off pending the German invasion of Yugoslavia and Greece. Soon after his arrival at Malta, Westmacott confided his first impressions to his diary:

"The main trouble here is transport. The bus service is not very convenient and there is a curfew at 2100, not that it worries us much! Only two private cars are allowed per squadron and motor bikes are scarce and expensive. From observations with one or two people I find that some of them are very scared of the 109s and morale could be better. I hope we shall be able to change all that. (4 April) Woke up still very sleepy after a bad night. Saw the CO who told me I would get another stripe shortly, which is cheering. Read all the orders and went on a recco flight to view the island. Shall be on operations tomorrow. Marshall, Kennett and I went into Valetta in the afternoon and ordered our kits. Then I went into the Union Club where I ran into Whittingham and Gray who were all set for a party, so I joined them having lost the others. Finally ended up in the Osborne very late and stayed the night there. (5 April) Had a bit of a thick head but felt better after breakfast. Went back to Mess for lunch. Did readiness from 1630 until 2000. Some of the pilots who have been here a long time are going tomorrow and are very pleased. I expect to stay about six months. (6 April) Got up at 0500 and did early watch and dawn patrol. One scramble during morning but enemy aircraft turned away from the island. Stayed in the Mess for the rest of the day. Played poker in the evening and lost – as usual."

Another pilot who was now settling in at Takali was Flg Off Imshi Mason, as described in a letter home:

"This is a very pleasant place. Quite a change to use English money and to see green fields and trees. The Mess is really the best I have been in. It is an old palace dating back before the 16th Century and the food is excellent. We live in a very pleasant house in the village nearby. Very quiet here now, with very little work to do. Quite a rest cure. Everything is very cheap here so will be able to save money. On my last leave from the desert I spent £47 in four days; actually £7 was for a watch so I only spent £40. I will be able to recuperate now. I have been here nearly three weeks and have only had one night in which I have not been out. There are dances or parties every night. However, will be glad to have a bit of activity. The work has been a great disappointment as I anticipated lots of activity here. But at present there is very little happening.

However, things may liven up soon. Though it is extremely pleasant here and a rest, I am angling for a rather special job which may be going and is right in my line. I consider myself rather a specialist in this type of work now and have my past results to back me up. I am already rather fed up with doing nothing. Have considered getting a motorcycle or car, but at present intend to go steady." [8]

In addition to being an ace pilot Mason was also an accomplished saxophonist:

"Month before last [February] I had a week there [in Athens, having ferried a Hurricane from Egypt to Greece] and did 15 minutes swing recital on the saxophone from Radio Athens. Went down excellently, although 30 minutes before I had no saxophone and finally found one belonging to the studio symphony orchestra in a corner of the studio! I swung it in all the cabaret bands there. Very low standard."[9]

The "special job" referred to by Mason may have been the same task on which Sgt Jim Pickering found himself:

"On a day of which I can't remember the date, two aircraft maintained a low level (wave top) patrol from dawn onwards, on a line 50 miles east of the island, with instruction to look out for an aircraft flying from Sicily to Tripoli outside and under the limit covered by radar. There were no specific instructions to shoot it down. It could be a civil or military plane and its attempted destruction was taken for granted. Transgression of air space was an act of hostility that warranted being shot down, but was not always performed. So what of a civil Italian or German airliner flying from Sicily outside Malta air space? We did not know at the time, but guessed afterwards, that we were looking for an aircraft with a VIP on board. It might have been Rommel or Kesselring. It was likely that Intelligence sources had picked up information of an aircraft movement of importance (it might have been an Enigma intercept). At all event, whether a plane found on this patrol had been military, civil, or Red Cross, a determined attempt would have been made to terminate its flight.

There were dilemmas. If, for instance, a plane carrying Rommel had been shot down and a Red Cross seaplane had been sent to rescue him from the sea, would the Red Cross plane have been a legitimate target? In discussion amongst ourselves afterwards, there were a variety of options. One was that it was wrong to shoot the Red Cross plane down before it picked up a VIP, but legitimate to do so when one was aboard. If a VIP rescued by a Red Cross plane had been injured, was he a legitimate target? Was he a target if uninjured? There was no agreed consensus. It remained an individual decision. On this occasion, however, the patrol was unsuccessful so no decision was necessary."

The arrival of the new Hurricanes and their pilots allowed a number of veterans to depart and, on 7 April, Sgts Jim Pickering, Jock Norwell, Harry Ayre and Drac Bowerman were flown from Luqa to Egypt in a Wellington. Next day, Flt Lt John Waters and Plt Off Allan McAdam left for Gibraltar aboard a Sunderland, on the first leg of the long journey home.

Flg Off Westmacott was on early morning duty again on the 10th:

"Did the 0600-0930 watch. Got sent off after a recce machine but did not catch it. Then I forgot about the new orders to land and stayed up much longer than I should. Spent the rest of the day in the Mess as I was on the night stand-by. Spent [the] night sleeping on a stretcher in the bus at dispersal point. There was no raid so we did not have to go up. Usually the two pilots who are on night duty sleep in the ambulance but the driver and the medical orderly who also sleep there worked up a terrific fug. Imshi Mason and I felt we could not cope with the smell of unwashed feet etc, so we dragged the two stretchers out."

The Messerschmitts of Oblt Müncheberg's 7/JG26, which had left Sicily for Taranto to participate in the invasion of Yugoslavia, had returned to Gela within a few days, and on 11 April escorted a reconnaissance aircraft to Malta in conjunction with MC200s of 17°Gruppo CT and six CR42s of 23°Gruppo CT. Pairs of Hurricanes were scrambled. Sgt Bert Deacon (Z3978) was up on one of the first patrols and encountered five CR42s but was unable to engage. He was airborne again (in Z3978) at about 1130, as part of an eight aircraft formation scrambled at the approach of Bf109Es and MC200s. About ten minutes after becoming airborne the Hurricanes, led by Sqn Ldr Lambert, had reached 10,000 feet and were eight miles east of Filfla when Deacon was attacked. Looking behind, he saw two formations of Messerschmitts and Macchis:

"I called a warning and attacked one of the enemy aircraft from quarter. Breaking away, I attacked a second from quarter again. No results were observed. A third I attacked from astern and he went into a vertical dive into the sea. Whilst watching him I was attacked from astern. A bullet smashed my windscreen and the cockpit was full of smoke. I thought I was on fire and decided to land at Takali, but the ground defences opened up on me and I turned back and landed at Hal Far. After running about 50 yards my undercarriage collapsed."

Sgt Deacon, who was credited with one destroyed and two damaged as a result of this combat, was slightly injured in the crash. Hal Far's Station Commander, Wg Cdr J.E. Allen, witnessed Deacon's combat:

"I personally observed Sgt Deacon's engagement. Enemy appeared to execute a stall turn ahead of him, at same time machine-gun fire was heard. Enemy aircraft (ME109) dived into sea five to eight miles south east of Malta. Sgt Deacon's aircraft was observed to circle spot enemy aircraft crashed. Whilst doing so he was attacked from the rear and the port quarter by two other ME109s. He avoided further action and flew off in direction of Takali."

The aircraft he saw crash into the sea was probably one of the Hurricanes being shot down since no Messerschmitts were lost. Two of the new IIAs, flown by Plt Off Peter Kennett (Z3036) and Sgt Peter Waghorn (Z2904), had intercepted an aircraft identified as a Ju88 and reported over the R/T that they had shot it down. It seems probable that their victim was a reconnaissance Bf110C (4U+ZK) of 2(F)/123 reported to have been shot down by fighters 30 miles north of Gozo, in which Lt Johann Scharringhausen and his gunner, Fw Hans Gericke, were lost. Within minutes however, both Hurricanes were bounced by Bf109Es flown by Oblt Müncheberg and Oblt Klaus Mietusch. Kennett managed to bale out and was seen by Sqn Ldr Lambert to be swimming and waving vigorously. As the raid was still in progress, however, there was a long delay in sending out a rescue launch (HSL107) and Kennett did not survive. Sgt Waghorn, meanwhile, struggled back to the island:

> "Carmen Fenech . . . recalled how a Hurricane approached from the direction of Bidnija to crash in fields opposite the road. It slid along on one wing before coming to a rest against her house . . . The dead pilot was close by, still strapped in his seat after having been thrown clear of the wreckage."[10]

Flg Off Westmacott wrote:

> "It is the same old story – no one was looking behind. It is frightfully difficult to make inexperienced pilots realise the necessity of even so small a formation as two aircraft keeping one up above looking out while the other is attacking the Hun . . . Not very long ago he [Kennett] told me he was sure he was going to be killed."

Two more Hurricanes returned to Takali badly shot up and both crash-landed: Plt Off Pip Mortimer was slightly injured when his aircraft (V7116) broke its back, while Plt Off Doug Whitney, who had also engaged a Bf109E, survived unhurt although his aircraft (V7418) was badly damaged; he noted in his logbook: "Left me with one strand of rudder wire. Attacked 109 but did not claim. Later reported crashed in sea." Other pilots were apparently credited with two CR42s probably destroyed, though the Italians recorded no losses. The Macchis strafed one of the airfields, presumably Luqa, and claimed one bomber destroyed on the ground and several damaged.

There occurred another success for the night flying Hurricanes when Plt Off Hamish Hamilton was scrambled just after midnight on 11/12 April. Wearing his pyjamas under his tunic, he soon spotted a Ju87, one of nine aircraft despatched by III/StG1 at intervals to harass the defences. Bombs fell at Takali, Siggiewi and Mgarr, killing four civilians and injuring a further six. Searchlights picked up Lt Werner Zühlke's aircraft, J9+BL of 9 Staffel, allowing Hamilton to close in and open fire. The dive-bomber crashed into a farmhouse at Il-Maghtab, near Gharghur, killing its crew and a young girl in the farmhouse (eight-year-old Rosaria Mifsud), seriously injuring another. Machine-gunners of 2/The Royal Irish Fusiliers also claimed a Stuka shot down, evidently the same aircraft.

There were four raids on Malta on 13 April, but only two interceptions. First off was a flight of Hurricanes led by Flt Lt Whittingham:

> "An air raid was in progress when we got to our planes. Asked Control if we were to take off. They said 'Yes'. Bombs started to drop very near; so rang up Senior Controller and asked if I was to wait until they had stopped dropping their bombs. He laughed but ordered the whole flight to take off. This was done and we escorted four destroyers into harbour."

Shortly thereafter, at about 1030, Flg Off Imshi Mason was up in Z2838 with Flg Off Westmacott providing cover by weaving above and behind. As Westmacott turned into one leg of his weave, Mason saw below him four Messerschmitts and, being well positioned up-sun, dived onto them:

> "I came out of the sun into them and got my chap beautifully. He dived straight down. However, as my other chap [Westmacott] saw no Germans, did not see me waggle my wings and go down to attack, but blissfully continued on patrol, I got no support there! As I broke away from my attack one of the other three got a lucky shot at me and hit my hand

and shattered my windscreen. I was now 15 miles from land, five miles high and helpless, so I had to fight my way back as best I could with this chap firing at me all the time. The instruments smashed up in front of me and the controls went funny, bullets flying through the cockpit. He kept firing from the beam. My right hand was numb. Finally, when I was twisting and turning a few feet off the sea, the motor stopped and the left side started burning. So I landed in the water, foolishly undoing my straps. I broke my nose on the windscreen frame and climbed out before it sank. The other chap flew over me, quite content with his victory and made no attempt to shoot me. The shore seemed a long way away (four miles it transpired later) and the blood was pouring out of my glove so I started to swim with one hand. I wasn't worried but very annoyed.

Anyway, both my victim and myself had been seen to crash, so, after 50 minutes, a motor boat [HSL107] appeared. I was shivering with cold so, after drying and warming me on shore and temporarily tying string round the artery and dressing the hand, I went in an ambulance to hospital. On the way I made the driver stop at the Mess and went in for a drink and had a photograph taken in borrowed pyjamas and blue flannel dressing gown. Injuries were bullet through wrist entering at the top and coming out at the palm . . . and severing the artery, and nicked a nerve. Left elbow was only through flesh. No pieces of metal at all . . . They also found shrapnel in skull and left leg, which I had not noticed. It was so deep they decided to leave it in."[11]

Since witnesses on shore reported seeing the Bf109 he had attacked come down, Mason was credited with a victory but, once again, the watchers were mistaken as no Messerschmitt was lost, however, and Oblt Klaus Mietusch returned to register his eighth victory. The raiders were back after dark, disturbing the sleep of many, including Flt Lt Whittingham:

"There was a big raid over our aerodrome at night. It sounded like hell let loose. About 40 bombs were dropped round the aerodrome, some falling about 30 yards from my bedroom window."

Next morning (14 April), Flg Off Westmacott and Sgt Bert Deacon were scrambled before dawn as an unidentified plot appeared on the radar, coming in fast and low towards St Paul's Bay. Westmacott saw tracer at low level in the direction of Luqa and thought it was enemy fire but it was in fact the airfield's defences. Deacon heard over the radio that an aircraft – reportedly a Messerschmitt 110 – was attacking Luqa and he intercepted, firing without obvious effect. However, a Ju88 of 7/KG30 was hit over Malta and crash-landed on return to Catania. Westmacott meanwhile headed for Kalafrana where he saw a large twin-engined aircraft below and under fire. Thinking it was a Ju88, he attacked, but suddenly realised his target was a Maryland and broke away. The aircraft was flown by Flt Lt Adrian Warburton, 69 Squadron's ace reconnaissance pilot, who was airborne on an early morning air test. With a damaged starboard engine and undercarriage, Warburton was obliged to belly-land the Maryland (AR735) at Luqa. This was not the first, nor the last, occasion that Warburton's Maryland was the victim of mistaken identity. On one occasion a Lewis-gunner fired a long burst at what he believed was an enemy bomber, putting a dozen bullets into the Maryland as it was coming in to land at dusk. On another occasion he was again attacked by a Hurricane shortly after a night take-off:

"Although, after the first attack, Warby correctly identified himself by firing off the colours of the day, the fighter persisted. After the Maryland had been hit, Warby had had enough. He told Paddy [Moren] in the rear turret to let him have it. Paddy's shooting was always first class and the Hurricane was so badly shot up that the wounded pilot had difficulty in getting back to Hal Far. Warby was also forced to return to inspect his plane's damage. On the ground they counted 36 bullet holes in the Maryland. Warby later sent a humorous message to the pilot in hospital and relations between 69 Squadron and the Hurricane squadrons were not impaired."[12]

The following week was relatively quiet for the defenders, with only the odd desultory engagement. Airman X of 261 Squadron at Takali wrote in his diary:

"16 April: Just remembered that I haven't filled this in recently. Since 27 March we have lost seven pilots and nine kites. Last Friday, German aircraft came over in moonlight and dropped bombs for 90 minutes. The same occurred Saturday, Sunday and Monday nights. But, after all this, only three bombs hit the drome."

On the night of the 17th, a Bf110C of 1/NJG3 ditched in the sea off Sicily after a sortie to Malta, Fw Wolfgang Goldecker and his gunner being rescued by an Axis ASR craft; the Messerschmitt was probably a victim of an unidentified Hurricane pilot who reported damaging a Bf110. A Ju88 of 7/KG30 was lost over the island during the same night, Uffz Arthur Paproski and his crew perishing. Two days later two Ju87s of III/SG1 were shot down by AA fire when attacking shipping in Grand Harbour, where a freighter was sunk. On 20 April the Italians were back, nine CR42s of 23°Gruppo CT and 15 MC200s of 17°Gruppo CT providing escort for three SM79sbis which bombed Grand Harbour. Two Hurricanes flown by Flg Off Charles Laubscher and Plt Off John Pain (Z3032) intercepted, as the former recalled:

"I was detailed with Tiger Pain to give top cover to the Squadron, and we were allotted two of the new machines [the IIAs]. Operations reported that a big raid was building up over Sicily, and shortly afterwards all the aircraft were scrambled. We took off towards Rabat as usual and, as we wheeled to the south-west, it was evident how well the Mark IIs climbed. Although laterally we were little more than abreast of the Squadron, we were already 600 or 700 feet above them. We held our climb at full throttle, Tiger on my starboard flank, and searched the sky for enemy fighters while trying to keep an eye on the Squadron to port and soon well below us.

I think we had reached about 11,000 feet when the barrage opened up over Valetta and, against the white puffs, I saw seven biplanes heading directly towards us in a shallow vic formation. CR42s! This was literally manna from heaven! For once we had height advantage, possibly only 300 or 400 feet, but sufficient, I believe, for their top mainplanes to conceal us from their pilots' sight. I wheeled left towards them and called Tiger on the R/T to take the outside man on their port flank while I took the leader. We closed rapidly and I opened fire at about 800 yards, sighting a little high at first to allow for the distance and then dropping my bead to centre on the machine. Things happen fast in a head-on attack and in two or three seconds we had passed directly over them. I immediately went into a steep turn to port to attack them again. I saw to my great satisfaction that the centre of the vic was empty and there were only two planes on the left, which probably meant that Tiger's target had also gone down."

At that moment two of the top cover, reported by Laubscher to be Messerschmitts, flashed past in a steep dive. His aircraft was not hit, and he again closed in on the remaining CR42s:

"The five survivors of the CR42 formation were swinging to their right, towards and below me, which made it difficult to attack the three planes nearest me, so I chose the outer of the two planes on their left, laid off a deflection and opened fire again. My tracer passed in line with the machine, but behind it and, rather than stop firing, I pulled back steadily on my control column until the tracers crept along the rear of the machine and into the cockpit. I knew immediately that the pilot was finished, and stopped firing. The CR42 hung on its side for a moment and then slipped gently into a dive. I did not watch him all the way but looked for another target. The sky now suddenly seemed clear except for a CR42 going down in a spin ahead of me. I gave him a full deflection burst for good measure and then my ammunition ran out. It was time to return home so I jerked the machine into a spiral dive, just in case the remaining CR42s or the two 109s were still in the vicinity, flattened out at about 800 feet and jinked my way back to Takali. It was a wonderful feeling to put up an affirmative two fingers as the mechanic helped me taxi in. That night Ops confirmed my claim for two CR42s shot down. Tiger also had his victory confirmed and the AA batteries claimed another – four out of seven destroyed – not a bad effort, we felt, particularly as the Squadron had spent their time in a defensive circle!"

Plt Off John Pain added:

"I got one confirmed and one unconfirmed. I was then attacked by six 109s and diced with them without anything firm being achieved other than preserving my own neck. When I got clear of them I went down almost to sea level and there were two 'holes' in the water about where my two would have gone in. There was no other sign of wreckage of any other aircraft. I did not see Laubscher's two get hit, probably because I was busy myself. He said later he saw the 109s and took off for home. He was down and refuelled and re-armed when I got back."

Italian records show only one CR42 missing on this date, Serg Giuseppe Sanguettoli of 74^Squadriglia being killed; the pilots of 23°Gruppo CT jointly claimed one Hurricane, while a Macchi pilot claimed a Hurricane damaged. It seems probable that it was Macchis rather than Messerschmitts that had attacked Laubscher and Pain. The following day Airman X of 261 Squadron noted in his diary:

"21 April: Since my last entry (16 April) our Squadron has shot down five German [sic] aircraft confirmed and three probables. We have not lost any Hurricanes. We have had several warnings each day and yesterday three Italian 79s came over with a fighter escort of 17 CR42s and Me109s. We claimed three fighters."

Airman X's information would appear to be slightly inaccurate on this occasion. Records suggest that the defences had claimed five or six enemy aircraft during the period 16-20 April, with the guns accounting for two of these. There was a further skirmish between a pair of 261 Squadron Hurricanes and 7/JG26 on 22 April, Flg Off Laubscher becoming a victim on this occasion, as he recalled:

"We were flying across the southern end of the island when Control came on the air with the warning that two bogies were in our area. The R/T was bad and I thought he said 'below you' so I concentrated on that section of the sky almost exclusively, leaving it to Dick to watch above us. Suddenly he swung up close to my port side, waggling his wings frantically and pointing downwards. I thought he had seen enemy aircraft and, as he winged over into a steep dive I followed him without question. Our speed built up rapidly and the inside of my cockpit started to mist up. I tried to pull the canopy back but it was impossible against the dive so I flattened out and throttled back. As my speed dropped I again tried to open the hood, fortunately with my left hand. Suddenly there was an ominous popping of cannon-fire behind me and little white balls seemed to float past on both sides of the cockpit. I dropped my right wing suddenly as if I were turning into the cloud and immediately swung over into a steep left-hand turn. There was a split second of violent clattering as cannon shells hit the machine and then I was clear, and in a 270° turn which took me back across my flight path and into the safety of that wonderful cloud. Even then I jinked from side to side as I pulled the hood back.

I gave myself a minute or two to get my nerves under control and ventured outside the cloud, briefly at first then more confidently when it was apparent that the danger had passed, for the sky was clear of aircraft. I looked at my port wing to judge the extent of the damage and saw some nasty holes there, while my instrument panel had also taken a slight hammering. It was obvious that my aircraft was not in a condition for any further fighting, and I flew a zig-zag course back to the drome, keeping a very watchful eye on the sky around me. When I landed and taxied to the dispersal point, an awed group of aircraftsmen crowded around the machine to examine the damage. I was told later by the Flight Sergeant that they counted five cannon and 30 7.62mm holes in the machine. One of the light calibre bullets had missed the top of my head by an inch and a half!"

Flg Off Laubscher had been attacked by Fw Wagner, who was credited with shooting him down. During the day a He111 of 5/KG4, one of several units passing through Sicily following action during the early stages of the Balkans campaign, force-landed in the sea after a raid on Valetta. The crew was later rescued. The crew of a returning Heinkel of 6/KG26 reported that their gunner had baled out over Malta for unknown reasons; there is no record of him landing safely.

On the evening of 23 April, the Messerschmitts of 7/JG26 escorted a reconnaissance aircraft to Malta, where they intercepted a Hurricane patrol, Oblt Müncheberg shooting down Plt Off Henri Auger's aircraft (Z3032) south-east of Hal Far. The French-Canadian baled out near Delimara Point, as noted by Plt Off Pain:

"He landed safely in the drink between Filfla and the main island, only a short distance from the cliff. He was seen to wave that he was OK to one of the other aircraft. He was not picked up by ASR largely due to the delay in allowing them to put to sea. We were given to understand that the ASR boats did not put out on the express orders of the AOC because they would be too vulnerable to air attack. This incident caused a very serious morale problem with all the pilots and a number of letters were written to the AOC stating our anger at the loss of Auger."

Hurricanes subsequently searched until nightfall, but no sign of the missing pilot could be found. A Hurricane patrol led by Flt Lt Whittingham narrowly avoided a similar fate two days later, as he recorded:

"I took L [Laubscher], D [Sgt Len Davies] and self up to 30,000 feet. I saw three 109s pass about 1,000 yards in front of us and slightly underneath. My oxygen was not working too well because by the time I had thought of pressing the [gun] button it was too late. I then began to patrol and did a rather sharp turn, not being used to high flying. This put me into a spin. This was fortunate because another section of 109s had seen me and was fastening itself on my tail. D [Davies] saw this but was a moment later attacked by two others. There had been two formations, one at 30,500 feet and the other, which I saw at 29,500 feet, circling the island about three miles from each other."

The night of 25/26th saw a heavy raid on the island, both Luqa and Takali being targeted. At the former aerodrome a Maryland and a Magister were destroyed; Sgt Len Davies noted: "Takali blitzed. 44 bombs on the drome. Took off at dawn, bomb craters and all!"

A further welcomed reinforcement arrived on the 27th, when 23 Hurricanes, under the codename Operation 'Dunlop' were launched from the *Ark Royal*. New Zealander Sgt Peter Jordan provided an insight into Operation 'Dunlop':

"In April, [Sgt] Ted Lawrence and myself were flown to Hendon (from Elgin in Scotland) and, under strict security arrangements, did 130 hours practising take-offs before reaching a white line across the strip, seemingly only a few yards ahead of us. The Hurricanes were fitted with new-fangled 45-gallon long-range tanks, non-jettisonable and fitted under the mainplanes with auxiliary pumps to pump fuel to the main tanks. We were told to use 15 degrees of flap for take-off, something completely new to us. On 16 April we left Greenock on the old aircraft carrier *Argus* with 24 Hurricanes, 25 pilots and an appropriate number of fitters and riggers, for Gibraltar, although we did not know our precise destination at the time. As far as I knew, we were originally bound for Greece or Crete, but it was too late for that. I remember that we were quite concerned that we might be expected to take off from *Argus*, as even the resident Swordfish seemed to have difficulty. Our aircraft – with mainplanes detached – overflowed from the hangar deck on to the quarter deck and it was one of the latter which was rendered u/s during the bad weather experienced in the Atlantic. On arrival at Gibraltar the aircraft were off-loaded onto the quayside and the mainplanes and long-range tanks fitted by the ground staff, with the doubtful assistance of the pilots to whom the particular aircraft had been allocated. They were then hoisted by crane onto the after end of *Ark Royal* and with little delay off we went into the Mediterranean. We were supposed to take off for Malta about 12 hours after leaving Gibraltar but, because of bad weather and, I think, intelligence reports about enemy activity around Sardinia and Sicily, we retraced our course and eventually took off about 36 hours out of Gibraltar."

Another of the pilots, South African-born Plt Off Douglas Robertson, recalled:

"Taking off from the deck of a carrier was to be a first time experience for all of us. We were told that after take-off we were not to attempt a landing back on the carrier under any conditions. Also that no rescue attempt would be made if we came down in the sea. It was explained that after all Hurricanes had become airborne, the carrier with escort ships would leave on a fast evasive course. I remember sitting in the cockpit, starting the engine and waving to some of the naval crew who were standing at the side. When it was my turn to take-off, I held back the control column, kept my feet pressed down on the brakes, then opened up the throttle until the aircraft tail came off the deck. I then eased off on the brakes and gave the engine full throttle. My forward acceleration seemed to be slower than I would have liked. Would I become airborne when reaching the end of the deck? Hurricanes ahead of me were in the air, so I figured that I could do it. The raised ramp at the end of the deck lifted my plane, only to sink towards the sea. The downward motion gave me the lift needed and I climbed away from the carrier. 'Oh boy, I made it.'"

The Hurricanes were despatched in three flights of seven, eight and eight (one had been rendered unserviceable en route) led by Flg Off N.P.W. Hancock, Flg Off N.A.R. Doughty and Flt Lt C.G.StD. Jeffries (Z4354) respectively, each flight escorted by a Fulmar for navigation purposes, while from Malta three Marylands and a Sunderland set out to meet the incoming formation and guide them in. Sgt Len Davies of 261 Squadron intriguingly noted in his logbook: "Dawn patrol. Leading Sgt Quinn. Had a slight argument with a Sunderland but left it OK." Whether he fired at the Sunderland or vice versa, or if they fired at each other, is unclear. Meanwhile, Flg Off Pat Hancock, who was leading the first flight of Hurricanes, met the Sunderland as planned, and reached the island without problem, although there were moments when individual pilots had doubts, as Plt Off Robertson noted:

"The easterly 500-mile flight was exceedingly boring. It was a beautiful sunny day, with the blue sky reflected in the water. So this was the blue Mediterranean. Most of the time there was no sight of land. Nothing but sea, sea and more sea. When my main tank fuel level dropped a bit, I tested my electrical fuel pump to transfer fuel from the long-range external tanks to the main tank. It was a relief to find that all worked well. There were moments when my imagination played tricks on me. I was worried as my engine sounded different. If there was a problem there was nothing I could do about it. After a few minutes when all returned to normal, I realised that my imagination was the problem and not my engine. We passed the Italian island of Pantelleria. There were supposed to be enemy aircraft there, but we saw nothing. A quick check of my fuel level gave me the confidence that I could make it to Malta."

As the Hurricanes approached from the south, the pilots watched the Sunderland descend and alight in Kalafrana Bay. At that moment, Flg Off Hancock saw two Bf109Es which he thought were about to attack the Hurricanes. Instead, Oblt Müncheberg and his wingman dived after the Sunderland, strafing as it taxied to its mooring. A fuel tank in the port wing was holed and a fire started. Within a short while the aircraft was on fire, which was eventually extinguished by the aircraft sinking; one member of the crew was wounded during the attack. This event marred an otherwise successful operation, with all the Hurricanes landing safely at Hal Far or Takali. Plt Off Robertson continued:

"It was a good thing that the enemy aircraft either did not see us or had finished their sortie. We were not equipped for operational activity. Even evasive action could have been dangerous as our fuel levels were so low. We did as instructed and landed at Takali airfield. The groundcrew there signalled for us to taxi to remote sandbagged or stone-walled pens. These were located outside the perimeter of the airfield. I left my aircraft and was directed to a Maltese bus for transport to our quarters. The maniac driver, bent on suicide, drove at high speed along narrow, twisting, stone-lined bumpy roads. There was barely enough room for a second vehicle to pass. We held on for dear life, hoping that nothing would come from the opposite direction. This was the most frightening part of our day's journey!"

Their arrival, soon after the earlier delivery, now presented the beginnings of an overcrowding problem at Luqa and Hal Far. The decision was therefore taken to base some of the fighters at Takali, while the lastest batch of pilots[13] was to be known as C Flight of 261 Squadron. Several of the new arrivals were experienced pilots including the detachment leader, Flt Lt Charles Jeffries – known to his close friends as 'Porky' due to his ample girth, and to others as Jeff – who had three victories to his credit, Plt Off Peter D. Thompson with four (one shared), Plt Off Bob Innes (four, two shared), Plt Off Alan Dredge (three, one shared), and Plt Off Richard Graves (one), while Flg Off Pat Hancock had fought in France and the Battle of Britain. But the majority were inexperienced.

The Messerschmitts were back again on 28 April, two Hurricanes being scrambled to investigate, as recalled by Flg Off Innes Westmacott:

"I was scrambled with a sergeant pilot, seeing a number of high-flying 109s about. Two of these began diving onto us and, at the right moment, I carried out a hard climbing turn, coming out behind one of the Messerschmitts as it began to pull up. I fired and it went down. Looking around for my wingman, I saw another Messerschmitt about to attack me, so repeated the same trick. This time the German dived away and headed off north."

Although Westmacott was credited with a victory, no Messerschmitt was actually lost. However, the Hurricanes did achieve a definite victory next day when Ju88s of III/LG1 carried out another early evening raid. Seventeen Hurricanes were scrambled and two of these, flown by Plt Off Tony Rippon and recently-arrived Plt Off Joe Hall (Z3034), engaged one of the bombers. Their victim, L1+BT of 9 Staffel, crashed near Ghain Tuffieha after Fw Rudolf Lenzer and his crew had baled out. One of the crew was captured at Pembroke Ranges and the other three rescued from the sea. They stated that their aircraft had been damaged by AA fire before the Hurricanes attacked. Meanwhile, the other Hurricanes tangled with the escorting Messerschmitts, and although both Oblt Müncheberg and Obfw Ernst Laube claimed victories, there were no known Hurricane losses. On the last day of the month two flights of SM79s from 87°Gruppo BT escorted by 27 MC200s attacked Valetta. Hurricanes were unable to intercept. However, five bombers returned with splinter damage from AA fire. The gunners achieved better success during the course of another raid when they claimed two Ju88s, one of which was possibly a He111 of 6/KG26 which failed to return.

The arrival of the new fighter pilots allowed some more of the old stalwarts to be rested, notably Flt Sgt Jock Robertson and Sgt Reg Hyde. Robertson's record was outstanding while on the island: he had participated in 189 interception sorties and been credited with ten confirmed, three probables and seven damaged. The New Zealander Hyde believed he had shot down five and damaged seven others, but was actually credited with only two destroyed and two probables. More postings and changes followed. Sqn Ldr Lambert was replaced by Flt Lt Derek Whittingham as commander of 261 Squadron; the latter recorded in his diary:

> "AOC came round. He asked me if I would like to take over the Squadron. He gave me a talk on the responsibilities I would be assuming. Heigh-ho for those carefree days as a Flying Officer."

On the last day of the month a new unit came into existence when C Flight of 261 Squadron was renumbered 185 Squadron, although official confirmation was not forthcoming until 12 May and, until then, it continued to operate as C Flight. The new unit was to operate with Hurricane IIs from Hal Far under the command of Flt Lt Mould, and comprised two flights:

X Flight	**Y Flight**
Flg Off H.W. Eliot	Flg Off I.B. Westmacott
Flt Lt C.G.StD. Jeffries	Flg Off N.P.W. Hancock
Plt Off C.E. Hamilton	Plt Off G.G. Bailey
Plt Off R.A. Innes	Plt Off P.D. Thompson
Plt Off J.E. Hall	Plt Off A.R. Dredge
Sgt C.S. Bamberger	Plt Off C.K. Gray
Sgt R.A. Ottey	Sgt C.G. Hodson
Sgt B.C. Walmsley	Sgt A.W. Jolly
Sgt E.V. Wynne	Sgt R.A. Branson

Promoted to Flying Officer, Jock Barber now left 261 Squadron for a brief rest before transferring to 69 Squadron:

> "I and other pilots of the Squadron had done single aircraft standing patrols over bomber airfields in Sicily, commencing in the early morning, with the idea of radioing back to Control when enemy bombers were moved out of their three-sided pens. A squadron of Beaufighters were on standby at Luqa, and the idea was to strafe the enemy bombers once they were clear of their protective pens. Needless to say, this was a nerve-racking experience but strangely the Italians ignored the single Hurricane circling the airfields, although admittedly at 20,000 feet. This led the AOC to put up a PR Hurricane."

In conjunction with newly promoted Sqn Ldr George Burges and Flt Lt Adrian Warburton, Barber was soon flying a locally modified blue-painted Hurricane I – V7101 – on short-range photo-reconnaissance sorties. Burges recalled:

> "We took out the guns, radio, armour plate, and anything else we could safely get rid of, and installed two cameras. Unfortunately, we didn't have the facilities to instal extra fuel tanks, and so we knew its range would be restricted to Sicily. What wouldn't we have given for one of the blue Spitfires the PR chaps were using in the UK! Incidentally, we painted our Hurricane blue, mainly to enable our gunners to recognise it! I actually got this aircraft up to 36,000 feet but I think by stripping so much out of it we had probably moved the centre of gravity too far back because at this height, if one wasn't careful, it whipped into a spin. I used to operate at about 30,000 feet and at this height could cover two or three targets in Sicily in one sortie."

Flg Off Barber was also to meet 69 Squadron's mascots, a marmoset monkey which used to accompany the Maryland crews on operational trips, and a seagull named Sammy. The latter had been hit by Warburton's aircraft on take-off and, while recovering from a damaged wing was adopted by the Squadron. Sammy's special treat was to be allowed to bathe in a bowl containing beer, as a result of which he usually ended up inebriated! Eventually, on full recovery and presumably with a clear head, he met a lady seagull and flew away.

May 1941

According to German sources, the Messerschmitts were back in force early on 1 May. Oblt Müncheberg and Lt Hans Johannsen reported sighting eight Hurricanes off the northern coast of Malta shortly before 0800, and bounced one flight of four over St Paul's Bay. Müncheberg's first victim dived away trailing smoke, while the second apparently burst into flames. At the same time, Johannsen shot pieces from a third Hurricane as the fourth attempted to get on his tail. This was chased away by Müncheberg, who then spotted another preparing to land which he reportedly shot down in flames. It has not been possible to relate this action to any known operations by the defenders[14]. Airman X noted: "Several scrambles this morning. Jerry kites came over and machine-gunned the deck at about 0900, one of our kites was shot up. Several warnings before midday."

Müncheberg was certainly at the head of his Staffel in the afternoon, when he reported meeting six Hurricanes over Luqa, one of which he claimed shot down from about 300 feet. A second was claimed by Lt Johannsen and a probable by Obfw Karl Kühdorf. Their opponents on this occasion were from 261 Squadron's C Flight led by Flg Off Chubby Eliot, Sgt Walmsley (Z3061) being shot down, as recorded in the unit diary:

> "Our first day of operations. During the morning some Me109s were seen but they had the advantage of height and sun and made no effort to attack. During the early evening, the Squadron was on patrol and was attacked by six Me109s. These again had the advantage of height and caused us to break up in all directions. Unfortunately, Sgt Walmsley didn't move quite fast enough and had to bale out as the result of damage to his aeroplane. P/O Innes [Z2900] was injured in his foot but not seriously. This was not discovered until he started to climb out of his cockpit. As he trod on the injured foot, he gave a loud howl and subsided onto the firing button which had been left to fire position and a hail of lead forthwith projected over to the hangars much to the alarm and consternation of all. Taken all round – not a brilliant start but we hope better may be expected."

Walmsley's Hurricane crashed close to Ghaxaq church, and the pilot was admitted to hospital with slight wounds. C Flight lost another aircraft next day, together with its pilot, but not due to enemy action. During a routine patrol Sgt Ray Ottey's Hurricane (Z3054) suddenly went into a steep dive while flying at high altitude and crashed into the sea. Ottey, from Leicester, did not survive and was probably a victim of oxygen starvation.

During the morning of 4 May, a section of two Hurricanes of C Flight led by Flt Lt Jeffries was patrolling over Kalafrana Bay at 29,000 feet when a Ju88 was spotted below. Plt Off Joe Hall (Z2904), who was flying as Yellow 2, reported:

> ". . . I saw a vapour trail and warned my section leader who manoeuvred for position, scanning the sky for enemy fighters. The section then dived down to attack, Yellow 1 going in on the starboard quarter, slightly above . . ."

Yellow 1, Flt Lt Jeffries (Z3060), added:

> "I finished my ammo from astern. Both engines were smoking and pieces fell from the port engine. I experienced about ten rounds of return fire and one bullet struck my starboard mainplane. I landed at 0825, my port wing covered with oil from the Ju88."

Meanwhile, Hall followed his leader into the attack:

> ". . . I dived down and made a quarter astern attack from below, opening fire at 400 yards and closing to 50 yards, giving e/a three three-second bursts. I then broke away because I saw two fighters above on the port side. On hearing 'Go to it, Rose Section – go to it' I decided it was Rose Section. On turning back to finish my ammunition on the Ju88 which was pouring smoke from the starboard engine, my aircraft was hit by return fire from the e/a in both sealing tanks. During the engagement AA bursts were exploding all round me,

my port mainplane receiving a near miss which made a large hole and spattered the aircraft with splinters, which injured my left elbow . . ."

Sgt Al Jolly of Rose Section also claimed a share in shooting down the Ju88: "I dived on the Ju88 and gave it two short bursts of approximately three seconds at 250 yards, before getting a cannon shell from behind in my port wing, apparently from a fighter above." It would seem that Jolly's aircraft was accidentally hit by a cannon shell fired by his No2 since no enemy fighters were present. Hal Far Station Commander, Wg Cdr Allen, observed the engagement from the ground and submitted his own report:

> "As the Ju88 crossed the coast between Zonqor Point and Delimara Point, it was making a strong visible vapour trail. As the enemy aircraft passed directly overhead, Yellow Section were seen to be chasing along the vapour trail, slightly higher than the e/a. Yellow Section engaged in succession when over Luqa – AA fire still continued, and only ceased as Hurricanes broke off the engagement. During the engagement, e/a altered course towards St Paul's Bay in a shallow power dive, leaving a slight trail of smoke. E/a then disappeared from view. Yellow Section Hurricanes were covered with oil from the Ju88 which proves their close-range engagement. Yellow Section are to be congratulated on their exhibition of determination in pursuit of the enemy, in face of our own AA fire. Yellow Section claim one Ju88."

The bomber attacked would appear to have been an aircraft of 9/KG30 which crashed on return, Lt Albrecht Irion and his crew of 4D+CT being reported to have died in the crash. The Hurricanes missed out next day (5 May) when a small formation of Ju87s from 9/StG1 carried out an attack on shipping in Grand Harbour. The guns shot one down into the sea: none of the crew survived; a second returned to Sicily so badly damaged that the crew were obliged to bale out.

The whole of the Mediterranean was a hive of activity on 6 May. In North Africa, Rommel had driven the weakened British and Commonwealth forces back across Cyrenaica into Egypt, while the Balkans were firmly in German hands following the fall of Yugoslavia and Greece, and an invasion of Crete seemed imminent. To allow the army in Egypt to challenge the Germans, a fast convoy carrying 295 tanks, 180 motor vehicles and 53 crated Hurricanes had been despatched from England, leaving Gibraltar on the morning of the 6th under the codename Operation 'Tiger'. A stiff fight was anticipated. Meanwhile, in an effort to subdue Malta's fighters, a fairly substantial Luftwaffe attack was launched against the island, including sorties by units based briefly in Sicily following the Balkans fighting. One of these units was III/JG27 led by Oblt Erbo Graf von Kageneck, an ace with 13 victories to his credit. Shortly before midday four He111s of II/KG26 approached the island escorted by elements of both III/JG27 and 7/JG26, C Flight being scrambled to intercept:

> "It never rains but it pours! After our previous misfortunes we were at least hoping to turn the tables on our friends across in Sicily. Today they certainly did not mean us to! A fairly small bombing force comprising six He111s was escorted by a considerably larger fighter force said to number between 30 and 40 Me109s. The boys got amongst them but were hopelessly outnumbered and only as could be expected, we suffered in consequence. Although we lost four aircraft, only one pilot was injured. P/O Dredge, after a gallant attempt to force-land after being shot up, unfortunately overran the aerodrome and crashed. His aircraft [Z3057] burst into flames but the prompt action of the fire tender crew probably saved him from much worse. Sgt Branson [Z3059] and P/O Gray [Z3060] both baled out, one in the sea and the latter on the roof of a house! Both are quite unhurt and returned to the Squadron in the evening in high fettle."

The fourth Hurricane damaged in this action, Z3034, was landed safely by Plt Off Peter D.

Thompson, who suffered a minor splinter wound in his leg. Contrary to the diarist's statement, both Gray and Branson suffered injuries, the former with a slight wound in his left thigh and the latter with minor burns to his right leg. He reported:

> "We were climbing up to engage . . . hoped to attack from behind when I noticed three 109s dead astern. I was about to signal 'Duck' and at the same time take action when I was hit. My machine caught fire and I was forced to abandon it."

Plt Off Dredge's burns were more severe and he was taken to hospital for treatment. It is believed that he had been shot down by von Kageneck, while Müncheberg claimed two Hurricanes in quick succession, probably Branson and Gray. The raiders returned in the evening:

> "At about six o'clock in the evening, the Hun again tried his hand. This time, with only three serviceable aircraft in the air, F/O Westmacott, F/Lt Hancock and P/O Bailey managed to intercept the bombers before the escorting Me109s had fully woken up to what was going on. A certain amount of damage was inflicted before our three Hurricanes had to break off and deal with the escort. One He111 was definitely seen to be damaged and a second was possibly damaged. This time we sustained no damage ourselves and altogether, after the morning show, it was indeed a very good start."

Westmacott reported that he attacked one Heinkel and shot it up. The bomber dropped from formation with smoke pouring from it and disappeared slowly out to sea. He could not follow as he was under attack by the Messerschmitts, but the Controller later reported that the 'plot' had disappeared from the radar screen halfway to Sicily, and Westmacott was awarded a probable. His attack on the Heinkel was witnessed by Sqn Ldr Whittingham, who wrote in his diary:

> "Westmacott put up a magnificent show by attacking a He111 with many 109s behind him. When attacked on three occasions he took evasive action and kept high to proceed after his target which he is believed to have damaged."

Westmacott subsequently received a personal letter from the AOC, who had also witnessed the action, congratulating him on his persistence in continuing to attack the bomber when under attack himself. II/KG26 reported that a Heinkel of 4 Staffel (1H+FM) crashed on return and was destroyed, Lt Eberhard Möller and his crew all being killed. This may well have been Westmacott's victim. As darkness fell another raid developed, Sqn Ldr Whittingham – who had formed a Night Fighter Flight within 261 Squadron – having an opportunity to put up a similar fine performance: "In the evening I went up with Pain. We had a field day – or rather night. I fired my guns four times. Afterwards, it was confirmed that I had shot down one for certain and very probably another, and damaged a third. Most gratifying result." His victims are believed to have been a He111 and two Ju88s, one of the latter – 8/KG30 (4D+FS) flown by Uffz Werner Gerhardt – crashing at Ospizio near Floriana, while a He111 of 4/KG26 crash-landed on return with a dead gunner. The guns were also were credited with hits on two bombers.

Following the intense activity of the previous day, 7 May was somewhat of an anti-climax for the Hurricane pilots, although a welcomed reprieve. It was not, however, without incident and when seven Hurricanes of C Flight scrambled during the afternoon on the approach of a reconnaissance Ju88, two collided, resulting in the death of Sgt Henry Jennings whose aircraft (V7365) crashed south-west of Fort Madliena. The body of the 23-year-old from Essex was recovered and buried in Capuccini Naval Cemetery. The other pilot, Sgt George Walker (V7548), was injured but managed to bale out into the sea, from where he was speedily rescued. At Malta, the 8th passed relatively quietly although Hurricanes were again up at night, albeit without success.

Axis units now concentrated on a convoy steaming from the west, which was defended by Fulmars of 807 and 808 Squadrons operating from the accompanying carrier *Ark Royal*. By the following morning (9 May) Malta's Beaufighters were also able to provide cover. Meanwhile, from Alexandria, the Mediterranean Fleet including the carrier *Formidable* had sailed to rendezvous with the convoy south of Malta, at the same time providing escort to another smaller convoy bound for Malta. It was while the latter ships were entering Grand Harbour that Ju87s from both II and III/StG1 launched an attack. Two Hurricanes of B Flight were vectored towards the Stukas as more Hurricanes were scrambled. Flg Off Charles Laubscher recalled:

"I was leading Sgt Peter Jordan on a patrol when we were vectored onto a flight of Ju87s which had attacked Grand Harbour. They had turned back to Sicily and I couldn't see a formation but spotted a straggler who, curiously enough, was flying diagonally across our line of approach and not heading pell-mell for home. He was only a 100 feet or so above the sea and we closed on him rapidly. I instructed Peter to keep a sharp lookout for enemy fighters and then to follow me. I started a quarter stern attack and had the unpleasant experience of flying down the middle of a cone of tracer from the rear-gunner. I held my fire until the enemy was in range. When I pressed the button there was the ripping noise that was characteristic of the Hurricane's eight guns and I saw strikes on the fuselage of the Stuka. The rear-gunner was killed by that burst, as his gun swung up in the vertical position as he slumped down. I tried to turn in behind him but found that I was going to overshoot and pulled away to starboard.

I swung in a wide circle around the machine, climbing slightly to lose speed and came in at him again from dead ahead and slightly above. The pilot of the Stuka had plenty of courage and pulled up his nose to have a crack at me with his forward firing guns. I was so surprised that I involuntary pulled up slightly and passed over him before I could get him in my gunsight again. At that moment Peter came in from the port quarter, misjudged his deflection by a fraction and blew off the Stuka's tail. When I turned I saw a long patch of fluorescent dye that the Germans carried staining the sea a light yellow-green, but could not pick out the pilot. Nevertheless, we circled the spot and radioed Control to get a radar fix on us and send out a crash boat. They never found him and I often wondered whether he went in with his machine and dead gunner, or whether he managed to bale out and was picked up by the flying boat they had stationed in Sicily for sea rescue work."

Sgt Peter Jordan added: "One of the crew baled out – nearly hit me in the process – but I didn't think his parachute would have opened properly from that height." His judgement of the situation would appear to have been correct, for this was undoubtedly Oblt Ulrich Heinz's aircraft (J9+GL) of 9/StG1, which was lost along with its crew. A second Stuka was claimed probably destroyed by Plt Off Hamilton, which Sgt Len Davies (in Z4261) apparently "finished off"; he reported:

"A battle was taking place over Grand Harbour and those of us who were off duty had gone to dispersal and taken off as a scratch flight. We attacked a Ju87 over the harbour at about 1,000-2,000 feet and the pilot or crew baled out."

185 Squadron's diarist wrote:

"During a scramble in the morning, P/O Hamilton found a stray brace of Ju87s which he warmed up to the extent of several hundreds of rounds before they made off in cloud. He was credited with one probably destroyed. On his way home he sighted a submarine in close proximity to some of our destroyers and, just to show there was no ill feeling, he delivered a burst at its conning tower."[15]

A 4/StG1 aircraft which crash-landed at Comiso suffering 70% damage was probably their victim. Messerschmitts continued their sweep over Malta, searching for Hurricane patrols or any other arriving or departing aircraft. On the 10th, Oblt Müncheberg spotted a Sunderland in Marsaxlokk Bay, which caught fire following his strafing attack. Next day, Sgt Arthur Todd of 261 Squadron reported damaging a Bf109 over Luqa as it attempted to strafe. Meanwhile, at sea, Fulmars from *Formidable*'s 806 Squadron continued to intercept and harass bombers and reconnaissance aircraft hunting the convoy with some success. However, one of the convoy was lost when the *Empire Song* struck two mines and sank, taking with her 57 of the tanks and ten of the crated Hurricanes. The four remaining freighters reached Alexandria safely.

Following the attack on the RN submarine on the 9th, Plt Off Hamilton was again in trouble two days later, as indicated in the unit diary:

"Early this morning the Squadron was scrambled and an aircraft was sighted flying low just off Delimara Point. Anti-aircraft bursts were seen in the vicinity of this aircraft, and led by P/O Hamilton the boys gave chase. For 20 minutes, having pulled everything in sight to try to get an extra mile per hour, the chase continued. After nearly 100 miles very little progress had been made and the leader gave it up. Sgt Wynne, however, with great gusto continued the chase single-handed and eventually closed to firing range. After putting all his ammunition into what he supposed to be a Ju88 he returned to land and reported he had damaged the aircraft in question.

All well and good – one probable Ju88 to the credit of the Squadron – but more to come! Some little time later an irate Glenn Martin crew arrived, looking for the Hurricane who had chased them halfway to Crete! After a good deal of explaining and apologies, everything was settled and a party ensued during which everyone concerned became very light-hearted about the whole issue. The evening ended with handshakes all round and a promise from the Glenn Martin crew to enter in their logbook – 'Affiliation exercises with Hurricanes'! Needless to say, not one hole was shot anywhere in the Glenn Martin!"[16]

Next day (12 May), 185 Squadron officially came into existence with newly-promoted Sqn Ldr Mould in command. Flt Lt Jeffries assumed command of A Flight (formerly X Flight) and B Flight (formerly Y Flight) continued to be commanded by newly-promoted Flt Lt Westmacott:

"Today the Squadron is officially born and we are now a separate unit to 261 Squadron. Signals of good wishes for the future were received. Although on its first day, the Squadron did quite a lot of flying, no engagements took place, and we passed a fairly peaceful day. During the evening a party got going in celebration, and our CO made a good start by getting very drunk!"

Meanwhile, 261 Squadron began to wind down preparatory to leaving the island and, with more Hurricanes imminently due from the UK, the unit was ordered to despatch six of its own aircraft without delay to Cyrenaica. The tide had turned against the British and Commonwealth forces in Cyrenaica and HQME needed all the aircraft that could be spared to reinforce the Western Desert Air Force. Flg Off Laubscher was called upon to lead the flight:

"I was given the unenviable task of leading a flight of six Hurricane Is, fitted with long-range tanks, from Malta to Mersa Matruh, a flight of about 600 miles. The Wimpy [crew] which navigated us across the Mediterranean had never flown in the area before and knew nothing of the compass deviations which had to be allowed for when travelling across the Mediterranean. Five and a quarter hours later we hit the coast ten miles away from Alexandria, about 180 miles farther east than planned, a fantastically long flight for a Hurricane. We naturally missed the flying boat waiting at Mersa Matruh to ferry us back to Malta but, when a second flying boat was laid on at Aboukir two days later, we missed that one as well due to a farewell luncheon of gargantuan proportions at the Petit Çoin de France."

Initial operations by 185 Squadron did not meet with great success. During the early afternoon of 13 May four Hurricanes were led off by Flt Lt Westmacott. They climbed above others, a flight from 261 Squadron, and at 8,000 feet were attacked by a number of Messerschmitts. The section evaded in cloud, whereupon it broke up. Westmacott then saw two 'red noses', which he thought were Hurricanes from his own flight. In fact they were Bf109Es from 7/JG26 led by Oblt Klaus Mietusch who opened fire on Westmacott's Hurricane (Z2837). With the cockpit filling with smoke and no response from the controls, Westmacott undid his seat straps and opened the hood, whereupon he was ejected into space. Fortunately, his parachute opened safely but, as he reached the ground, a 25mph wind pulled him over backwards and he was knocked unconscious. On coming to, he found himself surrounded by a hostile crowd of Maltese who had mistaken him for a German. Having made it clear that he was RAF, Westmacott discovered that he had been slightly wounded. He was taken to hospital, where a piece of shrapnel was removed from his elbow. Baling out over Malta had become a risky business, as Plt Off Doug Whitney recalled:

> "They [the Maltese] were so bitter about the bombing that they were inclined to treat anyone baling out as the enemy and this became so bad we all carried revolvers to protect ourselves until we could convince them otherwise. I remember a Rhodesian in our Squadron writing a long letter to the *Times of Malta* about this very subject, but I don't think it was ever published."

Other Messerschmitts from III/JG27 engaged the 261 Squadron flight during which Oblt von Kageneck shot down Plt Off Peter J. Thompson, a 20-year-old from Sussex, who was killed when his aircraft (V7115) crashed into the sea. The new pilots were paying a high price for their inexperience. On this occasion some of the Messerschmitts carried bombs – not a new rôle for III/JG27, which had operated as fighter-bombers in the Balkans during the previous month. This was probably an action in which Plt Off Douglas Robertson participated:

> "Three of us were jumped by Me109s. The Hurricane beside me was hit and burst into flames. I made a violent upward turn to try and get behind another attacker that was diving towards me, but he shot past in an almost vertical dive, and disappeared. Another 109 was circling above, so I followed his pattern as I was unable to out-climb him. I had learnt to fly in ever decreasing circles, and finally disappearing up my own empenage! I then started a turning dive, keeping the 109 in sight and waiting to see if he would come down to my altitude. With this distraction I failed to notice that the ground was getting dangerously close. When I became aware of this, a building loomed up in front of me. I pulled up and cleared the roof top by about 50 feet. This close encounter with solid stone gave me a fright. My saliva dried up around my lips. I brushed the back of my hand across my mouth. A radio message from HQ reported that all enemy aircraft were clear of the island, so I returned to Takali and landed."

After dark, Sgt Len Davies (Z4060) operating with 261 Squadron's Night Fighter Flight again attempted an interception but was hampered by lack of illumination. He was aware of enemy aircraft over the island but was unable to locate a target without the aid of searchlights. He flew a second sortie but again without success. Three nights later (in Z4385) he managed to locate an aircraft held by the searchlights but on this occasion was unable to make an attack owing to its low height and intensive Bofors fire.

Two fighter sweeps were made by the Messerschmitts during 14 May, the first occurring at about 0800. Four Hurricanes from 185 Squadron were scrambled with Flt Lt Jeffries (Z2840) leading, as noted in the unit's diary:

> "F/Lt Jeffries was observed to be having some fun and games with two Me109s at very low altitude. In spite of their determined efforts, he managed to outwit them and had not so much as one hole when he landed."

It was a different outcome in the afternoon, when four more 185 Squadron Hurricanes were scrambled to provide top cover for 261 Squadron as Messerschmitts from III/JG27 swept in. Oblt von Kageneck closed in on Plt Off Hamish Hamilton's Hurricane (Z2901), and shot it down. Critically wounded, the 20-year-old Scots pilot from Midlothian crash-landed his aircraft on Marsa Sports Club racetrack, where he died shortly afterwards. Extremely popular, Hamilton had only recently achieved acedom and had apparently been recommended for a DFC[17]. Sqn Ldr Whittingham wrote:

> "One of the finest characters I have met. It was he who always took extra watches when things were hottest . . . Dear old Hamish, you could almost smell the heather of Scotland when you spoke to him. Always so romantically dressed and so elusive. He was the scarlet pimpernel to the life.ß"

Plt Off Brian Cavan's 261 Squadron Hurricane (Z4087) was also hit in the skirmish and the pilot slightly wounded, while Sgt Ernie Wynne had attacked one Messerschmitt from below, but without observed results. Uffz Karl Kühdorf of 7/JG26 apparently claimed a Hurricane in this action but seems not to have had it confirmed, and may well have been the pilot responsible for the damage to Cavan's aircraft.

261 Squadron notched up a rare success – and its last at Malta – on the morning of 15 May, when two sections were sent off early to investigate an unidentified plot. Plt Off John Pain (Z4060) recalled:

> "This was on the morning pre-dawn patrol when I was scrambled for an unusual early morning recce. I chased him west along the south coast of the island and closed off Gozo. He went into the drink well out to sea off the island, by which time I was light on fuel and out of ammo. There was no doubt he crashed into the sea as I watched him hit, but I did not get confirmation of this as there was no one else to see it and RDF didn't seem to have much coverage up that way."

Although Pain thought his quarry was a He111, it may well have been an SM79bis of 32°Gruppo BT that failed to return from a sortie to Malta. Four more SM79bis were despatched to search for the missing aircraft but one ran out of fuel and had to ditch, the crew being picked up by an Italian hospital ship. There was no sign of the missing aircraft. 185 Squadron suffered another loss during the day when Sgts Cyril Bamberger and Ernie Wynne took off at midday to cover a flight of 261 Squadron, which had scrambled as Messerschmitts again approached the island. Without warning the top cover pair were bounced by Hptm Max Dobislav of III/JG27 who shot down Wynne's aircraft (Z3035), which crashed between Kirkop and Safi; the 22-year-old from Essex was killed. On landing, the shattered Bamberger, who had survived many weeks of combat, announced to one and all: "I'm not taking off from this bloody island again!" True to his word, he did not fly operationally again with the Squadron, being posted temporarily to Safi as a test pilot until the following month, when he was flown back to the UK via Gibraltar aboard a Sunderland[18].

Meanwhile, following five relatively uneventful days with only minor incursions, Malta lost another Hurricane to the Messerschmitts of III/JG27 when Oblt von Kageneck shot down Plt Off Tony Reeves of 261 Squadron, who baled out of N2673 with minor injuries. This proved to be III/JG27's last victory over Malta, as the Gruppe departed Sicily for North Africa. Following the shooting down of Flt Lt Westmacott, Flt Lt Pat Hancock had transferred to 185 Squadron to take command of B Flight, but his appointment very nearly ended prematurely, however, as the unit's diary reveals:

> "F/Lt Hancock ran out of main tanks and couldn't turn on reserve as his petrol cock had stuck. After wrestling with it several times, he decided to land with no engine. This is always a bit tricky and, as luck would have it, he pranged neatly on a wall on the edge of

the aerodrome and did his aircraft no good at all although, luckily, he was unhurt himself."

Further reinforcements for the Middle East were on the way from Gibraltar aboard a convoy, which included the carriers *Ark Royal*, *Eagle* and *Furious*. On board were 48 Hurricanes divided between 213, 229 and 249 Squadrons[19], the latter destined for Malta (although the pilots were unaware), the other two for Egypt. All aircraft were to refuel at Malta. The Hurricanes were to be guided and navigated by a specially formed flight of Fulmars called 800X Squadron under the command of Lt Cdr Geoffrey Hare DSC, who recalled:

"The Operations Officer of *Furious* and I carefully prepared diagrammatic charts for each Hurricane pilot of probable times, courses and distances so that they would not be lost should they become detached. This turned out to be a very wise precaution. The day before we arrived in Gibraltar we received a signal from Admiral Sir James Somerville of Force H, who was in command of the operation, saying that on arrival in harbour we were to berth stern to stern with *Ark Royal* so that some of our Hurricanes could be transferred to her and rolled off *Furious* direct onto *Ark Royal*. He also required 800X Squadron's Fulmar IIs to be transferred to Ark and they would be replaced as navigational escort to the Hurricanes by her Fulmar Is, which were teased out and no longer suitable as fighters. I protested, as CO of 800X, to the Commander Flying that the object of the operation was the safe delivery of the Hurricanes to Malta but my protest went unheeded.

During the night of 18-19 May, *Furious* arrived at Gibraltar and the exchange of aircraft took place; then both ships sailed in company. Next morning my senior pilot, Lt(A) P.J. Connolly, reported that the four Fulmar Is transferred to us were indeed in a very ropey condition but maintenance crews were working on them. He later reported that they were in worse condition than he had first thought and doubted whether they were fit for the job. I then went again to the Commander Flying and said I wished to report the fact to the Captain. He advised me not to do so as, he said, the Captain was a difficult man, and he had no intention of telling him himself. However, I insisted and he ushered me into the Captain's sea cabin. I didn't stay there long: I was told very forcibly that the job had to be done and to get the hell out of his cabin. I said I fully realised the job had to be done but I wished to protest against the shabby trick *Ark Royal* had played on us. This incensed the Captain even more and out of that cabin I got!"

When news of the imminent arrival of more Hurricanes reached Sqn Ldr Whittingham, he confided to his diary:

"Another squadron is booked to arrive and we are to move to the Middle East. We are all greatly cheered by the news. These past months have been a tremendous strain upon us all. It is sad to think back to that company and still sadder to recall the many boys, cheerful, youthful and optimistic, whom I knew so intimately and who are now gone forever."

Neither could reinforcements come soon enough for the survivors of 185 Squadron, whose diarist wrote:

"Our numbers grow smaller and smaller as the days go by. We are back to operating two aeroplanes now which are the sad remnants of the 18 Hurricane IIs which have been at Malta. As we ourselves have so few aeroplanes, let us hope that this anticipated stream of Hurricanes will bring forth a pleasant surprise for 185 Squadron."

Next day, the diarist was able to add:

"This was a great day [21 May] as 48 Hurricanes went through on their way to the Middle East. We were all very busy with refuelling both aircraft and pilots, and it was a great feat that although the first visitor did not land until nearly 0945, they were all ready and on their way by half past one. No raids occurred except a solitary recco first thing in the morning. All the Hurricanes reached their destination safely with one exception."

Although the Hurricanes had been safely delivered with the exception of that flown by 213 Squadron's Plt Off N.C. Downie[20], the operation had not been a success for the clapped-out Fulmars of 800X Squadron, and particularly not so for Lt Cdr Geoffrey Hare and his pilot:

"Pat Connolly and I were in the third Fulmar [N1994] and we joined up our range of Hurricanes with some left from the second range which had returned. In all I expect we were about a dozen strong. After going comfortably for nearly an hour, Pat reported that we were losing engine pressure. At that time we were flying about 4,000 feet and were 40 miles off the North African coast. A minute or two later Pat said he couldn't keep height for lack of power and we would have to ditch. I immediately gestured to the Hurricanes to carry on for Malta by themselves and we turned for the coast, losing height all the way. The morning was fine and the sea was calm. Pat told me over the intercom to stand clear as he was about to press the button of the destructor switch for the IFF gear. Nothing happened. I then burrowed into the cockpit to wrench the gear from its housing, but in so doing I became unplugged and did not hear the pilot shouting that we were ditching. I struck the IFF gear with my forehead with such force that my goggles, which I was wearing luckily, were shattered and my face badly bruised and bleeding profusely. I was scarcely conscious but Pat helped me out of the machine and, as the dinghy hadn't emerged after the ditching, we had to swim about 250 yards to the beach."

On reaching the beach they were greeted and then arrested by a party of Vichy French gendarmes and Arabs. Initially taken by boat to Bône, they were later transferred to Algiers, where Lt Cdr Hare received treatment for his facial injuries. A second Fulmar was also obliged to ditch, the crew fortuitously being picked up by a destroyer and taken to Malta. One of the Hurricane pilots, Flt Sgt Fred Etchells of 249 Squadron, also recalled the flight:

"All 24 of our Hurricanes were tightly crowded at the blunt end of the carrier and I remember the almost complete disbelief at the impossibly short runway. *Ark Royal* then opened her throttles and headed into wind at something like 30 knots, which meant a further 30mph by the aircraft would give us the 60mph needed for take-off. Conscious of the heavily-laden state of my machine, I was grateful for the great height of the flight deck above sea level, which had made me quite dizzy when looking over the side earlier in the journey. It meant no immediate necessity to climb until adequate flying speed was gained. I recall the joy of seeing the aircraft in front of me become safely airborne before reaching the end of deck at the sharp end. Many of our pilots swore they bent their throttle levers to ensure maximum possible revs!

Our Hurricanes were being led by a Fulmar, which was forced to return to the carrier after 45 minutes with engine trouble. But before long a replacement Fulmar met us and we turned round and again headed for Malta. After almost five and a half hours in the air, during which time two enemy aircraft crossed our track heading for Tunisia from Sicily, we saw Malta ahead – in the middle of a bombing raid. We had been briefed to circle a small island off the south coast called Filfla, in order to identify ourselves, but the state of our fuel gauges decided the issue and we flew straight in to land at the first aerodrome sighted – Luqa in my case and several others, though others landed at Hal Far and Takali." [21]

185 Squadron's diarist continued:

"We are pleased to hear that most of 249 Squadron pilots are here, and their place has been taken by members of 261 Squadron who took their aircraft on to Egypt for them. All that now remains is for some more Hurricane IIs to arrive for both us and 249. The present situation is that we are left with about 30-odd Hurricane Is, which we shall fly alternatively with 249 Squadron for the next week or so."

Whilst 185 Squadron was pleased to have the company, 249 Squadron did not view the situation with quite the same enthusiasm. Sqn Ldr Butch Barton and his pilots[22] were dismayed to learn they were to stay on the island, for they had no kit with them, all being aboard ship with the ground party bound for Egypt. Kit and groundcrew were not seen again by most of the pilots. Worse was to follow, for they were taken by bus to Takali where they were informed they were to fly the well-worn, battle-weary Hurricane Is left by 261 Squadron. One of the new arrivals, Flt Lt Tom Neil was not impressed with what he saw, and described the Hurricanes as: "A poor crowd of battered Mark Is – no squadron markings, some with Vokes filters, some not. A variety of propellers etc . . ." Another reported seeing tailwheel tyres stuffed with straw due to lack of spares, and the inherited Hurricanes were undeniably in a poor state of repair and serviceability. Plt Off John Pain agreed with the comment regarding the condition of the aircraft left behind: "By the time we left, aircraft were being repaired with dope-painted linen or cloth from anywhere, and metal repairs were made with the aid of 'Players' 50s tins. And, of course, cannibalisation where practicable." One of the departing pilots, Sgt Arthur Todd, recalled:

> "The Hurricanes we had on Malta had Vokes filters which we didn't really need, but they needed them in the desert so we did a swop. We flew ours with long-range tanks with electric pumps, navigated by a Wellington for five hours ten minutes, all over the sea, and then we did it all again – this time a six-hour flight to Mersa Matruh. Of course we had no proper maps, just a plan on a piece of roneod paper with a line on it and a course, and that was all."[23]

Soon joining the migration south was Flg Off Laubscher and his flight of five pilots, who had just arrived back at Malta aboard a Sunderland from Aboukir:

> "We arrived at Hal Far on the night of 21 May. When we got back to Takali we found that our dispersal area had been moved across the drome to the Rabat side. Although we had only just finished a nine-hour Sunderland flight we were put on readiness immediately. A scramble followed. After a few minutes the Controller reported that the bogies had gone away. I landed and then opened my throttle and ran across the drome, my tailwheel raised, to get back to dispersal for refuelling as soon as possible. I saw the erks standing around waiting for me as I throttled back and started braking. As I stopped the engine and was busy loosening my harness straps I suddenly realised that there wasn't a person near me. I looked to my left and saw a peculiar wisp of white smoke coming out of the ground about 50 yards away. I looked quickly to starboard and saw an enormous black column of earth erupt into the sky! I didn't even wait to undo my parachute but scrambled out of my machine, parachute thumping behind, and dived under a nearby lorry to find my fitter and rigger lying there. A Ju88 had appeared out of the blue and dive-bombed the dispersal point. I still believe he was trying to hit me personally – a most unfriendly gesture! Two days later we were again flying Hurricanes across the Mediterranean but this time they routed us directly to El Amriya, south of Alexandria. The flight lasted five and a half hours and we just made it with some aircrafts' tanks already showing empty."

261 Squadron had defended Malta since its formation from 418 Flight in August 1940, and had suffered severe losses in the period ending 21 May 1941, when it was effectively disbanded. Although the Squadron was credited with at least 100 victories in Malta's skies, 21 of its pilots had paid the supreme sacrifice[24]. The surviving pilots of 261 Squadron were not sorry to go, an entry in Plt Off Doug Whitney's logbook epitomising the feeling of most as the Hurricanes left Takali for the last time: "The finest sight of Malta I've seen . . ." It was not only 261 Squadron's Hurricanes that 249 Squadron inherited but also the departing pilots' girlfriends, as recorded by Flt Lt Ginger Neil shortly after his arrival:

> "I chanced to be in dispersal at Takali when a gharry, with the statutory straw-hatted nag,

creaked past in a swirl of dust. At the reins and dextrously flicking a whip with Beau
Brummell aplomb, was a pilot of 261 Squadron whom I knew would be shortly leaving,
and alongside him a delectable dark-eyed girl of about twenty whose name I later
discovered was Patsy."[25]

Also arriving at Malta at this time was Wg Cdr P.J.H. Halahan DFC, known as 'Bull' to his
friends, who had commanded 1 Squadron during the fighting in France in 1940. In more
recent times he had acted as RAF officer in charge of flying aboard *Ark Royal* during
Operation 'Dunlop' at the end of April. He was now to take up Fighter Control duties at
Air HQ. The surviving Fulmars of 800X Flight were destined for Crete, but with the
imminent fall of that island were retained at Malta and would find a new rôle as night
intruders. With the knowledge that an airborne invasion of Crete was imminent, Air HQ
placed some of 69 Squadron's Marylands on readiness to fly long-range sorties against the
troop-carriers, as the unit's CO, Sqn Ldr Titch Whiteley recalled:

> ". . . we were stood by to intercept transport aircraft proceeding from Italy to North Africa
> [*sic*]. Air HQ expected to detect these transports east of Malta at extreme range. I could
> spare some Marylands while still meeting the PR tasks. I remember sitting in the cockpit
> and being cooked by the sun for a few hours, but we were never scrambled."

The day after its arrival, 249 Squadron was split into two flights, one commanded by Sqn
Ldr Barton and the other by Flt Lt Neil. Each flight was to operate for half of each day,
allowing 50 per cent of the pilots to be off duty at any one time. 185 Squadron now moved
to Takali alongside 249 Squadron with its remaining ten Mark Is and two Mark IIs, leaving
Luqa and Hal Far free for use as staging airfields to Egypt, and bases for the bombers and
reconnaissance aircraft. Its introduction to the battle of Malta came as something of a
shock for 249 Squadron: a dozen Hurricanes were gathered round the dispersal tent at
Takali on the afternoon of 25 May when, just before 1400, the sirens sounded. Suddenly
Messerschmitts of 7/JG26 arrived with a crackle of gunfire, shooting-up the airfield.
Airman X wrote:

> "Machine-gunned by Me109s; eight of them came straight across our 12 machines on the
> runway, catching two on fire. They burnt out and three others were badly damaged. One of
> our groundcrew was badly injured and had eight bullets from the thigh downwards . . . A
> bad show, the Hurricanes should never have been on the deck, they should have been up to
> meet the 109s."

Flg Off Harrington's aircraft was hit by a cannon shell in the forward fuel tank, and another
lodged in his parachute pack; he was unhurt but his Hurricane burst into flames and was a
complete write-off. Sgt Colin McVean leapt from his cockpit and broke both legs, while
Flg Off Pat Wells suffered a bullet through his right ankle, as he recalled:

> "This was our first readiness in Malta and whilst sitting in the crew room we were
> astonished to hear the air-raid sirens howling – in the UK we had always been airborne
> before the sirens sounded. We rushed out to our aircraft and got ready for the scramble
> which never came. I noticed F/Lt Neil get out of his aircraft, obviously to go to the
> telephone. I am fundamentally lazy and decided that we would inevitably be scrambled, so
> it was less of an effort to remain in my aircraft and wait for it, helmet on and listening to
> the R/T. The next thing I saw was people running – I still could not hear anything due to
> my helmet – and on looking round saw the 109s starting their dive on the airfield. I tried
> to start the engine but the airmen on the starter battery trailer had fled, so I could not do a
> thing except huddle in the cockpit, waiting for the sensation of being hit. The aircraft was
> burning well and this, plus exploding ammunition, drove me out. Only when I got to the
> ground and tried to walk did I realise that I had a bullet through the top of my right ankle.

The ambulance came and I was filled with delicious brandy, but was instantly sick when I got to M'tarfa Hospital."

Four Hurricanes were claimed destroyed, two by Oblt Müncheberg and one each by Lt Johannsen and Obfw Karl Laube. It was believed that from an estimated 15 Hurricanes seen, six had been hit. In fact, two Hurricanes were totally destroyed, two others were considered irreparable and a fifth was less seriously damaged[26]. The débâcle came as a great blow to the confident pilots of 249 Squadron, as the reaction of Flg Off Harrington would demonstrate when, a few days later, a reconnaissance Maryland approached the airfield, looking for all the world like a Ju88. Harrington at once leapt into a slit trench in great haste, only to find it full of barbed wire which inflicted severe lacerations. Sympathy was not forthcoming from all quarters, as an entry in Airman X's diary reveals:

"The trouble with 249 is there is too much class distinction; every time we speak to an officer they try to make us stand at attention, but we soon cured them of that. The first day they came here, when the warning went and we all rushed to the shelter, one bright bastard said; 'Why do you brave crews run like rabbits when the siren goes?' Sunday's strafing showed them why. Very brave men the 249ers, they run like rabbits themselves now."

The attack on Takali by 7/JG26 was in effect a final fling by the Luftwaffe in Sicily, since German units had been steadily transferring to North Africa to assist Rommel's push in Cyrenaica. During its four months in Sicily, the Staffel had claimed 48 victories (46 Hurricanes, one Blenheim, one Wellington), of which 20 Hurricanes had been claimed by Oblt Joachim Müncheberg alone. During this period not a single operational loss had been sustained[27]. By the end of the month most German units had gone, leaving the Italians once again to defend their territory. The respite was most welcome in Malta and also allowed 249 Squadron time to settle in. The reduced Axis air activity enabled more offensive action be carried out and, on 27 May, six Blenheims from Malta attacked a convoy, losing two machines in return for an Italian freighter badly damaged. That night a formation of ten BR20Ms of the newly arrived 43°Stormo carried out a raid but without inflicting serious damage. They returned the following night and targeted Grand Harbour and Hal Far, but this time Hurricanes were able to prevent half of the bombers from reaching their targets, forcing them to return to base with their bomb loads intact.

This latest raid raised the total of alerts for the month to 98. According to official figures, in excess of 2,000 houses had been destroyed or seriously damaged since the outbreak of hostilities, and almost 12,000 people were now homeless. Fatalities amongst the civilian population were close to 300 with a further 250 seriously injured.

CHAPTER VI

THE HURRICANES REGAIN THE ADVANTAGE

June – July 1941

For Malta's defenders the tide had turned. The start of the new month saw the arrival of Air Commodore Hugh Pughe Lloyd MC DFC who took over as AOC from Air Vice-Marshal Maynard. Lloyd had been serving as SASO with 2 Group of Bomber Command in the UK. On arrival at Malta, Lloyd and the other passengers and crew of the Sunderland were fortunate to escape serious injury:

> "The final course was then set for Malta where we were fortunate to alight in Kalafrana Bay in one piece. The direction of the alighting was towards the island and our pilot overshot three times and went round again narrowly avoiding the high ground on each occasion. When we did alight the aircraft was swung so violently to miss a rock that all the passengers were thrown into a heap and battered in the process, all the crockery on board was broken and a wing float torn off. Fortunately I was sitting next to the pilot and only bumped my nose."[1]

The new AOC's promotion to Air Vice-Marshal soon followed. The change in fortunes – with the withdrawal of the Luftwaffe from Sicily and the arrival at Malta of Blenheim detachments from his old Group – enabled Lloyd to implement his main task, which was to organise an offensive against Axis Mediterranean supply routes to North Africa in support of Rommel's push in the desert.

For the first week of June there was little employment for the Hurricane pilots, although four of 185 Squadron were scrambled on 1 June in a failed attempt to intercept an aircraft skirting the island. The newly arrived Blenheims carried out a strike against a convoy on 3 June, although the operation cost the lives of the Blenheim CO and his crew. On the same date, Sqn Ldr Barton registered 249 Squadron's first victory over the island when he intercepted an SM79bis of 56^Squadriglia as it was flying from Sicily to Libya as part of the air cover for the convoy. Flying Z4043, he recorded: "SM79 shot down into sea – on fire off Gozo – no crew known to have escaped." Ten Franco Miscione and his crew did indeed perish. Having refuelled and re-armed, Barton led a section of Hurricanes to the scene of action and carried out an unsuccessful search for survivors. With the onset of darkness the raiders returned and both Sqn Ldr Mould and Flt Lt Jeffries were scrambled. One or two aircraft were illuminated by searchlights but the two pilots were unable to close in time, Mould being particularly unlucky as his intended victim disappeared from view as he was manoeuvring into position. On returning from one sortie, Plt Off Cliff Gray almost came to grief when he mistook the Sunderland flare path in Kalafrana Bay for the aerodrome runway, realising his error just in time to avoid landing in the sea. The next tangible encounter also occurred at night, during the early hours of 5/6 June, when Flt Lt Pat Hancock of 185 Squadron intercepted a bomber, which he identified as a He111:

> "Saw enemy aircraft illuminated south-west of Grand Harbour – attacked and observed tracer strikes – lost it, but then found it again by moonlight – attacked again and saw further tracer strikes. Out of ammunition and returned to base."

Hancock was credited with a probable. At this time 185 Squadron was redesignated as the island's night fighter unit, a move made possible by the arrival during the day of yet more reinforcements. Under the codename Operation 'Rocket', 43 Hurricane IIs arrived from the carriers *Ark Royal* and *Furious*. Those belonging to 229 Squadron, which was destined for Egypt, were exchanged for Malta's remaining old Mark Is, while those comprising 46

Squadron were to remain at Malta under the command of Sqn Ldr A.C. 'Sandy' Rabagliati DFC. Although the Squadron contained a sprinkling of experienced pilots who had seen action during the Battle of Britain, most were straight from OTUs[2]. One of the new arrivals was Plt Off Albert 'Andy' Anderson, a nephew of Captain Albert Ball VC, one of the leading aces of World War I; of this episode and his thoughts in general, he wrote home:

"I felt vaguely ill for the first two days on the water, it was cold and quite rough. Now the sea is smooth and ultramarine and the air warm. I feel fine. It's a bit late in the day, but I've become convinced that the thing that really matters, above everything else at the moment, is to fight this war with all we've got. Up till the time I started on this trip I'd tried to make the war affect me as little as possible and apart from my particular job wanted nothing to do with it, but merely wanted to be left alone to mess about with my cars. I don't seem to be able to work up a great deal of enthusiasm about cars now and it was that fact that shook me into realising that literally nothing matters now but to go all out and get the war finished. My conversation is a very small drop in the ocean, but I think sooner or later everyone will have to face it."

A few days later he again wrote to his parents:

"I expect the address will surprise you, as much as it did me when they decided to keep us here. How long we shall be stuck I don't know. The trip out was uneventful and everything went without a hitch, pretty good effort getting all those machines out here right under Jerry's nose. The air raids here are fairly heavy and we've been in the shelters every night to date. We've not had any action yet although we've taken off on several false alarms. I don't think we shall have to wait long . . ."

Meanwhile, a number of postings effecting the Hurricane units took place, with Flt Lt Chubby Eliot and Sgt Cyril Bamberger among others leaving for the UK. 249 Squadron received four new pilots on loan from 185 Squadron – Plt Offs Gay Bailey and Denis Winton, Sgts Fred Sheppard and Jock Livingston, while Plt Offs Brian Cavan, Douglas Robertson and R.T. Saunders joined 249 Squadron from the now departed 261 Squadron, and Sgt Al Jolly was attached to 46 Squadron from 185 Squadron.

There followed a period of relative inactivity by the enemy during daylight hours, though Italian bombers continued their night raids. On the night of 7/8 June, Sqn Ldr Barton (Z3063) again scored when he shot down a BR20M of 243^Squadriglia (243-4), which fell in flames at 0330 south-west of Qrendi; Barton noted:

"I well remember the BR20 I attacked flew for a long time on fire over Valetta and Malta, much to the delight of the local populace."

On his return to Takali, Barton set off with his section and carried out a search for survivors. There were only two – Ten Sergio Reggiani, the pilot, and his co-pilot M.llo Guglielmo Mazzolenis, both of whom came down on land; the remainder of the crew were lost. Mazzolenis later told his captors:

"The Hurricane came in from the direction of the moon. [We] could see him quite well. His attack was very determined and the gunner was unable to return accurate fire, as the Hurricane was weaving across [our] tail. The first burst hit one engine which went up in flames and from that moment the crew prepared to bale out."

A second of the unit's bombers was attacked by Flg Off John Beazley and Plt Off Titch Palliser (Z4028) jointly, and was believed to have gone down into the sea 40 miles from the island; the pair were credited with a probable, but in fact the seriously damaged aircraft succeeded in limping home having suffered some 50 bullet strikes. Among those to witness Sqn Ldr Barton's victory was Plt Off Andy Anderson:

". . . the night flyers brought down a large bomber in flames. It really was an amazing sight. I saw the whole thing from the time our fighter shot him up the backside. It lit up the sky as it came down and blew up with an almighty explosion; we also saw the Italians coming down in their parachutes by the glow of their plane. The searchlights here are really good, very different from in England."

On the morning of 9 June, four of 249 Squadron's Hurricanes led by Flg Off Harrington were sent to investigate aircraft some 50 miles out to sea, intercepting four SM79bis of 193^Squadriglia which were being ferried from Sicily to Castel Benito in Libya. Sottoten Marcello Weber's aircraft (MM21852) was shot down in flames, Sgt Jock Livingston being credited with its destruction although Sgt Dennis Rex (Z4087) also claimed one destroyed, while Flg Off Harrington and Sgt Roy Lawson claimed damage to the other two aircraft. Sgt Rex subsequently had to bale out, apparently due to a glycol leak, but was later rescued together with the pilot of the downed bomber. The commander of the rescue launch, Flt Lt Edward Hardie, recorded:

"We had a very vague idea of where he [Sgt Rex] was; we knew he was about 50 to 60 miles out . . . visibility was poor and we went on and on – we did not see anything and I was about to give up in despair when I saw something on the horizon that looked like wreckage . . . it was the wreckage of an Italian troopship. It was only the fact that I altered my course like that, that I came across the fighter pilot swimming like mad and, when I got him on board, I said, 'Where were you going?' and he said, 'I thought I would give you boys a helping hand in getting nearer Malta.' I told him that he had been heading for Benghazi! He told me that before he ditched he had shot down one of the Italian bombers and he did not know if any of the crew were still alive . . . we looked around and came across one of the wings of the Italian bomber, on which was the very badly burned pilot. He had torn strips off his clothing and bound himself up. When we threw a line and pulled him aboard, I had to restrain him because he wanted to shake hands with the boy who had shot him down. They had a lot of brandy together. I was now nearer to Benghazi than I was to Malta [53 miles out from Malta] and when I was on the way back I saw something in the water – a dinghy with two FAA officers in. They had ditched after running out of fuel whilst on a submarine patrol. We had picked up the FAA pilot before. So I went out for one and came back with four."

Weber's co-pilot, M.llo Luciano Fabbri was also rescued; the other four members of the crew were lost. The RAF Air-Sea Rescue launches went out after friend or foe alike, and achieved a remarkable number of rescues. One of these concerned a wounded Italian pilot, as recorded in the memoirs of Sybil Dobbie, the Governor's daughter:

"I knew a Naval surgeon-lieutenant who went out with a rescue launch to pick up a wounded Italian pilot some way out to sea. He said they pulled him on board and gave a first hasty dressing to his wounds, but the boy (he was very young) was obviously terrified of the reception he was going to get and had been brought up on appalling tales of British treatment of prisoners. A rather hostile crowd were awaiting when the launch came ashore, which apparently confirmed his fear, but he was hurried quickly away without incident to an ambulance and taken to hospital.

The Germans were a tougher proposition. One of them tried to escape. Considering Malta is an island and very closely guarded, he was something of an optimist, but he thought that if he could get down to the harbour he might be able to steal a small boat and sail back the 60 miles to Sicily. He had managed to save a little food from his rations. He broke a leg, however, getting over the high prison wall and so had no chance of putting his wild scheme into execution . . . one cannot withhold admiration for the spirit that prompted the German's disastrous effort . . ."[3]

With the end of operations on 10 June, Air HQ issued a communique on its assessment of enemy aircraft losses to Malta's fighters in the first year of war, which revealed initial credits for 99 shot down (possibly later adjusted to 111), plus 43 probables and 37 damaged, for the loss of 41 fighters and 23 pilots. The guns were officially credited with 28 victories and nine probables.

For 46 Squadron the first clash with the enemy over Malta occurred during the early morning of 11 June, when seven Hurricanes were scrambled on the approach of an SM79bis reconnaissance aircraft of 194^Squadriglia and 17 escorting MC200s from 7°Gruppo CT at 8,000 feet. Sgt Norman Walker, who was acting as 'weaver' above and behind the other Hurricanes, was the first to spot the SM79bis when it was 2,000 feet above him:

> "I was first to attack. I opened fire at 250 yards giving three-second burst and then closed to 100-50 yards, firing all the time. I observed pieces fall from starboard wing and white smoke started pouring from the port engine. I then broke away, at the same time observing five enemy fighters in front. These aircraft did not attack."

By now three other Hurricanes had arrived on the scene, Sqn Ldr Rabagliati (Z2680), Flg Off Peter McGregor and Plt Off Jack Grant all attacking the reconnaissance machine and setting its port wing on fire, following which it plunged into the sea. Four members of the crew were seen to bale out, but Ten Giorgio Pozzolini and his crew all perished. Escorting Macchis claimed two Hurricanes shot down by Ten Armando Cibin and Serg Facchini. One Hurricane, Z2480 flown by Flt Lt Norman Burnett, failed to return. The rescue vessel *Jade*, a former Hull fishing trawler captained by Mr William Fellowes, searched to within sight of the Sicilian coast but was unable to find any trace of wreckage or pilot. Two E-boats came out to challenge *Jade* and gunfire was exchanged, one crewman being mortally wounded but a hit was also registered on the larger of the two E-boats, which then broke off the action.

Two major engagements were fought over and around the island on 12 June. At 0721, 18 Hurricanes were scrambled – drawn equally from 46 and 249 Squadrons – to intercept an incoming reconnaissance flight which comprised a single SM79bis from 57^Squadriglia flying at 16,000 feet with an escort of 15 MC200s of 7°Gruppo CT, while 15 more from 17°Gruppo CT provided indirect support. The Hurricanes closed, Flt Lt Neil (Z2397) misidentifying his victim as a "Messerschmitt 109 with a light-coloured nose"; he continued:

> "I fired. My tracer with its familiar flicks of curving, whipping red, reached out and clutched both fuselage and wings in a brief rippling embrace. After which it had gone. Below my tipping wing. Downwards. Turning. Diving steeply. I followed, violently, keeping it in sight. I was aware of the sea directly beneath. Going like mad now, everything roaring and shaking. Firing! Then a small blob that was a parachute, detaching, a white streak at first, then developing, finally drifting sideways before rushing quickly in my direction and vanishing to my rear. Further below me still, a diminishing silhouette and a sudden slow-motion eruption of water which died quickly into a disc of pale green as the aircraft went in."[4]

Neil was adamant that his victim had been a Messerschmitt:

> "The aircraft I encountered alongside the Savoia had been a 109. I ought to know as I'd been shooting at the blighters for the last nine months! One or two, including Crossey and Etchells, agreed, but others were doubtful. You couldn't confuse a 109 with a Macchi 200; one had an in-line engine and the other a ruddy great radial. I found myself hoping that the chap in the parachute would be picked up, but by late afternoon there was no news."[5]

Sgt Jock Livingston claimed a probable in this fight, but 249 Squadron lost two Hurricanes, Plt Off Rioch Munro being killed when his aircraft (Z4043) crashed into the sea, while Plt Off Saunders (Z4385) baled out, wounded. Fortunately, he was located by Sgt Noel MacGregor of 46 Squadron who reported the position. Four Macchis circled overhead but did not intervene as Saunders was picked up by a rescue launch. A third Hurricane, flown by Plt Off Denis Winton, was damaged during the combat and forced-landed at Safi airstrip. 46 Squadron claimed two more Macchis. One was shared by Plt Off Peter Rathie and Sgt Harry Johnston, who each pursued the same fighter which was seen over Hal Far; Rathie reported:

"I gave chase and saw another Hurricane doing likewise about 500 feet below. As I had the advantage of height and speed I was able, or so it seemed to me, to get in between the two aircraft. The Hurricane, behind and to one side, started firing. The enemy aircraft turned into a tight turn to port, which I was able to keep inside, firing at intervals. The Hurricane behind was still firing. After some minutes the enemy aircraft turned to starboard and commenced to do a half-roll (the pilot was seen to hold his hands above his head). With the enemy aircraft in this position I was able to hit the pilot and the rear petrol tank exploded, and the pilot baled out. Two other aircraft and myself circled the pilot in the water for some considerable time."

The other Hurricane pilot involved, Sgt Johnston, later reported:

"I noticed a Macchi fighter heading north-west. I followed him down and, at about 2,000 feet opened fire, range 300 yards, closing in. He turned and I gave another burst. He went into a half-roll and baled out. The enemy aircraft burst into flames and dived. I then noticed another Hurricane behind him just before my second burst, and saw him firing as well."

Flt Lt Pip Lefevre had in the meantime climbed to 22,000 feet and saw Macchis and Fiats below him, heading for Sicily. Diving with two or three others, he closed on one MC200, fired a two-second burst and obtained strikes, but another Hurricane then shot down the Macchi at a height of just 100 feet above the sea. Observing another Macchi at the same level Lefevre fired his remaining ammunition into it, closing from 250 to 100 yards and reported that it crashed straight into the sea. Subsequently, he spotted a third Macchi trailing smoke and being chased by Hurricanes. 46 Squadron suffered no losses. Despite these detailed claims it seems that there was a fair degree of double claiming: Sottoten Umberto Curcio of 76^Squadriglia failed to return in MC200 MM5334, while Serg Antonio Tirapelle forced-landed near Agrigento on return. The SM79bis also returned in a damaged condition, having been hit by AA fire as it passed over the island and again during an attack by Sgt MacGregor of 46 Squadron who reported "hits but no result". Nevertheless, the SM79's centre engine was put out of action which resulted in the reconnaissance mission being terminated. For the Italians, the close escort pilots had less opportunity to engage in dogfighting than those of 17°Gruppo CT, and claimed just two Hurricanes shot down, while their colleagues submitted claims for no fewer than seven and two probables[6].

During the early afternoon, and for the second time that day, a red cross-marked air-sea rescue Z506B floatplane (MM45292) of 612^Squadriglia left Syracuse to search for the missing pilot, Sottoten Curcio, escorted by a section of CR42s from 74^Squadriglia. Hurricanes from 46 Squadron were again scrambled, intercepting the seaplane flying at about 200 feet some 45 miles from Grand Harbour. Sqn Ldr Rabagliati, who was leading the nine Hurricanes in Z2491, and his No2 Sgt Tom Hackston both fired at the Cant but broke away when they saw the markings, as the CO reported:

"Sighted one aircraft flying at sea level. Dived to attack, gave short burst. Saw it was a Red Cross machine and broke off; other fighters shot it down. Gave one short burst at CR42. No results observed. Gave another short burst at another CR42 and he turned sharply, coming at me head-on; gave a short burst from head-on and the aircraft fell to pieces in the air. Saw two other enemy aircraft shot down and one Hurricane. One enemy aircraft definitely a CR42. Orbited Cant seaplane after engagement, which was burning furiously on water but no aircraft in sight, so returned to base. One of the CR42s shot down Blue 1 (Sgt Walker)."

Sgt Hackston also reported meeting MC200s:

". . . dived to attack to give one short burst. Later I observed the Cant floatplane blazing on the water – another Hurricane broke away. Saw one CR42 dive into the sea. About five minutes [later] I was jumped on by three Macchis when I was at sea level. Had a running fight of about eight minutes. Put a long burst into one Macchi from a range of 200 yards, closing to 50 yards. Black smoke came out and one piece flew off. I did not see this aircraft crash into the sea as I was being engaged by the other two machines. I out-distanced them after two to three minutes."

Sgt Rocky Main followed up the attack on the Z506B and shot it down into the sea:

"Sighted one Cant seaplane at sea level. Close in to range from astern and fired three short bursts. Port engine burst into flames. Observed red crosses on wings after the attack. Others had attacked it previously. Climbed to 2,000 feet and fired one three-second burst from beam astern at CR42. Engine burst into flames and pilot baled out. Machine dived into sea. Saw another CR42 shot down."

One CR42 (MM7046) failed to return and Sottoten Vittorio Bartoccini was killed, while a second CR42 was damaged although the pilot, M.llo Germano Gasperoni reported that he had downed a Hurricane in return. He was undoubtedly responsible for shooting down Sgt Norman Walker (Z2900), who was posted missing. On return, Sqn Ldr Rabagliati was again soon airborne with his section to search for the missing pilot, but no trace of the Scot from Motherwell was found. Another Z506B rescue aircraft, bearing the civil registration I-POLA, was despatched when the first Cant and the CR42 failed to return. Nine CR42s provided close escort while 15 MC200s gave indirect support and nine flew a sweep over the general area. Nothing was seen and, on return, the escort left the seaplane about ten miles off Cape Passero where it was caught by seven Hurricanes of 249 Squadron which had been scrambled when the Italian formation appeared on the radar. Flt Sgt Fred Etchells recalled:

"On third scramble of the day I shot down a Cant Z506 near Sicily, which had red crosses on its wings and was apparently an air-sea rescue aircraft – S/Ldr Barton disapproved but AOC approved. I did not see the crosses on the wings at the time and do not know if it would have made a difference had I done so."

One man on board was killed and two wounded. On this occasion the survivors were successfully rescued by another Italian craft. Air Vice-Marshal Lloyd appeared to confirm his support for the actions of the pilots who had shot down the ASR floatplanes, when he wrote:

"Two of their fighters had been shot down into the sea only 15 miles from the Sicilian coast and, as it was certain that the Axis would come out with a naval floatplane complete with fighter escort to rescue the pilots, we awaited our opportunity. As soon as the floatplane came out, the Hurricanes shot it down. Undeterred by this event, the Axis sent out another with heavier escort; and when this second floatplane had been lost . . . we allowed them to make rescues as they chose."[7]

The Regia Aeronautica was conspicuous by its absence over the next few days, which proved fortuitous for the defenders as, on 14 June, there was another delivery of Hurricanes. On this occasion *Ark Royal* was joined by the new Fleet carrier HMS *Victorious*, which had on board 28 Hurricanes of desert-bound 238 Squadron. *Ark Royal* carried a further 20 such aircraft of 260 Squadron bound for the same destination, with Malta as the staging post. As the Hurricanes became airborne, Hudsons from Gibraltar arrived to navigate each batch of 12 to Malta. One Hurricane failed to take off, a second crashed into the sea, and a third suffered engine problems en route and was last seen heading for the North African coast, where it landed at Blida with fuel leakage problems; before he was taken prisoner the pilot set fire to his aircraft. As the remainder reached Malta, one (Z4356) overshot the runway on arrival and hit a wall, although Sgt Robert Wilson was unhurt. However, a second (Z4317) spun in and crashed north-west of Luqa, killing the pilot, Sgt Robert MacPherson, also of 260 Squadron. Meanwhile, Fulmars, rescue boats and Hurricanes of 249 Squadron were sent on a search for the two missing pilots, Flt Lt Neil finding 238 Squadron's Sgt Campbell in the sea some 40 miles from Kalafrana, from where he was safely picked up. The other pilot, Sgt A.D. Saunders of 260 Squadron, was also rescued. Flt Lt Neil provided an account of the rescue of Sgt Campbell:

> "Leaving [Flg Off] Crossey to circle the tiny yellow dot in the water, I returned and made contact with the rescue launch, which was crashing and bouncing its way towards us at maximum speed, and after pointing it in the right direction, flew backwards and forwards endlessly, acting as a guide. After hours, it seemed, we watched it successfully make a pick-up, after which we left, full of warm feelings. It was nice to be able to save a life for a change."[8]

No sooner were the aircraft refuelled than the first left for Egypt, 21 departing that day, followed by 13 more over the next two days. Only a handful remained as reinforcements, their pilots continuing to North Africa aboard Wellingtons or Hudsons. Meanwhile, on Sicily, reinforcements were arriving from the mainland including 4°Stormo CT equipped with MC200s, which relieved 1°Stormo CT.

At around this time, 249 Squadron became involved in a misadventure which had sad repercussions for the recently-arrived Wg Cdr Bull Halahan, the new Senior Fighter Controller, as recalled by Flg Off Tommy Thompson:

> "Several of us went into Valetta for the evening and went first to the Great Britain Hotel for a drink. Before we even got our drinks a party of Maltese policemen burst in and arrested all of us for riotous behaviour . . ."

It transpired that shortly before the 249 Squadron party had arrived at the hotel, a crowd of drunken sailors had been evicted and it was these whom the Maltese police should have arrested; Thompson continued:

> "We were frog-marched – in full daylight – up the main street to the Opera House which was then doing duty as the police station as the proper one had been bombed, and were slung into bare cells. No beds, no blankets, bare rock, very uncomfortable. Among those present were Butch Barton, our CO, W/Cdr Bull Halahan from Air HQ, Cassidy, Harrington, Beazley, myself and a couple of others who I cannot now recall. We were released at 8am next morning and the fighter strength of Malta was restored. It had been a very uncomfortable night indeed and one I would not like to repeat. I think it was a put-up job as Halahan was exceedingly unpopular with Hugh Pughe Lloyd, the AOC, and he (Lloyd) was looking for an excuse to get rid of him. It was said of him (Bull) that he would have done better to plot the fuckers than fuck the plotters!"

Despite the mix-up and attempted explanation, Wg Cdr Halahan nobly accepted full responsibility completely and took the full brunt of the AOC's wrath. He was gone, posted away, virtually within 24 hours, and transported to Air HQ RAF Middle East aboard one of the RAAF Sunderlands – a sorry fate for such a notable fighter leader.

Nine MC200s from the newly-arrived 16°Gruppo CT approached Malta during the early afternoon of 18 June. 249 Squadron was scrambled and an interception made about

20 miles north of Grand Harbour, Plt Off Titch Palliser (Z4041) and Sgt Fred Sheppard (Z4070) jointly claiming one Macchi shot down, while a second was claimed as a probable, possibly the victim of Plt Off Gay Bailey attached from 185 Squadron. The aircraft flown by M.llo Sigismondo was badly damaged and belly-landed on return to base, the pilot wounded in one arm. During the fight Sgt Jock Livingston's aircraft (Z4058) was either hit or suffered a malfunction. A particular friend of his amongst the ground personnel, Cpl John Alton, recalled:

> "He desperately tried to bring his aircraft back with a glycol leak. When he was over Takali the aircraft caught fire and he abandoned it, alas too late – a couple of hundred feet cost him his life. I was always saddened when we lost a pilot but Jock's death affected me for quite a while."

Following a few more days of relative inactivity, the last week of June was to prove a most active one for 46 Squadron in particular, which found itself engaged for six days out of the nine. It started with a skirmish on 22 June, when 17 Hurricanes of 46 Squadron were scrambled to investigate an Italian reconnaissance aircraft with a large escort comprising 30 Macchis of 10°Gruppo CT. Sqn Ldr Rabagliati was vectored onto a smaller plot which turned out to be two stragglers from the main formation. Rabagliati (Z2526) dived onto their tails:

> "I fired at the right-hand one which immediately half-rolled and dived 500 feet. Bandit was lost for a few seconds in dive, then picked up when he flattened out. Followed him down and fired from dead astern a short burst, closing to 100 yards. Bandit rolled over straight into the sea."

Rabagliati's observation was apparently at fault, since although his Macchi had been damaged, M.llo Bignami of 84^Squadriglia was able to reach Sicily. In return, Serg Roberto Steppi of the same unit claimed a Hurricane shot down. The following morning (23 June) Sqn Ldr Rabagliati (Z2680) led four Hurricanes to strafe the Italian seaplane base at Syracuse, where moored seaplanes – Z501s and Z506Bs – and other general facilities were shot-up, as Rabagliati reported:

> "At 0525 attack was delivered on six Italian flying boats at moorings in the following manner. Dived to sea level in bay just south of Syracuse, pulled up over neck of land between bay and machine-gunned three flying boats, barracks and blockhouses. Attack was delivered at 250mph. Turned east directly after attack and flew out to sea."

While several of 46 Squadron's pilots were gaining successes, Plt Off Andy Anderson had missed out, as his latest letter home revealed:

> "The Squadron's had quite a bit of action this week. I had the wretched luck of my machine being unserviceable both times, so I missed it. I could have wept the second time as I was up with the Squadron and had to come back with an oxygen leak. The Squadron's done pretty well, ten Italians shot down for two of ours. If we go on at this rate I'm afraid they'll fetch the Jerries back down to help them again and then it won't be nearly as pleasant. The other squadrons on the island have also been doing quiet well (not so well as us!) . . . I'm quite used to the Hurricane now and like it the more I fly it. From the fights the Squadron's had to date it's proved superior to the Italian fighters in performance. We only hope and pray they don't send any Messerschmitts down this way because the Hurricane doesn't like them one bit."

Plt Off Anderson had his first experience of combat early on 25 June, when a large incoming raid was plotted and 18 Hurricanes drawn equally from 46 and 249 Squadrons took off and hurriedly climbed to intercept. The intruding force comprised one reconnaissance SM79bis of 58^Squadriglia flown by Colonello Ranieri Cupini, 10°Stormo

BT commander, with an escort of no less than 48 Macchis led by TenCol Carlo Romagnoli although a dozen of the latter returned early. The remaining 36 Italian fighters continued towards Malta, stepped up from 18,000 to 25,000 feet, where they were intercepted by the nine 46 Squadron Hurricanes. Sqn Ldr Rabagliati (Z2481) led the attack, concentrating his own fire on the reconnaissance machine:

> ". . . sighted an SM79 above, proceeding north at an indefinite speed. Pulled everything and climbed as fast as possible. Commenced firing at 400 yards and closed to 100 yards in port attack. Undercarriage fell down and oil came back. I pulled up to do another attack into eight Macchi 200s and lost sight of SM79. Saw two Macchis dive straight into the sea when coming home."

Flying as No2 to Sqn Ldr Rabagliati was Plt Off Anderson:

> "I followed but gave up as it [the SM79] was faster than me and was higher up. I turned . . . and fired a short burst at a Macchi 200 which was climbing towards me – it turned away apparently undamaged. I then saw two Macchi 200s and turned to attack them. They both dived towards the sea and I was able to get on the tail of No2 of the section. I continued firing from 18,000 feet to sea level, when the Macchi crashed into the sea. At about 10,000 feet the Macchi assumed a much steeper diving angle which may have been the result of a bullet in the pilot."

Sgt Rocky Main was also successful, gaining his third victory in two combats:

> "Fired one short burst at Savoia 79 from beam astern. Dived on following flight of seven Macchi 200s. Fired repeated bursts from beam astern at 250 yards range. Macchi 200 was jumped by another Macchi and [I] chased the latter to within ten miles of Sicilian coast. When last seen it was diving steeply toward Sicily from 8,000 feet."

A third Macchi was claimed by Sgt Tom Hackston:

> "Attacked Macchi 200 at 20,000 feet over Valetta as it broke away from an attack on a Hurricane. Fired a deflection shot about five-seconds, closing from 250 yards to less than 50 yards. My bursts struck the cockpit, the hood coming off. The Macchi immediately flicked over on its back and went down into the sea."

Canadian Sgt Ted Copp also reported shooting down the Macchi he engaged:

> "I dived and managed to get within range about 10-15 miles off the Sicilian coast. Fired a four-second burst from dead astern and then another two-second burst from starboard beam. He turned to port and pulled his nose up high. I poured another two-second burst into the cockpit section. The Macchi then appeared to be out of control and dropped like a plummet."

Actual losses amounted to two Macchis of 16°Gruppo CT; M.llo Giovanni Bravin was killed, but M.llo Otello Simionato came down 20 miles off the Sicilian coast and was rescued by a Z506B. Ten Virgilio Vanzan of 90^Squadriglia claimed one 'Spitfire' shot down, while others claimed a single probable between them. On this occasion there were no RAF losses.

Two days later (27 June) 46 Squadron was again back in the thick of the action. During the late morning nine Hurricanes were airborne to intercept the usual heavily-escorted lone SM79bis reconnaissance machine, which approached Grand Harbour at 20,000 feet. The escorting Macchis kept the Hurricanes at bay, but at a cost. Sqn Ldr Rabagliati (Z2593) opened the scoring:

> "Turned sharply to port . . . developed into a stern chase. Fired a two-second burst at SM79, no results observed. Was attacked by three Macchis. One turned into me head-on and I

fired a short burst from 100 yards. Macchi burst into flames and crashed into sea ten miles east of the island. One Macchi was observed to crash on the island and I saw another crash into the sea close to the one I had engaged."

Sgt Ted Copp again claimed:

"Engaged Macchi at 16,000 feet above Grand Harbour. Fired two two-second bursts (beam attack). Macchi went down in a dive. Engaged a second Macchi over the island at 12,000 feet. Fired a three-second burst (beam attack). Macchi went down and pilot baled, chute did not open."

The body of the Italian pilot shot down by Sgt Copp – Serg Alfredo Sglavo of 90^ Squadriglia – was found near Ta'Karach, not far from Ghaxaq. Although wounded in the face, he had been killed by the fall when his parachute failed to open. Plt Off Andy Anderson, who was again flying No2 to Sqn Ldr Rabagliati, claimed his second victory in consecutive combats:

"I got on the tail of a Macchi and got in several bursts into the cockpit as the Macchi was doing a stall turn. It spun down with smoke coming out. Seen to crash by Sgt Hackston."

Meanwhile, Plt Off Len Barnes claimed two Macchis shot down:

"I was 4,000 feet above Squadron and climbed to 27,000 feet to attack escort which was stepped up to 26,000 feet, with two aircraft at approximately 30,000 feet. On delivering a diving beam attack on a Macchi, closing to astern quarter, the aircraft started to turn and went into an inverted dive and, as far as I could see, went into the sea. I attacked another Macchi at about 23,000 feet in a head-on diving attack. The enemy aircraft pulled up his nose, making it a head-on shot with little or no deflection. This pilot force-landed on the sea and I reported his position and circled until he was picked up by a Swordfish floatplane."

The fortunate pilot was Sottoten Neri De Benedetti, also from 90^Squadriglia. A sixth Macchi was claimed by Sgt Jolly, who was attached to 46 Squadron from 185 Squadron. It would seem that only two Macchis failed to return. Three Hurricanes were claimed shot down by pilots of 10°Gruppo CT although none was lost.

While 46 Squadron was thus engaged, 21 more Hurricane IIs arrived from the carrier *Ark Royal*. One crashed on landing, although the pilot was unhurt, and another (Z3554) went missing en route, Sgt D.R.O'R. Sherburne being rescued from the sea near the Sicilian coast by a Z506B of 612^Squadriglia. This delivery, codenamed Operation 'Railway I', was the first part of a much larger consignment of Hurricanes destined for Malta, and *Ark Royal* returned to Gibraltar to pick up more aircraft. Many of the new pilots were direct from OTUs, including Plt Off Harry Moon from Belfast:

"I had just finished OTU when I (and others) were recalled to do two flights in Hurricanes fitted with long-range tanks. Having completed these, we were told to entrain from Abbotsinch where, on arrival, we were taken to the docks where the carrier *Furious* was anchored. We were then told we were going to be flying Hurricanes from her deck.

On arrival at Gibraltar we and our Hurricanes were transferred to the *Ark Royal* and we were told we were going to Malta. I was due to take off in about the third position but, on starting up, my Hurricane [BV163] was enveloped in steam – the coolant cap had been left off. By the time the coolant had been replaced, all the others had taken off and were disappearing into the distance."

Nonetheless, Moon took off and was able to catch up, all Hurricanes arriving safely. Three days later, on 30 June, *Ark Royal*, with a further 26 Hurricanes, was back and this time accompanied by *Furious* with an additional 16 aircraft (Operation 'Railway II'). All 26 Hurricanes departed *Ark Royal* safely, but the second to take off from *Furious*, BV164 flown by Sgt Max Hare, swerved halfway along the deck, struck the navigating position and knocked off its long-range tanks which caused a large petrol fire. Two Naval officers and one rating were killed and four more officers and ten ratings seriously injured. Four RAF officers including Wg Cdr R.E. Bain, who was in charge of flying-off operations, and four sergeant pilots were also seriously injured, while Sgt Hare succumbed to his burns and injuries. Despite this serious mishap, the remaining eight Hurricanes of the first flight were all flown off safely but, with all six pilots of the second flight injured, no more aircraft were launched. All of the 35 Hurricanes that took off reached Malta safely.

46 Squadron was now renumbered 126 Squadron, since it was intended that a new 46 Squadron should be built around the ground party currently in Egypt. Thus renumbered, it moved from Hal Far to Takali. The Squadron's first interception under its new title was undertaken on the day of the move (30 June) when, at 1215, six Hurricanes were scrambled, including some of the new Mark IIs. Flg Off John Carpenter led the section up to 17,000 feet to the north of the island, from where three MC200s were observed diving for home. These could not be caught but, as he was returning to Malta, Carpenter saw six more enemy fighters:

> "I chased one of them to sea level and caught up when I pulled the emergency boost. I gave a three-second burst at 250 yards. The Macchi did not attempt to pull out of its dive and went straight into the sea."

A second Macchi was claimed by Sgt Alex Mackie:

> "I climbed and chased one Macchi to 20 miles south of Sicily when I shot him down with a three-second burst from astern and below from 15,000 feet. The Macchi's starboard undercarriage leg dropped about one foot and smoke issued from the engine and it went into a spiral dive straight into the sea without recovering."

Sgt John McCracken damaged a third:

> "When I sighted this aircraft it was about 2,000 to 3,000 yards away, steaming very fast. I dived onto it from about 15,000 feet and closed range considerably after chasing it for about seven minutes. I was about 25 miles from Sicily and about 500 yards behind. I opened fire and saw the tracer going all round him. It appeared to strike him many times. All ammunition was fired."

Only one Macchi was lost, Ten Armando Cibin of 7°Gruppo CT being reported killed. In return, Hurricanes were claimed by Cap Saverio Gostini and Serg Walter Omiccioli although, once again, none was lost. These latest victories brought 46/126 Squadron's tally since 11 June to a creditable 19 (14 MC200s, two CR42s, two Z506B and an SM79) for two losses.

During the month 69 Squadron had made good use of its two photo-reconnaissance Hurricanes, a modified long-range Mark II, Z3053, having been delivered to join V7101, but most reconnaissance work continued to be undertaken by the Marylands, which Sqn Ldr George Burges particularly enjoyed flying:

> "Our Marylands were lovely aircraft to fly and had an exceptional performance up to about 10,000 feet, then it fell off rather quickly so that we rarely flew above 15,000 feet. Unfortunately, they were not built to take much punishment. Our job was to keep watch on the enemy airfields and harbours to provide photographs for the Royal Navy and for our own bomber force. Generally, when we flew over a harbour or airfield, the enemy would send up fighters after us. Very often we could see them climbing up to intercept and, as we were at the most at only 15,000 feet, we had to get our photographs and get out to sea quickly. If we did get chased we would put the aircraft into a shallow dive and open up the throttles and revs, under which conditions we generally had the legs on the fighters. This

was all very nice but it meant that each target we had to photograph needed a separate sortie. This had given us the idea of putting cameras in a Hurricane, and I was given the job of sorting this out [greatly assisted by Sqn Ldr Louks, the Command Engineering officer]. We were given V7101. We took out the guns, radio, armour plate, and anything else we could safely get rid of, and installed two cameras. Unfortunately, we didn't have the facilities to install extra fuel tanks, and so we knew its range would be restricted to Sicily. What wouldn't we have given for one of those blue Spitfires the PR chaps were using in the UK!"

Sqn Ldr Louks however soon decided that the Hurricane's range could be extended with the help of a few local modifications:

". . . using crashed Wellington fuel tanks, put an extra 150 gallons within its standard parameters, with an extra 25-gallon oil tank in the leading edge of one wing. Additional oxygen, and two cameras plus a one-piece windscreen and a perspex panel in the floor, completed the mods. The windscreen was half a Blenheim astrodome, which looked about the right size. Again we were lucky. It was. The range was now a maximum of 1,500 miles, and the results so satisfactory, that subsequently we built several more to the same design."

Sqn Ldr Burges added:

"We painted our Hurricane blue, mainly to enable our own gunners to recognise it! I actually got the aircraft up to 36,000 feet but, I think by stripping so much out of it, we had probably moved the centre of gravity too far back because, at this height, if one wasn't careful it whipped into a spin. I used to operate at about 30,000 feet and at this height could cover two or three targets in Sicily in one sortie."

Burges flew four operational sorties in V7101, carrying out reconnaissances to Comiso, Gela, Catania, Augusta and Syracuse, before he left Malta in early June. Flg Off Adrian Warburton flew the Hurricanes almost as often as he did the Marylands during this period. On 28 June, while carrying out a recce of Gela airfield, he observed three MC200s taking off and shortly thereafter these approached him from below. Warburton dived the Hurricane towards them and they sheered away, allowing him to fly back to Malta safely. Two other 69 Squadron pilots, Flg Offs Roger Drew and Bob Wootton, also made their first flights in the PR Hurricanes during the month, while Flg Off Jock Barber (also ex-261 Squadron) had registered his first operational flight in V7101 at the end of May when he flew to Linosa and Lampedusa, subsequently undertaking 13 flights over Sicily during June (six in V7101 and a further seven in Z3053, the second converted Hurricane) visiting Comiso, Gela, Catania, Augusta, Syracuse, Gerbini, Messina, Reggio di Calabria, Trapani and Palermo. Sqn Ldr Louks was necessarily secretive about the unofficial modifications that had been carried out on V7101, but the secret could not be kept indefinitely:

"In the middle of this unofficial exercise, the Inspector-General arrived (Air Chief Marshal Sir Edgar Hewitt). I carefully arranged for the first model [V7101] to be hidden whenever he visited Luqa. I was attached to his visiting entourage and one day, on our way back to HQ from Luqa, he stopped the car and told the driver to go back. When we reached the tarmac, there was the PR Hurricane standing alone. We got out and, as he walked towards it, he asked me what it was. 'A Hurricane, Sir', was the limit of my imagination. I explained we had removed the guns to make way for extra tankage and gave details of the additional equipment. By then he was standing with one hand on the leading edge. 'You've forgotten one thing', he said, 'With all that extra fuel, it needs extra oil.' I explained that he had his hand on the extra 25-gallon tank. 'Does it work?', he asked. 'All the photographs you have been looking at at HQ were taken by it.' These included Naples and other fairly distant targets. Then, 'Have you told the Air Ministry about this?' 'No, Sir.' 'Well, if you haven't, I won't!' End of episode."

Some of the photographs referred to had been taken by Flg Off Barber on 25 June, during a sortie from Messina up to Naples, when he had sighted a convoy of troopships, as a result of which all available Marylands were bombed up and despatched to attack the convoy. One Maryland was lost during the operation, the victim of a successful interception by a Macchi.

Towards the end of the month an unusual aircraft arrived at Malta under cover of darkness, a German-built He115 which had seen service with the Norwegian Naval Air Force early in the war. It was one of four such aircraft that had escaped to Britain following the fall of Norway, all of which would eventually fly clandestine operations from Malta. The first to arrive, BV185, was flown by a Norwegian officer. On arrival at Kalafrana it was secreted away in a hangar under strict security, as part of Z Flight.

July 1941

With the three resident Hurricane squadrons reinforced by the influx of new arrivals, responsibility for the night defence of the island shifted temporarily from 185 to 249 Squadron although, within a few days, the Fulmars of 800X Flight would be officially designated Independent Night Fighting Unit (INFU) under the command of Lt(O) J.S. Manning. The unit's main task would be to undertake intruder sorties over Sicily, each aircraft carrying four 20-lb bombs. Malta's small strike force was kept busy during the first three days of the month, Tripoli harbour and its approaches being the main target for Wellingtons, Blenheims and Swordfish. Several ships were hit and damaged during these attacks.

For a short period, 1-4 July, 126 Squadron's Hurricanes were dispersed to the newly-constructed Safi airstrip, a very narrow landing strip hewn out of rock and bordered by anti-invasion devices consisting of poles topped with explosive charges, embedded in the ground, as they had been at Takali. Cpl John Alton recalled just how sensitive these charges were:

"... anti-airborne landing mines were placed in groups around the perimeter of the airfield. Following an airborne landing warning, these mines would have been placed at strategic points on the airfield. Once in position, a vertical antenna was fitted and deflection of this would set the mine off. It was the duty of squadron armourers to service these mines. One day, whilst this operation was being carried out, there was a very loud detonation followed by a cloud of dust. The armourers concerned had simply vanished and had to be posted 'missing', even though it was obvious what had happened."

Safi was not considered to be an ideal airstrip location, as Sgt Noel MacGregor remembered:

"Landing there in partial darkness and taking off for Takali before dawn was very dodgy indeed – Sgt Johnston, P/O Blackburn, Sgt Ormiston, Sgt Emery and P/O Baker all crashed, and Sgt Hackston went missing. It was that dodgy!"

It transpired that Sgt Tom Hackston's aircraft (Z3055) crashed into the sea shortly after taking off for an early morning air test on 4 July. The cause of the accident was undetermined (see Appendix VI). On a lighter note, Cpl Alton provided another anecdotal account of life on the airfields:

"Church parades were held regularly. The Padre would arrive from HQ at Valetta, drive to the point where the pilots and groundcrew were standing-by for an alert and would commence the act of worship. One airman would not be involved and it was his duty to man the telephone. On occasion the telephone would ring, closely followed by the airman shouting, 'Scramble! Scramble!'. Hymn books would go flying as groundcrew and pilots rushed to the aircraft; engines started and away would go the Hurricanes in a great cloud of dust. The Padre would collect his hymn books, climb into his vehicle and depart for Valetta. I often wondered what his thoughts were."

Later that morning 38 MC200s of 54°Stormo CT provided cover for a lone reconnaissance Z1007bis. The latter, however, was forced to return early. Rather than abort the whole mission, the Italian fighter leader decided to carry out a sweep instead. Four Hurricane IICs of 185 Squadron led by Flt Lt Jeffries (Z3495) were scrambled, encountering the Macchis north-east of Grand Harbour. Jeffries reported:

> ". . . saw e/a at 22,000 feet . . . attacked section of three, Nos2, 1 and 3 in that order. No2 dived away slowly and hood appeared to come off. No1 climbed away slowly. No3 turned on its back and started spinning down – I kept firing and at 8,000 feet it was spinning violently."

He was credited with one destroyed and one damaged. Another was claimed destroyed by Sgt Jolly:

> "I attacked a Macchi which was lagging – four-second burst and he turned over and spun into the sea ten miles north of Grand Harbour . . . circled oil patch . . . saw another 200 spinning down apparently out of control."

Two more Macchis were claimed damaged by Sgts Trevor Bates and Jock Sutherland to complete a successful sortie. The Italians reported being attacked twice by formations of four Hurricanes and claimed one probably shot down on each occasion. One 7°Gruppo CT Macchi failed to return, Ten Gian Paolo Mantovani being killed. His body was recovered by HMS *Gloxina* from the sea, to which it was returned with suitable ceremony.

Shortly before midnight 6/7 July, an INFU Fulmar crewed by Sub Lt(A) Mike Tritton and Lt(O) Manning set off on an intruder sortie. Patrolling over Catania at 1,500 feet, the Fulmar crew saw a large aircraft with its navigation lights on; this was a BR20M (MM21534) of 43°Stormo BT flown by Ten Carlo Natalucci, returning from a raid over Malta. Tritton attacked with a three-second burst and the bomber crashed in flames into the mouth of the River Simeto to become the first victim of the RN night fighter unit. Next morning (7 July), a reconnaissance Z1007bis from 176^Squadriglia carried out a sortie over Malta, escorted by 40 MC200s. The Italians reported a battle over the target area, Ten Maurer of 7°Gruppo CT claiming a Hurricane shot down. There were no reported RAF losses. Another nocturnal raider was shot down on the night of 8/9 July, when ten BR20Ms from 43°Stormo BT and six SM79bis from 10°Stormo BT raided Malta. 249 Squadron was currently tasked with night fighter defence and Flt Lt Neil (Z3498) was sent off on approach of the bombers. Although the searchlights soon found him a target, his own aircraft was illuminated before he could get into position:

> "I ducked down into the cockpit – for one, two, three seconds – before the brilliant eyes beneath, recognising their error, shifted their glare and I was straining my own eyes into the red darkness of light-scarred blindness. The beams ahead of me now, but there, to the left of the cone, a small dark shadow that was the bomber . . ."[9]

The bomber disappeared into the darkness, leaving a frustrated Neil to curse his luck. Next off was Flg Off Cass Cassidy. Amongst those watching was Flt Lt Neil:

> "A sudden flick of something extra and the beams caught the underside of a twin-engined [*sic*] aircraft. They'd got it. Immediately, every lance of light moved quickly onto the target. And held it. Cass must have seen it, surely, or been told. We continued to watch. And listen. Then, just above the horizon and far to the south a sudden flicker of light. Followed by a tiny shifting flare. Moving. Dropping. Falling. Not unlike a star, but much more slowly. He'd got it! Cass had hit it! It was on fire. In less than ten minutes Cassidy's Hurricane was back in the circuit. An aircraft emerged suddenly, almost silently, out of the darkness, before floating to the ground. He was down. Within minutes, Cassidy was being carried should-high around dispersal, grinning, but feeling much as he looked, totally

embarrassed. A BR20, he thought. Into the sea south of the island. Easy really. Caught fire so quickly. None of us gave the Eyetie crew a single thought – dead or alive!"[10]

Cassidy's aircraft recognition was at fault and what he thought was a BR20M was actually an SM79bis of 56^Squadriglia, MM22594 flown by Ten Vincenzo Petti. There were no survivors.

Next morning (9 July), four 185 Squadron Hurricanes were scrambled to investigate a radar plot near the island. They found four MC200s and two Z506B floatplanes, the crews of which were probably searching for survivors of the missing SM79bis. Flg Off Gay Bailey claimed one Macchi damaged – Sottoten Giuseppe Avvico of 54°Stormo CT was slightly wounded and crash-landed on return to base – while Sgt Westcott attacked one of the floatplanes. Four more Hurricanes were despatched on an offensive sortie in the afternoon when Sqn Ldrs Mould and Rabagliati, accompanied by Flt Lt Jeffries and Sgt Alex Mackie, carried out a strafing attack on Syracuse seaplane base; Sqn Ldr Mould (Z3495/GL-T) reported:

> "We approached the harbour from the east; entered the harbour through the entrance at about 50 feet and immediately did a steep right-hand turn and slipped into echelon port and opened fire at a cluster of three seaplanes (Cants). I was then at about five feet off the water. I saw my shells going low to start with and after raising my aim, one of the three seaplanes caught fire; the tail fell off another and I could see my shells going into the third machine. I then turned slightly and saw the remainder of my shells go into the hangar, but no definite damage was seen. I nearly hit one of the seaplanes and then the hangar and eventually nearly removed my starboard wing on some large building. There was quite a lot of AA but all burst at about 250 feet just before I started breaking away."

Flt Lt Jeffries (Z3456/GL-X) added:

> "I saw several seaplanes on the water. I opened fire on the nearest one and I observed several strikes. I then concentrated my fire on the slipway on which there were about five aircraft. I saw one floaplane burst into flames as my shots entered it. I sprayed the other aircraft and then fired a long burst into the hangar. Several men working there scattered. As I flew over the slipway I observed three aircraft on fire."

Another was claimed by Sqn Ldr Rabagliati (Z3498):

> "Gave one two-second burst on Cant floatplane, followed by another two-second burst. Fired at slipway in two-second burst and three men ran – two fell down and rolled into sea. Sighted train on mole when coming out and attacked. Saw hits on last coach and large pieces of wood fell off."

Rabagliati's No2, Sgt Mackie, reported:

> "I observed pieces flying off the seaplane and the centre of it appeared to collapse, but I had no time to observe further damage. I saw shells fired from S/Ldr Rabagliati's aircraft entering the last carriage of a train moving along the coast."

Six flying boats were claimed destroyed and four damaged as a result of this attack, but actual losses were one Z506B of 612^Squadriglia and one Z501 of the Ricognizione Marittima destroyed, and two more Z506Bs damaged. A Maryland sent to ascertain the effects of the Hurricane attack also carried out a strafe, the crew reporting setting fire to a He115 and damage to three more aircraft.

Two days later, on 11 July, the Italians struck back when they launched a fighter attack on Luqa, 11 Macchis led by TenCol Romagnoli attacking the airfield while 42 more provided cover. A dozen Hurricanes were scrambled by 185 Squadron, as humorously noted by the unit's current diarist, Sgt Butch Burton:

"Twelve Hurricanes from A Flight were scrambled about one o'clock against +3, 70 miles north towards the Gem of the Med [Malta]. Due to a dreamy pilot leaving his transmitter on, the R/T information received clearly was very scanty and may have saved half a dozen Macchis. Dreamy pilot please note. The +3 became +9, 35 miles north and then +16, 20 miles north. From the pilots' lines we can say that at least 40 e/a came over the island and, from a most trustworthy source, that eight Macchis essayed a low flying attack on Luqa, where one Wellington was set on fire and two others damaged. The Italians went home quickly, leaving three Macchi pilots and their machines in the drink north of Grand Harbour. This is confirmed by the Navy, who did the necessary fishing."

Despite the final comment by Sgt Burton, it would seem that 185 Squadron were credited with three probably destroyed and nine damaged in this action, the probables being awarded to Sqn Ldr Mould (Z3495/GL-T), Flt Lt Jeffries (Z4946/GL-E) and newly-arrived Flt Lt S.A.D. Pike. The CO reported:

"At 2,000 feet I noticed that someone in the formation had left his transmitter on. I carried on climbing, very fast, and when at 15,500 feet managed to receive a message from Banjo saying 15+, ten miles north of Zambuk [St Paul's Bay]. Within one minute I saw the enemy aircraft about 1,000 feet below and just in front of us. We were not well positioned for a decent formation attack, so I broke my formation up and dived into the middle of the rear formation. I aimed at the outside one of a vic of three, and they immediately broke in all directions. I followed one e/a in a steep diving spiral, firing bursts at intervals, at ranges varying from 75 to 20 yards, when I had to break away. I did not see the enemy hit the water, but I am sure that I damaged it badly. I then chased another Macchi 200 and fired several bursts into it at varying ranges with no visible result. I was then about 30-35 miles north-east of Grand Harbour. I returned home after finishing my ammunition."

Flt Lt Jeffries' report was similarly inconclusive:

"I engaged a Macchi and gave him a short burst. He tried evasive action and I let him go. I engaged two more Macchis without any visible results. I then picked on one aircraft and gave him five-seconds firing. He broke away, going down. I was firing from about 50 yards range. I then engaged another Macchi at sea level, closing to 100 yards. I fired about five-seconds burst into the aircraft. I am claiming this aircraft as damaged. My bullets were plainly visible as they entered the fuselage. The other aircraft mentioned before, I claim as probable. It should have crashed 30-35 miles north-east of Delimara."

Flt Lt Pike also claimed a probable:

"I opened fire about 150 yards from below. My shots went into it, raking it from just behind the cockpit to the tail. I could not hold on to the position owing to the height. I then attacked another from slight port quarter to astern. Some pieces came off as my shots entered the fuselage. I had run out of ammo and had no further interest in the proceedings."

Plt Off Cliff Gray and Sgt Jock Sutherland (Z2819/GL-W) each submitted claims for two damaged, but it is unclear who the other claimants were[11], while at least one Hurricane pilot reported being fired at by another, Sgt Burton commenting: "The practice of bouncing .303 ammo off another Hurricane to hit a Macchi, not held in sights, will be gently discouraged!" In the event, there were no Italian losses, although five Macchis returned with battle damage. Nor were any of the Hurricanes lost although four were claimed shot down by pilots of 10°Gruppo CT, Cap Franco Lucchini and M.llo Leonardo Ferrulli being amongst those credited with shares.

The next victory went to a Fulmar night fighter after Sub Lt(A) Tritton intercepted a BR20M returning from a sortie to Malta on the night of 16/17 July. The bomber crashed on its approach to Gerbini and was destroyed. One member of the crew was killed and two injured. The Italians responded with another large fighter sweep next day (17 July), the main purpose of which was to protect a reconnaissance Z1007bis. Forty-nine Macchis from 7° and 10°Gruppi CT took off at mid-morning but a third of these returned early when they became separated from the main formation. The remainder however continued and reached Malta. On their approach, eight Hurricanes from 249 Squadron were scrambled. Sqn Ldr Barton (Z3262) led the attack and shot down one Macchi, Plt Off Graham Leggett downed a second, while Flg Off Davis claimed a third as damaged. Two fighters of 10°Gruppo were lost, Serg Magg Enrico Botti (MM6500) being killed, while Serg Magg Natale Finito (MM5217) was rescued from the sea by an Axis ASR craft. The Hurricane (Z2818) flown by Sgt Maurice Guest failed to return and it was assumed that he had been shot down, while newly arrived Plt Off Bob Matthews[12] (Z2481) reported that a gun panel blew off his aircraft, damaging the fuselage and fin. Claims for Hurricanes were submitted by TenCol Carlo Romagnoli and Cap Franco Lucchini, while Serg Elio Miotto claimed two more.

Meanwhile, new pilots continued to drift in from various quarters, two experienced Battle of Britain veterans, Sqn Ldr George Powell-Sheddon[13] (four including one shared victories to his credit) and Flt Lt Don Stones DFC (11 including two shares) arriving aboard transit Blenheims from the UK via Gibraltar. 126 Squadron lost another pilot on the night of the 19th, when Sgt John McCracken was killed in a take-off accident in BV171. However, the Squadron saw the return of Plt Off Andy Anderson, who had been in hospital with sandfly fever. In a letter home, he wrote:

> "Our Flight's on readiness this afternoon waiting to take off if any Italians show up, everyone is hoping they will, of course, as we've been unlucky lately and missed the action that has been going. Actually I've only just come out of hospital . . . The weather's terribly hot now and we sink gallons of iced drinks: flying is awful low down, the cockpit gets just like a furnace with the hood closed. Every day is a flying day here, nothing like English flying. The sky nearly always cloudless and a brilliant blue, we can see Mount Etna whenever we go up, and that's 100 miles away. We get air raids with monotonous regularity, you get used to them and I always stay in bed . . . So far I've only been in two fights. I felt a mixture of fear and exhilaration. The most wonderful feeling in the world; only trouble is, you risk paying a very expensive price for the pleasure."

On 21 July, another convoy (a troopship and six freighters) set sail from Gibraltar, accompanied by *Ark Royal*, four cruisers and a strong escort of destroyers. As the convoy approached the island, empty vessels at Malta waiting to return westwards were to sail under the protection of the warships. Thus, during the ensuing few days, Italian attention was concentrated on the movements at sea, during which six of *Ark Royal*'s Fulmars were lost in return for shooting down six SM79s and a Z506B. This allowed Malta further respite, although a unit of the Italian Navy was about to launch an audacious attack against Grand Harbour.

Shortly after 1030 on the morning of 25 July, a lone reconnaissance Z1007bis from 9°Stormo BT approached with the obvious intention of photographing ships of the incoming convoy. Escort was provided by two groups of 26 and 21 Macchis. Twenty-two Hurricanes were scrambled by 185 and 249 Squadrons, the pilots mistakingly reporting two reconnaissance aircraft – a BR20 and an SM79. The misidentification would seem to stem from an unfamiliarity with the Cant Z1007bis. Those approaching from the rear saw the twin tail fins and reported a BR20, whilst those engaging from ahead saw the three engines and believed it to have been an SM79. The 185 Squadron formation (B Flight) was led by Flt Lt Hancock (Z2982/GL-O). Sgt Burton (the diarist) later noted:

> "F/Lt Hancock led the Squadron into the attack and was as furious as his naturally tolerant nature allows him to be when his cannon seized up after firing a few shells. His language

revealed a closer study and more thorough understanding of the basic thoughts than we have imagined. P/O Thompson and Sgt Forth have been credited with the SM79 and the other pilots share the BR20. P/O Barnwell also attacked the SM79 after the Professor [Thompson's nickname] and his No2 had been in with cannon and machine-gun respectively."

Plt Off Thompson (Z3456/GL-X) reported:

"I was flying as Blue 1. I was detached from the Squadron at 5,000 feet and ordered to climb fast with my No2 (Sgt Forth). I gained height and reached 28,000 feet when e/a were reported at 26,000 feet. I saw SM79 with three or four fighters and attacked SM79 from astern, closing rapidly to 100 yards, firing three bursts of cannon. I saw large pieces fall off starboard side and red flashes where the explosive shells hit also. The starboard engine began to smoke and the undercarriage fell down. I broke away, the guns having stopped firing. P/O Barnwell later saw this aircraft explode and crash into sea."

His No2, Sgt Jimmy Forth (BV162/GL-J), added:

"I followed astern and saw my No1 open fire. Pieces came away from the 'recco', though the rear-gunner continued to fire. When P/O Thompson broke away I opened fire at 200 yards. More pieces came away from the 'recco' and I believe my first burst put the rear-gun or gunner out of action, because though he opened fire at me, for the remainder of my first attack there was no counter fire. Having broken away I climbed into the sun and found the 'recco' at 16,000 feet with about three fighters. I delivered a second attack from beam, going to half astern, breaking away at about 150 yards when dived at by a fighter. During the flight I saw an aircraft dive vertically, but did not see it hit the sea. On my return flight I saw a large white splash mark."

Plt Off David Barnwell[14] (White 3) also attacked this aircraft:

"I did a front quarter attack followed by a stern attack. I saw pieces flying off and had to break for fear of collision, and in the subsequent turn, I spun. I believe this aircraft might have had twin tails. After my spin I attacked what I thought was the same aircraft, but it may have been another. I did four attacks and ran out of ammunition. The second aircraft was definitely an SM79 [sic], coloured mottled dark and light green with yellow engines. Two attacks on the beam and two stern attacks. It had previously been damaged, the undercarriage was down and starboard motor seemed to be giving white smoke. After running out of ammunition I followed close beside as there was no return fire, also did some dummy attacks. After about five minutes I saw flames behind starboard engine nacelle. The aircraft was continuously losing height, turning each way. It continued to fly for some time with the small fire on the starboard wing, and then turned towards the island, shortly after which the aircraft exploded and crashed into the sea. I saw one parachute fall into the sea and continued to orbit the wreckage for some time with White 1 [Plt Off Winton]."

The aircraft misidentified as a BR20 – in fact the same aircraft as attacked by Plt Off Thompson and his section – was set upon by a number of pilots. Plt Off Gay Bailey (Black 1 in Z3522/GL-A), reported:

"I made three attacks on 'recco'. Left it with starboard engine smoking and wheels down. Several other Hurricanes made attacks."

His No2, Sgt John Alderson (Z4946/GL-E), added:

". . . approximately six Hurricanes dived to attack from above me. I waited to allow them to complete their attack and then dived on the bomber which by this time was almost immediately below me. I fired 50 rounds from each gun at point-blank range and observed hits in the fuselage."

At the same time Sgt Ray Ellis (Black 3) was carrying out an attack:

"I opened fire at about 200 yards astern, closing to 50 feet. I broke away and made two beam attacks, and then one final beam attack. Upon this attack white smoke came from the starboard engine. My ammunition was then finished. There were two other Hurricanes making a beam attack just as I was caught in the slipstream, which turned me upon my back."

Sgt Bob Branson, Green 1, was also involved with his section:

"I made three attacks on BR20. As there was no return fire experienced, I was able to make a steady attack, closing to 50 yards, when I broke away. My No2 [Sgt Nurse] confirms that the starboard engine was left smoking. I carried out two more attacks, using all my ammunition and then returned to base. When I left it, it was smoking and diving towards the sea."

Green 2, Sgt Bill Nurse (Z2394/GL-H), followed his leader:

"I sighted the enemy and started firing at a range of 350 yards, and gave a three to four-second burst. I did not observe any hits. I then climbed and delivered a three-quarter attack, and noticed the undercarriage was down, and again gave a three to four-second burst, hits being observed on the fuselage. After breaking away, I climbed again and started to attack, opening fire from 200 yards, and closing to 75 yards. I noticed all my bullets entering the fuselage and starboard wing. I broke away very sharply, and when I noticed the enemy again, he was too far away to catch, but was being pursued by three Hurricanes. I noticed smoke coming from his port engine."

Sgt Ream (Z2592/GL-Y) had also followed the bomber out to sea:

"I tried to get into a position for a head-on attack. I failed to do this however, as several Hurricanes were attacking from astern and quarter, so I carried out a beam attack and saw him pass through my tracer. I broke away and, as three or four other Hurricanes were attacking, I started looking for something else, and failing to see any more enemy aircraft, I turned for home as I was about 40 miles out to sea. On the way back I saw a cloud of smoke above the water and some wreckage beneath, about 25 miles east of the island."

Both Plt Off Denis Winton (White 1) and his No2, newly arrived Plt Off P.K. 'Woody' Woodsend, carried out attacks on the aircraft, while Flt Lt Don Stones (Z2481) of 249 Squadron also had a "squirt":

"As I went in to attack, something fell away from our target and nearly hit me. I assumed he was jettisoning a bomb. We set him on fire and down he went into the sea. Only later did we discover that the object which had flown past me was the rear-gunner baling out. He survived."

The surviving crew member of this aircraft was in fact the observer, Magg Achille Torrerossa (an army officer), who was rescued from the sea and taken to hospital. His pilot, Ten Alfonso Cinieri, and the remainder of the crew perished[15]. Although only one aircraft was present, the destruction of two – a BR20 and an SM79 – was credited to the Squadron. Meanwhile, as the pilots of 185 Squadron converged on the aircraft, those from 249 Squadron engaged the escorting Macchis, three of which were claimed shot down. Sqn Ldr Barton (Z3492) and Plt Off Frank Hill reported that their victims fell into the sea, both probably having attacked the Macchi (MM6873) flown by Ten Silvio De Giorgi of 98^Squadriglia:

"When we were in sight of the island [Malta], I saw a certain number of aeroplanes that, higher and behind us, were diving in our direction. I believed that the planes were our indirect escort, but I was wrong. After the Hurricane assault, we scrambled all around. I was wounded and moreover I could see many bullet holes in the left wing of my aircraft. I started to feel pain in my leg, so I decided to go home. I wished to have someone help me, to spot me in case of a forced alighting on the sea, so I started to ramble around, looking for an escort.

Suddenly three aeroplanes appeared. The first was a Hurricane. I had the impression that the other [two] were Macchi 200s, and that the Hurricane was trying to attack them. I set aside my intention to return to base and fired a few warning shots towards the Macchis (this was our established signal to warn one another as we had no radio) and prepared to face the Hurricane, by now fully aware of my presence. At the first burst of fire from the Hurricane, I pulled up the nose of my aircraft as if he had hit me, then quickly changed manoeuvre and dived towards the sea, as if I had no control of the aircraft. This manoeuvre confirmed my plane had no structural damage. Now I could go back to Sicily even without an escort. But suddenly there was a burst of firing and I was surrounded by flames. The Hurricane, of which I had lost sight and which I thought I had escaped from, had instead followed me. There was no alternative but to eject myself. As soon as the parachute opened, an excruciating pain in my chest overcame me. I became completely blind and at that moment I thought my adversary had machine-gunned me. The pain in my chest was terrible and I could hardly breathe."

The wounded De Giorgi was subsequently rescued from the sea by a launch from Malta. Another pilot of 98^Squadriglia was not so fortunate. Sottoten Francesco Liberti (in MM8894) was shot down over Valetta by Plt Off Bob Matthews (Z2418), who wrote:

"We scrambled in the morning and at 23,000 feet intercepted one BR20 and 15 Macchis out of the sun. I was shot at. I turned away and then got on his trail. I climbed after him and, as he stall-turned, I got in a burst from 200 yards. He straightened up and I followed, closing to 50 yards. I then fired again and he did a slow roll. Then he went on his back, diving towards Valetta. I took another squirt and saw something fly away from the aircraft. A glove? The pilot began to get out. At first he was stuck, then he jumped and nearly ran into me. But his parachute did not open and he dropped straight down. His aircraft went straight down also and crashed in Strada Reale in Valetta, in a bombed house."

Wg Cdr Carter Jonas, Station Commander at Luqa, who was visiting Valetta, recalled:

"Out of the confusion of sound above us, something appeared, tangible and definite. It was a puff of white smoke. A little puff at first, but it grew rapidly and formed itself into a trail of white, like a comet. Then it faded away almost as rapidly as it had come. A moment later there was a new sound. Something terrifying which I could not describe. I had often wondered what a terminal velocity dive in an aircraft would be like. Now my wondering was to be answered. Just below where the first white puff had appeared was an aircraft diving vertically earthwards. I realised almost immediately that the aircraft would fall into Valetta. Also that it would fall very close to me. Probably fall on the very spot on which I was now standing. I argued to myself that it was too late to attempt to escape into the building, down the stairs to safety. I decided to stay and hope for the best, but now I realised also the meaning of the phrase 'rooted to the spot'. It appeared to be coming straight for my eyes. As it flashed by, diving slightly over the vertical, I recognised it as a Macchi 200. A moment later it hit the ground about 75 yards away. There was a loud report, then silence, followed by the sound of running feet and excited shouts of the Maltese. The pilot had baled out but his parachute had failed to open. He had fallen from the vast Mediterranean sky – in memory of Icarus. I straightened up slowly. I felt rather sick and, looking around, I saw that my Engineer Officer friend was laughing. As he had been running to safety, one of the rotten staircase steps had given way. There he was, jammed between two of the treads – his head and shoulders above, and his body and legs swinging below. Apart from a deep graze to each shin, he was unhurt."

Having witnessed much of the action, Air-Vice Marshal Lloyd later wrote:

> "I am not guilty of exaggeration when I say that as a result of that engagement it was almost a reasonable operational risk for aircrew to be seen in the streets, as they would be mobbed and carried shoulder high by a frenzied and excited populace. Every airman was the idol of the island and it was extremely embarrassing to be seen about after these events. Old ladies would remove themselves from the pavement to let us pass, or would curtsey, and the men would raise their hats; soon, all the traffic would come to a stop and shops would be emptied and crowds would form until it was impossible to go forward or back. Hundreds of smiling faces would then show the most sincere admiration for the Service in which we had the honour to serve. I have seen six aircrew carried shoulder high by a joyous and boisterous mob the whole length of one street. The aircrew were the modern Knights.
>
> As I drove along the 'ditch' I was given the customary salute by its young male inhabitants, ranging from three to seven years, and many of their beautiful Rubenesque faces reminded me of the cherubs in the religious paintings. All would line the roadway and salute me as I passed . . . These boys – and sometimes, I suspected, little girls as well – were always there, in sunshine and in rain, alert or no alert, and even when the Axis bombers were overhead . . ."[16]

It was at this stage, with all the vessels in Grand Harbour, that the Italians attempted their seaborne strike against Grand Harbour. The Italian Navy's 1,568-ton sloop *Diana* approached the Malta area before midnight. On board were nine explosive MTM motor boats and their one-man pilots. The sloop also towed a smaller electric-powered MTL motor boat carrying two SLC human torpedoes and their four crewmen. Accompanying the vessels were two 60-foot motor torpedo-boats (MAS451 and 452), the latter towing a small MTSM motor boat. *Diana* hove-to 20 miles north of Malta, from where the attack was to be launched. This was to coincide with a diversionary raid by BR20Ms.

Quite unknown to the Axis forces – or to many on the Allied side – the British were receiving messages through 'Ultra' sources concerning most enemy air and sea movements in the Mediterranean, and was the main reason for the successes of Malta's striking forces in finding and attacking their convoys. Thus, when *Diana* was detected by radar on arrival at her station, Malta's defences were immediately placed on full alert. The boats set off at 0200, reaching the final rendezvous an hour later. One SLC was found to be defective and was ordered to return to the mother ship but was lost with its crew. The attack finally got under way at 0430 on the morning of 26 July, 15 minutes after the bombers had commenced their raid. The MTMs, tasked with destroying the harbour boom net, were first into action but one failed to explode and another hit the pier and blew up together with its pilot. The force of the explosion brought down the west span of the steel bridge across the harbour entrance, which was now effectively blocked. As searchlights illuminated the scene, the shore defences added to the carnage.

Dawn was breaking as Hurricanes were scrambled by 126 and 185 Squadrons, these passing over the action at the harbour entrance to attack the four motor boats offshore. At about the same time MC200s from 7°Gruppo CT took off from Comiso with orders to escort the returning craft. *Diana* was already well underway. Although MAS451 and 452 (the latter still towing the MTMS) were following at full speed, they were soon caught by the Hurricanes. Flt Lt Lefevre (Z3498) of 126 Squadron attacked one – evidently MAS452 – with cannon fire, reporting that the crew signalled surrender, while pilots from the unit strafed the other craft with machine-gun fire. Plt Off Gay Bailey (Z3522/GL-A) of 185 Squadron reported:

> "I saw Bofors fire at sea level. I dived down and there were two large explosions. Two patches of oil appeared and on closer examination four survivors were counted in the water. I reported to Banjo and circled. About 20 minutes later was vectored onto two MTBs. I

attacked with machine-gun fire and one started turning in small circles and suddenly exploded, leaving a large patch of oil and wreckage [apparently MAS451]. I attacked the other and this also went into a small circle after attack. Being out of ammunition, I returned to Malta. [Later], in company with another Hurricane, I returned to the spot [where the] MTB was stationary and waving a white flag."

His second target was obviously the same as that selected by Flt Lt Lefevre. Another of the attacking pilots, Flt Lt Hancock (Z2982/GL-O), recalled:

"About 15 miles out I saw two MTBs travelling north very fast. I flew across to the west and turned, diving down to a few hundred feet. I opened fire on nearest MTB at about 800 yards, closing to 100 yards. I gave four bursts, my first falling short and the others striking the MTB. I then broke upwards and to starboard. Circling, I saw both MTBs engaged by other Hurricanes."

Closely following was Plt Off David Barnwell:

"I saw F/Lt Hancock's bullets striking all round the first boat which immediately swung to the left and slowed up. I attacked and saw my bullets strike. No return fire. I broke left and made another attack on the other boat. Just after this attack I saw a Macchi firing on a Hurricane from above. I broke upwards and managed to get behind the Macchi. I observed my fire striking the fuselage and starboard wing. I then saw a Macchi behind me, followed by a Hurricane. I broke left and was attacked by a third Macchi on the beam. He broke away and did not continue his attack. I then saw the first Macchi heading north at sea level, smoking profusely (black exhaust smoke). I managed to catch him and he took no evasive action until I was 200 yards away, when he did a medium turn to the left. I saw my bullets again striking his right wing and then ran out of ammunition and was forced to break off. On the return flight, I saw the first boat [had] sunk and the second was proceeding slowly, being attacked by about three Hurricanes. I was joined shortly after this by P/O Thompson and returned to base."

Flying No2 to Plt Off Barnwell was Sgt Peter Lillywhite (Z2402/GL-P):

"I followed my leader down and did a diving beam attack on the rear MTB, which was turning very slowly. I broke away and did an astern attack on the front MTB without visible effect. I turned and came in on a front attack on the same boat, and broke away again. The first MTB was stationary, with a small boat behind it. Just before I again attacked the front MTB, which was travelling fast and weaving, I saw an aircraft, which I took to be a Hurricane, dive vertically into the sea. I did a beam attack on the front boat and saw a flame from the starboard side."

Plt Off Peter Thompson (Z3456/GL-X), who was flying top cover with Sgt Jimmy Forth, watched as the Hurricanes attacked the MTBs:

"I remained at 18,000 feet and saw a Macchi attacking a Hurricane. I dived on the Macchi from astern and fired from 100-50 yards. I then broke away and attacked an MTB, my incendiary causing fire in the rear of the boat. I saw the Macchi again and fired from astern, causing smoke and pieces to fall off. The Macchi was seen to go into the sea by Sgt Westcott. I fired the remainder of my ammo into an MTB. I saw one MTB sinking and the other was seen by Sgt Lillywhite to be on fire."

Sgt Westcott added:

"I followed Red 1 down and while we were diving the MTBs broke up [sic]. We took the rear one and I closed to 50 yards after Red 1 [Flt Lt Hancock] had attacked, and saw the gun on the launch hanging vertically. After the first attack I did a steep climbing turn and upon reaching 1,500 feet I saw a Hurricane (P/O Thompson) attack a Macchi. The tracers entered the cockpit of this machine and I saw a red glow from the cockpit. The Macchi turned over on its back and dived into the sea. I made another attack on the MTB which had now stopped and seemed to be sinking slowly."

Two more Macchis were claimed shot down by 126 Squadron's Sgt Alan Haley, an Australian from Sydney, who reported that he attacked one from astern as it skimmed the wave tops on its way back to Sicily, where it dived into the sea some ten miles from the coast. His own aircraft was then hit several times and he saw another Macchi on his tail. Turning southwards, he was pursued for about five minutes before Plt Off Thompson came to his aid, forcing the Italian to break away and allowing Haley to get in a short burst, following which the Macchi crashed into the sea. Both pilots claimed its destruction. Two Macchis were lost during this combat; M.llo Avellino De Mattia of 98^Squadriglia baled out and being rescued from the sea by an Italian craft, but Serg Magg Ruggero Gallina of 76^Squadriglia was killed. Two other Macchis of 76^Squadriglia returned with battle damage. The Italians initially claimed seven Hurricanes but this was later reduced to three confirmed and two probables. As the Hurricanes headed back, it was soon realised that Plt Off Denis Winton (Z4946/GL-E) was missing. The 185 Squadron diarist, Sgt Burton, recorded:

"P/O Winton's adventures must be mentioned. Thirty miles or so out to sea, he was surprised by a Macchi and received such damage to his plane that the fan stopped. Using his speed to gain height he was able to reach 700 feet and then baled out, both parachute and dinghy doing all the things a kind-hearted MO likes them to do. For the next few hours he sunbathed, played with a friendly turtle, wondered who would have his motor cycle, and then spotted a stationary torpedo-boat [MAS452]. He paddled the dinghy with his hands and, finding progress slow, towed it and swam towards the boat. By climbing up the side he was able to peer into it and was confronted by eight very much dead Italians. Apparently cannon are not suitable presents for playful infants.

Taking possession of the boat was thus quite easy and he waited – he couldn't start it – flying the flag at half mast since he didn't know which side would rescue him. An Army rescue boat [actually a civilian-manned RASC launch] did a circuit round him – almost six hours after he had baled out on an empty stomach – and, thinking he was Italian and also that there was a .5 machine-gun handy on the boat, left him to cool his heels for a time. Before they could return, a Swordfish with floats dropped in to pay him a visit and gave him – and the flag – a lift home, where he again took possession of his motor cycle."

In the evening, Flt Lt Jeffries and Sgt Vardy were ordered to sink MAS452. Having flown to within a few miles of the Sicilian coast without making a sighting, they returned to Malta where they observed the MTB being towed into Grand Harbour by the converted trawler *Jade*. The commander of MAS452 was among those killed but 11 survivors had been able to transfer to the MTMS, subsequently rejoining *Diana*, while a number of survivors from MAS451 were later picked by an RAF ASR launch, bringing the total of prisoners to three officers and 15 ratings. Fifteen others had died in the gallant action.

185 Squadron continued its runs of successes with two more victories – SM79bis of 56^Squadriglia – on 27 July, as noted by Sgt Burton:

"F/Lt Hancock led a completely successful excursion 50 miles on a vector of 150°. The dénouement, officially, was the destruction of two SM79s by himself and the Professor [Plt Off Thompson]. For this unofficial record – which does not suffer from the anomaly of an apparently ignorant IO – it would perhaps be truer to say that Sgt Forth can claim half the Professor's lesson to the 'Vagina Aeronautica'. No doubt, and this seriously, with another plane or two down, P/O Thompson will be recommended for suitable recognition of his good work since he has now about seven to his credit."

Plt Off Gay Bailey (Z3522/GL-A) recorded:

"I was Black 1 and weaving and sighted two e/a about 8,000 feet below Squadron. I informed leader. Squadron turned and I made first attack from beam – no effect seen. Other Hurricanes attacked and one SM79 pulled up and burst into flames. I made second attack from beam, saw red flash – may have been rear-gun. Other Hurricanes attacked and e/a blew up in flames."

Flt Lt Hancock (Z2982/GL-O) continued:

"I led in astern of two SM79s in formation and engaged the starboard machine from 300 yards, closing to 50 yards. All cannon fired and large pieces broke off and port engine burst into flames. I climbed away to starboard, being struck in the starboard wing by a few bullets. The SM79 then climbed and stall turned, diving into the sea in flames. Sgt Cousens (Red 2) followed me after delivering an attack before the aircraft plunged into the sea."

As Sgt Dick Cousens (Z4942/GL-F) recalled:

"We encountered two SM79s flying below us at about 4,000 feet. My leader attacked on the beam, going into astern attack. I followed him in line astern. I opened fire at about 300 yards, and gave him four-seconds burst. His port engine was already on fire and his starboard engine now caught fire. As I pulled out, the enemy aircraft went straight up, climbing hard, and then went straight into the sea. I climbed up and did a beam attack on the port side of the second aircraft, firing all my ammunition. It hit forward of the wing with no visible result."

Meanwhile, other Hurricanes pursued the second aircraft, Plt Off Peter Thompson (Z3456/GL-X) leading:

"I was flying Blue 1. I led the attack on the second machine, closing to 100 yards, firing with four cannons. The machine blew up when I broke away."

Sgt Jimmy Forth (BV162/GL-J) added:

"I was flying No2 to P/O Thompson and stayed with him during the engagement. I saw one SM79 fall into the sea in flames. P/O Thompson and myself attacked the second bomber, I flying in No3 position, and I saw my second long burst entering the enemy bomber. P/O Thompson and I broke away together as the SM79 burst into flames, to fall into the sea a second later."

During the afternoon of 28 July, Hurricanes of 185 Squadron escorted pairs of Beaufighters – which had been operating from Malta since the middle of the month – on a strafing attack over Sicily. At Catania, where 11 MC200s, three BR20Ms and three CR42s were damaged, four Z501s were damaged at Marsala seaplane base, and a further four at Syracuse, while at Borizzo six SM79s, two CR42s and a Ca164 biplane trainer were damaged. Over Catania, one Beaufighter was attacked and damaged by a MC200 although it reached Malta safely. None of the enemy aircraft sighted were engaged by the Hurricanes.

On the last day of the month Sqn Ldr Barton of 249 Squadron had a narrow escape in Z3492:

"Engine failure on take-off. I crash-landed from 300 feet – almost impossible at Malta – my lucky day. Only suffered second degree burns from acid, glycol and petrol."

Flt Lt Ginger Neil and Flg Off Crossey went to see Barton after he was admitted to M'tarfa Hospital:

"Crossey and I visited him the day after and found him disfigured, shocked and trembling but profoundly thankful that things had turned out as well as they had. Few people had survived such an experience. Looking tiny and waif-like in his hospital bed, he was childishly relieved at his deliverance. As we left him behind, I was all too conscious of the Squadron's debt to the little man. Small and slight in stature, in no way an heroic figure and unassuming almost to a fault, he was one of the best leaders and fighter pilots it would be my good fortune to meet."[17]

At about this time, the Malta Night Fighter Unit (MNFU) was formed at Takali with eight Hurricane IIC and four IIBs[18]. This relieved the pressure on the soon-to-be disbanded Independent Night Fighting Unit whose Fulmars, though hardly suitable for the rôle, would be used for nocturnal intruder sorties over Sicily. Sqn Ldr George Powell-Sheddon returned from Egypt to command the MNFU and pilots were drawn from other Malta-based units. 249 Squadron provided both flight commanders, Flt Lt Don Stones and Flg Off Cass Cassidy, the latter a former night fighter pilot, in addition to Flg Off Tommy Thompson, Plt Offs Jack Mills and Douglas Robertson. From 126 Squadron came Plt Off Jack Grant and Sgt Alex Mackie, while 185 Squadron supplied Plt Offs David Barnwell and Denis Winton, and also Sgt Bob Branson. The unit's Hurricanes were painted matt black. Sqn Ldr Powell-Sheddon remembered:

"We operated only at night and dawn, and usually in co-operation with the searchlights. The Italians were scared of night fighter Hurricanes and would drop their bombs into the sea. Often they did not approach the island. I initiated the idea of hunting in pairs in unison with the searchlights, the Hurricanes switching on their tail lights to avoid collisions. On my first operation over the island I was illuminated by searchlights and shouted over the R/T, 'Turn those bloody things off!'"

Flt Lt Stones had a similar frustrating experience:

"I chased my first bomber on 31 July when he was illuminated by searchlights, which then lost him and blinded me before switching off, so my target got away. We decided to embark on an intensive programme of co-operation with the searchlight batteries and spent a lot of time flying towards the cones where their beams intersected. This got better and we began to have good illuminations of enemy aircraft."[19]

At the close of July, AHQ Malta issued its usual communique of results, crediting the fighters with 21 confirmed victories during the month[20], plus five probables and nine damaged, for the loss of three Hurricanes in combat, two pilots having been killed.

CHAPTER VII

HURRICANE SUMMER

August – October 1941

The first three weeks of August were devoid of major engagements, but activities continued with an increasing number of allied offensive sorties. During the first week Beaufighters struck at targets along the Sicilian coast and Wellingtons launched a night attack against Tripoli, while Fulmars successfully bombed and strafed Gerbini airfield during ongoing night operations over Sicily by the FAA.

The new MNFU enjoyed its first success during the night of 5/6 August when eight BR20Ms from 43°Stormo BT raided Grand Harbour. Flg Off Cassidy and Plt Off Barnwell intercepted, the former making for a bomber seen on the edge of the searchlight illumination concentration. He managed several bursts and knocked pieces off his target which rapidly lost height. Later, a signal from Catania HQ to Syracuse was intercepted, reporting the loss of the aircraft. Barnwell then attacked two bombers in quick succession. Two BR20Ms were actually lost, both falling soon after midnight: TenCol Nello Brambilla, commander of 99°Gruppo BT, was killed in MM21904, together with two members of his crew; two others were rescued. In the other machine, MM21920, there were no survivors from Sottoten Antonio Romeo's crew. This was the start of a successful but brief run of successes for Barnwell.

Life was relatively quiet for the Hurricane pilots in general, however, the lack of activity broken only by the occasional scramble or incident. 185 Squadron's Sgt Swire carried out a heavy landing at Hal Far on the 6th, writing off his aircraft in the process although he was unhurt. Next day the same unit scrambled when an unidentified aircraft was plotted but this turned out to be a PR Hurricane returning unannounced from a reconnaissance sortie. Then, during the evening of 9th, Sqn Ldr Rabagliati took Hurricane Z3462 on an engine test, flying as far as Cape Scalambri:

> "When at 5,000 feet sighted single enemy machine (seaplane) flying just over water, two miles offshore. I closed and recognised it as a Cant Z506. From astern two very short bursts were delivered and aircraft landed with port wing on fire. Four men got out and port wing subsequently fell off and aircraft sank."

On returning to Takali, Rabagliati refuelled and re-armed and undertook a search for the Italian aircrew, although he failed to locate them, nor did he sight any enemy aircraft or rescue craft in the area. Of Rabagliati's latest victory, Flt Lt Neil wrote:

> "I ran into Rags one evening who said with mild amusement that he had been on an air-test and had suddenly run into an Eyetie bomber [sic], which he had managed to shoot into the sea. Surprised, I replied that it sounded a pretty rum sort of air-test, to which, with his slow smile and drawling lisp, he admitted it had been – he had been flying alone at 1,000 feet along the southern coast of Sicily, some 80 miles away to the north. I couldn't conceal my astonishment. Since his squadron had joined us in Malta, Rags had never failed to amaze and amuse me. Being a squadron commander, he had rather more freedom of action than the rest of us; even so, he was clearly taking advantage of his good fortune and opportunities and was not only quite fearless in action but never seemed the least concerned wandering about over endless wastes of sea in aircraft that were anything but reliable."[1]

Another staunch admirer of Sqn Ldr Rabagliati's was Flt Lt Don Stones:

"Rags became a close friend of mine, even after I had thrown a folding metal chair at him one evening from our Mess verandah during a rather boisterous lunch-time party. The chair folded before I had properly released it and took the top off my small finger before it crashed beside him in the courtyard below. To get even, he would appear at our night dispersal hut before I did my night flying test and watch with glee as the medical orderly put new dressings on my finger, which took a long time to heal as I had to use it every time I squeezed the hand-grip which operated the brakes on the Hurricane. This gave Rags enormous pleasure."[2]

On the morning of the 10th, Hurricanes of 185 Squadron were again scrambled but made no interception. When some 35 miles from the island, Plt Off Oliver's aircraft (BV157) suffered engine failure and he baled out into the sea. Kalafrana was notified and Lt(A) Eyres was soon on his way in the Swordfish floatplane; Oliver was plucked from the sea and on his way back to the island within 30 minutes of baling out.

The MNFU scored another success after dark on 11 August, when BR20Ms from 43°Stormo BT raided the island, together with five SM79bis from 10° and 30°Stormo and a number of Ju87s. Two pairs of Hurricanes were scrambled with Sqn Ldr Powell-Sheddon in the lead. He sighted one bomber coned by the searchlights, and made two attacks, but was then illuminated himself, temporarily losing his night vision and failed to see Ten Livio Vercelli's BR20M (MM22626) burst into flames and fall into the sea. Although three parachutes were seen by watchers, no survivors were found. There was no damage from the bombing apart from a small fire in a warehouse at Marsa. However, next day Rome Radio broadcast a substantially different version of events:

"The naval and air bases of Malta have been made the object of another very heavy attack by the Fascist air force. Formations of bombers and dive-bombers brought themselves wave after wave over the more important military objectives of the island. A veritable shower of bombs was rained down on Mqabba [Luqa] aerodrome. Aerodrome buildings and other establishments, stores and aircraft dispersed on the airfield were hit by medium and heavy calibre bombs and hundreds of grenades which caused vast destruction and fires. The attack on the naval base of Valetta was extremely effective. Serious damage was caused to harbour installations and to the dry docks."

Blenheims and Swordfish were active during mid-August, attacking a variety of targets. Several successes were claimed against shipping but two Blenheims failed to return from one operation, as did a Maryland of 69 Squadron which was shot down by a Vichy French D520 off Bizerta. Frustrated by the lack of activity, Sqn Ldr Rabagliati organised and led another raid against Syracuse seaplane base shortly after dawn on 17 August. Ten Z506Bs were sighted at their moorings, two of which were claimed destroyed by Rabagliati (Z3512) and Plt Off Rocky Main. Four others were strafed and damaged by Flt Lt McGregor. Rabagliati commented:

"Attacked at sea level around mole from the east. Picked on one Cant 506 and it burst into flames, and was seen burning furiously. Weather good. Visibility 50 miles. AA fire very heavy but inaccurate."

Indeed, two Z506Bs of 612^Squadriglia were set on fire and four more were damaged. Later the same day Control telephoned Flt Lt Neil of 249 Squadron to tell him that an aircraft carrying a 'special passenger' (probably a VIP or possibly an SOE operative) was due from the direction of Greece. 249 Squadron was to provide a section to escort it to Malta. Neil led Plt Offs Jack Hulbert, James Stuart and Sgt Dennis Rex to a designated point north-east of the island, but en route his own aircraft developed an oil leak. Nevertheless, he decided to remain with his section:

"We soon sighted a twin-engined aircraft of some sort, low down, dark against the sea and flying in the opposite direction. I gave a rather low-key 'Tally-ho!' and, crossing over the top of it, all four of us turned and took station, two on either side, before straightening up. Then, dropping down a further 1,000 feet or so, we headed back towards Malta. For about ten minutes we flew back together, the four of us providing what was no doubt a comforting escort to the aircraft beneath, Control being advised of our progress from time to time and everyone in good heart. In the distance Malta hove into sight."[3]

Neil was somewhat surprised that the aircraft did not head for Luqa, but instead approached Kalafrana Bay:

"At this point, although I had no grounds for suspicion, the faintest shadow of doubt crossed my mind, causing me to look more closely at the aircraft beneath. Whilst I was toying with my doubts, something splashed down into the water and the aircraft upended itself in a steep turn to the right so that it passed directly beneath me."[4]

Although the aircraft was tentatively identified as a Ca312 floatplane, their 'charge' was in fact an SM79bis torpedo-bomber. On informing Control, Neil was ordered to shoot down the raider. Since he was unable to see clearly through his now oil-smeared windscreen, he detailed Plt Off Hulbert and Sgt Rex, who were flying cannon-armed Hurricanes, to take care of it. Despite using all their ammunition they were unable to deliver a *coup de grâce* and the bomber was last seen smoking and at sea level. When a subsequent reconnaissance by several Hurricanes of 249 Squadron found a trail of oil and wreckage, the destruction was confirmed on this evidence. However, it would seem that the badly damaged aircraft – possibly from 278^ or 279^ Squadriglia Auto AS from Gerbini – did in fact reach its base, with every member of its crew wounded.

During August, Macchis failed to appear in strength until the morning of the 19th, when a dozen 126 Squadron[5] Hurricanes led by Flt Lt Lefevre (Z4941) were scrambled to intercept a similar number of enemy fighters near Cape Passero. Four of the Macchis were chased towards the Sicilian coast, when six more were seen at the same height. Lefevre reported:

"After various vectors, 12 e/a were sighted by P/O Rathie five miles ahead. After closing, e/a sighted me and turned, but was able to put two or three-second burst into e/a which dived in an aileron turn with smoke coming from the cockpit. I broke upwards but was unable to find another target, but was then attacked by Macchi on return journey. After a short circle, I broke and returned. He did not catch me."

Another successful engagement was reported by Plt Off Pat Lardner-Burke (DG615[6]), who claimed two destroyed and one damaged:

"Was flying Yellow 1 when 'Tally-ho!' was given, and followed Red 1 who turned left towards Cape Passero. When island about five miles [away] I saw a formation of six aircraft at my own height, covered by six more about 2,000 feet above. Red 1 turned towards the lower formation which split up into two sections of three. I went for the tail man of the second and fired a short burst which appeared to hit the pilot. The machine turned over and spun towards the land. I climbed and turned towards the e/a and saw F/Lt Lefevre attacking and followed, and shot down my second e/a, which was seen by F/Lt Lefevre. The first was seen by Sgt Worrall. I [then] attacked second from astern as he pulled his nose up and the fire seemed to enter the cockpit. White smoke appeared and the machine spun downwards."

A probable was also claimed by Sgt Noel MacGregor. It seems that the Macchis were from 90^Squadriglia. Ten Soprana of this unit reported shooting down a Hurricane, while Cap Franco Lucchini and Serg Battista Ceoletta shared a second.

The policy of taking the fight to the enemy was continued next day (20 August), Sqn

Ldr Rabagliati (Z3512) leading an afternoon raid by six 126 Squadron Hurricanes against the seaplane base at Augusta, as he later reported:

"Attacked diving from 9,000 feet from the east. Four aircraft detached to attack balloons. Two cannon aircraft dived to attack petrol storage tanks on mole. I gave two-second burst on one storage tank and observed explosive shells hitting it but with no apparent effect. Dived between balloon cable and attacked Cant 506 on water but with no result. Three cannons failed during attack."

Sgt Jack Mayall shot down one balloon in flames and also fired at a seaplane; a second balloon fell to Sgt Alan Haley, and a third to Flg Off Carpenter. Flt Lt McGregor and Lefevre also fired, albeit without conclusive results. The latter then observed a boom defence vessel in the harbour, which he strafed, seeing strikes. AA fire was fairly intense but poorly directed, although one Hurricane sustained some damage. Two Z506Bs were reported by the Italians to have been slightly damaged during this raid. Air Vice-Marshal Lloyd noted this attack in his memoirs:

"As the Italians would persist in keeping their seaplanes and flying boats on the water at Syracuse and Augusta, which were just within range for the Hurricanes, and as these targets were made more appetising because they were moored in straight lines, it was asking too much to resist attacking them. The Hurricanes seldom returned with a kill of less than three. We then found that the Axis oil was stored in big tanks on the shore. They were as big as gasometers and the Hurricanes endeavoured to destroy them – only to discover that their bullets merely bounced off the structures.

The next development in this private war was the Axis attempt to protect the flying boat anchorages with balloons, but the Italians little realised that they would lose them as soon as they were flown. When the last three remaining balloons were lost on 20 August, the Italians abandoned the unequal contest and, after the Hurricanes had destroyed several of the small craft which were used to protect the anchorages, they decided to move their flying boats out of harm's way."[7]

Next morning (21 August) the Regia Aeronautica retaliated. Ten 10°Gruppo CT Macchis provided cover while six more strafed Hal Far but without great effect, as noted by Plt Off Peter Thompson (the new 185 Squadron diarist):

"The dawn watches were rudely interrupted at 6 o'clock. They were scrambled for a 3+ 25 miles north but, lo and behold, as they took off three Macchis flew across the aerodrome at 200 feet, firing into space and hitting precisely nothing. However, P/O Bailey leading P/O Reeves and Sgt Westcott happened to be directly underneath them and the Bofors, which were pooping off madly, seemed to be shooting at our three Hurricanes and, only by the grace of God, did they escape being hit. Ten minutes later three more Macchis attempted the same thing, with net result nil."

Later in the morning Sqn Ldr Mould took off with six others from 185 Squadron to investigate a three-plus plot, which materialised as a flight of Macchis. After pursuing these back to Sicily the Hurricanes returned to Malta, only for Mould to be rebuked for being over enemy territory without permisson. Next day Flt Lt Hancock and his flight were scrambled to intercept incoming aircraft, but the plot faded soon after they became airborne. On returning to Hal Far, Plt Off Thompson force-landed although he was not hurt.

Shortly before midnight on 24 August, a Sunderland alighted in Kalafrana Bay with passengers from Egypt including at least one replacement fighter pilot, Sgt Peter Simpson from the Middle East Pilots' Pool. He was posted to 126 Squadron, and soon found himself in action. The last major engagement of the month came two days later (26 August), when a dozen Hurricanes of 126 Squadron and eight from 185 were scrambled late in the afternoon. The latter were ordered to patrol over a ship about 40 miles west of the island.

Meanwhile, those from 126 Squadron engaged nine Macchis about 15 miles south of Sampieri. Sqn Ldr Rabagliati (V7103) reported:

"After Controller had informed us that e/a were three miles south of us, whole formation orbited to port and I sighted six Macchis about 5,000 feet below, and a further formation of three at the same height. I overshot in my first attack badly and climbed steeply. Saw one e/a diving towards Sicily. I chased him along the beach, giving it a short burst whenever possible. Eventually, after third two-second burst, his starboard wing caught fire and he crashed and burst into flames. Controller and information was excellent. I saw a patch of oil underneath the main battle and just east of main flight, and one mile off the Sicilian coast. One Hurricane missing."

P/O Lardner-Burke (Z2825) claimed another:

"I was flying Black 2 in weaving section below the Squadron when 'Tally-ho!' was given. I then moved into position to attack and followed Red 1 down. I noticed one e/a who broke away from the formation and followed him. He turned away and I had a deflection shot which missed, so I closed up and had another shot and his port wheel dropped. He dived very steeply towards the coast of Sicily. I followed him and got into very close range and fired a long burst. His tailplane broke up and he dived straight into the sea from 1,000 feet. The pilot appeared to be trying to abandon the aircraft but did not."

Two more were credited to Sgt Noel MacGregor and Plt Off Dicky Dickinson, the latter recording:

"I saw a Macchi heading for the coast of Sicily pursued by a Hurricane which, however, soon broke off and turned back. I dived down on the Macchi and finally caught it up about two miles off the coast. Coming up from dead astern at a height of 2,000 feet, I fired a burst of about two-seconds, opening at about 100 yards. Breaking away, I saw the Italian pilot bale out and his machine hit the water. I was then attacked from above by a second Macchi which I had not noticed but, on turning to give combat, he dived away to sea level and headed home. After following to just over the Sicilian coast I broke off and returned home."

Yet another claim was submitted by Sgt Bill Greenhalgh, who also reported attacking a Macchi and seeing one undercarriage leg drop, whereupon the aircraft fell away pouring white smoke. He was awarded a probable after losing sight of his target when he had to break to avoid a collision. One Hurricane (Z3498) was shot down in the engagement, Sgt John Maltby, a 19-year-old from Derbyshire, being reported missing. He did not survive. Italian sources indicate that five Macchis of 86^Squadriglia were engaged on an escort patrol south of Cape Scalambri. Two Hurricanes were claimed shot down by Sottoten Duca Gabriele Ferretti and Serg Walter Omiccioli, and a probable by M.llo Avellino De Mattia, for the loss of Sottoten Luigi Cantele's aircraft (MM5862). The Italian pilot baled out and was later picked up from the sea.

On the night of 26/27 August, Sqn Ldr Powell-Sheddon was on patrol with Flg Off Cassidy when they intercepted and attacked a BR20M. The bomber was last seen losing height with smoke pouring from the starboard side. They then jointly attacked another, shooting away part of the starboard engine. The damaged aircraft circled Gozo at 1,000 feet, with lowered undercarriage, before it headed back across the sea towards Sicily. Both BR20Ms were claimed probably destroyed, but in fact they got back, though badly damaged. The crew of one baled out near the coast, the pilot then making a forced-landing but the bomber caught fire and was destroyed. In addition to the genuine successes achieved by the MNFU, it was known to Air HQ at Malta that a number of the Italian bombers were experiencing problems, as later confirmed by Air Vice-Marshal Lloyd:

"There was one closely guarded secret, however, which arose from some imperfection in the Italian technical arrangements. As soon as the bomb-release trigger had been operated to drop a new type of incendiary bomb the aircraft would burst into flames. It was important that the Italians should not become apprehensive and as our claims were always published in the Press and given out over the radio in Britain, we had to say that the aircraft was, in fact, shot down. Colonel Nelson, who commanded the searchlights, knew the secret, as did a few others; but in order to keep it, the MNFU had to be given an entirely bogus credit of five victories."[8]

The MNFU's CO, Sqn Ldr Powell-Sheddon, confirmed this when he recalled:

"Once we saw bombs drop five miles from the island and someone commented – 'Another Wop lack of guts coming in' – but something had gone wrong with the aircraft's bomb release and it caught fire. I knew this but I couldn't tell others."

The last few days of the month were largely uneventful: On 29 August, Flg Offs John Beazley and Pat Wells (BV156) of 249 Squadron strafed a schooner in the Sicilian Narrows while returning from a reconnaissance to Pozzallo. Next day two Hurricanes of 185 Squadron collided when investigating a report of enemy fighters attacking some Wellingtons. Sgt Dick Cousens clipped Flg Off Len Murch's aircraft, as recorded by Plt Off Peter Thompson in the unit diary:

". . . some damage was suffered by F/O Murch when his No2, Sgt Cousens, knocked his empennage for a burton. L.C. [Murch] was unhurt and made a good landing, complaining that he could not make his elevators work. It is understood that Sgt Cousens apologised to F/O Murch; no doubt the CO had a few words with the aforementioned Sgt Cousens. We leave the two participants sucking inky fingers and glaring at sheets of paper headed – Sir, I have the honour to report . . ."

The end of the month brought the usual communique from Air HQ, which credited the fighters with a dozen destroyed, three probables and one damaged for the loss of one Hurricane and its pilot.

Within 69 Squadron there was a change in command, as Wg Cdr John Dowland GC arrived to replace Sqn Ldr Russell Welland. The new CO had won the George Cross the previous year for twice removing unexploded bombs from ships. A number of awards for the reconnaissance unit came through at this time including a Bar to Flt Lt Adrian Warburton's DFC, and a DFC for Flg Off Roger Drew. The CO of 185 Squadron, Sqn Ldr Peter Mould, also received a Bar to his DFC.

September 1941

The month began with a night attack of Comiso airfield by a Fulmar of the INFU. Late the next night, two more took off for another intrusion, both heading for Gerbini. PO(A) Bert Sabey arrived in time to see an aircraft approaching the airfield with its lights on, which disappeared before he could manoeuvre into position. Another was seen landing and was attacked with a short burst but with unobserved results. Climbing to 4,000 feet he chased a third out to sea, but lost track of this also. Another was then sighted, which he pursued and caught just south of Mount Etna. He fired a long burst and saw his target go down in flames. At that point he noticed three Italian fighters climbing towards him, so set course for Comiso where he released his bombs. The various aircraft Sabey had attacked were BR20Ms of 43°Stormo BT, returning from a raid on Malta. One bomber (MM22689) crashed in flames a few miles from the airfield; three members of the crew baled out but only two survived. A second bomber was damaged.

During the morning of 4 September, nine aircraft of 126 Squadron and nine from 185 were scrambled to investigate activity over the sea to the east of the island. Shortly before 1130 an estimated 16 Macchis were seen, aircraft of 10°Gruppo CT searching for signs of an allied ship reported to have been sunk by Italian Ju87s during the night. Sqn Ldr Rabagliati (Z4941/XL), leading the 126 Squadron formation, reported:

"When at 25,000 feet, sighted six e/a south of us 10-15 miles. Dived to 22,500 feet, which was their level, and engaged from behind. One pulled up and appeared to have seen us. I pulled up after him and gave a short burst. Strikes were observed and he half-rolled and disappeared with black smoke coming out, and streaks of white. I did a steep turn to the left and almost immediately observed three parachutes in the sky, although at the time it was not obvious whether they were enemy. One Macchi dived in, out of control. Sgt Simpson confirmed seeing the enemy aircraft I fired at going down on fire and out of control, but did not see it hit the sea."

A second Macchi was claimed by Flg Off John Carpenter. He was acting as top weaver some distance above the other Hurricanes and climbed after four Macchis providing high cover for their own formation. Accompanied by Plt Off Lardner-Burke, Carpenter attacked one Macchi from below and to port, whereupon all four dived in line astern. His fire struck the starboard aileron of the leading fighter and pieces flew off the wing. The Italian did a flick roll and turned, at which point Carpenter claimed to have shot him down. Lardner-Burke (Z3512), meanwhile, was concentrating on shooting down the second Macchi:

"Black 1 was attacking an e/a, with another on his tail. I engaged the latter and saw his wing disintegrate. I was using a cannon aircraft. The machine spun over and the pilot abandoned the ship. I then came down as my guns had ceased to operate. I also saw three parachutes descending and two other aircraft crash."

Another Macchi was credited to Flt Lt Lefevre:

"I slid to the right and attacked simultaneously with Red 1. One burst of three-seconds was fired, hits being observed. Aircraft went down vertically and hit sea. Pilot was not seen to bale out. Two men were seen to bale out of other machines and two splashes seen in the water."

While Plt Off John Russell reported:

"Fired a three-second burst from dead astern, closing from 400-50 yards and observed strikes. Overshot and turned, losing sight of e/a. Claimed as damaged. Sighted two other e/a diving steeply to the north. Closed one down to sea level and after several bursts from dead astern and rear quarter, e/a burst into flames near the cockpit and went into sea at high speed. No apparent survivor."

Plt Off Chas Blackburn had to be content with a probable and a damaged:

"I went into the attack on the starboard of my CO and selected the second in from the starboard side of the enemy formation as my target. I gave about a two-second burst and saw part of wing and other pieces fall from e/a; it promptly went into a steep dive (practically vertical). I then attacked another aircraft which appeared in front of me. I saw sparks coming off it and broke away from the attack as I was being fired at myself from behind. I was flying a cannon aircraft. Afterwards I saw three parachutes descending."

Sgt Noel MacGregor was also credited with a probable, and Sgt Peter Simpson (Z2418/C) with one damaged, the former carrying out a forced landing on return due to a burst glycol tank. Two pilots of 185 Squadron also joined the fight, Flt Lt Jeffries (Z3562) attacking one Macchi orbiting at 19,000 feet. He managed a short burst from very close range and saw hits around the cockpit. The Italian fighter dived vertically towards the sea and although Jeffries did not observe the crash, he claimed it destroyed but was awarded only a probable. Newly-promoted Flg Off Peter Thompson wrote:

"Jeff saw one lone aeroplane and thought it was a Hurricane, but on closer examination it proved to be a Macchi, so Jeff and [Plt Off] Oliver did their stuff in no small way and although it was only credited as a probable, 52 cannon shells delivered at 25 yards range rather leads one to believe that one little Macchi did not get home. Jeff was then the object of affection of four more Macchis, but believing discretion to be the better part of valour, he decided it was time for his morning cup of tea and promptly removed himself from the locality."

The Italians lost Sottoten Andrea Della Pasqua and the commander of 10°Gruppo CT, TenCol Carlo Romagnoli, a veteran of the Spanish Civil War and one of the Regia Aeronautica's aces. Two more pilots got back with damaged aircraft. Five Hurricanes were claimed shot down by all pilots jointly.

In the afternoon, 20 more Macchis from 54°Stormo CT, operating from Pantelleria and led by Cap Valentino Festa, and a further ten from 10°Gruppo CT led by Cap Franco Lucchini, covered a Z506B of 612^Squadriglia in a search for the missing pilots. Eight Hurricanes of 249 Squadron were scrambled to intercept. They met the Italians five miles off Cape Passero at 1546, and engaged them in a fierce dogfight at 1,000 feet. Sqn Ldr Barton (Z2794) later described it as the hardest fight of his career:

"We attacked, from above, a formation of Macchis escorting what I believe was an air-sea rescue floatplane. We had the advantage but somehow the Italians reacted strongly and an unhappy dogfight ensued – all low down close to the water. I ordered disengage – I doubt if anyone heard – and we ran for home. A most dangerous situation, hence our losses. We should have done better."

Barton himself claimed one probable and one damaged, while Sgts Dave Owen and John Parker each claimed one shot down. Plt Off Bob Matthews (Z3574) damaged another:

"We went down to attack and we came up astern of these four who were diving towards Sicily. I gave one on the right-hand side a burst with my cannon from about 200 yards, closing. He went on his back and flicked, but almost at once we went in amongst some more Macchis and I had to break off. This time the Italians stayed. They had the advantage of numbers and we were only five miles from Cape Passero. At 500 feet there is not much room to manoeuvre. We fought hard for about five minutes then I got followed around over the wave tops. I packed up from home at 240 ASI at sea level, zig-zagging. In the fight I saw someone take a squirt at the rescue flying boat and I saw a splash also of an aircraft spinning in. There were a lot of Macchis and several carried out very split beam attacks, but their shooting was bad."

249 Squadron lost two pilots. Plt Off George Smith (Z3056) and Sgt Jim Kimberley (Z3521) had apparently attacked the Z506B, which suffered a number of strikes, before both were shot down by the Macchis and killed. The Italians, obviously incensed by the loss of TenCol Romagnoli, thought they had been attacked by 25 Hurricanes and claimed no less than 16 shot down – again all jointly as no individual credits were awarded – plus one probable and eight damaged. One 10°Gruppo CT Macchi flown by Serg Luigi Contarini was lost, while two more, piloted by M.llo Avellino De Mattia and Serg Walter Omiccioli, were damaged.

The air battles of the 4th seemed to cool the ardour of the Italian fighter pilots, allowing the Hurricanes to concentrate on keeping the bombers at bay. Shortly before dawn next day, three Z1007bis of 9°Stormo BT attacked Hal Far, and were intercepted by two MNFU Hurricanes flown by Plt Off David Barnwell (Z2961/K) and Flt Lt Stones (Z3574/F). The latter recalled:

"Barnwell had a Hurricane with machine-guns, and mine had cannon. The enemy turned out to be a Cant 1007 when illuminated. Barnwell was a few miles nearer and attacked first, setting an engine on fire which gave me a perfect target to finish off with my cannons."[9]

Two of the crew of MM23332 were reported to have baled out. The rescue launch found only the pilot, who had been wounded in the chest, and who was rushed to hospital. Three nights later, shortly before midnight on the 8th, Plt Off Barnwell (Z2680) shot down another Z1007bis (MM23331), one of nine Cants of 9°Stormo CT, which raided Luqa and Takali:

> "I got into range just before he got out of the searchlights. I fired a few bullets – closed to about 50 yards. He was diving and I throttled back and went after him for he showed up as clear as daylight against the moonlight shining on the sea below. I gave him a few more short bursts and I saw burning lumps falling off the port engine. Other engine smoking and pilot, who seemed to know his business, making steep, diving turns to evade fire. Gunners meanwhile firing at me. Finally he dived straight down, levelled off and made a perfect landing on the sea."

At dawn, the crew of the Swordfish floatplane from Kalafrana saw four survivors of the Cant in a dinghy rowing towards Malta, although the rescue boat actually picked up all five. Barnwell, who now had four night bombers to his credit, later met the pilot.

On 9 September, the island welcomed a new delivery of Hurricanes from *Ark Royal* (codenamed Operation 'Status I'). Four Blenheims from Gibraltar were to have led the fighters in, but just two arrived, and with insufficient guides for the entire flight, just 14 of the 26 Hurricanes were flown off. These were actually reinforcements for Egypt, and next day they continued to their destination. *Ark Royal* returned on the 13th, together with *Furious*, and this time 46 Hurricanes left the two carriers (Operation 'Status II'). When taking off from *Furious*, Z5218 hit the carrier's island, caught fire and catapulted into the sea, taking Flt Sgt W.R. Finlay RCAF to his death, as noted by fellow Canadian, Plt Off Joe Crichton:

> "We had Blenheims from Gib fly down and do the navigating for us, as on *Furious* we could only get seven Hurris on deck to fly off at a time. I drew the last one in the last batch of three. The third plane in the first batch went over the side, Sgt Finlay, who was RCAF. One of the destroyers found his Mae West and that was all. Three hours and 55 minutes to Malta."

Among the many Canadians on *Ark Royal* was Plt Off Bert Houle:

> "Bill Swinden came over to my aircraft and asked me to sit on his raincoat. He had no room for it in his aircraft. As he was about ten inches taller than me, he could not sit on it himself; I agreed. It is alright after one gets safely home to say one wasn't scared, but I frankly admit I was. The big carrier turned into wind, and tense and fearful, those pilots near the front started their engines and waited for the despatcher's signal for the first aircraft to take off. It was lined up, the pilot ran the engine up, held the aircraft with full brakes and waited. Finally the flag was lowered, the brakes were released and the aircraft crawled across the deck. When it hit the ramp at the bow of the ship, the aircraft was thrown into the air but it had not gained flying speed and slowly sank from sight below the ship's deck level. We breathed a sigh of relief as it staggered into view and fought for altitude. Immediately the next aircraft was off, and next, and then it was my turn. I opened the throttle as much as I dared without putting my kite on its nose. The only danger with this would be the sudden swing when the brakes were released. My aircraft did swing slightly but I straightened it and before I knew it, the ramp threw me in the air and I was out smoothly over the blue waters of the Mediterranean."[10]

With a 700-mile flight ahead of them, the Hurricanes formed up into their assigned groups and set course. Houle continued:

> "By this time my kidneys were floating. There were no relief tubes in the Hurricane and it is doubtful if it would have been used anyway. We had heard stories of relief tubes whose outlet had been placed in a low-pressure area so that it created suction. If the private part got too close it was sucked in and one could easily believe that the extraction could be

painful. Getting relief in a fighter is no easy task. The pilot sits on his packed parachute with his dinghy as his seat. A looped nylon strap came up between his legs while a strap came around each hip, passed through the loop and fastened into the lower holes in the release buckle. A back strap came over each shoulder to fasten into the upper holes in the release buckle. The buckle was on a flap which came around the left side and the parachute opening D-ring was also attached to this flap. Over all this, one fastened the four straps of the Sutton harness, which held the pilot to his seat and which automatically locked tight if the aircraft was to decelerate. This prevented the pilot from smashing into the instrument panel during a crash. There was no way, outside doing it in your pants, to get relief without undoing all those straps and attempting to clear all clothing. For these reasons, it was certain that getting relief at sea level would be dangerous. My timing was good; relief was obtained and everything put back in place before we had to level out. Bill's raincoat had been completely forgotten. It collected a lot of salty moisture and showed a big brown stain until the end of the war."[11]

Among those destined for Malta were four American pilots: Plt Offs Howard Coffin, Don Tedford, 'Pete' Steele and Ed Streets. In a book he later wrote based loosely on his experiences, Coffin wrote:

"And then suddenly, out of a long, thin cloudbank, an Italian Z506 put in an appearance. I imagine he was as surprised as we were, finding himself abruptly in the midst of 200 [sic] British planes coming in over the sea. At any rate, he did not open fire, and neither did we. I caught a glimpse of his startled face as he slipped down below us; and only later did I remember those 100 rounds of ammo in my guns. He disappeared as abruptly as he had come. Everyone else experienced the same delayed reaction as myself. It was a good lesson, although I suppose none of us could be blamed; we were all green to combat, and just about out of gas."[12]

A young Yorkshireman aboard *Furious*, Sgt Ted Wood, wrote in his diary:

"I took off No5 [in Z4005], quite easy, at about 0745. Joined up more or less in formation, 12 Hurricanes and one Blenheim, quite a sight. Flew on quite happily, shot past Pantelleria. Bloody glad when Malta sighted after three hours 35 minutes flying. One of our formation missing, Sgt Lee. Found later he had landed in Tunis, asked the way and took off again after finding his position, just as local police rushed up to hold him. When he landed at Takali, landed down wind and wrote off his own machine and another one as well."

Sgt Bud Lee, a Canadian, was fortunate to survive the crash, which severed the fuselage of his aircraft just behind the cockpit and knocked off the underwing tanks, although these were by now empty and did not pose a fire hazard. The aircraft he hit was Z4360/G[13] of 126 Squadron, which was less seriously damaged.

Twenty-three of the Hurricanes were due to fly on to Egypt, with half departing on the 19th including two flown by Plt Offs Houle and Swinden, but Sgt Wood was obliged to return to Malta:

"Had to get up at 0600 to get machines from dispersal on to the drome. Took off about 0845 after Wimpy which flew round and round the island with Hurricanes streaming after it, finally leaving about 0900. Flew on for 1 hour 25 minutes, with the Yanks [in the group] making a lot of noise on the R/T. Tried electric pumps to find generator had packed up, extra tanks no use. Called up Wimpy and got course and ETA; turned round and set out for Malta about 200 miles away. No land anywhere else. Main tanks ran dry and engine cut, quite a flap as I was still out of R/T range. Switched over to reserve and climbed. Suddenly the electricity came back and was I glad! Finally arrived over Malta after a trip of about 3 hours 15 minutes. Caused quite a flap, everybody wanted to hear from me."

The second batch, including the inexperienced Sgts Wren, Swire and Horsey of 185 Squadron, took off for Egypt on the morning of the 25th, but Sgt Wood was again left behind when his aircraft was pronounced unserviceable. Another of the new pilots, Sgt Garth Horricks RCAF, who flew Z3767 to the island, remembered the gist of a speech given soon after their arrival by Sqn Ldr Rabagliati:

"A man ought to know what he's up against. Remember, the Germans have been preparing and planning this war for years. They are at their peak now. Our potential strength is almost unlimited; the enemy's full strength is on the battle line today. He must win quickly or not at all, and so he will use his strength in whatever way he thinks will help him to win. He bombs homes in order to paralyse the people; he has done it before and he will do it at Malta, if he can, until the island is nothing but rubble and the people are driven to live in holes. He kills our pilots who have baled out of their planes and he destroys our rescue boats because he knows we can replace our equipment but that it's much more complicated to replace a man trained in air combat, like ourselves. Forget glory. Don't be afraid to run for it if the enemy has superior altitude or number. And if you have to bale out, delay pulling your rip-cord as long as you can – and then pray to God. And above all, heads up – and hang onto your nerve."

There was little operational flying for the remainder of the month. The arrival of replacement pilots allowed some of the old hands to have a rest, as Flg Off Peter Thompson noted in 185 Squadron's diary:

"The CO has been feeling pretty ill for about a fortnight and has at last been persuaded to go off flying for a few days. What he really needs, together with several others, is to go off the island. That is the only cure. Pat Hancock, hearing that he would have to remain on the island for another six months, decided to apply for posting to ME with a view of going into Training Command in Rhodesia. He was in France in 1940, came home for the London blitz and, just when things were quieting down at home, he was posted to Malta just in time for the German blitz. Sgt Branson, ex-185, now in the MNFU, did some very low flying along the Sliema front for the benefit of a girlfriend. Unfortunately, the AOC was also an interested spectator and decided that Branson could do some more low flying – along the banks of the River Nile. Apart from the injustice of the punishment, it puts ideas into people's heads – if you want to get off the island, low fly along the Sliema front!"

Another who had an enforced rest was 126 Squadron's Sgt Noel MacGregor, who was among those sent to intercept some Macchis when they attacked Takali on 12 September:

"E/a strafing. Self scrambled [in Hurricane B] in thick dust and crashed off drome. M'tarfa Hospital for ten days [two fractured ribs]."

MacGregor's colleague, Plt Off Les Barnes, was more fortunate when the engine of his aircraft (BV173) seized, as noted by 249 Squadron's Flt Lt Neil:

". . . he ploughed through a couple of stone walls, miraculously surviving, someone jocularly remarking at the time that he had discovered the quickest possible way of slowing down. Such macabre humour was always in vogue at Takali."[14]

Although it had been a quiet period for the Hurricanes generally, there had been much bomber activity and many air battles out to sea as another convoy fought its way to Malta from Gibraltar. Blenheims and Swordfish had struck at Axis convoys off the Greek and Tunisian coasts and Blenheims had also raided Messina where they damaged the Italian cruiser *Bolzano*. During strikes off Tripoli on the 13th and 15th, six Blenheims failed to return, at least three of these falling to CR42s and MC200s. Two Italian freighters were sunk and several others claimed damaged in the attacks. Another Blenheim, and a Swordfish, were lost on the 21st, and a Wellington failed to return from a raid the following night. During this period a delivery Wellington was also lost, as was the Heinkel 115 (BV185) spyplane, and another Blenheim was shot down. It was a costly period all round, with two Italian 20,000-ton troopships – *Neptunia* and *Oceania* – being sunk by a Malta-based submarine, although casualties were few. The latest British convoy came within range of Sardinian-based bombers on the 27th, *Ark Royal*'s Fulmar squadrons bravely fighting off wave after wave of SM79 and SM84 torpedo-bombers, shooting down four of these and a Z506B for the loss of two Fulmars, both of which fell to ships' gunfire. One crew was lost, the other rescued. Next day, as the escorting warships headed back towards Gibraltar, the Fulmars accounted for another Z506B. Meanwhile, the convoy's eight remaining merchant ships (one having been lost), had come under the protection of Force K destroyers from Malta, with air cover provided by two Beaufighters and a Fulmar. By noon, they were safely berthed in Grand Harbour where unloading of supplies began in earnest.

Air Vice-Marshal Lloyd, a bomber man at heart and by experience, was keen to take the fight to the enemy, using whatever aircraft were deemed suitable for the task:

"Certain Sicilian airfields were within Hurricane range and these, which held numerous fighters and some twin-engined aircraft, were repeatedly attacked from low level – although we did not succeed in driving the aircraft away. The Axis then moved a good deal of flak around these aerodromes and, as the results of further attacks were unlikely to bear any relation to losses which were bound to occur, we had to find some way round the problem. The answer was the Hurricane bomber, and it was on Malta that this redoubtable and ubiquitous aircraft made its first appearance in that rôle. Twenty-four of them were fitted to carry eight 20-lb bombs and after the Axis had lost a few twin-engined aircraft it did not take them long to move the rest. The fighters were of a more sturdy quality and would not move."[15]

Locally-produced bomb racks were fitted to an equal number of aircraft from 126, 185 and 249 Squadrons, which allowed four 20-lb, 25-lb or 40-lb bombs to be carried under each wing; the small bombs were released individually by means of a bank of switches situated near the pilot's elbow. Flt Lt Neil commented: "Bombs! What next, mines and torpedoes? What were we, fighter aircraft or one-engined Blenheims?"[16]

Nonetheless, bombing practice began in earnest, the uninhabited islet of Filfla being the main target. Some fighter pilots were keen on this new form of warfare, others not. The first operation took place on the morning of 28 September, when six Hurribombers of 185 Squadron were led by Sqn Ldr Mould to attack Comiso airfield, covered by six fighters led by Flg Off Peter Thompson. No spectacular claims were made, but all bombs were safely released over the general target area and there was little opposition from the defences. However, during the return flight Plt Off Woodsend had to bale out of Z4946 when about eight miles north of Gozo, as recorded in the Squadron diary:

"Woody, on his way home, decided that travelling in an aeroplane that might blow up at any moment was not his idea of fun. He indicated this feeling to the CO by a well known gesture before making a rapid, if undignified, exit from his aeroplane. He was seen to make a safe landing in the water; unfortunately, and this seriously, his exact position was not made known and it was not until five and a half hours later that he was picked up by the rescue launch *Clive*. In the course of the search, two Swordfish, one Gladiator, two Hurricanes, one Fulmar, one cruiser, one destroyer, two motor boats and the rescue launch took part. When the *Clive* first spotted him, Woody appeared to them as if suspended in mid-air. This effect was due to the fact that he was jumping up in his dinghy and then falling in the water. When the CO went down to collect him, Woody was asleep; he returned to Hal Far dressed in a Naval tunic, with last war's medals, and grey flannels, but apparently none the worse for his adventure."

Meanwhile, the Hurricanes were refuelled and re-armed preparatory to another attack with

Mould again leading. On this occasion Flg Off Len Murch led the escort. There was another incident during the return flight. Flg Off Thompson:

> "Jeff [Flt Lt Jeffries] had one bomb hang up and try as he might he could not get rid of it, so he decided to land with it still attached but the bomb apparently had a mind of its own and, as Jeff approached the circuit, the bomb fell off and landed on Malta. Fortunately, or otherwise, it did no damage except kill a goat."

A third mission was subsequently flown, led by Flt Lt Pike. Again no aerial opposition was met but, after the raid, a plot of 20-plus appeared on the board. These were apparently Macchis orbiting Comiso. A total of 257 20-lb bombs had been dropped on or near Comiso in the three raids. Most pilots flew two sorties, one as a fighter-bomber and one as escort; Mould was the only pilot to bomb twice. During the attacks damage was claimed to have been inflicted on several buildings and it was believed that a number of parked aircraft were set on fire.

On the night of 28/29 September, PO(A) Arthur Joping of the INFU was again over Sicily in a Fulmar, as he recorded:

> "Operated as night fighter over Sicily. Proceeded to Trapani where flare path was on. Saw aircraft signalling to land – gave chase but lost it in the dark. Machine-gunned flare path and dropped four incendiaries, one causing minor explosions. Attacked AA battery of four guns with machine-gun fire, silencing two. Proceeded to Marsala and machine-gunned seaplanes and hangars without visible result. Drew heavy AA fire from Agrigento – caught napping here."

In the afternoon of 30 September, five Hurribombers of 185 Squadron again attacked Comiso, while six fighters provided top cover, the Hurribombers each carrying six 40-lb bombs and two 25-lb incendiaries. Having completed their strike, they were attacked by three of the newly-arrived MC202s[17] from 97^Squadriglia led by Ten Jacopo Frigerio, who shot down Plt Off Donald Lintern's Hurribomber (Z2514/GL-B). He was seen to bale out just north of Gozo. After returning to base and refuelling, five of the Hurricanes set off to escort the ASR Fulmar flown by Lt(A) Eyres on a search for the missing pilot. Patrolling Macchis carried out an attack and while none of the Hurricanes were hit it seems that the Fulmar came under attack from Ten Luigi Tessari and Serg Raffaello Novelli, who jointly claimed a fighter shot down into the sea. Tessari's aircraft was then attacked by a Hurricane and received numerous hits in the fuselage although it returned to Comiso safely. The Fulmar ditched but the crew managed to get into their dinghy, and were later picked up by the Swordfish floatplane. However, Plt Off Lintern[18] was not found. In the skirmish with the Macchis, Flt Lt Jeffries (BD702) claimed one probable (probably Tessari's machine), while Plt Off Peter Veitch and Sgt Al Jolly each claimed a damaged. Jeffries reported:

> "I, Red 1, was leading a formation escorting one Fulmar to try to locate P/O Lintern. We approached the Sicilian coast at 2,000 feet. When about ten miles off the coast I sighted one floatplane. Black 1, Sgt Jolly, went to investigate. We were engaged by five enemy fighters. I fired several bursts at close range. I then concentrated on one aircraft. He tried every evasive action but my machine was more manoeuvrable and had a better performance. I broke off the engagement over the Sicilian coast and returned with the Fulmar. I last saw the enemy aircraft going down at 800 feet with smoke and bits trailing behind."

Air HQ's September resumé listed eleven enemy aircraft confirmed, one probable and five damaged during the month by the fighters, but more importantly in three weeks of intensive operations against Axis convoys plying between Italy and North Africa, eleven ships had been sunk, six by air attack, totalling just over 23,000 tons. A number of decorations came through for the more successful Hurricane pilots, DFCs going to 185 Squadron's Flt Lt Jeff Jeffries, Plt Off David Barnwell of the MNFU, and the now departed Flt Lt Chubby Eliot.

October 1941

On the morning of 1 October, 9°Gruppo CT undertook its first sorties over Malta with its new aircraft, seven MC202s of 73^Squadriglia led by Cap Mario Pluda participating. At 1150, eight Hurricanes from 185 Squadron scrambled after the incoming bandits, climbing to 24,000 feet. At this height, 30 miles north-east of the island, they were jumped by the Macchis and Sqn Ldr Peter Mould (Z5265/GL-T) was shot down. In the Squadron diary Flg Off Peter Thompson provided an account of his loss and paid a heartfelt tribute:

"The CO was leading A Flight in a scramble after a +2. These he spotted and proceeded to give chase. As they were above him, he was compelled to lose speed in order to gain height. A further plot of +9 then appeared which he apparently did not hear about owing to R/T failure, and just when he was unfavourably placed – he had followed the +2 out of the sun – the formation was jumped by about a dozen Macchis and CR42s. F/O Murch was hit in the wing and several others, in an attempt to turn to engage, spun off. The situation was hopeless and our pilots broke off the engagement and returned to base – with one exception, the CO.

Immediately, the rescue services were put into operation – two motor boats, a float-fish [Swordfish floatplane] and three Hurricanes led by P/O Veitch went to search in the area where the CO was presumed to have crashed. A patch of oil was reported. As time went on and still no further definite news arrived, the grave faces of the pilots at dispersal reflected the general feeling that little hope could be held for the CO's rescue. Another three Hurricanes led by myself went out later in the afternoon but nothing was seen.

At about four o'clock Controller phoned Jeff and reported that Lt Eyres of the Rescue Service [in the Swordfish floatplane] had seen the patch of oil with flourescence in the middle of it, and much against everyone's will, the following conclusion had been reached – the CO had been killed. Everyone joins in offering their deepest sympathies to the CO's wife. The tragedy of his death is beyond real expression. He was the most courageous, popular and beloved CO – we count it a privilege and an honour to have been associated with him."

During the skirmish with the MC202s, Sgt Ernie Knight managed to get amongst the attackers, one of which he claimed damaged. Three of the 73^Squadriglia pilots, Cap Carlos Ivaldi, Ten Pietro Bonfatti and Serg Magg Enrico Dallari, jointly claimed two Hurricanes shot down and two probables in the first pass, although Ivaldi's aircraft (MM7723) was hit in its main fuel tank in return. With all fuel drained away, Ivaldi was obliged to force-land on a beach near Pozzallo on the Sicilian coast.

Following the loss of Sqn Ldr Mould, Flt Lt Pip Lefevre of 126 Squadron was promoted to take command of 185 Squadron. He arrived with Flg Off Charles Ambrose DFC, who was to take over B Flight. However, four days later both returned to 126 Squadron, following which Flt Lt Pike was given command, and Flg Off Len Murch was promoted to lead B Flight in his place. These comings and goings tempted Flg Off Thompson to comment: "S/Ldr Pike now takes over command of the Squadron – this is what should have happened in the first place – the way things happen in the Air Force is still a mystery!"

185 Squadron suffered a further loss on 4 October, when two Hurricanes were scrambled to investigate a reported six hostiles although there was no interception:

"Another catastrophe. This morning, P/Os Veitch and Allardice went up on a one section scramble; 30 minutes later a Hurricane was seen to come out of the clouds, which were down to 1,500 feet, in a terminal velocity dive and go into the sea about half a mile offshore. Five minutes later, P/O Allardice landed and told us the following story: he was up at 25,000 feet when he suddenly felt groggy. The next thing he remembers is pulling out of a dive at 500 feet. The trouble was oxygen, and therefore we must conclude that the same thing happened to Veitch, only unhappily he was unable to pull out in time. Veitch was very quiet and did not mix with the Squadron. He was a very capable pilot and his loss can be ill spared."

Plt Off Peter Veitch's Hurricane (Z2518/GL-Q) crashed off Benghaisa Point; the body of the 19-year-old from Sussex was not recovered. Although his death was attributed to oxygen failure, he may actually have been the victim of Serg Teresio Martinoli of 73^Squadriglia who apparently reported shooting down a Hurricane during the day.

After dark, Sub Lt(A) Mike Tritton of the INFU headed towards Sicily in his Fulmar on another intruder sortie. Over Trapani shortly before midnight he attacked what he believed was a Ju87. After a 15 minute chase, and in spite of gun stoppages, he eventually broke away with his target trailing black smoke. The unit's other serviceable Fulmar, flown by PO(A) Jopling, was meanwhile operating over Marsala where AA positions and seaplanes were strafed. Jopling claimed at least two of the latter severely damaged.

Following the successful strikes against Comiso, Air Vice-Marshal Lloyd agreed that other targets should be attacked by the Hurribombers, by day and at night:

> "The Sicilian trains, which ran within range, were another tempting target. The Hurricanes watched their movements, made out a time-table and set the trap. One operation sufficed as the trains never ran again in daylight. But there were other profitable and worthwhile targets, too, such as railway signal boxes, wagons in the sidings, cars and lorries on the roads, the lighthouse on the southern tip of the island, and even the occasional coaster which was courageous enough to venture out in daylight. I am at a loss to explain why the Axis did not come out and murder us for these activities and for those by the other types of aircraft. But operations over Malta were expensive in Axis casualties, and perhaps that had deterred them."[19]

On the night of 6/7 October, Flt Lt Neil (GN-R[20]) of 249 Squadron set out to bomb Gela railway station:

> "Fondly hoping that the Italians would reveal their known defensive positions by shooting at me with the red balls, they did nothing of the sort, obliging me to wander about endlessly over Sicily trying to discover exactly where I was. In fact I never did find the railway station but, by sheer good fortune, came across the railway line. I did a gentle dive in that direction and disposed of my load." [21]

That same night Comiso airfield was visited by Sqn Ldr Barton and Plt Off Titch Palliser (Z4016), who noted: "First dive-bombing in Hurricane. Target stood out well in moonlight. Bombs fell near dispersals and hangars in south-east corner." The two Hurricanes returned, refuelled and re-armed and set out again for the same target. This time Palliser recorded: "Set off at 4.30am. Much darker. Overshot target and bombed eastern side of Vittorio town, near Comiso." Hurricanes of the MNFU and the two Fulmars of the INFU also operated over Sicily that night, one of the latter being lost when it was forced to ditch in the sea off Syracuse. Its crew, PO(A) Arthur Jopling and Lt(O) Manning, were taken prisoner, as the former recalled:

> "Released four bombs on Catania, machine-gunned dispersed aircraft and AA positions. Attacked balloon barrage at Augusta and was hit by shell. Machine caught fire and was just able to make coast, though engine was useless, and about one mile east of Syracuse was compelled to land in the sea. Taken POW about three hours later."

During the night Malta-based Blenheims and Swordfish attacked shipping off Tripoli, where one 6000-ton freighter was sunk, but the Blenheims continued to take losses: two were shot down during a daylight operation on the 9th, and two more two days later. The Regia Aeronautica was also active, two Z1007bis from 9°Stormo BT carrying out a raid on Hal Far from which one failed to return, having presumably been shot down by the guns, or fallen victim to a faulty bomb-release mechanism. One of the MNFU pilots operating at this time, Plt Off Douglas Robertson, recalled:

> "The most thrilling tasks given to us were flights over enemy territory in eastern Sicily. These trips were nuisance raids, carried out on moonlight nights, to keep the enemy night bombers on the ground. The procedure was to fly near an enemy bomber airfield, at 500 feet, to avoid being picked up by radar. The assignment over Sicily was to stay there for one hour, then be relieved by another pilot from our Flight. Aircraft taking off were guided by a totem pole with lights. All these lights were shaded so that they could not be seen above a few hundred feet. The night landing at Takali was assisted by runway lights. Malta, of course, was otherwise blacked out.
>
>   [On one occasion] I flew towards an airfield near Catania, south of Mount Etna. Before reaching the airfield perimeter I turned sharply away. This tactic would be repeated by an approach to another side of the airfield. Each time I turned away, my rear-view mirror gave me a sight of the sky lit up with anti-aircraft fire. The operation proved to be successful as the enemy bombers did not attempt to take off while my presence kept them under air raid alert. Once I flew north of Catania and found myself uncomfortably close to Etna, so I moved away from the mountain. In the bright moonlight, when I was flying over what looked like a park, I could see enemy soldiers moving about amongst the trees. Small light flashes made me presume that they were shooting at me with their rifles. They must have been bad marksmen as I was never hit."

Plt Off Titch Palliser (Z4016) of 249 Squadron was again over Comiso on the night of 10/11 October:

> "Target stood out very well. Did very steep dive and straddled hangars, dispersals and billets. Intense flak. Two bombs on Comiso town. No results observed although aerodrome flak, five miles away, opened up again."

This was a relatively uneventful period for the Hurricanes, with sections from 126 and 185 Squadrons frequently scrambled to investigate plots, when they would search for an elusive enemy. The pilots of 185 Squadron had noticed a regular visitor to be a reconnaissance Macchi, which came over at a great height, causing Flg Off Thompson to comment in the diary: "The plot comes in so fast that we do not get sufficient warning, but we are still expected to climb to 30,000 feet in about ten minutes!"

   The PR Macchi 202 was frequently flown by Sottoten Duca Gabrielle Ferretti, a young nobleman serving with 86^Squadriglia CT; he had previously flown MC200s with the unit and had claimed a Hurricane shot down in August[22]. The calm at Malta was broken early on the morning of 14 October when six low-flying MC202s of 9°Gruppo CT strafed Luqa. From the safety of Takali, which was not attacked, Plt Off Bob Matthews of 249 Squadron was among those to witness the attack:

> "I was standing outside dispersal looking towards Valetta, over which the dawn made a yellow and red band and the sun edged above a low, dark bank of cloud. There were two dull flashes in the town, anti-aircraft. Almost at once I saw three aircraft in line astern dropping down from the darkness towards Luqa and Hal Far. The Bofors began to fire red balls of fire, which leapt from the guns, that seemed to float up towards their target. Machine-guns opened up, so did the aircraft. The air was full of flying red balls and black puffs. Bofors fired from all directions over the aerodrome. The second three Macchis came down. This last was windy and opened fire at 5,000 feet. An even more terrific firework display followed them out, but none were hit. They did no damage."

Five MNFU Hurricanes took off to intercept, led by Flt Lt Cassidy. They were followed by three each from 185 and 249 Squadrons. Flg Off Tommy Thompson of the MNFU had good reason to remember the occasion:

"My 21st birthday! Dawn – scramble! Low flying attack on Luqa by six Macchi 202s. P/O Barnwell and myself jumped. Barnwell [Z3512] shot down one but failed to return himself. The action took place at dawn and 249 Squadron were also scrambled – P/O Leggett fired at me over Grand Harbour. I seem to remember it cost him at least a couple of beers!"

A contemporary report of Barnwell's loss stated:

"[He] engaged enemy aircraft attacking the island. The Control Room heard his voice saying 'Tally-ho! Tally-ho! Got one! Got one!' Five minutes later his voice sounded again, 'Baling out, engine cut; am coming down in the sea.' A rescue launch searched all day until dark, but found no trace of the pilot."

Both 185 and 249 Squadrons joined the search for the missing pilot, Plt Off Titch Palliser sighting wreckage but seeing no sign of life. On a second search the same pilot reported what he thought was a dinghy but was unable to relocate it on subsequent sweeps. Sections of aircraft continued to search throughout the day, assisted by the ASR Swordfish floatplane, but to no avail. The search for Barnwell was called off next day. It would seem that the Macchi attacked by Barnwell was that flown by Sottoten Emanuele Annoni, but despite two cannon shell strikes in the fuselage, he was able to fly it back to Comiso. Claims for two Hurricanes shot down were made by Sottoten Bruno Paolazzi and M.llo Manlio Olivetti – obviously one or both were responsible for shooting down Barnwell. A probable was also claimed jointly by Serg Magg Luigi Taroni and Serg Gustavo Minelli.

Air Vice-Marshal Lloyd and his staff continued to intiate ways and means of harassing the enemy, as Lloyd wrote:

"We began to collect all the bits of information from various sources about the movement of aeroplanes employed on transport service from an aerodrome in the middle of Sicily to Africa, but we found that the route lay well to the west and traversed Pantelleria and Lampedusa. The Marylands and other aircraft which had seen them reported that they flew low and were unescorted – unfortunately this movement was too far away to be seen on our radar location sets. When sufficient information became available [including Ultra intercepts] to work out a rough schedule of the services, the Hurricanes were re-fitted with the long-range petrol tanks which had carried them to Malta, and with two Naval Fulmars, they were sent out to a patrol line 120 miles away . . ."[23]

As Flg Off Thompson made clear in 185 Squadron's diary, the pilots themselves did not necessarily agree with the AOC's latest suggestion:

"The Hurricane, originally a short-range interceptor-fighter, has since been converted into (1) medium bomber; (2) recce – long-range. The latest idea and/or inspiration is to make the long suffering Hurricane a long-range fighter, the idea being to add external long-range petrol tanks – then make equally long suffering pilots fly them for a long time, during which they are expected to shoot down Italian transport aircraft – rather long odds! It has since come to my ears that plans are afloat to convert the Hurricane into a heavy bomber. This, I imagine, will be done by removing the undercarriage, slinging on a 4,000-lb bomb and launching us into the air with a catapult!"

Neither were the pilots of 249 Squadron keen on the thought of flying long missions over the sea; Flt Lt Neil wrote:

"In line with our instructions to 'take the offensive', the second half of October saw 249 engaged in lengthy flights in search of transport aircraft. There was no question of us being controlled onto known targets, it was all a business of guess and hope. Four of our Hurricanes being fitted with two 44-gallon wing tanks each, Crossey and I were the first to go [on 15 October]. I had mixed feelings about the arrangement. The prospect of shooting down a few juicy Savoias or Cants was appealing enough, but going into action carrying what amounted to a primed bomb under each wing was less attractive. Our long-range tanks were simply not meant for fighting: they could not be jettisoned, they reduced the Hurricane's performance very considerably, and even when empty contained a lethally explosive mixture. Were we to encounter enemy fighters, our number would almost certainly be up as we could neither fight nor run, dire possibilities which sharpened our minds considerably when making plans. In the event, nothing much happened on that first trip."[24]

Next day (16 October) 185 Squadron provided two aircraft to the Lampedusa area, Sqn Ldr Pike and Sgt Jolly undertaking the duty. They returned three hours later having seen nothing, the CO reiterating his opinion that the whole idea was a "bloody waste of time". Having had to return next day after ten minutes due to Sgt Vardy's aircraft having developed engine trouble, Flt Lt Jeffries and Vardy set out again on the 18th to patrol west of the island on a search for the elusive transports, but none was seen. The Hurricanes at last achieved success, on 19 October, Sqn Ldr Barton (Z3155) and Plt Off Titch Palliser (Z4005) of 249 Squadron, flying exactly the same route as had Neil and Crossey on the 15th, spotted an SM81 transport aircraft 1,000 feet below; Barton reported: "The SM81 soon burned and there was little left by the time it hit the sea – not a pretty sight." During the afternoon, four Hurribombers of 126 Squadron carried out a strike on Comiso. Escort was provided by 249 Squadron including Plt Off Bob Matthews (BV156/Q) and his No2 Sgt Dave Owen. In his diary, Matthews wrote:

"We turned east when we were south of the aerodrome, over Vittoria. I was bottom weaver and had to flog along to keep up. We circled over the aerodrome and as we did so, I saw two aircraft going seawards which I thought were Hurricanes on their way home. We hung around a long time, too long. When we were about five miles out towards Malta, a single Macchi made a half-hearted head-on attack and raced overhead, turning hard. Another Macchi with an in-line engine joined and they followed us out, closing fairly rapidly.

The in-line Macchi [in fact both were MC202s] shot at Owen and burst his radiator. I then saw him [the Macchi] closing but I took it to be Owen catching up. I suddenly realised that it was a Macchi very close. He opened fire and at once hit my elevator. I skidded and banked left, put everything in one corner and I saw the tracer glowing and flashing over my starboard wing. I turned right sharply and called up on the R/T: 'Pinto leader, I am being attacked.' John [Beazley] turned left steeply with the rest of the formation. And the last I saw of the Macchi he was standing on his tail about two miles away to port.

I made for home, weaving and flying slowly as I knew I was damaged. I landed and inspected. One bullet went in the wing-root just near the trailing edge; it burst and made a hole about two inches long and half wide, with many splinter holes. The hard core went on and missed the petrol tank by half an inch. One bullet hit the port elevator a quarter inch from the outer bracket. It burst and split the elevator spar so that it was held by half an inch of aluminium. If this had broken I would have spun in. One bullet went through the starboard aileron and tore it badly. My lucky day!"

Despite the damage to his aircraft, Sgt Owen also got back and landed safely. The Macchis were from 73^Squadriglia, Serg Teresio Martinoli claiming two Hurricanes shot down while two more were claimed damaged by Ten Felice Bussolin and Serg Magg Pasquale Rossi.

185 Squadron's luck was also about to change. On 20 October, Flt Lt Len Murch and Sgt Peter Lillywhite took off at 1145 to patrol Lampedusa, Murch reporting:

"I had reached patrol line at 1230 and, at 1310, Sgt Lillywhite called my attention to six SM81 passing below us, heading north. Our height was about 2,000 feet and that of the e/a was about 50 feet. I turned to port and dived down on the formation. I found that I could not see through the windscreen [oil leak] so I passed behind the formation hoping to draw their fire while Sgt Lillywhite attacked a straggler from the starboard quarter astern. Fire was opened from the formation when he was at about 300 yards range and continued until he had broken away and was returning to base. The e/a which was attacked at first trailed smoke which later stopped. It was losing speed and height. It eventually hit the sea and exploded with no hope of survivors. The rest of the formation continued on course for Lampedusa. I fired a very short, haphazard burst while behind the formation but as I could not see the aircraft no results were observed."

The successful Sgt Lillywhite wrote:

"I closed in and opened fire from quarter astern at 300 yards and observed hits in the fuselage and engine. I closed to 25 yards, firing another burst and seeing a flame and smoke on the port side. I had to break away violently and as I did so I hit the slipstream of the next e/a in front. There was a flash and a puff of smoke and I saw petrol coming out of my starboard long-range tank and, at the same time, I found that the trimming gear was out of action. Set course for base with both hands on stick."

Flg Off Thompson added in the Squadron diary:

"Sgt Lillywhite nearly had heart failure when, on landing, it was pointed out that the bullet which had cut his trimming gear had passed through his hood, missing him by a mere couple of inches – phew!"

Flg Off Gay Bailey and Sgt Fred Sheppard of 185 Squadron undertook the long-range offensive patrol on the 22nd, but returned early, having had to evade three CR42s off Pantelleria. At about 1240, four Macchi 202s made a low-flying attack on Takali, as Plt Off Bob Matthews of 249 Squadron noted:

"I had just begun to get my machine ready for taxiing when the warning went and both 126 and 185 Squadrons were scrambled. So I waited and stood by my machine. Suddenly I heard machine-gun fire close to and imagined there was a fight. Then I saw the four Macchis diving down on the aerodrome and the pink tracer pouring down in streams, which swept across the aerodrome. I dived under the machine behind the armour plate and the slugs whacked into the ground all round us. The Italians zoomed over the aerodrome and climbed straight back to about 8,000 feet without turning. The ground batteries and machine-guns did not get off one shot until they were going away. The heavies put up a high barrage."

During the afternoon nine 249 Squadron Hurricanes scrambled on the approach of 14 MC202s, six of which were tasked with carrying out a strafing attack. The top cover dived on the Hurricanes as they climbed over St Paul's Island and shot down Sgt Dave Owen (GN-R). Sgt Alf Branch (Z4016) noted in his logbook: "Sgt Owen shot down into sea – circled him until picked up. Gave two short bursts head-on at a 202 – did not claim anything." Owen had been acting as a weaver in company with Plt Off Bob Matthews, whose aircraft (Z3756) was again hit, as he recorded in his diary:

"Just over St Paul's Bay, when we were at about 15,000 feet, we saw the enemy aircraft – seven down, [and] six above coming in very fast and diving apparently towards Takali. They were quite near when they turned towards us, still diving. They crossed us to the left of the formation and, as they came up, I pulled up my nose and gave a long burst so that the whole of the formation flew through it. They went over and all turned steeply to the left, while we nosed down and turned to the left also, trying to get some speed on the clock. We broke as they turned to fight and the whole sky filled up with aircraft milling around, and a few firing. Several Macchis stayed up and played the dive and climb tactics. As I circled after one Macchi, another jumped me and put a burst over my wings, both sides, so I turned and skidded away. I began circling to gain height, edging towards Valetta, which was darker than the west. And just as I was turning towards a couple of Macchis, another jumped me from above and got in a burst which hit me pretty badly. I could smell the incendiary and explosive as they hit. And again I turned violently. As I did so, I saw a Hurricane go down steeply in flames and eventually hit the water. I did not see anyone get out.

Again I began the circling climb racket with several other Hurricanes with me. One came up behind and I shied away in case it was a Macchi. Then suddenly the Macchis went and we were left at about 12,000 feet in the growing gloom. I came in and landed, just avoiding a wing dip on account of my damaged (leading) edge. Of course, there was an inquest on the battle. I had bullets all over the place. One went into my left wing and smashed two ammo tanks, exploding a lot of ammunition in them. One went down the semi-armour plate on the cowling and burst when it hit the glycol filler cap cones, and blew it open. Another hit my mainspar about one foot from the wing-root and almost blew it apart – the wing surface was blown open about six inches on either side of the strike. The last went through the trailing edge – a clean hole. So that was another day of near shaves. I admit that I felt pretty fagged when I landed, and very upset. I could easily have been sick. The day after that I caught sandfly fever and went up to M'tarfa [Hospital] for a week."

This was the second time in the last two outings that Matthews and Owen had been targeted by the Macchis, causing Plt Off Harry Moon to comment laconically: "Sgt Owen and P/O Matthews (weavers) consistently shot up and down!" The Macchi pilots were from 73^Squadriglia: two Hurricanes were credited to each of Ten Pietro Bonfatti and Sottoten Alvaro Querci, and one apiece to Cap Mario Pluda, Serg Mario Guerci and Serg Teresio Martinoli – his fourth victory of the month – while probables were awarded to Magg Antonio Larismont Pergameni and Cap Carlos Ivaldi. One Macchi returned with battle damage.

The Hurricanes unknowingly gained their first victory over the new Macchis on 25 October, as eight 185 Squadron aircraft led by Flg Off Gay Bailey were scrambled on the approach of four Z1007bis escorted by MC200s and MC202s. The bombers were misidentified as BR20s on this occasion. Bailey (BD835) reported:

"I was Red 1. When approaching Kalafrana from the south-east at 25,000 feet, I saw ack-ack bursts and then four enemy bombers. The e/a were heading towards us at about 20,000 feet. We dived for head-on attack. E/a turned and went out to sea. We caught them about six miles north-east of Grand Harbour. I opened fire on e/a on the left, fired one burst at 400 yards, and closed, firing. Broke off to the left and re-engaged and fired all my ammo. I noticed strikes on the starboard engine. Enemy fighters were circling above all the time. I was hit by a .5 bullet in fuselage."

Red 2, Plt Off Oliver, fired at the same aircraft and reported obtaining a few hits on its port wing and engine, but broke away when Macchis dived at him. Blue Section followed, Sgt Ream (Blue 1) only managing a short burst at the bomber before a Macchi attempted to get on his tail. His companion, Sgt Bill Nurse (Blue 2), also attacked the bomber:

"I opened fire from 300 yards astern, my bullets entering the fuselage. I opened fire again from 200 yards, giving a six-second burst, and observed strikes on the fuselage and port engine. I closed in again, firing until my ammunition ran out, and again observed my bullets entering the port engine and wing-root. I broke away at 50 yards, and I think I stopped the port engine."

Sgt Trevor Bates, leading Yellow Section, fired at the unfortunate bomber until his guns stopped. He reported that "something flew past me when I was about 100 feet away." The Z1007bis at the centre of all the attention was hit hard, its port engine being stopped, and it was considered to have been probably destroyed. In fact, the bomber managed to reach Sicily, where it belly-landed at Comiso with one dead and one wounded aboard. At this point, the Hurricanes were bounced by the MC202s and Sgt Ernie Knight (Z3456) was shot down. In return, Sgt Cyril Hunton fired several bursts into one and claimed it probably destroyed:

"I was flying as Yellow 2, when I saw on my starboard side, about five miles away, four enemy bombers. I followed my No1, who went in to attack one of the bombers. I was about 300 yards behind him when an enemy all-black fighter with an in-line engine came up to attack Sgt Bates and crossed my sight. I fired, and got on his tail, firing continually until I saw three Macchis attacking from above, when I broke off firing. As I turned towards the other fighters and fired, I ran out of ammunition. The first Macchi I attacked was leaving a thin trail of smoke when I broke off and came back."

Wreckage of the Macchi (MM7728) was later found floating in the water by Italian search craft, its pilot – none other than the commander of 4°Stormo CT, TenCol Eugenio Leotta – dead. Two Hurricanes were claimed shot down by TenCol Minio Paulello, one by Magg Larismont Pergameni and another by Cap Mario Pluda and Ten Pietro Bonfatti jointly, all of whom misidentified their opponents as Spitfires. Of the loss of Sgt Knight, a 20-year-old from Birmingham, Flg Off Peter Thompson wrote in the diary:

"Sgt Knight did not return from this engagement and in the subsequent search, which lasted all afternoon, no trace of him could be found. It is assumed that he was jumped by the fighter cover. Sgt Knight showed great promise as a fighter pilot. He was deservedly popular with everyone and it is with sincere regret that I have to record his death.

It has been impressed on pilots that they must maintain pair formation under all circumstances. No2s have been told to keep with their No1s. This also applies conversely: No1s must keep with their No2s. It so often happens that the No1 has the superior machine, and if he goes 'balls out', his No2 cannot keep up. It therefore behoves the leader of the section to maintain a speed which enables his No2 to hold formation comfortably. Sgt Knight, flying a heavy cannon machine, was probably left behind with the disastrous results that we all know."

185 Squadron suffered another casualty next day (26 October) but in vastly different circumstances, as Thompson recorded:

"In the evening, all the people who had been here six months foregathered in Valetta for the purpose of celebrating their survival. P/O Woodsend deputised for Jeff [Flt Lt Jeffries[25]] who was feeling very ropey. Later in the evening, after having had dinner, Woody felt rather out of things and wanted to leave. This request was, of course, refused and in the ensuing fun and games, Woody locked himself in a small room and then proceeded to climb out of the window on to what he thought was a balcony. Unfortunately, it wasn't, and he fell the odd 50 feet before coming to rest on the concrete floor. After some delay he was carted off to M'tarfa where he is likely to remain for some time. Woody sustained a badly broken pelvis and some superficial cuts. He was, however, lucky to get away with his life."

On the last day of the month Flt Lt Neil and Flg Off Crossey of 249 Squadron set off on another long-range patrol between Pantelleria, Linosa and Lampedusa, but nothing was seen. In the event, the two successes achieved earlier during the month were to be the only two, although patrolling Marylands of 69 Squadron had engaged Ju52/3ms of III/KGrzbV.1 on three different occasions and each time were credited with their probable destruction; at least one of the Ju52s crash-landed. The two Fulmars of the INFU engaged on long-range patrols failed to make contact with the transports. During their patrol Sub Lts(A) Mike Tritton and Hurle-Hobbs managed to evade several CR42s, presumably from Pantelleria. A day later CR42s attempted a further interception of the Fulmars but were spotted in time by PO(A) Sabey. However, these patrols gradually petered out and the appearance of CR42s effectively ended the chance of easy victories. Despite this singular lack of success, Air Vice-Marshal Lloyd nonetheless wrote glowingly of their achievements:

"They found magnificent targets. Scores of Italians and Germans were killed and there is every reason to believe that one of them was a German Air Force General who enjoyed considerable repute. But the operation could not last long – it was just too violent . . . the transport service was soon diverted via Greece."[26]

The final engagement of the month occurred during the night of 31 October/1 November, when night bombers – four BR20Ms of 116°Gruppo BT – again appeared over Malta. Plt Off Peter Rathie and Sgt Alex Mackie of the MNFU were up, seeing one bomber illuminated by searchlights. Misidentifying it as a Z1007bis, Mackie reported:

> "I was rather astonished not to be fired at as I made my first attack from astern from about 50 yards range, and also to find that the aircraft did not make the slightest attempt at evasive action. I made another attack from astern and below, still without being fired at from the enemy aircraft, which kept on its straight course. After the second burst it caught fire and went down. It was all rather too easy."

The radio operator baled out as the bomber (MM22248) burst into flames but the remainder of Ten Francesco Toscano's crew was killed. LAC Phil Chandler at Kalafrana noted in his diary:

> "An Italian bomber was shot down by a Hurricane near the camp in the early hours of this morning. He crashed in flames into the sea. I neither heard nor saw the incident, but many chaps were outside their billets and saw it. The big motor launch No129 [HSL129] went out to the rescue. There was only one survivor of the crew of four or five. He could only say, feebly, 'submarine, submarine.' No129 is of a rather peculiar design, and in the darkness his mistake was quite understandable."

For Malta it had been a period of relative calm, but all was about to change. The success of the anti-shipping campaign had resulted in the Italians suspending all sailings to Tripoli. During the preceding five months, the tonnage in Axis shipping losses had exceeded production. In the whole Mediterranean, this amounted to some 270,000 tons. On the Italy-North Africa supply route alone, 40 vessels totalling 178,577 tons had been lost, mainly in the period August-October. Twenty-four ships (101,894 tons) had been sunk by aircraft, but at a cost to Malta-based Blenheim units of at least 35 aircraft and most of their crews. Now, after many months of stalemate, the fighting in the Western Desert was about to escalate. It was imperative for the Italo-German forces to maintain an effective supply line: Malta had to be neutralised.

CHAPTER VIII

THE RETURN OF THE LUFTWAFFE

November – December 1941

On Malta all seemed well; there were plenty of Hurricanes and pilots, adequate supplies of fuel, ammunition and food – and no indication that any enemy other than the Regia Aeronautica would be faced for some time. During the first week of November two Wellingtons were lost to Italian fighters, one a Malta-based aircraft and the other en route to Malta from Gibraltar. A 69 Squadron Maryland was also shot-up by two MC202s while flying near the Sicilian coast. Meanwhile, pairs of Hurricanes from 185 Squadron were being sent daily to strafe railway targets in the south-eastern tip of Sicily, these generally escaping interception. However, a similar sortie by Plt Off Titch Palliser (Z4016) and Flt Sgt Fred Etchells of 249 Squadron on 4 November was intercepted by six MC202s after the pair had strafed Gela airfield, although they managed to evade their pursuers in cloud; Palliser noted:

> "Set out to bomb railway at Gela. Bombed railway bridge. No hits observed. Chased out by six Macchi 202s, but got away from them. Chased us for 15 minutes."

Two Hurricanes were also sent out by 126 Squadron on this date, their target the seaplane base at Syracuse where Plt Offs Andy Anderson and Howard Coffin strafed a number of Z506Bs, as the latter recorded in his diary:

> "P/O Anderson and myself made a low flying attack on Syracuse harbour. Damaged or sank four Cant 506Z [sic] seaplanes. Put out of commission an ack-ack gun, killing four Italians. Received plenty of flak from ground guns."[1]

One Z506B was actually destroyed. Six Blenheims from Malta attacked a convoy next day (5 November) but two failed to return. That evening, ten Ju87s, four BR20s and three Z1007bis attacked Valetta and French Creek. Two of the Ju87s, aircraft of 238^Squadriglia, were shot down by AA gunfire. Daylight on 6 November saw the arrival at Malta of a Sunderland of 10 RAAF Squadron, on board which were 14 Hurricane fighter pilot reinforcements including Wg Cdr M.H. 'Hilly' Brown DFC, a successful Canadian pilot who had served in France in 1940. He was posted to the island as Wing Leader, Takali, the post about to be vacated by Wg Cdr Rabagliati. Three days later another 10 RAAF Squadron Sunderland arrived with a further 15 fighter pilots.

After a two-day lull, 8 November proved to be the most eventful day for some weeks. A force of about 18 MC200s and MC202s from 4°Stormo CT escorted four Z1007bis to Malta at midday, four Hurricanes from 126 Squadron led by Flt Lt Carpenter intercepting. Again there was a complete misidentification of the bombers. This time the tri-motor configuration was viewed from above and reported as Z506B floatplanes. As the Hurricanes closed they were attacked by the MC202s, the pilots of which misidentified their opponents as Spitfires. Carpenter shot down one Macchi:

> "After I had broken away I saw two aircraft spinning down at my own level. I followed one down and saw the splash as it hit the sea. The second was in a flat spin and took much longer to come down. It was not going straight down but drifting out north. At about 6,000 feet it seemed as if something broke away as it went into a nose dive and went straight in. I could not see in what relation to the island very accurately as there was so much cloud about."

Another Macchi was claimed probably destroyed by Sgt Tom Worrall, while Sgt Allan Haley (Z3033), reported:

"As we were going for the bombers, the Macchis dived on us. I counted 16, and as I went after one of them, I saw the rest of the Hurricanes keeping engagements of their own. One of them was among six of the enemy, four of whom were on his tail. I put a few bursts into the one I was after, and his tail began to smoke. Then another attacked me from astern. I turned and saw this chap and flew straight at him. I expected him to turn, as the Italians usually do; but he didn't, he came straight on. Perhaps the pilot was killed and the Macchi was flying itself; anyway, I flew right into him, and the Macchi broke up in the air. There were pieces all over the place.

I am told that one of my wings broke off, but I don't know, for I didn't see the Hurricane again. I was in a spin and didn't need to jump, I just opened the lid and fell out. I thought I might have a broken leg. I was about 2,000 feet up at the time, and as I came down over the island I saw that I was going to land on a village. I hit the wall of a house, and landed on a flat roof right on top of a dog, which let out a terrific yell, jumped off the roof, and belted up the road."

Plt Off Pat Lardner-Burke also attacked a MC202 which he claimed shot down. He damaged a second before his own aircraft (BD789/G) was hit and he was shot through the back. Despite his injuries, he circled the aerodrome, landed and taxied to his dispersal point. Watching the air battle overhead and subsequent drama was 249 Squadron's Plt Off Matthews:

"All we could hear was machine-gun fire and the rise and fall of engines. Then a Macchi spun through the cloud behind M'dina and burnt. Next came an odd-shaped object which turned out to be a Hurricane minus tail and wing. It fell nearby and burnt; bits of fabric and wing followed it down. Later on the pilot came through on his brolly. Then another Hurricane came through the cloud trailing out a lot of smoke. He made an approach then staggered round again and made a landing. When he taxied up we saw that the side and top were blown for six and full of splinter holes. P/O [Lardner] Burke was the pilot. When he took off his mask we could see the blood trickle from the corner of his mouth. We hauled him out and as he went into the ambulance he was sick. An armour piercing bullet had gone through his [armour] plate, through the seat, through his left hand side and into the dashboard. The burst was nine strikes over the plating from close to. But he got the man he was chasing. For this he got the DFC."

Flt Lt Neil was also on hand to help:

"The propeller was still turning as I pulled down the retractable step and climbed onto the wing-walk, the slipstream clutching at my face and hair. The pilot still had his face mask attached but I recognised him immediately as Pat Lardner-Burke. Pat's head was bowed and his shoulders slumped. He undid his mask, clumsily. He was obviously in shock and pain. I sought to comfort him. Whatever its virtues, the Hurricane was not designed to enable a damaged pilot to be evacuated easily. About ten feet in the air, the cockpit did not have a side-flap, as did the Spitfire, so that to dismount, the pilot was obliged to climb out backwards, using first the cockpit rim then one of the steps, before walking down the wing-root and jumping to the ground. Needless to say, such gymnastics were beyond anyone crippled by wounds. Aware of the need to act quickly, I tried climbing onto the rim of the cockpit myself but found nowhere to put my feet. Then I thought about sitting on top of the open hood but saw immediately that I would not be able to reach down sufficiently to heave him up bodily. A pox on the man who designed this aircraft, I thought wildly, we would have to get a crane and winch him out. But there was no crane, or none that wouldn't take hours to find and fetch."[2]

Neil urgently explained the situation to the barely conscious pilot, who nonetheless managed to pull himself to his feet while Neil grasped his shoulders. With great difficulty they reached the ground and Lardner-Burke was stretchered away to a waiting ambulance.

Meanwhile, Neil returned to the damaged aircraft:

> "There was not much damage but what there was was frightening. Several bullets had hit
> the side of the aircraft behind the cockpit and one had punched a hole in the armour-plate
> as though it had been nothing more than a sheet of aluminium. After it had penetrated the
> back of the seat, it went completely through the pilot, before continuing through the
> dashboard and into the armour-plate and darkness beyond. Several other pilots joined me
> and breathed their horrified astonishment. Crikey! And we'd always thought . . .!"[3]

Two of the Macchis failed to return, MM7744 flown by Cap Mario Pluda, commander of
73^Squadriglia and the pilot involved in the collision with Haley's Hurricane; and
MM7736 piloted by Serg Magg Luigi Taroni of 96^Squadriglia. Both were killed. On this
occasion the Italian pilots claimed only one victory, by several members of 96^Squadriglia
jointly, plus two damaged. Haley's aircraft crashed near the AA gun position at Halq Dieri,
west of Zebbug, while Pluda's Macchi came down at Wied Qasrun, one mile north-west of
Dingli, the impact throwing up a cloud of dust and debris several hundred feet into the air.

Early next morning (9 November), two Hurricanes of 185 Squadron were despatched to
patrol over Force K destroyers returning to Malta. Three Italian torpedo-bombers were
intercepted as they approached the ships but Flg Off Gay Bailey (BD835), A Flight
commander, failed to return. It was assumed that he had been shot down by return fire. His
No2, Plt Off Oliver, later stated that he believed Bailey probably brought down the aircraft
he was seen to be attacking, and this theory was supported by a report from the captain of
one of the destroyers under attack, who confirmed that a Hurricane had engaged two of the
torpedo-bombers but then went straight into the sea from 200 feet. The aircraft caught fire
when it hit the water. However, Macchi pilots of 4°Stormo engaged Blenheims and
Hurricanes over the convoy during the day, claiming one of each type shot down.

That evening ten Italian bombers appeared over Malta. Between 1940 and 2038, newly-
commissioned Plt Off Alex Mackie of the MNFU was in the air, attacking a BR20M held
in the searchlights at 16,000 feet. He closed to 200 yards and fired, seeing flashes on the
aircraft and pieces fall off before it went into dive. Mackie attempted to follow but lost
contact at 3,000 feet. Two hours later Flt Lt Cassidy and Flg Off Tommy Thompson jointly
attacked another bomber. This, too, was hit, and was last seen shedding debris and losing
height. As another MNFU Hurricane scrambled to meet the intruders it suffered an engine
failure and crashed, as recalled by its pilot Flt Lt Stones:

> "I was taking off on a night interception from Takali when my engine blew up at 400 feet.
> You couldn't put it down because the fields on Malta are all like tennis courts so I baled
> out – just in time. The Hurricane was burning nicely in the next field as I was accosted by
> some Maltese who thought I was a German until I rapidly stripped off my flying overalls.
> Getting to a telephone, I rang ops and spoke to Cassidy who said 'I can't speak now, the
> commander of B Flight has just gone in!' I said, 'It's me you oaf!'"[4]

Sgt Wood of the MNFU wrote in his diary:

> "At 11.10pm Mackie and Stones went off – suddenly saw aircraft hit ground and burst into
> flames. Found it was Stones – feared the worst. Someone swore they saw a parachute but
> no proof. About half-an-hour afterwards, Stones himself rang up from Zebbieh. He was
> quite OK. Went to pick him up and found that his engine had cut dead from 500 feet so he
> left the 'office' pretty nippy and found himself an Army HQ and a bottle of whisky."

With the co-operation of Wg Cdr Sandy Rabagliati, Wg Cdr Hilly Brown planned an early
morning Hurribomber strike against Gela airfield using all available Hurricanes from 126
and 249 Squadrons, eleven of which were to carry bombs while ten would fly top cover.
At 0630 on the morning of 12 November, only three of the initial four Hurricanes took off
to strafe the airfield defences and parked aircraft prior to the arrival of the bomb-carrying

Hurricanes; they were flown by Wg Cdrs Brown and Rabagliati, who were to carry out the strafe while covered by Plt Off Don Tedford. The trio duly swept over the coast at very low-level and flew up a valley to the east of Gela, where Rabagliati (Z4005) saw a Ju87 flying low down in the same direction. As he came up behind it, the Stuka turned sharply and crashed into the hillside. As the Hurricanes reached Gela, so the flak opened up. On the first run across the airfield a parked CR42 was set on fire and a MC200 was also hit, at which point Rabagliati saw Wg Cdr Brown's aircraft (Z2397) apparently stall, break away and crash. It had been hit by ground fire and Brown was killed. After strafing some troops on horses – and with Tedford still on his wing – Rabagliati headed for home. Plt Off Bob Matthews (Z2526) was one of 249 Squadron's top cover:

> "Off in the dark and the whole show was to be over by sunrise. I was to be extra high cover at 25-30,000 feet, but the take-off was a little ropey at our end and I got off on Red 2 instead of White 2. Only six of the high cover formed up, so I weaved."

Down below, the Hurribombers followed the strafers in. As the Hurricanes approached Gela they were engaged by three MC202s of 97^Squadriglia led by Ten Jacopo Frigerio which had been scrambled from Comiso as a result of the earlier intrusion. Frigerio attacked one Hurricane without result, but the same aircraft – Z3158/HA-K of 126 Squadron flown by Sgt Peter Simpson – was then set upon by Sottoten Giovanni Deanna and Serg Magg Massimo Salvatore and shot down into the sea. Meanwhile, Flt Lt Carpenter claimed a Macchi in return, although no Italian losses were recorded on this occasion. Plt Off Matthews continued:

> "We weaved overhead, then turned out through very thick cloud and hailstorms. I only spotted Malta because the sun shone on its cliffs. Three Hurricane bombers joined us and we got back as the weather thickened. One of the bombers had been shot down by Macchis over the Sicily coast. This was, I think, an unsuccessful operation, unless the bombs did more damage than was seen."

On the journey back to Malta, with the Hurricanes skimming the wave-tops, Plt Off Harry Moon of 249 Squadron realised that one of his bomb switches was in the upright position. Assuming that he had caught it with his elbow, he flicked it down – thereby releasing a bomb which exploded barely 20 feet beneath his aircraft. Despite the deafening explosion, the Hurricane (Z4016) was not damaged and he landed safely at Takali, wiser for the experience. With the raids over, Sottoten Virgilio Vanzan of 10°Gruppo CT took off in a CR42 to carry out a search for the Hurricane pilot seen to bale out into the sea and Sgt Simpson was soon sighted and picked up by a launch.

While these offensive operations were underway, a further batch of Hurricanes were on their way. During the previous month 266 Wing under the command of Wg Cdr H.G. Maguire had been formed in the UK for service in the Mediterranean area. The Wing comprised 242, 258 and 605 Squadrons, 258's aircraft having been crated and loaded aboard the special transport HMS *Athene*, which could carry up to 40 Hurricanes with wings removed. The ground parties of all three squadrons, together with the spare pilots of 242 and 605 also went aboard this vessel, while the Hurricanes of these two squadrons were loaded aboard the old training carrier HMS *Argus*, which had carried the Hurricanes of 418 Flight to Malta the previous year. The ships docked at Gibraltar on 5 November, where a proportion of the Hurricanes were transferred to HMS *Ark Royal*. When the two carriers sailed a few days later they carried on board all the aircraft of 242 Squadron, and the larger part of 605 Squadron, a total of 37 Hurricanes. Meanwhile, at Gibraltar, 258 Squadron's crated aircraft were being erected with all speed, to be delivered with the balance of 605's in a second sortie by the carriers after their return.

Alloted the codename Operation 'Perpetual', the Hurricanes were flown off on 12 November in two batches under the direction of Wg Cdr W.B. Royce DFC. Each batch was to be met and escorted to Malta by four Blenheims from Gibraltar. During the take-off, Plt Off Howard Lester RAAF of 605 Squadron swung violently to port and broke *Argus'* flying-off flag, which was retrieved by another member of 605 Squadron and secreted aboard his aircraft – it later became a mess souvenir. Among those watching the first batch of Hurricanes taking off was Plt Off Oliver Ormrod, known as Sonny due to his youthful appearance:

"Our first flight took off from *Argus* when the Blenheims turned up at 10.15am. All took off OK except P/O Lester. Chuck had never flown a long-range Hurricane before. He swung violently to port. He nearly killed me and several others. His wing passed over Ricky Wright, Joe Hutton, Joe Beckett and me as he went off over the side a little higher up the deck. I just had time to think 'Thank goodness I've got fat Joe Hutton in front of me.' I then looked forward and down to see Chuck in the sea; but he wasn't – he was flying and his wheels were retracting too. Very lucky, for he'd broken off his tail wheel, which came off when he landed in Malta.

An hour later we took off with two more Blenheims which arrived from Gib; but not before I'd been choked by the fumes, for my machine BG713 was over the funnel. The apparent windspeed over the deck was 35-40 knots, so, though I had only 400-450 feet, I found the take-off easy enough. Joe Beckett did not take off with us, his generator failing to charge; however, he was sent off a little later and caught us up. The Blenheims really navigated very well. The visibility was bad. I think it was near Cape Bon that we went down to sea level and flew for some 200 miles at nought feet to avoid being fixed by the Italian radio locators. About 2.45 or 3 o'clock we came at last out of bad visibility over Gozo. Landed at Hal Far. I think I had 30 or so gallons of fuel left, though some of the others say they had as many as 70 gallons left over. Sgt [Alan] Wilson has landed somewhere else on the island – goodness knows why [he was short of fuel and headed for the first airfield he saw, Takali]. One of 242 [Plt Off Jimmy Tew in BG765] landed wheels up in front of me – he'd been unable to get them down."

Three 242 Squadron Hurricanes failed to reach Malta. One crashed at Colle in Sicily, the pilot setting fire to his aircraft before going into captivity; the other two came down on the North African coast, one two miles west of Tunis, this also being set on fire by its pilot, while the other crashed 12 miles north-west of Menzeltamine, where it was damaged beyond repair. The three Hurricanes were BE369, BE561 and BG712 flown by Sgts W.L. Massey, D.H. Jones and Donald Gray, all of whom were later reported to be prisoners. Apparently Massey had turned back to try to relocate the carrier. Next day, as the carriers headed back for Gibraltar, disaster struck. *Ark Royal's* charmed life came to an end as she fell foul of a salvo of torpedoes fired by German submarine U-81. Listing badly, the carrier was abandoned with the loss of only one life, and sank shortly afterwards. There was no question of the slow and vulnerable *Argus* making a second run alone, and the remaining Hurricanes and pilots stayed at Gibraltar, awaiting a replacement carrier. In the event they were never to reach Malta as, before a new vessel could arrive, the war in the Far East had broken out, and the rest of the party was redirected there[5].

On Malta, the respective COs of 242 and 605 Squadrons[6] were advised to await the arrival of their remaining aircraft from Gibraltar before continuing on to Egypt. In the meantime, the Hurricanes were deemed to be safe at Hal Far, where they were serviced by personnel of the resident squadrons. With the benefit of hindsight, the authorities were obviously awaiting developments in other parts of a volatile world before committing the advance elements of 266 Wing to combat. Significantly, its ground personnel were still at sea, while 258 Squadron was at Gibraltar with its Hurricanes.

Activities during mid-November continued at a somewhat reduced level, although small-scale fighter-bomber attacks continued against selected targets along the Sicilian coast. On the 15th, Flg Off Joe Hall[7] (Z3172) of 185 Squadron reported:

"Fighter cover with Tommy for two bomber Hurricanes and two cannon Hurricanes on Rhubarb. We join up. Tommy got bullet between glycol tank and bulkhead."

The Hurricanes piloted by Flg Off Peter Thompson and Sgt John Alderson were each armed with eight 20-lb bombs, their target being Noto Railway Station. Four Hurricanes provided cover. All returned safely. Thompson wrote:

"The weather was pretty duff but we arrived over Sicily according to schedule. [Sgts] Ellis and Lillywhite went in to shoot up the railway line, while Alderson and I proceeded to drop the odd bomb on Noto Station. I was attacked by a Macchi, which I did not see until afterwards, but suffered no damage. [But] some pongo marksman put one bullet through my engine cowling. Having dropped our bombs and after securing several hits, we went rapidly homewards, warming up some signal boxes on the way. Ellis caught the wrong train, but managed to shoot up a pier. 'Lil' had a quiet word with Ellis on their return home. In view of the weather, quite a successful do."

Delivery aircraft arriving from Gibraltar were still having to run the gauntlet of Italian fighters based at Pantelleria; a Wellington was shot down by CR42s on the 15th, while a Blenheim was damaged and subsequently crash-landed on arrival at Luqa. Malta's Blenheims continued to take the fight to the enemy but losses were severe, three returning severely damaged from an attack on a convoy near the Greek island of Cephalonia on the 17th, and three being shot down during an attack on a Libyan-bound convoy two days later.

To make up for the absence of daylight activity over Malta, the Italians now resorted to night intrusions. On the evening of 15/16 November, four bomb-carrying Reggiane Re2000s of the recently-formed 377^Squadriglia Aut CT took off from Trapani/Milo for their first offensive operation of the war. One pilot returned early due to technical problems, whilst another was attacked by a night fighter he identified as a 'Defiant' – presumably a MNFU Hurricane or an INFU Fulmar. He released his bombs in the sea and also returned. The remaining pair, led by Ten Giorgio Solaroli, dropped their bombs on Luqa. Four nights later another quartette of these aircraft headed for Luqa, led on this occasion by TenCol Tito Falconi of 23°Gruppo CT. Once more a night fighter intercepted, causing Falconi and one other to jettison their bombs whilst evading. The other two pilots pressed home their attacks at low level, reporting that they found the airfield lit up; all four Reggianes returned undamaged. Sgt Ted Wood of the MNFU noted:

"Went up at night, two scrambles, two hours. First one did not cross coast, second one came in and beat it, no illumination. The night was very dark, solid instrument flying. Dispersed aircraft. Just finished when Bofors opened up. Macchis [sic] shot up Luqa and Hal Far, an absolutely wizard sight, fireworks displays have nothing on it. Terrific barrage over Luqa way. One aircraft over our drome, plenty AA but not very accurate. Later found it was a Hurricane (126), poor bloke did not know what to do."

However, a BR20M flown by the CO of 276^Squadriglia, Magg Cesare Toschi, failed to return from a sortie. Next night another BR20M flown by Ten Arrigo Cesolini also failed to return, and a third was reported down in the sea near Castelvetrano while on its way to carry out a raid on Malta. These losses were possibly due to premature detonation of bombs.

During the late morning of 18 November, while returning from a recce sortie of Borizzo and Trapani where a total of 71 aircraft were observed on the airfields, Flt Lt Bob Wootton in one of 69 Squadron's PR Hurricanes (Z2332) was warned by Ops that two enemy fighters were approaching him from astern. These, however, were not sighted and he landed without incident. During a pre-dawn take-off from Takali, Sqn Ldr Powell-Sheddon experienced engine failure. The Hurricane came down on the Attard-Rabat road and hit a stone wall, Powell-Sheddon escaping with a severe shaking.

The Italians continued to repay Malta in kind by sending over fighter sweeps to attack targets of opportunity including the airfields. On 21 November, as Hurribombers headed for Sicily, a force of Macchis headed for Malta. Four Hurribombers of 249 Squadron had been detailed for the pre-dawn mission including one to be flown by Flt Sgt Fred Etchells, who recalled:

> "Unfortunately, the armourers bombing up my Hurricane found a technical snag, and it was almost dawn by the time I was able to take off, the other three being long gone. As I was more than half asleep, I suppose I must have expected the same to apply in Sicily, for after dropping my little load and strafing the railway target, and on gaining height again, our wonderful and normally unflappable Controller was almost screaming over the R/T for me to get home without delay.
>
> Being winter, there was a reasonable cloud cover which I used thankfully, but disliking instrument flying and wishing to see if I was nearing the island after some time in cloud, I descended – and found a Macchi 200 on my left and very close! Indeed, he was close enough for me to see that the pilot was wearing white goggles and had his cockpit closed. A little further away to my right was another Macchi. I don't believe either of them noticed the intruder in their formation, and I was back up into cloud and changing course in a jiffy. All my ammunition had been used in strafing, and I blessed the Italian pilots' poor airmanship for possibly saving my life. A minute or two after veering away from the Macchis, I cautiously broke cloud cover again. No enemy visible, so I nipped down to sea level, over the coast at just above rooftop height and straight into land without the formality of a circuit at Takali. After a tail-up, high-speed spot of taxying to the nearest slit trench and head down, I felt able to breathe again and waited for the strafing to stop."[8]

Meanwhile, four Hurricanes of 126 Squadron on dawn patrol attempted to engage the Macchis. Plt Off Noel MacGregor noted:

> "Self dawn patrol with three others when island attacked and strafed by 15+ Macchis. Terrific AA and e/a driven off and AA fired at us Hurricanes. P/O [Les] Barnes' machine holed through port wing."

Seven Hurricanes of 185 Squadron led by Sqn Ldr Pike were scrambled to challenge the Macchi attack on Hal Far, presumably attracted by the presence of 242 and 605 Squadron's Hurricanes based there. The Italian pilots claimed four Hurricanes and a Blenheim damaged on the ground before 185 Squadron engaged. No firm claims were made by the Hurricane pilots. Flg Off Peter Thompson wrote in the Squadron diary:

> "The raid came in at dawn. Some Macchis shot up Hal Far and Takali, doing hardly any damage. A Flight jumped part of the high cover at about 12,000 feet and a general dogfight ensued. During the fight five more Macchis joined in, making the odds 10-7 in their favour. Although A Flight did not claim any definitely destroyed, it is a safe bet to say that some little Macchi pilots did not have any breakfast this morning. The fight was watched from the ground with great interest. The Italians were seen to do some amazing evasive manoeuvres, including rolls off the top and bunting. The Italians on this particular occasion showed considerable initiative. They split up into two formations, one formation acting as stooges and the other as jumpers – they might have met with more success but for the skill of our pilots and the handling qualities of the old Hurricane. Sgt Nurse was attacked by an enemy 'Hurricane' (fitted with .5s) and received considerable damage to his ailerons and port petrol tank. Nurse landed OK."

Sgt Bill Nurse, whose aircraft was damaged in the skirmish, wrote:

> "One Macchi pulled up in front of me and I gave him a long burst from 200-150 yards and I saw my bullets appear to enter the fuselage. He rolled over and went down, presumably evasive tactics. I was later attacked by another machine which I thought was a Hurricane

and sustained hits in the tail and wings."

Sqn Ldr Pike also thought the aircraft which attacked him were Hurricanes with "red noses and a white roundel, rest of fuselage all black." The MC202 pilots of 97^Squadriglia reported fighting a dozen Hurricanes and Spitfires, claiming two Spifires shot down, one being credited jointly to Ten Jacopo Frigerio, Serg Raffaello Novelli and Serg Angelo Golino, and the other being awarded to Sottoten Giovanni Barcaro and Serg Magg Massimo Salvatore. Two more were claimed as probables. Plt Off Sonny Ormrod wrote in his journal:

> "We arose to the sound of much noise. The Italians were indulging in a low flying attack on this aerodrome at 7.15am. We went out to view the fun and were much pleased by the magnificent spectacle of the 'flaming onions' fired by the Bofors guns. Saw one stream of 'onions' pass through a vic of three Macchis. When the ack-ack had died down we witnessed a dogfight between seven of 185 Squadron and some Macchis. Apparently the 185 boys had jumped some of the enemy and had then been jumped in turn by more of the Italians. The Macchis powered by Daimler-Benz engines are superior to our Hurricanes in performance.
>
> It was most infuriating to see such a fight and we not in it. A fortune-teller told me I would survive this war, but if my survival is merely brought about by the misfortune to miss all the action, then I am indeed a most unfortunate individual. It would be better to die in action. To survive this war without ever having been in combat is most shameful for a fighter pilot."

69 Squadron's CO, Wg Cdr John Dowland, was shot down while carrying out low a level recce of the airfields at Gela, Comiso, and Biscari in Z3053. He observed three fighters taking off from Comiso and these evidently trailed the Hurricane. When just north of Gozo, Dowland was attacked by an unseen aircraft, which he shook off by taking violent evasive action. Five minutes later a second fighter (or the same one) attacked, bullets striking the armour plate behind his seat and the engine, which caught fire following a third attack. Although he thought his attackers were Messerschmitt 109s, they were in fact MC202s of 9°Gruppo CT. A pilot of 97^Squadriglia, Serg Alfredo Bombardini, reported shooting down in flames the reconnaissance aircraft. Dowland was able to bale out from 12,000 feet and came down in the sea. There was an immediate search, during which he was spotted by Plt Off Oliver of 185 Squadron, and he was rescued an hour later by Kalafrana's Swordfish floatplane flown by Sub Lt(A) Hurle-Hobbs. At Kalafrana, LAC Phil Chandler recorded events:

> ". . . the Swordfish rescue seaplane took off. We heard him coming in not very long afterwards and at the same time saw the ambulance pull up on the slipway. We dashed out on to the armoury roof. There were three people in the seaplane and only two had gone up. As the third man, who was wrapped in a blanket, was being helped out of the cockpit, our flight sergeant who had the binoculars trained on the scene, recognised him as a Wing Commander from Luqa. I don't know whether he was shot down in the earlier dogfight or crashed by accident. He seemed not much the worse, however; was carried ashore pick-a-back by one of the groundcrew and walked to the ambulance, with a word with some of our officers who had come on the scene. The Swordfish went out again early this evening, but was soon back."

Eighteen MC202s from 9°Gruppo CT, which returned to strafe in the afternoon, encountered four 185 Squadron Hurricanes led by Plt Off Tony Reeves engaged on convoy patrol. The Italians reported that there were a dozen Hurricanes, of which five were claimed shot down into the sea by Sottoten Alvaro Querci, Magg Larismont Pergameni, M.llo Rinaldo Damiani, Serg Magg Pasquale Rossi and Serg Raffaello Novelli. Only one Hurricane was in fact lost, 20-year-old Sgt Dick Cousens failing to return, his aircraft

ne of the original Hurricane pilots:

: Plt Off Jock Barber with his groundcrew.

dle left: Flg Offs John Waters and Peter Hartley of
Fighter Flight.

dle right: Plt Off Tommy Balmforth.

t: Plt Off Dick Sugden.

Top: One of the early Hurricanes over typical Maltese terrain.

Middle left: Sgt Reg Hyde (left) and Sgt Jock Robertson were both successful at Malta.

Middle right: Flt Lt George Burges with AOC.

Bottom: Two pilots of 418 Flight, with s[o] naval types. Both were killed flying Hurricanes at Malta. Sgt Bill Timms (le[f]) was KIA 11 January 1941 and Sgt Roy O'Donnell on 15 August 1940.

: A squadron pet in unfamiliar pose.

om: Relaxed Readiness at Luqa, *i*mn 1940. From left, Sgts Dennis

Ashton, Eric Kelsey and Drac Bowerman, all to be killed in action 1940-1942.

A few 261 Squadron studies:

Top left: Sgt Cyril Bamberger.

Top right: Hurricane 'N' landing at Luqa.

Middle: Hurricanes at Luqa including P3731/J.

Bottom left: Sgt Jim Pickering.

Bottom centre: Sgt Harry Ayre.

Bottom right: Sgt Reg Hyde.

Top: Sgt Deacon's Hurricane P3978 after being shot up by Messerschmitts.

Abo e: The result of bombing at Luqa 1940.

Left: Sgt Bert Deacon, with six victories to his credit during 1940, claimed his seventh at Malta.

Top: Sqn Ldr Lambert (with pipe) accompanied by some of his pilots, Takali March 1941. From left to right (rear): Sgt Dexter, Plt Off McAdam, Sqn Ldr Lambert, Flg Off Bellamy, Sgts Todd and Norwell. Front:?Plt Off Rippon, Flt Lt Peacock-Edwards and Plt Off Barber.

Bottom: Another Takali grouping. From left: Unknown, Sgt Deacon, Plt Off McAdam, Plt Off Eliot, Sgt Goode. Front: Flt Lt Peacock-Edwards, Army Officer and Flg Off Bellamy.

left: Sgt Reg Hyde, 261 Squadron.

right: Sgt Jock Robertson on the award the DFM – Malta's top-scoring ricane pilot.

Bottom: 261 Squadron pilots, Barber (back to camera), Bamberger, Hamilton, MacLachlan, Taylor and Hyde.

Top left: Flt Lt George Burges.

Top right: Sgt Jock Robertson.

Middle left: Plt Off John Pain.

Middle centre: Flg Off Timber Woods.

Middle right: Plt Off Hamish Hamilton.

Abo e right: Plt Off Tony Rippon.

Right: Flg Off Eric Taylor.

Far right: Flt Lt James MacLachlan, pictured in 1942.

Veterans of 261 soon to depart from
~~~ta, April 1941. Left to right: Sgts
~~ering, Hitching (?), Norwell, Jock
~~ertson, Bamberger, Plt Off Counter (?),
Sgt Bowerman, Plt Off Whitney and
Sgt Kelly(?).

Bottom: Plt Off Percy Mortimer's
Hurricane V7116 shot down, 11 April 1941.

Top: A Flight, 185 Squadron, May 1941. From left (rear): Flt Lt Jeff Jeffries, Sgt Cyril Bamberger, Plt Off Hamish Hamilton, Plt Off Chubby Eliot and Sgt B.J. Vardy; front: Sgts Al Jolly, Claude Hodson and Fred Sheppard.

Bottom: 185 Squadron Hurricane Z2402 GL-P.

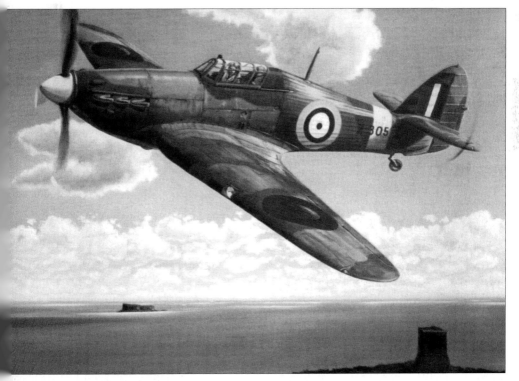

left: Sgt Tom Hackston of 126
adron, lost on 4 July 1941.

right: Sgt Jock Livingston of 249
adron, KIA 18 June 1941.

Bottom: A painting by Rens Biesma
(in colour) for the Takali Aviation Museum
of Tom Hackston's Hurricane Z3055.
The aircraft is now being restored
(see Appendix VI).

Top: A Group of 249 pilots, September 1941. From left (front): Flg Off Beazley, Sqn Ldr Barton DFC, Flg Off Harrington and Plt Off Leggett; standing: Plt Offs Tedford and Palliser, Sgt Rist, Plt Off Matthews, Sgt Skeet-Smith (behind), Sgts Branch and Parker, Plt Off Hill, Sgt Owen and Flg Off Davis.

Bottom: May 1941. Soon after arrival 24 Squadron lost three Hurricanes to grour strafing Bf109s.

Top: 185 Squadron, July 1941. From left: front: Flt Lts Pike and Jeffries, Sqn Ldr Mould DFC, Flt Lt Hancock and Plt Off ?. Thompson; middle: Plt Off Oliver, ? Bates, Plt Off Bailey, Sgt Cousens, Sgts ?ywhite and Sutherland, Plt Off Reeves and Sgts Nurse and Vardy; rear: Plt Off Allardice, and Sgts Jolly, Ream, Hunton, Alderson, Forth, Knight, Hayes and Horsey.

Bottom: 185 Squadron Hurricanes. Sqn Ldr Peter Mould DFC was lost in Z5265/T on 1 October 1941.

Top: New arrival lands downwind.

Middle: New arrival Z3757 also landed downwind.

Right: New arrival (Sgt Bud Lee) collides with a 126 Squadron Hurricane.

Top: Three 249 Sergeant Pilots – Dave Owen, John Parker and Alf Branch.

Middle: Plt Offs Graham Leggett and Bob Matthews of 249 Squadron.

Left: Flt Sgt Fred Etchells about to mount his aircraft.

Top left: Sgt Ted Wood of 1435 Flight KIA 27 April 1942.

Top right: Plt Off John Russell of 126 KIA 25 January 1942.

Bottom left: Sgt Jack Mayall RAAF of 126 KIA 10 March 1942.

Bottom right: F/Sgt Jack Fletcher RCAF of 185 KIA 28 April 1942.

: Wg Cdr Sandy Rabagliati with Plt Off
ry Moon (right), 249 Squadron.

om left: Plt Off Lardner-Burke of
Squadron.

Bottom right: A trio from 242. From left, Plt
Off Bill Hay, Sgt Jock Gardiner and Flt Lt
Nigel Kemp DFC.

Damaged Beyond Repair...

Top: Pilots of 605 Squadron. From left, Plt Off Peter Lowe (KIA 15/2/42), Flt Lt George Allen (KIA 12/2/42), and Plt Offs Chuck Lester, Ian McKay and Phil Wigley.

Left: Plt Off Oliver Ormrod DFC, 605 Squadron, KIA 22 April 1942.

Top: Z2961/K of 185 Squadron.

Middle: Plt Off Bill Hollis Hallett in 'Death Warmed Up' of 126 Squadron.

Bottom: Bill Greenhalgh's damaged Hurricane Z2491 HA-D of 126 Squadron which was brought down strafing Comiso airfield.

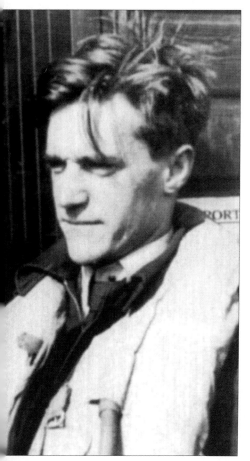

left: Sqn Ldr R.A. Barton DFC.

right: Wg Cdr A.C. Rabagliati.

dle centre: Flt Lt J.M.V. Carpenter

Middle right: Plt Off D.U. Barnwell DFC.

Bottom, far left: Plt Off P. Lardner-Burke DFC.

Bottom left: Sgt G.E. Horricks DFM.

Bottom right: Plt Off G.R. Tweedale DFM.

Bottom, far right: Plt Off J.L. Boyd DFM.

Flt Lt Andy Anderson of 126 Squadron, fighter pilot and artist.

Top: Remains of Sgt David Roy's 229 Squadron Hurricane BM964, 6 May 1942.

Bottom left: Sub Lts (A) Colin White, Ernie Pratt and Reg Elliott (front) flew Hurricanes on fighter bomber and ASR sorties, 1942.

Bottom right: Unidentified Hurricane suffers a crash-landing.

(Z2813/GL-L) presumably having been attacked by several of the Macchis before they carried on to complete their strafe and returned without loss. Luqa was their target, as Cpl John Alton recalled:

> "Four Hurricanes were scrambled and, as was customary, the fitters and riggers sat around on the starter trollies awaiting the return of the aircraft. Four aircraft were seen approaching, which at a glance looked like our Hurricanes. This was a gross mistake, because they were Macchi 202s and, before anyone could move, explosive bullets were churning up the ground. Then, just as quickly, they were gone. Not a soul was so much as scratched."

The Regia Aeronautica's attack was stepped up next afternoon (22 November), when ten Ju87s from 101°Gruppo B'aT set out with an escort of 61 MC200s and 202s drawn from 54°Stormo CT and 9°Gruppo CT. The close-escort MC200s became unco-ordinated and returned early, but the MC202s which were providing indirect cover reported engaging 40 British fighters. In fact 21 Hurricanes had scrambled, all available machines of 126 and 249 Squadrons led by Wg Cdr Rabagliati. They saw a force of fighters north of Gozo at 26-30,000 feet, identified variously as 15 Macchis or 24 Macchis and Messerschmitts (there were no Bf109s). Flt Lt Carpenter of 126 Squadron was leading the top cover and hurriedly climbed with his section:

> "While flying as Yellow 1 and escorting 249 Squadron, we were told that bandits were coming in from the north at heights varying from 20,000 to 32,000 feet. I was doing high cover for my own Squadron with a section of three. I saw the two squadrons engage in a dogfight so I stayed above for some time. When I was sure there were no enemy aircraft to come down on them, I joined in the dogfight. I engaged the last Macchi in a formation of four, in line-astern. He was straggling and I got in a five-second burst at 200 yards dead astern. His hood fell off and something else I could not distinguish. I thought he was going to bale out so I kept on firing just in case. He did a very slow roll and disappeared."

He was unable to follow as he now became engaged in another violent dogfight. Meanwhile, Sgt Ted Copp attacked a Macchi in a steep turn, whereupon it began to pour smoke. Flg Off Jack Kay and Plt Off Noel MacGregor claimed damage to the aircraft they attacked, while Plt Off Rocky Main claimed two more as probables. None of the 126 Squadron pilots was able to make any confirmed claims. Wg Cdr Rabagliati was attacked twice by flights of Macchis but he, too, managed to escape. Plt Off Joe Crichton recalled:

> "We intercepted 16-plus Macchi 202s. Three of us were top cover at 32,000 feet and we got jumped. Had one on my tail and could not turn inside him nor could he get a shot at me – finally lost him in cloud at 17,000 feet. Climbed back up but couldn't get high enough before they headed for home. There sure was a great dogfight going on and not a bullet hole in any of our aircraft."

Meanwhile 249 Squadron, at a lower altitude, had better success as the Macchis swooped down on them. Sqn Ldr Barton (Z3764) claimed one eight miles north-east of Gozo; the pilot was not seen to bale out. Flg Off Davis claimed a second and then shared another probably destroyed with Sgt Alf Branch (BV156/GN-Q), the latter noting:

> "Sqn Ldr Barton was leading us when we intercepted 12 Macchi 202s at 18,000 feet. Flg Off Davis and myself shared a probable 202. Sgt Skeet-Smith got shot up in the tail and spun down out of control. Machine levelled out and he landed OK."

There were no Hurricane losses, only damage to the 249 Squadron machine. Plt Off Bob Matthews (Z4941) also participated in this fight:

> "I was, as usual, bottom weaver. We saw the bandits, who split up, one lot going north, the other south, both climbing. We turned north, then west, then south; the bandits attacked.

But before this I had spotted a bandit coming up behind us. When he was 400 yards away, I turned away from the rest of the formation and attacked him head-on; he turned down and away at once and I lost him. By now I was some way below the formation, so I followed them weaving violently. The sky was empty, then full, all machines milling around. I saw a Hurricane on the tail of a Macchi about ten yards away, going down. I took a look as the Macchi went down and saw the Hurricane barely miss another machine below. A Macchi dived down across my nose. I followed him round, keeping inside his turn and getting good deflection. When I got enough [deflection] I opened up and gave a long burst, allowing myself to come down dead astern of him. He jerked over on his back and went straight down through the cloud and I did not follow. I weaved around a little and then we were recalled, so I pancaked. It was a good day for us, three destroyed, two probables, five damaged. Our losses nil with one machine damaged."

Only one MC202 (MM7748) was reported lost in the action, Ten Pietro Bonfatti of 73^Squadriglia being killed. Claims made by the Macchi pilots were extremely wild and inaccurate, no fewer than eight 'Spitfires' being claimed: Ten Fernando Malvezzi (two), Cap Ezio Viglione-Borghese (one), Sottoten Emanuele Annoni (one), Sottoten Giovanni Barcaro (two), Serg Magg Dante Labanti (one), and one claimed jointly by all pilots of 9°Gruppo CT.

No further daylight attacks were launched against Malta for the remainder of the month, all further engagements occurring as a result of offensive action by the RAF. On the 23rd, five Hurricanes of 126 Squadron carried out a fighter-bomber raid on Comiso, but it was not particularly successful and Flt Sgt Bill Greenhalgh was brought down. He crash-landed Z2941/HA-D and was taken prisoner, his aircraft being salvaged by the Italians and stored in a hangar. Of his loss, Flt Sgt Fred Etchells of 249 Squadron recalled:

"A fellow Flight Sergeant pilot was thought to have been shot down whilst strafing an airfield and, as no news came through to report his being taken prisoner, we mourned the loss of another comrade. Ten years later I was a guest at a golf club dinner, when the sight of my 'late' comrade, alive and well, brought me to a fully sober condition in one second flat! It appeared that whilst strafing what he considered to be the enemy's officers mess from across the airfield, he touched the ground with his propeller, which disintegrated. He skidded across the airfield, coming to a halt just short of the building he'd been attacking, and thus quickly changed his status to that of a POW."[9]

Other losses during the last few days of November included a Maryland, two Wellingtons and an Albacore, although Blenheims were successful in severely damaging a tanker off the western coast of Greece. A 242 Squadron Hurricane was also written off as a result of a crash-landing at Hal Far when in the hands of Plt Off Bill Hay, as noted by Plt Off Ormrod:

"One of 242 Squadron had a spectacular crash this afternoon; however, he was uninjured. Came in to land in bad visibility and did not hit off the longest run. Brakes failed to produce any effect, the ground being so muddy. He went on, through hedges, barbed wire, and so forth."

December 1941

December opened quietly although there were several changes amongst key personnel in the squadrons. Sqn Ldr E.B. Mortimer-Rose DFC[10] arrived from HQ Middle East to take over 249 Squadron from Sqn Ldr Butch Barton, while Sqn Ldr S.C. Norris DFC[11] took over the reins of 126 Squadron from Sqn Ldr Pip Lefevre. Sqn Ldr Powell-Sheddon handed over the MNFU – which was now renamed 1435 (Night Fighter) Flight – to Sqn Ldr Innes Westmacott, and took command of Takali, being promoted to Wing Commander at the same time. Wg Cdr Rabagliati[12] also departed briefly for HQ Middle East, returning within a few days to take command of the Takali Wing. Of Sqn Ldr Barton's[13] departure,

Flt Lt Neil wrote:

"Butch Barton slipped away one night aboard a Sunderland in Kalafrana Bay bound for
Gibraltar and home. There was no departing binge or palaver, he just went. Quietly.
Without fuss. Disappearing as he had always fought, with unassuming distinction. I suspect
he was glad to leave; he had been on the go since September 1939 and was beginning to
believe that his luck would shortly run out."[14]

There remained a certain air of complacency among the Hurricane pilots, who felt they
were coping adequately with the infrequent Italian fighter sweeps and occasional bomber
raids. The Hurricane force had been built up and there was a surplus of pilots, while the
newly arrived pilots of 242 and 605 Squadrons, awaiting the arrival of those still at
Gibraltar, expected to soon continue their journey eastwards. Had the resident pilots
known of the imminent arrival in Sicily of 85 of the latest Bf109F-4s of JG53, one of the
Luftwaffe's premier Geschwadern, there would have been cause for grave concern. The
Luftwaffe was returning to Sicily – in force. Due to commitments in North Africa, the
Germans had decided to reinforce the Luftwaffe in the Mediterranean despite the fact that
heavy fighting was continuing in Russia. The onset of winter there would restrict air
operations in any event, and consequently elements from the Eastern Front were released
for operations in the south, their first duty being the subjugation of Malta. Feldmarschall
Albert Kesselring, commander of Luftflotte 2, was designated Commander-in-Chief
(South), while II Fliegerkorps headquarters moved from the Moscow Front to Messina in
Sicily. On 2 December 1941, Hitler issued Directive No38:

1. In order to secure and extend our position in the Mediterranean, and to establish a focus
of Axis strength in Central Mediterranean, I order, in agreement with the Duce, that part of
the Luftwaffe no longer required in the East be transferred to the South Italian and North
African areas, in the strength of about one Air Corps with the necessary anti-aircraft
defences. Apart from the immediate effect of this improvement on the war in the
Mediterranean and North Africa, efforts will be made to ensure that it has a considerable
effect upon further developments in the Mediterranean area as a whole.
2. I appoint Feldmarschall Kesselring to command all forces employed in these operations.
He is also appointed Commander-in-Chief South. His tasks are:
   (a) To secure mastery in the air and sea in the area between Southern Italy and North
Africa in order to secure communications with Libya and Cyrenaica and, in particular, to
keep Malta in subjection.
   (b) To co-operate with German and allied forces engaged in North Africa.
   (c) To paralyse enemy traffic through the Mediterranean and British supplies to Malta
and Tobruk, in close co-operation with the German and Italian Naval forces available for
this task.
3. Commander-in-Chief South will be under the orders of the Duce whose general
instructions he will receive through the Commando Supremo. In all Air Force matters,
Commander-in-Chief Air Force will deal with Commander-in-Chief South. In important
matters the Ober Kommando der Wehrmacht (OKW) is to be simultaneously informed.
4. The following will be subordinate to Commander-in-Chief South.
   (a) All units of the German Luftwaffe stationed in the Mediterranean and North Africa.
   (b) The air and anti-aircraft units put at his disposal for the execution of his tasks by the
Italian Armed Forces.
5. German Naval Forces in the Central Mediterranean remain under command of
Commander-in-Chief Navy.
For the execution of the tasks assigned to him, Commander-in-Chief South is authorised to
issue directives to the German Admiral Group South (for the Eastern Mediterranean).
Operations orders will be issued by the Naval Headquarters concerned in agreement with

the Commander-in-Chief South.

Requests by Commander-in-Chief South for combined operations by allied naval forces will be made exclusively to the German Admiral with the Italian Naval High Command.

(signed) Adolf Hitler

* * *

Of his new appointment, Feldmarschall Kesselring later wrote:

"I first became really interested in the Mediterranean theatre when Jeschonnek [Generaloberst Hans Jeschonnek, Luftwaffe Chief of Staff] rang me up one day in September 1941 and asked me how I liked the idea of going to Italy or Africa. He was sure we should very soon have to make a much greater effort in that part of the world if we wished to prevent the collapse of the Italian position in North Africa.

I flew to Berlin and reported to the OKW [Oberkommando der Wehrmacht – Supreme Command of the Armed Forces] and Luftwaffe GHQ for my instructions. The title proposed for me, C-in-C South (Oberbefehlshaber Süd), seemed appropriate in view of the scope and nature of my task. I was given a final briefing by Hitler in the presence of Göring and Jeschonnek. The unfavourable situation of our supply line to North Africa, I was told, must be remedied by the neutralisation of the British sea and air key-point, the island of Malta. When I objected that we ought to make a thorough job of it and occupy Malta, my interruption was brushed aside with the flat statement that there were no forces available for this. I arrived in Rome in advance of my staff on 28 November 1941.

The salient feature of the military operations at the end of November 1941 was the inadequacy of our communications system across the Mediterranean. Every day showed more plainly the naval and air supremacy of the British in these waters. Malta had assumed decisive importance as a strategic key-point, and my primary objective at the beginning was to safeguard our supply lines by smoking out the hornets' nest. Time was required to build up our ground organisation in Sicily, to bring forward our air formations and the supplies needed to smash Malta's naval and air bases, as well as to secure the co-operation of the Italian air force in our offensive. For the moment it was impossible to do more than reinforce the air umbrella over the most indispensable convoys."[15]

Comiso was being prepared to house Stab (Maj Günther von Maltzahn) and II Gruppe (Hptm Walter Spies) of JG53, whose aircraft were due to arrive on the 15th; I Gruppe (Hptm Herbert Kaminski) was to operate from Gela and III Gruppe (Hptm Wolf-Dietrich Wilcke) from Catania, although the latter would not arrive until the end of January. Among the Gruppen were many experienced fighter pilots with impressive tallies of air victories[16]. Following closely in the wake of JG53 were the first elements of five Gruppen of Ju88s and one Stukagrup; I/KG54 landed at Gerbini, II and III/KG77 at Comiso, KüFlGr606 and KGr806 at Catania (a total of 86 bombers), while the Ju88C-equipped I/NJG2 had flown to Catania a few weeks earlier. Although trained for night fighter duties, the Ju88C crews were obliged to provide convoy protection and long-range offensive fighter patrols during daylight hours. Other units would follow in due course including old adversaries from earlier in the year, III/ZG26 with its Bf110s, while the Bf109Fs of II/JG3 would be withdrawn from the Eastern Front to assist JG53. Towards the end of November ten six-engined BV222 flying boats had arrived at Taranto to assist with the air transport run to North Africa. In his memoirs, Air Vice-Marshal Lloyd wrote:

For this contest with 400 German and Italian bombers and a similar number of fighters we could muster 81 serviceable Hurricanes, plus another 29 which might be made serviceable if only we could get the spares. It looked a ridiculous contest with our outmoded fighters; a sledge hammer to crack a nut. The momentous problem was whether, and for how long, the Hurricanes could retain the mastery of the air which was vital to the continuance of the activities over the sea; the one was as complementary to the other as Achilles' shield to his sword. If that mastery was lost, the strikes would suffer and our eyes would be blinded."[17]

The first Luftwaffe sortie of the new offensive against Malta was an armed reconnaissance by a Ju88 from KüFlGr606 on 3 December. Meanwhile, Malta's small force of Blenheims continued to take the fight to the enemy, four aircraft attacking ferryboats at Messina on the 4th, before bombing the marshalling yards at Villa San Giovanni, the mainland port opposite Messina. One Blenheim failed to return, shot down by Macchis. Other Blenheims went after the 10,000-ton German tanker *Reichenfels* which had just arrived at Tripoli, at least one bomb hit being claimed. Wellingtons were also out after darkness, 20 aircraft raiding Naples. One was shot down by a CR42 from which two of the crew survived to be taken prisoner. Over Malta on the night of 7/8 December, Flt Lt Don Stones of 1435 Flight attempted to intercept an intruder caught in the searchlights, which he identified as a Ju88 – an aircraft of I/NJG2 – but his guns failed to fire. The Ju88Cs were active over Malta that night including R4+HH of 1 Staffel flown by Lt Wilhelm Brauns, a six-victory ace. After dropping his bombs he reported shooting out two searchlights with machine-gun fire before returning to Sicily, where he was diverted to land at Comiso owing to a crashed aircraft on the runway at Catania. Airman X of 185 Squadron wrote in his diary:

"Air raid all last night. A Ju88 dropped a stick of bombs across our billets. We were all in bed. He killed one soldier and injured six – that was about ten yards from our block, shook us all up. Then just as we were getting dressed to hurry and help the soldiers, the Jerry kite came round and machine-gunned the drome. Think I'll sleep in the shelter for a few nights."

Two Blenheims were lost during a raid on Catania on the 8th when they collided in bad weather. Another was lost next day and a fourth failed to return on the 11th from a raid on Argostoli harbour, another victim of CR42s. Two Blenheims also raided Catania harbour on this date, their bombs striking a transport. However, three more Blenheims were lost on the 13th, two apparently falling to Ju88Cs of I/NJG2. The first two weeks of the month had proved relatively uneventful for the Hurricane pilots, although small-scale fighter-bomber sorties were flown over the southern tip of Sicily, 249 Squadron's Flt Lt Neil (GN-J) flying one such sortie to bomb Ragusa railway station on the 7th.

On the morning of the 11th, Plt Off Tony Reeves (Z2402) and Sgt Garth Horricks (Z5158) of 185 Squadron were scrambled after an unidentified aircraft, but were unable to intercept what turned out to be a Ju88. Later, while awaiting the arrival from Gibraltar of a flight of Wellingtons, one of which was carrying Flt Lt Sidney Brandt, a replacement flight commander for 249 Squadron, news was received that the Wellingtons were under attack by CR42s from Pantelleria. Ten Hurricanes of 185 Squadron led by Sqn Ldr Pike (Z5326) were scrambled but too late to intercept the Italian fighters which had by then shot down two of the bombers and damaged that in which Brandt was flying. Flt Lt Neil of 249 Squadron, due to be replaced by Brandt, also scrambled in company with Flg Off Crossey but they, too, failed to make contact with the enemy.

Sqn Ldr Pike (Z5326) was again at the head of 185 Squadron when it provided fighter cover for Hurribombers of 126 Squadron bombing Comiso next day, where AA fire was reported to be "very good for its height but 200 yards astern". All Hurricanes returned safely. German reconnaissance aircraft continued to make their presence felt over and around Malta. Sgt Alf Branch (BD834) of 249 Squadron chased a Ju88 during a dawn patrol on the 13th but was unable to catch it when it entered cloud. Night intruders returned to harry Malta's defences after dark on the 15th. The Hurricane pilots tasked with night fighting duties were beginning to realise just how difficult it was to engage intruders without the benefit of airborne radar. While on a patrol to the west of Malta on the 16th, Flt Lt Peter Thompson (Z4014) of 185 Squadron, accompanied by Sgt Brian Hayes (Z3766), encountered a Blenheim over Lampedusa which opened fire on them.

Fortunately, neither Hurricane was hit and both returned to Hal Far, landing at 1640. Plt Off Bob Matthews of 249 Squadron also flew a patrol to the west of the island, sighting a convoy off Kerkennah and two CR42s over Lampedusa. At this time Sqn Ldr Pike of 185 Squadron upset the other squadron commanders when it was discovered that he had unofficially authorised the exchange of old ferrying tanks with long-range, self-sealing fuel tanks belonging to aircraft of 242 and 605 Squadrons. Although Pike argued that his squadron was often required to fly long-range offensive sorties to Lampedusa and other points south-west, he still had to return the tanks.

The first Hurricane success of the month was achieved on the 18th. Four aircraft of 185 Squadron led by Plt Off Phil Allardice were sent to patrol over the destroyers of Force K protecting an incoming convoy to the south-west of the island. At 1105, three Italian bombers identified as BR20s were encountered preparing to attack the convoy. The Hurricanes engaged, Plt Offs Allardice (BD702) and Oliver (Z3758), and their No2s, Sgts Brian Hayes (Z2823/GL-U) and Bill Nurse (Z4943), claiming damage to the two aircraft they attacked. Although Allardice's Hurricane was hit in the tail by return fire he was able to return safely to Hal Far. It would seem that the two bombers were SM84s of 259^Squadriglia, three of which had been despatched to attack the British convoy. These were intercepted and one shot down: Sottoten Antonio Galati's aircraft (MM22487) crashed into the sea with the loss of all but one member of the crew; a second Savoia limped back to Sicily with a mortally wounded man on board and a second less badly wounded. Members of this crew stated they had been attacked by Hurricanes. However, an unusual encounter took place during the afternoon when Lt Brauns' Ju88C R4+HH of I/NJG2, which was on an offensive sea patrol against RAF fighters between Malta and Tripoli, intercepted two Italian aircraft identified as a Savoia SM63 and a Savoia SM86, which were attacked after failing to respond to recognition signals. The reason for this act of aggression by Braun stemmed from an earlier encounter with Italian G50s off north-east Sicily, when, in spite of repeated recognition signals, the G50s attacked. The crew was disgusted with their "gentleman allies for whom we are leaving our bones", as Obgfr Erwin Hesse, the gunner, later related, and "we decided to shoot on sight next time." The result of this action is unknown.

On 19 December the Luftwaffe finally made its anticipated daytime appearance over Malta. During the morning a reconnaissance Ju88 appeared over the convoy as it was arriving at Grand Harbour. Hurricanes of 126 Squadron intercepted and claimed damage to the intruder. Somewhat later, at 1045, three Ju88s were seen approaching and on this occasion four Hurricanes of 249 Squadron intercepted, as noted by Sgt Alf Branch:

> "The new CO [Sqn Ldr Mortimer-Rose] together with Smudge [Sgt Skeet-Smith], Alan [Sgt Cairns] and Risty [Sgt Ron Rist] chased three Ju88s. CO attacked one Ju88 and Alan and Smudge attacked another. Alan was hit by cannon and machine-gun but landed OK. Risty did not fire. One Ju88 later confirmed and we collected the tail, guns and wings from the kite."

The Ju88s were from I/NJG2, which were also flying daylight sorties. Sqn Ldr Mortimer-Rose's victim was Lt Brauns' R4+HH which crashed in terrace fields in the San Blas Valley in north-east Gozo. W/Op Gfr Johannes Mattuschka was killed, and Brauns seriously injured[18], while Obgfr Heese suffered only slight injuries. Examination of the wreck revealed Italian markings. Heese told his captors that their task had been to remain over Malta for about an hour and attack any aircraft encountered. The aircraft engaged by Sgts Skeet-Smith and Cairns limped back to Catania where it crash-landed and was further damaged although the crew survived. Shortly thereafter, Flt Lt Peter Thompson and Sgt Trevor Bates of 185 Squadron were scrambled; Thompson noted:

> "Sgt Bates and myself came to readiness. We had three scrambles. On the first one we successfully intercepted an Albacore 'bandit' which we refrained from shooting down. We

also chased a Ju88 back to Sicily but could not catch him."

During the afternoon Hurricanes of 126 Squadron were scrambled at the approach of enemy aircraft. This time it was the Geschwader-Stabsschwarm of JG53 led by Maj Günther von Maltzahn on a free chase mission in conjunction with Ju88Cs of I/NJG2. The German pilots reported an engagement with seven Hurricanes over the island shortly before 1700, during which Maj von Maltzahn recorded his 50th victory. His victim would seem to have been Plt Off Pete Steele, one of the American pilots, who baled out over Grand Harbour while his aircraft (Z3764) crashed in the sea off Delimara, as noted by 605 Squadron's Plt Off Ian McKay: "The aircraft hit the sea and when the air sea rescue arrived found a dinghy but no pilot. The Ju88s are getting very bold with these daylight attacks." However, Lt Peter Laufs of I/NJG2 reported that his starboard engine was shot out by a Hurricane but, as he turned, the fighter overshot and promptly disintegrated under the power of the Ju88C's front armament. Possibly he fell victim to both Lauf's Ju88 and von Maltzahn's Messerschmitt. Either way, the first of 126 Squadron's four American pilots was killed.

The real challenge to the Hurricanes came next day (20 December), when four Ju88s returned during the morning to attack shipping in Grand Harbour, but this time with a strong escort of 11 Bf109Fs from Stab and 1/JG53. Apparently MC202s from 9°Gruppo CT were also present. A dozen Hurricanes from 249 Squadron were scrambled at 1036 to meet the incoming raid; Plt Off Titch Palliser (Z2904) attacked one Ju88 head-on, opening fire when only a few yards away from a collision. He saw his shells hit its starboard engine and reported that the wing then broke off. As the stricken bomber fell, it was lost from sight in cloud. Before Palliser could follow he was attacked by a number of Messerschmitts, one of which he believed he probably damaged. In the meantime the bomber was seen to crash into the sea by coastwatchers. All three of the remaining bombers were claimed damaged before the escorting Macchis and Messerschmitts intervened.

The aircraft (Z2418) flown by Sgt Howard Moren was believed to have collided with the Ju88 shot down by Palliser, although its seems more likely that he fell victim to a Messerschmitt flown by Oblt Friedrich-Karl Müller, who claimed a Hurricane at 0923, his 23rd victory; 21-year-old Moren, from Surrey, was killed. Meanwhile, Flg Off Crossey, having had a shot at one of the Ju88s, fired at a Macchi, hitting its starboard wing. He reported that it gave a "quick flick" and went straight down. Another Macchi was attacked by Sgt Hugh McDowall, who reported that it spun down apparently out of control, disappearing into cloud. The Squadron suffered a second fatality when Plt Off Brian Cavan's Hurricane (BV162) was shot down from 20,000 feet. The aircraft fell like a stone and 20-year-old Londoner Cavan was killed, the victim of either Hptm Kaminski (his 6th) or Lt Werner Schöw (his 4th), or both. Both Plt Off Sonny Ormrod and Plt Off Ian McKay recorded these actions in their respective diaries, Ormrod writing:

"There have been various air raids lately in honour of the convoy. This morning just after breakfast, out of a sky spread with clouds, an attack was made. We had had warning that a plot of 50+ was on board, so we were up on the roof to see the fun. Wish we'd been up in the air but we are not here for that. Soon the barrage was in full blast. An 88 dived down from the sun and we saw its bomb falling from it (at about six or seven thousand feet I suppose). Then it went off through the thick of the barrage. Some bursts were very close, but it kept on going and passed out of sight. Only saw this one 88; but after a lull of a quarter of an hour, three more attacked. I missed seeing these, having gone inside. 249 destroyed an 88 and a 109 [sic], possibly another 88 too, but lost an odd Hurricane or two, being jumped by the escorting fighters that formed the majority of the plot. This was all out of our sight. Anyway, it shows that the Huns have returned from Russia and mean to spend a happy winter in the Mediterranean. Not too good for the Hurricane boys here, 109s having a much superior performance to old Hurricanes."

Plt Off McKay noted:

"The excitement started earlier today. We have had two air raids already this morning and it is not yet noon. The first was by two Ju88 flying about 5,000 feet. They were engaged by anti-aircraft fire (which is, I might say, really good) but then dropped a few bombs. The second attack was by four 88s and again they were flying quite low and had a hell of a time trying to dodge the flak. I think two of the six were shot down. I have found out since that the Hurricanes from Takali were jumped by 50 109s. They lost two and got three 109s and two 88s [*sic*]."

With the return of the Messerschmitts, Air Vice-Marshal Lloyd's worst fears were realised:

"The Hurricanes were easily outnumbered and their performance was not equal to that of the new 109s, which had now appeared on the scene from the Belgian and English Channel coasts and were flown by pilots who had fought against the Hurricanes and Spitfires in the Battle of Britain. Our answer too should have been the Spitfire, but not one, so far, had been allowed out of Britain."[19]

During the late morning of 21 December there was another raid, comprising four Ju88s and 20 escorting fighters – again both Bf109s and MC202s. Ten Hurricanes of 185 Squadron and eight from 249 Squadron were scrambled, led by Wg Cdr Rabagliati in Z4005, who claimed one Macchi shot down. A second was claimed probably destroyed by Flg Off Davis of 249 Squadron, while Bf109s were damaged by Flt Lt John Beazley and Flt Sgt Fred Etchells also of 249 Squadron. However, 185 Squadron's Sgt Brian Hayes, a 21-year-old from Essex, failed to return, as noted by Flt Lt Thompson:

"When we were at 17,000-18,000 feet we met six 109Fs head on. I chased two of them up to 25,000 feet but could not catch them. The squadron joined up again and we started to come down. Sgt Hayes did not return and it is assumed he was jumped on the way down. With the Huns about, losses are to be expected, but it is with deep regret that I have to record the death of Brian Hayes, a sound and efficient pilot but perhaps not quite experienced enough."

His aircraft (Z2823/GL-U) was observed falling into the sea some five miles out, probably the victim of Maj von Maltzahn of Stab/JG53 who claimed a Hurricane at midday for his 51st victory, although two 249 Squadron Hurricanes were hit in the action. Flt Sgt Dave Owen made a dead-stick landing at Luqa, while Plt Off Graham Leggett's aircraft (DG615) was also hit in the engine:

"Attacking three Ju88s, I became entangled with half a dozen 109s. Shot up and half blinded by engine oil, I baled out near Luqa and my Hurricane dived straight in a mile or so to the east of the airfield, in a small ravine and quite close to a gun site."

Plt Off Ormrod witnessed the crash:

"This morning we got a beautiful view of another attack on the Grand Harbour. Three 88s dropped several bombs, successfully running through the barrage again. The 88 is a very fine aircraft. After their dive attack they climb like the devil. The bombs seemed to send up clouds of dust, so think they missed the harbour. At the same time the fighters must have been having a fight above the broken clouds which the 88s had used so well for cover. At the end, one Hurricane came gliding back. Looking through my glass I could see its wheels were down. Looked to be OK. Then suddenly it dived. A little lump, which I took at first to be a puff of smoke, flew off behind. The aircraft dived into a hillside facing us, about one-and-a-half miles away, and immediately blew up in flames. The thing I thought was a puff of smoke turned out to be the pilot. He was only at about 1,500 feet but his parachute opened and set him down OK. In the evening the clouds cleared away and I took a walk across the country to see the crushed Hurricane. The remains had been removed. Learnt from a soldier beside whom the pilot landed that the pilot was P/O Leggett of 249. The aircraft had landed across a stone wall so had not imbedded itself in the earth."

The Germans were back again next day (22 December). In the afternoon Hurricanes from both 126 and 249 Squadrons were scrambled when reports were received that enemy fighters – apparently both Messerschmitts and Macchis – were shooting up fishing boats off Grand Harbour. Plt Off Bob Matthews of 249 Squadon went after one of the strafers. Plt Off Coffin of 126 Squadron wrote:

"Matthews got the Messerschmitt as it climbed from the sea for new altitude, but another German was hard on his own tail chasing him towards shore. Matthews was hit and crashed into the sea wall at Valetta, where his aircraft exploded and started to burn."[20]

This account is not strictly correct, however. It would seem that Matthews pursued and damaged an aircraft, thought to have been a Macchi, before being engaged by Messerschmitts. His aircraft (BV156/GN-Q) did not crash into the sea wall at Valetta, as suggested by Coffin, but was shot down from about 20,000 feet, as testified by on-the-spot witnesses including Plt Off Ormrod:

"This morning an 88 made an attack on the neighbourhood of Valetta. It was a good surprise attack, making use of the sun, but in the face of some ack-ack he did not seem to press it home. The weather today is excellent. Sunny, with very few clouds, but not too hot. Was wandering from 1.00pm to 4.45pm. I saw part of a dogfight between Hurricanes and enemy fighters. Only saw aircraft when they flashed in the sun. Saw one come down in flames. Dived straight in, no parachute was seen. Am afraid it looked like a Hurricane. 249 were up."

Another was Plt Off McKay, who wrote:

"This afternoon there was a terrific dogfight directly over us and we saw a Hurricane go straight in. Apparently he was shot up at about 20,000 feet and the pilot must have been killed and fallen over the stick for he didn't get out and the aircraft came down nearly vertically. It must have been going about 600mph when it went in. It also exploded. We are beginning to think we will be staying here now seeing Jerry is getting busy again and they need some replacements for the squadrons that are here. I don't care much what we do so long as we get doing something."

In fact, Plt Off Robert Matthews' Hurricane crashed near Defence Post M33 just west of Addolorata Cemetery, on the outskirts of Paola, the victim of either 2/JG53's Oblt Klaus Quaet-Faslem, who claimed a Hurricane at 1436 (his 10th), or Lt Heinrich von Schwerdtner who claimed one 14 minutes later (his 6th). The other Hurricane was that flown by Sgt Ted Copp of 126 Squadron, who landed safely despite having been shot up. I/NJG2 lost another of its aircraft when R4+KK of 2 Staffel, flown by Fw Ernst Ziebarth, failed to return from a sortie over Malta with the crew being reported missing, presumably the victim of AA fire.

The alarm sounded again on 23 December as an estimated 22 raiders approached Grand Harbour, although the plot materialised into two Ju88s escorted by Bf109Fs of II/JG53, which had also now reached Sicily. Hurricanes of 126 Squadron were sent off to intercept, one Messerschmitt being claimed damaged in which Lt Hans-Jürgen Frohdien (flying Black <2) was slightly wounded, although he was able to return to Comiso safely. Two of the Hurricanes were also hit – Sqn Ldr Lefevre, imminently due to leave the island, force-landed at Hal Far with his engine and hydraulics shot to pieces and his canopy shattered, while Plt Off Noel MacGregor, with a shrapnel wound in his foot, force-landed Z5118/HA-S having been jumped by an aircraft he never even saw. One of these was the victim of Lt Hans Möller of 6/JG53 who claimed a Hurricane shot down at 1120 for his fifth victory.

Again Plt Off Ormrod recorded these events, writing:

"A sunny day. 249 Squadron [in fact is was 126 Squadron] were jumped by 109s more or less over this district. We saw them split up with undignified haste. The 109s were practically invisible, being camouflaged silver; some are black I believe, and at that height are only to be seen if the sun's rays glint off them. Most of the fighter activity is invisible because they fight in the sun, the result of each trying to get up-sun of the other. A little after first being jumped, a Hurricane came from over the sea to the south. His engine was u/s but he made a beautiful landing on the aerodrome. He'd glided down from 20,000 feet, having been hit by cannon shells in engine and tail. His oil tank had been holed. The pilot was a Squadron Leader ... Hear we're to operate here – sentiments mixed. Far better than nothing. Don't know now whether we'll move on or not eventually. The Hurricanes already operating here need reinforcement. Up to yesterday they'd lost seven in four days!"

One of 69 Squadron's PR Hurricanes – Z3173 which had replaced Z3053 lost the previous month – narrowly escaped a similar fate when Plt Off Smith was pursued by a MC202 while attempting to reach Trapani. As the Macchi closed, Smith dived the Hurricane from 23,000 feet down to 8,000 feet where cloud enabled him to escape. With the onset of darkness, Hurricanes of 1435 Flight took over.

Christmas Eve 1941 brought four alerts, but only one interception when Wg Cdr Rabagliati led off 17 Hurricanes of 126 and 249 Squadrons after four Ju88s of II/KG77 which dive-bombed Grand Harbour. This was the 25th raid in seven days, and indicative of the level of activity following the arrival of the Luftwaffe. 249 Squadron's CO, Sqn Ldr Mortimer-Rose, had decided that his aircraft should take off and climb in pairs to make it appear that there were more Hurricanes available than was actually the case. Plt Off Harry Moon recalled:

"I was one of the last to take off and, as I climbed, I could see the CO's aircraft virtually standing on its tail as he fired at a bomber. A pencil-thin line of smoke or vapour appeared from one of its engines, but this had ceased before I lost sight of it."

Mortimer-Rose was joined by Plt Off Titch Palliser (Z2904) and the Ju88, 3Z+EP of 5/KG77, was sent crashing into the sea in flames some 20 miles east of Zonqor Point, Lt Siegfried Tack and his crew all perishing. A second Ju88 was claimed shot down by the combined attacks of Flg Off Crossey and Flt Sgt Fred Etchells, who were also joined by Palliser. Their victim had apparently been damaged by AA fire and when last seen, five miles north of Malta, was losing height with smoke pouring from both engines. It seems probable this was M7+HK of KGr806 flown by Uffz Werner Lessner, which failed to return. A third bomber was pursued to Sicily by Plt Off Moon (Z2546/GN-D):

"I saw a Ju88 leave the formation. I was 2,000 feet below and chased it towards Sicily but before I could catch up, it entered a thundercloud. I followed, held steady and luckily met it on the other side. I fired at long range, but nothing observed. Fired again and the 88 started weaving. I caught up and fired again, saw strikes and it fell away. My No2, Sgt Lawson, then appeared and I told him to follow it down to observe the crash but, when I got back, I found that he had followed me instead."

This was clearly an aircraft of 4/KG77 flown by Fw Otto Bude which crash-landed on return to Catania, one member of the crew (Obgfr Paul Müller, the observer) having been fatally wounded during the combat. During the attack on the bombers Palliser's aircraft had been hit in the glycol tank although he landed at Takali safely. Wg Cdr Rabagliati and 126 Squadron had been unable to reach the bombers, being intercepted by the escorting Bf109Fs of II/JG53 with the result that 25-year-old Geordie Sgt Dick Emery (BD830) was shot down, apparently by Oblt Kurt Brändle of 5 Staffel (his 29th victory). Sgt Ted Wood of 1435 Flight noted:

"Got up for sirens about 10am. Five 88s dived-bombed harbour. 126 and 249 stayed out of way of 109s. Two 88s confirmed shot down and one probable without loss. AA also claim one. Saw this happen. It was coming straight down and suddenly turned violently and went away. Heard the machine-gun fire. About 1.30pm another attack by 88s on Grand Harbour and Luqa. 126 up but could not get in because of AA. Nothing brought down. Heard my room mate Dick Emery was missing; no one knows what happened but AA say they saw a Hurricane chase and shoot down an 88. A pity, and Christmas Eve too. Charlie and Ted [Copp] very cut up, the latter did searches until his petrol ran out."

Plt Off Ormrod gave a slightly more detailed account:

"This morning I saw an attack on the island by 88s, about four of them. They seemed at first to be making for Luqa; but the barrage was good and rather shook them. At least one was hit, though not brought down until the Hurricanes joined in. Believe the Hurricanes destroyed two and damaged one. They were at the right height, about 1,000 feet higher than the bombers and don't seem to have been jumped by the 109s, who would be much higher still. Believe some Hurricanes were covering from above. After luncheon more 88s made an attack on the Grand Harbour. The barrage was up again and the fighters came down as they were leaving; but I know not with what result . . . 242 Squadron are preparing to operate with some of their aircraft, but we have been told nothing – suppose we are to do nothing. I am very vexed. This business is shaming our honour. Might just as well be civilians for all we do. I am ashamed when I find us mere spectators of dogfights. If only we would move off on the operation that brought us here without more delay, or become operational here for a time until the time for our move comes – it would be a mistake to fritter us away and so imperil the outcome of that operation; but it is a mistake to reduce us to slackness by remaining so long inactive. Little did I think that, on becoming an operational pilot, I should spend seven months inactive. If only circumstances would permit me to go into action with one of the other squadrons until the time comes to move."

Ju88s paid a visit to Malta after dark on Christmas Eve, their presents not very charitable under the circumstances with bombs falling on Hal Far among other places, as noted by Sgt Wood:

"Had a wizard dinner at night followed by a glorious binge, all officers and all B Flight present, mostly under the influence, even the SCO. Finished up by nearly a free fight, quite a few blows struck. Why? I don't know. Came back with Ted and Charles and had a drink in their billet, and so to bed. A bomb was dropped about 50 yards from dispersal on the drome, just missing the kites but only made a couple of holes in one aircraft. P/O Mackie was just taxiing in and one of the airmen was signalling him when the bomb fell right in between them without causing a scratch."

The next day he wrote:

"Christmas Day. Just managed to get up for breakfast and then sorted out Dick's kit [Sgt Dick Emery]. Did not go down to the Officers' Mess for a drink but Reg [Fowler] did. Had lunch and then went to the Airmens' Dining Hall to serve dinner. It was quite hard work but had a few drinks with the lads. Finished this about 3.30pm, had some tea and got ready to go on. Very strong cross wind, did an air test and went on, 30 minutes. Everybody was annoyed about it but officers brought some beer back. P/O Mills was a bit tight and caused bags of laughter all night so had very little sleep. A few bombers over the island but AA engaged. Heard that Charlie had been in the NAAFI and broken the place up; the CO was after him."

On Christmas Day nine Hurricanes of 185 Squadron's A Flight led by Flt Lt Peter Thompson were scrambled after a small plot which failed to materialise. On their return they overflew a football match then in progress, as recorded in the diary of Airman X of 185 Squadron:

> "Went to a fancy dress soccer match. Our Hurricanes went up and dropped toilet paper on the soccer pitch. Had a wizard dinner, then slept in the afternoon. Gave concert in the evening, went down very well."

Pilots of 185 Squadron also enjoyed the festive celebrations, as recorded by Flt Lt Thompson, who had been responsible for the predetermined attack on the footballers:

> "A Flight at readiness had a scramble for a 3+ which mercifully faded. A Flight then showed their appreciation of the Officers v Sergeants football match then in progress by bombing the bums with bog-bumff. Other Xmas Day festivities included the presentation to Jimmy Forth of the one and only German Gremlin in captivity, said Gremlin being brought here under close escort by Sgt Sutherland. Chief of Gremlins Forth showed his appreciation in the manner usual to Gremlins. Sgt Alderson was seen to run around the dispersal hut indecently clothed. The Squadron foregathered in the dispersal hut in the evening and spent a very pleasant three hours sitting round the Yule log (stove in Maltese) yarning and telling 'feelthy' jokes, drinking sherry thoughtfully provided by the CO, and eating cake which had belonged to Brian Hayes. Altogether, a most successful day."

Plt Off Ormrod had learned unofficially from his CO that 605 and 242 Squadrons were not continuing to the Far East to rejoin their ground echelon, but were now to remain at Malta prior to re-routing to North Africa:

> "Our business here is following its usual fluctuations of prospects. Now 605 and 242 are said each to be operating one section only. That we will eventually move is now again the case. Our position is now this – we are now free for other employment. This would probably mean a move, after some delay, whilst they decide what to do with us; but it so happens that at the moment the fighter squadrons of this island are in need of reinforcement and we are the obvious reinforcement. But they can only use us in so far as they can get groundcrews to service our aircraft – an irritating limitation, there being insufficient on the island for all needs of the service.
>
> Late this afternoon 242 wrecked another Hurricane in a taxiing accident – went off the taxi track at the corner of a hill. Airscrew splintered to pieces and one leg of undercarriage practically wrenched away, besides lesser damage [this was BE402/LE-S]."

After observing a peaceful Christmas Day, the Germans and Italians returned with a vengeance on Boxing Day, as summarized in the official communique:

> "During the course of the day five alerts have been sounded. During the first and second alerts enemy aircraft crossed the coast, but dropped no bombs. In the third alert a number of enemy bombers escorted by fighters crossed the coast and were engaged by our fighters. One enemy bomber was definitely destroyed and two others were damaged. One enemy fighter was destroyed and another damaged."

The first clash came late in the morning when Maj von Maltzahn led an escort for a reconnaissance Ju88, two sections of 242 Squadron Hurricanes being scrambled, as noted by Plt Off McKay:

> "Today dawned very bright and rather warm. Ron Noble and I walked down to 242 dispersal and just as we arrived they were scrambled. F/Lt Kemp listened in on the R/T and could hear Paddy Kee say he was after an 88. About ten minutes after we heard gunfire directly above and then saw two 109s coming down on the four Hurricanes. Sgt Neale was hit by cannon and machine-gun fire and for a few seconds we thought he had bought it but he got his kite under control and managed to land it wheels and flaps up. He was able to

get out of the machine by himself but had a lot of shrapnel in both legs and one arm. The aircraft's starboard side was literally filled with holes. The office was covered in blood and oil. The hydraulic system was completely shot away. Sgt Neale was a very lucky man, some of the cannon and machine-gun burst were really close."

Sgt Donald Neale was indeed lucky, having been attacked by Maj von Maltzahn, who claimed the Hurricane (BE555/LE-X) as his 52nd victory.

The mid-afternoon raid was again directed against Luqa and caused much devastation. Four Wellingtons were destroyed including one which blew-up, while a Maryland and PR Hurricane (Z2332) of 69 Squadron were severely damaged. Both 126 and 249 Squadrons were up and were engaged by Bf109Fs of Stab/JG53. 126 Squadron lost an aircraft to the Messerschmitts with Sgt Ted Copp baling out of Z2680, slightly wounded, while Sqn Ldr Mortimer-Rose crash-landed at Luqa with a dead engine and shrapnel lodged in his heel. Both pilots were taken to hospital for treatment. Their victors were Maj von Maltzahn, who claimed his second victory that day and his 53rd overall, and Lt Preu, also of Stab/JG53, whose tally was now four. On taking command of 249 Squadron, Sqn Ldr Mortimer-Rose had changed the standard line abreast formation to line astern, with two weavers at the rear. Although the unfortunate weavers were shot down from time to time, he was convinced it was the fault of the weavers themselves rather than the formation flown. Determined to prove the point, on this occasion he flew as one of the weavers rather than as leader and was attacked and badly shot-up from astern by a Messerschmitt which he had not seen! Sgt Ted Wood's diary contains an account of the action as he witnessed it:

"Came off [duty] at dawn and had breakfast. Stayed in mess until 1.00pm. Got a couple of letters. An attempted attack in the morning but nothing seemed to come down. The sirens went about 2.00pm and the biggest attack yet developed, 25 Hurricanes airborne. Two separate attacks by 88s were made on Luqa, three or four quite large fires were started, probably aircraft. The Hurricanes were all together, very low down and did not intercept but AA opened up and covered the sky. The 88s went straight down through the clouds. Saw about six 109s nipping on top of the clouds, just above us. AA opened up and shrapnel just missed me as I took some photographs of the fires. Went down to mess for tea. Sirens went again, 21 Hurricanes up for 40+ fighters. Saw one top weaver jumped and he force-landed at Luqa. Saw another one attacked and glycol streamed out, the aircraft did some queer antics, finally the pilot baled out and the kite crashed not far away. Learned that it was Ted Copp; he was OK apart from shock and a flesh wound. The other chap was the CO of 249."

It was becoming painfully obvious that the Hurricanes and their pilots were completely out-classed by their German opponents; Plt Off Ormrod:

"After tea there was another warning. The Hurricanes went up a little higher this time. It seemed to be a fighter sweep by 109s. A pair came up behind a squadron of Hurricanes in full view of us at Hal Far House. The weavers never noticed them. The 109s attacked with the greatest calm and simplicity. Formated on the Hurricanes, fired and then breaking away raced off up to the sun, whilst the Hurricanes were left wondering what happened. I've never seen aircraft move so fast as these 109s on their break away, or at least they gave that impression. I believe they are the latest make of 109s. One of the Hurricanes landed with a crash-landing at Takali, I believe."

As darkness descended, another raid came in and 1435 Flight scrambled five of its night fighters; Sgt Wood:

"About 6pm, just at dusk, another attack. One 88 came below cloud and was illuminated. All the Bofors opened up, a wizard sight but no apparent hits. Our A Flight were up – five of them, three [with] cannon and two twelve machine-gun jobs – and learned later that they were just behind but could not get in for AA."

During the morning of the 27th, Hurricanes from 126 and 249 Squadrons led by Flt Lt Carpenter were ordered off in good time for the third alert of the day. Climbing to 24,000 feet, the Hurricanes patrolled for some 40 minutes before being vectored on to a reported four of five Ju88s at 16,000 feet, five to ten miles east of Kalafrana. There were in fact just three bombers of KüFlGr606, with an escort of 20 Bf109Fs from I/JG53. Carpenter was able to dive on the last Ju88, probably the aircraft flown by Uffz Johann Krause, as his subsequent Combat Report revealed:

"While leading Wing at 24,000 feet for 40 minutes, we were given a vector. The cloud was 10/10th at 7,000 feet and we spotted them against it at around 16,000 feet. There were four or five Ju88s in loose formation with some 109s a little above. I dived down on the last one and opened fire at 300 yards from abeam, turning to him astern. I closed right up till there was a risk of collision and broke away down and to the left. In the quarter attack the Ju88 kept on a straight course but turned around soon after. He dived for cloud cover and I managed to get in another two attacks from astern before he got to it. His engine was on fire and I did not get any return fire from the rear-gunner."

Although Krause and his observer were both wounded, the damaged bomber returned safely to Catania. By this time the rest of the Hurricanes were engaged with the escort, and Plt Off Rocky Main attacked one Messerschmitt from 50 yards and set it on fire. Although initially claimed as a probable, this was subsequently upgraded to confirmed when it was learned that a Messerschmitt had crashed into the sea off Ragusa, although the Germans maintained that this particular machine, from which the pilot was rescued, had run out of fuel. Other pilots claimed damage to two Ju88s and another Bf109, the latter credited to Flg Off Davis and Plt Off Tedford, as noted by Sgt Alf Branch (Z2698) who was among the 249 Squadron pilots scrambled to meet the raid:

"We joined up with 126 Squadron and climbed to 25,000 feet. CO [newly promoted Sqn Ldr Beazley] then left formation as his engine was cutting. Four attacked one Ju88 and destroyed it. Risty [Sgt Rist] had his first squirt in action. F/O Davis and P/O Tedford had a poop at a 109 and believed to have damaged it. F/Sgt Owen had his time cut out getting out of the way of 109s. F/Lt Carpenter of 126 Squadron claimed a Ju88 with 249. One Hurribox shot up, but no damage or casualties apart from this."[21]

Plt Off Coffin, the pilot of the shot-up Hurricane (Z3984), carried out a successful forced-landing at Takali. Two Hurricanes were claimed by pilots of I/JG53, one being credited to Oblt Karl-Friedrich Müller (his 24th) at 1205, while Lt Walter Zellot claimed his 13th two minutes later. The diary of Plt Off Ormrod offers further detail:

"The morning alert was a little earlier than usual. The Hurricanes were overhead when I went down to breakfast at 8.30am. A pair of 109s came sneaking up through broken cloud and would probably have jumped the Hurricanes; but they were chased off by the anti-aircraft guns. There was more activity after breakfast. A pair of 109s, camouflaged black [sic], insolently cruised up and down the coast at a low altitude, varying from a couple of thousand feet to sea level. The ack-ack let off at them from time to time, but was always behind. The Hurricanes stayed over the island. They got one 88 above cloud. Don't know where it crashed, but it jettisoned its bombs in the sea here. In the afternoon there was another air raid alarm. We were occupied marking out letters on the aircraft. BG713 will become my third 'O' when she's lettered."

Ju88s were back over Malta after dark. Hurricanes of 1435 Flight were airborne including a pair flown by Flg Off Denis Winton and Sgt Ted Wood, who wrote in his diary:

"Went into Valetta to buy a few things and had to get a gharry back because of an air raid; just made it in time to go on readiness. On an air test some 88s came in but did not come below cloud. AA was firing. The first scramble got a very good illumination. Bofors opened up just as we were closing but F/O Winton went straight in and fired all his ammo. Just as I went in, the starboard engine burst into flames so I did not fire but flew alongside and watched it burn. Finally it went into the sea just off the coast and blazed out. Saw somebody bale out and followed the parachute down but he was not heard off again. Did two more scrambles but saw nothing except sticks of bombs on the island."

This was undoubtedly Hptm Eberhard Stahle's 3Z+BM of Stab II/KG77. Flg Off Winton (Z3570/D) simply annotated his logbook: "Scramble. Good illumination. Broke my duck. One Ju88 destroyed."

249 Squadron had scrambled shortly after 1300 on the 28th when Ju88s and their escorts were reported approaching the island. Sgt Alf Branch (flying Z3757 on this occasion) recalled:

"Saw Ju88 but jumped by Messerschmitts as unable to get height. Squirted at by 109. Dave Owen had a nasty experience. Shot up by 109s, he baled out and landed in a very rough sea five miles out. Kalafrana rescue launch kept on and finally found him, after two of the crew had been knocked out and the boat battered to blazes. Lucky man Dave. This makes the second time in three months and he still has 27 pieces of shrapnel in his shoulder."

This was, in fact, the fourth time in three months that Flt Sgt Owen had been shot up or shot down. On recovery he deservedly left Malta, having done his bit for the island. Meanwhile, Plt Off Ormrod wrote in his diary:

"In the afternoon a Ju88 flew over high escorted by 109s. Saw them clearly right overhead. Did not drop any bombs, so suppose only a reconnaissance. Then later, about sunset, three 88s came over. I got out of the mess to see one of them go right over with Bofors guns sending streams of 'flaming onions' after him."

The bombers were back that night, one falling victim to AA fire, as recorded by Plt Off McKay:

"Tonight was rather exciting. A Ju88 was on the way down to bomb Hal Far and he was caught in the searchlights. It flew down one searchlight and tried to machine-gun it but failed and the searchlight held him all the time and the anti-aircraft guns opened up. One Bofors gun was right on and got direct hits and then the kite burst into flames and came down on the edge of the aerodrome and blew up. The bodies of the crew (three) were found in four different fields. The aircraft must have been travelling at a terrific speed for it went through four stone fences and the wreckage was spread all over the place. I got a cannon shell and a couple of pieces of it."

Ormrod also rushed over to the scene of the crash:

"Reaching the near side of the aerodrome we could see the flaming wreckage on the other side. Paused a little to see if any bombs onboard were going to explode and then raced off. Arrived a little breathless in the vicinity of the wreckage, which was a good deal scattered. It was soon realised that there were no survivors. A soldier took me to see one of the corpses lying at the side of the road. The poor devil had been disintegrated. I was shocked by a Maltese workman dancing round a stray leg. Those airmen died nobly for their country and their Führer even though they be our enemies. They were military airmen whatever else. Personally the corpses moved me little more than a bird I might have shot down. After all why should they? They are fundamentally the same. It is weakness of nerves that sees more to it than that. Tomorrow I am to be attached to 242 Squadron. I go on readiness with them at 9am. I am very pleased. For some reason one of their pilot officers is not to fly – I'm replacing him for the day."

29 December was to see the heaviest day of fighting over Malta and a costly one for the defenders, since the return of the Luftwaffe. There were five scrambles during the day, three of which developed into major combats. After the first plots, which were in fact Bf109s of II/JG53 searching for signs of the missing Ju88, the first attack occurred soon after 0945 when an estimated 36 aircraft – apparently two Ju88s escorted by II/JG53 – approached. Seven Hurricanes from 185 Squadron and four from 242 Squadron were scrambled. During the action, two aircraft from the latter unit collided in the air, Plt Off Merton Blanchard[22], an American in the RCAF, losing his life in BE343 and Flt Lt Andrews (BE344) baling out into the sea, from where he was rescued by HSL129. The remaining Hurricanes engaged the Ju88s and escorting Messerschmitts, one of the latter being claimed destroyed and a second damaged; in return three Hurricanes were damaged. Plt Off McKay's account of the action is revealing:

"This morning we were told that we were to be ready to leave by the 31st, so Chuck Lester and I walked up to our dispersal to check our aircraft. Just as we arrived there was an air raid warning and five minutes later we could see the 109s at about 10,000 feet and two 88s just below them. The 88s dropped their bombs on Luqa and then the Hurricanes engaged the 109s and dogfighting followed, during which one 109 was shot down by F/Lt Thompson [Z5326]. F/Lt Andrews and Tiny Blanchard were jumped by 109s and Tiny must have been shot up for he came right down on Andy and they collided. Tiny's tail was knocked off and one of Andy's wings. Andy baled out into the sea and was picked up by the air sea rescue but Tiny's kite went right in and he didn't get out.

When Chuck and I came back from our aircraft to the aerodrome we found two crashed aircraft, riddled with bullet holes and cannon fire, in the middle of it. One was F/Lt Thompson whose undercarriage had been shot away and had to land wheels up. It was not bent though. And the other was P/O Macnamara who had been jumped by 109s and was shot up very badly. He was unhurt but nearly every longeron was shot away. After being shot up in the air he was on his way in to land when two 109s came down over the drome and machine-gunned him. The aircraft [LE-C] was hit but again he was unhurt. It almost seems a miracle that he was OK cause there was hardly a square foot of the kite without a hole in it. Sonny [Ormrod] was also jumped but only got a couple of bullet holes in his wing and he got a good long burst at the 109 but only the two starboard cannons were working and he missed. It was damned hard luck."

Of his first taste of action, Plt Off Ormrod (BE351/LE-Y) wrote:

"I was to fly as P/O Macnamara's No2. We had not long to wait for action. We got 'stand-by' at about 9.30am and were scrambled about ten minutes later. Off we went after 185 Squadron. Had just reached them and were about to form up on them when the bombers, Ju88s, approached. We were on the point of attacking, but down came the Messerschmitts before we could. I saw them, little silver specks, above us. 'Duck' was shouted – half the formation to turn steep to port and the other half steeply to starboard. This was a dangerous manoeuvre for we had to turn into sun and for a moment or so I could not even see my No1. Picked him up again but next time we passed into the sun I just caught sight of 109s diving down; looked at them, looked back for my No1, blinded by sunshine and could see nothing; out of the sun again, didn't know which of the Hurricanes was my No1. Cursed myself for losing him. Hurricanes passing at all angles, think 109s had come and gone by now – was turning very steeply and slipping violently from side to side, twisting around to keep a good look out behind as far as possible.

The mêlée dispersed. I was over Hal Far at 7,000 or 8,000 feet. Some Hurricanes were weaving about in different directions at the same height. Wandered around looking for my No1. The R/T was telling someone to land. I couldn't make out who. I was not going to until I'd met something. I waited around by myself hoping something would turn up. I think I'd rather tired of weaving violently and straining my neck to look at my tail – a dishonourable occupation, though admittedly most necessary when you are in an old Hurricane and the enemy is the latest Messerschmitt. This solved my question of what to do – somebody found me! I heard machine-gun fire mixed with the fire of one cannon. I heard it rather closer that I'm normally accustomed, so I looked around, and there beside me, to be sure ,was a little silver-grey Messerschmitt with big black crosses. Not very good shooting, I thought. My turn now. He was passing me very fast on my starboard side about three wing spans away. The silly ass turned across me in a steep, climbing turn as I moved my sights on his receding personage.

I pulled up my nose and gave him a burst with deflection at 250 yards. Unfortunately he was climbing fast and to keep my sights on, my nose had to be pulled high, bringing me to the stall; and only the two starboard guns fired. The recoil of cannon being on one side only caused the aircraft to skid. The 109 flicked and for a moment I wondered if I'd hit him; but I saw no trace of hits on him and think I missed, but that I got near enough to make him feel anxious. If my other cannon had fired I should possibly have got him. Anyway, his continued climb was too much for me and, after this burst, I could keep my sights on him no longer. Stalling completely, I went over in a vicious spin. Came out in a vertical dive. Knew my ailerons were OK. As to whether he'd shot up my tail it remained to be seen. Eased back on the tail trim and we flattened out OK at about 4,000 feet right over Hal Far aerodrome. Climbed up to about 8,000 feet and stooged around for a while – weaving this time but nothing attacked me and I saw nothing to attack.

On approaching the aerodrome I saw three aircraft wrecked on it. Landed between them and saw 'C', my No1's aircraft, up on its nose, the most spectacular. Found I was the only one of the four to return in one piece, though I had two explosive bullets through my starboard wing. Thanked God for my safe return. Apparently my luck was even better that I supposed, for people saw my scrap with the 109 from the ground – the 109 had his No2 with him behind me, and that No2 followed me down in my spin a little way. He probably thought I was finished, as did those on the ground, when I span. The starboard mainplane had to be changed. One of the bullets pierced the main spar; however, it stood up to a vertical dive with full throttle."

Sgt John Alderson, who had taken over as 185 Squadron's diarist, added:

"The Squadron was ordered to land as quickly as possible. Two 109s seemed to think we weren't landing quick enough so they shot us up as we were coming in. They got three aircraft which were luckily already on the ground and caused bags of panic to people in the middle of the drome who were making noises like pieces of rock. P/O Oliver, in a power dive from 8,000 feet, looked like catching them but when they saw him they opened their throttles – and he seemed to be going the other way."

Apart from Macnamara's and Thompson's damaged aircraft – the latter having been hit by Bofors fire as he returned to Hal Far, necessitating a one-wheel landing – that flown by Plt Off Oliver (Z2982/GL-O) of 185 Squadron had also been damaged by Bofors fire as he was closing in on the two Messerschmitts that had attacked him. He was not hurt and his aircraft not seriously damaged. Sgts Jolly (Z5158) and Vardy (Z2819/GL-W) of the same unit also returned with damaged aircraft. Although no Hurricanes were lost, four were claimed shot down by the pilots of 6/JG53, Oblt Otto Böhmer opening the score with his eighth victory at 1005, followed two minutes later with another by Obfw Rudolf Ehrenberger (his 16th). Two more were claimed at 1010 by Oblt Helmut Belser (14th) and Uffz Paczia (his first). There was further action in the afternoon, as noted by Plt Off McKay:

"After lunch two 88s went over, and three 109s, but there was no activity. About three o'clock there was another raid and another terrific dogfight. We stood and watched S/Ldr Pike take on three 109s. His chances of living were about 1 to 109, but he put up a damn good show and got away with it."

The action in which Sqn Ldr Pike battled alone with three Bf109s had resulted in him becoming separated from the remainder of his squadron (185), nine of which had taken off under his leadership to intercept the fighter sweep. Pike (Z2815) claimed damage to all three of his assailants, while Flg Off Rhys Lloyd[23] (Z5155) claimed to have shot down one of the two he engaged. It was on returning from this scramble that Sgt Forth lost control of his Hurricane (Z4943) and crashed at Hal Far, being killed instantly. Airman X of 185 Squadron witnessed the demise of the popular Sgt Forth:

> ". . . one of ours dived straight in on the drome. The pilot was Sgt Jimmy Forth; he was a wizard bloke, flat out for us erks. We found him minus head and legs. There wasn't much left of his Hurribird."

Next day AHQ sent a signal to Hal Far wishing to know the name of the pilot who had used obscene language over the R/T when calling for assistance! It read:

> "Forward name of 'Mustang' pilot [Mustang was 185 Squadron's call sign] who used following language over R/T yesterday, south of Hal Far: 'You shits, assholes, assholes . . .'"

The offending pilot was of course Sqn Ldr Pike but in view of his fine performance and lucky escape, the name of 185 Squadron's CO was not proffered. Sgt John Alderson wrote in the diary:

> "The CO spent an amusing half hour trying to extract a confession from various people. We came to the conclusion that the offender was the CO himself, but it afterwards appeared that the signal was an example of the Wingco's low humour."

At about 1500, 249 Squadron scrambled four Hurricanes led by Flt Lt Sid Brandt to investigate a report that Messerschmitts were attacking the Gozo ferryboat, the *Marie Georgette*. On arrival over the Gozo Channel they saw that the schooner was in fact on fire and that German fighters were still in the vicinity. These engaged and Lt Joachim Louis of Stab/JG53 promptly shot down one of the Hurricanes (his first victory), but failed to notice another, flown by Plt Off James Stuart, closing in on his own tail; Louis was wounded but managed to reach Comiso and land safely in Black <4. Meanwhile, Oblt Gerhard Michalski, 4 Staffelkapitän, succeeded in shooting down a second Hurricane. Plt Off Ormrod was among those watching the action:

> "The Hurricanes fought bravely but had little chance. They had gone out to assist one of our submarines that 109s were strafing[24]. After a little while one Hurricane returned in an undignified hurry, weaving to look behind. Saw the rest dogfighting. One Hurricane went into the sea with a splash. No sign of the pilot was seen. His machine had, I think, been hit and as he was coming back losing height one of the Messerschmitts had followed up behind him. We plainly saw the flash of the enemy's armament that caused the Hurricane to go in. Several 109s proceeded to mob the remaining Hurricane (don't know what happened to the fourth). One could see him twisting and turning below them as they climbed up and dived on him from all angles, he trying to meet them head-on. At last he burst into flames. We cheered when we saw a parachute open and drift slowly down. He landed in a dignified manner beside his aircraft that still burnt on the water. Saw the rescue launch [HSL129] go out and search around the first crash. Perhaps he was picked up by another launch, the second crash being a few miles north of the Bay up the coast."

At the first opportunity an RN Swordfish was despatched from Hal Far to search for the missing pilots, but returned after a fruitless three hours. Despite the search and rescue attempts, both Flt Lt Brandt[25] and Sgt Roy Lawson, a 20-year-old from Cheltenham (in BD834 and Z2829/G), were lost. The damaged ferryboat, which normally carried a crew of ten, also had on board a dozen passengers. When attacked, Marcel Theuma, the skipper, had rushed to the bridge, taken the helm and succeeded in heading the vessel towards St George's Trenches. The Messerschmitts returned to the attack and Theuma was struck by a bullet; one of the crew was killed as was a passenger. The vessel was beached and the survivors jumped into the sea. All bar one were saved as rescuers – soldiers in the vicinity – formed a human chain to get them ashore. The severely wounded master was taken to St Patrick's Military Hospital where he died the following day.

During the late afternoon four Ju88s raided Luqa, with the escort provided by a dozen Bf109Fs from I/JG53; Plt Off McKay recorded:

> ". . . the siren had barely stopped when it went again and, in about ten minutes, I saw four Ju88s just above the clouds directly over Luqa where they dropped their bombs. The ack-ack opened up with everything they had on them but they all went right through it. Apparently some Wellingtons getting ready for operations were hit – there isn't anything as loud as a Wellington with a bomb load going off."

Another witness to the raid was LAC Phil Chandler at Kalafrana:

> "Soon after tea we heard gunfire, and dashed out of the armoury to see the familiar black smoke going up from Luqa, the sky full of shell-bursts and three Ju88s flying towards us. One of them seemed to be in trouble; he came lower and lower, right over us, while every gun on the Station opened up. He passed behind the buildings, banking slightly and still descending. We heard later that he was down in the sea five miles off Valetta, having evidently turned north in an attempt to get home. The barrage was about the biggest I have yet seen – the sky being almost invisible for the shell-burst. The fire at Luqa seemed to be serious. Time after time during the evening the windows were nearly blown in as bombs went off. We heard later that ten Wimpys and the bomb dumps were hit. The fire was burning long after dark. The Swordfish went out after the raid but brought nobody back. HSL129 came back after dark, so it was impossible to see who was aboard, but the ambulance was waiting on the slipway. HSL129 has made about four trips today."

At Luqa about 15 aircraft had been destroyed, including nine Wellingtons; others were damaged. Fires had broken out in an area where several bombed-up Wellingtons were dispersed, and where a bomb dump was situated. Flt Sgt A.J.M. MacDonald, in charge of the Luqa Fire Section, attempted to extinguish the flames of one of the burning bombers with a portable fire hydrant. He was successful, thereby saving two other nearby Wellingtons from destruction. For this and other actions following raids on Luqa he was later awarded the BEM. It had been a very costly day for Malta's rapidly dwindling air force. Apart from the aircraft destroyed on the ground at Luqa, five Hurricanes had been lost in the air and a further six damaged, three of which had suffered additional damage during crash-landings.

In the afternoon 242 and 605 Squadrons were told to prepare to move on the 31st, necessitating the fitting of long-range tanks in readiness for the flight across the Mediterranean to North Africa. However, that evening the AOC over-ruled the signal owing to the serious losses sustained by the resident Hurricane squadrons and advised the squadron commanders that 242 and 605 were to remain to support them.

The last combat of the year occurred during the morning of 30 December. Just before midday ten Hurricanes from 126 and 249 Squadrons – the Takali Wing led on this occasion by Wg Cdr Bill Satchell[26], Takali's new Station Commander – were sent off as a raid approached. The bombers – five Ju88s of KGr806 – made for Luqa, Takali and the Dockyard, the Hurricanes intercepting. Wg Cdr Satchell (Z3766) chased one:

> ". . . alone I pursued the Ju88 out to sea and, unable to catch it, fired really well out of range but to my surprise immediately saw smoke pour from its starboard engine. Getting short of

fuel then, I returned to Takali. Later, the pilot of a PR aircraft reported seeing a Ju88 smoking from its starboard engine, in approximately the area where I had broken off the attack, crash into the sea. I was therefore credited with its destruction."

This aircraft may have been M7+AL flown by Oblt Georg Lust, which failed to return from the raid, although 249 Squadron submitted claims for one Ju88 destroyed and a second probably destroyed, as revealed in the official communique:

"Another Junkers which was set on fire by a Sergeant Pilot [Sgt Dennis Rex] was also seen to crash into the sea. Black smoke was pouring from another, which was trying to make for home after it had been attacked by another Sergeant Pilot [Sgt Hugh McDowall]."

The AA guns and Royal Navy gunners each claimed damage to Ju88s, to conclude a fairly successful day for the defenders, about which Plt Off Ormrod wrote:

"At noon another merry raid developed. 88s bombed Luqa once more and another Wellington burnt out. Four of these [Ju88s] passed over us afterwards. They flew solemnly across a little below 10,000 feet. As they passed right overhead I supposed they had something for us and edged back towards the shelter. However, nothing dropped on us. A few minutes later a terrific hullaballoo caused us to look up and over came an 88 at perhaps less than 2,000 feet. Everything seemed to be firing at him and two Hurricanes were attacking. One was closing in from behind and was, I fancy, rather put off by the Bofors guns, which were behind their target as is usually the case (due to obsolete predictors). The guns did stop to give the fighters a chance to close eventually. This the fighters had difficulty in doing, as their speed was insufficiently in excess of the bomber to allow nicely positioned attacks. They disappeared into cloud with the bomber."

The Ju88s also bombed Kalafrana and Hal Far; Ormrod continued:

"The others have just told me of their humorous actions when a bomb whistled down this evening. Heard it screaming down and soon we heard the loud whistle of the bomb coming our way. I fell prone outside the room in the hall. Wiggles [Plt Off Phil Wigley] rushed inside on all fours. Lowe [Plt Off Peter Lowe] shot back through the front door and skidded past me on his belly. The others fell in the dust outside. The bomb, however, burst at the other side of the aerodrome."

By contrast, the last day of the year proved relatively uneventful, with only one small raid by three Ju88s shortly after lunch, as Sgt Ted Wood recalled:

"Just after lunch at least three Ju88s dived-bombed camp with very little opposition. Saw the first aircraft just pulling out and a moment later heard the scream of bombs. Stones and rocks went hurtling up and came down around me as I crouched up against the mess wall. Others exploded just off dispersal. Found that they had gone off about 100 yards away, one right against a billet wall. Only the roof came in slightly. Another landed right outside the door but did not explode. Two more made terrific holes nearby. Caused quite a stir. People could not get down shelter for crowds on top. One person injured by shrapnel."

With the close of December, AHQ reported that during the month the fighters had been officially credited with nine destroyed, eight probables and eight damaged, taking the totals for the 18 months since the start of hostilities in June 1940 to approximately 190 destroyed, 78 probables and 79 damaged, including those claimed by the Gladiators, FAA Fulmars and Beaufighters operating from Malta. The AA defences were credited with an additional 50 destroyed/probably destroyed. Against these claims, a variety of figures were subsequently published for the Axis air forces which provide some measure of comparison, bearing in mind that the quoted Italian losses of 105 (57 bombers and dive-bombers, two torpedo-bombers and 46 fighters) were to both fighters and AA fire, while Luftwaffe losses

– 33 Ju88, 29 Ju87, ten He111, four Bf110, two Bf109, and three Ju52/3m – were due to all operational causes.

On the debit side, 47 Malta fighter pilots had been killed in action or had died as a result of enemy action, including one FAA pilot. Six were killed in flying accidents and three were taken prisoner. Additionally, about 15 pilots had been lost while ferrying Hurricanes to Malta, including those lost on the first ferry flight way back in June 1940. A further 12 pilots had been seriously wounded. One Gladiator, at least 90 Hurricanes and three Fulmars had been lost in action, while many more had been destroyed on the ground. A further ten Hurricanes and two Fulmars had been written-off in accidents. Italian fighter claims against Malta's defenders are unknown, but the Luftwaffe claimed 84 RAF aircraft shot down over or around Malta during 1941: 76 Hurricanes, two Gladiators (actually a Swordfish and an Albacore), two Blenheims, one Wellington, one Sunderland, and two unspecified types.

At about three minutes before midnight on the night of 31 December/1 January, a single Ju88 appeared over Takali airfield in bright moonlight and carried out half a dozen strafing attacks. Five minutes later a repeat attack was made to welcome in 1942. Sgt Wood was up in his black Hurricane shortly into the New Year but had no success:

> "Went on at night. New Year's Eve. Weather cleared and nearly a full moon. Just wishing everybody a Happy New Year at 0001 hours when the dispersal was shot-up and bombs dropped near SHQ. Two more came just afterwards and dropped more bombs in dispersals. Getting quite shaky but things quietened down a bit. I did one scramble but saw nothing."

For the Hurricane squadrons in particular, 1942 would be a grim and costly year.

CHAPTER IX

AGAINST THE ODDS

January – February 1942

New Year's Day proved relatively quiet and uneventful, perhaps due to the night's celebrations on the various Sicilian airfields. There was only one alert, shortly before midday, when three Ju88s and at least a dozen Bf109Fs of II/JG53 approached Malta, bombs falling along the southern coast and damaging a number of fishing vessels. Hurricanes from 126 and 249 Squadrons scrambled, Blue Section (Plt Offs Les Barnes and Andy Anderson) of the former unit engaging one Ju88, as Anderson subsequently reported:

> "I dived head-on at one Ju88 as he was doing his dive. On seeing me he released his bombs. No strikes observed. I then came up astern and fired continuously, closing from 350-200 yards. Continuous return fire from 88's lower rear-gun. Numerous strikes observed on 88 including some on port engine nacelle. I then attempted to get the pilot by diving, and then climbing vertically under the 88, giving deflection shots; strikes also seen on fuselage. I then lost 88 in cloud but he came out of cloud in a good position for beam attack, which I carried out. No results observed as ammo gave out almost immediately button was pressed. While making these attacks, P/O Barnes was doing beam attacks on the same machine and also observed strikes from his fire."

After dark the raiders returned, one of which dropped bombs on the little town of Gzira in the heavily-populated area around Grand Harbour, killing 27 civilians and wounding eight others. Air Vice-Marshal Lloyd, who had been dining with squadron and flight commanders in a small restaurant in Valetta, had a narrow escape when a heavy bomb – described as a rocket bomb – exploded nearby, causing extensive damage. A number of night fighter Hurricanes were up including one flown by Wg Cdr Satchell but no interceptions were made.

Sqn Ldr Peter McGregor, who had just taken command of 185 Squadron from tour-expired Sqn Ldr Pike, was soon in action with his new unit. At 1515 on the afternoon of 2 January, he led ten Hurricanes to intercept an incoming raid; two formations comprising four Ju88s and an estimated dozen Bf109s being engaged about ten miles north-east of Grand Harbour. McGregor (BD702) and his No2, Sgt Archie Steele (Z2840), believed they jointly inflicted damage on a Ju88, while Sgt Jock Sutherland (Z4014) chased a Bf109 back to Sicily and claimed it probably destroyed but his own aircraft was hit and he suffered slight wounds: "I tackled a 109 and another tackled me so I gave one a headache and the other gave me a sore leg containing some cannon shell splinters. I got a probable for the first 109." In Grand Harbour the target of the bombers, the supply ship *Breconshire*, sustained some damage although she was able to sail six days later. Guns claimed damage to both a Messerschmitt and a Ju88.

By night, Hal Far and Luqa were the targets for an estimated 26 intruders, most of which were Ju88s but including five Z1007bis of 9°Stormo BT. Flying throughout the hours of darkness in relays, the Ju88s would dive on Luqa to drop a single bomb, climb and fly out to sea, only to return for another attack until their bomb loads were exhausted. Three Wellingtons were burnt out. All hands were required to clear the rubble and hundreds of butterfly bombs, and to fill-in bomb craters. Even the AOC and members of his staff lent a hand. Two civilians were killed and six injured on Malta, and a further two killed and five injured on Gozo. Night fighter Hurricanes were up for the first alert and the latter part of the third alert, but there were no illuminations.

At 0840 on the 3rd, seven Hurricanes each from 126 and 249 Squadrons scrambled from Takali. They were followed ten minutes later by eight more from 185 Squadron led by Flt Lt Lloyd. Climbing to 20,000 feet, newly promoted Flt Lt Les Barnes leading the 126 Squadron formation spotted two Ju88s over Luqa about 5,000 feet below. The unaccustomed height advantage was not to be wasted and Plt Off John Russell engaged one of the Ju88s which was heading westwards, having dropped its bombs, before being obliged to break away by one of the escorting Messerschmitts. He later reported:

"On patrol as Yellow 2 at about 18,000 feet. Sighted two Ju88s over Luqa. Attacked one steering west at about 12,000 feet with full beam shot, broke away and returned to attack from beam following to quarter from above. Broke away because of 109 on tail. One engine caught fire and one parachute left aircraft. Sighted Red 1 delivering attacks. Aircraft crashed near Takali after three more parachutes left the aircraft."

The American Plt Off Ed Streets (Red 1) took up the attack:

". . . saw one Ju88 over Luqa, [also] three or four 109s. Attacked Ju88 immediately after Yellow 2 delivered attack – followed enemy until all types baled out, firing at all time from quarter to stern until it span in and burned up; followed it down to 0 feet. Return fire from rear-gunner until he baled out."

The same aircraft was also attacked by Sgt Garth Horricks (Z5158/V) and Sgt Ray Ellis (Z2982) of 185 Squadron, the Canadian noting in his logbook:

"I attacked Ju88 from rear quarter and set its port engine on fire. It crashed near Takali. Rear gunner put ten bullets in my plane. I was hit in left arm."

A pilot of 249 Squadron, Plt Off John Hulbert, followed the bomber attacked by Horricks and opened fire at close range. He reported that its port engine was already on fire when he attacked, and he was now able to gain strikes on the other which then poured black smoke; the aircraft was last seen in a dive, and was credited as probably destroyed. The victim of all this attention was M7+AK of 2/KGr806, flown by Oblt Viktor Schnez, which eventually crashed in a field near Zebbug and exploded. Its approach was witnessed by Maltese civilian John Galea:

"I spotted a Ju88 coming towards Zebbug, smoking and getting lower and lower. I counted three aircrew bale out. The pilot still controlled the aircraft – it was nearing my village but luckily just clear of the buildings. The plane turned over, the pilot came out and his parachute opened almost at once as otherwise he would not have survived – he was very low . . . Soldiers and policemen arrived with the crowd which was not in a friendly mood. The pilot was brought along the narrow streets surrounded by the soldiers. A woman had some hot coffee in a tin and threw the stuff at the German but hit a couple of soldiers instead."[1]

All of the Ju88's crew survived. A further account is provided by Sgt Ron Gillman, a Blenheim pilot, who wrote:

"He [the Ju88] was almost above us when the Hurricane, which was closing fast, opened fire. There was a long deep trill of the guns and the Jerry went into a steep turn to the left. The fighter swung wide, and then tightening its turn he came round on the bomber's tail again. The machine-guns rattled again and a puff of smoke shot from the starboard engine of the Junkers. Shouts and cheers went up from the growing crowd on the balcony . . . a further long burst from the fighter extracted a tail of flame from the damaged engine. More shouts went up from the watching crowd as three black dots fell from the crippled machine. Then the white canopies of their parachutes blossomed . . . The dark grey Junkers flicked on to its back, the nose dropped gracefully, then it went into a vertical spin which became more vicious with each turn, the black smoke twisting into a corkscrew shape behind it . . . The fourth body was hurled from the spinning aircraft. It fell for several seconds, then the parachute cracked into shape behind it. An involuntary cheer went up from the onlookers."[2]

Another graphic account of the demise of Schnez's aircraft came from Maj Francis Gerard:

"The Ju88s were coming in much lower than usual. Two of them were turned by the harbour barrage and swung right-handed. One of them, at about 2,000 feet, was heading straight across us up the Birkirkara Valley. A Hurricane came sweeping across the sky in a long, graceful curve. We heard the sudden crackle of its eight machine-guns and then the bomber was flying with a plume of smoke in its wake. Another squirt from the fighter . . . Quite suddenly the bomber tucked its nose between its legs and rushed towards the earth, flaming like a torch. The impact as it struck was plainly audible. We watched the second Ju88 which had turned away towards Hamrun. There were two fighters on his tail. We heard later that they had shot him down."[3]

Plt Off Howard Coffin, another of 126 Squadron's American pilots, also attacked one of the Ju88s – possibly the aircraft flown by Oblt Kurt Kehrer. As he saw his fire hitting home, he was set upon by a pair of the escort, which he mistakenly identified as Italian fighters, apparently being shot down by Oblt Michalski Staffelkapitän of 4/JG53:

"Shot down by two Macchis who hit me from behind just as I was closing in on a bomber for a squirt. They used cannon shells and almost blew my ship out of the sky; it was riddled with holes. I was hit in the arms and legs by shrapnel. Gas began pouring out of my tank and I was afraid it would catch on fire. When I pancaked, a wheel came off and I crashed. I woke up 24 hours later. They had pulled a couple of pounds of shrapnel out of my legs and arms and I guess shot me full of dope because I felt all right. I tried to get up but my legs wouldn't work. The doctor came along – 'Got a date in Valetta', I mumbled."[4]

While Coffin was carrying out his crash-landing at Takali, the fighting raged overhead. Sgt Horricks also had a pot shot at the second Ju88, as did Sgt Dave Howe of 605 Squadron who was flying with 185 Squadron on his sortie, but the unit suffered the loss of Z5155 when Sgt Westcott was shot down by Bofors fire, baling out and landing in the sea with slight wounds. He was picked up almost immediately by the rescue launch from Kalafrana; his aircraft crashed near the Officers' Mess at Kalafrana. He later related how one cannon shell had entered his cockpit from over his shoulder and then struck the bullet-proof windscreen from the inside but without piercing it. Another pilot of this unit, Plt Off Reeves, reported seeing a Messerschmitt blow up when hit by AA fire and, in fact, Uffz Werner Mirschinka of 4/JG53 (White 12) was lost. On the ground at Luqa, a Wellington and a Whitley were destroyed by bombs, and a second Wellington was strafed by a Bf109 and destroyed. Plt Off McKay witnessed Uffz Mirschinka's demise:

". . . the port wing and also the starboard wing came off and came down in pieces. The fuselage came down, turning over very slowly until it hit the deck. No one got out . . . After this, the Hurricanes all came back to the drome and while they were re-arming and refuelling – we were all standing around – we heard and saw three 88s at about 8,000 feet coming towards the drome. Everyone just stood there for a moment and then made a mad dash for the nearest shelter. This was quite a jam, and seeing everyone wanted to be first in, when I arrived I had to walk (should I say run) over a couple of the boys lying in the doorway. I didn't get any farther than the door. This was the first time I had ever looked up and seen a bomb whistling straight down at me, and I must say it didn't help my consti- tution any. The bombs fell all around the drome and some very near the aircraft which were not dispersed. My kite had three holes in it made by bomb splinters, so was again unserviceable. After this raid the AOC arrived and gave us a little fireside chat on how important it is that the air defence is kept up. We came to think of healthier places to be."

Although there were no casualties, 605 Squadron's Sgt Doug Robb was badly shaken when a bomb landed outside the Sergeants' Mess near to where he was standing. Now it was the turn of the night raiders. An estimated 20 bombers crossed the coast between 2220 and 0530 on the 4th, and dropped bombs in widely scattered locations, although Luqa was again the main target, where two Wellingtons, a Maryland and a Blenheim were badly damaged, while 69 Squadron's PR Hurricane Z3123 sustained repairable damage. During the raid, as working parties continued filling craters, a bomb exploded amongst one team killing four airmen. A number of 1435 Flight Hurricanes vainly attempted interceptions but only Flg Off Tommy Thompson briefly engaged a Ju88 in a head-on encounter, claiming some damage. Although the guns reported shooting down one raider and probably another, apparently just one Ju88, B3+CA of Stab I/KG54, returned to Sicily having been hit by AA fire which wounded the pilot.

There were two raids during daylight hours of the 4th, the first comprising 30 aircraft which were reported heading for Luqa. This latest threat was met by three Hurricanes from 185 Squadron led by Flt Lt Peter Thompson, two from 605 (Plt Off Joe Beckett and Sgt Howell) and one from 242 (Sgt Tony Boyd), all hastily scrambled from Hal Far. These were at once engaged by ten escorting Bf109Fs of II/JG53. During the ensuing skirmish, strikes were claimed on a single Messerschmitt while two Hurricanes suffered minor damage in return including BG753 flown by Sgt Vardy of 185 Squadron, which was hit in the radiator causing a bad oil leak. One Hurricane was credited to Obfw Herbert Rollwage as his 12th victory – his first over Malta, and two more were claimed by Oblt Helmut Belser (15th) and Oblt Kurt Brändle (30th). AA gunners claimed another Ju88 shot down and indeed Lt Friedrich Müller's 7T+KH of KüFlGr606 went down off the Sicilian coast with the loss of the crew. Plt Off McKay, who was not flying, noted:

> "Some 88s and 109s were over and dropped a packet on Luqa again. The Hurricanes engaged them but none were shot down. Joe Beckett got a squirt at a 109 but saw no effect. Sgt Howell came down and there were two bullet holes in his windscreen and a side panel had been shot away. He didn't see anything . . . This afternoon we were told we are going to stay here and operate. I certainly knew of healthier places after watching that raid of 54+ coming in this afternoon. The sky was absolutely filled with 109s and they aren't the easiest thing to fight with if you are in a Hurricane. The raid wasn't very successful and most of the bombs landed in the sea."

Although both 242 and 605 Squadrons were to remain at Malta, the latter unit's two senior pilots did not. The CO, Sqn Ldr Reid, was troubled by defective eyesight while Flt Lt Bird felt he was not up to leading the Squadron into battle; both departed for the Middle East forthwith. To make good this shortfall, Flt Lt Syd Andrews of 242 was promoted and posted to command 605, while newly promoted Flt Lt Titch Palliser arrived from 249 Squadron to command A Flight; within the unit, Plt Off George Allen was promoted to take over B Flight, and within 242 Plt Off Paddy Kee was promoted to fill Andrews' vacated position.

Demonstrating Malta's continuing ability to hit back, a force of 11 Blenheims set out to raid Castelvetrano airfield during the afternoon. Following take-off, one Blenheim developed engine trouble as its pilot struggled to gain height. Fearing a crash, the pilot ordered the bombload to be jettisoned. These narrowly missed the Sergeants' Mess at Takali. Jubilant crews returning from the raid believed they had destroyed at least 30 aircraft on the ground and damaged many more. Three Wellingtons repeated the assault on Castelvetrano after dark. One failed to return, probably the victim of a Ju88C of 4/NJG2. As a result of these two attacks five SM82 transports, four Z1007bis, a CR42, a Ju52/3m and a Luftwaffe SM82 were all destroyed, and no less than 42 other machines damaged. This would seriously hinder the Axis air ferry service to North Africa. An immediate retaliatory raid was launched by the Luftwaffe, Takali being selected as the main target. There were no military casualties but three civilians were killed. LAC Metcalf recalled:

"The old sod gave us what for at Takali. The third stick set the petrol bowser on fire and the Service Police kicked us out of bed and down the Madhouse shelter. Seven Hurricanes were damaged by bomb splinters . . ."

Storms which had raged over Sicily during the past few days now reached Malta, and Takali was soon waterlogged and rendered unfit for flying. Operations from Sicily and Malta were severely restricted, but the conditions did allow a heavily escorted, southward-bound, Italian convoy to reach Tripoli. Neither did the poor weather prevent 69 Squadron's reconnaissance aircraft from ranging far and wide, the Marylands were now supplemented by the arrival of a Beaufighter. Two enemy convoys were located off Taranto and near Tripoli and, after dark, three torpedo-carrying Swordfish and a similar number of Albacores were despatched to carry out attacks, sinking one freighter and possibly damaging a second. Although there was little operational flying during the next few days, aircraft continued to arrive from Gibraltar, using Malta as a staging post for destinations further east. Not all of those making the long and arduous 1,000 mile journey arrived safely. Some were lost due to various problems en route, others missed landfall, and some fell victim to German and Italian fighters. Two Beaufighters, two Blenheims and a Hudson were all lost during this enforced break in operations. On Malta, some of the pilots and aircrew took the opportunity to live it up, as recorded by 185 Squadron's Sgt Jock Sutherland:

"On the evening of the 9th we had a party in the dispersal hut. We had champagne and beer to wash down sausages and eggs fried by Tommy, ably assisted by a few keen types. During the course of a hilarious evening we amused ourselves by putting Very cartridges in the stove, and shooting at a bottle placed on a window ledge with a .38 revolver."

The Hurricanes' next contact with the Messerschmitts was on 12 January when 242 Squadron scrambled a flight to intercept a small fighter sweep. Cloud and rain prevented any conclusive results, although strikes were claimed on two of the Messerschmitts. In return Plt Off Jimmy Tew's Hurricane was slightly damaged. Next day, 69 Squadron suffered the loss of its CO, Wg Cdr Dowland, and his air gunner when their Maryland was shot down by two Bf109Fs off Tigne Point. Only the observer was able to bale out. Lt Hans-Volkmar Müller of 5/JG53 was credited with this, his seventh victory. It was mistakenly thought that one of the attackers was shot down by the Maryland's gunner before his own demise. Later, a small force of II/KG77 Ju88s raided Hal Far, where two Hurricanes including Z2592 of 185 Squadron were severely damaged on the ground, and Plt Off Ormrod's BG713/UP-O and 185's GL-N were both slightly damaged by bomb splinters. Two Skuas and a Swordfish were, however, destroyed, and there were a number of casualties including two soldiers and a civilian. AA gunners were successful in shooting down Oblt Walter Biemer's 5 Staffel aircraft, 3Z+CN falling into the sea with the loss of the crew. On the morning of the 14th, during a patrol over shipping south-east of Kalafrana, Flt Lt Carpenter of 126 Squadron encountered a lone Ju88 which he claimed to have damaged in a series of attacks before the aircraft was lost in cloud.

69 Squadron almost lost another Maryland to Messerschmitts on the afternoon of 15 January, when it was attacked by a pair of Bf110s of III/ZG26 as it returned to Malta. Although severely damaged, the pilot managed to belly-land the Maryland at Luqa, during which two of the crew suffered injuries. Pairs of patrolling Hurricanes were unable to make contact with any of the raids during the day despite six attempted interceptions. The heaviest raid was directed against Hal Far where a Swordfish and a Skua were hit and set on fire. Luqa was also targeted and a Blenheim there was damaged beyond repair, while a submarine was damaged at its base at Manoel Island. Next day (16 January), 21 Hurricanes from 126, 242 and 249 Squadrons were sent after an estimated 15 bandits. While patrolling in two formations at 12,000 and 16,000 feet, three Ju88s were seen far below, going west at about 8,000 feet, with a close escort of two Bf109Fs. Despite the numerical and height

advantage, the best that could be achieved was a few strikes on one bomber by Plt Off Andy Anderson of 126 Squadron.

A late afternoon raid by three Ju88s, on the 17th, brought a similar inconclusive result for Wg Cdr Rabagliati. After pursuing one bomber down to 1,000 feet, firing at and stopping its starboard engine in the process, he was engaged by the escorting Messerschmitts and forced to abandon his quarry. Not so fortunate was an intruding Ju88C of 4/NJG2. At 0645 on the morning of the 18th, R4+MM flew into a hillside at Ghar Mundu near Rabat. The pilot, Lt Felix-Dieter Schleif, apparently lost his bearings in 10/10th cloud. He and his crew were killed. The following night a second Ju88C was lost over Malta while trailing a returning Wellington, R4+AH being shot down into the sea with the loss of Lt Herbert Haas and his crew, which included a war correspondent.

After a period of relative quiet for the Hurricane pilots, 19 January proved to be a day of intense aerial activity. Frustrated at being on the receiving end of continuous attacks, and in order to lift flagging morale, Wg Cdr Rabagliati led a mini pre-emptive, early morning strike against Comiso airfield, home to the bombers of KG77 and Bf109s of II/JG53. With him were Sqn Ldr Beazley and Flt Sgt Fred Etchells of 249 Squadron, and Plt Off John Russell of 126 Squadron. Each aircraft was armed with eight 20-lb fragmentation bombs. Drums of aviation fuel were set on fire and two Ju88s were claimed probably destroyed on the ground, but Sqn Ldr Beazley's aircraft (BV174) suffered engine problems and he was subsequently forced to crash-land at Luqa on return. Before midday Wg Cdr Rabagliati was off again. While leading a patrol from 249 Squadron over a convoy approaching Grand Harbour from the west, he spotted and attacked a twin-engined aircraft which he initially identified as a Ju88. It was in fact a PR Beaufighter (T4705) returning from a reconnaissance of the Cyrenaican coastline, whose crew reporting being attacked five times by a Hurricane patrol and also being fired upon by ships of the allied convoy. The attacks only ceased when the colours of the day were fired by the Beaufighter, which was piloted by the renowned Flt Lt Adrian Warburton. Plt Off Harry Moon was involved in the attack:

> "There was a steady stream of Ju88s and 109s in thick cloud. Saw twin-engined aircraft and attacked but thought it might be a Blenheim and broke away. Later heard that a dinghy was seen and feared that I had shot down the Blenheim after all, but it turned out to be the crew of an Albacore shot down by 109s. The aircraft I attacked was in fact a Maryland [*sic*] flown by Flt Lt Warburton. I later apologised but Warburton seemed unconcerned."

When Wg Cdr Rabagliati also apologised to Warburton over a drink, the latter allegedly responded:

> "I don't mind, sir, that you don't know the colours of the day. You opened fire on me. I took evasive action, and I think it is rather a poor show that when inspecting my aircraft, I found only one bullet hole in my left aileron!"[5]

Meanwhile, II/JG53's Messerschmitts were busy over the sea lanes, shooting down an Albacore[6] on an anti-submarine patrol off Pantelleria and, later, damaging a Swordfish on its landing approach to Hal Far, before being chased away by a Hurricane patrol from 242 Squadron. Sgt Ray Harvey (LE-R) claimed one of the Messerschmitts probably destroyed, and Plt Off Len Hall (BG698/U) fired at the other but made no claim. Shortly after midday a 70-plus raid was plotted, obviously heading for the incoming convoy. Hurricanes from 126, 242 and 249 Squadrons were patrolling as the Ju88s from KüFlGr606 arrived. Sqn Ldr Norris of 126 Squadron and his No2 Sgt Jack Mayall were joined by Flt Sgt Fred Etchells of 249 Squadron in attacking one of the bombers, but could only claim damage; Norris' aircraft was hit by return fire and he force-landed at Takali with a dead engine. Two others from his squadron, Flg Off Jack Kay and Plt Off Rocky Main, enjoyed greater success during a combined attack on another Ju88. Making several passes, they last saw their victim losing height at 2,000 feet with one engine stopped. They were credited with its probable destruction. This was undoubtedly Uffz Waldemar Nicolay's 1 Staffel aircraft (7T+GH) which failed to return and was reported by other crews to have been shot down by fighters. Plt Off Main also claimed damage to another Ju88, one more being hit by Flg Off Ces Baker. Due to the prompt intervention by the Hurricanes, no co-ordinated attack could be made on the convoy by the raiders and none of the ships was hit.

As the Hurricanes returned to Malta, Plt Off Graham Leggett and Sgt Alf Branch (Z3757/GN-R) of 249 Squadron were attacked from astern by three Bf109Fs over Luqa; the latter noted: "Jumped by three 109s at 2,500 feet and had starboard aileron control shot away. Got two bursts at 109. Claimed damaged – landed at Luqa OK." Nevertheless, his Hurricane was claimed shot down by Oblt Kurt Brändle of 5/JG53 as his 31st victory. Although the convoy escaped damage, Malta did not. Ju88s dropped their bombs indiscriminately over the island, hitting Kalafrana, Rabat, Zebbug, Takali and Mosta. At Takali four airmen were killed when their rock shelter received two direct hits, while a Hurricane and two Blenheims were damaged. During the raid 13 civilians were killed and four others later died from their injuries. While the raids were in progress, low-flying Messerschmitts hunted for targets of opportunity. Two strafed a submarine as it approached the entrance of Grand Harbour but inflicted only minor damage. Air Vice-Marshal Lloyd summed up the opening weeks of the new year:

"In the first twenty days of January, approximately 1,000 bombers had dropped their bombs upon our three aerodromes. By the end of the month the total was 1,500. As a rough estimate, 80 percent of the bombing was at night; the remainder was divided between aircraft using cloud cover and formations of three or four bombers heavily escorted by fighters. The Hurricanes were holding the enemy against great odds, and that was about all."[7]

There was little activity for the Hurricanes during the next two days, all three airfields being waterlogged after torrential rain. On the 21st, however, Ju88s raided Hal Far during the morning and three Hurricanes were damaged by shrapnel. Next day heralded better weather. Although Hal Far was still unfit for flying, conditions at Takali were improving and Luqa was serviceable. The first raid approached just after 1100, three Hurricanes from 126 Squadron, six from 242 and seven from 249 being scrambled. Three Ju88s from I/KG54 and five escorting Bf109Fs – misidentified on this occasion as MC202s – were sighted at 10,000 feet, ten miles east of Kalafrana. In an attack with his No2 (Sgt Harry Hale), Flt Lt Nigel Kemp (BG756/W) of 242 Squadron was able to claim one of the escorts as probably destroyed, while Sgt Jock Gardiner (LE-O) damaged one of the bombers. The leading section of Hurricanes then joined in, Plt Off Rocky Main attacking another Ju88 and seeing smoke pour from both its engines. His own aircraft was then hit in the engine by the rear-gunner and he was forced to break away. A third bomber was claimed damaged by the joint efforts of Plt Off Joe Crichton (Z2481) of 126 Squadron and two pilots of 249 Squadron, Flg Off Davis and Plt Off Don Tedford. Of the action, Crichton reported:

"Mixed squadron of 249/126 intercepted three 88s over Kalafrana at 15,000 feet, meeting enemy aircraft head-on. Enemy aircraft went into their dive and we followed them down. I got on the tail of one 88 and opened fire about 250 yards and closed right in. No return fire from gunner after my first burst; saw small pieces fly off the starboard engine. I broke away as I went past him and F/O Davis attacked enemy aircraft and it went into cloud. I gained height again and followed F/O Davis and again got into position and opened fire, but before I could get close I ran out of ammo so returned to base. P/O Tedford followed aircraft and when he last saw it, it was down to ten feet but both engines were still going."

Following debriefing, it was decided that two of the bombers had possibly been too severely damaged to reach their bases in Sicily, but in fact only Oblt Hans Schumacher's B3+GH failed to return, probably the victim of all four pilots.

At 1400 there was another scramble, five aircraft from 242 Squadron providing cover for six from 249 and two from 126. When just south of Filfla, the latter spotted three Ju88s and a dozen Messerschmitts, although the fighters were again misidentified as Macchis. Meanwhile, to the south-west, the top cover saw two more bombers and three fighters at 12,000 feet. Flt Lt Paddy Kee, leading the 242 Squadron flight, engaged the escort and claimed one damaged, while Sgt Tony Boyd (LE-P) went after the bombers, one of which he claimed destroyed after shooting out its starboard engine; he was granted a probable. As the Hurricanes drifted back to Takali the airfield gunners, ever-fearful of being surprised by strafing Messerschmitts, misidentified the returning fighters and opened up, hitting Sgt Donald Neale's aircraft (BE346). The 19-year-old Londoner, with much of his Hurricane's tail unit shot away, struggled to keep it under control as he attempted to land, but eventually spun in and crashed; he died instantly. Although his Hurricane was also hit, Sgt Ray Harvey managed to land his damaged machine without further incident. He later told an enquiring Plt Off Ormrod that all the fabric on the back of his aircraft was shot away, as was one elevator. To fly level he had to keep the stick forward but nonetheless made a safe landing. During these raids a number of bombers evaded the defending fighters and AA to attack Hal Far yet again. Several aircraft, including one Hurricane, were riddled by shrapnel.

While two Hurricanes patrolled over Luqa during the afternoon of 23 January, ten others from 126 and 249 Squadrons practised tactics until being called into action after ten hostiles were reported approaching Kalafrana. Five Ju88s and many Bf109Fs were seen, Flt Sgt Fred Etchells of 249 Squadron claiming possible damage to one of the bombers. Meanwhile, Flg Off Jack Kay of 126 Squadron attacked a Messerschmitt which emitted black smoke before he was chased away by other Bf109s. Flg Off Ces Baker claimed damage to a twin-engined aircraft he identified as a Do215, but was possibly an escorting Bf110 from III/ZG26. The fast Ju88s were very difficult to catch; of this frustrating period, Flt Sgt Etchells commented:

> "On several occasions, as I recall to my disgust, I saw an odd Ju88, unescorted and just asking to be shot down, but with all the power on, and nose down by 15 degrees, it was able to increase its distance between us. In retrospect, I realise that Malta had to take very low priority for good and modern fighters, and fear that a lot of our time was taken up by attempting to survive in well-used Hurricane Is, and later IIs, again very second-hand . . . We were quite aggressive as a fighter squadron, but soon learned that it was more necessary to keep a good look-out behind and above than looking for victims, as the 109s in particular had many thousands of feet advantage over us, plus an enormous speed advantage."

Both Luqa, where a Maryland was destroyed, and Hal Far were again raided, the airfields being left covered with bomb holes. The afternoon of the 24th saw further raids on Luqa and Hal Far, during which 15 Hurricanes (four/126, six/242, five/249) took to the air led by Wg Cdr Satchell. These were followed by a further eight from 185 Squadron led by Wg Cdr Rabagliati which intercepted three Ju88s from III/KG77 and eight Bf109Fs at 17,000 feet. Sgt Garth Horricks (BD704/H) attacked one bomber, chased it towards Luqa and shot out its port engine. He broke away when his own aircraft was attacked from astern by one of the escorting Messerschmitts. In an effort to escape, he rolled the badly damaged Hurricane on to its back and dived, landing at Hal Far without further incident. Meanwhile, Sgt Al Jolly of 185 Squadron pursued the same bomber. He had seen two fighters behind it, but thinking they were Hurricanes, he had cut across them in order to reach his target. It was only when the fighters shot at him that he realised they were Bf109s. He returned fire as they sped past and believed he had damaged one. 249 Squadron's Plt Off Harry Moon also engaged the bomber, gaining strikes, before his aircraft (DG612/H) was shot up by a Messerschmitt:

> "The cockpit filled with smoke and I opened the hood, ready to bale out, but the smoke cleared so I glided back to Luqa with a dead engine and landed with the wheels down. One

propeller blade had a cannon hole through it the size of a man's fist, and a bullet hole through the canopy beside my head."

One of the Hurricanes had evidently been attacked by Oblt Michalski of 4/JG53, who claimed one shot down at this time. Meanwhile, the radar blip indicating the bomber Horricks, Moon and Jolly had jointly attacked ultimately faded and they were credited with its destruction. This was undoubtedly an aircraft of 8/KG77 which crashed on returning to Castelvetrano, in which Lt Ernst Fischer and his crew were killed. Wg Cdr Satchell also reported being in a dogfight with one of the Messerschmitts, albeit without result.

Earlier in the month Sqn Ldr Westmacott, CO of 1435 Flight, had suggested to the AOC that, as Hurricane pilots were experiencing great difficulty in catching the fast Ju88s over Malta, his pilots might carry out night intruder sorties over Sicily to catch them over their own airfields. He suggested utilising some of the dozens of long-range fuel tanks which had been discarded by Hurricanes after use on ferrying operations. Fitted to the Flight's aircraft these would give them sufficiently increased endurance to enable intruder sorties to be undertaken. Air Vice-Marshal Lloyd enthusiastically agreed, particularly as he was also aware of an agent operating in Sicily who desperately required money and supplies to be dropped by air. The AOC enquired if Westmacott could help. Working with his ground staff, Westmacott devised a cylinder fitted with a small parachute which could be released via the Hurricane's flare tube. After several practice drops, the system was shown to work. The responsibility for these early secretive flights would fall upon Westmacott personally, but a number of other senior and experienced pilots would later also be involved, including Wg Cdr Satchell, Wg Cdr Hugh Dawson[8], and Flt Lt Don Stones.

Although practice flying had resulted in restricted manoeuvrability, Sqn Ldr Westmacott declared his unit ready to commence intruder operations as from the night of 24/25 January, and five Hurricanes set out after dark to patrol over the Sicilian airfields at Comiso and Catania. After half an hour over Comiso, Flg Off Palmer saw a Ju88 take off and promptly attacked; he reported that it disintegrated in the air. A second Ju88 was then seen taxiing on the airfield and this was also attacked and claimed damaged. None of the other pilots saw any suitable targets.

The defending fighters were hit hard next day (25 January), when a maximum effort was called for to cover two empty supply ships, which were departing the island with an escort of destroyers. To ensure minimum interference as the eastward-bound ships left Grand Harbour, Flt Lt Peter Thompson led off four 185 Squadron Hurricanes. He was closely followed by three more from 242 Squadron led by Flt Lt Kee, while eight others from 126 and 249 Squadrons provided top cover, although three of the latter were forced to return early, including that flown by Plt Off Harry Moon who managed to glide back to Takali with a dead engine when the supercharger sheared in BD789/G. As the ships passed Delimara Point, the northern promontory of Marsaxlokk Bay, four Ju88s and a dozen Bf109Fs (of 6/JG53) were seen approaching. Bouncing the top cover, Maj von Maltzahn's JG53 Stab flight of five Bf109Fs rapidly shot down three of the five Hurricanes, before diving to attack those at lower level, being joined by pilots of 6 Staffel. Plt Off Ormrod recorded what he witnessed of this epic one-sided contest:

"Could hear the fighters up in the sun. Thought it a dogfight, but could not be sure. The sun shone brilliantly from a clear blue sky. After a short time the flash of sunlight on aircraft fuselages attracted attention in the sky above Safi. The fighters had moved out of the sun. There was a fight in progress at an altitude in the neighbourhood of 15,000 feet, or a little less. Suddenly saw that a pilot was descending by parachute. At that height it appeared not to fall but be suspended in the air like some cloud or celestial body. He swung gently from side to side at the end of the shroud lines. The strange part was that we had noticed no crashing aircraft, nor could we see one now. Then an aircraft came spinning down viciously. Supposed it must be his – but no – it stopped its spin and continued diving vertically as another pilot made an exit from its cockpit and proceeded to descend gracefully by parachute. We were glad to see he was out, for the aircraft was a Hurricane.

Noticed another aircraft gliding down in wide spirals in the vicinity of this second pilot. Looked at it with my glasses. It was a Hurricane also. It was gliding inverted – most remarkable. It continued its inverted spiral glide until it disappeared from view shortly prior to striking the ground. This must have been the aircraft the first pilot baled out from. He most likely rolled on his back, to assist his departure from the machine which, being well trimmed forward, continued gliding in this position. Since the second parachutist baled out several thousand feet below the first, and since this aircraft was only losing height slowly, it was quite possible for it to come past the second parachutist, although he had baled out an appreciable time after the first, whose aircraft it was. Well, that was two Hurricanes down already and we had not long to wait to see more follow.

Another formation of Hurricanes curved round to our north. A single 109 was rapidly overtaking them from behind. Two peeled off towards this enemy; but the Messerschmitt flashed past them before they were fully turned and one, trying to turn too tightly, flicked into a spin. The Messerschmitt carried out the now considered obsolete No1 attack. He dived down and zoomed up underneath the tails of the Hurricanes. He fired at several and then appeared to pass through the middle of them all. After that I don't know where he went for I was watching a Hurricane that had fallen fast below the rest. It was crashing. The pilot baled out. The machine hurtled in a total velocity dive and though we could not see where it crashed, the sound reached my ears shortly after it had disappeared from my view – a thud mixed with a dull roar. Saw with regret that there was something amiss with the parachute. It opened to some extent; it was not streaming, but it twisted somehow as if a shroud line had passed over the top. Since he still had some distance to fall, and since it was slowing his descent, it was hoped that the pilot would untangle it. But he did not. I now suppose that I was witnessing the end of P/O Russell of 126 Squadron, though at the time I did not know who the pilot was."

Russell's aircraft (Z2827) fell into the sea and he was killed. 126 Squadron lost two more aircraft when Plt Off Chas Blackburn (BD828) baled out wounded, followed by Plt Off Andy Anderson (BG765); the latter came down over the island while Blackburn, having baled out over Hal Far, drifted out to sea from where he was soon recovered by a rescue launch from Kalafrana. Anderson wrote:

"I got shot down and had to make an undignified and hurried exit from my aeroplane. I'm still full of aches and pains but fortunately didn't damage myself. That's the third time I've baled out so I'm getting quite practiced at it now! Things are certainly lively around here nowadays."

Plt Off Charlie Sluggett (BV158), a Canadian from 242 Squadron, also drifted down safely to terra firma despite a badly burned face and a bullet through his left shoulder. He later related that he remembered the cockpit being full of oil. He tried to get out but at first was unable to do so due to his wound. When he finally undid his straps he just fell out as the dive of his aircraft was then over the vertical. The next thing he remembered was sitting on the ground. Two other 242 Squadron Hurricanes of the lower flight sustained damage and both crash-landed at Takali; Plt Off Morrison-Jones was unhurt but Flt Sgt Charlie Alpe had a number of shrapnel wounds, his aircraft having been "shot to pieces". Meanwhile, Flt Lt Thompson (Z5147) baled out near Hal Far:

"The enemy plots were estimated at being 20+ and 30+ and the Controller decided to scramble every available Hurricane. I was elected wing leader. We finally got together as a wing and then I think the Controller got the two plots mixed up. Certainly he put us down sun with the incoming plot above and behind us. Then my R/T packed up and I looked at my No2 to indicate my problem, but to my surprise his place had been taken by an Me109!

I took immediate avoiding action and hopefully set course for home when I saw bomb bursts on Hal Far airfield running from east to west. It was therefore easy to spot the bombers and they were at about 3,000 feet. With a height advantage I was able to catch them up. I had a go and was subsequently credited with a probable. It was only a few seconds after I had opened fire that I was severely clobbered. I had no option but to go ahead as the engine had been hit, as I also was [a bullet wound in his right arm]. I was then hit a second time and the aircraft caught fire. I baled out at very low altitude and the aircraft and I landed up very close to each other. I must add that the Ju88 probable was claimed for me by someone who apparently saw the action. For my part, I was in hospital and had lost all interest in the day's happenings."[9]

Thompson's Hurricane was probably that which crashed at Hal Tartarni near Dingli; another came down near the south-west perimeter of Qrendi airfield, a third in a field just south of Qrendi village, and a fourth near Zejtun. Two more Hurricanes were damaged in this extremely successful action by a handful of German pilots, although neither of the pilots, Flt Lt Crossey of 249 Squadron nor Sgt Doug Eastman (Z4014) of 185 Squadron, was hurt. Apart from the probable credited to Flt Lt Thompson, only Flt Lt Kee managed to make any form of claim against the attackers, believing that he had damaged one. The Messerschmitt pilots claimed eight Hurricanes shot down, two being credited to Maj von Maltzahn as his 54th and 55th victories, while Lt Franz Schiess (15th), Lt Joachim Louis (2nd) and Lt Karl-Heinz Preu (5th), all of Stab, claimed one apiece. The other three went to 6 Staffel pilots Oblt Otto Böhmer (9th), Obfw Rudolf Ehrenberger (17th) and Lt Dr Heiner Jörg (his first). Maj von Maltzahn later recalled his Stab's part in the mauling of the Hurricanes:

"I drew towards them [the Hurricanes] from behind with my five aircraft. Then, coming at them from the rear from out of the sun in wide curves, I set up the first attack against the five Hurricanes. This worked out well. We came in unnoticed, with me attacking the Hurricane laying on the extreme left. She was hit, went down immediately, and broke up in flames into the sea. Whereupon I collected together my flight and set up a second attack. The Hurricanes increased speed over the land and tried to climb above us. I allowed a little time in order to let my planes end their attack. Just then I saw two somewhat higher situated Hurricanes had curved around, apparently in order to position themselves behind us. But they didn't do this, though – to the contrary, they flew towards land. As a result I was able to push forward with the second attack without any harassment. Again I fixed my sights on the plane laying on the extreme left, thus allowing my comrades also to get going once more. Again the Hurricane received a direct hit. The pilot baled out. I saw him immediately afterwards, falling away from me over my cabin roof. At the same time two other Messerschmitts were attacking two enemy planes, which were likewise shot down and broke in flames on land. So that was three brought down.

The third attack I set up against the large squadron of 12 [sic] Hurricanes, of which two had already peeled off inland. Bringing in my aircraft from behind, I once more directed my attack on the left-hand plane. Now a real hurly-burly broke out, in the course of which I was no longer able to make out the fate of the shot-down plane. For sure, though, a further Hurricane was brought down by Lt Louis. The other planes went into a nose-dive in order to break away from us. They succeeded in this, except that they then had the bad luck to come into contact with the fighter escort [6/JG53] of our bombers which were just then flying a mission to Malta. As a result, two Hurricanes were shot down which, in their turn, plunged burning into the sea. Two more went down in a spin, trailing black smoke, but unfortunately it was not possible to observe their crash. On the other hand, Lt Preu pursued a Hurricane as far as the immediate vicinity of the coast, where he caught her and dealt with her at a height of 600 metres [possibly Flt Lt Thompson]. This was the eighth shooting-down. We must put it down to good luck that we came out of this combat completely unharmed, and returned to base without a casualty."

The overwhelming superiority of the Bf109F over the Hurricane had again been brought home. Ormrod continued with his observations:

"We were all very intent on watching the fighters and had not noticed the AA barrage behind us. Then someone noticed it and directed our attention to it, and we saw four Ju88s right above our aerodrome. Down into the shelter we went. Ron Noble called out the bombs were already falling, but would fall clear of us. Next moment there was a series of heavy explosions. We felt the blast. The bombs having been dropped, we emerged from the shelter once again, they'd dropped a stick down the aerodrome, eight or so bombs. A Swordfish, a new one, was blazing. Clouds of black smoke arose from it and it was hoped the torpedo would not explode. The aerodrome looks truly battered now, for besides the crashed Hurricanes strewn around and this burnt Swordfish and the bomb craters, there is another Swordfish lying on its belly."

Among the aircraft destroyed in the raid on Hal Far was Plt Off McKay's Hurricane, Z4315/UP-Y. Surprisingly, the Germans did not follow up their assault next day, thereby allowing the shocked Hurricane pilots time to recover and prepare for what the morrow might bring. Mid-morning on the 27th saw Wg Cdr Rabagliati leading a Hurricane patrol over an incoming convoy. Ju88s and Bf109s had been harrying the ships, but these departed with the arrival of the Hurricanes. Flt Lt Kemp (BG752) of 242 Squadron was apparently shot down on this occasion, as recalled by Plt Off McKay:

"F/Lt Nigel Kemp was shot up at about 15,000 or 20,000 feet south of the island. His aircraft caught fire and he baled out. The report around the dispersal hut after the scramble was that no one had seen him descend in his parachute and it was presumed that he had bought it. Late the following day, the ASR launch [HSL128] stationed in Valetta [*sic*] was informed that one of the pilots on a flight had seen a yellow dinghy some miles south of the island. The ASR launch was ordered to make a search, which it did, I believe rather unwillingly because of strafing by 109s. The yellow dinghy did in fact contain Nigel Kemp, who had managed to paddle for almost 24 hours and stay within reasonable distance of the island. When he appeared at Hal Far Mess he looked not unlike a lobster. His face and hands were severely sunburned. He had nothing to protect his head from the sun during the whole period."

As Malta was enjoying a welcome break from the constant raids, six Bf109Fs of 6/JG53 swept over Takali half an hour before dusk just as Hurricanes of 1435 Flight were preparing to take off for night flying practice. Plt Off Alex Mackie had just got into the air when three of the Messerschmitts closed in. It seems there followed a brief exchange of fire – onlookers thought one of the Messerschmitts fell into the sea – but Mackie's aircraft (Z3571/J) had been hit and crashed in a valley near St Catherine's church[10]; the Scots pilot was severely wounded and later died in hospital. Plt Off Jack Grant's aircraft was also shot up although he was unhurt. Following this harrowing experience, the unit carried out its practice flying at varying times throughout daylight hours and was never again caught in such a manner. Sgt Ted Wood wrote:

"Took off for air test, going along happily when I saw a column of smoke behind and just heard 'Three 109s' over R/T. Turned into sun and saw one in cloud, too far away. Heard that it was P/O Mackie, shot down with nothing on the board. Controller knew nothing about it. He was badly injured and died in hospital, one of the best lads I know. P/O Grant was also shot up."

The successful German pilot, Oblt Otto Belser, reported his victim as a Battle, presumably having been confused by the appearance of the black-painted Hurricane. Undaunted by the event, seven night fighter Hurricanes set off individually for Sicily at intervals, the first departing at 1725. One of the pilots was Sgt Wood, who patrolled a line between Catania and Comiso, commencing at 1925:

"Took off at 1915 for Catania. Uninteresting trip until I got there and then it scared me no end, heavy and light AA. Stayed there about an hour while they wasted ammunition. On the way back I saw the drome at Comiso lit up. Went towards it just in time to see an aircraft take off with lights on. Followed it round circuit up to 5,000 feet, got to within 50 yards and let him have it. First burst hit the engines and I hit the slipstream. Straightened up and a piece of burning wreckage just missed me. I fired again and blew the tail off. Broke away and saw it crash in flames. Mac's revenge. Came back and was congratulated."

Oblt Wolfhelm Dronke's 5/KG77 machine crashed near the airfield resulting in the deaths of two of the crew, including Dronke, the Staffelkapitän; the two survivors were both injured. About two hours later, Plt Off Grant saw a twin-engined biplane flying south of Augusta with its cabin lights on, and shot this down into the sea in flames. From the reported activity of vessels in the area, noted next day by a reconnaissance aircraft, it was assumed that some person or persons of importance had been aboard. Possibly the victim was a communications or training aircraft or even a civil machine. Another of the intruder Hurricanes, Z3562 flown by Sqn Ldr Westmacott, was slightly damaged in one wing by flak, following which he decided to circle Mount Etna for a break, only to have his aircraft hit by a bullet fired from the darkness below. On the conclusion of this successful night, marred as it had been by the death of Plt Off Mackie, Sqn Ldr Westmacott was gratified to receive, on behalf of the Flight, a message from the obviously delighted AOC; the signal read:

"My heartiest congratulations on the splendid performance of all pilots of the MNFU on night of 27th/28th January. A brilliant performance of which you may feel justly proud. Well done."

On the morning of 28 January, a reconnaissance Hurricane of 69 Squadron was lost. Sgt R. Ballantyne had set out for a sortie over southern Italy but his aircraft (Z3173) was hit by AA fire near Catanzaro; Ballantyne baled out, coming down near Marcellinara, where he was taken prisoner. Six Hurricanes of 605 Squadron were scrambled during the morning when an aircraft, believed to have been a Ju52, was reported heading towards the North African coast from Sicily, but this wisely skirted the island. As the Hurricanes returned, they were fired upon by the guns which had mistaken them for Messerschmitts. Plt Off Ormrod, one of the six pilots, wrote later:

"So long as one is not hit, only one's aircraft, one has the opportunity of baling out and becoming one who has had the experience of a parachute descent in an emergency without the dishonour of having been shot down by the enemy. There could be no disgrace in being shot out of a formation by friendly AA guns. One would have no right to expect them to fire."

Hal Far was on the receiving end of a sharp raid by three Ju88s and a number of Bf109s, the latter strafing the airfield. Although the gunners believed that they hit one of the bombers causing it to crash into the sea, all returned safely to Sicily; one Hurricane was destroyed on the airfield during the attack. Although the Hurricanes seemed almost powerless against the Messerschmitts, one or two of the German pilots had narrow escapes at this time, although it was AA fire which almost brought down ten-victory ace Lt Jürgen Harder of III/JG53, who wrote to his girlfriend at the end of the month:

"Don't be alarmed, something almost went wrong today, but our four-leaf clover was with me and my guardian angel helped me as he often has in the past. Wilcke [Hptm Wolf-Dietrich Wilcke, Gruppenkommandeur] and I were chasing two Hurricanes over Malta. We couldn't close with them because the anti-aircraft fire was too heavy and we flew round the rocky island at a height of five meters. Suddenly there was a huge bang – my cockpit filled with smoke and the engine quit. My windscreen was covered with oil, to my right was the coast of Malta. Flak! Five metres below me the water! Wilcke shouted that I should try to get closer to the coast so as not to come down in the water so far from shore. But I didn't want to, instead I pulled my smoking kite up and – oh wonder! – the engine started to pull again a little. There was a 90% chance that I would land in the water, but the 10% was with me and my machine and I made it. It was a less than pleasant feeling. Now Wilcke and I are off to the Geschwader; we're celebrating my lucky escape."[11]

During the afternoon Ormrod was ordered to scramble when a 'Heinkel' was reported flying low just south of Dingli. As he dashed to his aircraft, contemplating an easy first victory, he was recalled. Apparently someone had misidentified the ASR Swordfish floatplane for a He115 seaplane.

There was a small raid during the daylight hours of 29 January. Bombs were scattered over a wide area, some falling on the village of Qrendi, close to where a satellite airfield was under construction. One bomber jettisoned its load over Gozo. The guns were credited with damaging one of the raiders. The month ended for the Hurricane pilots with a relatively successful intrusion into the night sky above Sicily; on this occasion Flg Off Denis Winton (Z3580/B) engaged a Ju88 over Comiso. Firing from long range before his target was lost in the darkness, he reported:

"Comiso patrol. Saw one Ju88 and damaged it. Got illuminated and quite a lot of light AA. Saw another aircraft with lights on but could not contact it. Shot up a car which disappeared into ditch."

Another of the intruder Hurricanes was flown by the ever-keen Wg Cdr Satchell, but he was recalled when the weather closed in.

The weather throughout January had been poor. Indeed, the end of the month found both Hal Far and Takali waterlogged to the point of unserviceability with only Luqa providing runways fit for use. Similar conditions in Sicily had restricted Axis activity over Malta, and had certainly delayed the major air assault which was daily anticipated. Nonetheless, Malta had experienced more than 100 attacks during the month – in excess of 1,800 tons of bombs being dropped on the island. Some 800 bombs had landed on the three airfields where more than 50 aircraft had been destroyed or seriously damaged. With such an attrition rate, priority attention was therefore given to drawing up plans for the better dispersal of aircraft around the airfields, and for an intensive programme of building work to produce blast and splinter-proof pens. To construct dozens of such pens around the periphery of each of the main bases was a herculean task. The AOC appealed to the Army for help, since few airmen could be spared. The response was immediate and overwhelming. Up to 3,000 men were provided at once, while the Navy contributed all its available personnel not otherwise engaged on priority tasks. Hundreds of Maltese civilians also volunteered. In a matter of weeks, structures appeared in profusion as land was requisitioned around Luqa, Takali and Hal Far. The ground was levelled or filled as necessary by the hard sweat of manual labour – there being no bulldozers on the island – and 84 large pens built for the Wellingtons and Marylands, and more than 200 smaller versions for the Hurricanes and FAA aircraft, others for petrol bowsers, control vehicles and even the steam-rollers so vital to keep the runways repaired. Initially the pens were made with sandbags and rubble, a method soon superseded by the use of discarded four-gallon petrol cans, which were available in vast quantities. These were filled with earth or limestone rubble, and used to create walls up to 14 feet high. It took 60,000 such cans to construct three walls to house a Wellington and, it was estimated, 200 men working 18 hours to produce one such structure.

February 1942
The month opened with high winds and torrential rain, which effectively put a stop to all

flying. The weather continued in this vein for the next two weeks, the low cloud and almost continuous rain restricting the intensity of air raids. By the beginning of the month only 28 Hurricanes remained serviceable; many of the damaged machines had been cannibalised to keep others operational, but lack of spares was becoming a major problem, as was the shortage of aviation fuel and .303 ammunition for the Hurricanes. The skies cleared sufficiently on 2 February to allow three Ju88s to sneak in during the early afternoon and attack Hal Far. Little damage resulted although one Hurricane – Z2509 of 605 Squadron – was destroyed on the ground. Two aircraft from 605 Squadron had been scrambled on the approach of the bombers, Plt Off Ormrod (UP-G) and Sgt Alan Wilson intercepting a single Ju88 south of the airfield:

> "I was at 9,000 or 10,000 feet with Sgt Wilson weaving a little below and behind. Saw the Junkers diving very steeply. I don't think he'd seen us, for we must have been coming right out of the sun. He turned southwards over Hal Far as he eased out of his dive, and it was then I fancy he saw us. At 300 yards, as he cut my ring-sight, I opened fire with a short burst – I think the deflection I gave was probably insufficient; but it was only a short burst. I passed into a stern attack and withheld my fire until I'd drawn closer. I was not gaining very fast, in fact irritatingly slowly, though I had everything pulled. Gave another burst at 250 yards, holding the pip in the centre of my sight-ring just over the port engine. Could see the strikes on the engine and, as the sight wandered a little when I hit the slipstream, along the wing-root, inboard of the engine, and on to the cabin. There was return fire from the top rear-gunner, so I lowered my seat. As I gradually closed I gave further bursts. Again there were strikes on the cabin, wing-root and engine. Was perturbed by the little apparent effect my bullets were making. After four or five bursts I'd closed to about 100 yards. He seemed to be slowing a little. There was now no more return fire. I closed to 50 yards, hoping to give the *coup de grâce*, but found my ammunition gone. I flew on behind him at 50 yards or so for a moment or two. I actually thought of ramming him – fouling his elevators and rudder with my airscrew; but I looked at the sea. I couldn't glide back to land – was too far out. Switched over to transmit: 'Close right in, Blue 2. Close right in before you fire.' To my annoyance Blue 2 did nothing of the sort. He seemed to go up to 100 yards or so astern, and then break away after me. We returned to land at Hal Far."

It transpired that while Ormrod had been attacking the bomber from astern, Sgt Wilson had in fact made a number of beam attacks. The damaged bomber reached its base safely. Both Hurricanes had received minor damage, Ormrod's aircraft having been hit three times by the rear-gunner, one bullet piercing the oil tank; Wilson's aircraft had one bullet strike in its wing. With their return, two more Hurricanes flown by Plt Off Chuck Lester and Sgt Doug Robb were scrambled to search for the damaged Ju88, but were forced to give up after a fruitless 25 minutes. Shortly after they had returned to Hal Far, three Ju88s swooped down over the airfield and released their bombs; yet another Hurricane went up in flames. There was another incident of mistaken identity during the day when a Beaufighter suddenly appeared without warning over a convoy being protected by Hurricanes, one of which immediately engaged the intruder, mistaking it for a Ju88. Fortunately, the Beaufighter was not hit.

The raiders returned after dark, an estimated 20 aircraft roaming over the island. One Ju88 dived out of the clouds and dropped its bombs on a Sunderland which was being prepared for a flight to Egypt; one of the bombs shattered its tail and rear fuselage. The night fighter Hurricanes were up, but were busy on their series of intruder sorties over southern Sicily, where Flt Lt Stones strafed a military car near Modica, setting it on fire. Another of the pilots, Flg Off Tommy Thompson, spotted an aircraft off Gela which he identified as a Z506B floatplane; he reported that after he had shot off one float it spun into the sea near Licata harbour. An aircraft with its lights on was observed in the distance by Wg Cdr Satchell, but these were quickly extinguished on his approach, and the aircraft was lost in cloud.

Three Ju88s, with the usual fighter escort, swept in to raid Hal Far and Kalafrana during the morning of the 3rd, meeting a patrol of Hurricanes from 242 Squadron. One of the bombers was claimed possibly damaged during the pursuit, Plt Off Thady Macnamara firing at it from long range, AA gunners claiming hits on a second. A single raider dived from cloud and scattered more than 100 incendiaries in the Kalafrana area, one of which pierced the hull of a BOAC flying boat which had just arrived but the fire was promptly extinguished and the craft was able to depart at dusk. The black-painted Hurricanes went out over Sicily again after dark, including one flown by Wg Cdr Satchell who returned almost at once due to a faulty radio. Changing to another aircraft, he set out once more for Comiso airfield but failed to locate any worthwhile targets, whilst at the same time experiencing heavy AA fire and his Hurricane collected some shrapnel from near misses. In the area of Comiso he saw a single motor car which he duly strafed. Meanwhile, Flt Lt Stones had the task of dropping a container of messages to the agent based in eastern Sicily, the dropping zone being halfway up Mount Etna. On returning from these nocturnal sorties, another pilot crashed Z3570 on landing at Takali, but was unhurt.

On 4 February, several raids were made on the island, culminating in a heavy bombing attack on Takali. At 1125, four Hurricanes from 249 Squadron and two from 126 Squadron scrambled after Ju88s south of Kalafrana. One of the bombers was attacked by Flt Lt Davis, who gained hits on both engines before Sqn Ldr Beazley and Plt Off Don Tedford joined in, the Junkers finally escaping in cloud. This was possibly an aircraft of 2/KGr806 which crash-landed at Scalea; one crew member was injured. Meanwhile, six Blenheims had been despatched to carry out an attack on shipping in Palermo harbour, only two of which returned. Six of 249 Squadron's Hurricanes were ordered to cover the return of the Blenheims, taking off at 1350, three more from 126 and 242 Squadrons providing support. During the operation, Flt Lt Carpenter of the former unit spotted a lone Ju88 at 6,000 feet over Kalafrana – obviously a reconnaissance machine – which he attacked and claimed damaged before it disappeared in cloud. This may have been an aircraft of 8/KG77, 3Z+ES flown by Lt Eberhard Dammbrück and his crew failing to return from a sortie to Malta.

An hour later another scramble was ordered, 11 Hurricanes from 126, 242 and 249 Squadrons taking off but they failed to meet the bombers which had commenced an attack on Takali. Serious damage was caused to airfield buildings and there were a number of casualties. One section of Hurricanes was bounced by Bf109Fs from Stab and 6 Staffel and all three were shot down: Z4003/GN-S and Z4016 of 249 Squadron fell into the sea with the loss of Plt Off John Hulbert and Sgt Hugh McDowall, while 126 Squadron's Plt Off Rocky Main was killed in BV167. Lt Karl-Heinz Preu of Stab claimed the first, followed three minutes later by Maj von Maltzahn, with Lt Herbert Soukup gaining his first victory seven minutes later, probably the 126 Squadron machine. The only damage noted by the Luftwaffe was slight AA shrapnel damage to a Messerschmitt of 6 Staffel. Plt Off Harry Moon of 249 Squadron narrowly missed a similar fate:

"Flt Lt Crossey shot up into the clouds but the first I knew of an attack was when I looked either side and saw both Hurricanes falling in flames [Plt Off Hulbert and Sgt McDowall]. Two Messerschmitts sped past without hitting me and I became involved in a series of dogfights for about 15 minutes, squirting at several 109s. Once they had departed, Control ordered me to orbit the oil slicks where the Hurricanes had gone in. I said there was no point, there were no survivors, but was ordered to remain as a rescue launch was on its way. After about 15 minutes I called Control who told me to return since the rescue launch had been shot up by 109s."

Four Hurricanes, two Swordfish and HSL129 had been sent out to search for the missing pilots, the launch heading for a point four miles south-south-east of Benghaisa Point. Near Filfla, however, two Messerschmitts of 6 Staffel swooped on the launch, killing two of the crew, mortally wounding the skipper and wounding two others. Silent spectators gathered at Kalafrana as HSL129 limped slowly into view, engines faltering and backfiring, and the forward gun cupola splashed with blood.

A delivery Wellington, on the last leg of the long flight from Gibraltar to Malta, was intercepted by two Bf109Fs of 6/JG53 off Sicily at daybreak on the 5th, but managed to evade with minor damage although Obfw Otto Göthe claimed it shot down. Later in the day a reconnaissance Maryland was engaged by two Messerschmitts but also managed to escape. A further pair of Messerschmitts from 6 Staffel carried out a surprise strafe of Kalafrana seaplane base, catching a He115 spyplane[12] at its moorings, where it was set alight by Lt Hans Möller and damaged beyond repair; he surprisingly misidentified the seaplane as a Dutch Fokker T-VIII. Plt Off McKay noted:

> "Two 109s did some low flying attacks and set fire to the Heinkel 115 which sunk. It was really quite a sight to see them come down. They were going at least 400 [mph] when they went over. The Bofors opened up but they didn't touch them."

Plt Offs McKay and Wigley were in fact in a rowing boat in Marsaxlokk Bay when the Messerschmitts swooped over, Ormrod commenting:

> "One passed low across country behind Marsaxlokk and another skimmed the bay. Wigley pulled very hard for the shore – so hard that the fork of one of the oars broke and he fell over backwards. We were all highly amused, including the Wing Commander who'd turned up. The 109s succeeded in destroying the Heinkel. Only its inverted floats now protrude on the surface of the water."

On the morning of 6 February, the Dockyard and submarine base were subjected to heavy air attack, Ju88s from both I/KG54 and II/KG77 taking part. Hurricanes were scrambled but failed to make any interceptions. The guns, however, were more successful on this occasion and shot down an aircraft of 2/KG54, from which three of the crew baled out to become prisoners, and also hit another from II/KG77 which returned to Sicily on one engine. Hal Far was again attacked during the early afternoon, an Albacore being destroyed at its dispersal; one of the strafing Messerschmitts was claimed shot down by the ground defences, but none was lost. The Messerschmitts scored another demoralising victory during the afternoon, when a trio of Blenheims returning from a sortie to the North African coast ran into aircraft of 6/JG53, and all three were shot down into the sea not far out from Filfla; there were no survivors. When news reached the grounded Hurricane pilots at Malta, Ormrod commented:

> "Did not know that Blenheims were being shot down close at hand. Words do not describe the feelings of Lester, Wigley and I when we heard. We want to attack the enemy for the sake of our honour and because we're tired of inaction. Oh! for Spitfire Vs. With them we would soon regain aerial superiority here."

Shortly before midnight Sqn Ldr Westmacott set course for eastern Sicily, a package containing 500,000 Italian Lire for the agent stowed in the Hurricane's flare tube. As he approached the dropping zone on the north-eastern slopes of Mount Etna, the weather closed in and, as the whole area was shrouded in low cloud, the mission was abandoned. Undeterred, however, Westmacott cruised over the darkened landscape looking for suitable targets to attack, and soon spotted an electric train when just south of Taormina, his cannon-shells causing a "spectacular display of blue-white flashes" as he strafed.

Next morning, Messerschmitts roamed over and around Malta searching for targets of opportunity, catching one of 69 Squadron's Beaufighters as it returned from a reconnaissance sortie; it was attacked and set on fire although the pilot managed to crash-land at Luqa. A little over an hour later, a pair of Messerschmitts similarly intercepted a returning Maryland but this evaded the attack and landed safely, while one Bf109 was claimed possibly shot down by machine-gun fire from a submarine at anchor in Grand Harbour. HSL107 was sent out to look for the German pilot but was recalled when four more Bf109s appeared. However, one Messerschmitt did fail to return, Obfw Otto Göthe of 6/JG53 being shot down by Hal Far's ground defences as he swept in to strafe parked Hurricanes; Plt Off McKay was among those who witnessed the event:

> "About eleven o'clock two 109s shot-up Luqa and were just on their way to shoot-up Hurricanes on the line at Hal Far but the Bofors hacked one down. The tail was shot off and it went straight in about 300 miles per hour. The pilot (what was left of him) was scraped up."

Hurricanes from Takali were sent up to meet and escort another returning Maryland, these driving away yet a further pair of Messerschmitts which attempted to intercept. During all this fighter activity around the island three Ju88s managed to avoid the Hurricanes and targeted Hal Far once again, where an already damaged Albacore was completely destroyed and eight airfield personnel injured.

After dark Sqn Ldr Westmacott again departed for Sicily in his Hurricane and, on this occasion, made a successful drop to the agent, who subsequently reported safe receipt of the container. On the return flight Westmacott spotted a truck near Catania airfield, which he duly strafed. So began a series of such flights which would continue over the next ten months at monthly intervals, only terminating when the agent was ultimately caught and executed. During this period not only money but clothes, batteries and even a bicycle were dropped to the agent, albeit via a proper underwing container which had been fitted in place of one of the long-range fuel tanks. Whilst Westmacott had been away raiders had again been active over Malta; Hal Far, Kalafrana and Safi dispersal area all being targeted and a Blenheim and a Wellington destroyed. One Ju88 was illuminated by the searchlights, as Plt Off McKay noted:

> "He jettisoned his bombs right over our Mess at Marsaxlokk and, as luck would have it, one dropped on the Mess and one right beside it. Joe Beckett and Sonny [Ormrod] were in the bar at the time and that is the only room that was unhurt, the floors coming down in the others. S/L McGregor, Ron Noble and Wiggles [Plt Off Wigley] were outside and, of course, laying flat. They had just left the dining room to get some lamps, seeing the lights had gone out, or they would have all been killed."

Six alerts during the hours of daylight on 8 February brought but a single scramble at 0850 by four aircraft of 126 Squadron. A little later Sqn Ldr Norris crash-landed at Luqa with the engine of his Hurricane on fire, having been hit by return fire from a reconnaissance Ju88 which his section had intercepted, and which itself was claimed damaged. One of the day's raids was carried out by three bomb-carrying Bf109Fs of 10(*Jabo*) Staffel of JG53, which had been established a few days earlier under the leadership of Oblt Werner Langermann; most of the pilots selected for the new unit had limited experience of fighter-bomber operations against England in the autumn of 1940. The dire winter weather continued to restrict operations, although Takali suffered another raid next day, when six civilians, a soldier and an airman were killed. Plt Off James Stuart of 249 Squadron was also killed when his Hurricane (Z5326/GN-F) dived into the ground at Takali during an air test; Stuart, a former school chum of Ormrod's, died from a skull fracture. The weather was even worse on the 10th, although four Ju88s braved a raging storm to penetrate the defences in an attempt to bomb Luqa. With the crews unable accurately to pin-point the target, bombs aimed in the general direction of the airfield fell on nearby Qormi village instead, where 16 civilians were killed and a further 28 injured.

With the rapid attrition of the Hurricanes, all airworthy aircraft were now concentrated as one squadron, with the pilots from Takali and Hal Far to take over from each other every 24 hours. This did not satisfy Plt Off Ormrod, who was keen to see more action:

"All the Hurricanes and their pilots, even the night fighters, are pooled here [at Takali] now. Thus, this gave us nearly 20 serviceable aircraft. Two squadrons have to provide pilots at a time. There are five squadrons and the MNFU [1435 Flight] so that I shall only be on once in three days, if that, since not all pilots of two squadrons are needed at a time. This will not suit me, I want to do more."

The dismal weather still restricted flying, Plt Off Andy Anderson of 126 Squadron making mention of this in his latest letter home:

"We've had a bit of a respite today as the weather is so appalling that even Jerry, with all his enthusiasm, thought it too bad to take off. There's no doubt about it, the Hun is really keen on war, he just loves it and worst of all he never seems to take time off for meals. In the old days the Italians would never think of coming over in the breakfast or dinner hour, but these days, when you sit down for a meal, you'll probably have to take off just when you're getting to the oyster bit! Frightfully annoying, but it does make me really hate the Germans and I suppose that's a good thing."

Not until 11 February was any serious engagement recorded for the month, when a substantial force of Hurricanes was led off by Wg Cdr Rabagliati (Z4005/S) at 1015, their task to provide cover for incoming warships. Twenty-five minutes after take-off the Hurricanes had reached 16,000 feet and were eight miles north of Gozo. Some 10,000 feet below, a formation of six Ju88s with four escorting Bf109Fs were seen heading towards Sicily. Rabagliati led the Takali pilots down in a steep diving attack on the bombers, personally opening fire on one and seeing many strikes. His No2, Plt Off Howard Coffin of 126 Squadron closely followed him down:

"My stomach went tight as we came on them. Rags [Wg Cdr Rabagliati] started to take his man apart with short deadly bursts and then the other Ju88 was round on my tail. His bullets ripped through my port wing. I began to shake and froze to my stick . . . I was suddenly clear and steady again. I came up in a half-roll and the 88 dove under me. Rags led him away and then I had a chance to get square on his tail; I gave him a long burst and he slid off and began spinning down in flames."[13]

It would seem that Coffin's victory was actually the same aircraft as that attacked by his leader – Obfw Heinz Bösch's 3Z+JR of 7/KG77 – which also came under further attack from Plt Off Noel MacGregor, who recalled:

"Had good long bursts from very close range at Ju88, recording hits. Self hit in starboard wing and aileron by rear-gunner, and attacked by 109 but evaded. Ju88 afterwards confirmed destroyed."

Meanwhile, Flg Off Jack Kay and Sgt Ted Copp attacked another Ju88, evidently an aircraft of KGr806, which subsequently crash-landed at Catania, badly damaged by fighter attack. Kay's aircraft also sustained damage from return fire but he landed safely. The 60 miles across the sea to Sicily must have seemed more like 600 miles to the desperate crew aboard Obfw Bösch's crippled Junkers as the pilot struggled to keep the aircraft flying, before finally losing the battle when it splashed into the sea. Bösch and one of his crew died in the crash but the other two, although both injured, were picked up by a rescue craft from Sicily. This unfolding drama was not witnessed by the victorious Hurricane pilots and consequently only a claim for the aircraft's probable destruction was submitted by them on return. Confirmation of the bomber's loss was soon forthcoming, however, via the RAF's Y Service which subsequently reported that two more bombers had been damaged. Despite their success on this occasion, the Hurricanes had been unable to prevent an attack on the Naval vessels, one of which suffered some 20 casualties. A destroyer in Grand Harbour was sunk after dark following a direct hit from a bomb dropped by one of four Ju88s reported over the island, and bombs also fell on Hal Far where a Swordfish was badly damaged.

With the coming of dawn on 12 February, Messerschmitt pilots from III/JG53 were up early and succeeded in intercepting three delivery Beaufighters as they approached Malta, shooting one down into the sea. A little later a second Beaufighter was shot down by Bf110s from III/ZG26. Aircraft were not despatched to go to their aid but, during the late morning, a dozen Hurricanes (ten pilots from 605, two from 185) were scrambled on the approach of another raid, Sqn Ldr Andrews (Z5140/C) at their head. Two Bf109Fs were seen at sea level but these were not attacked as it was assumed that they were decoys for others higher up. Then, when about 20 miles north of Grand Harbour, a lone Ju88 and a Do24 flying boat with escorting Messerschmitts appeared. Plt Off Chuck Lester (UP-P) was the first to spot the Ju88 – 3Z+DD of 7/KG77 flown by the Staffelkapitän, Oblt Herbert Loerz – and gave chase, followed by Plt Offs Wigley (Z3757/UP-R) and McKay (BG698/LE-U), the latter recording:

"Chuck, Wiggles and I were weaving and we saw it first and immediately turned towards it, and then the rest turned. It fired a white and green recognition cartridge to make us think it was friendly but turned and started off out to sea. Everyone pulled the tit, put on full revs and gave chase. Wiggles and Chuck were a bit above and a little ahead and got there first. Wiggles attacked first, then Chuck and then I opened up. I could see my bullets enter the rear-turret and rip the fuselage. I almost shot Chuck down 'cause on his attack he went down and then came up right in my sight (50 yards) and I was firing but stopped in time. He had one bullet in his port aileron. Everyone had a shot. Sonny Ormrod finished it off with cannon and it went straight in (three jumped)."

Sqn Ldr Andrews also managed to get in a shot – seeing further strikes on its port engine – before Plt Off Ormrod, who was flying BE351/LE-Y, a cannon-armed IIc, the only one of the twelve aircraft airborne, completed the job:

"Opened up full throttle and revs. Immediately I drew away from my CO. I brushed through other Hurricanes trying to attack, deciding the cannon Hurricane had the right of way. The other Hurricanes had already done damage and I saw that the port engine was smoking. Saw one of the crew bale out. I opened fire at 150 yards. Immediately flames shot up from the starboard engine. Large pieces of the aircraft were blown off. Oil smothered my aircraft as I pulled hard on the stick to avoid colliding with the enemy. I skimmed just over the top of him, knowing that I'd delivered the *coup de grâce*. Could see sideways all right and watched the enemy aircraft, with both engines on fire and the starboard wing also on fire, crash into the sea.

I still could not see through my windscreen. I'd already tried to put my hand out to wipe off the oil; but had only had my arm seized by the slipstream and hauled violently back against the fuselage, hurting me and nearly pulling me out of my seat. Indeed, for a moment I thought I wouldn't be able to pull it back inside the cockpit . . . and then, to my amazement I saw a big black object. It was a flying boat escorted by 109s. I approached it at once, hardly able to believe it was really a Do24. Too good to be true. I flew over the top and looked at the markings, just to make sure of my aircraft recognition. I flew beside the Dornier about 150 yards to the right and 100 feet above, reduced speed to 140mph and tried again to wipe my windscreen. I made an attack but found I just couldn't see my sights against the oil, let alone the Do24 through it. Stopped this attack and closed in looking out of the port side. When I did not think I could miss this sitting shot, still looking out of my port side, I fired my remaining rounds, not many. All the rear-gunner's fire had been pouring past my starboard side, but as I'd got my face out the other side it did not worry me, until just after my fire ceased I felt a bang on the aircraft, and she lurched. Decided I'd been hit. Broke away and met an angry looking 109 with yellow paint underneath his nose, as if he'd spilt egg on his chin at breakfast. Had to do something, he seemed very close. Expected to be blown to pieces by his horrid cannon. He shot past without firing. I wished him goodbye very hurriedly, and experienced a few unpleasant moments climbing for cloud."

Ormrod was awarded a half share in the destruction of the Ju88, but 605 Squadron's newly promoted Flt Lt George Allen (Z2527) failed to return. He was seen scrapping with two of the escort, one of which it was believed he damaged before he was shot down by Lt Hans-Volkmar Müller of 5/JG53 (his 8th victory); Allen was heard to call over the R/T that he was baling out. Two Messerschmitts attacked Plt Off Lester but his aircraft was not hit, and he claimed one damaged as it overshot. Ormrod continued:

"We found Georgy Allen to be missing. Someone had heard him say that he was baling out, but no one saw him do so. We were not greatly perturbed because we thought he would be picked up fairly easily. No one knows why he baled out. None saw his Hurricane crash."

Despite a search by ASR, no sign of Flt Lt Allen was found. Some thought, and hoped, that he might have been picked up by the Do24, but this was not the case. The bombers had inflicted much damage during their attacks, both Hal Far and Luqa being on the receiving end; a Hurricane and a Swordfish sustained damage, while indiscriminate bombing destroyed a number of houses at Paola, Luqa village and Tarxien. There were 31 known fatalities including three soldiers, with about 100 injured.

Ju87s returned to the skies over Malta next day (13 February), Grand Harbour being targeted although one bomb hit Valetta Palace, the Governor's headquarters, necessitating an evacuation of his staff to his residence at San Anton. One bomb hit a house in South Street, Valetta, where Flt Sgt Bill Nurse of 185 Squadron, who happened to be on the roof at the time, was injured, suffering shock, concussion and a broken leg. Hurricanes were not scrambled on this occasion, the guns having a clear field of fire and claimed a Ju88, a Ju87 and a Bf109; the Ju87 at least was shot down. Bomb-carrying Bf109Fs of 10(*Jabo*)/JG53 carried out a surprise attack on Takali and, although the pilots had received very little in the way of bombing technique training, they nonetheless accurately placed their bombs on various buildings, inflicting much damage, as LAC Bill Metcalfe noted:

"What a hell of a day it has been too. In Takali's share this morning the M/T section was wrecked and the pottery badly knocked about by blast. Five casualties including Cpl Barfoot of our Armoury Section."

Axis attention was now focused on an incoming convoy; the only assistance Malta was able to provide coming by way of Beaufighter patrols, but these were unable to prevent severe damage being inflicted on all three freighters which comprised the convoy; two of these were abandoned and subsequently sank, while the other diverted to Tobruk, thereby depriving Malta of much needed supplies.

The aftermath of the convoy actions, however, brought one of the most active days of the month for Malta's small air force; four raids during the daylight hours of 15 February kept the island on constant alert for 20 hours commencing at 0800. Luqa was raided 15 minutes later by seven Ju88s of II/KG77, two Wellingtons and a Beaufighter being destroyed, while two Wellingtons, two Beaufighters and two Blenheims were damaged. AA shot down one Ju88 (3Z+FP of 7 Staffel), claimed a second and damaged a third. Again there was an absence of Hurricanes. Airman X of 185 Squadron witnessed the demise of the Ju88:

". . . as one of their Ju88s was diving in flames, the air gunner baled out. But the last time our motor launch went out to pick up a Jerry airman, 109s shot it up, killing two of our men and injuring all the rest. The air gunner baled out about 1145 and he was still seen swimming at dusk. Bet the water was cold, poor bugger."

There followed a lull before the next raid, five Beaufighters taking the opportunity to continue their intended journey to Egypt. As they cleared Malta, Bf109Fs were reported approaching but only two aircraft heard the recall. Of the other three, one was shot down by Messerschmitts of newly arrived II/JG3, while the remaining pair were fortunate to evade and reached their destination safely.

An hour later Wg Cdrs Satchell and Rabagliati took off at the head of a force of a dozen Hurricanes, flown by pilots of 242 Squadron and 1435 Flight, on the approach of another raid. Three Ju88s and five Bf109Fs were seen low down over the sea, heading towards Sicily, and a diving attack was made on the fighters, as Satchell (flying the cannon-armed BE351/LE-Y) reported:

> "I was leading a formation of 12 aircraft when I saw three Ju88s approaching the island from the north-east at approx 15,000 feet. Our formation was on patrol at about the same height to the south-east of the island. I turned towards the island and as I crossed the coast at Kalafrana I saw AA barrage round the Ju88s and lost sight of them in the smoke puffs. Controller told me they had turned south-east so I turned about and got the formation to the east of the island at 17,000 feet. We were warned of fighter bandits up sun of us but none were sighted. Suddenly I saw three Ju88s at about 4,000 feet to the north-east of the island, flying north. I warned all aircraft to keep a good look out astern and led a diving attack towards the bombers. Ahead of the bombers was some very heavy cloud towards which they were making.
>
> Suddenly, I saw two 109s astern of the bombers, flying west. I realised that we would probably not get to the bombers before they reached cloud cover, so again warning the formation to look out for fighters behind, I increased my dive, pulled the plug, and dived flat out on one of the two 109s. They saw us coming and also dived, taking violent evasive action. They dived down to about ten feet off the water and headed in a north-westerly direction at high speed. I was by this time diving at a very high speed and managed to get within about 350 yards of one of them. I saw that I was not any longer decreasing the range so I opened fire from astern and slightly above (I was at about 50 feet) with two short bursts of cannon fire. I did not observe any strikes but the 109 at which I fired suddenly put his nose down, hit the water, somersaulted and went straight in and disappeared from sight immediately. My No2, P/O Mills, chased the second 109 but could not keep up with me nor catch the 109 and therefore could not fire. He told me he saw the 109 at which I fired crash as described above. I fired a total of 20 rounds. The remainder of the formation were involved with other 109s and W/Cdr Rabagliati shot one down. I had a dogfight with one but did not get into position to fire again, so returned to base."

Wg Cdr Rabagliati (Z4005/S) reported that two Messerschmitts, flying in line astern, attacked him but the leading aircraft overshot, allowing him to turn to port and attack the second. He believed his quick burst probably killed the pilot, and reported that the fighter turned over and dived into the sea. It seems probable that both Satchell and Rabagliati attacked the same aircraft, believed to have been from II/JG3, the pilot apparently being rescued from the sea[14]. A second aircraft from this unit force-landed near Sciacca on the south-east coast of Sicily. Messerschmitts from II/JG53 were also involved, Oblt Kurt Brändle of 5 Staffel claiming a Hurricane shot down at this time for his 32nd victory.

At 1715, Sqn Ldr Beazley led off a mixed formation of a dozen Hurricanes to cover the return of a 69 Squadron Maryland, with Sqn Ldr Westmacott leading a section from 1435 Flight. Flying south to the rendezvous point, the Hurricanes failed to locate the Maryland, so turned north but were then jumped by a *Schwarm* of Bf109Fs which were escorting a small number of Ju88s, three Messerschmitts chasing Sqn Ldr Westmacott back to Malta. Several pilots engaged the enemy fighters, Flg Off Peter Rathie of 1435 Flight claiming damage to one, but Plt Off Peter Lowe of ʊ05 Squadron was shot down when his aircraft (BG755) was hit by a Messerschmitt flown by Hptm Heinze of Stab JG53 which dropped out of low cloud. The Hurricane dived straight into the sea, thereby raising Heinze's personal score to 11. The Maryland also fell victim to the Bf109Fs and ditched in Kalafrana Bay from where the crew was rescued, but the crew of a second Maryland perished when their aircraft was also shot down by Messerschmitts. Plt Off Phil Wigley, who was flying with Plt Off Lowe, recalled:

"P/O Lowe and myself, flying one of 242 Squadron's aircraft [LE-H], flew with 249 Squadron to assist a photo-reconnaissance Maryland which was approaching Malta from the east under attack from 109Fs – we did not find the Maryland but the 109s found the two Hurricanes. One slipped down out of the low cloud cover, shot down Peter Lowe and made off at high speed. On the return to Malta, a 109F (probably the same one) attacked me off Delimara Point in similar fashion but was spotted in time, out-turned and seen off by the light AA guns on the Point."

Plt Off Ormrod, who was not flying on this occasion, wrote:

"Later this evening, after dinner, heard that Lowe was dead. The Squadron was going full speed, and so unable to weave, in an endeavour to save the Maryland. They were flying just below thick cloud. S/Ldr Beazley looked back and counted his aircraft, saw that there was one too many and shouted 'Look out' and turned violently. Though his quick action must have saved others of his pilots, it was too late to save Lowe who was, I believe, flying on the outside, No2 to Wigley. He must have been killed by the enemy aircraft's fire for he went straight down into the sea. Thus passed P/O Lowe. Once again I am the youngest pilot of 605 Squadron."

Air Vice-Marshal Lloyd picked out the 15th as a warning example of the way the battle was progressing. He was a very worried man, with just cause:

"The day's fighting brought out the stark truth; unless we could get on better terms with the Axis there was no doubt whatever that such a load of bombs would be dropped on our aerodromes that we would never leave the ground again. Our few Hurricanes had fought through December and January and the losses of the most experienced fighter pilots had been very heavy. The odds, indeed, against any one of the pilots surviving seemed overwhelming. We began February with 28 serviceable aircraft, and the 15th with 26, but at the end of that day the only Hurricanes left serviceable were 11. The defence was a cruel task, quite beyond our capacity. One raid would follow so quickly on the other that it was impossible to land the Hurricanes and re-arm and re-fuel them for the next contest. It was a non-stop performance. The Hurricane was a wonder in manoeuvre and would out-turn an Me109 with ease, but it lacked the speed and the fire-power. It was clean out of its class. We wanted more speed, more aeroplanes and a heavier armament as the task was to kill. We were not interested in damaging the bombers. But once the Hurricanes were out of the battle and could not fly again, the battle for Malta would have been as good as lost; once Kesselring's hordes dominated the Malta sky they would soon be dominating all the activity on the ground and that would have been the end of it."[15]

A Sunderland flying boat alighted in Kalafrana Bay during the early hours of 16 February, bringing eight fighter pilots to the island, all of them Spitfire trained. The party comprised Sqn Ldr Stan Turner DFC[16], a Canadian who was to take command of 249 Squadron; Flt Lt Laddie Lucas and Flg Off Raoul Daddo-Langlois (a Channel Islander) both of whom had been serving with 66 Squadron; Plt Off Harry Fox, Plt Off Bob Sergeant and another American, Plt Off Tex Putnam RCAF, plus Sgts Tom Freeman RAAF and Tim Goldsmith RAAF; Flt Lt Lucas wrote:

"I could see at once that Stan Turner, with experience of France, the Battle of Britain and sweeps over Northern France behind him, thought little of this motley crew. Casually, and with some disdain, he flicked open my unbuttoned greatcoat and looked at the left breast of my tunic. A deprecating glance told me unmistakenly that a flight lieutenant without a decoration wasn't worth a damn. We reached the Rock [Gibraltar], and its circus of lights, in the evening, and after the inevitable visit to the bar at the Bristol turned in for our last quiet night's sleep for weeks. The Sunderland pilot bided his time at Gibraltar until next evening. Then, flying through darkness and one electric storm after another, we made our way eastwards down the Mediterranean, landing in Kalafrana Bay as the sun began to rise above the eastern horizon."[17]

Sgt Goldsmith, an Australian from New South Wales, wrote of their arrival:

"At about 4.30 in the morning I made my way to the Flight Deck to see what our position was. Standing in the cockpit behind the skipper I could see several searchlights about 40 miles north of us.
'Where are the searchlights?' I asked him.
'Malta', he replied.
'Well, why aren't we headed that way?'
'Because there's a bleeding air raid on, chum, and we don't want the bleeding machine smashed around our bleeding ears!'
Feeling rather squashed I clambered back to the gunner's hatch to watch the proceedings. For two hours our machine circled north of the island until the All Clear was given to us by wireless, just as dawn broke."

While the new pilots swelled the ranks of those available, they were in fact awaiting the arrival of the first Spitfires now imminently due, although their presence allowed some of the time-expired to depart. However, it was the rapidly diminishing number of Hurricanes which caused gravest concern. As the weary new arrivals made their way to the mess for breakfast, the sirens heralded the first raid of the day; Flt Lt Lucas continued:

"In a moment or two a section of four manifestly old Hurricane IIs passed overhead, strung out in V formation, labouring to gain height over the island. High up above them, eight Messerschmitt 109s, flying fast and purposely in pairs in line abreast, swept southwards across the brightening sky, dominant and unchallenged. It was a different world from the Spitfires of Fighter Command and the sweeps over Northern France. Turner watched in silence, and gathering apprehension, as the Hurricanes disappeared into cloud. 'Good God,' he exclaimed, turned on his heel and strode on towards the mess."[18]

Following further raids on Luqa and Takali later in the day, when a Wellington and a PR Mosquito were both damaged, fewer than a dozen Hurricanes could be made serviceable and ready for operations. However, some respite was forthcoming when the weather again intervened, and over the next four days gale force winds and torrential rain severely restricted flying activities. Takali and Hal Far were flooded and became temporarily unserviceable, the Hurricanes moving to Luqa as a result. Meanwhile, new arrivals Sgts Tim Goldsmith and Tom Freeman presented themselves to the Adjutant for allocation:

"I was attached to 126 Squadron while Tom went on the strength of the MNFU [1435 Flight]. Sqn Ldr Wells commanded my squadron and, when he interviewed me, showed plainly that he was very disappointed that I had not flown a Hurricane. His pilots had more than enough work to do, but no Hurricanes could be spared to enable me to get experience in handling them. He put me in the capable hands of Flt Lt Paddy Kee, who taught me the cockpit drill of a Hurricane, promised me a flight as soon as he could possibly arrange it, and dismissed me. Pooling experiences in the evening, I found that Tom had found things very much the same."

There was much consternation on Malta during the early hours of the 17th, when five delivery aircraft failed to arrive from Gibraltar. Severe weather had caused several to fly too far north resulting in two Wellingtons being shot down by Ju88 night fighters; another was hit by AA fire from Sicilian ground defences and subsequently carried out a force-landing near Castelvetrano; a fourth force-landed in North Africa, and a Hudson crashed off the Sicilian coast. Hurricanes were airborne providing protection for the delivery aircraft that did reach Malta, one patrol being led by recently-arrived Sqn Ldr Ron Chaffe, the new CO of 185 Squadron, flying his first operational sortie from the island. There was no contact with the enemy although the patrol was not without incident as Plt Off Ormrod noted:

> "Chuck's hood blew off. Such things should not occur, and illustrates the ropey nature of the old aircraft we fly. It took a large chunk of fabric off his starboard tailplane and pieces out of the fin. Luckily it did not damage the control surfaces."

That evening Flt Lt Peter Thompson, who had just been awarded the DFC, threw a party at the Officers' Mess at M'dina, not only to celebrate his award but to say goodbye to his colleagues since he had been advised of his posting from the island; Flt Sgt Jock Sutherland wrote in the Squadron diary:

> "Tommy invited us for a drink as he had learnt that he would be leaving shortly. Well, we had a drink, and another and another, and so it went on. It is believed that F/Lts Lloyd and Thompson were in cahoots, and endeavoured to make every sergeant pilot well and truly tight. In a few cases they succeeded. Sgts Jolly and Ellis were found at 1130 in the Cathedral Square burrowing for gremlins or something, while Sgts Vardy and Alderson had to retire early, probably due to electrical failure as they seemed well lit up. During the evening, W/Cdr Ragbags gave us an exhibition of a Zulu dance, to which S/Ldr Andrews and Sgt Wilson of 605 replied with a Maori war dance. F/Sgt Fletcher of 605 did a few things of his own, or maybe they originated from the American Indians. It was a pity our own Indians, Sgts Horricks and Eastman, were not there, or they might have shown us something. None of our pilots were required [next day] so we spent most of the day recuperating."

There were few encounters involving Malta's Hurricanes during this period of inclement weather, although Ju88 reconnaissance crews vigilantly overflew the island, gathering information. A number of Ju88s individually intruded over Malta on 20 February and, although several interceptions were made, the Hurricanes could not prevent bombs falling on Takali, Kalafrana and the Dockyard area. At 0930 Plt Off Wigley (605 Squadron) and Sgt Finlay (242 Squadron), encountered a Ju88; Wigley recalled:

> "Intercepted a Ju88 at about 10,000 feet over Filfla. Fortunately my aircraft [Z4002/M of 1435 Flight] was armed with 20mm cannon and hits were scored on the fuselage and port engine before it reached cloud cover – it was later revealed that the 88's radar plot abruptly disappeared and a 'probably destroyed' was awarded. In view of the known hitting power of 20mm ammunition, this seemed to be a fair decision."

Wigley may, indeed, have accounted for 7T+FH of 1/KüFlGr606 in which Uffz Hermann Ehehalt and his crew perished, reportedly as a result of fighter action. Alternatively, the Ju88 may have fallen foul of other Hurricanes, for just over one and a half hours later, Plt Off Ron Noble (BG756/LE-W) led six more Hurricanes flown by 605 Squadron pilots after another reconnaissance aircraft, which was intercepted at 10,000 feet. Plt Off Ormrod was flying on this occasion:

> "For some reason F/Lt Stones' aircraft did not start up, so P/O Noble led us. Gained height over the island until above the clouds, 12,000 feet. Control ordered us to orbit for quite a while. P/O Noble circled slowly and we all weaved around him. At last P/O McKay saw a Ju88 passing below and behind us, down sun from us. P/O Noble turned and led us against the enemy, who seemed quite unaware of our presence until Noble opened fire. We must have attacked him right out of the sun. Whilst Noble and his No2, Sgt [Ray] Ellis of 185

Squadron [Z5140/HA-C], attacked, I positioned myself for a full beam attack. Unfortunately I was unable to execute this for fear of hitting Sgt Ellis, who was behind the enemy. I therefore made a quarter attack. My fire caught him beautifully. I saw the majority of it strike the fuselage just behind the wing root, though some of it did, I think, strike the engine. Then I passed astern and closed in, firing into the port engine, which was already smoking, I fancy as a result of Noble's and Ellis' fire.

As my first burst from astern struck the port engine, the black smoke more than doubled in volume. I continued to fire into it as I closed in. I remember seeing the rear-gunner's fire passing on my port side, tracer leaving, as it appeared, small smoke trails. I crouched lower in my cockpit; but my seat did not lower at the first attempt and, being otherwise engaged, I did not try further, having got my head as low as was consistent in using the sight efficiently. I continued to close until, when at least within 75 yards, oil from the engine of the enemy sprayed my windscreen. Unable to see forwards, I then ceased fire and broke downwards to starboard. My No2, Sgt [Cyril] Hunton [Z2840/GL-T], who'd attacked just after me, now passed on my starboard side. Then I dived down and landed at Luqa in a heavy rainstorm. Everyone else returned all right. Found my machine had a bullet through the port mainplane and aileron."

Wg Cdr Rabagliati (Z4005/S) and his No2 had scrambled from Takali at about the same time, intent on intercepting another or the same Ju88, but were prevented from engaging owing to the Messerschmitt escort. This was undoubtedly the same aircraft intercepted a little later by Flt Lt Don Stones (flying Z3562/C of 1435 Flight), who had been delayed taking off. At the head of four more Hurricanes, he opened fire at long range. Although it may have been hit and damaged, the Ju88 was able to escape due to the prevailing weather conditions.

During the early hours of the 21st, another Sunderland arrived from Gibraltar following an 11-hour flight, carrying more fighter pilots[19]. Again, all the new pilots were Spitfire trained and were part of the advance echelon awaiting the arrival of the first Spitfires, soon to be despatched from England. The flying boat was due to leave again that night with a number of time-expired pilots, and was being prepared for departure when a Bf109F swept in at low level with guns blazing. Damage was inflicted to the starboard wing and tail section, causing the Sunderland to keel over; she sank two days later. Hurricanes scrambled to meet the first raid of the day although no interceptions were made, but a second plot – which turned out to be a lone reconnaissance Ju88 – was engaged by four Hurricanes flown by 1435 Flight pilots led by Flg Off Peter Rathie, as Sgt Ted Wood noted:

"Went over to Luqa, missed first scramble. Took off with four others on next effort. One 88 came in, we talley-hoed over Hal Far and had to fly through AA barrage. I got in second and fired a burst at 250 yards. Then I had to go full out to catch it again, saw the rear-gunner's tracer going past me but fired a long burst with no apparent effect. Then I broke away. It was smoking a bit and was then about 20 miles off the coast. Came back smartly and found I had fired 150 rounds from each gun and that I had an AA splinter in the mainplane and a cannon shell in the tailplane. It was given as a probable."

Flg Off Denis Winton (Z4002/M) and his No2 Sgt Reg Fowler also engaged the aircraft and were jointly credited with a share in its probable destruction, the former noting: "Intercepted one Ju88. My starboard cannon did not fire, port cannon fired five rounds." Intruders again breached the defences an hour later to bomb Hal Far and Luqa: a Swordfish was destroyed, a Hurricane (BG744) written off, a second Hurricane blast damaged, as were five Wellingtons; in addition an irreplaceable streamroller – vital for runway repairs – was damaged as were two petrol bowsers.

At 1135 on the morning of 22 February, eight Hurricanes manned by 126 and 249 Squadron pilots were scrambled on the approach of three Ju88s from I/LG1 – a newly arrived unit – and their escort from II/JG3 and III/JG53, which were encountered at 16,000 feet over Filfla. Plt Off Eddie Streets of 126 Squadron saw strikes on the bomber he attacked before being chased away by the escort, while Flt Lt Les Barnes put a burst into a Messerschmitt, seeing pieces fly off before he was forced away by others. Plt Off Harry Moon (Z4002/M) of 249 Squadron attacked the right-hand bomber of the trio but saw no results before he, too, was chased away:

> "Squirted Ju88 but got shot up by a 109. Landed OK even though tyre on tailwheel shot to pieces. Some bullets had glanced off the armour plate and passed under the seat, others had glanced off the foot rest."

Moon's No2, Sgt Alf Branch, pursued the same bomber, closing from 300 to 75 yards, but the tail of his aircraft (BE583) was damaged by a Messerschmitt, and he broke away: "Got four bursts into one 88 – saw strikes. Got shot up by 109, landed OK." A third Hurricane was damaged when Sgt Alan Cairns attacked another, or the same, bomber, while Sqn Ldr Turner and Flt Sgt Fred Etchells each reported strikes on the Messerschmitts with which they became entangled. One Messerschmitt returned to Sicily with fairly substantial damage, while Uffz Leopold Münster of II/JG3 claimed one Hurricane shot down for his 10th victory, Lt Fritz Dinger of 4/JG53 claiming a second for his 13th. Two hours later the Hurricanes were again scrambled, led by Wg Cdr Rabagliati, seven aircraft flown by 185 Squadron pilots engaging over Hal Far three Ju88s escorted by Bf109Fs from 9/JG53. In the ensuing scrap Flt Sgt Jock Sutherland (BD826/A) shot down Uffz Walter Schwartz, whose aircraft (Yellow 10) crashed at Wied is-Sewda near Qormi; Schwartz died in the cockpit. Sutherland later wrote:

> "We jumped the 88s as they were pulling out of their dive, but only one is claimed damaged (by self). I managed by a lucky shot to fix up a 109 who was about to tackle Sgt Westcott, who later observed his late attacker spin down minus a wing."

Sgt Doug Eastman (Z2840/GL-T) also engaged the bombers, as reported in the *Times of Malta* next day:

> "Another Sergeant Pilot [Eastman] attacked in turn two Ju88s and two Me109s. His tracer bullets ripped into the fuselage of one bomber, the underneath side of the other and hit the rear-gunner in the second. Bursts of tracer also hit both the fighters."

However, the Squadron lost its new CO when 27-year-old Sqn Ldr Ron Chaffe was shot down in Z3452/GL-B. It seemed he had been so intent on getting his first victory that he failed to see his attacker and was forced to bale out. He was observed at the time of the action in his dinghy four to five miles south of Delimara Point, but was not found by the rescue services. Another Hurricane (UP-N) landed badly shot up although Plt Off Oliver was unhurt. For the loss of one of their own, the Messerschmitt pilots claimed two Hurricanes, Uffz Max Nairz claiming one for his third victory, while Obfw Heinz Hipper was credited with another (his seventh) but his Messerschmitt (Yellow 1) crashed on the beach near Scoglitti as he attempted an emergency landing when short of fuel; Hipper was killed. Again Plt Off Ormrod's journal provides an account:

> "Saw some of them dive to attack a Ju88 amongst the clouds over Luqa, which aerodrome the enemy was bombing. Soon they were mixed up with the escorting 109s. One of the enemy fighters with one wing shot away fell to the ground. I myself did not see it fall, but saw the explosion as it hit the ground. Soon 185 were returning to land and it became quite exciting for all concerned as 109s, facilitated by a thin layer of cloud that lay over the aerodrome at 500 feet, joined in the circuit of the aerodrome. Saw one Hurricane in a spin at a low altitude south of the aerodrome. Thought he'd had it, but he just managed to pull out for, by great luck, he was over the valley between M'dina and M'tarfa and pulled out

of his spin in the valley below the level of the high ground on either side – a miraculous escape. 109s were dashing through the thin cloud, a suspended bank of haze, all round and over the aerodrome. I betook myself to an army post on the edge of the aerodrome, determined to shoot at them from the ground if I couldn't fly against them as I wished. I saw two passing through a small gap in the clouds close at hand, and blazed off a few rounds after them with the twin Lewis gun. Don't suppose the bullets caught them up.

The Hurricanes all landed safely except one – S/Ldr Chaffe is supposed to have baled out off Kalafrana Point. P/O Oliver landed streaming glycol fumes. His aircraft was much shot about. It had large cannon shell holes in the port wing and much of the port aileron had been shot away. Inside the fuselage there was damage to the glycol pipes and inside the cockpit a bullet had cut through his R/T plug just beside his seat. Something had also passed through his trouser leg, luckily without wounding him, and his trousers were soaked in glycol. It was he who had spun and escaped so miraculously. He had been attacked by two 109s from opposite sides, at the same time, so that he could not attack both head-on. He turned into one; but that forced him to turn his tail to the other which did the damage. Escaping from these unhurt, he considered landing. It was as he was approaching the aerodrome with this intent that he was again attacked. He knew he would probably spin on account of his aircraft being damaged. He pulled the stick into his stomach. His aircraft spun out of the turn at once. He was low. He began to attempt to bale out, but decided he was too low. The ground was so near that he had to pull up forcibly, risking a spin in the other direction. His aircraft immediately flicked the other way but luckily came out at once and thus he just got away with it . . . I spoke to [Harry] Moon in the Union Club this afternoon. He says he was down at Marsaxlokk with [Flt Lt] Palliser when S/Ldr Chaffe was shot down. He saw Chaffe chasing a Ju88. He was a long way behind it and only overtaking it slowly. Some 109s saw him, overtook him and shot him down, whilst he was still intent on his pursuit of the Junkers. Moon did not see anyone bale out, but Palliser said that he thought he saw someone do so. Just before dark four of 185 went off to try and find Chaffe. They had not really started to search the sea off Benghaisa Point when they were recalled. 109s pursued them back. The rescue launch did not go out on account of enemy fighters. It has not done so since 109s shot it up recently, killing some of the crew. The search was postponed until night. Poor show."

At 0915 next morning (23 February), Flt Lt Rhys Lloyd, temporarily in command of 185 Squadron, led ten Hurricanes to escort a Maryland setting out to continue the search for Sqn Ldr Chaffe's dinghy. As the Hurricanes climbed they were attacked by two Bf109Fs and broke formation. Two Ju88s of I/KG54 and four more Messerschmitts were then seen approaching from the south-east and were individually engaged by the Hurricanes. Sgt Garth Horricks (Z5140/C) attacked one bomber and saw his fire hitting home before he was forced to break away to take on a Bf109F; this was attacked at close range and he was credited with its probable destruction; this was later upgraded to confirmed. Flt Lt Lloyd (BG769/LE-W) got several bursts in at one of the Ju88s, gaining strikes on its wing roots, rear fuselage and starboard engine, which began to smoke. This aircraft was considered unlikely to have reached its base although it did, B3+KH crash-landing at Catania. Others engaged the escort, and Sgt Archie Steele (Z4011/HA-B) chased a Messerschmitt down from 10,000 feet to sea level, claiming several strikes on his victim which he believed he shot down; Sgt Doug Eastman (Z2840/GL-T) attacked another, observing a trail of white smoke as it escaped. One Hurricane (BD826/A) force-landed at Hal Far, Flt Sgt Jock Sutherland reporting that the engine had suddenly cut-out and stopped. It is not clear if this was due to combat damage. During the next raid a Ju88 of I/KG54 was shot down by AA fire, B3+CH falling in flames into the sea between Filfla and the coast; Ormrod:

"The AA guns shot the tail off a Ju88. Am told that three of the crew baled out. Saw some Holy Fathers on a neighbouring roof raking an unholy delight in watching enemy airmen crashing to their deaths."

The rescue launch was sent out and recovered two seriously injured airmen and the body of a third, but Messerschmitts were again encountered by Hurricanes searching for the missing Sqn Ldr Chaffe, although they came off second best on this occasion when Sgt Tony Boyd (LE-P) of 242 Squadron shot down Gfr Otto Butschek (White 4) of 10(*Jabo*)/JG53, while a second was claimed damaged by 126 Squadron's Sgt Jock Gardiner; Boyd reported:

> "Did search for dinghy, then joined remainder of Squadron to intercept 6+. Saw enemy aircraft and peeled off alone to attack as others did not see them. Fired short burst at one 300 yards from astern. Saw no results. Then got into position under a second and fired four-second burst from stern quarter below. Obviously got him. Two others in line of fire. Cannon fire whizzing by so returned at 0 feet. Sgt Gardiner shot at one on my tail."

Gfr Butschek was seen to bale out but did not survive. Nor did the missing Sqn Ldr Chaffe. During the day's raids all three airfields were attacked; two Wellingtons, an unserviceable Blenheim and a Hurricane were badly damaged at Luqa, as was another Hurricane (BG754) at Takali.

Next day (24 February) there was another Ju88/*Jabo* raid directed against Takali, from where Hurricanes had just scrambled, including one flown by Sgt Ted Wood of 1435 Flight:

> "A wizard clear day, but nothing happened until 1200 noon with the next scramble. Just after we had gone off, four 109s bombed the drome and got a direct hit on the dispersal. Poor old Mac was killed. On the scramble I could not keep up and as four 109s and two 88s were close, I broke away and came to land. On coming down I had a terrible job pulling out and found that the fabric on the elevators and behind the cockpit had torn away."

Flg Off Denis Winton of 1435 Flight was also on the scramble, flying GL-E of 185 Squadron:

> "Intercepted two 88s 1,000 feet above. Chased them 45 miles to Sicily but could not get in range. Fired long burst 400 yards from below astern. No damage seen."

On returning to Takali the pilots discovered the full extent of the damage inflicted by the *Jabo* attack; their dispersal hut had been hit by a 250-lb bomb dropped by a Bf109F. A witness, LAC Bill Metcalfe, recalled:

> "Plt Off Macnamara was killed; four more injured. We were all leaning against the wall when the Messerschmitt dropped a bomb but he had to give us a burst of cannon fire, which told us what to expect. We all dived for the hole and just made it. Truscott, who was the only chap behind me, was badly hurt."

Although Plt Off Thady Macnamara of 242 Squadron was the only fatality, Flt Lt Lloyd was among the injured. Command of 185 Squadron passed to Sqn Ldr Mortimer-Rose, now recovered from his wounds whilst leading 249 Squadron at the end of December.

> "It is most sad that it should have been Macnamara. There are many whom I would exchange in death for him. Lloyd and Macnamara were lying beside each other when the bomb fell on the roof. The blast killed Macnamara, but appears only to have dazed Lloyd, who has been dug out of the debris."

So wrote 19-year-old Plt Off Sonny Ormrod, who listed his 'Principles of Life' as: War – supreme object of man's existence; Women – diversions to be avoided; Wine – man's downfall, and also held very scathing opinions about some of his contemporaries. He seemed to fail to understand that many wished to unwind, let off steam and live for the day; his journal records many events and incidents that did not meet with his approval:

"I was being introduced to F/Lt S and this clever fellow asks how many drinking hours I've got. I told him I did not drink. This fellow rather prides himself on his drinking. Take him to be one of those fellows whose only reason for being a fighter pilot is to get a line to shoot and an excuse to drink. I have no use for such fellows. I fancy his type is more interested in having a good time, and thinks the chief object of a fighter pilot is to attract women."

"F/O T was quite amusing, ending up falling asleep on the ante-room floor, warming his bare feet at the fire. His uniform bore German eagles, iron crosses, etc. marked on in white chalk. S/Ldr Andrews says he's met him numerous times before, but only on one of those occasions was he sober, and then because he was about to fly."

"P/O B was too drunk again last night to find the place, and now has decided to move to other apartments. He really is a disgrace. One night he shouted with foul language to be let in when intoxicated at three in the morning."

"Last night F/Lt S, F/O T, P/O M and F/Lt T, being intoxicated, were a menace, I hear, with their revolvers, shooting at electric light bulbs etc. They find their .38 revolvers a great help in getting meals served late, for they threaten the Maltese servants with them. It annoys me to hear them spending their time singing vulgar songs instead of contemplating how to outwit the enemy. I for my part think constantly of my few experiences and what I did wrong and why I failed to shoot down an enemy aircraft. How combat fills my thoughts. I have much to learn. I have learnt much, but I lack immeasurable experience."

Plt Off Ormrod was in for an even greater shock, as were his colleagues in 605 Squadron, when Sqn Ldr Andrews was suddenly banished to the Middle East following an incident in a Valetta night club which upset the Provost Marshal. Ormrod wrote:

"The others went to Valetta last night, leaving here at twenty minutes to midnight. Ridiculous. Joe came back and tells us that Stones and the CO are under arrest for hitting somebody; but it turned out that it is not quite so bad as that. Wigley told me all about last night's affairs. They had pitched the proprietor of the Great Britain out of his hotel once or twice in the early hours of the morning, because he was rude, and had dealt with a wingless Squadron Leader who'd interfered. The Provost Marshal took their names, but seemed to side with them. It was all very funny as described by Wigley."

In fact the Provost Marshal did not see the funny side of the incident. Plt Off McKay provided additional detail:

"On this particular night they gathered in the lobby. The elevator to the fourth floor was inoperative, and they carried on their party there. A gentleman in a rather loud bathrobe appeared, having walked down four flights of stairs, demanded that the noise cease forthwith. Andy, backed by his dauntless fighter pilots, informed the unidentified individual to leave (I am putting this in as gentlemanly manner as possible), which he did. He returned some ten minutes later in the uniform of a Wing Commander, informed the gathered gentlemen that he was Judge Advocate General of Fortress Malta, and that the four gentlemen were under arrest. The following day they appeared before him. The three junior officers were given a severe reprimand. Andy was informed that he would be transferred to Cairo immediately. He in fact was flown out of Malta the following day. We learned some weeks later that Andy was probably overjoyed that he had been transferred to Egypt. The very attractive barmaid whom he had been seeing rather frequently for some months was noticeably pregnant."[20]

That night I/LG1 despatched a number of Ju88s into the darkened skies above Malta, individual aircraft orbiting Luqa and Hal Far, releasing bombs at opportune moments. Hurricanes were sent up and one intercepted Lt Georg Sattler's aircraft; unable to shake off the night fighter despite a series of violent manoeuvres, Sattler was only able to evade due to the speed of his bomber and set course for Sicily. The Hurricane pursued the fleeing Junkers northwards, almost as far as Catania, but was unable to close.

Having witnessed the way in which the Hurricanes attempted to carry out their battle climbs with Messerschmitts sitting above, waiting to pick them off, Sqn Ldr Turner immediately implemented new tactics, as Laddie Lucas reported:

> "Stan Turner's impact on the day fighter operations in Malta was immediate and lasting. Taking over 249 at Takali when things were close to their worst, he sized up the situation in a couple of days. He put the case bluntly to Grp Capt Woodhall, the operations controller, with whom he had worked closely at Tangmere. Either we get Spitfire Vs on the island in days – not weeks – or we're done. Woodhall understood immediately. He in turn was equally forthright with Air Vice-Marshal Lloyd, who knew the score anyway.
>
> Stan Turner's other lasting accomplishment was to change the squadrons' style of flying on the island. The effect upon him of having seen, on his first morning, that section of four Hurricanes clambering up in straggling V formation, with the 109s thousands of feet above, had been profound. Within a week, pairs and fours in line abreast had become the only battle formation flown on the island. Vs and line astern were out. Apart from the change in style of flying, the tactics employed in promoting the interceptions were radically overhauled. No longer were the sections, even with the old Hurricanes, vectored straight on to the approaching enemy aircraft, with the manoeuvring climb left to the leader's own discretion. Instead, the few serviceable aircraft were got off the ground much earlier, as the raids began to move in from Sicily. In place of the climb northwards towards the enemy – or, at best, sideways to the east or west – the instructions to the pilots were to use the extra time in gaining altitude to the south of the island, right away from the course of the attackers. It gave much more elbow room."[21]

But first, Sqn Ldr Turner would have to learn the hard way, which almost cost him his life. At 1510 on 24 February, radar screens picked up the blips of approaching aircraft and eight Hurricanes manned by 249 Squadron[22] pilots were scrambled, these separating into pre-arranged pairs. Sqn Ldr Turner and his No2 Plt Off Don Tedford were vectored to the reported height of four 'hostiles', but were unable to see them. The Controller informed Turner that they were dead ahead, but had apparently confused the two plots on the radar. The four 'hostiles' – Bf109Fs from Stab/JG53 – were in fact behind, and the Hurricanes were consequently bounced. Tedford's aircraft BG771 was shot down into the sea by Lt Franz Schiess (his 16th victory), while Turner's Z3580 took hits in the cockpit and engine, which caught fire. Unable to open the damaged cockpit hood to bale out, the slightly wounded Canadian dived his aircraft steeply, whereby the flames were extinguished, enabling him to make a belly-landing at Luqa. What the irascible Turner later told the unfortunate Controller has not been recorded. One of Tedford's American friends, Plt Off Howard Coffin, wrote in his diary:

> "Two 109s intercepted Sqn Ldr Turner DFC. Crash-landed wheels-up at Luqa aerodrome. Bullet clipped his goggles from helmet. Plt Off Tedford, one of the four Americans on this bloody island, shot down and last seen to have crashed in the sea. Words cannot express how I feel at this moment. I've lost a buddy and the Air Force has lost a wizard pilot."[23]

Apparently Tedford had called Control to say he was wounded and baling out. When Coffin heard the news, he went off in search of him:

> "Nobody ever blamed me for leaving my post of duty that day. At Takali I managed to get a plane into the air that was no good for fighting, but was serviceable for patrol, and went looking for Tedford. I searched the sea until dark. I found no sign of life down below."[24]

For the next week or so there was a slackening in the intensity of the raids, partly due to further storms and torrential rains. This allowed some of the new pilots to familiarise themselves with local terrain – essential to improve their chances of survival in combat, and to sharpen and refresh their reflexes for the coming fight. Whilst the Luftwaffe's respite was most welcome, all felt this was but a temporary pause – the lull before the storm.

Newly-arrived Flg Off Raoul Daddo-Langlois, attached to 185 Squadron pending the arrival of the Spitfires, damaged Hurricane UP-P on the 25th when he crash-landed at Hal Far. A little later two Ju88s carried out a sneak raid on Takali, suddenly appearing out of low cloud. Two patrolling Hurricanes flown by Flt Lt Don Stones (GL-P) and Flt Lt Laddie Lucas (Z2824/HA-H) intercepted one of the bombers, Stones getting in a burst which caused it to jettison its bombs; one of these fell on a farmhouse, injuring an occupant. A second pair of Hurricanes flown by Plt Offs Ormrod (BG698/LE-U) and McKay (Z3757/GN-R) covered their attack, as the former noted:

> "I was leading my section on the starboard side of Stones, so that I might keep watch on him and into the sun, where there might be enemy fighters. Suddenly he began turning steeply to starboard. I looked round to see what he'd seen and saw a Ju88 about 2,000 feet above us and coming our way. It had just emerged from a huge bank of cloud that towered several thousand feet, like a huge rock, above the level of the main cloud layer. The Ju88 turned, diving steeply. We gave chase, McKay and I keeping a sharp look-out behind in our mirrors. I cut the corner of the Ju88's turn and was approaching to attack from the back when he disappeared in cloud. Stones had opened fire from astern, but outside the effective range for machine-guns."

Sqn Ldr Westmacott was also airborne, meeting the same pair of bombers which he chased back towards Sicily. Luqa was the target for a similar raid next day (26 February) where another Wellington was severely damaged; two of the precious petrol bowsers also went up in flames. The last engagements of the month occurred to the 27th, as five Hurricanes intercepted Ju88s and escorting Bf109Fs over Grand Harbour during the late afternoon. Flt Lt Bud Connell led a trio of 126 Squadron pilots, while the other section comprised Plt Off Ormrod (GN-E) and Plt Off McKay (Z2480/GL-T) of 605 Squadron, the former describing the somewhat chaotic events leading up to the successful interception of one of the Ju88s:

> "At about 5 o'clock, 185 Squadron came to replace us. Luckily P/O Allardice was slow in changing over with me. And in the middle of the change over there was a scramble. Not being ready himself, he told me to go and strapped me in. I taxied out to Stones' aircraft, but only found Steele getting out. Stones had already handed it over. Three other aircraft were now at the end of the runway waiting for someone to give them a lead. I would have done so myself but I had no code card, having lent mine to Stones. At last someone took off and the rest of us followed. We formed up into two sections of two aircraft. Somebody was calling himself Red 1 [presumably Flt Lt Connell] and Control gave him instructions. As we climbed south towards the sun another aircraft, GL-T flown by McKay, caught up.
>
> From Control we continually received positions of the enemy fighters. They were higher than us. We kept climbing and looking around. Expected to be jumped at any moment. Had to keep climbing further and further out to sea. Dared not turn our backs to the sun and return towards the island. Suddenly I saw three single-engined aircraft in line astern swing round in a left-handed turn about 500 to 1,000 feet below and some 500 yards away, between us and the island. I called out, 'Three aircraft approaching from astern'. I then made up my mind that they were 109s and peeled off in a steep left-handed turn to engage them as they attempted to attack. I think it was the middle one I chose. He was only 50 yards away, banking past me, so that I saw his plan view from above. My tracers appeared to be going right into the top of his cockpit; but tracer is deceptive, so I cannot be sure. Anyway, when next I was able to take stock of the situation only two of the 109s were continuing the game, so I suppose I'd got him.
>
> I led the other two aircraft that were with me back towards the island. I saw an aircraft

some distance behind and thought it was a Hurricane catching us up. Thought wrong. I had dismissed this aircraft from my mind, when shells started bursting on my port side between myself and the next fellow. Decided I'd better turn round and see what was happening. Saw the enemy aircraft climbing away towards the sun, issuing a trail of black smoke. Called out over the R/T, 'Rotten shooting, you little bastard'. He'd opened fire at extreme range into the middle of our formation, hitting no one, instead of sneaking up to a more favourable position and picking off one of us. By opening fire at such a range he gave warning of his presence soon enough for McKay to turn round and meet him head-on, as I afterwards learnt. McKay believes he hit the Messerschmitt."

The 126 Squadron trio also engaged the Messerschmitts but only Plt Off Howard Coffin was able to make a claim, the American now showing increasing confidence:

"Intercepted three 109s and two 88s . . . Had three-second burst at one 109. Damage claimed. The 109s aren't so hot when you can see them."[25]

Ormrod now found himself alone over Malta, with Control warning that bandits were still around. On enquiring if there were any bombers in the vicinity, he was advised of a plot approaching St Paul's Bay from the north:

"I was at 4,500 feet when I saw the AA engaging five Ju88s over St Paul's Bay – could see the 109s above them. The bombers began to dive towards the east. I whistled off to meet them at the bottom of their dive, which would be over the Grand Harbour area. I kept glancing behind and into my mirror until I was within range of the Junkers. As I approached, he turned, giving me a head-on view. Now I couldn't see whether he turned his head or his tail towards me. Suddenly I realised he was approaching me. The range was therefore closing quickly. I was about 1,000 feet above the enemy aircraft. I pushed forward my nose, but it would not go as far as I desired. I fired a burst, which I could not hold, from above and in front. I was in the middle of all the flak, too.

Passing the enemy, I turned steeply to starboard and back after the Junkers. I took a shot from a quarter astern at about 300 yards. I then held my fire until I was about 200 yards astern. I fired at both engines. Smoke began to emerge from both engines. All this time the confounded Bofors guns fired up past my nose and behind the Junkers, from which I was therefore separated by a stream of 'flaming onions'. One shell burst close on my port bow. The Junkers was losing height in a shallow dive. I fired my last rounds into him from about 100 yards astern, a couple of hundred feet above the sea this side of Filfla. The enemy aircraft had then lost a great deal of speed and was not going at much of a pace. The sea being below, I broke away above him. I had no ammunition left and returned to Takali."

After he had landed he was congratulated by several who had watched his attack, including Flt Lt Stones, Sqn Ldr Wells of 242 Squadron and Wg Cdr Rabagliati, who told him that Sqn Ldr Turner had also witnessed the action from Safi and saw the Ju88 drop its undercarriage and disappear behind Filfla. He added that he thought he had seen a flash, such as a small explosion would produce. In fact the bomber – M7+DK of KGr806 flown by Lt Wilhelm Schmidt – failed to return and evidently crashed into the sea; there were no survivors.

A big disappointment at this time was the delay in the arrival of the promised Spitfires. Rumour was rife at Malta – Spitfires were said to be on their way but the old sweats had heard it all before. This time though, the optimists were about to be rewarded although the first batch were experiencing technical problems with the experimental auxiliary fuel tanks fitted to each aircraft, and it would be another week before they actually arrived. Following Grp Capt Woodhall's approach, Air Vice-Marshal Lloyd, perhaps more disappointed than most, signalled the AOC-in-C accordingly, outlining the current grave situation:

"Daylight attacks on aerodromes very serious. Little work being done owing to continuous alerts. Much minor damage to aircraft sufficient to make them unserviceable for night operations. They are repaired next day and then hit again. Deliveries are serious problem as they are damaged if they stay here during day. The longer they stay, the more the damage. Have 17 Wellingtons in this category, including those damaged in landing on arrival here with further minor damage due to air action. To avoid this, the Wellingtons are passed through same night as arrival with relief crews. This is difficult with continuous intruder raids, but we can take it. Must have more fighters as soon as possible. Delay in Spitfires is annoying . . ."[26]

For Malta the situation was going to get worse, much worse. During the month Feldmarschall Kesselring had called a conference at II Fliegerkorps' HQ at Messina to discuss preparation for the overdue air assault on Malta:

"When I inspected the formations I found them confident and eager. The basic idea of II Air Group's orders was to surprise then neutralise the enemy's fighters, or at least to cripple them so much that they would not be any considerable danger to the ensuing bombing assault, while the three airfields were to be attacked at short intervals with heavy bombs, light anti-personnel bombs and machine-gun fire in order to destroy the aircraft on the ground and to render the runways at least temporary unserviceable.

The objectives of further bombing raids were the airfields and harbour installations and shipping: the town itself [Valetta] was to be spared. Daylight attacks were to be concentrated and incessant, and given such powerful fighter protection that the British fighters would be kept away from our bombers and pursued until they were wiped out. At night continual nuisance raids by single aircraft were to hinder clearing up the wreckage and repairs. An additional part of the programme was the sinking of the few supply ships making for the port by dive-bombing attacks, and the blocking of the harbour entrance by dropping mines."[27]

The die was cast.

CHAPTER X

SPITFIRES JOIN BATTLE

March 1942

On 1 March there was a midday scramble involving nine Hurricanes flown by 242 and 605 Squadron pilots, followed by another four manned by 185 Squadron, which intercepted the usual trio of Ju88s (from 8/KG77 on this occasion) and escorting Bf109Fs from II and III/JG53. The two formations clashed over Benghaisa at 14,000 feet, one section of Hurricanes managing to evade the escort, Flt Lt Stones, Plt Off Phil Wigley (GL-C) and Flt Sgt Dave Howe (Z3756) inflicting considerable damage to the bombers they attacked, Stones having carried out a solo attack while Wigley and Howe jointly engaged a second; Oblt Erich Behr crash-landed his damaged aircraft at Donnafugata on return, resulting in its total destruction with all members of the crew sustaining injuries, while a second bomber flown by Uffz Heinrich Gassmann crashed near Santa Cruse and was also totally destroyed, the injured pilot being the only survivor from this aircraft. Immediately following his attack on the Ju88, Howe's aircraft was hit and the Canadian baled out, breaking a leg when coming down at Marsaxlokk.

Another of the 605 Squadron pilots, Plt Off Chuck Lester, managed to manoeuvre on to the tail of one unsuspecting Messerschmitt and launched an attack; as a result, Fw Alexander Kehlbuth of 5 Staffel was wounded and subsequently force-landed his damaged fighter at Syracuse, where his aircraft suffered further severe damage. A second Messerschmitt – from 6 Staffel – crash-landed at Comiso in a damaged condition, possibly as a result of combat with a 242 Squadron Hurricane flown either by American Plt Off Jimmy Tew Jr or Canadian Flt Sgt Ray Harvey, both of whom failed to return. Tew died when Z2824/H was shot down over the east coast, while Harvey attempted to abandon his burning aircraft (Z4002) at low level, but was killed when it hit the sea five miles off Delimara Point; apparently he had unfastened his seat straps ready to bale out and his body, which was later recovered by HSL107, had been thrown clear. LAC Phil Chandler at Kalafrana witnessed the return of the launch:

> "Saw a Hurricane spin into the sea just behind married quarters. Then a parachute opened behind Fort St Lucien – whether theirs or ours, I can't say [this was obviously Flt Sgt Howe]. 107 picked up a Hurricane pilot this afternoon – protected by Hurricanes, for Messerschmitts were lurking. The pilot was lying on the deck of the launch when they returned. His legs were badly burned and his face just a mass of blood. They covered the body with a blanket and rowed him ashore, while the deck of the launch was washed down."

One of these three Hurricanes fell to Lt Hermann Neuhoff (his 36th victory) of 7/JG53 and a second to Lt Hermann Münzert of 9/JG53 for his 14th victory; the third Hurricane may have been the victim of the wounded Fw Kehlbuth, although he was not credited with it. As soon as the battle receded, Flt Lt Stones and Plt Off Wigley took off to search for the missing pilots, but only Flt Sgt Howe had survived this latest clash with the Messerschmitts. Plt Off Ormrod, although not flying, recorded what he saw from the ground:

> "Was about to clean my teeth in my quarters, when I decided to postpone it to watch a dogfight, which I could hear above. Unfortunately, clouds obscured it. Something hit the water in Kalafrana Bay and bombs burst in the neighbourhood. Suddenly to the north-east a pilot hanging from a parachute emerged from cloud. A Hurricane circled round to protect him, so concluded him to be one of our pilots. Then saw two 109s attack a Hurricane at no great altitude below cloud near Hal Far. The Hurricane (learnt afterwards it was Nigel

Kemp) only just turned out of their way in time.

I went down to the slipway and went out with the crew, commanded by an officer, in a rowing boat to one of the smaller launches. In this we sped at a great pace across Kalafrana Bay and into Marsaxlokk Bay, where we thought the pilot might have landed. No sign of him in the water, however. Found he'd landed just on the shore near the guardroom at Marsaxlokk. I disembarked. An ambulance was arriving, so the speedboat returned to Kalafrana. Found the pilot was F/Sgt Howe of my squadron, though I did not at first recognise him, he wearing a khaki battledress he'd acquired for himself, being unable to get a blue one. He had hurt his left ankle, but was otherwise all right.

Howe was flying No2 to F/Lt Stones. Stones attacked the first Junkers and Howe attacked the second from underside and on the beam, giving plenty of deflection and then allowing it to pass through his burst. He is sure he raked it from stem to stern. The last thing he knew was that he'd lost control of his own aircraft; that the instrument panel was smashed and that fabric all around him was torn. He did not know what had hit him. He decided to bale out. He did so but forgot to undo the oxygen tube. This held him, at first, half out of the cockpit, but it then broke. He allowed himself to fall to the clouds before pulling his ripcord. His parachute opened in cloud. He worked hard on the shroud lines to prevent himself falling in the water. Unfortunately in succeeding to fall on land he hurt his ankle. Otherwise he was uninjured. When he last saw the Junkers it was spiralling down, issuing white smoke. He claims half share, having seen another Hurricane [Plt Off Wigley] on its tail."

Hal Far and Luqa were both on the receiving end of raids during the daylight hours of 2 March, and although Hurricanes were up they could not prevent five Ju88s of KüFlGr606 from bombing the target area. Later in the day six Bf109F *Jabo* raided Luqa while three Ju88s of II/KG77 attacked Safi and another from I/KG54 bombed Kalafrana. Darkness brought much activity over both Malta and Sicily as ten Wellingtons from Luqa targeted Palermo, where a number of ships were sunk or damaged, while a similar number of Ju88s dropped bombs on Luqa and Kalafrana, one bomb damaging the Officers' Mess and a building where some of the officers were sleeping; Plt Off D'Arcy Milburn had a lucky escape when half the room collapsed on his bed without injuring him. One Ju88 was shot down by the guns, M7+CH from KGr806 falling into the sea with no survivors from Lt Heinz Jesek's crew, whereas all the Wellingtons returned from their very successful operation.

Eleven Hurricanes were scrambled after six Ju88s of KGr806 during the early afternoon of the 3rd, with Sqn Ldr Wells of 242 Squadron leading. Two of the bombers were claimed damaged before the escorting Messerschmitts forced the Hurricanes away. Bombs fell on Luqa were a Wellington was hit and burnt out. Meanwhile, six *Jabo* attacked Hal Far. During a later raid by two Ju88s of I/KG54, Luqa was again targeted and this time four Wellingtons and a PR Beaufighter were damaged; in addition, a submarine was strafed by a single Bf109F as it entered harbour, although damage was slight. Ju88s droned over the island during the night, dropping the occasional bomb. One Hurricane (Z3562) piloted by Flg Off Denis Winton took off but failed to make contact. He had a lucky escape when his engine cut as he came in to land; Sgt Wood wrote: "Watched pretty breathless for a minute, saw the aircraft go in and burn – and [then] saw a parachute by the light of the fire. He was quite OK and landed in Rabat."

The Hurricanes were back in the thick of the action on 4 March, all available aircraft being scrambled during the early afternoon when five Ju88s approached from the north. Sqn Ldr Wells of 242 Squadron again led the mixed formation and attacked a Ju88, setting its port engine on fire; the same aircraft was targeted by his No2 Sgt Jock Gardiner. Flt Lt Kee of 242 Squadron went after another bomber and saw pieces fall off its port wing as a result of his attack; meanwhile, Plt Off Ron Noble of 605 Squadron gained strikes on the tailplane, fuselage and one engine of his target before his own aircraft (Z2414/E) was hit by return fire. Yet another Ju88 was damaged by Flt Sgt Jack Fletcher (BD826/A) with strikes observed on the rear-gunner's turret and on the fuselage, but the German doggedly returned fire and damaged the Canadian pilot's Hurricane, forcing him to break away; one bullet penetrated his armour plating and another struck the windscreen. Two of the escorting Messerschmitts were claimed damaged, one by Plt Off Marcus Kidson, who saw pieces fly of his victim's tail unit, forcing it into a shallow dive, while Sgt Alan Wilson (Z3757/R) claimed the other. One aircraft from 3/JG53 force-landed at Gela on return, and one from 2 Staffel returned badly damaged and overturned on landing although Lt Günther Hess survived unhurt; these were possibly the victims of Kidson and Wilson. One Messerschmitt failed to return, Plt Off Ormrod possibly shooting down Fw Hans Stockmann of 2/JG53:

> "I noticed an aircraft on my tail just coming into range on me. I turned in my dive and just as I was pulling out to climb up, I skimmed over the top of a Ju88, which was lagging behind its friends. It was too late for me to turn and engage it, so continued after the fighter above. We were approaching head-on and I almost fired when I realised it was a Hurricane. I later discovered that it was F/Sgt Fletcher, my own No2. He had lagged behind, owing probably to his aircraft being slower than the rest. He passed me and attacked the Junkers.
>
> Turning round again, I met three 109s in line astern. They came from my starboard bow and turned across close in front of me. I opened fire on the last, giving him plenty of deflection. My first rounds were in front of him, but he was soon in my fire. I saw my de Wilde [tracer] strike on his underside, but could only hold him thus in my sights for a brief moment. I followed on his tail and fired a second burst into him at 250 yards – he was filling the crossbars gap on my sight – and again saw my de Wilde striking. He was now diving gently and seemed to have lost touch with his fellows. I could not stop to see what happened to him owing to the presence of more of the enemy. I doubt he reached his aerodrome, for I think I may have finished the pilot, or anyway jammed his elevators for he took no evasive action. I expect he went into the sea at the same angle of dive. I don't believe he would know what hit him, for I had the sun behind me."

Fw Stockmann later wrote:

> "Lt [Günther] Hess' *Schwarm*, in which I was a wingman, climbed into the sun off to one side of the bombers. From a height of 7,000 meters we dived in the direction of Malta and arrived just in time to rescue a lone Ju88 from a pack of Hurricanes. As we dove I saw the following: the Ju88 was flying north, 400 meters below to the left of a Hurricane. Above and to the right of the Ju88 another Hurricane and, directly behind the tail of the Ju88 was a third Hurricane. Lt Hess attacked the last-mentioned Hurricane from the right rear and then dived away. I could see from the smoke trails that the Hurricane was still firing. I at first found myself directly behind the Hurricane but could not fire for fear of hitting the Ju88. So I swung out to the left a little and opened fire with all weapons from a range of 80 meters until I was forced to pull right up to avoid a collision. The Hurricane went down. I did not observe it crash."[1]

As Stockmann pulled away, his aircraft was hit from behind by another Hurricane:

> "I put the nose down, picked up speed and slowly climbed to 2,000 meters. By applying left and right rudder I was able to determine that there were no enemy aircraft behind me, however I was leaving a white smoke trail – the cooling system had been hit. As far as I could ascertain in the time available to me, my machine had sustained a fist-size hole in the left radiator flap, two holes level with the left radiator and a hole in the rear of the cockpit. This bullet had glanced off the head armour plate."[2]

Having informed Sicily of his plight, course and position, he set off over the sea to put as much distance behind him as possible, intending to carry out a ditching off the coast of Sicily:

"I approached the surface of the water in such a way that I could set down parallel to the waves. I touched down at about 150 kpm, braced myself against the windscreen with my left hand and drew up my legs. The shock of landing was much less than I expected. After releasing my harness I jumped out onto the right wing still wearing my parachute, and from there into the water. I had to get rid of the parachute at once as it forced my head under water. At the same time I opened the compressed air bottle on my life vest. I opened the upper belt of the inflatable raft before I tried opening the CO_2 bottle. The raft popped out of the container without difficulty."[3]

Once aboard his life raft he fired a signal flare to let his circling comrades know that he was all right, but had to wait until next morning before he was located and picked up by a Do24 of 6 Seenotstaffel. This was one of the few occasions when Malta's Hurricanes came off better. During another raid by Messerschmitts of II/JG3, Uffz Benedikt Wegmann's aircraft (Black 3) of 5 Staffel was hit by AA fire and crashed on rocks at the Pembroke Ranges; Wegmann baled out and came down into the sea just offshore, from where he was able to swim to safety and into captivity. That made two Bf109Fs shot down and two badly damaged for the day. The run of successes continued after dark when Sgt Ted Wood of 1435 Flight chalked up his second night victory by shooting down a Ju88 of 2/KüFlGr606 which had been illuminated by searchlights. Uffz Albert Degenhardt and his crew of 7T+JK perished when their aircraft crashed in flames near Siggiewi:

"Took off on a night flying test and a plot came in. Stayed up and was vectored around but saw nothing at all; was very close at least six times. The Controller congratulated me on my efforts, said it was good work. Took off on another scramble and was again vectored around; followed one in but got fogged. I was going across the island when I saw an aircraft firing at the searchlights, going the other way. I turned towards it and it was illuminated. I closed very fast and hit its slipstream at about 300 yards, so I could not get my sight on. I straightened up and just had time for about 15 rounds from each cannon, and saw strikes. I broke away and just missed the tail and port wing, then lost it. The rear-gunner was shooting off everything he had, finally a lot of coloured lights like Very cartridges were shot off. Next minute I saw it crash in flames near Dingli, where it burned for a long time. Most people seemed a bit jealous of my luck but I felt satisfied."

Ten-year-old Anthony Busuttil visited the scene early next morning with a friend:

". . . big parts of the Junkers were scattered all over the area. About eight soldiers were collecting parts of the bodies in sandbags. My friend and I found a foot with the big toe missing. We left it on the ground as the soldiers sent us away because they said that there may be some ammunition which may have been dangerous."[4]

Just before midday on 5 March, six Hurricanes manned by 242 Squadron intercepted five Ju88s of II/KG77 and ten escorting Messerschmitts north of Grand Harbour; Sgt Tony Boyd (LE-P) went after the bombers:

"I attacked rear three in turn, causing black smoke to pour from engines of two, and strikes seen on the third. First one attacked slowed up and lost height. Jumped by Messerschmitts throughout and lost P/O Kidson."

Boyd was credited with two of the bombers damaged, one of them from 4 Staffel in which the observer was wounded. Plt Off Marcus Kidson (Z2402) was indeed shot down and killed, the victim of Obfw Heinrich Leschert of 3/JG53 (his 7th victory); his aircraft was seen to plunge into the sea about eight miles from Grand Harbour, and he was not seen to bale out. It is believed that Kidson may have intercepted a Do24 ASR flying boat just before being shot down, this machine returning to Syracuse with a dead air gunner (Fw Erich Liebick) aboard, although one pilot reported that he had last seen Kidson chasing what he thought was a Ju88. Luqa was again heavily raided, one Wellington being totally destroyed, with another sustaining damage as did a Maryland and two unserviceable Blenheims. The Ju88s were back after dark, yet another Wellington being destroyed and three other aircraft damaged.

Midway through the afternoon of 6 March, eight Hurricanes were scrambled, Bf109Fs (possibly from II/JG3) being encountered west of Filfla. Flt Lt Stones (BG770/GL-D) attacked one and got in a long burst, raking it from nose to tail before losing sight of it. Shortly afterwards a parachute was reported coming down to the north of the island and on the strength of this sighting Don Stones was credited with a victory, his 15th including five shared; he wrote:

> "I was convinced that deflection shooting was an art I would never learn and that those pilots who had it were born bird-shots who had probably been given a shotgun when still in their prams. We discussed many times the theory of deflection shooting, particularly for the fleeting targets of turning 109s. The theory was well known – setting wingspan of the enemy aircraft and its estimated speed on one's reflector sight, aiming off a ring or so ahead of the nose, but I seemed to have no time to fiddle with my reflector sight in close fighting. Perhaps I needed a rest. My depression endured until 6 March when leading 605 Squadron into an attack on the usual mob of Ju88s. My No2, Joe Beckett from my old school, shouted on the R/T: '109 right behind you!' A glimpse of him in the rear-view mirror, panic evasion turn and reaction shot as he overshot me, turning the wrong way. It was more of a spray than accurate shooting, but the pilot baled out. Blind luck, and I had not hit the cockpit or he would not have baled out. Not satisfactory but a 109 destroyed nevertheless. I was very grateful to Beckett."[5]

Plt Offs Wigley (BE583) and Ormrod (GL-X) were also involved in this action, the latter recording:

> "Soon after crossing the south coast we were attacked from behind by a Messerschmitt. I turned right and pressed the button at the same time. He passed through my burst but, at that speed, would of course only pick up a few bullets. I then turned after him – he turned to starboard slightly in his dive. I fired a short burst from a fine quarter position; saw the tracers going nicely in front of him, think he must have met the bullets, couldn't see. Stopped firing as there were others on his tail from the four in front. Wiggles fired a short burst. Stones delivered a longer burst from his port quarter and then astern. Enemy aircraft began to smoke and was subsequently confirmed as destroyed. Wiggles and I did not consider it worth a report, having been able to get in a short burst and left the victory to Stones, whose it was more than anyone else's. Fletcher, as my No2 having lost me, had a thrilling fight with two 109s. He did not get a shot at them, but they got a number at him, luckily missing him each time."

About an hour later, four bomb-carrying Messerschmitts from 10(*Jabo*) Staffel swept in over Takali at low level, sharp-shooting Bofors gunners shooting down Oblt Hermann Raab's Yellow 4; the pilot was lucky to bale out and landed near Mosta while his aircraft crashed near Rabat.

Meanwhile, the aircraft carrier HMS *Eagle* was again on its way from Gibraltar, with 16 cannon-armed Spitfire Vbs. In preparation for this historic and much-anticipated event, there had been considerable movement of pilots between the squadrons following the recent spate of new arrivals aboard the Sunderlands. Since 249 Squadron was to be the first to re-equip, most of these reinforcements, all Spitfire-trained, were now being concentrated into this unit. The arrival of the Spitfires was in the nick of time. Since the beginning of February, 17 of the island's remaining Hurricanes had been destroyed in the air or on the ground, and at least 14 more damaged; current availability was just 21 machines.

At 0700 on the morning of 7 March, the first Spitfire launched from the deck of *Eagle*, followed within the hour by 14 more; one had become unserviceable and did not take off. Ahead of the pilots was a 700-mile flight, a 45-gallon slipper auxiliary tank bolted beneath the fuselage of each aircraft supplying additional fuel required for the long journey, which proved to be uneventful. Hurricanes covered the Spitfires as they arrived and landed at Takali, but of the Luftwaffe there was fortunately no sign. Four Beaufighters followed them in; these were AI-equipped night fighters which were to take over the rôle of night defence from the Hurricanes of 1435 Flight.

The first the new arrivals were to see of the Luftwaffe was a raid by an estimated 27 aircraft on the three airfields between 1515 and 1910, but it seemed that the Germans were as yet unaware of these formidable new reinforcements. At Hal Far a single Hurricane (Z2819 of 185 Squadron) was destroyed on the ground, while Z2815 of 126 Squadron was written off at Takali. Oblt Otto Böhmer, Staffelkapitän of 6/JG63, returned to Sicily slightly wounded and with his aircraft damaged after having been hit by AA fire. There were no raids at all during the daylight hours of the 8th, the main event being the arrival of three delivery Blenheims for which eight Hurricanes flown by 242 Squadron pilots provided escort. These were met some 30 miles west of Gozo and guided to Luqa without event. Darkness saw the return of the Italian night bombers. Seven BR20Ms of 55°Gruppo BT raided the airfields, joined in this task by an estimated dozen Ju88s. Around midnight, Sqn Ldr Westmacott of 1435 Flight scrambled in Z4004/L and was brought in behind a Ju88 by Ground Control. However, conditions were hazy and he had to pursue the intruder south for about 40 miles before he was finally able to get within range and open fire. Having lost sight of his opponent, he then spotted what appeared to be a flame on the surface of the sea, but did not think it was the Junkers; nonetheless, he was credited with its possible destruction. It seems that the same aircraft – believed to have been a Ju88C of I/NJG2 – was also attacked by one of the newly-arrived Beaufighters, the crew of which reported shooting down a Junkers in flames into the sea. This was R4+V8 in which Oblt Heinz Schulz and his crew perished.

At 0700 on the morning of 9 March, Wg Cdr Rabagliati led seven Hurricanes manned by 242 Squadron pilots to meet and escort an incoming Blenheim. During this flight Sgt Tony Boyd (Z2961/K) saw an aircraft approaching him from behind: "I turned slowly, thinking it was a Hurricane. By the time I realised [it was a Messerschmitt] he was 400 yards ahead. Gave him a futile burst. Followed another plot. No interception." An hour later more Hurricanes were sent out to meet and guide in more delivery Blenheims, on this occasion without incident, but at 1030 the island came under attack once more when three Ju88s and nine Messerschmitts approached. A total of ten Hurricanes was scrambled, led by Wg Cdr Rabagliati, and the two formations engaged east of Delimara. Two of the bombers were claimed damaged, one by Flt Sgt Fletcher (Z2414/E) and the other jointly by four pilots from 242 Squadron – Flt Lts Kemp and Kee, Plt Off Morrison-Jones and Sgt Harry Hale, while Flt Lt Stones (BG770/GL-D) attacked another but with unobserved results; Stones also engaged a Bf109F which he claimed probably destroyed, and another was attacked by Wg Cdr Rabagliati (Z4005/S), who observed pieces break away from its tail unit and flames coming from its engine; he was awarded a probable. Plt Off Ormrod (BG711/G) also attacked a Messerschmitt:

"I was flying beside Stones when I saw two 109s diving on us. I called him over the R/T but apparently he did not hear, and then I turned to engage the enemy fighters. In the short combat that ensued I fired a couple of bursts at a Messerschmitt and I think I damaged it. These bursts were full deflection at 250 yards. Stones and Fletcher had just opened fire on the Junkers when they were attacked by 109s. One 109 presented Stones with its belly at close range and he hit it and thinks he probably destroyed it. A couple of 242 also damaged 88s and Rabagliati, who was leading, destroyed a 109. On the way back I hung over the coast as the other Hurricanes came back below me, hoping some 109 would offer me a target, but no enemy followed the Hurricanes in this time. I was one of the last to land.

Heard that Sgt Finlay had been badly shot up. Later I went to see his aircraft [BE583/T]. It amazes me that he managed to fly back. Some 109 pilot will certainly be impressing upon his superiors, juniors and equals how he blew large lumps off a Hurricane this morning and destroyed it. One would hardly believe a machine could fly in this one's condition. Half of the rudder and half of each elevator is missing. There is a great hole behind the cockpit in the fuselage, where several square feet of fabric are missing and where the woodwork has been destroyed. In fact the fuselage is about one quarter cut in half. There are bullet holes in two of the airscrew blades. Cannon shells have rent holes in wings and flaps. I would like to have spoken to Finlay as he was my No2, but he's already gone to hospital, though not badly hurt, as might have been supposed; only suffering from a cannon shell splinter in his leg."

Sgt Colin Finlay was probably the victim of Lt Joachim Louis of Stab/JG53 who claimed a Hurricane shot down during the morning for his third victory. The Germans were back in greater strength soon after midday, an estimated 18 Ju88s from KG54 and 26 Messerschmitts from III/JG53 raiding Luqa, Safi and Hal Far between 1220 and 1550. Ten Hurricanes – six from Takali led by Sqn Ldr Stan Norris of 126 Squadron and four from Hal Far led by Flt Lt Keith Lawrence of 185 Squadron – were scrambled; Flt Sgt Jock Sutherland of 185 Squadron recorded:

"It was one of the biggest scraps yet. Sgt Steele had a day out as he shot down a 109, damaged an 88 and hit a second 109 – without however observing any damage [to the latter]. Sgt Tweedale, our new Digger, did marvellously well in the scrap, his first action out here, as he sat on the tail of an 88 and gave it all he had from close range in spite of the attentions of at least three 109s. Unfortunately, he was slightly hurt when his kite was hit, and a small piece of cannon shell hit him in the foot. His kite was in a slightly dilapidated condition so he had to crash-land. At the same time, a 109 attempted to shoot him up but Sgt Steele, who was coming in with his wheels and flaps down, scared him off with a few rounds of .303 in his belly. Sgt Baines, our Armourer Sgt, had mounted his pet twin-Brownings on top of the Ops dug-out and blazed off the odd 40 rounds at our friend without, however, any effect being seen."

The wounded Sgt Gordon Tweedale (UP-H) noted: "Dived on six Ju88s after they had dropped bombs. Emptied ammo into one Ju88, then a Me109 filled me full of holes. Crash-landed on drome with cannon shell hole in left foot. I'll learn![6]" Meanwhile, the 126 Squadron contingent also engaged the bombers, Sqn Ldr Norris leading Plt Offs Joe Crichton (BG792) and Howard Coffin in an attack on one, on which serious damage was believed to have been inflicted. It was last seen diving towards the sea with its starboard engine on fire. During his attack, Coffin's Hurricane was hit in the engine by return fire and he was obliged to carry out an emergency landing between Safi strip and Gudja village, his aircraft sustaining serious damage: "Shot down today for third time. Rear-gunner of Ju88 put a slug through my engine. One stitch put in my head and received cut over eye."[7] Flt Lt Anderson attacked another bomber:

"Squadron dived to attack e/a which were about 10,000 feet below, over Hal Far. I chose an 88 and did a deflection shot from starboard and closed on it until I was dead behind its tail, squirting continuously. There was a very large explosion and pieces flew off in all directions and then it went into a steep left hand spiral with black smoke pouring out. I was unable to follow it down as there was a 109 on my tail and I had to take evasive action. I had turning matches with two separate 109s, firing, and fired at by both 109s. No visible results."

He was credited with its destruction, although it would seem that this was the same aircraft as that attacked by Sgt Tweedale. Flg Off Ron West reported strikes on the two bombers he attacked, while Plt Off Hollis Hallett tangled with two of the Messerschmitts:

"I saw a Ju88 and several 109s – as these were nearer I went for them. I attacked one from abeam, allowing deflection, and gave him about three-seconds burst. There was a large red flash from under his fuselage, accompanied by a big puff of black smoke. I had to stop firing as three Hurricanes were about to cross my line of fire. I also had to take avoiding action from a 109 on my tail. Later, I did a head-on attack at another which was about 200 feet above me. I fired, pulling my nose up as I did so. A few small pieces came off the trailing edge of the port wing. He was also firing at me. Later, I saw an aircraft flying low over Kalafrana Bay towards Hal Far, probably trying to shoot up aircraft landing. This had yellow leading edge, so I had to hold my fire until he got up beside me. I saw it was a 109."

One Ju88 failed to return from this raid, B3+KH of I/KG54 in which Lt Herbert Müller and his crew were lost, probably the main target of the Hurricanes. On this occasion the Messerschmitt pilots overclaimed somewhat, Obfw Werner Stumpf of 9/JG53 with two Hurricanes for his 29th and 30th victories, while Uffz Hans Schade of 8 Staffel claimed his 12th victory and Uffz Gerhard Beitz of 9 Staffel his first. A third intrusion was plotted at 1615 when a single reconnaissance Ju88 appeared, soon to be followed by an estimated dozen bombers complete with Messerschmitt escort, and again Hal Far, Luqa and Safi were bombed. No Hurricanes were available on this occasion, but guns managed to shoot down Oblt Gerhard Becker's Ju88 of 6/KG77. Becker, the Staffelkapitän, baled out into the sea but was not picked up; the observer was seriously injured when 3Z+JP crashed near Hal Far airfield, while the W/Op survived to be taken prisoner. The bombers were back after dark, the first raid coming in at about 2200, when the airfields were again raided, one Hurricane being destroyed. Of the late afternoon raid, Plt Off Phil Wigley wrote:

"I was with the crater-filling personnel at the time near the south side of the airfield. Two crew members of the Ju88 baled out at low altitude and landed about 100 yards from me. They were only a few yards from each other. A machine-gun with a circular bullet-proof glass screen was lying nearby. Both men were unconscious but showed no outward signs of wounds. They were taken to Station Sick Quarters before they could become victims of the unfriendly intentions of local people."[8]

The risk to German airmen – and sometimes even to RAF pilots – from the Maltese population was all too real. Wg Cdr Stan Turner alleged that while visiting a tiny café in M'dina one day he enquired of the owner the contents of three large clay pots displayed behind the bar, and was horrified when a severed head was produced from one. Apparently it was the head of a German airman who had baled out safely over Malta, but who had then been butchered by a crowd of Maltese civilians. This may have been connected with an account written by Plt Off Howard Coffin of 126 Squadron:

"The Nazi pilot had landed in his parachute and they were swarming over him with shovels and rakes and hoes and knives; I heard one sharp cry; and then the voices roared louder than ever. They cut off his head and spiked it on the gate-post of a ruined house in Mosta; I saw it when I went over a few days later to catch a bus to Valetta. There were three dogs sitting on their haunches and howling up at the head. I felt a bit sickened but I paused a moment to study the man's face. Death, I suppose, strips away all the corruption of thought that activates such a man. His features seemed, in death, somewhat the same as ours; it was a young face, rather woeful. I walked away slowly."[9]

At last, on the morning of 10 March, came the moment for the Spitfires' debut over Malta. This occurred at 1020 when seven took off in company with eight Hurricanes from Takali and four from Hal Far. The Spitfires climbed to 19,000 feet. Sqn Ldr Norris led four of the Hurricanes to 18,000 feet while the others remained at lower altitude. Nine Ju88s were observed below, the Spitfires bouncing the unsuspecting escort, one of which was shot down; two more were claimed probably destroyed and a fourth damaged. Four Hurricanes flown by 185 Squadron pilots led by Flt Lt Lawrence engaged six Messerschmitts over Filfla and claimed two damaged, one each by Plt Off Noble (UP-N) and Sgt Steele. The Squadron's current diarist, Flt Sgt Jock Sutherland, wrote:

> "At 10,000 feet two 109s attempted to jump us so we turned towards them. I was so ham that I spun down and took no further interest in the proceedings. A Spitfire shot down one of the 109s and Sgt Steele had a good burst at the belly of the other. Archie [Steele] then attacked one of the three bombers over Luqa and made him jettison his bombs, the other two making off without bombing at all. A second 109 tried to attack but Archie made a head-on attack and used the rest of his ammo on him, without any apparent effect, however."

Plt Off Hollis Hallett of 126 Squadron claimed damage to one of the Messerschmitts and Plt Off McKay (UP-F) observed strikes on the bomber he attacked, but Sgt Jack Mayall of 126 Squadron, who was flying No2 to Sqn Ldr Norris, was shot down in Z5140/C, his aircraft crashing near Qormi; the Australian was killed, the 13th victory for Uffz Hans Schade of 8/JG53 who mistakenly identified his victim as a Spitfire. Sgt Tim Goldsmith noted in his diary:

> "My very good friend Jack Mayall was killed. Dogfighting above Takali with two 109s at about 10,000 feet he was caught unawares by a third which bounced him out of the sun. Following a long burst of cannon fire, Jack and his Hurricanes came screaming down like a bomb, and crashed near the outskirts of Hamrun."

A second Hurricane was caught in the landing circuit and Flg Off Ron West had to crash-land, which he survived unhurt; Plt Off Ormrod wrote:

> "This morning we saw a fine dogfight. The Spitfires were in it. First time that Spitfires have operated over Malta – historic occasion. I saw a Spitfire, a tiny speck, above some 109s. Then I heard cannon fire and a Messerschmitt fell down issuing white and black smoke and disintegrating. Saw a lone Hurricane attack three bombers, Ju88s, that had crept in during the dogfight, unobserved. This Hurricane, I have since learnt, contained Sgt Steele of 185 Squadron . . . I hear two Hurricanes attacked [a Spitfire]. This is understandable, because the Hurricanes here are not accustomed to hesitate to shoot at any machine not clearly one of their own. They cannot afford to do so, and from some directions the Spitfire is somewhat similar to a Messerschmitt – especially when seen suddenly in a mêlée. Now the Spitfire pilot was so annoyed that he turned round and fired at the Hurricanes. An enemy pilot looking on must have been a bit bewildered as to which he should engage. Luckily, neither side scored hits.
>
> Was told how this morning an impudent Messerschmitt had played around Takali aerodrome as the Hurricanes were returning to land. Luckily he did not manage to get any, somehow they always saw him at the last moment and turned out of the way. He actually had the nerve to do a loop over Takali and roll off the top, thus coming down on a Hurricane's tail – a beautiful, if bold, manoeuvre. As Rabat stands on its hill above Takali, to those in the M'dina mess the Messerschmitt was much of the time below them or on the same level. The AA guns did not open fire on him until he went away, presumably they feared lest they should hit the Hurricane beforehand. I am filled with genuine admiration for the boldness of this German pilot. He has set us, his enemies, a high standard of daring to follow and, if it pleases God, to surpass."

Attempts to intercept two more raids during the mid part of the day failed, during the second of which Hal Far was heavily attacked, three casualties being inflicted. Then, at 1620, 40 more enemy aircraft were plotted approaching from the north. Ju88s from I/KG54, II and III/KG77 and LG1 attacked Luqa and Hal Far while Bf109Fs from II/JG3 provided cover. Eleven Hurricanes were scrambled together with four Spitfires. A section of three pilots from 242 Squadron – Flt Lt Kee, Plt Off Morrison-Jones and Sgt Tony Boyd (HA-F) attacked one of the bombers, as Boyd reported: "I attacked the Ju88 after F/Lt Kee had caused explosion with cannons. I followed it ten miles, using all my ammo and causing smoke from both engines. Claim one-third of it." Two more of the bombers were claimed damaged by Spitfire pilots but one Spitfire was shot down by Hptm Karl-Heinz Krahl, the Kommandeur of II/JG3, for his 24th victory. One Ju88 of 4/KG77 returned to its base in Sicily with two wounded crew members on board including the pilot, Fw Josef Neumann, while an aircraft from 2/KG54 crash-landed at Gerbini.

There was only one raid during the daylight hours of 11 March when, at 1135, two Ju88s of 5/KG77 and six Bf109Fs approached the coast. Sixteen Hurricanes – a dozen from Takali led by Sqn Ldr Wells of 242 Squadron, and four from Hal Far manned by 185 Squadron pilots – were scrambled, together with four Spitfires, but first there was a little excitement at Hal Far as Plt Off Ormrod later recorded:

"Ron [Noble], Joe [Beckett], self and [Flt Sgt] Fletcher were scrambled. As we were taxiing down the field to take off from the other end into wind, there was a loud explosion. I thought I'd burst a tyre yet my aircraft continued to taxi all right. Then I saw Joe's aircraft stopped and him out of it. Supposed he'd burst a tyre. Then for some reason I looked right and behind us and saw a huge pillar of dust raised by a bomb. I thought that in that case we were being bombed, but as no more fell I supposed it was a delayed action one from a previous raid. Ron was wondering what to do. Joe was out of his aircraft. I had my R/T switched on already and could hear that 242 were airborne, so I waved Ron off and followed. The others caught us up over Luqa where we joined 242 and the Spitfires."

The Ju88s turned back without bombing, and one crashed on landing at Comiso in which the crew perished, but a number of dogfights ensued with the Messerschmitts. The Spitfires claimed a probable and a damaged for no losses, while Ormrod (Z2840/T) also claimed one damaged:

"Imagine my surprise, when on emerging through a thin layer of cloud, I found myself zooming right at three 109s who happened to be passing along above the cloud. It seemed too good to be true. For a moment I hesitated, but they were 109s all right. The cause of my slight hesitation being the red spinners like ours. However, I also saw the black crosses and yellow under the nose. I opened fire on one from almost vertically below and saw strikes on the engine. Then, as he passed, I rolled slightly on my back and continued the attack with an inverted low quarter astern. I was then attacked by the other two 109s, so having come to the top of my zoom and, having little speed left for steep turns in a mêlée, I rolled completely over and went back into the cloud layer in the bottom half of the loop. The other two failed to hit me and I lost them in cloud. I expect I destroyed this Messerschmitt as having hit his engine I would likely have damaged his petrol injection system. Being out of sight of the coast I don't know what happened. No one would have seen him crash here. Indeed, one is lucky if one gets a victory confirmed here."

There was a lessening of air activity over the next few days, particularly as far as the Hurricane pilots were concerned. During a scramble by six Hurricanes at 1100 on the 12th, Sgt George Mulloy of 242 Squadron claimed a Bf109F damaged, part of the escort to six Ju88s of II/KG77 which carried out a raid on Takali, where seven Hurricanes were slightly damaged by blast and debris, and against Luqa where an unserviceable Wellington was destroyed. A further raid during the mid afternoon was not challenged by the fighters, Takali again being targeted where a Hurricane and a Spitfire were both slightly damaged, while at Luqa another Wellington was burnt out. After dark the raiders, which included four BR20Ms of 55°Gruppo BT, returned. Three night fighter Hurricanes were scrambled as was a Beaufighter, the latter shooting down a Ju88 of 1/KüFlGr606. Next day (13 March) brought with it a further raid on Takali where a Hurricane and a petrol bowser were burnt out. Although 13 Hurricanes were scrambled they failed to make contact with the bombers and were themselves attacked by numerous Messerschmitts although no claims or losses resulted. The guns put up their usual heavy barrage and succeeded in damaging a Ju88 of 6/KG77.

The first intrusion on the morning of 14 March came at around 0830, when a reconnaissance Ju88 and two Bf109Fs of 3/JG53 appeared over the island, and were greeted by some sharp shooting from AA gunners on Gozo who claimed damage to the Ju88 before shooting down the Messerschmitt flown by Lt Walter Seiz, which collided with the other flown by Uffz Heinrich Blum; Seiz was able to bale out but the unlucky Blum crashed to his death. Two hours later three Ju88s of II/KG77 and an estimated 20 Messerschmitts approached, and a further 15 fighters were observed searching the sea for the two missing pilots. Hal Far was again targeted, and another Hurricane was set on fire while three more sustained damage, as did a Swordfish. Plt Off Ormrod was amongst those who tried in vain to save the burning Hurricane:

> "I took out the fire truck at once to the burning Hurricane and tried to save its tail; it was obviously impossible to save the rest. We extinguished the fire on the tail, the wind blowing the fire forward. However, the reserve petrol tank blew up and the oxygen bottles did also, thus the tail was relighted and burnt. It was a very fierce fire, ammunition exploding and shooting out in all directions, sometimes to a considerable distance from the aircraft."

Four Spitfires, the only fighters to have been scrambled, engaged three Bf109Fs of 7/JG3 orbiting Gozo, one of the Messerschmitts being shot down into the sea, from which Uffz Adolf Jennerich baled out. During the afternoon no less than 29 enemy fighters were reported off the coast, searching and patrolling, accompanied by a Do24 which was seen to alight on the sea. Both Seiz and Jennerich were rescued. Spitfires were up again, skirmishing with two Messerschmitts, one of which was claimed damaged. Shortly before nightfall, two Axis flying boats were reported off the coast to the south-west, obviously still searching for the missing Blum. These were allowed to complete their task unhindered.

Shortly before lunchtime on 15 March, three Ju88s with fighter escort provided by III/JG53 raided Luqa and Valetta. Four Spitfires and seven Hurricanes were airborne and intercepted the raid in low cloud. Results were inconclusive, the Spitfire pilots claiming damage to a Ju88 and a Bf109. For the Hurricanes, Plt Off Ron Noble (Z2480/T) also claimed a Messerschmitt damaged when he saw strikes near the cockpit and on its fuselage, as noted by Plt Off Ormrod:

> "Ron attacked a Messerschmitt and also just avoided one's attack when he heard on the R/T: 'Look out, Hurricane', from one of the others, probably a Spitfire [pilot]. He saw a 109 behind and turned in time out of the way."

Plt Off Phil Wigley (BG711/G) joined forces with a Spitfire in attacking another Bf109, which was claimed damaged, and 242 Squadron's Sgt Tony Boyd (HA-H) pursued a Ju88:

> "Mixed it with two Messerschmitts at 14,000 feet, then ten more appeared so lost height. I was climbing at 4,000 feet and saw one Ju88 over Grand Harbour, 2,000 feet above me. Chased it halfway to Sicily; two long bursts at 400 yards. Being still alone, broke off and returned while possible."

Oblt Belser of 8/JG53 claimed a Spitfire during the action, and a second was claimed by Obfw Stumpf of 9 Staffel, and although none were lost, two were damaged. At 1320 three Ju88s escorted by seven Bf109Fs raided Zabbar, and were met by four Spitfires which shot down one of the bombers, probably M7+ML of 3/KGr806 in which Uffz Rudolf Alex and his crew were reported missing. Four hours later three more Ju88s, from 3/KüFlGr606, and six Messerschmitts (evidently from II/JG3) approached the coast while an estimated 19 fighters patrolled out to sea. On this occasion six Spitfires and eight Hurricanes were scrambled, the latter led by Wg Cdr Satchell. The Hurricanes went after the bombers, which were then ten miles off Delimara Point, one being claimed damaged by the combined efforts of Plt Off Phil Allardice, Flt Sgt Trevor Bates, Sgt Doug Eastman and Sgt Garth Horricks. No return fire was experienced and it was believed the rear-gunner was killed; however, the bomber escaped serious damage. Flt Sgt Jock Sutherland of 185 Squadron wrote in the unit diary:

> "One of the Ju88s was intercepted at 16,000 feet. He jettisoned when the fighters attacked and dived to sea level. The Hurris had the odd squirt but could not catch the enemy aircraft, so they started back home. Just then, the 109s decided to hurry them up and chased the boys back. Bates had four on his tail pooping at him, but they did not damage him at all. Twitch was flying around, though. The rest were also fired at but no one was hit."

Meantime, Wg Cdr Satchell, together with two Americans Plt Offs Howard Coffin and Sandy McHan (HA-M), attacked another bomber, but were forced to break away when Messerschmitts dived on them, as reported by Satchell:

> "I was leading the Malta Hurricane Wing at approximately 17,000 feet to the east by north-east of the island on a northerly course when I saw a Ju88 on my starboard bow, flying south-west about 4,000 feet below. Warning the Spitfires above and behind to keep a good look out for fighters, I led the Hurricanes in a diving attack from quarter ahead. There were three aircraft in my section and four more to starboard and slightly astern. The three of us all opened fire and I observed strikes from my cannon shells on the Ju88's starboard wing. The enemy aircraft immediately jettisoned his bombs into the sea. We turned – still in vic formation – and delivered another attack from astern on the bomber which was now diving to the south-east. Messerschmitt 109s, of which I had seen twelve not far away, then took a hand in the proceedings and we broke off the attack and reformed. Whilst reforming I noticed what at first I took to be a Hurricane join up in formation on my No3's [McHan] port side. Suddenly I realised it was a 109 and I pulled up into a steep left-hand climbing turn to attack, but the 109 dived away. Owing to this and the close proximity of other 109s, the formation became split up. I then saw the Ju88 again some distance to the south-east and fairly low. I saw two or three fighters in its proximity astern of it, which I took to be Hurricanes, so I dived to attack it again. As I came up astern suddenly one of the 'Hurricanes' pulled up and across my bows and I clearly saw the black crosses on its wings!
>
> I immediately went into a very steep left-hand turn and succeeded in turning inside the 109 and got a good burst in. I saw strikes on the fuselage. Then suddenly the whole tail unit fell off! The remainder of the aircraft then shot straight upwards. I could not watch it as I saw tracer coming uncomfortably close and continued my steep turn and finally got a bead on a second 109. I commenced firing but only fired about five or six rounds from each cannon when they stopped; whereupon I zig-zagged down to water level and headed all out for the island. Three 109s chased me for a while then disappeared, and I returned to base and landed. I learnt afterwards that my No2, P/O Coffin, had been not far away and flying to join up with me the whole time. He saw the tail unit of my 109 hit the sea. A considerable amount of ammunition was expended by the enemy in our direction but, except for two small holes in my starboard wing caused by shrapnel from their self-destroying cannon shells, neither Coffin nor I was hit."

Since JG53 did not report any losses or even damage to any of its aircraft during the day, it is assumed that the Messerschmitt shot down by Wg Cdr Satchell came from II/JG3. A Ju88 from 3/KüFlGr 606 which crash-landed on returning to Catania was possibly the other victim of his attack. A total of 130 sorties had been directed against the island during ten alerts, inflicting about 50 casualties (mainly civilian) of which at least seven were fatal. AA gunners claimed damage to three Ju88s and two Bf109s.

The 16th proved to be a quiet day for the few Hurricanes and Spitfires still serviceable, although there were 16 separate raids by Ju88s against the island with all three airfields receiving visits. Hurricanes were scrambled on two occasions, meeting a couple of Messerschmitts but no conclusive action resulted. There was greater activity next day, following a night of continuous bombing, when four Spitfires and 11 Hurricanes were sent off. The Spitfires climbed to 20,000 feet where six Ju88s and many Bf109Fs were encountered, one of the latter being claimed destroyed. The Hurricanes meantime went after five Ju88s escorted by ten Messerschmitts at 15,000 feet, catching the bombers as they began their dives. Sqn Ldr Wells, who was leading, and Sgt Harry Hale each claimed one damaged and Sgt George Mulloy saw strikes on two more. Both Flt Lt Stones and Plt Off Ron Noble carried out head-on attacks against Ju88s but made no claims, while Plt Off Joe Beckett tangled with a Messerschmitt, and the American Plt Off Sandy McHan (LE-E) reported: "Attacked Ju88 from front and below. [It] almost dropped bombs on me!" Flt Lt Nigel Kemp, leading the other flight of Hurricanes, led an attack on four of the escorting fighters, seeing strikes on one, but the skirmishing was inconclusive. Following this raid, one Ju88 of 6/KG77 crash-landed at Comiso on return, possibly due to damage sustained. Plt Off Ormrod had watched part of the battle:

> "I had just got to the waterside at the bottom of Marsa Creek when several 88s arrived and bombed Grand Harbour. Several Hurricanes were close upon them and there was much firing heard. Twice I saw Hurricanes spin, but on each occasion they pulled out. I have since heard that one of these was Mad Mulloy – a most amusing Sgt Pilot in 242 Squadron. Apparently, Mulloy met a Ju88 above him going in the opposite direction. So, regardless of his speed, he just pulled back on the stick and fired. Of course, he span off the top. On landing he observed that he had not quite enough speed to get round. It is probably he whom Wigley saw loop and roll off the top when jumped by 109s some days ago, when we were flying behind 242. He's a delightful fellow. Always makes me laugh. Can talk utter nonsense."

At 0955 seven more Ju88s and four Bf109Fs crossed the coast, and one of four intercepting Spitfires was lost. During the afternoon and early evening, an estimated 50-plus raiders approached at intervals, bombers attacking Grand Harbour and all three airfields. At Takali two Hurricanes were damaged and two civilians killed. Hurricanes, with Spitfires as top cover, were scrambled; 185 Squadron's current diarist, Flt Sgt Sutherland, noted:

> "This afternoon the first scramble (four aircraft) was led by W/Cdr Reilly, the new Station CO. Owing to his not having flown for some time, he was rather unsteady, but realised it himself and apologised handsomely for it afterwards. We managed to intercept an 88 and a Heinkel 111 [sic] but owing to their speed very little damage was done to either aircraft. Sgts Steele and Broad had long-range squirts at the 88, while only the Takali boys fired at the Heinkel, which Steele swears was a Maryland. However, according to Ops, no Marylands were airborne at the time.
>
> The second scramble of the afternoon was led by F/Lt Lawrence. We were actually sent off to disperse below cloud as it was thought it was Hal Far's turn to be bombed. We made one circuit of the island below cloud base (2,000 feet) and watched the AA guns firing and bombs bursting all over the island. When we were over Hal Far on our first lap, Archie Steele sighted an 88 about 4,000 feet above us and to one side, being fired at by the Bofors which hit him once in the starboard engine. Backed up by self, Archie chased the 88 about 15 miles out to sea and succeeded in closing to firing range. He (Archie) hit him with three bursts, then his ammo finished and he returned to base, so I took over and also hit him. I made three attacks then started for home. On the way back I met a 109 on his own, 2,000 feet up, so made an attack on him and saw him turn on his back, diving towards the sea. Later, Fighter Control confirmed the 88 so it is shared between the Bofors, Archie and myself. The 109 was given as a probable."

Although a Ju88 of 3/KüFlGr606 crash-landed on return to Catania, and was totally destroyed, Luftwaffe records imply this loss was caused by a landing accident rather than enemy action; Obfw Wilhelm Heipe and his crew of 7T+BL were all injured in the crash. The identity of the aircraft assumed to have been a He111 is not clear. It was however attacked and claimed damaged by Flt Lt Ces Baker and Sgt Alan Cairns of 126 Squadron, the latter, formerly with 249 Squadron, noting that he had "shot away part of its tail" and it was left severely damaged. Of the afternoon's action, Ormrod noted:

> "Learnt that the Station Commander, W/Cdr Reilly, flew on one scramble with 185 Squadron this afternoon. He was shocked to see a sergeant pilot pour 2,000 rounds of .303 into a Ju88 and only thereby produce sparks – Oh! for cannon."

Since Ormrod had not been flying, he took the opportunity during the day to visit the cemetery where two of his friends were buried:

> "Eventually I found an old lane under the directions of the inhabitants and came to the cemetery. An old Maltese labourer, the chief gravedigger it seemed, showed me the registration books and I found the names of James Stuart and Macnamara, poor dears. Macnamara was buried nearest the gate in Grave No90. Then I saw Stuart's grave, No15, and was rather disgusted to find him and another fellow, a pilot officer from Kalafrana, were buried in the same grave. I was sorry to see the graves so bare. No cross, no name, just a number. The old Malt explained that all would be attended to after the war and that for the present the tombstone markers were all employed in government work and that, anyway, since the war with Italy, the marble supply had been cut. Think they might have at least had wooden crosses. I gave the old man 10/- and instructed him to take especial care of these two graves. He promised that he would procure flowers for them this very day. This place is, methinks, more of a repository for corpses of no further use than a graveyard for gallant pilots.
>
> I'd known James so long at Wellington and we shared so many common memories of school days, as is natural when two boys enter the same house at the same school on the same day, and eventually leave together to join the same service at the end of the same term. If he had to die here, I wish it had been in action rather than on active service. Poor James.
>
> Macnamara was one of the most upright, honest gentlemen I've ever known. Everyone here liked him. He was a first-rate pilot. Yes, I am truly sorry he is dead. However – 'Those whom the gods love die young'. And indeed they must have loved Macnamara. Perhaps he is in a better place now. He deserves to be. In our imagination he will never grow old. Poor Macnamara – everyone misses you. Oh! why did it have to be he? He did not lack courage. I would suppose him braver than most. Fate seems cruel."

Little did he realise that he, too, was fated soon to join his friends in their last resting place.

18 March saw the official disbandment of both 242 and 605 Squadrons; the ground echelons of these squadrons had arrived in the Far East and had subsequently been lost with the fall of Java. Of the pilots remaining at Malta, those from 242 Squadron were absorbed into 126 Squadron including Sqn Ldr Wells, although he was soon to be promoted to Wing Commander and posted to Air HQ, while those of 605 Squadron became part of 185 Squadron[10] and were temporarily labelled C Flight under Flt Lt Stones, who wrote:

> "The Hurricanes were getting worn out, but there was a promise of more Spitfires to come. Morale amongst the Hurricane pilots and groundcrew, who still bore the brunt of the fighting, was still amazingly high, but signs of wear and tear, and above all exhaustion, were beginning to be noticeable. There was little rest at night, either for air crew or groundcrew, many of whom volunteered to help in the nightly job of clearing a path through the bomb craters for the fighters to take off next day. The only advantage in being such a small and compact target as Malta was that we were all in the same boat, civilians

too, and there was nowhere to hide from the noise and shrapnel on the ground or the flying metal in the air.

One of our armourers now had a brilliant idea which would keep the wind-blown sand out of our 20mm cannons. He had somehow procured, we suspected from his friend a medical orderly, a box of a certain contraceptive which he proposed to put on each of the cannons. It was a good fit and perfect protection. Many were the ribald remarks amongst us, as to what impossible outrages we were going to carry out on enemy aircraft and crew with guns so sheathed. Alas, the practice was not to last long, at Hal Far anyway, because our armourer dropped a handful in a gusty wind and many were blown across Kalafrana Bay to land on a private beach occupied by one of Malta's most noble families who were bathing there. Being staunch Catholics, a strong protest was made, and our cannons flew naked again."[11]

Despite Flt Lt Stones' comment regarding the high morale amongst the Hurricane pilots, Plt Off Sonny Ormrod was still having difficulty in reconciling the lack of respect and discipline displayed by some of his fellow pilots, particularly the NCOs. On one occasion . . .

". . . I asked Sgt Wilson to take my aircraft across to be refuelled. He replied that he had his own to do and that it was usual for pilots to do their own in the Squadron. I was very angry and ordered him to do as he was told. These colonials [Sgt Alan Wilson was a New Zealander] don't know the meaning of discipline. Whether the order was unfair or not he should have obeyed it and damn his impertinence for replying in that familiar manner to an officer, and rudely. These colonials fail to realise that sergeants are not the equals of officers, whom they address by the Christian names or nicknames. How is one to expect obedience in the air without it on the ground?"

Of another incident, he wrote:

"Ron [Noble] was waiting for LE-Y [BE351], the cannon Hurricane, to become serviceable. At last it was serviceable. Then [Sgts] Robb and Wilson turned up. Ron told Wilson that he could have the machine he had, after he had moved his kit into Y. To my amazement Wilson replied to P/O Noble as if he were his equal saying he saw no reason why Noble should move into the cannon aircraft, that it was unfair as he already had an aircraft. Why should he take the cannon one? Why should not he, Wilson, have it? I seethed with rage at this insolence to the senior officer. I had suspected that the familiarity and slack manner of the sergeants would lead to such indiscipline as this before long. Sgt Wilson seems to forget that he's a sergeant and not an officer. The leader usually flies the best aircraft. When we were sergeants we never supposed that we should be other than at the bottom. Ron has served over a year with the Squadron. Wilson has served only a few months. I've never known such blasted indiscipline."

18 March was again a day of heavy combat, which began around 0900 when two Bf109Fs crossed the coast at low level, covered by four more higher up, and strafed the Gozo ferry boat *Royal Lady* which had just docked at Marfa with 209 passengers aboard. Fortunately, only two civilians and one soldier were wounded. Spitfires were scrambled at lunchtime when five Messerschmitts patrolled off the coast, while another four Spitfires took off to escort a returning Maryland. Two enemy fighters were engaged and claimed damaged, one by newly promoted Wg Cdr Turner.

Eleven Hurricanes joined four Spitfires to intercept an evening raid by two dozen Ju88s from I/KG54, KüFlGr606 and KGr806, in five waves, escorted by many Bf109Fs. All three airfields were targeted and an Albacore was destroyed at Hal Far, and three damaged Wellingtons at Luqa were destroyed. A Messerschmitt shot down a Spitfire and a Spitfire shot down a Messerschmitt, the British pilot being killed and the German being captured. Two Hurricanes were also claimed by pilots of III/JG53, one each by Obfw Werner Stumpf (his 32nd victory) and Lt Hermann Neuhoff (37th) and, indeed, both Plt Off Chuck Lester (Z2840/T) and Sgt George Mulloy (Z5213) were shot down. It seems that the latter was the victim of Neuhoff, who related:

"Everything was going according to plan. We have half the trip behind us already, when my *Katschmarek* [wingman] reports engine trouble and has to return home. I am alone – now what? Turn back too? No, I don't feel like doing that, especially as enemy fighters have been reported. I am going to rely on my experience acquired in over 400 missions against the enemy and continue flying as a blind *Rotte* [pair]. Already we are over Malta. The bombers are preparing to dive. They dive very calmly because they know their Messerschmitts keep a look-out. Everything seems to be going well when, at the beginning of the dive, there, overhead – the Tommy! Shooting wildly they dive into our group. Behind me are three Spitfires, wanting to sniff my pants! Now I have to watch out – first let them come close, then go hell for leather and turn! The Spitfire is no longer in a position to fire. On the other hand, I have got dangerously close to the last one. They are immediately aware of the situation and dive straight down.

I am just about to return to the bombers when I discover a Hurricane 100 metres below me. Now with the stick forward the Messerschmitt dives swiftly towards the Tommy. He sees me coming and wants to escape. But too late, I have already pressed the buttons and my MGs and cannons bark hoarsely. He sees that there is no escape and has to engage in an air battle with me. Now things are really hotting up. Ten times I was unable to get into position, the sweat pouring from my head. Then I was successful. I curved around and managed to get behind him and filled him so full of lead that he momentarily flew straight and level. It was enough – once more let him fill my sights and fire with all barrels. I was 50 metres behind the Tommy when I saw him break up. Half of the left wing broke off, so that the bird spun twice on its own axis right in front of my nose and disappeared into the waters like a U-boat. Now one more turn around the spot, but nothing else showed. There was nothing more I could do, so I turned back and went home."

No sign of Sgt Mulloy could be found despite two searches, but the Australian Lester, although severely wounded, was picked up by HSL128 within an hour. Of the fight and the shooting down of his close friend, Plt Off McKay wrote:

"We climbed out over Gozo and then the 109s started to bother us. We then had to turn and go back across the island after the 88s. We did this by going straight for a minute then turning around after the 109s. We eventually did get to the 88s and some of us had a squirt at them. The 109s were coming down on us all the time and it's damn dangerous to fly straight and level for any length of time. Hal Far was bombed – and Luqa – so Don Stones, Fletcher and I came back and landed at Takali.

We then heard that Chuck Lester had been jumped by four 109s and, not having any ammunition left, had to go down to sea level to get away from them, but one got him eventually through the leg and he hit the sea and was thrown out. The next thing he remembered he was holding on to his dinghy but couldn't get into it 'cause both his legs were u/s. He is pretty badly shaken up. He has a compound fracture in one leg and a cannon shell in the other, and his face is badly bruised. It is amazing how he ever got out of his aircraft; he was going at least 220mph when he hit the water."

Flt Lt Stones (Z4942/GL-Y) engaged and damaged a Ju88 which was also attacked by Plt Off Ormrod and by a Spitfire (flown by Flg Off Norm Lee), and then attacked two others without apparent result, while Flt Sgt Fletcher (BG770/UP-D) reported seeing strikes on the port engine of the Ju88 he engaged. Ormrod wrote:

"The Ju88 which Stones followed was indulging in a most startling series of steep S turns for an aircraft of its size in its endeavour to evade us. I was annoyed to find that we were hardly overtaking it. I gave it a short burst from 200 yards astern and I think my rounds struck it. Then, to my annoyance, a Spitfire just walked past me straight up behind the Junkers, fired and broke away, whilst Stones and I were still going full throttle trying to catch it up with little success. Stones had the cannon Hurricane and I flew a little behind him to protect him as he attacked, for there were plenty of 109s coming down behind us. I saw him fire at one 88 and then go down on a second. Then I lost him whilst I was dealing with 109s – firing at them to distract them from protecting their Junkers. I engaged three 109s with my fire although I saw many more. I only gave the first two short bursts. The third I fired at from a quarter astern below, getting semi-inverted in the process, and then a long burst from astern 150 to 250 yards – I'm sure I hit him. I was beautifully on his tail, but I could not hold him. He just sped away from me. I fancy I merely made a few bullet holes in the back end of his fuselage."

At 1830, Takali was again raided and a Hurricane, the cannon-armed Z4942/GL-Y, was destroyed; another and two unserviceable Spitfires sustained damage. AA gunners reported hits on two of the raiders; one Ju88, B3+EH of I/KG54, crashed on returning to Catania.

There was but a single raid by seven Ju88s on the 19th, this directed against Takali, where a Beaufighter night fighter was destroyed. A second was damaged as were two Hurricanes and a Spitfire. Escorting Messerschmitts strafed the Polish submarine *Sokol* as it was heading for Grand Harbour. Although hit by eight 20mm cannon shells, little damage was inflicted. The AA gunners were again on target, scoring hits on two of the raiders, one Ju88 of 7/KG77 crashing near Comiso on return, in which all the crew perished.

Four Spitfires and a dozen Hurricanes were scrambled at 0805 on the morning of 20 March, the Spitfires encountering Messerschmitts of III/JG53, an aircraft of 7 Staffel being shot down for the loss of a Spitfire and its pilot. The guns were again spot on with their shooting, hitting a Bf109F of 6/JG3 which crashed near Gela on return; the pilot was killed. But this was just a skirmish when compared to what was next in store for Malta and its defenders.

In view of the increasing losses being suffered by individual or small formations of aircraft, particularly since the arrival of the Spitfires, the Luftwaffe decided upon new tactics. Now RAF fighters were to be attacked on the ground. It was planned that two of three Staffeln of Messerschmitts should be sent over half an hour before the main attack was due in an attempt to get the defending fighters into the air. More Messerschmitts would arrive and circle the airfields to pick off the Spitfires and Hurricanes as they entered the landing circuit. Commencement of these attacks was delayed until photo-reconnaissance could confirm that the Spitfires and Hurricanes were concentrated mainly at Takali, and sufficient bomber crews were available to carry out the proposed mass formation raids. The first such raid was planned for the evening of 20 March, Feldmarschall Kesselring having called for every aircrew with night flying experience to participate. As dusk fell, the island's radar screens showed large numbers of aircraft assembling over Sicily before heading towards Malta. By 1830 the vanguard of some 63 Ju88s drawn from II and III/KG77, I/KG54, KüFlGr606 and KGr806 began crossing the coast, escorted by Bf110s of III/ZG26, Ju88Cs of I/NJG2 and a few Bf109Fs. No defending fighters rose to oppose the aerial armada, but AA gunners claimed four Ju88s shot down and another damaged. Although one aircraft of KüFlGr606 crash-landed at Catania on return, there were no other recorded losses. Ormrod observed the raid from the comparative safety of Kalafrana:

"This evening I witnessed, just on dusk, a great attack by the Luftwaffe on Takali, presumably for the benefit of the Spitfires. At least 20 Ju88s attacked. There may have been as many as 50 aircraft. The barrage was intense, both heavy AA and Bofors. In the twilight the effect was like a fireworks display."

Sgt Alf Branch, formerly of 249 Squadron but now attached to 126 Squadron, wrote in his journal:

> "I was on watch and I must say Jerry is getting to be a nuisance. The drome was dive-bombed by Ju88s and He111s [*sic*], making the fourth day in succession. Approximately 30 bombs dropped in one go during one raid. The Mess had a near shave; at the same time an amusing thing happened. The two bombs dropped close to the Mess were approximately 1,000-lb each. These bombs were very close to an old well and the blast sucked all the mud and water out of it – and poured it down on the building, shaking the occupants who thought the lot was coming down on top of them."

Takali was rendered unserviceable following this onslaught, when in excess of 114 tons of bombs were directed at the airfield. German crews reported good accuracy, with explosions being observed among quarters, hangars and aircraft blast pens. A number of aircraft were damaged but not as many as would have been expected. Bombs fell on neighbouring Naxxar, Mosta, Zebbug and Attard, killing ten civilians.

The Luftwaffe's all-out assault on Takali was repeated during the morning of 21 March, a total of 106 Ju88s, plus one Bf110 for observation duties and a large fighter escort – over 200 aircraft in all – appearing between 0845 and 1015. The airfield was again heavily cratered (182 tons of bombs being released here), and many delayed-action bombs were dropped in the first example of carpet-bombing the island had experienced. Despite a complete lack of opposition in the air, only two persons were killed and seven injured on this occasion, the AA claiming one bomber shot down and two damaged.

Soon after the bombers had departed, eight Bf110s of III/ZG26 swooped down to bomb and strafe Hal Far under an umbrella of Bf109Fs. Two Hurricanes, two Beauforts and a Spitfire were damaged, but six of 185 Squadron's Hurricanes were up, led by Sqn Ldr Mortimer-Rose, ostensibly to cover the arrival of more Spitfires flying in from the west, as recorded by Flt Sgt Sutherland in the Squadron diary:

> ". . . the CO led them out over Gozo. There they found eight aircraft flying in a vic, and the CO, thinking them to be Hudsons, thought that Control must be wrong about the Spits. However, a closer inspection was made when the eight 'Hudsons' made an ugly pass at Takali armed with many bombs, and were discovered to be Messerschmitt 110s, so the Squadron piled in. In the ensuing fight, much ammo was expended on our side and more on the other side with the result that four 110s went in the drink."

Sqn Ldr Mortimer-Rose (Z2961/K) reported shooting down one in flames, which fell into the sea. As the remaining aircraft headed towards Sicily they were pursued by the Hurricanes, Plt Off Phil Allardice (BG711/G) catching one:

> "I first sighted the bandits about 2,000 feet above and to port . . . I turned and dived to port as they came down and gave some short bursts from astern, scoring hits on one bomber from 200 yards. As we went out over St Paul's Bay I could not close, so I turned my attention to another bomber which was below me at about 50 feet. At the same time I saw two other Hurricanes making attacks on another bomber still further to port at same level. I did quarter attacks and then sat behind him giving long bursts until ammo ran out. I saw pieces fall of the fuselage, clouds of smoke and aircraft staggered badly and my aircraft covered in oil. When later seen, aircraft was very low and flying erratically."

Plt Off Joe Beckett (Z2824/HA-H) and Sgt Doug Robb (Z3767/B) engaged another, as Beckett reported:

> "Fired at second last enemy aircraft in formation – hits on fuselage and tail – smoke and sparks – last seen losing height over the sea. Saw another 110 go in about five miles off St Paul's Bay."

The final victory was credited to Plt Offs Phil Wigley (BG770/D) and Sonny Ormrod

(BG769/J), the latter writing in his journal:

> "I heard some shouting on the R/T about Messerschmitt 110s. My R/T was not very strong, but I clearly heard 110s. Couldn't believe it, because Control had given us no information concerning them. Looked in front and there were eight twin-engined aircraft. As we were expecting friendly aircraft, I hesitated to fire, thinking first they were Blenheims leading Spitfires and then, when I had looked at all, [thought] they might be some new aircraft such as Mosquitos. Withheld my fire until I saw a cross on the fuselage of one and then engaged the rear aircraft with a quarter attack as it passed. Turned after them as they began to dive. Got on the tail of one, 150 to 200 yards behind, and fired a good burst into him as he dived steeply. Saw their bombs go. They were trying to bomb Takali. Took a quick glance behind to be sure that no 109s were on our tails. Then, on looking forward again, I could not see the enemy aircraft at once against the landscape of the island. Then AA shells burst close in front of me. I swerved and called into the R/T 'Oi, we're friendly'. Then I continued after the 110s which were leaving the coast towards Sicily, passing over St Paul's Bay. I was catching them up very slowly. I attacked one from the quarter. It had another Hurricane on its tail. My first burst on this aircraft passed mostly just in front of its nose. I'd allowed too much deflection, but it must have shaken the pilot to see tracer in front of his face. I took off a little deflection and hit the front of the enemy aircraft and his port engine with my last rounds. Then I broke away and returned to Hal Far."

Amongst the many upturned faces on the ground watching the battle overhead was newly-arrived Australian Spitfire pilot Sgt Ray Hesselyn, who wrote:

> "Eight Me110s came out of the sun in a shallow dive . . . but all the bombs fell short and none hit the aerodrome. The Me110s machine-gunned the aerodrome as they passed over . . . saw four Hurricanes diving out of the sun onto the tails of the bombers, which were straggled out in line abreast. The Hurricanes opened fire as the bombers crossed the coast, apparently taking the 110s by surprise. It was point-blank range, and almost simultaneously four of the 110s dived seawards. Two of them burst into flames, flicked over and fell straight into the drink. The other two lazily rolled on their backs and dropped straight into the sea. The remaining four 110s at once broke, and began weaving, each steering a different course for home. Splitting up, the Hurricanes gave chase to the 110s, shooting down two more before returning to base."[12]

Yet, despite the apparent eye witness report of the destruction of at least four and possibly six of the Bf110s, available German records indicate but a single loss – 3U+FT of 9 Staffel, together with the crew, Lt Hans Hufnagel and Uffz Emil Camler.

As the engagement with the Bf110s was underway, the first elements of the second delivery of Spitfires, from the aircraft carrier *Eagle*, were approaching the island, all nine aircraft landing safely at Takali despite the damaged runway. The new arrivals, who were absorbed into 126 Squadron since this unit was also to be fully re-equipped with Spitfires, were swiftly greeted to a display of German might when, at 1435, the third major raid to be centred on Takali within 24 hours began as 70 Ju88s arrived over the island. Bombs fell over a wide area, one of which fell just outside the front door of the Point de Vue Hotel in Rabat, which had been requisitioned to billet RAF officers stationed at nearby Takali. A number of officers were gathered there of which six were killed outright including two Hurricane pilots – Flt Lt Ces Baker and Plt Off Bill Hollis Hallett of 126 Squadron – and two Spitfire pilots of 249 Squadron, while 126 Squadron's Plt Off Eddie Streets, who lost a leg and was blinded, succumbed to his injuries in hospital. Others were fortunate to escape serious injury including Flt Lt Buck McNair, now flying Spitfires with 249 Squadron:

> "When I came to I didn't know where I was. I didn't feel I was dead, but I didn't feel whole. My eyes were open but my jaw and chest didn't seem to be there. There was no pain

. . . As I became more conscious, I found I was upstairs. Then I realised I had been blown upstairs either through a door or through an opening at the turn of the staircase. I'd been blown up 20 or 30 feet. I went down the main staircase which was barely hanging in place. I saw the bodies lying at the foot of it. They were in a heap. Heavy dust covered the bodies. One was headless . . . I heard a moan, so I put my hand gently on the bodies to feel which of them was alive. One of them, I noticed, had a hole, more than a foot wide, right through the abdomen. Another's head was split wide open into two halves, from back to front, by a piece of shrapnel . . . How the man managed to be still alive I don't know. I thought of shooting him with my revolver. I heard Bud Connell's voice behind me. Ronnie West appeared. We decided to get drunk. When we got over to the Mess the orderly refused us anything to drink and wouldn't open the bar. We broke our way in and each took a bottle of White Horse. We drank gulps of it straight."

Another who grieved for the loss of a close friend was Plt Off Howard Coffin, who wrote in his diary:

"Our hotel was bombed. P/O Streets, the third of the four Americans to go. This day will never be forgotten. Four ships sunk in the harbour. Hospitals bombed, churches and town after town cleaned out. What a slaughter of human lives. Unless help comes soon, God save us. No food, cigarettes, fuel. They are doing a lot of evacuating of English wives."[13]

Once again there were no fighters up to intercept, but the AA gunners claimed three Ju88s shot down and three others damaged. One of the raiders, 7T+FK of KüFlGr606, crashed on the island. The pilot was killed but his crew managed to bale out and were soon rounded up. A second Ju88, 3Z+FN of 5/KG77, also failed to return; there were no survivors. A third bomber crash-landed at Catania on return. At Takali two Spitfires, four Hurricanes and three other aircraft were destroyed, while five Spitfires and 15 Hurricanes were damaged in this latest attack. However, many of the Hurricanes were non-operational machines, having been severely damaged in earlier raids. Takali appeared to be so severely bombed that returning German bomber crews reported that the base looked as if it had been subjected to a volcanic eruption. Around the Takali area, Mosta had been particularly hard hit with 35 houses destroyed, and 31 civilians killed and 80 injured. Air Vice-Marshal Lloyd, when he came to look at the destruction for himself, had to agree that Takali reminded him of a World War I battlefield, and feared that it would remain unserviceable for at least a week. Notwithstanding the immense task, troops worked throughout the night and all next day and, by the evening of the 22nd, all serviceable Hurricanes and Spitfires were able to be flown to Luqa.

At 0950 on the morning of 22 March a raid comprising six Ju88s and 20 Bf109Fs approached, but just seven Hurricanes were all that could be mustered from Hal Far. The leading trio, Plt Off Allardice (BG711/G), Plt Off Wigley (BG770/D) and Sgt Doug Robb (Z2824/H), attacked three Ju88s over the sea to the south of the island, as Phil Wigley recalled:

"The Ju88s got away quite easily – they had jettisoned their bomb loads just as we attacked and, by diving away at full power, they lived to fight another day. Plt Off Allardice was shot down by crossfire from one of the Ju88 rear-gunners. We were both attacking 88s at the same time – there were no 109s anywhere in sight at the time."

Plt Off Phil Allardice's aircraft was seen to dive straight into the sea. An escorting Bf109F pilot, Lt Wilhelm Ruge of 5/JG53, claimed as his eighth victory what he thought was a Spitfire at this time, so it is possible that Plt Off Wigley was incorrect in his assumption.

Over the next few days the Luftwaffe in Sicily, aided not only by the Regia Aeronautica but also by their colleagues based on Crete, concentrated its efforts against an important convoy making for Malta from the east. The convoy comprised three merchantmen (*Clan*

Campbell, *Talabot* and *Pampas*) and the supply vessel *Breconshire*, loaded with 26,000 tons of urgently needed supplies including fuel oil, kerosene, .303 ammunition, bombs, AA shells, grain and coal. Escort was provided by four cruisers, 16 destroyers and six submarines. The convoy's arrival was vital to the island's ability to hold out in the face of the increasing intensity of air attack, which many thought was a premption to an invasion. Indeed, plans were being laid in Sicily for just such an event. But first, Malta's defences had to be subjugated. And the convoy had to be destroyed.

Having weathered the storm so far, the *Breconshire*, being faster than the others surged ahead and made a dash for Malta in the early hours of the morning of 23 March, but she was spotted and attacked by three Bf109F *Jabo* from JG53 led by Oblt Werner Langermann, the Staffelkapitän, effectively bringing her to a halt about nine miles from the entrance to Grand Harbour. But not all was lost since Malta's fighters were now able to provide assistance and protection for her, no fewer than 14 Spitfires and 11 Hurricanes being made available and ready for action. These were divided between island defence and convoy protection, with pairs operating over the ship at approximately half-hourly intervals. Encounters were reported during the day involving at least 60 Ju88s and 25 Bf109s, the first at 0815 when Flt Sgts Jock Sutherland (BG769/J) and Ray Ellis (Z3767/B) of 185 Squadron came across a Ju88 darting from cloud to cloud. Ellis managed to get in a good burst and was credited with a damaged. Close on an hour later, at 0910, another pair of Hurricanes attacked a Ju88 two miles south of Kalafrana at 1,000 feet, Sgts Garth Horricks (Z2961/K) and Doug Eastman (Z5118/S) taking turns to fire at the bomber which was last seen very low down over the water; they were granted a probable.

This may have been an aircraft of KüFlGr606 which returned to its base in a damaged condition. At about the same time two Spitfires of 249 Squadron encountered another Ju88 which fired a recognition flare of three red stars – presumably the crew thought the approaching fighters were Messerschmitts. The Junkers, almost certainly F6+CH of 1(F)/122, was promptly shot down into the sea. Just over an hour later Flt Lt Lawrence (BD826/A) and Sgt Ernie Broad (GL-U) encountered another Ju88, which they incorrectly identified as a He111, five miles east of Kalafrana at 5,000 feet. This was similarly treated, as Broad recorded:

> "Got burst in head-on. The enemy aircraft then did a diving turn and released bombs. I then did a beam attack as the e/a turned, seeing strikes on the port engine. E/a then flew east, gradually losing height. I did a rear quarter attack, seeing strikes along fuselage. E/a flying very slowly and I was able to do another beam attack at 500 feet, when I saw the e/a dive into the sea."

The bomber, believed to have been 7T+KK of 1/KüFlGr606 flown by Lt Walter Kipfmüller, was also attacked by Lawrence and they were jointly credited with its destruction. Members of the crew were seen to scramble into their dinghy. Sqn Ldr Mortimer-Rose (Z2961/K) and Sgt Eastman (Z5118/S) had a long-range shot at another Ju88 which was being engaged by two 249 Squadron Spitfires, but made no claims. A little later two more Spitfires from the same unit intercepted a further pair of bombers, both of which were claimed damaged. One of these may have in fact been shot down, since B3+LL of 3/KG54 flown by Lt Hermann Janzik failed to return, reportedly the victim of Spitfires. It had been a successful morning for the defenders. There were several more skirmishes in the early afternoon, most Ju88s escaping serious damage by seeking sanctuary in the heavy cloud. At 1300 Plt Off Wigley (BG770/D) and Flt Sgt Fletcher (GL-S) claimed damage to one bomber, while shortly afterwards Plt Offs Ron Noble (BG769/GL-J) and Joe Beckett (BD704/H) intercepted two more Ju88s. The next pair, Plt Off Ormrod (Z2961/K) and Sgt John Alderson (GL-U), failed to engage the enemy:

> "Some enemy aircraft were hanging around a few miles away, but we did not meet any over

the convoy. Actually, there was not much remaining of the convoy. Some of the ships had safely reached the Grand Harbour and we were patrolling off Delimara Point, where the *Breconshire* was stopped, having been engaged. Destroyers were patrolling the sea in her vicinity. In the Bay there was another ship. A good deal of oil seems to be emerging from it. Just off the Point there was much bubbling and a white swirl on the sea as if a ship had been sunk there."

In fact, the *Clan Campbell* had been caught by Ju88s when still some 20 miles from Malta. Her master and five of the crew were lost when the freighter sank, but the remainder were rescued by an escorting destroyer. Meanwhile, *Pampas* and *Talabot* safely reached Grand Harbour. But the *Breconshire* was still at the mercy of the Luftwaffe. One of the bombers returning to Sicily damaged from these encounters was an aircraft of II/LG1, in which the gunner had been wounded. In another aircraft from the same unit, flown by Lt Gerd Stamp, the hydraulics had been damaged by gunfire from ships' AA, and the aircraft was then pursued northwards by Hurricanes until Messerschmitts arrived and drove them off. On arrival at Catania, Stamp crash-landed the bomber, almost colliding with a concrete wall; he and his crew survived unhurt. The last success of this successful day for the fighters occurred when two Spitfires of 126 Squadron shot down another Ju88, an aircraft from 3/KGr806, while Beaufighters from Gambut shot down a second from the same Staffel. On Malta, at the end of this hectic day, although no fighters had been lost, only five remained fully serviceable. By a tremendous overnight effort, the hard-working groundcrews had a total of 18 Spitfires and Hurricanes operational by dawn next day. They were aided during the night by the supply of a number of Merlin engines and other aircraft spares from the two ships.

At first light on 24 March, the bombers were back and attacked the *Breconshire* and the destroyers and tugs assisting her, sinking a destroyer which had already been damaged when she struck a mine, but missing the crippled freighter. Ju88s and Ju87s also attacked the vessels in dock although both escaped damage. The first interceptions were reported soon after 1040, when two Spitfires of 126 Squadron claimed two Bf109Fs shot down off Kalafrana Bay. Within an hour some 40 Ju88s and 25 Messerschmitts appeared, heading for Grand Harbour in what was to be the most damaging raid of the day. Six Hurricanes and three Spitfires challenged the raiders, but only the latter engaged. Between 1420 and 1800, 30 more Ju88s, 30 Ju87s and 25 Bf109s again approached, four Spitfires and four Hurricanes being scrambled. One of the 126 Squadron Spitfire pilots claimed a Ju87 shot down, as did the guns, but the Hurricanes failed to engage. Hal Far was on the receiving end of one Stuka attack, a bomb falling near to the dug-out where Sqn Ldr Mortimer-Rose was manning the twin-Brownings. He was buried in debris up to his waist and his ear drums were pierced. Having been rescued, he cycled off to sick quarters, from where he was taken to hospital. Two Hurricane pilots, Sgt Ernie Broad and Tim Goldsmith, had a grandstand view as they sheltered in the entrance to the Ops Room, as graphically described by the Australian:

"Puffs of brown smoke from Delimara Point across the bay indicated that the 3.7s were going into action before their bark floated across to us, but we still could not see the bandits. Suddenly I looked straight above, then clutched Ernie's arm: 'Look, there's a Hurricane coming straight down with its undercart lowered'. Ernie took a swift look: 'Hurricane be buggered – that's a flaming Stuka!' Suddenly we could see them all. About a dozen Ju87s were diving on Hal Far from three directions, while roughly 20 more upstairs were queuing up waiting for their turn. Above them Messerschmitts laced the sky and then we heard the rattle of machine-gun fire. Apparently the Hurricanes [*sic*] were there, too. Then all hell broke loose as the sharp, fast explosions from surrounding Bofors guns mixed with the crash of the heavies, were overriden by the high-pitch scream of the falling bombs. We leaped down the Ops burrow like a couple of rabbits just as two terrific explosions above indicated a very near miss. The raid continued for 15-20 minutes, winding up with some strafing by three enemy fighters.

We came forth blinking in the sunlight to survey the results. The Officers' Mess had been flattened altogether, with part of the Airmens' Quarters. On the other side of the drome a Swordfish blazed furiously inside its dispersal bay. The wreckage of a Stuka smouldered in a field, the pilot smouldering with it. The gunner had managed to bale out. I learned later that he was taken prisoner by the crew of a Bofors gun near which he had landed. It was not until we had looked around and taken all this in that we noticed two craters where the nearby air raid shelter had been. Apparently the two eggs which landed just after we leaped for shelter had caused the damage. Together with the others, we raced for spades and shovels and set work excavating, or rather exhuming. Several hours later, when the job was completed, 23 bodies had been recovered. In addition, five badly injured airmen had been transferred to hospital. Three of these later died."

Shortly after this devastating attack, at around 1700, four Hurricanes from 185 Squadron scrambled on the approach of a further raid. Eight Ju88s were encountered and Plt Off Joe Beckett (BD704/H) led a diving attack, observing strikes on the two bombers at which he fired, one of which Sgt Ernie Broad (BG753/V) then attacked and damaged further before being driven away by a Bf109F. Plt Off Ron Noble (Z2961/GL-K) and Flt Sgt Jack Fletcher (GL-A) jointly attacked another and hit its starboard engine, which began smoking. Noble fired at two more which were seen to jettison their bombs, but his own aircraft was hit eight times by one of the rear-gunners. He managed to land safely, as did two of the other Hurricanes similarly damaged. One of the bombers may have been 3Z+CT of 9/KG77 which failed to return, and was reported down in the sea about 20 miles south of Comiso; Lt Heinz-Karl Müller and his crew did not survive. By the end of the day Malta was again down to nine serviceable fighters.

Early on the morning of 25 March, tugs managed to attach tow lines to the stricken *Breconshire* and by midday had succeeded in towing her to Marsaxlokk Bay. Rather surprisingly, there was little hostile activity over Malta until mid afternoon, when at least 30 Ju88s, 25 Ju87s and a dozen Bf109Fs of II/JG3 made their presence felt. The Stukas went after *Breconshire* but failed to hit her, while *Pampas* and *Talabot* were repeatedly attacked in Grand Harbour but also escaped damage. To meet these raids eight Hurricanes and six Spitfires were scrambled. Sgt Horricks of 185 Squadron wrote in the diary:

"F/Lt Lloyd brought about a wonderful interception. There followed a terrific air battle, one of the largest Malta has seen. Hurricanes, Spits, 109 and Ju87s totalling about 40 aircraft. And when the sky had cleared and everyone had returned and told their tale, it could clearly be seen that the German Air Force had received the dirty end of the stick. We later learned that 12 enemy aircraft went off the plot, and we feel certain that most of the probables never got home. However, they were not seen to go in so cannot be counted as destroyed. Everyone is quite happy as it was our first clock at 87s. Here's to many more."

Of his own performance, he noted in his logbook:

"Attacked 30 Stukas. I attacked one abeam and killed the rear-gunner, then went astern and hit engine. It went down towards the sea smoking badly. Probably destroyed. Attacked No2 and killed rear-gunner and saw strikes on fuselage. Damaged. Attacked No3 and hit it in starboard wing. Ran out of ammunition. Damaged. Ten holes in my plane. Down OK."

Two Stukas and two Messerschmitts were claimed shot down by the Spitfires, while the Hurricane pilots were credited with one Stuka destroyed and several probables, one being credited jointly to Plt Offs Wigley (GL-S) and Ormrod (GL-U), the latter confiding to his journal:

". . . we were just approaching Kalafrana when the first Stukas dropped like stones from the clouds towards the *Breconshire*, now lying in Kalafrana Bay. We all shrieked joyous

Tally-ho's and dashed to the counter attack. Oh, what joyous moments followed – perhaps the happiest in my life; no, couldn't be happier than moments I've had with the hounds, but particularly happy all the same. Several Stukas pulled out of their dives across my front. I chose one and stuck to it. I was determined to destroy one without doubt. I kept him as my target, having once fired at him, in spite of other 87s passing between us. I opened fire with a burst from about 250 yards, which may have killed the gunner as I experienced no return fire. I closed the range. The e/a tried to evade my fire by diving and zooming. I sat behind him, giving bursts from astern, whenever he altered course in front of me. Pieces were falling from the e/a and his engine was smoking. Then another Hurricane appeared from below; inverted, it almost entered my fire and then fell away. This later proved to be Wigley finishing an attack on my Stuka from below.

I continued after my Stuka which waddled away north-eastwards. As I came still closer, it ceased to take evasive action and went on in a steady glide pouring out white smoke. I closed in to about 15 yards or less then broke away to starboard. I climbed up again to attack afresh with a *coup de grâce* and looked for my Stuka. Wondered where it had gone and then found it on my tail. It had moved so slowly that I'd pulled up again in front of it. I then pulled away and I flew across it, watching it going down to the sea below me. I knew it was finished. I saw another and decided to attack it, but first I looked back to see my first Stuka hit the water, but it must have already done so, for the white trail of smoke had stopped abruptly at sea level. I now turned my attention to this next Stuka. I gave it a full beam attack with a short burst which hit the engine, which also gave out white glycol smoke. I finished my last few rounds from astern and left the e/a also to glide towards the sea. I returned to base. Can only claim these two as a very probable and a probable as I did not actually see them strike the sea. Hope some shore batteries saw them go in, so that I shall get them confirmed."

Another Stuka was claimed probably destroyed by the combined efforts of Sgt Doug Eastman (HA-D) and the New Zealand pair, Sgts Doug Robb (GL-C) and Alan Wilson (HA-A). Yet another was damaged by the combined attacks of Flt Lt Lloyd (GL-A) and Plt Off D'Arcy Milburn (Z2698/GL-L). However, despite all these claims for Ju87s shot down or damaged, only T6+CC piloted by Lt Klaus Heemann of III/StG3 failed to return; a second aircraft from this Gruppe returned with a wounded rear-gunner (Uffz Georg Claus).

Heavy cloud and low fog had favoured Malta during the last few hours, allowing the unloading of the freighters to get underway but, during the morning of 26 March, the clouds lifted and German reconnaissance crews soon spotted the anchored vessels, the first raiders approaching at 1220. Within minutes a total of 24 Ju88s and 20 Ju87s were reported over Grand Harbour. *Talabot* was the first to be targeted and received several direct hits, sinking with only a small fraction of her cargo having been unloaded. *Pampas* and most of her cargo followed. *Breconshire* escaped this onslaught, but a destroyer and a submarine were both sunk in this deluge of bombs.

The initial wave of bombers was engaged by seven Hurricanes of 126 Squadron which had scrambled at 1210, led by Sqn Ldr Jumbo Gracie, the new CO. He attacked a Ju88 at point-blank range, last seeing this slowly heading out to sea. His own aircraft was hit by return fire as he broke away, so he returned to Takali where he landed safely. Another Ju88 was claimed damaged by Plt Off Joe Crichton (HA-A):

"Saw two Ju88s just at top of cloud so went into attack. Picked out one and followed him, gradually catching up with him, the 88 dodging in and out of cloud. I got within 200 yards and he started to turn, so I gave him a full deflection shot, a short burst, then another very short burst as both my cannons had stopped. Saw one strike on starboard wing. Didn't see any result. F/L Anderson and P/O McKay both saw black smoke from the starboard engine. P/O McKay last saw 88 at 1,000 feet with black smoke pouring from it, in a gradual dive."

Four Spitfires – the only fighters immediately available – went up to engage the next raid, the pilots being credited with two Ju87s and a Ju88 shot down. Then, between 1630 and 1857, came a second major series of raids. A total of two dozen Ju88s, 18 Ju87s and many Messerschmitts were reported coming in over Kalafrana. One Ju88 dived out of the evening sun and planted its bombs on the crippled *Breconshire* and the supply vessel finally gave up the fight, heeled over and settled in the shallow water. Four Spitfires and six Hurricanes had been scrambled to challenge this raid. Sgt Archie Steele of 185 Squadron, flying a cannon-armed Hurricane (GL-P), closed in on one Ju88 and saw his fire striking its starboard engine which caught fire, followed by an explosion in the fuel tank. The Junkers glided into the sea, and he saw the crew scrambling into their dinghy before he returned to base. Other Hurricane pilots also engaged, Flt Sgt Jack Fletcher (HA-A) chasing a Ju87 into cloud before firing at a Messerschmitt, both of which he claimed damaged. North-east of Grand Harbour Sgt Ernie Broad (GL-S) damaged another Stuka with a short burst before being chased away by one of the escorting fighters. Having evaded this, he attacked a second Stuka head-on, claiming some damage to this also. Plt Off Ron Noble (Z2698/GL-L) used his ammunition on two Ju88s and two Ju87s, believing he probably caused some damage to all four aircraft, while Sgt Tim Goldsmith (Z3993/X) recorded in his diary:

> "I became airborne as fast as I could but found I had lost sight of my formation, so pushed the throttle through the gate and headed for where I had last seen them. There was thin, broken cloud at 2,000 feet and just before I entered it I saw the four Spits from Luqa pass across beneath me, climbing hard. When I emerged above the cloud a few moments later, the Spits were above me, heading south. Then I saw the Hurricanes near St Paul's Bay, but they were heading back so I climbed in circles until they passed me and then slipped into position on the extreme starboard. We were now at about 8,000 feet. Six 109s flashed across 1,500 feet above. We turned about, expecting to be attacked but nothing happened for a moment or two, then down they came. I pulled up my nose to engage one head-on when Keith [Flt Lt Lawrence] called up: 'Look out, boys, they're coming in behind – get under the mattress'. I half-rolled, then pulled the stick back and with full starboard rudder, aileron turned down until I had reached the cloud, underneath which our section reformed, and we flew east for a few miles before starting to climb.
>
> We climbed up through the clouds near Kalafrana, and when we had reached 10,000 feet, saw 30-odd Ju88s just north of Grand Harbour, weaving slightly through the flak. The majority of them peeled off and streamed down on Grand Harbour, but the remaining ten kept on until they were over Hal Far, then swung into line astern and slid down towards the *Breconshire* in Kalafrana Bay. We nosed down and angled in to join their dive, but they were travelling too fast for us. I fired a deflection shot at one as he drew away from me, then squirted at the kite behind him. At that moment the close escort arrived, interrupting our little party and sending us into tight steep turns. Suddenly the Huns had gone and we were alone again."

The Hurricanes circled Hal Far until the Controller warned of more bombers approaching Grand Harbour. Goldsmith continued:

> "Once more we poked our noses upwards and gathered angles. This time we reached 11,000 feet without fighter interference, although the Spitfires could be heard having more trouble than they wanted. We were above Luqa when the 87s arrived and tumbled down through the barrage to let loose their bombs on the ships in the harbour, three of which were already blazing like torches. Keith led us down in a dive that converged with the track of the dive-bombers and met at the bottom, just as they were pulling out and raising their dive brakes. A Stuka silhouetted itself against the sky 70 yards ahead of me and slightly above. I fired six seconds of machine-gun fire at him and watched the tracers ripping into

his fuselage, but he kept on flying. Then another one appeared from above and at about 50 yards range. I gave him three-seconds fire and had the satisfaction of seeing glycol pouring from his radiator, as he lost height towards St Paul's Bay. Tracer from behind reminded me where I was and I broke sharply down, just as a silver Messerschmitt flashed past. My ammunition was exhausted and my tanks nearly empty, I flew back to Hal Far and made a very ropey landing, but feeling pretty pleased with myself nevertheless. I was credited with a Ju87 probably destroyed, although I felt convinced that he could not possibly have crossed the 60 miles of water with no engine coolant."[14]

Plt Off Ormrod was on this scramble but his aircraft suffered damage to its engine when hit by either an unseen Messerschmitt or AA fire, probably the latter. With spluttering engine he landed at Luqa, with the underside of his aircraft covered in oil, and a large hole in the rudder. Although no Hurricanes were lost, two were claimed by Obfw Rudolf Ehrenberger (his 19th) and Uffz Paczia (his second), both of 6/JG53. The Spitfires engaged Ju88s and claimed four damaged, one of which crash-landed on returning to Comiso. One of the Spitfires was flown by Plt Off Sandy McHan, who had been flying Hurricanes with 1435 Flight, his aircraft being peppered by shrapnel from over-zealous AA gunners, though he was able to land safely. During the day's raids the AA gunners had optimistically claimed two Ju88s and a Ju87 shot down, and one Ju87 damaged. Although all three supply ships had been sunk, all were in shallow water and, during the coming weeks no less than 3,100 tons of cargo was salvaged from *Pampas* and 80 tons from *Talabot*, while several hundred tons of oil were pumped from *Breconshire*'s capsized hull.

Following the attacks on the ships there was a reduction in activity for a few days. Few interceptions were attempted while efforts were made to restore some semblance of numerical strength to the weakened fighter defences. During the daylight hours of 27 March there were seven alerts but no interceptions. Only one significant raid developed, 30-plus bombers appearing over Grand Harbour and the airfields but little damage was inflicted. The day was marked, however, by a limited but valuable and morale-boosting reinforcement when ten cannon-armed Hurricane IICs were flown by pilots of A Flight of 229 Squadron from El Firdan via Gambut[15]. These were led by the unit's New Zealand-born CO, Sqn Ldr Derek Kain, and flight commander Flt Lt P.C.P. Farnes DFM. An eleventh Hurricane had been forced to return when Plt Off Len Malthus RNZAF discovered his aircraft had a faulty fuel pump:

"229 was to be flown over to Malta from the desert in two batches, at pretty well deck level in order to avoid being picked up by Jerry radar or their R/T. I was on the first batch, so we set off and, of course, we had pretty concise instructions to behave ourselves and, among other things, we were told if we had any engine trouble or mechanical trouble of any kind, we had to make up our minds before the point of no return – the halfway mark. Beyond that one would have to carry on towards Malta. This was the correct thing to do. And, of course, we had long-range tanks just to get us over there, and they couldn't be jettisoned at all, which made the aircraft very cumbersome to fly and very heavy on petrol. About a third or two-fifths of the way across I tested my pump to get some petrol – and it wasn't working. I tried it several times and this gave me quite a fright. I wasn't halfway so I did the only possible thing and turned back. I eventually landed back in the desert, very, very short of petrol indeed. The main pump was found to be faulty, very much to my relief, though I wasn't very keen to try again."

Flt Lt Paul Farnes, a veteran of the fighting in France in 1940 and the Battle of Britain, had until recently been an instructor at 73 OTU in Aden:

"My posting took place under rather a large cloud and was precipitated after I had woken the Station Commander in the early hours of the morning by placing a bulbous motor horn against his ear and playing it rather loudly – the horn having been taken from a taxi which had brought us back to camp. Needless to say, he was not amused and I duly left Aden as a Pilot Officer. On arrival at 229 Squadron I found I knew the CO and was astonished to be promoted to Flight Lieutenant in charge of A Flight."

Following their arrival at Malta, Sqn Ldr Kain became unfit for operational flying duties and command of the Squadron effectively fell upon the shoulders of Flt Lt Farnes until a new CO could be appointed.

The remaining days of the month were relatively quiet for the defenders, allowing the cargoes to be salvaged almost unhindered, while the few fighter aircraft were serviced, repaired and patched-up for the onslaught which was certain to come. There was only one interception on the 28th, four Spitfires catching a lone Ju88, presumably on reconnaissance, but it managed to escape. Next day (29 March) saw the arrival of seven more Spitfires which had flown off the deck of the carrier *Eagle*, the balance of the second batch. Their arrival did not go unnoticed and soon after midday nine Ju88s approached, crossing the coast singly and in pairs. Four Spitfires and four Hurricanes were scrambled, the former probably destroying one of the intruders. The Hurricanes did not make contact. The weather remained poor on the 30th, the only action occurring when two Spitfires attacked and damaged a Ju88 in the afternoon.

The last day of the month began with a raid as the first intruders approached, in cloud, at 0650, and Ju88s and Bf109s continued to appear in small numbers throughout the day until 1515. Two Hurricanes flown by Sgts Archie Steele and Ernie Broad were scrambled after Ju88s in cloud but, while flying at cloud base, four Messerschmitts suddenly appeared behind them, the encounter recorded by Sgt Horricks:

> "Archie Steele, it appears, was a bit slow in turning and one of the 109s shot him down. Broad had a quick squirt at one of the 109s but observed no results. Sgt Steele's death came as a great blow to the Squadron. He was one of the most skilful and keenest pilots on the island. He can be ill spared during these hard times. I know everyone agrees with me when I say he was a damn good fellow."

Sgt Steele's aircraft, Z5302, crashed into a field not far from the Tas-Silg AA battery near Marsaxlokk, apparently the victim of Lt Herbert Langer of Stab II/JG53 who claimed his aircraft as a Spitfire, his first victory. The body of the 26-year-old from Lanarkshire in Scotland was recovered from the wreck and interred in Capuccini Naval Cemetery. His commission came through shortly after his death.

During the late evening a force of about 20 Ju88s made an attack on Grand Harbour, Hal Far and Luqa. Naval AA claimed hits on two of the bombers but could not prevent the wrecked *Talabot* taking another hit. Four cannon-armed Hurricanes were scrambled. Six Ju88s were seen by the pilots in the moonlit sky, each pilot selecting a target. Plt Off Ormrod claimed one damaged but Plt Off Wigley's guns jammed almost immediately. Sgt Eastman (GL-W) saw a Ju88 being attacked by two Hurricanes and attacked the same aircraft, closing to 100 yards. He then attacked another, making two passes and again closing in to 100 yards. This also was claimed damaged. Plt Off Ormrod wrote:

> "On seating myself in my aircraft, I found the pin for fastening the safety harness was missing, so though I do not like my harness other than perfect, I made do with a piece of string instead. Wigley and I took off in formation straight down the aerodrome in spite of there being a strong wind behind us. We got off OK though, so did the other two following us. Climbed to gain height, as much as possible, before the arrival of the enemy. There were three large hostile plots approaching, in all probability some 30 aircraft. Passed through a thin layer of cloud. Above it we were greeted with the last glow of a beautiful sunset to the west, whilst to the east rose the moon almost full. Had some difficulty in easily knowing where exactly I was since the island lay in darkness below and hidden by much cloud as well.

Suddenly, just as I was concentrating to endeavour to see at what the Grand Harbour barrage was firing, Milburn cried out that there were enemy aircraft behind. Turned, as Ju88s – four or six in number – passed behind in a shallow dive towards the island from the southeast. I attacked from his starboard and then from astern the last Junkers. He twisted and turned as I fired, and drew clear. He began a slight dive and I fired. I then got on his tail again and still fired, though dazzled by the very bright tracer, golden white, which his rear-gunner was firing at me. Then he went into a very steep dive, which I could not follow, and disappeared into the darkness and clouds below. I thought he'd gone in. Later, I saw so many bursts on the ground and some fires at Hal Far that I began to think perhaps I was mistaken.

I was flying slowly, straight and level, at about 1,000 feet, parallel with the southern coast and a couple of miles inside it. Furthermore, I was a single-engined aircraft, so I took a pretty dim view of some Bofors guns that proceeded to engage me. Luckily for me, they were rotten shots, the tracer from one passing in front of me and that from another, behind me. I switched over to transmit and poured forth some strongly-worded abuse of AA guns in general, Bofors in particular. Heard Wigley call over the R/T, 'Keep your shirt on, Olly'. I was then illuminated by searchlights and I wiggled my wings. They switched off and the Bofors stopped. I circled once round Takali and then landed in the moonlight without a flare path. Taxied in and found glycol to be streaming from my aircraft. Something had hit my aircraft somewhere, but it was too dark to see, no one having a torch. A few glim lamps had been lit and laid out in a line when Wigley and Eastman came in. Each made a perfect three-point landing."

The four pilots retired to the Officers' Mess at M'dina for dinner, Sgt Eastman being invited to join them, where there was a minor celebration taking place since a number of pilots had just learned they were soon to leave the island. Ormrod recorded one humorous incident:

"There were not many in the Mess tonight. 'Sproggit' (P/O Leggett) and Crichton, the big Canadian, however, made up for the absence of the majority. They were celebrating the reception of the news that they were to leave the island tomorrow night. They were very drunk and very merry.

Crichton said to Sproggit: 'Buy me a drink'.

Sproggit replied: 'No, you are drunk'.

'I'm not drunk, yer bastard', retorted Crichton as he picked up the detachable top of a stool and cracked it hard upon Leggett's head; Leggett held his head, with an uproariously funny expression on his face.

'Oh, I haven't hurt you, have I, Sproggit?' asked Crichton.

This sort of foolery continued an hour or more until I went to bed at 11 o'clock. Morrison-Jones was in the Mess. He tells me that Wells, Kemp, Kee and Sgt Gardiner are going home soon. I am very sorry to hear that we will lose them."

Another about to leave the island was Flt Lt Andy Anderson, who was posted to 73 OTU at Aden as an instructor, much to his chagrin:

"The thought of flying around with someone else doing the flying scares me stiff! I'm afraid if I'm stuck here too long I'll stagnate and lose interest in the war altogether . . . Looking at Malta in retrospect my admiration for it has gone up considerably; no praise is too great for the Maltese people, a thing we used to forget at the time, but remember now, is that it was their island and their homes that were being smashed up which makes the way they're taking it doubly creditable."

During March the island had suffered 186 alerts which brought an estimated 1,230 incursions by Ju88s, Ju87s and Bf109s. The defending fighters had claimed 31 aircraft shot down, 20 probables and 65 damaged, for the loss of ten Hurricanes and four Spitfires. The guns claimed a further 28 destroyed, three probables and 31 damaged, while Naval AA claimed one probable and four damaged to add to the tally.

CHAPTER XI

HURRICANE SWAN SONG

April – May 1942

At the beginning of April, Feldmarschall Kesselring at last unleashed his strike force:

> "The main assault was begun on 2 April 1942. II Air Group Messina did a splendid job in planning and the execution of the attack. Temporary interruptions of the air assault against Malta were caused by switching the attacking forces to convoys, the sinking of which was an indispensable preliminary to success against the island. In bitter battles these convoys, except for a few ships, were destroyed."[1]

229 Squadron carried out its first sorties over Malta on 1 April, Flt Lt Farnes leading Plt Off Carter, Sgts Pauley (HB-J) and Potts to attack three Ju88s at 1045, although no results were observed. There were several more raids during the afternoon, Spitfires shooting down a Bf109F of 8/JG53 flown by 13-victory ace Fw Hans Schade, who was killed, while a Spitfire force-landed with a slightly wounded pilot. Later, six Hurricanes manned by 185 Squadron pilots joined Spitfires intercepting 15 Ju88s of I and II/KG77, two of which were claimed shot down by the Spitfires, one pilot reporting that he had shared in probably destroying another with a Hurricane. In fact, Plt Off Ian McKay (GL-Z), who was celebrating his 21st birthday, recorded sharing a Ju88 with Plt Off Joe Beckett (Z4942/GL-Y), so perhaps all three attacked the same bomber. McKay's aircraft took a hit in the centre of its armoured windscreen without inflicting injury, but causing the Canadian to comment: "Almost couldn't say 'today I am a man!'" Both Plt Off Ron Noble (Z5118/S) and Flt Sgt Jack Fletcher (GL-W) reported attacks on other bombers, Noble claiming his victim damaged while Fletcher thought his would fail to get back to Sicily.

There was a lull before the next raid, although the antics of Flt Lt Don Stones, who was acting as Visual Controller from the top of the Palace Tower, from where he had a grandstand view of air fighting above Grand Harbour, almost caused a panic. On realising it was April Fool's Day, he decided to play a joke on the Ops Room:

> "I cranked our telephone and when Ops answered, I said: 'Visual Controller here. 30-plus approaching over St Paul's Bay.' I expected the man to say: 'There's nothing on the radar,' and I would say: 'April Fool. Keep awake!' But he hung up without speaking and the next second all the sirens were wailing air-raid warnings. Desperately I cranked the telephone many revolutions before it was answered. 'April Fool practice, only a joke. Cancel the warnings. April Fool,' I yelled. 'You're the bloody fool,' came the unknown voice and he slammed his receiver down. Gradually the sirens cried themselves to sleep. The telephone rang. 'Stones?' asked Woody. No first-names today. 'G/Capt Woodhall here. Come and see me at five o'clock in my office.'
>
> At the Ops room, Woody had the earphones on and was controlling on the R/T. When he had finished he came over to me and said: 'Get into that office.' He sat. I stood. 'That was the bloody stupidest thing to do. We nearly scrambled the entire Wing. Have you finally gone completely mad, even more so than usual?' I muttered an apology, while he glared at me. He picked up a piece of paper from his desk and thrust it at me. 'You'd better read that. From Air Ministry.' How could he have ordered a court martial so quickly? I could hardly bear to read it. It said that F/Lt Stones had been awarded a bar to his DFC a few days previously. I looked at Woody, glad to see he was grinning. 'Sit down. You are a bloody idiot,' he said, and then: 'Get that tit sewn on your gong and I'll take you up to Takali tomorrow evening for a drink with the boys.'"[2]

At 1630, a Do24 flying boat was observed five miles north-east of Grand Harbour under an umbrella of Bf109Fs, apparently searching for the missing Fw Schade. Four Spitfires and one Hurricane were sent to investigate. The Spitfires engaged the enemy fighters, claiming two shot down and two damaged; Uffz Gerhard Kitzenmaier of 5/JG53 was killed. No sooner were the Spitfires down than another raid approached including an estimated 50-plus Ju87s, which headed for the Dockyard and Hal Far. Two Hurricanes of 229 Squadron had been sent up at 1700 to cover the returning Spitfires, and these were joined by five more from 185/605 Squadron, followed by five Spitfires half an hour later. The defending fighters encountered formations of Ju87s and Ju88s – and their escorts – over Grand Harbour, the Hurricanes claiming one Stuka destroyed by Flt Sgt Jack Fletcher (GL-W), who also claimed a probable. Sgt Ned Pauley (HB-J) of 229 Squadron also claimed a probable, which was "last seen gliding, smoking" – and a second damaged, while Plt Off McKay (Z4942/GL-Y) claimed yet one more damaged, and Flt Sgt Tony Boyd (GL-M) another probable: "Attacked Ju87 – probable. Had a dogfight with it, several bursts, left it pouring white smoke from port side. Also attacked two 109s (shot up)." Plt Off McKay's Hurricane was also hit and damaged by a Messerschmitt following his combat with the Stuka:

> "I had a good crack at one 87 and think it went in but couldn't see 'cause I had to break away when two 109s came down on me. My birthday nearly ended in disaster after breaking off engagement with the 87. I then went to sea level and came back over the island. I was just about over Luqa when I felt and heard my aircraft being hit, which made me turn steeply to port. A 109 had come up behind me and taken a good squirt at me. There were two large cannon holes in my wing and several machine-gun bullets. I had to land without flaps 'cause the starboard one was all shot away."

Oblt Helmut Belser of 8/JG53 claimed a Spitfire at 1701 for his 20th victory, but it seems likely his victim was in fact McKay's Hurricane. When the Spitfires arrived on the scene they claimed three more Ju87s, two probables and a damaged, while the AA guns claimed two more of the dive-bombers together with a Bf109, to make a grand total of six Ju87s and one Messerschmitt destroyed, five Ju87s probably destroyed and three damaged. Two Stukas failed to return, T6+FN of 8/StG3 crashing on Delimara Point with the loss of the gunner, Gfr Wilhelm Neubauer. His pilot, Uffz Winfried Günther, managed to bale out and was blown out to sea. A second Stuka from the same unit came down in the sea five miles north-east of Valetta. Oblt Kühn, the pilot, was later rescued from the sea by an Axis air-sea rescue craft but the gunner, Gfr Helmut Suchlich, was lost. A third aircraft, from 7 Staffel, returned with a wounded pilot, Obfw Kurt Auer. Despite the determination of the defenders many Stukas got through to attack shipping in Grand Harbour, where two submarines and a minesweeper were sunk, and another submarine and a minesweeper were damaged together with an oiler and three tugs.

From Kalafrana, Flt Lt Crockett immediately set out in Seaplane Tender *ST338* and within minutes had picked up Uffz Günther, who was still struggling to release his parachute harness when help arrived. The Messerschmitt shot down by the gunners was Black 11 of 5/JG53 which had swooped low over Luqa to strafe AA batteries; its pilot, Uffz Hans Pilz, was able to belly-land in a nearby field at Paola. There was a tragic sequel to this raid when, later that evening as military personnel were inspecting the remains of the Ju87 which had crashed on Delimara Point, a bomb on board exploded and killed at least five RAF AMES personnel and seven soldiers and wounded two others, one of whom later died of his injuries.

The second day of the month brought a resumption of the heavy assault. At 1010 an estimated 50 Ju88s and Ju87s began crossing the coast under their usual cover, again to bomb the Dockyard area and Hal Far. Four Hurricanes of 229 Squadron led by Sqn Ldr Kain were first off, followed by four Spitfires of 126 Squadron and seven Hurricanes of

185 Squadron, the latter led by Flt Lt Lloyd. The Spitfires attacked the Ju88s, two of which were claimed probably damaged and a third damaged. Sqn Ldr Kain landed again almost immediately due to mechanical problems, and Flt Lt Farnes took over as section leader, personally claiming damage to a Ju88 before the escort intervened. Having avoided contact with the Messerschmitts, Plt Off Joe Beckett of 185 Squadron and Sgt Ned Pauley (HB-H) of 229 Squadron jointly attacked a Ju88 which they claimed damaged before it escaped. Pauley then orbited the parachute of a Spitfire pilot down in the sea (Plt Off Don McLeod, an American of 126 Squadron) until a launch arrived to rescue him, a deed for which he received an official congratulations. It seems that Bf109Fs of II/JG3 formed part of the fighter umbrella, Oblt Walter Dahl claiming a Hurricane shot down for his 18th victory – although this was not officially credited – and, indeed, Plt Off Taffy Andrews' BV174 was badly shot up by a Messerschmitt but, although slightly shrapnel-wounded in both feet, he succeeded in landing at Luqa. The Spitfires, meanwhile, had also tangled with the escort and were overwhelmed; two were shot down with one pilot losing his life, the other being rescued from the sea, while a third landed with more than 20 bullet strikes. Pilots of Stab I, II and III/JG53 were responsible.

Meanwhile, Lloyd led the 185 Squadron Hurricanes after the Ju87s but there was time only for snap shots before the escorting fighters intervened; nonetheless, two Stukas were claimed damaged by Lloyd (BG770/D) and Plt Off Wigley (Z4942/GL-Y), while Plt Off Milburn reported the probable destruction of a Ju88 and Sgt Gordon Tweedale (Z5140/C) damaged a second: "Caught an 88 diving on Grand Harbour. Knocked a chunk off him then followed him out to sea. Tons of flak around." Tweedale had only just returned to the Squadron following his sojourn in hospital and had not been officially passed fit to resume operational flying, so should not have scrambled to join the battle. One Stuka sustained serious damage, the 9/StG3 aircraft landing with a wounded gunner. Flt Lt Lloyd also damaged a Bf109F while Plt Off Ormrod (Z2698/L) damaged a Ju88:

"Four aircraft of 229 Squadron took off, but their CO [Sqn Ldr Kain] subsequently landed owing to something being wrong with his undercarriage. Of the remaining three, one [Plt Off Andrews] climbed up to 20,000 feet alone and was damaged by a 109, his No2 having lost him. One other [Sgt Pauley] eventually joined us when we took off. We climbed to about 8,000 feet and were engaged by about 20 Messerschmitt 109s. We entered into a mélêe with the 109s, managing to dodge them successfully. I kept in formation for as long as possible until I had to break to avoid colliding with other Hurricanes. I then did steep turns alone over Luqa, keeping on a little top rudder and thus eventually getting to 9,000 feet. Two 109s made a pass at me, but I out-turned them and got a squirt at one. Then I saw the Ju88s attacking Grand Harbour. I caught one and attacked him head-on as he broke southwards out of the barrage, and then turned eastwards. I almost collided with him, passing very close. Then I turned and gave him a squirt from astern as he passed out over Zonqor Point. I was very disappointed that there had been no spectacular results. I had thought a head-on attack would fix him at once. The bullet-proof glass on the front must be very tough.

Anyway, I cannot have missed the next one. Attacked him head-on and my tracer went right in him. He was in a slight climb and I in a slight dive. About 100 yards in front of him, I pulled up my nose, rolled over, pulled the stick into my stomach and raked him from stem to stern along his back as he passed. Pulling out behind him and a little below, I followed him a little way, firing from astern. He jinked about in front of me. Then, knowing full well how little one can do to a Ju88 from astern with machine-guns, and knowing what happens to Hurricanes which fly straight and level for too long with 109s about, I gave up the chase. He went out to sea between Grand Harbour and Zonqor Point, losing height with Bofors guns firing at him. Another Hurricane had appeared from below me and was firing at an 88 from astern. I turned round now, luckily. Met a 109F coming hell-for-leather to pick me off the Junkers' tail. I fired at him as he passed, turned and fired again as he receded and he, thinking discretion to be the better part of valour, decided not to bother about the other Hurricane. I returned across the coast and headed for Hal Far which, I could see, was being attacked by Stukas. However, I could not get there in time. Two more 109Fs made a pass at me and I avoided them. They did not try very hard. Asked Control if they had any more bombers for me. They told me to land, so returned to Takali."

On landing, he discovered that the other Hurricane pilot was Sgt Tweedale:

"Sgt Tweedale is not supposed to be flying for medical reasons – however, he had brought an aircraft over from Hal Far and joined us when we scrambled, without orders. It appears to have been he who attacked the Ju88 after me, though he did not see me or the 109. He claims to have knocked pieces off the tail of the 88. He is very keen to fight."

Twenty-six Ju87s and 29 Ju88s were back at 1625, bombing Grand Harbour, Kalafrana, Hal Far and Luqa, where an unserviceable Wellington was burnt out. At Kalafrana a hangar and a repair shop were hit and badly damaged, an Albacore under repair being destroyed and another damaged. Hal Far took another battering, as noted by Flt Sgt Horricks:

"The bombers again attacked Hal Far and left it badly shaken; many more bomb holes, planes damaged and buildings shaken. One 100-pounder landed on our dispersal hut, but didn't explode. However, one end of the hut fell out. No one will be able to complain of not having sufficient air in the dispersal hut now."

Six of the escorting Messerschmitts strafed and sank the schooner *Anna Docoutros* while on her way to Gozo. There was no opposition from the defending fighters. Next day (Good Friday of the Easter weekend) found the island with few serviceable fighters. There were three major raids, the airfields again being targeted with the result that a Hurricane was destroyed at Hal Far and a Spitfire at Takali. Spitfires of 249 Squadron were up to meet one raid, a Ju88 being engaged without tangible result. More raiders appeared during the night of 3/4 April and two of 1435 Flight's Hurricanes were scrambled, but Sqn Ldr Westmacott soon returned with an unserviceable radio while Flg Off Peter Rathie intercepted one bomber without success.

When the Luftwaffe next put in an appearance, on the morning of 4 April, only the gunners opposed the bombers as they approached Grand Harbour, shooting down one Ju87 of 7/StG3. The next two raids, in the afternoon, were also unchallenged by fighters but, as evening drew on, four Spitfires and six Hurricanes were made available to meet the final daylight raid. One Ju88 was claimed shot down by the Spitfires and two more damaged, while the only success for the Hurricanes led by Plt Off Ormrod was achieved by Sgt Potts of 229 Squadron, who claimed damage to a Ju88. Ormrod wrote:

"We had six serviceable aircraft – all that can possibly be scraped together on the island. F/Lt Farnes of 229 Squadron was to lead us. When it came to taking off, Farnes' aircraft was u/s, so I led in his place. Five aircraft took off but two of these landed almost immediately, one having a burst oil pipe and another something else wrong. So only three of us were left airborne. There were however four Spitfires up. The three of us climbed up to 20,000 feet and were unhindered by 109s, there being none about. At last I viewed enemy aircraft approaching. I dived on them from 10,000 feet above them and out of the sun.

I made to do a head-on attack on a Ju88 but found that my windscreen was covered by oil, which obscured him from my view. For once we had even excess speed over the 109s but, though we'd jumped them beautifully, it was no good to me. I could not see to fire. I twice overtook 109s and, being able to also out-turn them, should have been able to shoot them down had I been able to see to fire. We must have reached 300mph in our dive. The 229 sergeant [Sgt Potts], flying his cannon aircraft, damaged the Ju88 on one engine. Wigley [Z4942/Y] also fired at the 88. Of course, they did not have such a good chance as myself, who was leading.

On my way back, I reduced the speed to 120mph and tried to wipe my windscreen. In this, however, I was unsuccessful, so, knowing a large plot to be approaching, I landed at Luqa. Taxied to the dispersal hut. Called an airman. Gave him a handkerchief and made him wipe my windscreen, and took off again. Took off in such a hurry with flaps down but it did not matter. I climbed to 6,000 feet and then Control asked me how many I had with me. I answered none and they told me to return to base."

When 40 Ju88s and 15 Ju87s attacked under a large fighter escort during the early afternoon of the 5th, four Spitfires and four Hurricanes were scrambled, the former returning with several successes but the Hurricanes had a hard time; 229 Squadron's Plt Off Taffy Andrews was again shot up and this time was seriously wounded in the left arm by a cannon shell. In spite of his severe injury he was able to land at Luqa, but his aircraft (BM964) then ran off the runway due to damaged brakes and he was further injured. It would seem that he had been erroneously attacked by another RAF fighter, according to Ormrod:

"One Hurricane was shot down today. It appears that it was shot down by another Hurricane or a Spitfire. The pilot was the same pilot officer of 229 Squadron that was shot up by Messerschmitts last Thursday. He did very well to get down at Luqa where he crashed over into the ravine at the end of the runway. His aircraft was practically uncontrollable. Noble, who was there, thought it was a Spitfire. He's pretty sure it was. F/Lt Farnes witnessed it from the ground and is sure that there were no Me109s there at the time. He thought it had been shot down by another Hurricane."

Interestingly, there were no claims by Messerschmitt pilots during this action. Flt Sgt Tony Boyd (Z2698/L) also found himself involved with the escort:

"One Hurri shot up before engaged. I attacked two Ju88s – strikes. Dogfight alone with four 109s out over sea. Definitely damaged one. Was attacked in the circuit by two 109s, but evaded OK. One bullet through starboard wing and one clipped bottom of seat and parachute cover. Phew!"

The other two Hurricane pilots – Plt Off Ron Noble (Z4942/Y) leading Plt Off Ian McKay (GL-Z) – also engaged the bombers, the latter reporting:

"The bombers came in over Grand Harbour and we all split up and went in. I think I got one 88 but couldn't see what happened to it because I had to break away when four 109s attacked. I have never seen so many 109s in my life before; they went all over the place, even in the circuit. God knows how any of us came back seeing it was 12 to 1 odds against. There were 83 enemy planes and seven of us. When we landed Ron, Boyd and I split an 88 three ways destroyed."

Their victim was probably M7+JL of 3/KGr806 which crash-landed one mile west of Catania, having limped back to Sicily on damaged engines. The pilot, Uffz Hugo Paul, and two of his crew sustained injuries. They reported, however, that their aircraft had been damaged by AA fire rather than fighter attack. No fighters were available to meet the final raid at 1705, when 28 Ju88s targeted Grand Harbour. With nightfall, Sqn Ldr Westmacott scrambled in a Hurricane but, as he was vectored onto a Ju88, a hydraulics pipe burst and he had to give up the chase, landing at once.

There was only one major raid on Easter Monday (6 April) – again unopposed by fighters – Grand Harbour and Luqa being the main targets; on the airfield five Hurricanes (Z3757, BE349, BE351, BG698 and BG764) and two Spitfires were damaged beyond repair. At Hal Far several aircraft also sustained blast and debris damage. The guns put up their usual barrage and one Ju88 was hit, crash-landing on return. LAC Bill Metcalf at Takali recorded in his diary:

"This Easter has been one that I'll never forget (should I be one of the lucky ones to get away with it!). From dawn to dusk wave after wave of 88s, 87s and other gash kites to make the weight have bombed and better bombed. During one lull I bobbed my head above the slit trench and suddenly spotted a fresh wave of 88s coming in over St Paul's. I counted 27 but when their leader put his nose down and started a power dive straight for my slit trench – what a sensation – I could neither speak nor move! Luckily he came a few feet too low and the bombs went over the top of the trench. What a hell-hole! And still they came, in all their might. God in heaven alone knows what's going to happen next and where this is all going to end. It's a pity we haven't got some fighter protection, but what we do have has done wonderful work and each pilot deserves a VC at least. To send the last few up alone would be murder in the first degree. The ack-ack boys too are great and I hold my hand out to each of them."

There could hardly have been a more opportune moment for the arrival of reinforcements as B Flight of 229 Squadron[3] led by Flt Lt M.A. Beatty finally flew in from Gambut. One of the nine aircraft was flown by Plt Off Len Mathus, who had failed to complete the earlier flight:

"Since we had to fly at deck level to avoid detection and we couldn't do our own navigation at that level, we were given an escort of a Beaufort, and we had to form up on this and fly along with it escorting us. We had been flying for a long time and begun wondering when the Beaufort was going to turn to port, because we had to do a dogleg to keep well away from Jerry territory; we had to fly north and then west to get to Malta, and we wondered when the Beaufort was going to make its turn. Suddenly, we picked up Malta's frequency on our VHFs, and they told us that we were flying in the wrong direction, and that we were heading directly for Sicily. We couldn't make radio contact with the Beaufort, so two or three of us flew alongside, waggled our wings violently and turned away. I suppose we did this four or five times but the Beaufort crew paid not the slightest attention, so we turned off for Malta. We could see Malta from a long way off because there was an air raid going on. As we approached we could see the palls of smoke from the bombing. We landed at Hal Far in the middle of an air raid but got down safely. I never heard any more of the Beaufort – it was possibly shot down or landed in Sicily."

Many intruders were over the island during the night, including seven BR20Ms of 55°Gruppo BT, which dropped 400 small anti-personnel bombs but caused little damage. Two of 1435 Flight's Hurricanes were up on patrol, Sgt Ted Wood encountering a Ju88, which he claimed damaged. One of the Beaufighters was also up, the crew reporting the destruction of another, or the same, Ju88. Of his latest success, Sgt Wood wrote in his diary:

"Told that I was on tonight. I went with the CO to Luqa to pick up an aircraft and spent four hours finding one in the dark and getting a crew organised; meanwhile, there were a few wizard illuminations. Finally took off to find a hopelessly u/s aircraft so I landed at Takali. After a while I did two more scrambles. On the second one I had a wizard visual at 5,000 feet of an 88 going the opposite way. I turned after it and lost it, then saw it again alongside me. I gave a short burst and it did a steep diving turn then pulled up into a climbing turn. Getting behind it I gave it a good squirt and then spun off, pulling out at 1,000 feet. It went straight home and no more came in; a 'damaged', anyway. Came off at dawn and the CO was in a terrible mood."

7 April found the fighters grounded once again. The day's first raid concentrated on Grand Harbour, although Kalafrana was also targeted. Later raids also went after shipping in Grand Harbour where two destroyers were attacked but not hit. The journal of Sgt Wood records:

"In the morning they did a baby blitz, only ten, on Takali. About 2pm, 80 bombers and 45 fighters raided the harbour, Luqa and Kalafrana. No fighters up. At 6pm about 100 bombers from all directions did the same again. The AA didn't stand a chance and never know where the raid is intended for. I was absolutely disgusted. The fighters wanted to go off but were not allowed; it is pathetic watching the havoc caused. The morale of the groundcrews and pilots is terrible, no effort being made by the authorities to do anything and the aircraft are being written off on the ground, time and time again. The pilots are keen to have a try but the people up top just sit on them and let them go to pot on the ground."

Following desperate efforts by groundcrews, a number of fighters were serviceable to offer some resistance next day (8 April), although none were available to meet the morning raids. However, as a dozen Ju88s and 20-plus Bf109Fs, including some *Jabo*, approached at 1330, three Spitfires and six Hurricanes (flown by 185 and 229 Squadron pilots), rose to meet the challenge. While the Spitfire pilots claimed a Ju88 destroyed, and a Bf109 probable, Flt Lt Lloyd (GL-W) led the 185 Squadron Hurricanes after the bombers, but Plt Off Ormrod (GL-T) had a torrid time:

"When we'd climbed several thousand feet and were awaiting the approach of the enemy, I found that I could not see through my windscreen forwards, it being covered by oil. I tried to get my hand outside to wipe the oil, but could not do so. Since I could not see to fire and would therefore be of no use, I told Lloyd I was leaving the formation."

As Ormrod dived towards Hal Far to carry out an emergency landing he observed two Messerschmitts over Delimara Point, but considered he could get down before they arrived:

"However, as I was coming in with wheels down, these two came racing along the Kalafrana road and over the camp in the opposite direction to me, with guns firing. I pulled up my wheels and flaps, turned and chased them off towards Filfla, though unable to fire. Saw them disappearing out to sea at great pace and turned back when I reached the coast, thinking I would land before they came back. I was just 300 feet above the ground with wheels and flaps down again and speed 100mph, when I saw one cross the coast behind me. I just turned out of his fire in time, for, instead of hitting the fuselage and probably me, his fire entered my starboard wing. I nearly hit the ground, but pulled out all right and, seeing him turn in front of me, I straightened out for a moment and fired a burst as the aircraft passed in front. I was now nearly at Luqa. My wheels and flaps were already down and I was only at a couple of hundred feet, so I landed at once, down wind, on the big runway."

It would seem that Ormrod's assailant was Lt Ernst Kläger of 8/JG53, who claimed a Hurricane shot down for his 12th victory. Meanwhile, Flt Lt Lloyd claimed to have damaged one of the bombers and a Messerschmitt. Flt Sgt Tony Boyd (Z5118/S) was again in the thick of the action:

"Our section of three Hurricanes attacked incoming bombers head-on; I attacked one head-on, seeing strikes, then attacked a second from about 100 yards. My tracers entered him from nose to tail (two seconds), and small pieces like fabric flew off. I made second attack on same aircraft from astern as he dived and poured two-seconds in from astern, definitely striking – claimed damaged. Next I saw a Ju88 6,000 feet below and dived vertically on him, shooting from above to astern, 50 to 100 yards, and then a couple more bursts. His starboard engine immediately poured black smoke and must have stopped, as he slowed up, but 109s made me break off. As I looked back there was a large splash. Claim – very probable. Position approximately six miles north of Zonqor Point. Flt Lt Lloyd noticed a long line of foam in sea looking like a large aircraft going in, four miles north of Zonqor."

It seems likely that both Boyd and one of the Spitfire pilots had attacked the same aircraft at the same time – a Ju88 of KüFlGr606 ditching in the sea after being hit by fighters, the crew later being picked up safely by Axis air-sea rescue craft. The 229 Squadron section failed to engage.

A bigger raid developed at 1500, no less than 57 Ju88s and 26 Ju87s being reported together with many fighters. Three Spitfires were joined by nine Hurricanes, one of the former being shot down by AA fire over Grand Harbour, although the pilot survived. Two of the bombers were claimed damaged by the Spitfires and two more by the Hurricanes, Flt Sgt Tony Boyd (Z5118/S) believing his victim was probably destroyed:

"We caught first raid as it dived on Grand Harbour. I went round barrage to north and attacked one Ju88 coming out. Beam shot, four seconds, 100 yards; stern shot, 150 yards, six seconds. Port engine poured white smoke, then both engines black smoke. Left him in dive just north of Grand Harbour. Me109s made me break off. Strikes observed going in both engines and fuselage. In second wave, attacked one Ju88 from below astern. Saw strikes. No other results."

The other Hurricane claim was submitted by Plt Off Ron Noble (GL-P), who commented: "Armed only with .303 Brownings, I merely succeeded in damaging one." One Ju88 of 6/KG77 crash-landed at Comiso, damaged by fighters. Nocturnal intruders began appearing two hours after the last daylight raid, a Hurricane and a Beaufighter being scrambled, the latter intercepting a Ju88 of I/NJG2 which crashed near Safi; none of the crew survived.

The first major raid on 9 April was in the early afternoon, the airfields being targeted on this occasion by 40-plus Ju88s and 16 Ju87s, while an estimated 40 Messerschmitts provided cover. Luqa and Grand Harbour were again the main objectives. The defending fighters remained on the ground but were scrambled to meet the next raid, at 1630, when an estimated 60 Ju88s and a dozen Ju87s returned, attacking Takali. Here, a Hurricane under repair was destroyed and two other aircraft damaged. Nearby Mosta Church, famous for its large dome, was struck; one bomb penetrated the vast structure but failed to explode. Meanwhile, the Spitfires and Hurricanes engaged waves of bombers, claiming a total of eight damaged of which three were credited to the Spitfire pilots. Two of the claims by the Hurricane pilots were for probables, one of which was submitted by Plt Off McKay (GL-P):

"There were ten Hurricanes and two Spitfires against a plot of at least 100, about 50 bombers and the same number of Me109Fs. It seemed futile but we did manage to put a lot of bombers off their target and then a terrific dogfight ensued. The dogfight went on for some time and we were having trouble getting in to land 'cause there were 109s around trying to get you when you got your wheels and flaps down. I had two bullet holes in the port wing and one through the perspex. I got a Ju88 I think."

Another probable was credited to Flt Sgt Tony Boyd (BN118):

"I attacked a Ju88 front port quarter to abeam, 150 yards, with three-second burst of cannon, and broke off quickly for the next. My No2 – Sgt Tweedale – who watched my attack, saw a stream of pieces fly off the Ju88, which went down in a steep dive still streaming pieces. A gun-post observer, who watched the engagement, saw a Ju88 engaged by a Hurricane about same position, and the Ju88 did not pull out of its dive. Claim one Ju88 damaged – or on the evidence of the gun-post – probably destroyed."

Three more Ju88s were claimed damaged by Flt Lt Lawrence (GL-W) and Flt Sgt Jack Fletcher (Z5118/S) of 185 Squadron, and Flt Sgt Lucien Brooks of 229 Squadron. However, Sgt Ned Pauley of the latter unit was shot down in Z3505/HB-S, baling out off Grand Harbour:

"We intercepted them as they approached the east coast and attacked them from 17,000 feet. I damaged a Ju88 and silenced the rear-gunner and set the starboard engine smoking heavily. But a couple of tracers crossed in front of me and one hit the side of the cockpit near my right thigh and knee. But now I had to act quickly. I unbelted, pushed the cockpit cover back and commenced to get out as fast as I could. Because of the terrific speed and wind pressure, I got jammed halfway out. Then my head hit the tail of the plane and I saw stars, and perhaps had a slight black-out. Once again, because of the speed, I was unable to get my hand down to the ripcord.

Eventually my parachute opened with a pleasant 'bang' and I was suspended in the silent atmosphere probably no more than 100 feet up and I could see my plane disappearing into the sea. I did not open my dinghy and just as well, as a Me109 twice made a low level pass near me, but did not see me. When the enemy plane had finally gone, I unhooked the dinghy, inflated it and climbed in – and waited. By now my right thigh and knee were sore and stiff from the shrapnel of the explosive bullet. I was beginning to give up hope of being rescued. I was not too far from shore – about two miles off Grand Harbour. Eventually a rescue launch did appear and Oh! what a relief. I was taken to hospital."

Sgt Gordon Tweedale (BN182) narrowly avoided a similar fate: "Had six Me109s gunning for me. Did not get a shot but got shot up [in] both mainplanes. Bags of Messerschmitts in circuit." Four Spitfires were claimed by the Messerschmitt pilots, although one was obviously Pauley's Hurricane and another Tweedale's Hurricane, two victories being credited to Lt Hermann Neuhoff of 7/JG53 as his 39th and 40th; newly promoted Hptm Helmut Belser of 8/JG53 claimed another for his 21st, while Maj Günther von Maltzahn registered his 61st.

The first raid on 10 April came in at 1245 but met no defenders; bombs fell on Luqa and destroyed an already damaged Wellington and damaged two Hurricanes. The bombers returned in great strength at 1745, an estimated 65 Ju88s and 20 Ju87s attacking Grand Harbour, Hal Far and Takali. To meet this mighty onslaught eight Hurricanes flown by 185 Squadron pilots were scrambled, followed by four more from 229 Squadron and four Spitfires, although three of the Hurricanes returned early as did one Spitfire. The remaining three Spitfires took on ten Ju88s, shooting down one and probably a second, and probably destroying a Stuka. One Spitfire pilot (Flg Off Buck Buchanan) dived out of the sun on a Messerschmitt over St Paul's Bay as it was pulling up after firing at a Hurricane. He fired from long range and rather to his surprise, the aircraft burst into flames and the pilot baled out. However, Flt Sgt Garth Horricks (BD826/A) of 185 Squadron reported chasing a Messerschmitt from 17,000 feet down to sea level, four miles west of Grand Harbour:

"While the other fellows were having their good, clean fun, I was also having games with eight 109s. But I guess I'm a poor sport because I got mad and hit one of them with my cannon, and he thoughtfully exploded and came down in flames."

Only one Messerschmitt was lost, piloted by none other than III/JG53's leading *Experte*, Lt Hermann Neuhoff (Yellow 1), who baled out to become a prisoner. Only the previous evening he had been promoted to lead 6 Staffel in place of Hptm Belser. Neuhoff told his interrogators that his No2 had failed to protect his rear when he dived to attack a Hurricane and that he was then attacked by a Spitfire. He subsequently asked to meet his victor and was introduced to Flg Off Buchanan, though the evidence suggests that he was actually brought down by Horricks. However, much later, Neuhoff claimed:

"I was flying with my *Schwarm* over Malta. Suddenly, my second *Rotte* disappeared. Instead, three Spitfires appeared. I shot at one aircraft as it flew in front of me. At the same time I was hit. Leutnant [Werner] Schöw reported his first [*sic*] victory – unfortunately it was me! He had mistaken me for a Hurricane. I stayed with my aircraft because I knew that if I came down in the drink I would be fished out again. However, when the fire spread I jettisoned the cockpit hood. Shortly afterwards the 109 exploded. It was lucky for me that I had released my harness and got rid of the cockpit hood. I ejected from the aircraft at 2,500 metres altitude and deployed the parachute at 400 metres and belly-landed near Luqa."[4]

After the battle, Flt Sgt Horricks updated the Squadron diary with an account of the actions:

"Twelve took off. By the time we were at 15,000 feet there were nine left. Things suddenly happened and every Hurricane found himself surrounded by seven 109s. Then more things happened. We tried to get to the bombers but the 109s didn't think we should. A great argument ensued, resulting in too many private dogfights to count. The first section led by F/Lt Lloyd and with P/Os Ormrod and Wigley got at the bombers while Yellow Section led by F/Sgt Eastman and Sgts Finlay, Broad and myself more than contacted the Me109s. In the first few minutes of the fight Sgt Broad was forcibly ejected from his aircraft [Z3766] by anywhere from one to fifteen 109s."

Sgt Tim Goldsmith, watching the battle from the ground, saw Sgt Broad's aircraft shot down:

"Four Hurricanes came in from the beam and attacked. Three of them followed downhill after the bombers, but the fourth seemed unable to keep up with his target. As he slipped further behind, we saw a 109 creeping up behind and below him. Each moment we expected the Hurricane to whip round to meet the danger but he kept on after the 88, until we heard the rattle of the Hun's cannon. The Hurri curved peacefully round to the left, then its nose fell and it went into a crazy, uncontrolled dive to the earth, 15,000 feet below, where it crashed and burst into flames on the hill behind Naxxar, on the far side of the aerodrome.

'Poor bugger', said someone, but an excited cheer from one of the Maltese spectators drew our attention to his arm pointing to the sky. A parachute seemed suspended there, as the little figure beneath it swung to and fro like a pendulum, eventually to come to earth near Mosta village. It was in the evening that I learned it was Ernie Broad. He had been rescued by the army and taken to St Andrew's 45th General Hospital, with his left calf well-filled with shrapnel. I was surprised that Ernie should have got himself caught like that, but very pleased to hear that his injuries were not serious."

Flt Sgt Horricks' narrative continued:

"F/Lt Lloyd [GL-W] had a whack at the bombers but was set upon by some 109s. He played with them for a while, and after shaking off his alloted ten Messerschmitts he landed at Luqa with only a few holes in his plane. P/O Ormrod also landed at Luqa but in a much different manner. He was cruising around in between 109s when he suddenly spied five or six Ju87s in line astern diving on a target. He thought they were playing so he got in behind the third one and played too. Only he played with .303 and probably got one of the 87s. Meanwhile, the boys flying the 87s behind him thought he was rude butting in like that, so proceeded to shoot at his Hurricane [BG756/GL-M] till it caught fire."

Plt Off Ormrod also recorded events:

"We climbed up to about 15,000 feet, dodged some Messerschmitts, and attacked the Ju88s, about 20 or 30 in number. I followed Lloyd in two or three beam attacks on a Ju88. Saw my strikes on the e/a but no effect. I thought I should stay with Lloyd as long as possible, but he disappeared whilst I was making my last attack. I saw a Hurricane returning towards the coast, but too high for me to catch up. This was probably Lloyd, but I saw another going in the same direction, only lower. I caught up this aircraft and found that it was Wigley. He dived down to ground level and I tried to formate on him, but he did not realise this and nearly wrote me off on a domed building. Then he signalled me to lead him. I did so, but never saw him again. Was now in a great mix-up of 109s and Hurricanes. Saw a pilot shoot down a Messerschmitt in flames. Its pilot baled out and floated down past me. I called over the R/T, 'Well done, Hurricane boy'. I called up in order to confirm it for him.

Now I heard Controller say that there were Ju87s approaching Grand Harbour. Climbed up and saw the Stukas diving in line astern as usual. I got into the middle of the AA barrage, climbing just above the height of the parachute mines, and met the Ju87s where they were coming out of their dives. Two turned around me, dropping their bombs, and I therefore turned the other way and met one head-on. He received a considerable portion of my fire into his engine and almost collided, passing very close. Was unable to see what happened to him, No2 passing across my front, and, to turn after No1 would have meant sticking my tail under the nose of No2; besides, No2 presented me with a good target and I hoped No1 had already received enough to finish him.

Now No2 went into a most peculiar sort of upwards corkscrew. We both went up almost vertically it seemed, hanging on to our airscrews and I, all the time, firing at him from underneath his tail. Meanwhile, there was another Ju87 hanging on to my tail. I suppose there were about 20 Ju87s, and I was the only Hurricane amongst them, so I was a bit outnumbered. My engine suddenly stopped and I fell away. I saw No3 firing at me with his front guns as I fell past him. I pulled out. My engine seemed to be working again, but felt a great deal of heat coming from somewhere, so I made straight for Luqa with glycol fumes entering the cockpit and blurring my goggles. There were Me109s and Hurricanes flying low down and shooting at one another, and I hoped none shot at me. I lowered my undercarriage, made an S turn to lose a bit of speed, and came over the west end of the long runway at 140mph. I didn't like to slow down as a 109 had seen me. Luckily it is a long runway and even though I came in at 140mph until over its end, I had room to float until I touched down without flaps. As I completed my landing run, flame suddenly burst forth from under the instrument panel. The cockpit was enveloped in flame. I stood on the seat. Pulled off my helmet and jumped out on the runway before the aircraft stopped. It must have been burning as I was bringing it down, but luckily it did not really blaze up until I was completing my landing. It was now burning furiously and, after a short while, the petrol tank exploded with a flash, bang and puff of black smoke. When it finished it was completely burned out.

So ended my third forced-landing in three consecutive days. My only injuries are singed eyebrows and lashes, and a minute blister on the end of my nose. A terrific dogfight was now in progress, at nought feet. Me109s were strafing and trying to catch low flying Hurricanes. Some of the fire tender crew came across to my aircraft, thinking I was still in it. I am most grateful to them for the risk they took even though it is expected of them. They came right across the aerodrome, a considerable distance, with the 109s strafing and the bombers overhead. These are their names – Cpl Clawson, LAC Spencer, LAC Mitchison, and LAC Hunter. I shall recommend them to higher authority."[5]

Another Stuka was engaged and badly damaged by Plt Off Phil Wigley (GL-P), whose aircraft was then attacked by several Messerschmitts:

"After about 30 minutes, and many attacks by Me109Fs on me, and several by me on them and the bombers, my Hurricane was hit in the coolant system and hot liquid sprayed about the cockpit, probably from the damaged header tank. Of course the engine over-heated and so I tried to land, first at Hal Far, but was attacked by a 109F, then at Luqa where the same thing happened. I therefore thought my best action would be to bale out as the engine was losing power and flames were beginning to appear. As the German fighters had complete control of the air over Malta that evening, I did not want to risk being shot up while hanging below my parachute. I considered a low bale out over the sea to be the best option – ditching a Hurricane is not recommended because of the prominent radiator under the fuselage.

I headed south towards the sea, but the engine had almost completely lost power and the fire situation was now becoming a problem. The last altitude I noticed on the altimeter before I jumped was 700 feet. This would have been set at zero at Hal Far, so I would have been about 900 feet above sea level. However, I was losing height gradually and also lost valuable seconds getting rid of the cockpit hood. Also, I hung onto the radio mast behind the cockpit before I finally let go, pulling the rip-cord when clear of the rudder and tailplane, probably at about 400 feet above the ground. The parachute opened perfectly, although the shroud lines briefly entangled my feet, and I landed on rock after 10-20 seconds. I heard the aircraft hit the ground, or it may have been the fuel tanks exploding in the air, very soon after I pulled the rip-cord. The remains of the Hurricane were only about 20 yards away from my point of landing [a shallow gorge near Ghar Lapsi].

A corporal of the Maltese Army arrived with a Tommy-gun in case I was German or Italian and led me up a rocky slope to a path which led to a RAF RDF station. On the way I met the oldest Maltese lady in the world who was charming and shook my hand for about five minutes! I was well looked after at the RDF station and later taken in a truck to Siggiewi to await collection from Hal Far. By then it was dusk. I was taken into the little police station and treated very kindly. However, some local people thought I was an enemy airman and I was obliged to go to the door and show them my wings. If I had been German or Italian anything could have happened."[6]

Meanwhile, another Hurricane was pursued across Luqa aerodrome by a Messerschmitt, which then opened fire. The damaged Hurricane, BN142 of 229 Squadron, belly-landed in a small field where it ended up on its nose, the pilot (Sgt Pendlebury) being lucky to survive. Shortly afterwards, another damaged 229 Squadron Hurricane (BN122/HB-W) carried out an emergency landing at Luqa, its pilot, Sgt Norm Vidler, having claimed a Ju88 damaged before being set upon by the Messerschmitts. Flt Sgt Horricks summed up the traumatic day for the Hurricane pilots:

> "Everyone was tired by now, having either been shot up or shot down. We then shot our lines to the IO and gathered in the Sergeants' Mess at Kalafrana and drank many bottles of champagne and whisky to celebrate everybody shot up but not killed. We are all very proud of today's do. We attacked 100 bombers and 50 fighters and got away without losing a man."

Nonetheless, three Hurricanes had been destroyed, plus one crash-landed and another two damaged, in this one action. The German pilots claimed nine Hurricanes and one Spitfire, Obfw Rudolf Ehrenberger of 6/JG53 alone claiming three, while single victories were credited to Lt Joachim Louis (Stab I/JG53), Oblt Friedrich-Karl Müller (1 Staffel), Oblt Wilfred Pufahl (7 Staffel), Lt Hans Möller (6 Staffel), Hptm Walter Spies (II/JG53) and Lt Friedman (II/JG53), with Fw Alfred Seidl (8 Staffel) claiming the Spitfire. Oblt Müller reported of his 23rd victory:

> "I took off at 1735 with three aircraft of 1 Staffel. We undertook a *Freiejagd* and gave cover for bomber formations which were attacking the port and airfields of Malta. We attacked enemy fighters several times without any success. I then attacked a Hurricane coming from the east above the airfield hangar (at Hal Far). After a short burst with MG and cannon the plane burned immediately and went down vertically north of the airfield. Witness from the air: Obfw Krause."

During the next few days the defending fighters – few as they were – were not able to achieve much. Soon after midday on 11 April, bombers again attacked Grand Harbour and the airfields. One Ju88 of 6/KG77 was shot down by AA guns off Marsaxlokk, the gunners also claiming a Ju87 and another Ju88 damaged. During these raids heavy damage was inflicted on the airfields, and a Hurricane was destroyed at Luqa, another burnt out and two damaged at Hal Far, and a fifth damaged at Takali. Three more Hurricanes were written off during an evening raid on Luqa, including the two damaged 229 Squadron machines (BN122 and BN142) which had landed there earlier.

Next day (12 April) saw the arrival of Air Marshal Sir Arthur Tedder, AOC Middle East, for a brief stay in order to gain first-hand knowledge of Malta's plight. Of this visit, Air Vice-Marshal Lloyd was to write:

> "There was a raid at Takali as soon as Tedder arrived there, and from the verandah of the

Officers' Mess he was able to get an excellent view of the enemy tactics and the encircling patrol of 109s as it closed on the aerodrome below us to dive on every sign of movement. They even made some dives at Tedder as he was standing on the verandah, and a photographer who was trying to photograph the Chief and a 109 on the same plate found discretion preferable to valour when he saw another 109 flying straight at him with cannons firing.

The visit to Luqa, however, was better timed, as a few minutes before Tedder had arrived there, the Axis had dropped a few more hundred tons of bombs, making it a shambles. Pilots, observers, radio operators, air-gunners and airmen and soldiers were busy moving the stone and filling the holes, all of them as happy as sandboys [!] I have never seen Tedder so delighted with any scene, and pointing with the stem of his pipe to a group of men who were busy filling holes and then to some of the men surrounding him, as if to add emphasis to his comment, he said – very quietly: 'That is the spirit of Malta.'"[7]

Tedder's visit to Hal Far later was also interrupted by ground strafing Bf109s, one of which was shot down by the defences, Plt Off McKay writing:

"Air Officer Commanding Middle East gave us a pep talk and told us we were doing a magnificent job, but we all wished he would go up in one of our Hurricanes against the Me109s that outnumbered us at least ten to one! There was a raid just after the talk and then the 109s started ground strafing. One was firing on its way over the aerodrome when it was hit by ack-ack and it went straight in. There was a terrific explosion and huge sheet of flame. The engine rolled at least two hundred yards away from the wreckage. The pilot was more or less swept up."

Another of the oil and sweat-stained pilots assembled to meet the AOC laconically commented: "When Tedder passed this way we shook him rigid. I thought he was going to get out his wallet and give us ten bob each to buy a new shirt." While Flt Sgt Horricks commented in the Squadron diary:

"Air Marshal Tedder shook hands with us all and said we were doing a marvellous job of work and were making history. Of course, we already knew that, but it was nice to hear it from him. It shows our work is recognised and appreciated."

In addition to the Messerschmitt, the gunners claimed a Ju87 shot down and two Ju88s damaged. Some damage was done to the airfields and a number of aircraft were destroyed or damaged, including Hurricane BE562 which was burnt out at Hal Far. Only reconnaissance flights bothered the radar operators and controllers at Malta on the 13th, allowing maintenance personnel unexpected and uninterrupted valuable working hours, and all a welcome respite from the hitherto continuous bombing. In spite of the explosions of bombs and blasts of guns that shook and wracked Malta's very foundations from dawn till dusk, and then throughout the night, life went on as normal for some of the island's residents, Plt Off Ormrod noting in his travels: "Saw some puppies that were born in the fort [Fort St Lucien], which reminds me I saw a cat that had newly born kittens in the clothing store at Kalafrana, amongst the Mae Wests!"

However, not all the island's feline population was as fortunate, as noted by Mgr Emmanuel Brincat, Archpriest of Senglea:

"Food was so scarce and cats were wild with hunger. They had been left behind by their masters and roamed about in the streets looking for something to eat. One morning we were roused up by the sound of rifle-shots and when we came out to see what it was, we saw the dockyard defence soldiers, with rifle in hand, chasing these unfortunate creatures . . . in wartime sometimes it is kindness to be cruel, and deliver those poor animals from hunger and sure death."[8]

On 14 April, the main attention was directed out to sea, where a heavily-escorted Italian convoy bound for North Africa was attacked by Beauforts and Beaufighters operating from Bu Amud in Cyrenaica. On completion of their sorties, the strike aircraft were to land at Luqa for refuelling and re-arming before returning to their base. However, Malta did not escape attack. The first raid came in at 1045 and was intercepted by three patrolling Spitfires, one of which was shot down into the sea. The pilot baled out and HSL128 was despatched to the rescue, cover being provided by two Hurricanes. As the launch stopped to pick up the pilot, two Messerschmitts appeared and attempted to attack but were driven off by the Hurricanes, Flt Sgt Jack Fletcher (BV163) claiming damage to one.

The Beaufort operation against the convoy proved disastrous. Escorting Bf109Fs and Bf110s intercepted the strike force, shooting down into the sea five of the eight torpedo-bombers; a sixth belly-landed at Luqa. Only two carried out normal landings, one of which was badly shot up. As the Beauforts approached the island at 1645, four Hurricanes of 185 Squadron had been scrambled to go to their aid, followed ten minutes later by two more from 229 Squadron. Plt Off Phil Wigley (Z4005) recalled:

> "One Beaufort was spotted too late – it was at sea level and under attack from two 109s – and before the Hurricanes could reach it, it was shot down a mile short of the relative safety of Malta. 185 felt badly about the loss of the Beaufort crew so close – unfortunately the Hurricanes had been ordered to climb after take-off and, of course with the benefit of hindsight, a sea-level patrol would have been more appropriate and the Beaufort might have been saved."

Plt Off Ormrod (Z5325) takes up the story:

> "Wigley had seen the Beaufort crash. I saw the Me109s. Dived down upon them. Wigley was, I think, just ahead of me, because he managed to deliver a beam attack on one. There were two 109s. After our dive we had quite a bit of speed. Horricks and I each set ourselves on the tail of one of them and with everything pulled managed to hold them at approximately 300 yards range for some five miles. We fired, but the range was a little too great and their camouflage even at that distance made them hard to distinguish against the sea. If we'd had cannon we might have got them. If we'd been flying Spitfires we definitely could have done. As it was, we could not decrease the range below 300 yards, and after some seconds the enemy aircraft began to draw away from us."

Despite the difficulty in closing the range, Flt Sgt Horricks (Z4004) nonetheless claimed damage to a Messerschmitt he pursued, and two more were claimed damaged in the skirmishing by Flt Sgt Gordon Tweedale (BV163) and Sgt Bob Lees, the latter from 229 Squadron. Meanwhile, HSL128 was despatched to search for survivors, the Hurricanes providing cover as Messerschmitts made repeated attempts to attack it. Wreckage of the Beaufort was sighted and a body recovered. Ormrod continued:

> "Well, there were now four of us flying round the rescue launch and two 109s were flying around us. We reached Filfla without interruption. I had been flying across the rescue launch's track, stall turning and crossing back again, all the time watching the 109s, whilst the others weaved around according to fancy. The two 109s made one attack on a Hurricane. This Hurricane had been up to the wreckage and was flying back past Filfla when they dived down behind him. I shouted a warning and at that moment he turned just in time out of the way of a line of black puffs, made by the shells of the e/a's cannon. I now noticed that the others did not seem to be about, and was wondering whether they had gone home, when black puffs very close to my starboard side made me do rather a steep turn to port.
>
> Things now moved rather fast and furiously. I took several short bursts at 109s as they whistled past, and several times I saw the shell bursts first and turned afterwards. I did not fire long bursts, since I knew my ammunition was rapidly being exhausted. Once I fired at

a 109 and it rolled over on its back and dived vertically. It pulled out without hitting the water. Horricks reports a 109 at which he was firing doing the same thing, so we must both have engaged this one – it was about over the launch. Once one of the varmints appeared just off my starboard wingtip. I saw the flame of his cannon emerging from the spinner of his airscrew. I thought we might collide. He passed very close across my front. I pressed my button, but the speed of passing was very great and he was too close for me to follow with my sights. Only a few rounds came out and then my guns stopped. Only Wigley and myself were left defending the boat now. My engine spluttered – main tanks empty. I changed to reserve. Wigley and I kept flying backwards and forwards along the coast, which the launch was now hugging."

Despite the efforts of the Hurricanes the launch was again attacked, during which five members of the crew were wounded, one seriously, forcing the craft to take shelter under the cliffs until dark, when it made its way back to Kalafrana. Ormrod continued:

"The 109s suddenly all dived on us. Saw black puffs in front of me again. An e/a was attacking head-on, but seemed to have opened fire too far away as his shells exploded just before reaching me. His No2 was a little to one side of him, but seemed more interested in following his No1 than in firing at me, and turned away after No1 broke off his attack. I now called Control and said I had expended my ammunition and had little fuel remaining. I asked them to send reliefs, as I thought one of the others might have refuelled and re-armed by now. I was told to land. I started back, but seeing Wigley remaining alone, I returned. However, my reserve tank was fast emptying and I expected to have to dodge 109s before I could land. I returned at nought feet, skimming over small fields and villages, and skimming over the ridge I put myself down at Hal Far. Wigley landed at Luqa 15 minutes after me. He had tried to land here, but the 109s prevented it. His action today was most gallant. He landed with but eight gallons of petrol remaining. His bravery and contempt for the enemy almost at times approaches madness. If ever a pilot in this war deserved a DFC, I consider P/O Wigley to deserve one. No odds deter him."

During the course of the day the AA defences were kept busy as Ju88s and Ju87s raided the island and Messerschmitts strafed the airfields. Claims were submitted for two Ju88s, two Ju87s and two Bf109s, but only one of the latter flown by Hptm Karl-Heinz Krahl, Kommandeur of II/JG3, was shot down. The 24-victory ace was killed when his aircraft crashed north-east of Hal Far.

With Malta's defences on the brink of being overwhelmed, it was an appropriate day for the Governor, General Dobbie, to announce that HM King George VI had awarded the George Cross to the 'Island Fortress', the first (and only) time in British history that such an award had been made to a community. Adverse weather – heavy cloud and high winds – now brought flying to a virtual standstill over Malta and Sicily for the next three days. Reconnaissances by small groups of Messerschmitts were made each day but no offensive operations were undertaken. 185 Squadron now received the services of four of the redundant Spitfire pilots, Flt Sgt Dave Ferraby, a Yorkshireman, Sgt Bob Sim RNZAF, Flt Sgt Wilbert Dodd RCAF, and Sgt Jack Yarra RAAF, who wrote:

"The trouble seems to be that there are too many fighter pilots for the aircraft: it meant that we should do readiness about once a week. We spent most of our spare time building pens from sand bags and trying to make the existing pens blast proof. After I had been at Takali for about a week, I was transferred to 185 Squadron at Hal Far. This was a Hurricane squadron and as I had flown Hurricanes I welcomed the transfer as it meant I would get quite a lot of flying done as 185 Squadron was very short of pilots. Sim, Ferraby and Dodd were going with me."

A number of awards came through for the Hurricane pilots at this time, DFCs being announced for Flt Lt Rhys Lloyd and Plt Off Sonny Ormrod, and DFMs for Flt Sgt Tony Boyd and Flt Sgt Garth Horricks, who also received his commission, as did Flt Sgts Jack Fletcher and Doug Eastman. Ormrod, who had just celebrated his 20th birthday, wrote:

"Went to Kalafrana for dinner and met Wigley. As I left Kalafrana for Marsaxlokk, I passed W/Cdr Reilly with G/Capt Chick. They stopped me and started congratulating me. I begged to be allowed to know the cause of these sudden congratulations and they seemed surprised that I didn't know I'd been awarded the Distinguished Flying Cross. Could hardly believe it. However, these two are hardly likely to be mistaken. They told me that it had just come through this evening. Imagine my joy, though I can still hardly believe it . . . it will so please my dear mother. One thing saddens me. Wigley is not mentioned, and I think he deserves it before me."[9]

The Luftwaffe was back with a vengeance on 18 April, making four raids against the airfields, but still no fighters were available to intercept them. At Hal Far two Hurricanes were destroyed, while at Luqa there were a number of casualties. The gunners claimed a Ju88 shot down, and probably a second, in addition to a Ju87. Next day (19 April), another Hurricane was destroyed at Hal Far, and again the guns put up an intense barrage, shooting down two Ju88s, one from 5/KG77 and the other from 1/KüFlGr606. It had now been five days since Malta's dwindling number of fighters had been able to operate, and the situation was truly desperate. Although more Spitfires were on their way, the first new arrivals were six more Hurricane IICs of 229 Squadron which flew in from Gambut led by Flt Lt R.C. Dafforn DFC. Of the long and arduous flight, Plt Off Tom Lawrence wrote to his parents:

"We travelled 720 miles over nothing but water hoping we shall strike this very small island which is only 60 miles in circumference. However, as the sun sank slowly behind the horizon – of which I was glad because we had been flying for about two hours with it in our eyes – there, in the distance, was a column of black smoke and then the outline of the island itself, and a raid was in progress. Well, that was no joke! Long-range tanks, which means no manoeuvrability, very little gas left, and the only three aerodromes may be cratered, and feeling exceptionally tired, we came in uneasily. However, with an odd 109 and an 88 still about, we came in and landed. One chappie who landed with me had only five gallons left (about seven minutes flying). Another chap went over on his back. They had to get a crane to extricate him, and out he walked with a broken wrist – lucky fellow!"

The injured pilot, who had overshot the runway in BE636, was Plt Off Patterson, who had indeed escaped lightly. The flight leader, Flt Lt Bob Dafforn, had only recently joined the Squadron, and on arrival at Malta was promoted to command vice the sick Sqn Ldr Kain. He was an experienced operational pilot, having flown in France and the Battle of Britain. Another of the flight, Wt Off Douglas Corfe, had also flown during the Battle of Britain, when he had been shot down twice, having been wounded on the second occasion[10]. Although this handful of Hurricanes was welcome, more effective help was imminently at hand.

While the delivery of the two initial batches of Spitfires to Malta had brought some relief, it was obvious that the small numbers involved would not allow sustained operations to be maintained for long – as had indeed been the case. To help overcome the problem of supply, Prime Minister Churchill had persuaded US President Roosevelt to make available the large aircraft carrier USS *Wasp* to ferry up to 50 Spitfires into the Mediterranean; in fact, she took on board 52 Spitfires and two complete RAF squadrons, 601 and 603. By the early hours of the morning of 20 April, *Wasp* and her entourage were at the launching position, about 660 miles west of Malta, and began flying off the Spitfires. Within an hour 47 were in the air – all that could be made serviceable – and the leading elements were well on their way to the besieged island.

Malta had already experienced one raid that morning when 70 Ju88s and 20 Ju87s attacked Valetta, Hal Far and Kalafrana. Amongst the damage inflicted was the destruction of Hurricane BE710 at Hal Far, three others sustaining blast and debris damage. The first of the new Spitfires arrived at around 1000, although it was 1230 before the next raid came in, 32 Ju88s and 20 Ju87s attacking all three airfields; at Takali one of the new Spitfires was badly damaged, three more and a Hurricane being slightly damaged. With the approach of this raid, three Hurricanes and six Spitfires were scrambled. The Spitfires claimed damage to several of the raiders, while two of the Hurricanes also managed to engage the Ju88s, Plt Off Ron Noble (Z4011/B) reporting strikes on one. Meanwhile, Flt Sgt Tony Boyd (Z2698/L) went after a flight of four and gained strikes on the belly of one from 100 yards. He also reported strikes on the fuselage and port wing of a second, then hit a third, but this appeared to receive a direct hit from AA to be shot down. The aircraft in fact limped back to Sicily, although two of the Stab III/KG77 crew baled out, one of whom landed near Rabat, critically injured, and died 15 minutes later. The other fell into the sea and was not recovered. The Hurricanes then attempted to provide cover for the Spitfires as they came into land in the face of strafing Messerschmitts.

For many months Malta had been almost a Luftwaffe preserve by day, but this situation was about to change. 4°Stormo CT had returned to Sicily, its 9° and 10°Gruppi now based at Castelvetrano with new MC202s; other units had also arrived including those equipped with MC200s, CR42s and Re2000s, plus six squadrons of bombers and a further five with torpedo-bombers. Macchis of 10°Gruppo had already undertaken a straightforward acclimatisation flight, but had lost one of its aircraft when the pilot baled out due to trouble with his oxygen supply, a not infrequent problem. On this date (19 April), 19 Macchis of 10°Gruppo had taken off for what should have been its first operational mission over Malta. However, two of the Macchis collided and fell into the sea off Porto Empedocle, one pilot losing his life, and the mission was subsequently aborted.

Spitfires dealt with the afternoon and early evening raids of the 20th, two pilots being shot down during the course of the latter including Plt Off Tex Putnam, who had briefly flown Hurricanes when he initially arrived at Malta. Putnam, an American, was killed. The other pilot, a Canadian, was seen to be shot down into the sea. An ASR launch was despached on a search, while three Hurricanes flown by 185 Squadron pilots and two from 229 Squadron provided cover. These encountered a number of Ju88s, two of which Flt Sgt Gordon Tweedale (Z4011/B) claimed as probably destroyed:

> "Bags of 109s about. Caught 88 diving on Takali – finished astern and left him burning. Second one head-on, busted his hood off and raked the fuselage. Messerschmitts did not worry us much till landing."

Flt Lt Lloyd (Z22698/L) and Flt Sgt Lucien Brooks claimed damage to two more Ju88s, but Sgt Jack Yarra (HA-D) crash-landed at Hal Far after his aircraft had been shot up by a Messerschmitt, probably that flown by Obfw Ehrenberger of 6/JG53 who claimed a Spitfire, possibly having misidentified Yarra's Hurricane.

Only 27 Spitfires could be made serviceable by dawn on 21 April to oppose the anticipated onslaught on the airfields, the first bombers approaching at 0730. An estimated 37 Ju88s and 34 Bf109Fs began a series of attacks on Grand Harbour, the Dockyard, Luqa and Takali. Ten Spitfires and five Hurricanes (three/185, two/229) were scrambled, the former claiming three Ju88s and a Messerschmitt for the loss of one of their own. One of the 229 Squadron Hurricanes (BN278) was also shot down with the loss of Sgt John Fullalove, whose aircraft is believed to have fallen near Fort San Leonardo. In return, two Messerschmitts were claimed damaged by the Hurricane pilots, one by Sgt Colin Finlay (Z2698/L) and the other by Plt Off Garth Horricks (BM905/J), who also claimed a Ju88 probably destroyed; and Flt Sgt Gordon Tweedale (Z4011/B) had another lucky escape: "Jumped at 19,000 feet by Me109s. My elevators jammed so had to return. Pulled out at 3,000 feet. Phew!"

Only Spitfires were called upon to meet the afternoon raids, two being shot down in return for several claims although both pilots survived. Six more Spitfires were damaged in combat during the day, while six more were damaged on the ground, two being written off. In addition, five Wellingtons were destroyed on the ground at Luqa. Most of the Wellingtons were in transit, but would now never arrive at their intended destinations. Amongst aircraft that did depart Malta under cover of darkness was a Wellington in which were embarked six fighter pilots[11] who had been instructed to fly to El Ballah airfield near Heliopolis in Egypt, from where they were to collect reinforcement Hurricanes for 229 Squadron, and to ferry them to Malta.

The handful of Hurricanes were stood down until the late afternoon of 22 April, sufficient numbers of Spitfires being available to deal with the earlier raids during which a Ju88 and a Bf109F were shot down for the loss of one Spitfire. At 1720, however, Plt Offs Ormrod and Wigley scrambled in their Hurricanes together with six Spitfires to challenge an estimated 50 Ju88s and 20 Ju87s, with the airfields and Grand Harbour as their prime targets. At least one Ju87 was claimed destroyed plus two probables, but one Spitfire was shot down and its pilot died from his injuries. Meanwhile, the two Hurricane pilots became engaged, Plt Off Wigley (Z4942/Y) claiming a Messerschmitt probably destroyed; his victim was possibly an aircraft of 4/JG53 which crash-landed at Comiso, badly damaged, but Plt Off Ormrod failed to return. He was seen to pursue a Ju88 through the Grand Harbour barrage just before his aircraft (Z4011/B) crashed into the sea off Valetta, his demise having been unwittingly witnessed by his young Maltese friend, Edgar Smith, whose parents owned the former hotel where Ormrod was billeted:

> "The German bombers approached from the east with the Grand Harbour their intended target. A curtain of steel was awaiting them. The gunners let loose well before the first plane flew through it. It seemed an impossibility to fly through all that inferno and come out in one piece, but through it they came. A Hurricane was flying in pursuit; but the barrage did not distinguish a Hurricane from a Junkers. As I stood watching on a hill together with a friend, to our horror, the Hurricane came to an abrupt stop and plummeted to earth [sic]. My friend and I saw the pilot coming out of the plane and rolling down, with no parachute open. Presumably he was killed instantly. In the evening of that day, Sqn Ldr Mortimer-Rose came over to see me and asked: 'Have you heard about Sonny?' I was momentarily choked and could not answer."

HSL128 went out and searched one and a half hours for Ormrod, but no trace could be found. After dark, the craft went out again when a light was reported at sea, but once more there was no sign of the missing pilot[12]. The ASR crew were particularly distressed by his loss, as he had often flown cover to their launch, and while on such duty lived at the Kalafrana Mess with them. Of the nine claims submitted by the Luftwaffe on this date, five were credited to JG53, the remaining four claimed by returning bomber crews. During this final raid, two Spitfires were claimed but only one Hurricane, and it would seem that Plt Off Ormrod fell victim to Hptm Wolf-Dietrich Wilcke, Kommandeur of III/JG53, as his 36th victory, although his aircraft may also have been hit by AA fire, the latter view being held by his colleagues. Flt Lt Rhys Lloyd wrote to his mother:

> "His sense of duty and gallantry was outstanding, and he was a real example to the Squadron. It is unfortunate that little evidence exists as to how he met his death. It occurred at the height of a big raid, and I think he must have been hit by anti-aircraft fire when pursuing an enemy machine through the barrage. I do not think he was shot down by the enemy, as he was a first-class pilot and had gained a lot of experience on the island. Several pilots have had the misfortune of being shot down by our own AA fire."

The final entries in his journal had found him in profound thought:

"I wonder what it's all leading to. Are the Bosch going to content themselves with smashing the island by means of aerial attack, so that it will take all summer to repair before it is any more use to us? Or are they going to invade? At the moment fighter defences are in abeyance and the AA must be running short of shells. If they start to turn their dive-bombers from the present targets onto the batteries and army shore defences, I shall know that invasion is coming. At the moment the odds seem against it, because I would not imagine the enemy could spare the effort here when he will need so much of his strength in Russia soon. Nor would the enemy, if he actually intended invasion, go to such trouble to destroy the dockyard from the air. He would not trouble so much about damaging the surfaces of our aerodromes either. He would attack aerodromes certainly, but his aim would be at the aircraft and ground defences, not the surface that he requires for transport aircraft. Time not reason will nevertheless tell the true secret of the plans of the German General Staff. We must wait and see. Hope for the chance to again take [to] the air."

At least his final wish was granted. When news of Ormrod's fate reached his Canadian friend Ian McKay, who was spending four days' leave at St Paul's Bay Rest Camp, he wrote in his diary:

"Joe Beckett arrived tonight for his leave and told me that Sonny Ormrod is missing. It is a damn shame 'cause he was a grand kid and had just received the DFC. Out of the four that roomed together when we arrived here, I am the only one left."

With the arrival of more Hurricane IICs, at least two were made available for 1435 Flight to resurrect its night intruder work; Sgt Ted Wood, who was becoming increasingly frustrated by the lack of flying, managed to log a sortie:

"In spite of all the bomb holes on the 'drome, we were able to operate at night. I did an hour. A Wimpey did three trips over Comiso. I saw one fire it started 60 miles away. No Huns were over the island all night, only a few Italians. Came off at dawn and went to bed until I was shaken out by the first Hun hate [raid] on all the usual places."

The morning of 23 April opened with a small fighter-bomber attack, followed at 1035 by a major raid involving an estimated 42 Ju88s and 15 Ju87s. At Takali a number of aircraft pens were damaged and two unserviceable fighters – a Spitfire and a Hurricane – were destroyed; a second Hurricane was destroyed at Hal Far. Six Spitfires and a similar number of Hurricanes were scrambled to oppose this raid, the aggressive Flt Sgt Gordon Tweedale (Z2698/L) shooting down a Stuka over Kalafrana Bay despite being under attack by Messerschmitts. The Stuka, S7+CM of III/StG3 flown by Uffz Jürgen Schwengers, ditched in Marsaxlokk Bay but sank almost immediately in 12 feet of water and the pilot was drowned; his gunner, Gfr Franz Netelnbeker, baled out but was also lost. For some time afterwards the wreck could clearly be seen on a calm day, with the body of the unfortunate pilot still in the cockpit. Of his first confirmed victory, the Australian noted:

"Jumped a mob of Ju87s in their dive for Hal Far. Had 300 [mph] on the clock and got a lovely burst at one from dead astern. Then an AA shell in the barrage blew half the hood off and pushed the side in apart from making a lot of holes. Plenty of 109s about but they only had one squirt at me. Landed OK."

Another Stuka was claimed damaged by Flt Sgt Wilbert Dodd (Z2396/D), while Plt Off Phil Wigley (Z4942/Y) damaged one of the escorting fighters:

"On this occasion it was noticed that several Ju87s jettisoned their bombs in the sea north of Grand Harbour when attacked by fighters, thus incidentally sparing them from dive-bombing through the Grand Harbour AA barrage. The barrage was a spectacular sight though it must have been a nerve-shattering experience for the Luftwaffe crews who were not lacking in courage – only very rarely did one see a bomber break away from the barrage without attacking."

Of the shooting down of the Ju87 by Flt Sgt Tweedale, he added:

> "The pilot was probably wounded and tried to ditch in the bay. His aircraft hit the water, turned over immediately and sank, leaving some wreckage on the surface. I went out in a motor boat with an airman . . . to look for survivors, but there were none at all. All I saw was a tyre floating on the sea."[13]

Two Hurricanes returned from this sortie having suffered combat damage including Z4942/Y flown by Sgt Colin Finlay, although he landed safely and was not hurt. His victor was probably Hptm Helmut Belser of 8/JG53 who claimed a Hurricane shot down as his 23rd victory. Four Hurricanes and two Spitfires were scrambled to meet an afternoon raid but only the latter engaged, claiming two Ju87s shot down. As the Spitfires returned to Takali, the Hurricanes provided cover as Messerschmitts tried to catch them with their wheels and flaps down. During the early evening nine Ju88s and 21 Bf109Fs carried out an undisputed raid on Luqa, where another Spitfire was destroyed on the ground, the 13th to meet its end in such a manner in the last four days. The situation was again becoming very serious for the defenders.

At least 30 Ju88s pounded Grand Harbour and the airfields on the morning of 24 April, while up to 20 Messerschmitts patrolled overhead. At Luqa two Hurricanes and a Wellington were destroyed. Four Spitfires scrambled at 0730, followed five minutes later by four Hurricanes of 185 Squadron and two from 229 Squadron, but these could not prevent the Gozo ferryboat from being strafed; five civilians were wounded during the attack. The Spitfires engaged the bombers over Grand Harbour and claimed two probables and two damaged, the Hurricanes being intercepted by the escorting fighters as they attempted to reach the bombers. Flt Lt Lawrence (Z4942/Y) claimed damage to one Messerschmitt and Plt Off Jack Fletcher (GL-C) damaged a Ju88 before the escort pounced, while Flt Sgt Tony Boyd (Z2698/L) experienced another successful engagement, recording:

> "At 10,000 feet we were attacked by four 109s. I turned into these and gave the last one a short burst 250 yards from astern. Lost remainder of formation in doing so. Flying alone at 7,000 feet [I was] attacked by two 109s (three machine-gun bullets in port wing and rudder controls shot away). Took evasive action and fired a [one] second burst into one from stern quarter. 100 yards. Observed strikes with tracer. Saw a pair of 109s diving on a Spitfire. Caught one as he pulled up. Two-second burst, saw strikes from astern on fuselage [and] two puffs of black smoke from his engine before he pulled the tit. Proceeded to manoeuvre in a circle with six 109s at 5,000 feet near Hal Far. Fired at one pair, abeam, below. No result. Caught another one at 50 yards, from starboard beam. Fired remainder of ammunition. Saw strikes all along fuselage and starboard wing. He pulled up very steeply, rocking from side to side."

It is possible that the two Messerschmitts which Boyd reported hitting were aircraft of JG53's 6 and 7 Staffel which crash-landed at Comiso on return, although both reportedly due to engine failures. The Hurricanes were not called into action when the next raid arrived, but three were scrambled just after midday when an estimated 32 Ju88s started bombing Grand Harbour and the airfields. The Hurricane trio led by Sqn Ldr Dafforn, flying his first sortie from Malta, skirmished with the escort, Plt Off Nixon claiming one damaged. While they were airborne, bombers raided Hal Far and destroyed two of 229 Squadron's Hurricanes. The last raid of the day was by 34 Ju88s and 15 Ju87s against the airfields, a single Spitfire being burnt out at Takali. Four Spitfires and four Hurricanes scrambled, the former claiming a Stuka shot down and two damaged for the loss of two of their own which crash-landed. Meanwhile, over Grand Harbour at 10,000 feet, Sgt Colin Finlay (Z2698/L) saw a formation of Stukas and attacked one from 250 to 200 yards, observing strikes on its tail and cockpit. He then attacked a second with which he almost collided, seeing strikes on its engine cowling, then a flash of flame before it dived away.

As Plt Off Ron Noble (Z2396/D) endeavoured to engage the bombers he was attacked by a Messerschmitt, a cannon-shell blowing a hole in his port elevator although he was able to land safely.

Up to 85 Ju88s and 15 Ju87s were reported attacking Luqa on the morning of 25 April in a raid unopposed by fighters. Much damage was inflicted during which five soldiers were killed and an RAF officer and four airmen were injured. Bofors gunners were successful in shooting down a low flying Messerschmitt, the 5/JG53 pilot baling out to be taken prisoner. Soon after midday a further 80 Ju88s and Ju87s returned, and 14 soldiers were killed when bombs fell on St George's Barracks, with over a dozen more seriously injured, while a dozen gunners where killed when a bomb scored a direct hit on the HAA battery at Spinola. On this occasion six Hurricanes and three Spitfires were scrambled at 1225, followed half an hour later by four more Spitfires. One Spitfire from the trio was shot down in return for claims for three or four Stukas damaged, while the Hurricanes attempted to intercept a formation of ten Ju88s and ten Ju87s. Sgt Colin Finlay (Z4942/Y) was again successful, claiming two Ju88s damaged over St Paul's Bay, while Flt Sgt Wilbert Dodd (Z2396/D) claimed a Ju88 damaged and a Ju87 probably destroyed. He reported that he engaged the latter as it came out of its dive and that it disappeared into cloud pouring black and white smoke. Another Ju88 was damaged by Plt Off Phil Wigley (Z2481), while Flt Sgt Gordon Tweedale (Z2698/L) claimed a Bf109F shot down:

> "Jumped the Ju88s at the bottom of their dive. Got three good squirts in. Broke away over Takali and got a Me109 during a circuit. Knocked his engine and probably him. Followed him out to sea pretty slow and absolutely gliding. Tons of Messerschmitts around but they didn't bother me much."

These successes for the Hurricane pilots came at a cost, however, and 24-year-old Cheshireman Wt Off Douglas Corfe was shot down and killed in BE708. As the Hurricanes returned to Hal Far, a number of Messerschmitts joined the circuit and attempted to shoot them down as they came in to land. When two Spitfires arrived to provide cover, two Hurricanes tried to land simultaneously, only for one to misidentify the other for a Messerschmitt and pull away, while the other Hurricane pilot mistook the two Spitfires for the enemy and also hesitated. One of the Spitfire pilots, Flt Lt Buck McNair, called over the R/T that he would himself shoot down the over-cautious pilots if they did not land quickly. Thus encouraged, both Hurricanes promptly put down and taxied to safety.

The Luftwaffe was back again in the evening when 57 Ju88s and 24 Ju87s attacked Takali and Luqa. Four 185 Squadron Hurricanes were airborne as the raiders came in, two more (from 229 Squadron) and four Spitfires being scrambled to assist. Plt Off Ron Noble (Z2396/D), leading the 185 Squadron quartet, went after the Ju88s: "Fired at two Ju88s – no results seen. Dogfight with Me109. Cannon-shell in starboard wing. One Me109F destroyed." Plt Off Jack Fletcher (Z2698/L) gained better success against the bombers, reporting that his victim would be lucky to get back to Sicily. A Spitfire pilot claimed a second Ju88, and indeed two aircraft of KGr806 were badly hit. Lt Werner Schrader's 3 Staffel aircraft (M7+LL) crashed near Vittoria on return, the crew all suffering wounds or injuries, while M7+FK of 2 Staffel returned badly damaged with a dead rear-gunner. In addition, Lt Wolfgang Herkner's aircraft of 5/LG1 crashed on landing at Catania, possibly due to combat damage.

One of the two 229 Squadron aircraft, flown by Flt Sgt David Roy, was obliged to return early and Flt Sgt Lucien Brooks (BN182) decided to carry on alone, a brave but foolish decision. It was believed that he shot down a Ju87 before being attacked by four Messerschmitts over St Paul's Bay. Watchers on the ground saw the Hurricane's port wing come adrift before it dived into the ground on Bajda Ridge, taking the Canadian pilot to his death. It seems probable that he was the victim of Hptm Wolf-Dietrich Wilcke, Kommandeur of III/JG53, the same pilot who had possibly shot down Plt Off Ormrod, although he may have been another victim of ground fire. Flt Lt Denis Barnham, a Spitfire pilot with 601 Squadron, witnessed events from the RAF rest camp at St Paul's Bay:

"Four 109s appeared on the hill on the opposite shore of the bay – a lazy note of their engines. The leading two climbed suddenly and turned out to sea, the second pair followed. A machine roared out from a fold in the hills, it turned violently to the right and disappeared back from where it had come – there was a burst of machine-gun fire – a pause then I saw the machine again – it appeared from round the side of a hill, its left aileron breaking away, it turned upside down then it struck the ground. A bubble of crimson flame seared up where it struck and a smoking shape bounced down the hill, then it stopped and burst into flames also. Two large fires were now burning on the opposite hillside and thick black smoke was rolling back from the flames. Was it a Hurricane or a Messerschmitt? I think it was a Hurricane.

The fires were gradually dying out, the first had stopped completely but black smoke still oozed from the second fire. Little flames were still dancing among the rocks, and through the field glasses we could make out several figures running down from a scarlet building further up the hill. The sea was a peaceful deep blue and lapping quietly on the rocks; the hillside was yellow and white – the noise of engines had now died away . . . Some army officers were coming down the paths from the house; they came through the archway where the honeysuckle was, onto the terrace: 'We brought these along,' they said. 'They are all the things we could get from the pilot. He was badly burned about the head and he had a cannon-shell through the pelvis.' They produced a torn fragment of battle dress burnt on all sides but the wings were intact, and a letter badly charred, but from which we could establish his identity."[14]

After dark, Sqn Ldr Westmacott set out in BE347/D for an intruder sortie over Catania and Comiso, hoping to catch the night bombers but to no avail. However, he took the opportunity to strafe a train south of Catania, on which he saw cannon strikes before it took refuge in a tunnel. On return, the Hurricane was refuelled and re-armed, and taken over by Sgt Ted Wood, ever keen to strike at the enemy: "We are going on intruders again with the moon. The Hun began bombing what are either AA positions or coastal batteries and continued in all raids, up and down the coast." Wood's brief was to intrude around Gerbini but, as he arrived in the vicinity of the airfield, his aircraft was shot down by flak and the 21-year-old Yorkshire pilot was killed. His commission was announced shortly after his death.

There was little activity over Malta next day (26 April) until the early afternoon when, from 1430 onwards, a total of 55 Ju88s and 15 Ju87s were reported, bombs falling on Valetta and military installations. Six Spitfires and four Hurricanes were scrambled. For the loss of one pilot mortally wounded and a second seriously wounded, the Spitfires could claim but one Stuka shot down before the Messerschmitts pounced. The Hurricanes did not fare much better, Sqn Ldr Dafforn crash-landing at Hal Far in BV163, with shell fragments in his right leg, lower back and arm. A second Hurricane landed showing clear signs of battle damage. Only Plt Off Garth Horricks (Z4942/Y) and Sgt Bob Lees reported any success, the Canadian claiming a Bf109F damaged while Lees claimed a Stuka damaged, although Plt Off Doug Eastman (Z2698/L) fired at both a Ju88 and a Ju87. The bombers returned that evening to attack Kalafrana, but the fighters were not scrambled on this occasion.

The remaining fighter strength was now so reduced that little resistance could be offered to two raids on 27 April. Defence was left to the guns which again did well, shooting down a Ju88 of 4/KG77 and another from 4/LG1, and inflicting slight damage to three Z1007bis during a later raid. By dawn next morning a handful of Spitfires and Hurricanes had been made available to face the first challenge of the day, three Spitfires being scrambled at 0740, followed ten minutes later by four Hurricanes of 185 Squadron. As they became airborne an estimated 43 Ju88s, 20 Ju87s and large fighter escort appeared. One Stuka was claimed damaged by a Spitfire pilot, the dive-bombers also being targeted by the

Hurricanes including Plt Off Ian McKay (Z2396/D):

> "I think I got two Ju87s. A few holes made by some keen types [in his aircraft]. Hope they
> don't get any more practice. Jack Fletcher, Tony Boyd and myself got in a scrap with some
> Ju87s and some Me109Fs. Fletch [Z2698/L] apparently was jumped by 109s and hit – tried
> to jump and is thought to have pulled the cord too soon because eight panels of it were
> ripped out and, of course, he went down very fast and was killed."

Flt Sgt Boyd (BD826/A) reported firing at two Ju87s and a Ju88, although he did not submit
any claims. Meanwhile, Plt Off Phil Wigley (Z3462) had become separated from the others
and attacked a Ju88, which he claimed damaged, but was also set upon by the escorting
Messerschmitts. Plt Off Fletcher's body was recovered about 500 yards from the wreck of his
Hurricane, which crashed in a field south-east of Dingli. A second Canadian pilot was killed
later in the morning when 229 Squadron's Plt Off Tom Foley crashed to his death when the
engine cut while air testing BE555, as recorded by his friend Plt Off McKay:

> "He tried to get into the aerodrome, but just didn't make it and spun just off the boundary;
> the aircraft turned over and burst into flames. I was quite near at the time and saw it all
> happen. I rushed down with the airmen to see if we could get him out but it was impossible.
> I think he was dead and likely never knew his aircraft was burning."

Raids next day (29 April) proved to be much smaller affairs, but they brought about some
heavy fighting nonetheless. Seven Ju88s and eight Bf109Fs raided Hal Far at 1445, five
Spitfires being scrambled, followed somewhat later by four Hurricanes. The Spitfires shot
down one Ju88 and possibly a second, the bombers also being engaged by the Hurricanes,
one of which was claimed damaged by Flt Sgt Tony Boyd (BD826/A), who noted:

> "Leader's R/T packed up so I led the flight. Very successful interception five miles east of
> Kalafrana at 18,000 feet. Bombs still on. Damaged one Ju88. Upset bombing. Well-strafed
> by 109s as I touched down. Machine riddled with MG. Armour plate saved my back."

A second Ju88 was claimed damaged by Plt Off Ron Noble (GL-C), who reported: "Fired
cannons at Ju88 formation. Big yellow flash." Sgt Norm Vidler (Z2481/HB-D) of 229
Squadron claimed damage to a third Ju88 following which he was attacked by a Bf109 and
upon landing at Hal Far overshot the runway, severely damaging his aircraft. The
Australian pilot was, however, uninjured.

April ended with two raids on the 30th, the first by 20 Ju88s, 18 Ju87s and a number of
Bf109F Jabo, which attacked Hal Far and Luqa just after 1100. Eight Spitfires were
scrambled and claimed a Ju88 shot down and a Messerschmitt probable for no losses,
although several Spitfires were attacked in the landing circuit. Tangible help came from an
unusual source on this occasion – Wg Cdr Satchell on the ground at Takali:

> "I was manning a pair of Vickers K guns – which I did most days in company with [Sqn
> Ldr] Westmacott and others, who helped with the loading etc – when a 109 came in behind
> one of our remaining Spits [flown by the CO of 603 Squadron], who had his wheels down
> for landing. I aimed the gun directly at [the Spitfire]; the deflection of the speed was just
> right. I fired and had the satisfaction of seeing the 109 pull straight up, stall, and crash on
> the far side of the airfield. It was very spectacular indeed."[15]

One Spitfire was destroyed on the ground during the raid, further reducing the meagre
number of fighters available to the defenders. Despite the strong reinforcement of only ten
days earlier, no more than seven Spitfires and a handful of Hurricanes remained
serviceable. Indeed, 229 Squadron had effectively ceased to function owing to shortage of
aircraft, although more were imminently due. With the hospitalisation of Sqn Ldr Dafforn,
Flt Lt Farnes was promoted to take command. There were other personnel changes towards
the end of the month; many pilots had left the island or had been posted elsewhere,

including Wg Cdr Stan Turner, of whom Flt Lt Laddie Lucas wrote:

> "Stan Turner only led 249 and the Takali Wing for a couple of months or so before they took him off operations. His nervous system was already strung tight after two continuously hard operational years during which he had had no rest. The signs were there for all to see. He was leading faster and faster in the air. Too fast, in fact. He never took a day off. He was becoming more edgy all round, and he had started fidgeting about with details which didn't matter and which, anyway, could well have been left to the flight commanders to handle. Exhausted, he was now transferred to Headquarters."[16]

During April there had been 170 alerts by day, which materialised in an estimated 3,547 bomber sorties, and a further 182 alerts at night. Indeed, on only two days – when the weather had been particularly bad – had the island not reverberated to the thud of explosions. In what was to be described as 'the cruelest month', 339 civilians and 208 servicemen had been killed in the raids, and 550 civilians injured, while an estimated 6,727 tons of bombs had fallen on the island. Twenty Spitfires and 16 Hurricanes had been lost in combat during the month, and at least 22 Spitfires and 19 Hurricanes destroyed on the ground. In return, the fighters claimed 53 enemy aircraft shot down, 29 probables and 118 damaged, while the guns grossly overestimated their claims as 102:12:69 during the same period.

May 1942

The month opened with a number of small fighter sweeps. The first of these was intercepted around mid morning by two Spitfires of 249 Squadron which shot down a Bf109F of 6/JG53, the Messerschmitt ditching in the sea off Cape Scalambria; the German pilot was rescued by a Do24. Late afternoon saw the appearance of five Z1007bis over the island, escorted by MC202s of 9°Gruppo CT. Four Spitfires of 603 Squadron attempted to intercept but were engaged by Messerschmitts of 6/JG53, one Spitfire being shot down from which the pilot baled out. Night raids were again becoming a frequent occurrence and, with darkness, nine Ju88s were plotted crossing the coast. Luqa and Hal Far were bombed, one of the Beaufighter night fighters being destroyed. Four of 185 Squadron's Hurricanes were sent off at 2025 to intercept, Flt Sgt Tony Boyd (Z5140/C) returning early when the tail trim of his aircraft jammed. Meanwhile, Sgt Yarra (HA-B) attacked a Ju88 illuminated by searchlights just off the coast: "Picked up exhausts, closed and squirted Ju88 – probably destroyed – disappeared from plot." The radar plot had indeed faded some 38 miles north of the island, and the intruder was considered to have been probably destroyed. However, available Luftwaffe records do not verify this loss.

Next day the air defence of the island was left to the Spitfires, but only one inconclusive combat occurred. The handful of worn-out Hurricanes were not called into major action over the next three days, Spitfires intercepting intermittent small raids by Messerschmitt-escorted Ju88s and Ju87s. Nonetheless, Sgt Norm Vidler of 229 Squadron recorded that his cannons jammed when attacking a Ju88 on 3 May while, next day, he "squirted" at a Messerschmitt without success. 229 Squadron now received a minor reinforcement in the guise of five replacement Hurricanes which flew in from Gambut during the late afternoon of the 5th, with Flt Lt Connell at their head. Another Hurricane would arrive the following evening, Plt Off Sandy McHan having been delayed due to engine problems. Whilst these new machines would briefly resurrect the Hurricane unit, their presence would have little effect on the outcome of the present series of air battles.

6 May therefore saw 229 Squadron once again operational, four of the unit's aircraft and four 603 Squadron Spitfires scrambling to intercept ten Ju88s and ten Bf109s at 0945. Three of the bombers were claimed damaged by the Spitfire pilots, and one by Sqn Ldr Farnes. Another Hurricane pilot, Flt Sgt David Roy (BD702), also attacked a bomber but his engine was hit by return fire and he crash-landed at Hal Far. The Hurricane collided with a stone-built torpedo store at the far end of the runway, causing large blocks of

masonry to fall upon the aircraft. Fortunately for Roy, the torpedoes had been removed to an underground store the night before, and he suffered only minor injuries. Not so lucky was Sgt Bob Lees, who failed to return. He was seen to ditch his Hurricane (BN181) five miles off Benghaisa Point, but when HSL128 was called out to pick him up, only wreckage could be found. A Spitfire of 126 Squadron, covering the returning Hurricanes, was also shot down by the Messerschmitts, the pilot baling out with wounds and burn injuries. It seems that Lee's Hurricane and the Spitfire had fallen foul of II/JG53's Messerschmitts, Obfw Rudolf Ehrenberger having claimed one fighter identified as a Spitfire at 1003 (presumably the Hurricane), and Lt Herbert Langer a second at 1014.

At 0945 on the morning of 7 May, a pair of Hurricanes were despatched to search for a missing launch, but these were recalled early when two *Jabo* Messerschmitts attacked Kalafrana. One of the bombs struck a petrol storage barge, which contained 30,000 gallons of fuel, one-third of the precious liquid being lost before the fires were extinguished. Towards evening five Z1007bis and 15 MC202s approached the island, while at least 20 Bf109Fs patrolled over the coast. Six Spitfires and eight Hurricanes were scrambled, four of the latter flown by 185 Squadron pilots. Only Flt Sgt Tweedale (Z2394/GL-F) reported a successful engagement, claiming a Messerschmitt probably shot down at 1925.

After several relatively quiet days, 8 May brought more hectic activity, particularly for the Hurricanes. Spitfires carried out early interceptions, claiming a Bf109F shot down, before seven Hurricanes of 229 Squadron and four Spitfires were scrambled at 0900, followed by four more Hurricanes in the hands of 185 Squadron pilots some 40 minutes later. Their adversaries were six Ju88s of KGr806 and 15 Ju87s of III/StG3 escorted by MC202s from both 9° and 10°Gruppi, and the usual umbrella of Messerschmitts. Sgt Potts of 229 Squadron managed to evade the escort and attack one of the Ju88s which he claimed damaged, while the Spitfires engaged the fighters, two Bf109Fs being claimed damaged. The Italian fighter pilots claimed four Spitfires in return, but none was lost. However, it was the 185 Squadron quartet led by Flt Sgt Tony Boyd which emerged victorious, as recorded in the Squadron diary:

> "B Flight was still on readiness with four aircraft this morning. The four were scrambled at about 9pm. They made a wizard interception on some of Joe Kesselring's 88 boys. 'Tweedle' [Flt Sgt Tweedale in Z2394/GL-F] went to town with a vengeance and proceeded to shoot up everything in the sky, with the result that one Ju88 and one Me109 'went for a Burton' and another 109 probably emulated the other two kites. Flt Sgt Boyd (Z4942/GL-Y) also scored a probable Ju88 while Flt Sgt Dodd (Z2698/L) managed to intimidate an 'Ice Cream boy', who was stooging about in a Macchi 202, to such an extent that he probably went into the drink."

Flt Sgt Tweedale was credited with one Messerschmitt destroyed and a second probably so, while the Ju88 was also credited as probably destroyed. Only Sgt Colin Finlay failed to make a claim. He was attacked by a Messerschmitt whilst approaching to land, being obliged to belly-land BD789/GL-T at Takali, the incident being recorded by Flt Lt Barnham:

> "The fight took place at low level all round Takali, with Spitfires chasing 109s up into the sun while other 109s dived in from other directions, a free for all, but despite being outnumbered four or five to one, only one of the Hurricanes, whose landing we were trying to cover, was hit; I glimpsed it staggering to the ground, crashing on its belly on the edge of the aerodrome – the pilot got out unhurt."[17]

There seems little doubt that Flt Sgt Tweedale had shot down M7+KL of 3/KGr806, flown by Uffz Gerhard Andrea, which ditched near Pozzallo; Andrea and his crew were posted missing. This was probably the same aircraft as that attacked by Flt Sgt Boyd, who reported:

> "I led our flight. We jumped six Ju88s out of the sun at 18,000 feet. I got one, both engines

etc. Mixed it with ten Macchis 202s; came down, mixed it with 109s at zero feet. Hit in engine by cannon, glycol tank blew up. Drenched me. Belly-landed at Takali."

The ever-aggressive Flt Sgt Tweedale may have shared with AA in shooting down Uffz Heinrich Becker of 8/JG53, who baled out to be taken prisoner, his aircraft (Black 3) crashing on Marsa racetrack. One of the Hurricanes had been attacked by Oblt Michalski of 4/JG53, although he identified his victim as a P-40. The Macchi engaged by Flt Sgt Wilbert Dodd was that flown by Ten Giovanni Barcaro of 97^Squadriglia, the Italian pilot returning to base having been wounded in the right arm. Thus, for 185 Squadron the Hurricane era ended on a high note. Following this successful action, the remaining Hurricanes were handed over to 229 Squadron in anticipation of the arrival of more Spitfires on the morrow. However, most of the old Hurricanes were promptly destroyed or damaged on the ground, leaving only two operational machines.

The raiders were back at 1325 when five Ju88s and 18 Ju87s attacked Luqa and Takali, while Hal Far was targeted by five Z1007bis. Messerschmitts and Macchis provided close escort and top cover but, in the event, no fighters rose to challenge. Half a dozen Spitfire pilots were caught in the open at Takali, Flt Lt Connell being wounded while the CO of 601 Squadron had a lucky escape when a bullet pierced his hat without wounding him.

On the morning of 9 May, 64 Spitfires destined for Malta took off from the decks of the carriers USS *Wasp* and HMS *Eagle* and, this time, Malta was ready for them. The AOC decided that if the aircraft arrived in moderately serviceable condition and in daylight, it should be possible to re-arm and refuel them within ten minutes, thus avoiding a repetition of the damage inflicted following the previous delivery. Five groundcrew were to be allocated to each aircraft pen. As soon as the long-range tanks were removed and the fighter refuelled and re-armed, it would take off, this time with an experienced 'Malta hand' at the controls.

Enemy activity over Malta commenced at 0720, when a reconnaissance Ju88 and five Bf109Fs crossed the coast, only the AA guns engaging them. When another Ju88, five Cants, 16 Macchis and up to 45 Messerschmitts appeared two hours later, however, nine Hurricanes (six from Luqa and three from Hal Far) took off to provide some protection for the first batch of Spitfires, which were then imminently due. Two of the Hurricanes collided in mid-air in the mad scramble to get airborne although both were able to land safely. Neither Sgt Norm Vidler (BN362) nor the other pilot involved was injured. The Hurricanes were followed by six 603 Squadron Spitfires, both formations seeking to provide maximum cover for Takali. As the first of the new arrivals appeared they went in to land at once, the Hurricanes endeavouring to hold the enemy fighters at bay. As one Spitfire lowered its wheels and commenced its slow approach, a Bf109F raced towards it. Sqn Ldr Farnes of 229 Squadron immediately intercepted, turning violently with the Messerschmitt as it attempted to avoid his fire; he claimed some damage and succeeded in driving it away. In a letter to his parents, one of his pilots, Plt Off Tom Lawrence, later wrote:

"I did not engage, but when I was coming into land I was strafed by Messerschmitts. On the point of landing, with wheels and flaps down, I was jumped by 109s. Controller called up other pilots to give me protection for I was helpless, but it was really too late, and the next thing I heard was the Controller let out a groan. Well, I thought, I have had it! But I managed to race along the end of the runway and turned the aircraft with my back to the sea (to take advantage of the armour plating, as I knew they would be coming from that direction) and stopped, with my head well down in the cockpit. There was a roar and a babble all round me, and I looked up and saw the Messerschmitt climbing for height. Well, I got out of that one alright."

The 603 Squadron Spitfires enjoyed better success and claimed two Messerschmitts for one loss. Meanwhile, the initial batch of Spitfires had got down safely; a few were refuelled within four minutes, the remainder within seven, with pilots strapped in the cockpits ready to scramble. At 1055, eleven of the new aircraft took off, now flown by 249 Squadron pilots, and almost immediately encountered a formation of Messerschmitts. One of the enemy fighters was claimed shot down and two others probably so, but one Spitfire was lost with its pilot, Plt Off D'Arcy Milburn, who had until recently been flying Hurricanes with 185 Squadron.

At 1115, Spitfires were again scrambled, a total of 31 taking to the air as more reinforcements approached the island. Most of the new arrivals were still waiting to land as an estimated 40 Messerschmitts appeared at 12,000 feet, shepherding a dozen Ju88s and five Cants. Their target was Hal Far, which soon disappeared under a cloud of dust and smoke. Two civilians and three soldiers were killed, while the airfield was rendered unserviceable for several hours. One Spitfire pilot, who had just landed, immediately tried to take off again to assist a comrade who was being attacked but struck the top of a dispersal pen, crashed and was killed. Only two of this latest batch of Spitfires failed to arrive. Throughout the rest of the day Axis forces returned repeatedly in an effort to catch the new Spitfires on the ground. At 1315, some 15 Ju88s and 18 Bf109Fs attacked Hal Far and Takali, and were met by 24 Spitfires, six of which were flown by Hurricane pilots of 185 Squadron, as recalled by Plt Off Phil Wigley:

> "Most of the pilots had never flown Spitfires before and it had been originally intended that they should not fly them immediately on operational flights. However, the few survivors of 185 were not prepared to accept this decision without protest, and an appeal to Air Vice-Marshal Lloyd soon reversed it – those without Spitfire experience had been shown the cockpit drills by Plt Off McKay, who had."

In such desperate circumstances, it was an understandable decision to allow Malta-experienced pilots the opportunity of flying the new machines into action. But it would ultimately prove to be a tragically unwise one. From this initial action, Plt Off Ron Noble returned to Takali slightly wounded and had to crash-land his Spitfire, which was written-off. The 185 Squadron pilots were airborne again at 1620 as Ju87s carried out attacks on Luqa and Grand Harbour, and although they gained some successes, Flt Sgt Gordon Tweedale was shot down and killed, his Spitfire crashing at Lija. Thus died one of Malta's more successful Hurricane pilots. He had claimed six victories (of which two were shared) and three probables in a short period of time.

On 10 May the defenders were ready for the raiders as never before. Two early morning reconnaissance flights saw Spitfires scrambled, but it was 1020 before a major raid approached, some 20 Ju87s and ten Ju88s making for Grand Harbour. First off were 20 Spitfires, followed shortly thereafter by a further 17. For the loss of two Spitfires and one pilot, claims were submitted for the destruction of nine Ju87s, four Ju88s and a Bf109F. The Hurricanes were not required on this occasion, but six of 229 Squadron were scrambled at 1400, in company with 20 Spitfires, when more Ju88s again raided Grand Harbour. One Ju88 was shot down by the Spitfires, others being damaged. Two Hurricanes returned slightly damaged, having been jumped by Messerschmitts of III/JG53. In the early evening there was another raid and ten Spitfires were scrambled to investigate. This time five Z1007bis escorted by 20 MC202s and ten Re2001s, were followed by 20 Ju87s and a large formation of Bf109Fs. More Spitfires were scrambled, while six Hurricanes of 229 Squadron were sent up to provide cover for the airfields and returning Spitfires. One Cant and one Macchi were shot down and two other bombers badly damaged; in addition, claims were submitted for one Ju87 and two Messerschmitts, plus several probables, for the loss of one Spitfire from which the pilot baled out. Plt Off Tom Lawrence of 229 Squadron noted:

> "Scrambled three times today. I protected a launch as it went out off Kalafrana Point to pick

up, as we thought, one of our pilots. He turned out to be a Hun, and there was I circling and diving gently (so as not to frighten the pilot!) in order to direct the launch to him."[18]

This had been a serious, meaningful defence, which many believed, with some justification, to have been the turning point in Malta's fortune. Undeniably there were many months of hard fighting still to come, but never again would the defenders be reduced to mere handfuls of fighters. Luftwaffe losses did not quite match Malta's claims, nonetheless four Ju88s failed to return, another was written off on returning to base, four Ju87s and two Bf109Fs were shot down, and another Messerschmitt crashed on return.

Somewhat surprisingly, it was by this date that Feldmarschall Kesselring believed that his forces had won the air battle for Malta:

"On 10 May I could regard the task as accomplished . . . it was accomplished with comparatively small losses. Several factors made the battle against the island fortress difficult. There were natural shelters hewn out of rock on the perimeter of the airfields and around the harbour. The concentration of powerful British anti-aircraft defences on the shores, supported by naval AA guns protecting the harbour, put up a barrier of fire to be penetrated only by stout hearts and at the loss of many aircraft. The vulnerable moments in the dive-bombing attacks were going into the dive and then flattening out afterwards. These movements throttled the aircraft's flying speed and broke up the formation. Here we suffered losses which could only be minimised by sending in fighters to dive at the same time and by detailing special fighters to protect them at the flattening-out level. The British fighters deserve recognition for their bravery and manoeuvring skill, especially in the perfect handling of their aircraft when diving from high altitude through the middle of the closed German bomber formations.

Thanks to its success, our ascendancy at sea and in the air in the supply lanes from Italy to Africa was assured. It would have been easy to capture the island after the bombing assault. That this did not happen was a grave mistake on the part of the German-Italian Command. It is to the credit of the Luftwaffe that it restricted the battle to purely military targets. With the success of the attack the OKW considered the tension so far relaxed that it transferred the greater part of our air forces to the Eastern Front. Of course, sufficient forces were left in the Mediterranean to keep watch on Malta, to curb the activity of the enemy's sea transport and to protect our own communications, without having to call on the forces of the AOC Africa."[19]

There was a noticeable reduction in aerial activity next day (11 May). At 0725 a reconnaissance Ju88 with fighter escort approached, four Spitfires being despatched to investigate. Shortly before 1030 15 Ju88s and about 40 Bf109Fs were plotted, a total of 23 Spitfires being scrambled. Two of the escort were claimed shot down and a Ju88 probably so. In the early evening three Ju88s targeted both Hal Far and Luqa, where two Spitfires were badly damaged on the ground. There were several skirmishes during which two Spitfires collided, both pilots managing to bale out safely. A section of Hurricanes was up during one raid, Sgt Norm Vidler (BN184) engaging a Messerschmitt but without result. In the main, the Hurricanes were not required, now being mainly reserved for airfield defence and cover for returning Spitfires, and to escort ASR launches.

Two Hurricanes were up, just before midday on 12 May, as escort to HSL107, called out for a Spitfire pilot (Flt Sgt W.C. Conway of 185 Squadron) in the sea just offshore as a result of being hit by return fire from a Ju88 he had been attacking. The rescue was successful. It was late afternoon before the next raid developed, reported to comprise four Ju88s and three Z1007bis escorted by two dozen Messerschmitts and Macchis. The Italian bombers were in fact SM84s and their escort included Re2001s in addition to Macchis. Thirty-six Spitfires were scrambled and in the confusion to get off the ground two collided, though neither pilot was hurt. On this occasion six Hurricanes were also ordered off, as Plt

Off Tom Lawrence remembered:

> "We scrambled this afternoon at 1745 and, as usual, just when eggs were being dropped. Climbed to 14,000 feet and, after skying, dived for 88s. As we dived after them – they were dive-bombing Grand Harbour – we were diverted to Messerschmitts which went by in front of us heading north of the island. We had to divide to get through a little of our own ack-ack. Two 109s dived at me. One turned away as I turned with them, but the other was plucky, and came on. I manoeuvred the kite in such a way that the Hun did not like it and he zoomed a little faster, climbing for height. I was extremely annoyed as I could have put my hand out and touched his plane. I tried my hardest to get my sights on him, but couldn't. If I could have done so, I would have literally blasted him out of the sky. As I dived down, the Controller called up to say 13 Italians were over the island, but they wouldn't come down."

In the ensuing series of dogfights the Spitfire pilots claimed two of the Italian bombers, one of which crashed near Dingli, two of the Reggianes (both of which crash-landed on return to Catania), plus a Macchi and a Ju88 as probably destroyed. Three Spitfires were lost; one pilot was killed and a second wounded, while the third baled out safely. The Italian pilots claimed three Spitfires shot down in this action, while pilots of III/JG53 alone claimed ten Spitfires during the course of the day.

The Stukas were back at lunchtime on the 13th, 16 aircraft of III/StG3 raiding Hal Far where three Hurricanes were damaged, including BE716 which was written off. Only one Stuka was claimed damaged by the Spitfires, although one pilot reported shooting down two of the escorting Messerschmitts. Although the Spitfires claimed a total of six Ju88s and five Bf109Fs destroyed on the 14th, three pilots were killed in action against the Messerschmitts of III/JG53, two of these being the Hurricane veterans, Flt Sgt Tony Boyd and Sgt Colin Finlay, the Australian's aircraft crashing at Luqa while Finlay's body was recovered from the sea off Wied Zurrieq. Boyd had claimed five victories of which two were shared, plus six probables. At the height of the battle six Hurricanes were sent off. Once again Sgt Vidler (BN362) found himself a target but managed to return safely. He was scrambled again sometime later in BN283, another Messerschmitt pilot making a passing shot at his aircraft without scoring any strikes. The Hurricanes were not called into action again until the early hours of the 17th, the pilots enjoying some local leave while the Spitfires dealt successfully with the intermittent raids, Plt Off Lawrence recording in his diary:

> "An off-day. Went again to Sliema via Valetta and returned at midday. Signed a girl's autograph book in Valetta and her mother wrote under my signature 'Malta's Hope.' Believe me, I've been through the Battle of Britain, but these folks, who have been through the Battle of Malta, have had it worse. We have had five pilots of our Squadron killed and four hospital cases since we've been here."

During the early hours of 18 May, a number of Italian MAS (motor torpedo boats) and German E-boats were reported to be operating off Grand Harbour[20], about four miles from Madalena Fort, and the guns opened fire but without positive success. Four Hurricanes of 229 Squadron were sent to investigate at 0330, although these failed to see any signs of the craft. At 0515 four more Hurricanes took off, one of which returned early. The remaining three located one of the MAS about five miles east of Malta, and carried out a thorough strafing. The craft was left disabled, with no signs of life. By daylight, however, the MAS were still at sea and 16 MC202s and eight Re2001s were despatched to cover their return. Four Spitfires were scrambled to intercept and subsequently claimed three Reggianes shot down.

At 0930, with the presence of the MAS having been confirmed, four more Hurricanes were despatched to attack them. As they were searching, a big Luftwaffe fighter sweep began to form up and 18 Spitfires were scrambled to intercept this and cover the Hurricanes, which were now recalled. One Spitfire was quickly shot down, the pilot baling out into the sea, and two Messerschmitts were also claimed, one German pilot being seen to bale out into the sea. HSL128 was despatched immediately to pick up the Spitfire pilot, with Hurricanes providing cover, but these then came under attack. One Messerschmitt latched on to the tail of Sgt Jim Pendlebury's machine (BN362), as recalled by Plt Off Lawrence: "We lost our fifth kite on patrol. Six to eight Messerschmitts dived on us and shot poor old Jimmy down. He went right into the sea." Plt Off Ken Lee fired at the attackers and claimed one damaged; Sgt Norm Vidler fired at another head-on but made no claim. The skipper of HSL128 wrote:

> "At 11am we had a call out for a Spitfire pilot said to have baled out off Hal Far, about 100 yards out. Sounded like a piece of cake, for even though enemy fighters were plentiful in the vicinity, the position given was close to the island and we now had Spitfires on the job as well as Hurricanes. Getting on the given bearing we steamed 100, 200, 300 yards – still nothing seen – and kept on going, though enemy activity was getting more and more lively overhead. After we had steamed out about three miles, one of the escorting Hurricanes was shot down a couple of miles ahead of us. It was while we were investigating this wreckage that Jerry got closest to us, but even then the bullets only churned up the water over a hundred feet away. As there was no survivor from this crash, and still no sign of the original pilot for whom we had been called out, I decided to make for base, but on our way back we saw another fighter crash about six miles over to the westward, and a parachute drifting down. We picked this pilot up within a few minutes of him hitting the water, and he turned out to be a Hun [Uffz Johannes Lompa of 4/JG53] – a cheery soul, who advised us to get back ashore before we were hurt. As we were then fairly well out I decided to run out and then come in on our original bearing from a distance of about ten miles, as even the worst possible estimate of distance could hardly be over ten miles. We actually found the Spitfire pilot in his dinghy about nine miles from the island, and the German pilot insisted upon shaking hands with him as we welcomed him aboard."

229 Squadron's Plt Off Tom Lawrence commented: "We picked up a Jerry pilot. Why we picked him up, I'm dashed if I know, because the other day the Huns shot up one of our boys on the water, and then beat it."

During the afternoon a further 17 Spitfires arrived at Malta, having flown from the deck of the small aircraft carrier HMS *Eagle*. Their arrival coincided with a reduction of Luftwaffe strength in Sicily, as the Libyan and Eastern Fronts were now given priority over Malta. The Bf109Fs of II/JG3 and the Ju88s of II and III/KG77 had already returned to Northern Europe, II/JG3 soon being redeployed to the Eastern Front, where it was shortly joined by I/JG53; meanwhile, III/JG53, I/NJG2, III/ZG26 and III/StG3 began to deploy across the Mediterranean to Cyrenaica, and I/KG54 was transferred to Crete. Hence, only II/JG53, KüFlGr606 and KGr806, plus ASR and reconnaissance units were to remain in Sicily. A number of Italian formations in Sicily also moved to North Africa with their places being taken by units from the mainland.

The reduction of Axis strength on Sicily was immediately felt in Malta. The Spitfires were now able to adequately deal with the latest small-scale incursions, and generally were more than a match for the Italian fighters that ventured over Malta. During the next few days the Spitfire pilots claimed two Z1007bis, one Ju88, two Bf109Fs, two MC202s and two Re2001s for just one loss, while night fighter Beaufighters accounted for three BR20Ms. With no more requirement for the Hurricanes, preparations were made for the majority of the airworthy machines to be flown to North Africa, but not before one of the 229 Squadron pilots, Plt Off Tom Lawrence, had a lucky escape – but this time on the ground:

> "Only a couple of very light raids by bomb-carrying Messerschmitts. I was up at the time of one of these raids. Later one of these filthy little jobs dropped his egg a little too close. Legs and arms all over the place. I managed to do a graceful swallow dive into some debris and before I pancaked I barked my shin on an extremely hard piece of rock."

With sufficient Spitfires now to hand and with more on the way, the remaining pilots of 229 Squadron were ordered to return to the Middle East. A dozen departed at 0500 on the morning of 27 May in an assortment of patched-up Hurricanes, each fitted with long-range tanks, escorted initially by Spitfires of 185 Squadron. Sqn Ldr Farnes, who led the group, recalled:

> "Although the weather was not particularly favourable, bearing in mind that for this long journey we really needed a tail wind, we were nevertheless ordered to leave. I had given strict orders to all pilots that they were not to use their R/T under any circumstances for fear of the enemy obtaining a fix on our position. The first part of the journey was flown at sea level to avoid enemy radar at Sicily, then I was instructed to fly at 2,000 feet. At this height we were in thick haze and were on instruments for two and a half hours. During this time a Heinkel passed in front of us at a similar height, but there was nothing we could do about it. What was left of the Squadron finally landed at Sidi Barrani after four and a half hours flying, and with precious little fuel left, possibly enough for another five or ten minutes flying."

Three of the Hurricanes failed to arrive, both Flt Sgt Norris Ganes and Plt Off Ken Lee being taken prisoner following crash-landings; Ganes (Z2982) recalled:

> "En route I was separated from the Squadron, and flew along the coast of North Africa until I ran out of fuel. As we were flying just above the water to avoid radar contact, I crash-landed. Later that day I was picked up by a German patrol."

Plt Off Lee (BE642) had experienced electrical problems, neither his R/T nor fuel pump working, and he was therefore unable to transfer fuel from the long-range tanks to the main tank. Deciding to head for the coast, he anticipated making for Tobruk where he hoped to reach British forces. Before breaking away he noticed another aircraft drop out of the formation. En route he met about half a dozen Ju87s and made an attack on these without result. The rear-gunners put up a tremendous barrage of fire at him although the Hurricane was not hit. He continued flying towards Tobruk but when his fuel ran out was forced to carry out a crash-landing in scrub about 20 miles west of El Hania. He walked westwards for two days and a night, his intention being to steal a boat, but was spotted by Arabs and later that evening turned over to the Italians[21]. The third missing pilot, Sgt George Wilcox (Z4005), had similarly become separated and attempted to follow the coastline to safety, only to encounter a MC202 which shot down his aircraft. He was able to carry out a forced-landing and, after several days of evading enemy patrols, reached British lines. Another of the Hurricane pilots, Plt Off Len Mathus, later summed up the reasons for the failure of 229 Squadron to play an effective rôle on Malta:

> "In the first place, a Hurricane squadron should never have been sent to Malta at this stage of the blitz. Hurricanes were much slower, and could not cope with the 109s. Secondly, a green squadron, with many pilots having little or no operational experience, should never have been chosen."

Although it was an ignominious ending for Malta's Hurricanes, which had so valiantly held the island against great odds since June 1940, it was not the end of the story of the air battle for Malta. It was now the turn of the Spitfires to continue the good work performed by the Hurricanes, to revenge the Hurricane pilots lost in the struggle and to win the final battle[22].

CHAPTER XII

NOT QUITE THE END: SECOND-LINE DUTIES

June 1942 – 1943

While most of the airworthy Hurricanes had by now left Malta, there remained at least one which continued to play an important rôle – the all-black personal Hurricane (possibly BG766) in the care of Wg Cdr Hugh Dawson, who maintained the series of nocturnal supply-drops to agents in Sicily. One of the many characters seemingly attracted to Malta, during daylight he would be seen riding his white horse about the airfield, reins in one hand and fly-swat in the other!

At the beginning of July, Malta received a new AOC, Air Vice-Marshal Keith Park MC DFC, who arrived aboard a Sunderland from Egypt to relieve Air Vice-Marshal Lloyd. In response to the new AOC's call for a more offensive attitude to be adopted whenever possible, Wg Cdrs Dawson and Turner approached the AOC and requested permission to resurrect small-scale Hurricane fighter-bomber intruder sorties against targets in Sicily. Park readily agreed and a handful of redundant Hurricanes were serviced and prepared for limited operations. On 23 July, Z2825 crashed during a test flight and Plt Off David Kent of 185 Squadron was killed. Undaunted, three aircraft were eventually made available and, after dark on 26 July, the Hurricanes, flown by Wg Cdr Dawson, American Sgt Claude Weaver RCAF and Sgt Len Reid RAAF (BN408/E) of 185 Squadron, each with two 250-lb bombs slung underwing, set off to bomb Gela, taking the advantage of bright moonlight. The mission was not a success, however, as Weaver could not locate Gela and returned with his bombs intact, while Reid was unable to reach the designated target owing to heavy fuel consumption and released his bombs in the vicinity of Scicli instead. Only Wg Cdr Dawson actually arrived over Gela and although the two bombs were dropped on the airfield from about 3,000 feet, no results were observed. Buildings and vehicles were strafed by Dawson, who reported a lack of opposition from the defences.

At least seven[1] of the few remaining Hurricanes at Takali, most of which were unserviceable, were badly damaged during an air raid in 25 July, and two days later three more[2] were damaged. Nonetheless, three aircraft were available for Wg Cdr Turner and Sgts Weaver and Reid (BN408/E) to carry out an intruder sortie that night to Comiso. Two of the pilots dropped their bombs over the south-west corner of the airfield from 4,000 feet, but the third was unable to release his bombs and returned with them intact. Light and accurate AA was experienced on this occasion although none of the Hurricanes was hit.

There followed a brief lull in such operations until late in the following month, when three redundant FAA Albacore pilots at Hal Far requested permission to fly fighter-bomber sorties. Once again the AOC gave his approval and three pilots – Sub Lt(A) Reg Elliott and two New Zealanders, Sub Lt(A) Ernie Pratt and Sub Lt(A) Colin White – were soon in business. Following a short conversion course on the type, they were ready but BG770 was promptly rendered unserviceable when Elliott carried out a crash-landing at Hal Far when the undercarriage jammed. Although so few aircraft were unlikely to have much effect on the course of the war, it was felt that any attempt to harass the enemy was worthwhile, particularly as recent reconnaissances of Sicilian airfields revealed about 150 fighters – Messerschmitts, Macchis and Reggianes – at Gela, Biscari, Comiso and Pachino, while in excess of 100 Ju88s were counted at Trapani. Well aware of the chaos, confusion and damage the bomb-carrying Messerschmitts had caused to Malta's airfields, the volunteers considered any offensive operation would be worth the effort. Having carried out night flying and dive-bombing practice, the Naval pilots prepared themselves for their first operation – a daylight strike against Gela.

Hence, during the afternoon of 23 August, the three bomb-laden Hurricanes[3] set out for Gela, escorted by eight Spitfires of 249 Squadron and four from 229 Squadron. One Hurricane (Z4941 flown by Pratt) suffered engine trouble shortly before reaching the target area and turned back, the pilot jettisoning his bombs en route. The other two found 10/10th cloud over Gela, White deciding to drop his bombs on a small collection of buildings north-east of the airfield, while Elliott (Z2691) bombed Biscari airfield with unobserved results:

> "I found some aircraft near a hangar and went for them and then flew out on the deck – I could not see what the result was, but Colin White joined up with me as we crossed the coast and flew in formation with me back to Hal Far. He indicated that one of my bombs had hung up, and was secured by the back clamps of the bomb rack. The Controller at Hal Far gave me the option of baling out, having viewed the bomb through binoculars. I decided to land, and unknown to me, the whole aerodrome staff ducked behind shelters! Fortunately, the landing was one of my best and, as I got out, I noticed the bomb down at an angle so that the spike only just cleared the ground. As it had been released from the main securing lug it was, of course, primed. Had I known, I would have baled out!"

Italian records suggest that four civilians were killed at Gela and three injured. Two days later a repeat Hurribomber raid was attempted, the three FAA pilots briefed to attack Biscari while Spitfires again provided the escort. When just under way the Hurricanes were recalled owing to adverse weather conditions, the pilots ordered to jettison their bombs in the sea. One again experienced a hang-up but the bomb was finally released near Malta and fell into the midst of a group of Maltese fishing boats. There was no reported damage. Next day (26 August), two of the Hurricanes, flown by White and Pratt, again set out for Biscari escorted by Spitfires. The Hurricanes dived out of cloud and planted their bombs in the middle of the airfield from 6,000 feet, before strafing with two of the Spitfires. No aircraft were seen on the airfield. The defences put up stiff resistance and as Pratt swept in at low level his Hurricane (Z4941) was hit twice in the port wing by machine-gun fire. In turn, a group of soldiers were strafed, the pilots believing they had inflicted considerable casualties.

As Spitfires carried out another strike on the 27th, the Hurricanes were called out to fly ASR launch protection sorties. During one such patrol Pratt spotted a body in the sea and he guided HSL128 to the spot. The body turned out to be a badly decomposed, unidentifiable Axis pilot. With nightfall on 28 August, Elliott and White departed for Sicily to carry out nuisance raids on Gela and Comiso, Elliott (Z4941) visiting the former airfield where he released his two bombs without observing any results. Meanwhile, despite intense flak over Comiso, White (BE110) succeeded in dropping his bombs. Both Hurricanes returned safely. All three Hurricanes set out the following night, targeting Comiso, where they each made a bombing run from north to south, diving from 9,000 feet to release their bombs. They faced intense AA fire and the results of their attacks were not observed in their haste to get away. Despite the hot reception all three returned unscathed.

Just as the Naval Hurricane pilots and their RAF Spitfire colleagues were starting to get a taste for the offensive forays, orders were received from London effectively curtailing such freelance operations since it was necessary to conserve fuel. With bomb-carrying Spitfires now available at Malta, the Hurricanes were again relegated to the occasional ASR launch protection rôle, the three Navy pilots returning to their main duty of flying Albacores, more of which had reached the island.

By the beginning of October the Luftwaffe had returned to Sicily in some force for what was to be its last effort to subjugate the island: there were nine Gruppen of Ju88s, one with He111s, together with five Gruppen of Bf109Fs including one *Jabo* Gruppe. In addition, the Italians had strengthened their contingent which now comprised nine squadrons of MC202s and three with Re2001s, two squadrons of Z1007bis, four with SM79, two with SM84bis, and two with Ju87s. But Malta was now confident that it could counter any Axis threat, having established five full squadrons of Spitfire Vs with plenty of replacement aircraft and pilots available. The new blitz opened on 11 October. The fighting was fierce but brief and by 17 October the assault was effectively over, Feldmarschall Kesselring calling a halt to the bomber offensive after his units had suffered severe losses.

During the mini blitz the three Naval pilots had been assigned to fly ASR protection sorties and to search for downed pilots. Amongst their achievements during this period was the sighting on the 12th by Elliott (BE110) of a Spitfire pilot (Sgt W.B. Knox-Williams of 1435 Squadron) in the sea some 12 miles north-east of Grand Harbour, who was then safely picked up by the HSL directed to the scene by Elliott; another Spitfire pilot who owed his life to the vigilance of a Hurricane pilot (Pratt) was Flt Sgt C.A. Long of 126 Squadron, who was rescued on the morning of the 14th. Two days later the three Hurricane pilots were again despatched on a search for downed airmen. All that was spotted, however, were Spitfires of 229 Squadron orbiting oil patches off Kalafrana, where a pilot in his dinghy was waiting to be picked up. As Sub Lt(A) Pratt approached, a Spitfire broke away from the formation and attacked his aircraft (BE110), damaging the starboard wing before his assailant realised his mistake. The Hurricanes were on occasion joined by ASR Do24s, out searching for German survivors.

On 17 October, the Hurricanes continued to search for survivors of shot down aircraft. Patrolling an area from St Paul's Bay to Kalafrana, six to ten miles out to sea, they covered the rescue of two survivors of a II/LG1 Ju88 crew shot down earlier in the day ten miles north-west of Delimara. Elliott then sighted a parachute in the sea three miles off Zonqor Point, to which he directed the HSL, but no survivor was found. With the blitz now effectively over, stock could be taken of the momentous few days of intense activity, Air Vice-Marshal Park signalling the Marine Rescue Section:

> "The AOC sends personal congratulations to the Air/Sea Rescue Unit on their fine achievements during the recent battle of Malta when they made 36 trips and rescued 12 British and 16 enemy pilots [*sic*]. All pilots and aircrews are grateful for your efficient Air/Sea Rescue Service."[4]

The three Hurricane pilots had participated in many of these rescues. All three would be decorated with the DSC for their services, which included a number of Albacore sorties. Elliott rejoined his unit shortly thereafter, but both White and Pratt continued to fly the Hurricanes on various duties. On 26 October they were despatched to search an area north of Gozo following a clash between Spitfires and Messerschmitts, when one of the latter was claimed shot down. The Hurricane pilots sighted a body in a partially inflated dinghy, the HSL being directed to investigate.

With a lessening of enemy air activity over Malta, time was found on 10 November to officially open the new airfield which had been constructed at Krendi, Air Vice-Marshal Park beating up the strip in his personal Hurricane coded OK-2[5]. The AOC was a familiar figure at all the airfields, flying his Hurricane on quick-stop visits and immediately identifiable by his white flying helmet.

The RNAS Hurricane pilots continued to find employment and, on 3 December while on shipping reconnaissance, Sub Lt(A) White's aircraft was attacked from astern by a Ju88, which overshot without inflicting any damage, allowing White to open fire before it was lost from sight. The Ju88 was claimed damaged. Three days later, on 6 December, when Sub Lt(A) Pratt was returning to Malta from a trip to the Middle East via Lampedusa, his Hurricane (BE110) was attacked by a Spitfire patrol from 185 Squadron led by Sgt Walker. One of the Spitfire pilots involved was Sgt Johnnie Houlton RNZAF, who later wrote:

> "Our briefing from HQ advised that no Allied aircraft would be anywhere near Lampedusa, and that we should be on the lookout for enemy aircraft from the island. But what began as an interesting patrol ended in a kind of personal nightmare. The patrol went as planned as we

turned and dived in wide line abreast over the aerodrome, where only a couple of twin-engined Italian aircraft were to be seen on the ground. As we crossed out very fast at 200 feet a violent barrage of light flak chased us. I glanced ahead and saw a single-engined aircraft with floats, flying low to my left, visible in the bright glare of the sun off the water, and about 500 yards away. Giving a quick call to the section leader, I turned in and down, opening fire at 200 yards. For once both cannons fired, pounding into the sea ahead of the target, while the pattern from the four machine-guns was churning the surface slightly behind it; so I pulled through to hit the wing-root, cockpit and engine area with the machine-guns. Simultaneously I glimpsed a roundel on the fuselage and recognised the target as a Hurricane, with long-range fuel tanks under each wing, which I had mistaken for floats.

I broke away and screamed over the R/T to the other pilots who were turning into attacking positions. From start to finish the sighting and attack were over in about six seconds; then began 45 minutes of the ultimate form of self torture for any fighter pilot. The Hurricane was well riddled in the wing-root and lower cockpit area, a sizable chunk of the wing leading edge was missing and the pilot's airspeed was down to 120mph as he nursed the aircraft along, right down to sea level. I realised the Hurricane came from the small RNAS unit at Hal Far which operated anti-shipping Swordfish and also possessed a couple of Hurricanes.

Malta appeared out of the haze after what felt like several lifetimes. The Hurricane pilot lowered his wheels and landed straight in at Hal Far, slithering round to the right and stopping in a great cloud of dust on the edge of the field. By the time I completed a circuit and landed, the ambulance was disappearing towards the camp hospital, which screwed my anxiety level right off the clock again. I arrived at the hospital breathless and knocking at the knees to find the Naval Lieutenant pilot unhurt, which testifies to the benevolence of both our guardian angels on duty that day. He had been returning from a courier flight to the Middle East. To relieve the boredom of just stooging over hundreds of miles of ocean, he had detoured to Lampedusa to strafe shipping in the harbour beside the aerodrome. Pulling out from his last attack the wing of his Hurricane had hit a schooner, and he just staggered away amongst a storm of flak when we arrived on his back. He said his worst moment was when the tyre of his starboard wheel had been blown apart beneath his right foot, and he had no idea he was being attacked by a fighter until I pulled up alongside him. The Lieutenant very decently said that he had asked for trouble by attacking the harbour without orders; and we both had enormous strips ripped off us by the authorities, in my case for 'bloody awful' aircraft recognition. A check on my aircraft showed that the 20mm guns were, in fact, incorrectly harmonised well above the machine-guns, which had been the best of good luck for both of us."[6]

Strangely, another of those who participated in this patrol, Canadian Sgt Jerry Billing, provides a different – and probably slightly erroneous – account:

"Red Walker, Twitch Bolland, John Houlton and myself were flying low level, Walker leading just above the water, when Bolland screamed 'Break port, Jerry'. I stood on the rudder and pulled as hard as I could. The old Spit was juddering madly. Looking back, I could see bullet splashes just inside and below me. I pulled through a 360 degree turn, gaining height, and rolled inverted to see Twitch was shooting hell out of a Hurricane. The poor chap had mistaken us for Me109s and attacked. At the dispersal I thanked Twitch for saving me, however, he was not feeling well about the whole episode."[7]

While Sub Lt(A) Ernie Pratt was fortunate to survive this encounter, he was unfortunately killed in a flying accident while piloting a Spitfire on 19 January 1943. By early 1943, Wg Cdr Innes Westmacott had returned to Malta and was posted to Air HQ. Frustrated by inactivity, he requested permission to fly a Hurricane on night intruder sorties over Sicily, as he had done the previous year. Permission was granted and Hurricane BG766 was made serviceable. By late February, Westmacott had carried out three practice bombing sorties and a night-flying test in BG766 and on the night of the 22nd, armed with two 250-lb bombs, he set out for Sicily, noting: "Intruder sortie SE Sicily (1.35) nearly 10/10 cloud – bombed cement factory at Francofonte for want of anything better. Returned early, bad weather. Found out later that target was not Francofonte!" During the first two weeks of March he continued practice attacks in BG766[8], but these came to an abrupt halt when he was appointed to command the newly constructed airstrip at Safi on 20 March.

Ultimately, the island's Hurricanes were relegated a non-essential rôle and until well into 1943 were being used to ferry pilots on leave to Tripoli. One such flight was undertaken by Flt Lt Hal Knight and Flt Sgt Jerry Billing, as the latter recalled after he had been shot down in March:

> "For my wounds I was given one week's leave and a Hurricane to fly to Tripoli. Old Knight was to accompany me [in another Hurricane]. On arriving at Castel Benito aerodrome, Knight called me over and gestured to where a Lodestar was readying for take-off. 'Let's ask the old chap over there if he is going to Cairo. Maybe we can hitch a ride'. He was an old pukka type AVM – switch and all – named Saul [Air Vice-Marshal R.E. Saul]. 'Of course lads, hop in, we're leaving swiftly'. Old Saul gave us oranges to eat and acted a very fine host."[9]

The two Hurricanes remained at Castel Benito and, after a few adventures, both Knight and Billing returned to Malta aboard a Dakota. Eventually, after further such one-way ferry flights, few airworthy Hurricanes remained on the island. One of these, BG770, was finally written off when it undershot while landing at Takali on 29 June, possibly the last Hurricane accident to occur on the island. Another exception was Air Vice-Marshal Park's personal machine (OK-2) which he flew to La Marsa near Tunis, via Pantelleria, for a meeting with Air Marshal Sir Arthur Tedder, AOC-in-C RAF Mediterranean and Middle East, in August 1943. When Park finally left Malta in January 1944, he left behind his beloved OK-2. Its ultimate fate is unknown[10].

* * *

Today, the Aviation Museum Association located at the former RAF Station at Takali (Ta'Qali) is rebuilding Hurricane II Z3055, the engine and cockpit area of which were salvaged in 1995 from the sea off Malta's south coast where it had crashed on 4 July 1941 with the loss of its pilot, Sgt Tom Hackston of 46 Squadron (see Chapter VII). When completed, it will serve as a fitting memorial to a venerable warhorse and all who flew it and kept it flying (see Appendix VI).

APPENDIX I

ROLL OF HONOUR 1940-42
Hurricane and Fulmar Pilots

Propositi Insula Tenax Tenaces Viros Commemorat
An Island Resolute of Purpose Remembers Resolute Men
(Latin epigram on the Malta Memorial, Valetta)

16/7/40:	Flt Lt Peter G. KEEBLE	Fighter Flight	Hurricane P2623
15/8/40:	Sgt Roy O'DONNELL	418 Flight	Hurricane N2716
26/11/40:	Sgt Dennis K. ASHTON	261 Squadron	Hurricane N2701
11/1/41:	Sgt William J. TIMMS	261 Squadron	Hurricane N2622
18/1/41:	Sub Lt(A) Arthur S. GRIFFITH RN	806 Squadrn FAA	Fulmar
19/1/41:	Sgt Eric N. KELSEY	261 Squadron	Hurricane P2629
30/1/41:	Plt Off Ian R. CURRIE	261 Squadron	(non-flying)
12/2/41:	Flt Lt Gerald WATSON	261 Squadron	Hurricane N2715
25/2/41:	Flg Off John J. WALSH (Canadian)	261 Squadron	Hurricane V7346
26/2/41:	Flg Off Frederic F. TAYLOR DFC	261 Squadron	Hurricane V7671
	Plt Off Charles E. LANGDON (New Zealander)	261 Squadron	Hurricane V7474
	Plt Off Philip J. KEARSEY	261 Squadron	Hurricane V7121
2/3/41:	Lt(A) William L. LeC. BARNES DSC RN	806 Squadron FAA	(non-flying)
5/3/41:	Sgt Charles W. McDOUGAL	261 Squadron	Hurricane V7102
22/3/41:	Flg Off James H.T. FOXTON	261 Squadron	Hurricane P2653
	Plt Off Dennis F. KNIGHT	261 Squadron	Hurricane V7358
	Flg Off John S. SOUTHWELL	261 Squadron	Hurricane V7799
	Plt Off Thomas B. GARLAND	261 Squadron	Hurricane V7493
	Sgt Richard A. SPYER	261 Squadron	Hurricane V7672
11/4/41:	Plt Off Peter KENNETT	261 Squadron	Hurricane Z3036
	Sgt Peter H. WAGHORN	261 Squadron	Hurricane Z2904
23/4/41:	Flg Off Henri F. AUGER RCAF (Canadian)	261 Squadron	Hurricane Z3032
2/5/41:	Sgt Raymond OTTEY	261 Squadron	Hurricane Z3054
7/5/41:	Sgt Henry H. JENNINGS	261 Squadron	Hurricane V7365
13/5/41:	Plt Off Peter J.A. THOMPSON	261 Squadron	Hurricane V7115
14/5/41:	Plt Off Claud E. HAMILTON	185 Squadron	Hurricane Z2901
15/5/41:	Sgt Ernest V. WYNNE	185 Squadron	Hurricane Z3035
11/6/41:	Flt Lt Norman W. BURNETT	46 Squadron	Hurricane Z2480
12/6/41:	Plt Off Rioch H. McK. MUNRO (Rhodesian)	249 Squadron	Hurricane Z4043
	Sgt Norman McD. WALKER	46 Squadron	Hurricane Z2900
18/6/41:	Sgt Alexander LIVINGSTON	249 Squadron	Hurricane Z4058
4/7/41:	Sgt Thomas HACKSTON	126 Squadron	Hurricane Z3055
17/7/41:	Sgt Maurice GUEST	249 Squadron	Hurricane Z2818
19/7/41:	Flt Sgt John D. McCRACKEN	126 Squadron	Hurricane BV171
26/8/41:	Sgt John F.E. MALTBY	126 Squadron	Hurricane Z3498
4/9/41:	Plt Off George V. SMITH	249 Squadron	Hurricane Z3056
	Sgt James C. KIMBERLEY	249 Squadron	Hurricane Z3521
29/9/41:	Plt Off Donald W. LINTERN	185 Squadron	Hurricane Z2514
1/10/41:	Sqn Ldr Peter W.O. MOULD DFC+	185 Squadron	Hurricane Z5265
4/10/41:	Plt Off Peter J.B. VEITCH	185 Squadron	Hurricane Z2518
14/10/41:	Plt Off David U. BARNWELL DFC	MNFU	Hurricane Z3512
25/10/41:	Sgt Ernest G. KNIGHT	185 Squadron	Hurricane Z3456
9/11/41:	Flg Off Graham G. BAILEY	185 Squadron	Hurricane BD835
12/11/41:	Wg Cdr Mark H. BROWN DFC+ (Canadian)	Takali	Hurricane Z2397
21/11/41:	Flt Sgt Richard A. COUSENS	185 Squadron	Hurricane Z2813
19/12/41:	Plt Off Edward E. STEELE (American)	126 Squadron	Hurricane Z3764
20/12/41:	Flg Off Brian M. CAVAN	249 Squadron	Hurricane BV162
	Sgt Howard MOREN	249 Squadron	Hurricane Z2418
21/12/41:	Flt Sgt Brian HAYES	185 Squadron	Hurricane Z2823
22/12/41:	Flg Off Robert H. MATTHEWS	249 Squadron	Hurricane BV156
24/12/41:	Flt Sgt Francis R. EMERY	126 Squadron	Hurricane BD830

29/12/41:	Plt Off Merton C. BLANCHARD RCAF (American)	242 Squadron	Hurricane BE343
	Flt Sgt Alfred J. FORTH	185 Squadron	Hurricane Z4943
	Flt Lt Sydney BRANDT	249 Squadron	Hurricane BD834
	Flt Sgt Roy W. LAWSON	249 Squadron	Hurricane Z2829
22/1/42:	Sgt Donald T. NEALE	242 Squadron	Hurricane BE346
25/1/42:	Plt Off John K. RUSSELL	126 Squadron	Hurricane Z2827
27/1/42:	Plt Off Alexander S. MACKIE	1435 Flight	Hurricane Z3571
4/2/42:	Plt Off John G.K. HULBERT	249 Squadron	Hurricane Z4003
	Sgt Hugh J. McDOWALL	249 Squadron	Hurricane Z4016
	Plt Off Basil W. MAIN (Canadian)	126 Squadron	Hurricane BV167
9/2/42:	Plt Off James R.A. STUART	249 Squadron	Hurricane Z5326
12/2/42:	Flt Lt George ALLEN	605 Squadron	Hurricane Z2527
15/2/42:	Plt Off Peter LOWE	605 Squadron	Hurricane BG755
22/2/42:	Sqn Ldr Ronald I. CHAFFE	185 Squadron	Hurricane Z3452
23/2/42:	Plt Off Thady B. MACNAMARA	242 Squadron	(non-flying)
24/2/42:	Plt Off Donald A. TEDFORD (American)	126 Squadron	Hurricane BG771
1/3/42:	Plt Off James D. TEW Jr (American)	242 Squadron	Hurricane Z2824
	Flt Sgt Ray V. HARVEY RCAF (Canadian)	242 Squadron	Hurricane Z4002
5/3/42:	Plt Off Marcus W.T. KIDSON	242 Squadron	Hurricane Z2402
10/3/42:	Sgt John M. MAYALL RAAF (Australian)	126 Squadron	Hurricane Z5140
18/3/42:	Sgt George F.R. MULLOY	126 Squadron	Hurricane Z5213
21/3/42:	Flt Lt Cecil H. BAKER	126 Squadron	(non-flying)
	Plt Off William C. HOLLIS HALLETT	126 Squadron	(non-flying)
	Plt Off Edward E. STREETS (American)	126 Squadron	(non-flying)
22/3/42:	Plt Off Philip McL. ALLARDICE	185 Squadron	Hurricane BG711
31/3/42:	Plt Off Archibald C. STEELE	185 Squadron	Hurricane Z5302
21/4/42:	Sgt John K. FULLALOVE	229 Squadron	Hurricane BN278
22/4/42:	Plt Off Oliver O. ORMROD DFC	185 Squadron	Hurricane Z4011
25/4/42:	Wt Off Douglas F. CORFE	229 Squadron	Hurricane BE708
	Flt Sgt Lucien D. BROOKS RCAF (Canadian)	229 Squadron	Hurricane BN182
27/4/42:	Plt Off James E. WOOD	1435 Flight	Hurricane BE347
28/4/42:	Plt Off John W.S. FLETCHER RCAF (Canadian)	185 Squadron	Hurricane Z2698
	Plt Off Thomas G. FOLEY RCAF (Canadian)	229 Squadron	Hurricane BE555
6/5/42:	Sgt Robert J. LEES	229 Squadron	Hurricane BN181
18/5/42:	Sgt James R. PENDLEBURY	229 Squadron	Hurricane BN362
23/7/42:	Plt Off David W. KENT RCAF (Canadian)	185 Squadron	Hurricane Z2825

APPENDIX II

COMBAT CLAIMS & CREDITS

Hurricanes, Gladiators and Fulmars 1940-1942

Date	Name	Squadron	Serial No	Claim(s)
11/6/40:	Flg Off J.L. Waters	F/Flt	Glad N5520	SM79bis (credited as probable)
	Flg Off W.J. Woods	F/Flt	Glad N5519	MC200 probable
13/6/40:	Flg Off J.L. Waters	F/Flt	Glad N5520	SM79bis (credited as probable)
22/6/40:	Flt Lt G. Burges	F/Flt	Glad N5519	SM79bis
23/6/40:	Flt Lt G. Burges	F/Flt	Glad N5519	MC200
27/6/40:	Flg Off W.J. Woods	F/Flt	Glad	SM79bis
3/7/40:	Flg Off J.L. Waters	F/Flt	P2614	SM79bis
7/7/40:	Flg Off W.J. Woods	F/Flt	P2653	SM79bis
9/7/40:	Flt Lt G. Burges	F/Flt	P2645	SM79bis
10/7/40:	Flg Off W.J. Woods	F/Flt	P2653	SM79bis
	Flg Off F.F. Taylor	F/Flt	P2645	SM79bis
16/7/40:	Flt Lt P.G. Keeble	F/Flt	P2623	CR42 (Keeble also KiA)

31/7/40:	Flg Off W.J. Woods	F/Flt	Glad N5520	CR42
5/8/40:	Plt Off.T. Balmforth	F/Flt	N2484	SM79 probable
6/8/40:	Fighter Flight absorbed into 418 Flight			
13-14/8/40: (night)	Plt Off R.H. Barber	418 Flt	N2715	SM79bis
16/8/40:	261 Squadron formed from Fighter Flight and 418 Flight			
24/8/40:	Flg Off F.F. Taylor	261		CR42
	Sgt R.J. Hyde	261	N2715	CR42 (apparently later reduced to probable)
2/9/40:	Sgt H.W. Ayre	261	N2715	CR42
	Sgt F.N. Robertson	261	P2653	MC200 probable (apparently credited as destroyed)
5/9/40:	Flt Lt J. Greenhalgh	261		CR42
7/9/40:	Flt Lt R.N. Lambert	261		
	Flt Lt. J. Greenhalgh	261		SM79bis
	Plt Off R.H. Barber	261	N2622	
17/9/40:	Plt Off R.H. Barber	261	N2484	Ju87
	Sgt H.W. Ayre	261	P3731	Ju87
	Flg Off W.J. Woods	261		CR42
18/9/40:	Plt Off T. Balmforth	261	N2715	CR42
25/9/40:	Flg Off F.F. Taylor	261		CR42
	Sgt F.N. Robertson	261	N2484	CR42 probable
4/10/40:	Sgt R.J. Hyde	261	N2715	MC200
8-9/10/40: (night)	Flg Off F.F. Taylor	261		SM79bis

10/10/40: Air HQ issued a statement which credited Malta's fighters with the destruction of 22 enemy aircraft (nine SM79bis, seven CR42, four MC200 and two Ju87) and eight probables (five SM79bis, two CR42 and one MC200); these figures do not tally with those listed above.

16/10/40:	Flg Off J.L. Waters	261	P2645	SM79bis
27/10/40:	Flg Off F.F. Taylor	261		MC200 probable
2/11/40:	Flt Lt G. Burges	261	Glad N5520	CR42 probable
	(Plt Off A.G. McAdam)	261		MC200
	Unknown pilot	261		MC200 probable
12/11/40:	Unknown pilot	261		MC200
23/11/40:	Flt Lt G. Burges	261	N2622	SM79bis
	Sgt F.N. Robertson	261	V7474	CR42 probable
	Sgt R.J. Hyde	261	N2672	CR42 (apparently later reduced to probable)
26/11/40:	Sgt D.K. Ashton	261	N2701	CR42 (Ashton also KiA)
28/11/40:	Flt Lt J. Greenhalgh	261		CR42
	Sgt F.N. Robertson	261	V7346	SM79
	Unknown pilot	261		CR42

Air HQ stated that fighters were credited with nine victories plus 5 probables during November; therefore one or two missing from above list.

18-19/12/40: (night)	Sgt F.N. Robertson	261	P3731	SM79bis

At the end of the year Air HQ announced that fighters had been credited with 30 victories (13 SM79bis, nine CR42, six MC200 and two Ju87) plus 11 probables; again, the tallies vary with the above list and it seems that some aircraft initially claimed as probables were upgraded to destroyed, and others claimed destroyed were downgraded to probable.

9/1/41:	Flt Lt J.A.F. MacLachlan	261	V7474	2 MC200
	Flt Lt F.F. Taylor	261		2 MC200
16/1/41:	Lt(A) W.LeC. Barnes	806	Fulmar	Ju88, Ju88 probable
	Sub Lt(A) G.A. Hogg	806	Fulmar	2 Ju88

	Sub Lt(A) S.G. Orr	806	Fulmar N1884	Ju88
	Fulmars operating from Hal Far			
18/1/41:	Flt Lt G. Burges	261	P3731	Ju87
	Flg Off F.F. Taylor	261		2 Ju87
	Plt Off C.E. Hamilton	261		Ju87
	Sgt C.S. Bamberger	261	P2629	Ju87
	Sub Lt(A) A.J. Sewell	806	Fulmar	Ju87
	Sub Lt(A) A.S. Griffith	806	Fulmar	MC200 (Griffith also KiA)
19/1/41:	Sgt J.H. Pickering	261	V7548	Ju87 probable, Ju88 probable
	Flt Lt J.A.F. MacLachlan	261	V7546	2 Ju87
	Flt Lt G. Burges	261	P3730	2 Ju87
	Plt Off A.G. McAdam	261		Ju87
	Sgt C.S. Bamberger	261	V7370	Ju87
	Sgt H.W. Ayre	261	V7474	Ju87
	Sgt F.N. Robertson	261	V7474	Ju87, CR42 probable
	Flt Lt J.A.F. MacLachlan	261	V7545	Z506B, Ju87
	Flt Lt G. Burges	261	V7546	Ju88 probable (apparently upgraded to confirmed)
	Sgt F.N. Robertson	261	P3731	CR42, CR42 probable
	Sgt H.W. Ayre	261	V7474	Ju87 probable
	(Plt Off C.E. Hamilton)	261		Ju87 probable

Air HQ announced that fighters had shot down nine Ju87, two Ju88, one CR42 and one Z506B during the course of the day's operations, taking the score for the 16th, 18th and 19th to 24 for the fighters and 16 for the guns.

23/1/41:	Plt Off R.H. Barber	261	V7072	SM79 probable
24/1/41:	Sub Lt(A) A.J. Sewell	806	Gladiator	Ju88
	Unknown pilot ⎫	261		
	Unknown pilot ⎭	261		Z506B
26/1/41:	Unknown pilot ⎫	261		
	Unknown pilot ⎭	261		Ju88
1/2/41:	Sgt F.N. Robertson	261	V7116	CR42
	Flt Lt C.D. Whittingham	261		CR42
	Plt Off J. Pain	261	P3731	Ju88 (claimed as damaged, crashed Sicily)
4/2/41:	Sgt F.N. Robertson	261	V7116	Ju88
	Plt Off R.H. Barber	261	V7671	Ju88 probable
	Sub Lt(A) S.G. Orr ⎫	806	Fulmar N1884	
	Sub Lt(A) J. Roberts ⎭	806	Fulmar	Ju88 (claimed as Do17)
8-9/2/41: (night)	Flt Lt J.A.F. MacLachlan	261	V7671	He111 (claimed as Ju88), Ju88

10/2/41:   Air HQ's latest summary gave the fighters credit, since the outbreak of hostilities, for the destruction of 63 enemy aircraft (15 Ju87, 13 CR42, 12 Ju88, 11 SM79bis, ten MC200, two Z506B), plus 19 probables (seven SM79bis, four CR42, three Ju87, three MC200 and two Ju88).

12/2/41:	Plt Off J. Pain	261	P3731	Bf109 probable
21/2/41:	Plt Off C.E. Hamilton	261		Bf110 (claimed as Do215)
	Unknown pilots	261		Bf110 (claimed as Do215)
25/2/41:	Flt Lt C.D. Whittingham	261		Bf110 (claimed as Do215)
	Plt Off C.E. Hamilton	261		Bf110 (claimed as Do215)
	Plt Off R.H. Barber	261	V7102	Bf110 (claimed as Do215)
26/2/41:	Plt Off H.W. Eliot	261		Ju87, Ju87 probable
	Flg Off J.H.T. Foxton	261		Ju87, Ju87 probable
	Flt Lt F.F. Taylor	261	V7671	Ju87 probable (Taylor also KiA)
	Plt Off J. Pain	261	V7114	Bf110 probable (claimed as Do17)
	Unknown pilot	261		Bf110 probable (claimed as Do17)
5/3/41:	Sgt C.W. McDougal	261	V7102	Ju87 (McDougal also KiA)
	Sgt F.N. Robertson	261	V7116	Ju88, Bf109

Date	Pilot	Squadron	Serial	Claim
	Plt Off J. Pain ⎱	261	P2645	
	Plt Off A.J. Rippon ⎰	261		Bf110
	Sgt H.W. Ayre ⎱	261	P3731	
	Plt Off J. Pain ⎱	261	P2645	Bf110
	AA ⎰			
	Plt Off A.J. Rippon	261		Ju87
	Sgt H.W. Ayre	261	P3731	Ju88
9-10/3/41: (night)	Plt Off A.J. Rippon	261		Bf110
18/3/41:	Plt Off J. Pain	261	P3731	CR42, CR42 probable
22/3/41:	Plt Off D.M. Whitney	261	V7797	Bf109
28/3/41:	Sqn Ldr R.N. Lambert	261		Ju87
	Flt Lt S.R. Peacock-Edwards	261	V7115	Ju87
	Plt Off A.J. Rippon	261		2 Ju87
	Plt Off D.M. Whitney	261	V7561	Ju87
	Sgt R.J. Hyde	261	V7370	Ju87
	Sgt F.N. Robertson	261	V7495	2 Ju87
10/4/41:	Sgt A.H. Deacon	261	Z3978	Bf109
	Plt Off P. Kennett ⎱	261	Z3036	Ju88 (Kennett also KiA)
	Sgt P.H. Waghorn ⎰	261	Z2094	(Waghorn also KiA)
11-12/4/41: (night)	Plt Off C.E. Hamilton	261		Ju87
13/4/41:	Flg Off E.M. Mason	261/274	Z2828	Bf109
17-18/4/41: (night)	Unknown pilot	261		Bf110 (claimed as damaged, but FTR)
20/4/41:	Flg Off C.J. Laubscher	261/274		2 CR42
	Plt Off J. Pain	261	Z3032	CR42, CR42 probable
28/4/41:	Flg Off I.B. Westmacott	261	Z3063	Bf109
29/4/41:	Plt Off A.J. Rippon ⎱	261		Ju88
	Plt Off J.E. Hall ⎰	261	Z3034	
4/5/41:	Flt Lt C.G.StD. Jeffries ⎱	261	Z3060	
	Plt Off J.E. Hall	261	Z2904	Ju88
	Sgt A.W. Jolly ⎰	261		
6/5/41:	Flg Off I.B. Westmacott	261	Z3035	He111 probable
6-7/5/41: (night)	Sqn Ldr C.D. Whittingham	261		Ju88, He111 probable
9/5/41:	Flg Off C.J. Laubscher ⎱	261/274		Ju87
	Sgt P.L. Jordan ⎰	261		
	Plt Off C.E. Hamilton ⎱	261		Ju87
	Sgt L. Davies ⎰	261	Z4261	
15/5/41:	Plt Off J. Pain	261	Z4046	SM79bis (claimed as He111)
3/6/41	Sqn Ldr R.A. Barton	249	Z4043	SM79bis
5-6/6/41: (night)	Flt Lt N.P.W. Hancock	185		He111 probable
7-8/6/41: (night)	Sqn Ldr R.A. Barton	249	Z3063	BR20M
	Flg Off H.J.S. Beazley ⎱	249		BR20M probable
	Plt Off G.C.C. Palliser ⎰	249	Z4028	
9/6/41:	Sgt A. Livingston	249		SM79bis
	Sgt D.C.H. Rex	249	Z4087	SM79bis

10/6/41: At close of play, Air HQ assessed that the fighters (excluding Beaufighters) had destroyed at least 100 enemy aircraft during the first year of hostilities, with 43 probables and 37 damaged, which included 36-24-10 since 10/2/41.

11/6/41:	Sqn Ldr A.C. Rabagliati	46	Z2680
	Flg Off P.R. McGregor	46	SM79bis
	Sgt N.McD. Walker	46	
	Plt Off J.M.C. Grant	46	
12/6/41:	Flt Lt T.F. Neil	249	Z2397	MC200 (claimed as Bf109)
	Sgt A. Livingston	249		MC200 probable
	Flt Sgt F.A. Etchells	249	Z506B	
	Plt Off P. Rathie	46	
	Sgt H.J. Johnston	46	MC200
	Flt Lt P.W. Lefevre	46		MC200
	Sqn Ldr A.C. Rabagliati	46	Z2491	CR42
	Sgt T. Hackston	46		MC200 probable
	Sgt B.W. Main	46		Z506B, CR42
18/6/41:	Plt Off G.C.C. Palliser	249	Z4041	MC200
	Sgt F.G. Sheppard	249	Z4070	
22/6/41:	Sqn Ldr A.C. Rabagliati	46	Z2526	MC200
25/6/41:	Sqn Ldr A.C. Rabagliati	46	Z2481	SM79 probable
	Plt Off A.G.S. Anderson	46		MC200
	Sgt B.W. Main	46		MC200 probable
	Sgt T. Hackston	46		MC200
	Sgt W.E. Copp	46		MC200 probable
27/6/41:	Sqn Ldr A.C. Rabagliati	46	Z2593	MC200
	Sgt W.E. Copp	46		MC200
	Plt Off A.G.S. Anderson	46		MC200
	Plt Off L.G. Barnes	46		2 MC200
	Sgt A.W. Jolly	46		MC200
30/6/41:	Flg Off J.M.V. Carpenter	46		MC200
	Sgt A.S. Mackie	46		MC200
4/7/41:	Flt Lt C.G.StD. Jeffries	185	Z3495	MC200
	Sgt A.W. Jolly	185		MC200
6-7/7/41: (night)	Sub Lt(A) A.M. Tritton	INFU		BR20M
8-9/7/41: (night)	Flg Off E. Cassidy	249		SM79bis (claimed as BR20)
11/7/41:	Sqn Ldr P.W.O. Mould	185	Z3495	MC200 probable
	Flt Lt C.G.StD. Jeffries	185	Z4946	MC200 probable
	Flt Lt S.A.D. Pike	185		MC200 probable
16-17/7/41: (night)	Sub Lt(A) A.M. Tritton	INFU		BR20M
17/7/41:	Sqn Ldr R.A. Barton	249	Z3262	MC200
	Plt Off P.G. Leggett	249		MC200
25/7/41:	Plt Off P.D. Thompson	185	Z3456	
	Sgt A.J. Forth	185	BV162	SM79bis
	Plt Off D.U. Barnwell	185		
	Plt Off G.G. Bailey	185	Z3522	
	Sgt J.R.R. Alderson	185	Z4946	
	Sgt R.J.F. Ellis	185		
	Sgt R.A. Branson	185		BR20M
	Sgt W.E. Nurse	185	Z2394	
	Sgt T.J.M. Ream	185	Z2592	
	Flt Lt D.W.A. Stones	249	Z2481	
	Sqn Ldr R.A. Barton	249	Z3492	MC200
	Plt Off F.C. Hill	249		MC200
	Plt Off R.H. Matthews	249	Z2418	MC200
26/7/41:	Plt Off P.D. Thompson	185	Z3456	MC200
	Sgt A.H. Haley	126		2 MC200

27/7/41:	Flt Lt N.P.W. Hancock ⎱	185	Z2982	SM79bis
	Sgt R.A. Cousens ⎰	185	Z4942	
	Plt Off P.D. Thompson ⎱	185	Z3456	SM79bis
	Sgt A.J. Forth ⎰	185		

Air HQ credited the fighters with 21-5-9 for July, which included 4-2-0 during the attack on Syracuse seaplane base on 9 July.

5-6/8/41:	Flg Off E. Cassidy	MNFU		BR20M
(night)	Plt Off D.U. Barnwell	MNFU		2 BR20M
9/8/41:	Sqn Ldr A.C. Rabagliati	126	Z3462	Z506B
11-12/8/41:	Sqn Ldr G.ff. Powell-Sheddon	MNFU		BR20M
(night)				
17/8/41:	Plt Off J.G.K. Hulbert ⎱	249		SM79bis
	Sgt D.C.H. Rex ⎰	249		
19/8/41:	Flt Lt P.W. Lefevre	126	Z4941	MC200
	Plt Off H.P. Lardner-Burke	126	DG615	2 MC200
	Sgt A.N.C. MacGregor	126		MC200 probable
26/8/41:	Sqn Ldr A.C. Rabagliati	126	V7103	MC200
	Plt Off H.P. Lardner-Burke	126	Z2825	MC200
	Sgt A.N.C. MacGregor	126		MC200
	Plt Off E. Dickinson	126		MC200
	Sgt W.D. Greenhalgh	126		MC200 probable
26-27/8/41:	Sqn Ldr G.ff. Powell-Sheddon ⎱	MNFU		2 BR20M probable
(night)	Flt Lt E. Cassidy ⎰			
2-3/9/41:	PO(A) A.W. Sabey	INFU		BR20M
(night)				
4/9/41:	Sqn Ldr A.C. Rabagliati	126	Z4941	MC200
	Flt Lt P.W. Lefevre	126		MC200
	Flg Off J.M.V. Carpenter	126		MC200
	Plt Off H.P. Lardner-Burke	126	Z3512	MC200
	Plt Off J.K. Russell	126		MC200
	Plt Off C.A. Blackburn	126		MC200 probable
	Sgt A.N.C. MacGregor	126		MC200 probable
	Flt Lt C.G.StD. Jeffries ⎱	185	Z3562	MC200
	Plt Off G.M. Oliver ⎰	185		
	Sqn Ldr R.A. Barton	249	Z2794	MC200 probable
	Sgt D. Owen	249		MC200
	Sgt J.G. Parker	249		MC200
4-5/9/41:	Plt Off D.U. Barnwell ⎱	MNFU	Z2961	Z1007bis
(night)	Flt Lt D.W.A. Stones ⎰	MNFU	Z3574	
8-9/9/41:	Plt Off D.U. Barnwell	MNFU	Z2680	Z1007bis
(night)				
30/9/41:	Flt Lt C.G.StD. Jeffries	185	BD702	MC202 probable
14/10/41:	Plt Off D.U. Barnwell	MNFU	Z3512	MC202 probable (Barnwell also KiA)
19/10/41:	Sqn Ldr R.A. Barton ⎱	249	Z3155	SM81
	Plt Off G.C.C. Palliser ⎰	249	Z4005	
20/10/41:	Sgt P. Lillywhite	185		SM81
25/10/41:	Flg Off G.G. Bailey ⎱	185		
	Plt Off G.M. Oliver ⎰	185		Z1007bis probable
	Sgt W.E. Nurse ⎰	185		
	Sgt T.H. Bates ⎰	185		
	Sgt C.L. Hunton	185		MC202 probable (crashed)
31/10-	Sgt A.S. Mackie	MNFU		BR20M
1/11/41:				
(night)				

8/11/41:	Flt Lt J.M.V. Carpenter	126		MC202
	Sgt A.H. Haley	126	Z3033	MC202 (by collision)
	Plt Off H.P. Lardner-Burke	126	BD789	MC202
	Sgt T.C. Worrall	126		MC202 probable
9/11/41:	Flg Off G.G. Bailey	185	BD835	SM79bis probable (Bailey also KiA)
12/11/41:	Wg Cdr A.C. Rabagliati	Takali Wg	Z4005	Ju87
	Flt Lt J.M.V. Carpenter	126		MC202
22/11/41:	Flt Lt J.M.V. Carpenter	126		MC202
	Plt Off B.W. Main	126		2 MC202 probable
	Sqn Ldr R.A. Barton	249	Z3746	MC202
	Flg Off C.C.H. Davis	249		MC202
	Sgt A.T. Branch ⎱	249	BV156	MC202 probable
	Flg Off C.C.H. Davis ⎰	249		
18/12/41:	Plt Off P.McL. Allardice⎱	185	BD702	
	Sgt B. Hayes	185	Z2823	SM79bis
	Plt Off G.M. Oliver	185	Z3758	
	Sgt W.E. Nurse ⎰	185	Z4943	
19/12/41:	Sqn Ldr E.M. Mortimer-Rose	249		Ju88
	Plt Off E.E. Steele	126	Z3764	Ju88 probable (Steele also KiA)
20/12/41:	Plt Off G.C.C. Palliser	249	Z2904	Ju88
	Sgt H. Moren	249	Z2418	Ju88 probable
	Flg Off J.T. Crossey	249		MC202 probable
21/12/41:	Wg Cdr A.C. Rabagliati	Takali Wg	Z4005	MC202
	Flg Off C.C.H. Davis	249		MC202 probable
24/12/41:	Sqn Ldr E.M. Mortimer-Rose ⎱	249		Ju88
	Plt Off G.C.C. Palliser ⎰	249	Z2904	
	Flg Off J.T. Crossey ⎱	249		
	Flt Sgt F.A. Etchells	249		Ju88
	Plt Off G.C.C. Palliser ⎰	249	Z2904	
	Plt Off H.H. Moon	249	Z2546	Ju88 probable
27/12/41:	Flt Lt J.M.V. Carpenter⎱	126		Ju88
	Sgt R. Rist ⎰	249		
	Plt Off B.W. Main	126	Bf109	
27-28/12/41:	Flg Off D. Winton	1435 Flt	Z3570	Ju88
(night)				
29/12/41:	Flt Lt P.D. Thompson	185	Z5326	Bf109
	Flg Off R.M. Lloyd	185	Z5155	Bf109
30/12/41:	Wg Cdr W.A.J. Satchell	Takali Wg	Z3766	Ju88
	Sgt D.C.H. Rex	249		Ju88
	Sgt H.J. McDowall	249		Ju88 probable

By the end of 1941 it was assessed that the fighters had destroyed between 184-196 enemy aircraft.

2/1/42:	Sgt J.W. Sutherland	185		Bf109 probable
3/1/42:	Plt Off J.K. Russell⎱	126		
	Plt Off E.E. Streets	126		Ju88
	Sgt G.E. Horricks	185	Z5158	
	Sgt R.J.F. Ellis ⎰	185	Z2982	
	Plt Off H.M. Coffin ⎱	126		
	Plt Off J.G.K. Hulbert	249		
	Sgt G.E. Horricks	185	Z5158	Ju88 probable
	Sgt D.J. Howe ⎰	605		
19/1/42:	Sgt R.V. Harvey	242	LE-R	Bf109 probable
	Flg Off J.K. Kay ⎱	126		Ju88
	Plt Off B.W. Main ⎰	126		
22/1/42:	Flt Lt N.L.D. Kemp ⎱	126	BG756	Bf109 probable
	Sgt H. Hale ⎰	126	BG787	

	Plt Off B.W. Main ⎫	126	
	Plt Off J.M.S. Crichton ⎬	126	Z2481	Ju88
	Flg Off C.C.H. Davis ⎪	249	
	Plt Off D.A. Tedford ⎭	249	
	Sgt J.L. Boyd	242	LE-P	Ju88 probable
24/1/42:	Sgt G.E. Horricks ⎫	185	BD704	
	Plt Off H.H. Moon ⎬	249	DG612	Ju88
	Sgt A.W. Jolly ⎭	185	
24-25/1/42: (night)	Flg Off F.R.W. Palmer	1435 Flt		Ju88
25/1/42:	Flt Lt P.D. Thompson	185	Z5147	Ju88 probable
27-28/1/42:	Sgt J.E. Wood	1435 Flt		Ju88
	Plt Off J.C.M. Grant	1435 Flt		t/e biplane
2-3/2/42: (night)	Flg Off A.R.F. Thompson	1435 Flt	Z506B	
4/2/42:	Flt Lt J.M.V. Carpenter	126		Ju88
11/2/42:	Wg Cdr A.C. Rabagliati ⎫	Takali Wg	Z4005	
	Plt Off H.M. Coffin ⎬	126		Ju88
	Plt Off A.N.C. MacGregor ⎭	126	
12/2/42:	Plt Off P. Wigley ⎫	605	Z3757	
	Plt Off H.C. Lester ⎪	605	UP-P	
	Plt Off J.I. McKay ⎬	605	BG698	Ju88
	Sqn Ldr S.E. Andrews ⎪	605	Z5140	
	Plt Off O.O. Ormrod ⎭	605	BE351	
15/2/42:	Wg Cdr W.A.J. Satchell	Takali Wg	BE351	Bf109
	Wg Cdr A.C. Rabagliati	Takali Wg	Z4005	Bf109
20/2/42:	Plt Off O.O. Ormrod ⎫	185		
	Sgt C.L. Hunton ⎬	185	Z2840	Ju88
	Plt Off R.F. Noble ⎪	185	BG756	
	Sgt R.J.F. Ellis ⎭	185	Z5140	
21/2/42:	Flg Off P. Rathie ⎫	1435 Flt		
	Sgt J.E. Wood ⎬	1435 Flt		Ju88 probable
	Flg Off D. Winton ⎪	1435 Flt	Z4002	
	Sgt R.J. Fowler ⎭	1435 Flt		
22/2/42:	Flt Sgt J.W. Sutherland	185	BD826	Bf109
23/2/42:	Sgt G.E. Horricks	185	Z5140	Bf109
	Flt Lt R.M. Lloyd	185	BG769	Ju88 probable
	Sgt A.C. Steele	185	Z4011	Bf109
	Sgt J.L. Boyd	185	LE-P	Bf109
27/2/42:	Plt Off O.O. Ormrod	185	Z2414	Ju88
1/3/42:	Flt Lt D.W.A. Stones	605	UP-D	Ju88 probable (both Ju88s, from 8/KG77, crashed on
	Plt Off P. Wigley ⎫	605	Z5149	Ju88 probable returning to Sicily
	Flt Sgt D.J. Howe ⎭	605	Z3756	and were total losses.)
	Plt Off H.C. Lester	605		Bf109
4/3/42:	Plt Off O.O. Ormrod	605	Z2414	Bf109
4-5/3/42: (night)	Sgt J.E. Wood	1435 Flt		Ju88
6/3/42:	Flt Lt D.W.A. Stones	605	BG770	Bf109
7-8/3/42: (night)	Sqn Ldr I.B. Westmacott ⎫	1435 Flt	BE402	Ju88
	Beaufighter ⎭		
9/3/42:	Flt Lt D.W.A. Stones	605	BG770	Bf109 probable
	Wg Cdr A.C. Rabagliati	Takali Wg	Z4005	Bf109 probable
	Sgt A.C. Steele	185		Bf109

	Flt Lt A.G. Anderson ⎫	126		Ju88
	Sgt G.R. Tweedale ⎭	185	UP-H	(claimed as damaged)
10/3/42:	Flt Lt E.H.C. Kee ⎫	242		
	Plt Off C.R. Morrison-Jones ⎬	242		Ju88 probable
	Sgt J.L. Boyd ⎭	242	HA-F	
15/3/42:	Wg Cdr W.A.J. Satchell	Takali Wg		Bf109
17/3/42:	Sgt A.C. Steele ⎫	185		
	Flt Sgt J.W. Sutherland ⎬	185		Ju88
	Bofors AA ⎭			
	Flt Sgt J.W. Sutherland	185		Bf109 probable
19/3/42:	242 and 605 Squadrons' operational pilots absorbed by 185 Squadron			
21/3/42:	Sqn Ldr E.M. Mortimer-Rose	185	Z2961	Bf110
	Plt Off P.McL. Allardice	185	BG711	Bf110
	Plt Off J. Beckett ⎫	185	Z2824	Bf110
	Sgt D.J. Robb ⎭	185	Z3767	
	Plt Off P. Wigley ⎫	185	BG770	Bf110
	Plt Off O.O. Ormrod ⎭	185	BG769	
23/3/42:	Sgt G.E. Horricks ⎫	185	GL-K	Ju88 probable
	Sgt D.E. Eastman ⎭	185	Z5118	
	Flt Lt K.A. Lawrence ⎫	185	Z3758	Ju88 (claimed as He111)
	Sgt C.E. Broad ⎭	185	BM905	
24/3/42:	Plt Off R.F. Noble ⎫	185	Z2961	Ju88 probable
	Flt Sgt J.W.S. Fletcher ⎭		Z3758	
25/3/42:	Sgt G.E. Horricks	185	BD704	Ju87 probable
	Plt Off O.O. Ormrod	185	BM905	Ju87 probable
	Plt Off P. Wigley ⎫	185	GL-S	Ju87
	Plt Off O.O. Ormrod ⎭	185	BM905	
	Sgt D.E. Eastman ⎫	185	HA-D	
	Sgt D.J. Robb ⎬	185	GL-C	Ju87 probable
	Sgt A.S. Wilson ⎭	185	HA-A	
26/3/42:	Sgt A.C. Steele	185	GL-P	Ju88
	Sgt A.P. Goldsmith	185	Z3993	Ju87 probable
1/4/42:	Flt Sgt J.W.S. Fletcher	185	GL-W	Ju88 probable, Ju87, Ju87 probable
	Sgt J.B. Pauley	229	HB-J	Ju87 probable
	Flt Sgt J.L. Boyd	185	BG756	Ju87 probable
	Plt Off J.I. McKay	185	GL-Z	Ju87 probable
	Plt Off J. Beckett ⎫	185	Z4942	
	Plt Off J.I. McKay ⎬	185	GL-Z	Ju88
	Spitfire ⎭			
2/4/42:	Plt Off H.A. Milburn	185		Ju88 probable
	Plt Off O.O. Ormrod	185	Z2698	Bf109 probable
	Plt Off P. Wigley	185	BE583	Ju87 probable
5/4/42:	Plt Off R.F. Noble ⎫	185	Z4942	
	Plt Off J.I. McKay ⎬	185	GL-Z	Ju88
	Flt Sgt J.L. Boyd ⎭	185	Z2698	
8/4/42:	Flt Sgt J.L. Boyd	185	Z5118	Ju88 probable
	Flt Sgt J.L. Boyd ⎫	185	Z5118	Ju88
	Spitfire ⎭			
9/4/42:	Plt Off J.I. McKay	185	GL-P	Ju88 probable
	Flt Sgt J.L. Boyd	185	BN118	Ju88 probable
10/4/42:	Flt Sgt G.E. Horricks	185	BD826	Bf109
	Plt Off O.O. Ormrod	185	BG756	Ju87 probable
20/4/42:	Flt Sgt G.R. Tweedale	185	Z4011	2 Ju88 probable
21/4/42:	Plt Off G.E. Horricks	185	BM905	Ju88 probable

22/4/42:	Plt Off P. Wigley	185	Z4942	Bf109 probable
23/4/42:	Flt Sgt G.R. Tweedale	185	Z2698	Ju87
25/4/42:	Flt Sgt W.G. Dodd	185	Z2396	Ju87 probable
	Flt Sgt G.R. Tweedale	185	Z2698	Bf109
	Plt Off R.F. Noble	185	Z2396	Bf109
	Plt Off J.W.S. Fletcher	185	Z2698	Ju88
28/4/42:	Plt Off J.I. McKay	185	Z2396	2 Ju87 probable
1-2/5/42: (night)	Sgt J.W. Yarra	185	HA-B	Ju88 probable
7/5/42:	Flt Sgt G.R. Tweedale	185	GL-L	Bf109
8/5/42:	Flt Sgt G.R. Tweedale	185	BV163	Bf109, Bf109 probable
	Flt Sgt J.L. Boyd ⎫	185	Z4942	Ju88
	Flt Sgt G.R. Tweedale ⎭	185	BV163	
	Flt Sgt W.G. Dodd	185	GL-L	MC202 probable

While no official figures were released, it would seem that the Hurricanes, Gladiators and Fulmars were credited with between 230 and 250 enemy aircraft destroyed, and at least 115 probables.

APPENDIX III

HURRICANES FOR MALTA

The reinforcement of the Middle East with Hurricanes had already begun just before the entry of Italy into the war, but initially these were not intended for Malta, the defence of the main Fleet base at Alexandria enjoying a higher priority.

On 6 June 1940, six Hurricanes were assembled at 10 MU at RAF Hullavington, together with a group of seven pilots (including one spare) under the command of Sqn Ldr C. Ryley. As related in Chapter I, two of these (P2614 and P2645) were eventually retained for service at Malta, having arrived on 21 June. In the meantime, orders had been issued by the Air Ministry for a dozen more Hurricanes and a similar number of Blenheims to be flown to the Middle East via Malta as further reinforcements, before the route across France was lost. The Hurricanes were drawn from stocks held at 10 MU (two), 20 MU (six) and 27 MU (four), while the pilots came from 4 Ferry Pilots' Pool at RAF Kemble. One of the Hurricane pilots, Plt Off Dick Sugden, recalled:

"The four of us had just got back from Cirencester – Reg Carter, Pat Collins, Arthur Maycock and myself – and over supper were arguing about whether we should visit the local 'hop'. Before we reached any decision, however, someone shouted something about all Hurricane and Blenheim pilots were wanted down by the hangar. We sauntered off, to find a crowd of blokes lounging and smoking, all taking about a buckshee trip to Egypt, It looked as though we might be doing something exciting – most of us were pretty browned off with the usual sort of trip [mainly ferrying Hurricanes to various squadrons]. Anyway, [Sqn Ldr] Jimmy Wilde soon appeared and we were told that 12 Blenheim pilots and 12 Hurricane pilots were needed to ferry machines to Egypt at a moment's notice. Somewhat to my amazement, I found myself volunteering and being accepted. The other three [Carter, Collins and Maycock] were also chosen and there was a mad rush to our tents to pack a few odds and ends . . ."

The Hurricanes and Blenheims assembled at RAF Aston Down, where they were tested and the Hurricanes fitted with long-range, underwing fuel tanks. In overall command of the formation was the Blenheim leader, Sqn Ldr G.A.M. Pryde DFC. It was decided to divide the aircraft into four flights, each consisting of three Blenheims and three Hurricanes:

A Flight

Blenheim L9351	Hurricane P2653 Plt Off R.H. Barber
Blenheim L9314	Hurricane P2584 Plt Off A.G. Maycock
Blenheim L9315	Hurricane P2651 Plt Off C.R. Glen

B Flight
Blenheim L9320   Hurricane P2544 Plt Off R.W.H. Carter
Blenheim L9319   Hurricane P2642 Plt Off M.A. Sims
Blenheim L9316   Hurricane P2648 Plt Off J. Mansel-Lewis
C Flight
Blenheim L9263   Hurricane P2623 Plt Off W.P. Collins
Blenheim L9335   Hurricane P2629 Plt Off W.R.C. Sugden
Blenheim L9318   Hurricane P2626 Flg Off J.C. Smyth
D Flight
Blenheim L9300   Hurricane P2625 Plt Off C. Haddon-Hall
Blenheim L9317   Hurricane P2650 Plt Off G.D.H. Beardon
Blenheim L9334   Hurricane P2641 Plt Off A.G. McAdam

All the guns were removed from the Hurricanes and carried by the Blenheims. This was necessary partly because of the difficulties of fitting both tanks and guns, and partly owing to the question of load with the additional fuel aboard. It would have been possible to retain six guns but the fuel pipes to the outboard tanks would have passed very close to these and, if used, there might have been the chance of fire. The guns and ammunition would have added another 250-lbs extra weight which, though possible, was highly undesirable.

Nine Blenheims and nine Hurricanes departed from Aston Down for Tangmere during the afternoon of 17 June, followed by the remaining six aircraft in the evening. They were to set out on the first leg of the flight early next morning, their proposed route across France to start at Cap Frehel and then on to Nantes, Bordeaux, Castres and Marignane; and then across the Mediterranean to Tunis, El Djem and on to Mersa Matruh, but at about 2230 the crews were advised a change of route was necessary as a result of information received from Bordeaux. They were now to fly to Perpignan from Bordeaux instead of to Castres, and from there to Sétif (Tunisia) and then to Malta. An hour later Sqn Ldr Pryde received a further call, changing the route to Cap Frehel-Marignane-Sétif-Malta. It was the Air Ministry's intention that in flying to Marignane the aircraft would keep to the route laid down in the written orders – i.e. via Nantes and Bordeaux, although the aircraft were not to land at the latter for refuelling purposes. However, Sqn Ldr Pryde understood the change to mean that Bordeaux should be cut out altogether, with the aircraft expected to fly directly from Cap Frehel to Marignane; this instruction was subsequently given to his flight commanders, and furthermore, that beyond Marignane the route was to be Tunis to Malta. This course had two disadvantages: it passed over Monts d'Auvergne, where weather conditions were likely to become more difficult than the route via Nantes and Bordeaux which led along the coast and thence by the valley of the Gironde; secondly, it would bring the formation nearer to the advancing Germans.

Day 1
Orders were given for the aircraft to be ready to start at 0430 on the morning of the 18th, and the majority were ready at this time. However, some of the Hurricanes had not arrived until late the previous evening and refuelling had not been completed, while further delay had been occasioned by the changes in route. As a result, take-off commenced at 0630. The orders called for aircraft to take off in flights, but this was not complied with since no attempt had been made to form up correctly on the ground. In the case of D Flight, the Blenheim leader found that his R/T was out of order and ordered the other two Blenheims to take off with the rest of the formation, and for his three Hurricanes to remain behind with him. The three Hurricanes of C Flight were also delayed, partly because they were not refuelled in time, and partly because they had formed up behind the D Flight leader and could not get past. The result was that eleven Blenheims and six Hurricanes (A and B Flights) left at 0645.

The aircraft endeavoured to get into formation before they left Tangmere's airspace, but owing to the absence of those left on the ground, the formation was irregular and all aircraft flew in one big gaggle although spread out fairly widely; generally, the Blenheims led and the Hurricanes followed. The weather was excellent as far as the French coast and for some 50 miles beyond. Then it began to get hazy and visibility deteriorated. Some 70 miles south of the Loire, when beginning to approach the Monts d'Auvergne, they encountered heavy and continuous cloud reaching from ground level up to 16,000 feet. Soon the cloud became so thick that it became impossible for the pilots to see their own wingtips, and broke formation to avoid collisions.

Four Blenheims including that flown by Sqn Ldr Pryde, and two Hurricanes (Plt Offs Glen and Carter), eventually arrived separately at Marignane. Of the missing aircraft, two Blenheims had returned to Tangmere, one of which had initially force-landed on a sandy stretch of beach at Plage Des Blanc Sabonsfinisterre, where the crew were immediately arrested by French troops. After convincing the troops of their nationality, obtaining petrol from a nearby garage and refilling their aircraft using a rubber tube and two jugs, they managed to take-off once the tide had gone out and flew back to Tangmere. However, disaster had overtaken the remaining five Blenheims including all three of A Flight. All crashed in France at different locations, with the loss of all members of the crews. Of the four missing Hurricanes the news was somewhat better: Plt Off Jock Barber had returned to Tangmere in company with one of the Blenheims, and Plt Offs Mansel-Lewis and Sims had landed at Angouleme, where they would spend the night. The fourth pilot, Plt Off George Maycock, was not so fortunate. Having lost sight of the others in the appalling weather conditions, he found himself alone:

"My aircraft then flew into a clearing in the clouds and I flew in a complete circle so as to give the other aircraft time to reappear. Almost immediately a Blenheim appeared and I, now having no idea as to my exact position, altered course and flew towards him. I tried to contact him but was unable to do so owing to the electrical interference, and I took a quick look at my compass and realised that he was flying on an easterly course, which was in the direction of enemy-held territory. Increasing my speed I flew alongside him in order to point out his error. Unfortunately, he was unable to understand my signals, and I broke formation with him."

Maycock eventually found himself over the village of Loudon. He was about to land nearby when he noticed, to his consternation, that the village was being bombed. Next moment he spotted an aircraft closing on his tail. He tried to take evasive action, but the fighter – a Messerschmitt Bf109E – opened fire, a short burst hitting the tail of the Hurricane and damaging its controls. Maycock attempted to land but hit a hedge and the aircraft flipped over onto its back. Shaken but unhurt, he made his way to the local French Army command post where he learned that the Germans were only about ten miles away. After setting fire to his wrecked aircraft (P2584), Maycock managed to reach Bordeaux from where he boarded a Royal Navy cruiser and arrived in England three days later.

Meanwhile at 1745, Sqn Ldr Pryde, having discussed the situation with French officers at Marignane, decided that his group of four Blenheims and two Hurricanes should fly to Calvi on the island of Corsica before heading for Tunisia. However, Pryde's Blenheim suffered engine failure on take-off and ended up in the boundary fence, although no-one was hurt. The five remaining aircraft reached Calvi at 1900, where they stopped for the night.

While this disastrous progression was underway, the remaining Blenheim and six Hurricanes which had been left behind at Tangmere, had followed at 0930. Initially these too had found the weather very good over France, but on approaching Monts d'Auverge they encountered the same bad conditions as had the earlier flight. Plt Off Dick Sugden recalled the treacherous conditions:

"The cloud base was down to 2000 feet, which we found by cautious exploring. All the time we were dodging those damn clouds, keeping the Blenheim and each other in sight. After about three hours flying it became obvious that we should not get through to Marseille. The mountains were hidden in dirty grey fog, getting worse. I kept peering down at what land I could see, wondering what were the chances of a forced-landing. My petrol gauge had ceased to function so every half hour I switched on my overload pump and trusted to luck. It was now raining all the time and visibility was wretched. Suddenly, we made a turn to port and there in front of us lay an aerodrome. Not a pukka thing with runways and rows of hangars but a large, wet-looking field on top of a hill, with one miserable-looking shed. Still, any port in a storm . . ."

The airfield was near the village of Ussel, situated about halfway between Clermont-Ferrand and Brivé. The field, although on high ground, was found to be boggy and the second Hurricane to put down, P2626 flown by Flg Off Smyth, tipped up on its nose; the other five landed safely. After a brief conference with the French authorities, it was discovered that there was no food available so, after a collection among the pilots, bread, ham and cheese were purchased from the nearby village. An inspection of Smyth's Hurricane revealed that it was only slightly damaged and was deemed to be flyable. Following their meal the pilots sought to refuel their machines, as Plt Off Sugden recalled:

"All this time various French aircraft were taking-off and landing, some of them unbelievably ancient-looking wrecks. There were some large twin-engined biplanes standing around, either Breguets or Blochs, the most ramshackle machines I have ever seen. Of course, all the French pilots were very impressed with the Hurricanes and Blenheims, and I shot the best line that my French was capable of. When we had eaten our lunch we started on the business of refuelling. It was a business too, as each machine had to be taxied to a pump through what resembled a bog. As all the French machines were nosing in front of us, it was each man for himself. And, bless me, it started to rain in torrents. It was like a nightmare, pushing aircraft through mud nearly a foot deep, arguing in French and then having to unscrew the fairings off those infernal overload tanks. Just when my machine was being filled there was a cloudburst; everybody huddled together under the mainplanes, while I tried to shield the petrol tank with my body, whilst rain was pouring in cascades down the mainplanes. I don't know how much water got into the tanks, but it must have been a hell of a lot. I had long ceased to care, everything seemed so bloody awful. We knew that if the rain kept on, then we should never get those Hurricanes off the ground, let alone move them. At about 1700 the rain stopped. Everybody's machine had been more or less refuelled."

It was now too late to continue, and accommodation was found for the night. Meanwhile, Plt Off Jock Barber of A Flight, having returned to Tangmere at noon in company with a Blenheim, was ordered to take off again:

> "We landed back at Tangmere after being airborne for five hours. We had a bite to eat in the Mess and then reported to S/Ldr Blake, the briefing officer, and told him we couldn't get through, particularly with no oxygen to overfly. He didn't think much of this and implied we were pretty useless, and that we were to get airborne[1]. So we took off [at 1500], having decided to try to fly underneath the cloud. When we got over France we again found the weather bad although there was a slight improvement. My problem was that after about four and a quarter hours flying I was unable to use the fuel in my long-range tanks and that my wing tanks were reading practically zero. We were by then threading our way through the Alps and I looked around for somewhere to land."

Finally he spotted a small field on a mountainside and, after a couple of approaches, dropped the Hurricane onto the ground. Unfortunately, the force of the landing broke off the tail wheel assembly, thereby causing damage to the underside of the rudder and rear fuselage. He had landed close to the village of Monde, and was able to reach habitation on foot with ease. A curious crowd formed, none of whom were English-speaking. Fortunately, there were a number of Belgian refugees present and Barber, a South African, was able to understand the Flemish speech due to its similarity to Afrikaans:

> "I introduced myself to a young boy, Jan, and we were able to strike up a means of communication. As it was getting late, Jan took me to meet his friends who lived in some barrack huts, where I met old grandma and an exceedingly attractive young girl who could speak a little English and provided the romance. I shared their meagre food – some good bread and home-made jam – and fiery brandy, and they gave me a straw mattress on which to sleep. I might add that by this time I had stuck up a very reasonable acquaintance with this very good-looking young lady, who wanted to accompany me out of France – I was sorely tempted but it wasn't really on."

Day 2

Early in the morning Barber set out for Monde with his new-found friends and 'borrowed' a 12-volt car battery. With power provided by the battery, fuel from the long-range tanks was pumped up into the wing tanks. The Hurricane was then turned in the direction of proposed take-off, and was started by hand-cranking – no mean feat. Revving the engine hard against the brakes to raise the broken tail quickly, he got off safely and flew to Marseilles, landing at the civil airport which caused further damage to the tail. No fuel was available there and he was advised to fly to the military base at Marignane, where he landed at 1120.

At Ussel meanwhile, due to the previous day's torrential rain, all aircraft were found to be bogged down. However, the six Hurricanes were manhandled to firmer ground but, as the Blenheim taxied out, it stuck fast and all efforts to free it were to no avail. Resolved to go on alone, the Hurricane pilots taxied into wind but Flg Off Smyth again stood his aircraft (P2626) on its nose, this time causing serious damage to the propeller. Plt Offs Collins and McAdam got off safely, followed by Plt Off Sugden but, in taking off, the latter lost his maps from the cockpit. He circled the airfield waiting for the others to join him but, realising what had happened, Flg Off Haddon-Hall called him over the R/T to land again. Meanwhile, Collins and McAdam flew on to Marignane, arriving at 1210.

Leaving Flg Off Smyth and the Blenheim crew to make their way back to England, and Plt Off Barber to sort out his damaged aircraft, Flg Off Haddon-Hall, Plt Offs Sugden and Beardon eventually took off for Marignane, but en route ran into heavy rainstorms and were unable to find their destination. While circling in an effort to find the airfield, Plt Off Beardon became separated. Subsequently, Haddon-Hall and Sugden landed at Toulon – the first sizeable airfield they could find. After lunch they were shown around the base, seeing in one hangar an Italian CR42 biplane fighter, which had recently been brought down during a raid on the airfield[2]. Meanwhile, Beardon had found Marignane alone, and landed there shortly before the two Hurricanes of Mansel-Lewis and Sims arrived from Angouleme, where they had spent the night.

At about 1730, Sqn Ldr Pryde, who had commandeered another Blenheim having detailed its crew to make its way back to England, set out again from Marignane and was accompanied by five Hurricanes (Plt Offs Collins, McAdam, Mansel-Lewis, Sims and Beardon). Under normal circumstances, Pryde would probably have waited until the next morning. However, the French feared an air attack on Marignane if the Germans became aware of the presence of British aircraft, and he had been pressurised by the authorities into leaving at the earliest possible opportunity. Collins and McAdam turned back after about an hour owing to problems with the feed pumps on the underwing tanks – similar trouble to that experienced by the earlier reinforcement flight. The remaining three Hurricanes followed Sqn Ldr Pryde's Blenheim south-eastwards. Bad weather was encountered soon after leaving Marignane. The formation passed over Corsica and kept to the east of Sardinia. Dusk approached about half way across and it was quite dark before the African coast was reached, where they were greeted by thunderstorms.

Approaching the coast, Sqn Ldr Pryde's aircraft fired a Very light, presumably as a signal to the French, but shortly afterwards it crashed into the sea and turned over onto its back. Pryde and his gunner were killed instantly, and the navigator died two days later. Plt Off Mansel-Lewis tried to pancake his Hurricane (P2648) near the Blenheim but his aircraft turned on its nose and sank at once. His parachute, which was still in its pack, kept him afloat until he could inflate his life-jacket. He swam in the direction of the Blenheim, where he found one body, and then set out for the coast which he reached three hours later. In the morning he was found by Arabs and taken to Bizerta. Meanwhile, Plt Off Sims had reached the coast, only to be fired on by machine-guns. Completely lost in the darkness, he baled out of P2642; he too was picked up by Arabs and joined Mansel-Lewis in Bizerta. The third Hurricane (P2650) crashed on the beach nearby and Plt Off Derek Beardon was killed. Both Mansel-Lewis and Sims were taken to Casablanca by the French, where they met some Fleet Air Arm officers from *Ark Royal*. They were flown out to the carrier, which took them to Gibraltar that same night. From there they were shipped back to England.

While this drama was unfolding, back at Marignane Plt Off Barber had set out for the nearby village of Estres to recruit the aid of the local blacksmith. A tail skid was swiftly fabricated from an old car spring, taken back to the airfield and bolted to the damaged Hurricane's rudder sternpost. A test flight resulted in the collapse of this lash-up on landing, but a new skid using double the number of spring leaves was made and fitted. Rather than risk a further collapse, Barber decided to await his next destination – Tunis – to make the test. He was joined by the returning Hurricanes of McAdam and Collins and, later still, by Haddon-Hall and Sugden from Toulon. They decided to continue next day.

Day 3

The five Hurricanes left Marignane at 1400 and set course for Tunis. After half an hour they ran into a heavy rainstorm and became somewhat disorientated. Landfall was however made after about three hours, but Haddon-Hall, leading the flight, turned east along the coast instead of west. Realising that he was wrong, Barber flew ahead, waggled his wings, and turned westwards. The others followed and all soon landed safely at El Aouina at about 1730. There they were shocked to learn that Sqn Ldr Pryde's flight had not arrived.

Day 4

Following a good night's sleep, the five pilots prepared to fly to Medjez-el-Bab, from where they would embark on the final leg to Malta. First off was Haddon-Hall but his engine cut and his aircraft (P2625) crashed through the airfield boundary fence. He was unhurt apart from minor cuts and abrasions to his face, but he now had to be left behind. On landing at the dusty Medjez airstrip, the remaining four were delighted to find two more Hurricanes – those of Plt Offs Glen and Carter – and three Blenheims. Refuelling was very slow, taking about three hours due to inadequate equipment. Four tankers were used in succession but each either broke down or ran dry. Furthermore, Carter's Hurricane refused to start until a magneto adjustment had been made. By then it was too late to set out for Malta. No accommodation was available at Medjez, so the airmen were driven into Tunis for the night.

Day 5

Next morning, at 1050, the Blenheims and two Hurricanes (Carter and Glen) finally took off for Malta, where they arrived safely at 1300. Two more Hurricanes (Collins and McAdam) followed at 1230, but they turned back when Collins' aircraft again developed fuel problems. They took off again at 1445, landing safely at Luqa two and a quarter hours later. This left two Hurricanes at Medjez, where Plt Off Sugden could not get the engine of P2629 to start, as he recalled:

"The batteries of course were flat and Jock [Barber] and I took turns in cranking it with the starting handle. For about an hour and a half we cranked my wretched engine – starting a hot engine is always a bit tricky – and at last it started. We were both absolutely dripping, and I felt very sick. The sun was blazing down out of a cloudless sky. And so we set off on the last lap, across the bluest sea I had ever seen. Jock had the only map – a chart of the Mediterranean – and I flew in line astern, trying to crouch down out of the sun's rays. We flew over the tiny islands of Linosa and Lampedusa and then, like a white biscuit in the sea, appeared Malta."

They landed at Luqa in darkness (see Chapter I). All the stranded Hurricane pilots and Blenheim crews, who had fallen along the way, eventually returned to England by one means or another, but it had been a disastrous operation. Following a Court of Inquiry, Air Chief Marshal Sir Robert Brooke-Popham reported:

"Apart from the weather, the chief causes of the failure of the Flight were:
    (a) The great importance of the time factor which necessitated all preparations having to be made at high pressure;
    (b) The daily, if not hourly, change in the situation in France, causing changes of instructions up to a few hours before the departure of the Flight;
    (c) The inadequate attention paid during the preparations to the operational side, as distinct from

the administrative side;
>   (d) The issue of meteorological route forecast so incomplete as to be misleading;
>   (e) The amount of work that fell on the shoulders of S/Ldr Pryde before the start;
>   (f) Unwise airmanship on the part of the commander."

Recommedations were suggested to prevent such a disastrous operation being repeated. However, Plt Off Jock Barber believed there was another major factor contributing to the loss of the Hurricanes:

> "Apart from the weather, the major cause of the failure of the long-range tank refuelling in the Hurricanes was due to the engines turning at too low rpm for the generators to cut in. We had been briefed that for maximum range we were to fly in coarse pitch and low boost, and with the extra drag of the drop tanks, this gave us engine revs in the order of 1,200 or so. Had we but realised this at the time, all that would have been necessary would have been to select fine pitch when operating the electrical fuel pumps in the drop tanks!"

* * *

The next Hurricane delivery came via the aircraft carrier HMS *Argus* on 2 August 1940 (see Chapter II and Appendix IV), and the vast majority of all future deliveries arrived in this manner; a few others were flown to Malta from Egypt, and a dozen arrived in crates aboard a freighter.

Date	Operation	Carrier(s)	Hurricanes Launched	Hurricanes Arriving	
2/8/40	'Hurry'	*Argus*	12	12(1)	418 Flight
17/11/40	'White'	*Argus*	12	4	8 lost en route
3/4/41	'Winch'	*Ark Royal*	12	12(1)	
27/4/41	'Dunlop'	*Ark Royal*	24	23 ⎫	1 lost en route
21/5/41	'Splice'	*Ark Royal*	23	23 ⎭	213/249/229(part) Sqns
		Furious	18	17	1 lost en route
6/6/41	'Rocket'	*Ark Royal*	24	24	46/229 (part) Sqns
		Furious	19	19	
14/6/41	'Tracer'	*Ark Royal*	19	19(2) ⎫	2 lost en route
		Victorious	28	28(1) ⎭	238/260 Sqns
27/6/41	'Railway I'	*Ark Royal*	22	21(1) ⎫	1 lost en route
30/6/41	'Railway II'	*Ark Royal*	26	26(1) ⎭	
		Furious	10	9	1 crashed on take-off
9/9/41	'Status I'	*Ark Royal*	14	14	
13/9/41	'Status II'	*Ark Royal*	24	24	
		Furious	22	21	1 crashed on take-off
12/11/41	'Perpetual'	*Ark Royal*	21	18 ⎫	3 lost en route
		Argus	16	16 ⎭	242/605 Sqns
			346	330	(7 of which crashed on arrival)

Figures in brackets indicate aircraft that crashed on landing on arrival at Malta; two others had crashed on take-off, and 16 were lost en route. Approximately 150 of the Hurricanes delivered to Malta flew on to North Africa, including those comprising 213, 229, 238 and 260 Squadrons. Hurricanes which arrived by means other than from carriers were:

10/1/41 12 crated Hurricanes arrived aboard MV *Essex* ('Excess' Convoy)
29/1/41 6 Hurricanes (ex-HMS *Furious*, Takoradi) from Gazala, Cyrenaica
6/3/41 5 Hurricanes (ex-HMS *Furious*, Takoradi) from Gazala, Cyrenaica
17/3/41 6 Hurricanes of 274 Squadron (Amriyah) from Benina, Cyrenaica
27/3/42 10 Hurricanes of 229 Squadron – from Gambut, Cyrenaica (1 crashed on arrival)
6/4/42 9 Hurricanes of 229 Squadron – from Gambut, Cyrenaica
19/4/42 6 Hurricanes of 229 Squadron – from Gambut, Cyrenaica
5/5/42 5 Hurricanes collected by Malta pilots – from Gambut, Cyrenaica
6/5/42 1 Hurricane collected by Malta pilot – from Gambut, Cyrenaica
Therefore, between June 1940 and May 1942, approximately 250 Hurricanes arrived at Malta for the defence of the island; only a handful survived to be flown to North Africa at the end of May 1942.

* * *

MALTA HURRICANES

It is believed that the Hurricanes listed herewith served at Malta, sometimes with more than one squadron, particularly during early 1942 when stocks were dwindling and aircraft were pooled. Details in the main extracted from squadron ORBs, casualty records, logbooks, combat reports and Air-Britain Registers, all of which contain possible errors; therefore, these lists are undoubtedly open to revision:

Fighter Flight/418 Flight/261 Squadron: N2484, N2622 (crashed 11/1/41), N2672 (s/d 10/4/42), N2673 (s/d 20/5/41), N2700 (DBR 2/8/40), N2701 (s/d 26/11/40), N2715 (s/d 12/2/41), N2716 (s/d 15/8/40), N2717 (SOC 9/10/40), P2614 (DBR 5/8/40), P2623 (s/d 16/7/40), P2629 (s/d 19/1/41), P2645 (s/d 7/3/41), P2653 (s/d 22/3/41), P3730, P3731, P3733 (s/d 12/2/41), V6648, V6747, V7072, V7101 (to 69 Sqn, converted to PR), V7102 (s/d 5/3/41), V7103 (SOC 13/5/42), V7114, V7115 (s/d 13/5/41), V7116 (s/d 11/4/41), V7117, V7121 (s/d 26/2/41), V7297 (DBR 28/3/41), V7346 (s/d 25/2/41), V7358 (s/d 22/3/41), V7365 (collision 7/5/41), V7370, V7373 (lost en route 17/11/40), V7374 (lost en route 17/11/40), V7405, V7413 (lost en route 17/11/40), V7418, V7430 (s/d 28/3/41), V7472, V7474 (s/d 26/2/41), V7475 (lost en route 17/11/40), V7485, V7487 (lost en route 17/11/40), V7488 (lost en route 17/11/40), V7490, V7493 (s/d 22/3/41), V7494 (lost en route 17/11/40), V7495 (s/d 22/3/41), V7497, V7545, V7548 (collision 7/5/41), V7549 (lost en route 17/11/40), V7560, V7561, V7564, V7670, V7671 (s/d 26/2/41), V7672 (s/d 22/3/41), V7731 (s/d 16/2/41), V7768, V7769, V7771 (to Egypt 13/5/41), V7787, V7797, V7799 (s/d 22/3/41), Z2563, Z2825, Z2837, Z2838 (s/d 13/4/41), Z2840, Z2900, Z2901, Z2902 (DBR 11/4/41), Z2904 (s/d 11/4/41), Z3032 (s/d 23/4/41), Z3034, Z3035, Z3036 (s/d 11/4/41), Z3054 (crashed 2/5/41), Z3057 (DBR 6/5/41), Z3059 (s/d 6/5/41), Z3060 (s/d 6/5/41), Z3061 (s/d 1/5/41), Z3063, Z3082, Z3766, Z3978, Z4025, Z4028, Z4041, Z4047, Z4053, Z4060, Z4068, Z4071, Z4087, Z4261, Z4269, Z4315, Z4354, Z4385, Z4612, Z5118, BD791.

185 Squadron (GL): V7418 (ex-261 Sqn), V7797 (ex-261 Sqn), Z2339/G (SOC 1/5/42), Z2394/H/F, Z2396/D (SOC 7/7/42), Z2398, Z2402/P (lost 5/3/42), Z2414/E, Z2418/C, Z2421, Z2481, Z2509/N, Z2514/B (s/d 29/9/41), Z2518/Q (s/d 4/10/41), Z2527, Z2592/Y (DBR 13/1/42), Z2698/L (s/d 27/4/42), Z2813/L (s/d 21/11/41), Z2815, Z2819/W (DBR 7/3/42), Z2823/U (s/d 21/12/41), Z2824/H, Z2825, Z2827 (s/d 25/1/42), Z2837 (s/d 13/5/41), Z2840/T (ex-261 Sqn, s/d 18/3/42), Z2892, Z2900 (ex-261 Sqn), Z2901 (s/d 14/5/41), Z2940, Z2961/K, Z2982/O, Z2983, Z3035 (s/d 15/5/41), Z3063 (ex-261 Sqn SOC 5/9/41), Z3172 (DBR 25/7/42), Z3452/B (s/d 22/2/42), Z3456/X (s/d 25/10/41), Z3462/C/Y, Z3495/T, Z3498 (s/d 26/8/41), Z3512, Z3522/A, Z3580/XJ, Z3757/R (DBR 6/4/42), Z3758, Z3766 (ex-261 Sqn, s/d 10/4/42), Z3767/B (SOC 20/5/42), Z3837 (s/d 13/5/41), Z3993/X, Z4004, Z4005/S, Z4011/B (s/d 22/4/42), Z4014 (SOC 2/9/42), Z4016, Z4041 (ex-261 Sqn), Z4060 (ex-261 Sqn), Z4068 (ex-261 Sqn), Z4315/Y (DBR 25/1/42), Z4360/G, Z4380, Z4389, Z4428, Z4941/XL, Z4942/F/Y (DBR 8/5/42), Z4943 (crashed 29/12/41), Z4946/E (s/d 28/9/41); Z5140/C, Z5147/C (s/d 25/1/42), Z5155 (s/d 3/1/42), Z5157, Z5158/V (SOC 15/7/42), Z5213, Z5259, Z5265 (s/d 1/10/41), Z5302 (s/d 31/3/42), Z5325 (lost 11/5/42), Z5326, BD702 (DBR 6/5/42), BD704/H, BD826/A, BD828/O (s/d 25/1/42), BD835 (lost 9/11/41), BE542, BE563/F (SOC 26/7/42), BE583/T, BG711, BG719 (DBR 25/7/42), BG744/Y (DBR 21/2/42), BG745, BG755, BG756/M (DBR 10/4/42), BG765 (s/d 25/1/42), BG769/J (SOC 21/5/42), BG770/D (DBR 29/6/43), BG784/H, BG789/T, BG792/W, BG794 (DBR 27/7/42), BV157 (conv from L1581: crashed 10/8/41), BV158/K, BV163/F (conv from R2683: DBR 27/4/42), BV167 (conv from P3521: s/d 4/2/42), BV174/B (conv from P3216: s/d 2/4/42), BM905/U/J.

249 Squadron (GN): V6629 (DBR 25/5/41), V7103, V7732 (DBR 25/5/41), V7747 (DBR 25/5/41), V7797, Z2349, Z2388, Z2395, Z2397, Z2411, Z2414, Z2415, Z2418 (s/d 20/12/41), Z2455, Z2481, Z2522, Z2526, Z2527, Z2546/D, Z2578, Z2639, Z2663, Z2665, Z2678/E (SOC 25/7/42), Z2680, Z2684, Z2698, Z2794 (SOC 20/5/42), Z2818 (s/d 17/7/41), Z2825, Z2829/G (s/d 29/12/41), Z2904, Z2941, Z2961, Z2981, Z3033, Z3056 (s/d 4/9/41), Z3063, Z3148, Z3155, Z3176, Z3262, Z3452/B, Z3453, Z3462, Z3492 (crashed 31/7/41), Z3498, Z3505, Z3512, Z3521 (s/d 4/9/41), Z3562, Z3570, Z3571, Z3574, Z3580 (DBR 24/2/42), Z3730, Z3756, Z3757/R, Z3761/M (SOC 6/2/42), Z3764, Z3769, Z3993/T, Z4002/M, Z4003/S (s/d 4/2/42), Z4005, Z4016 (s/d 4/2/42), Z4025, Z4028 (SOC 7/9/42), Z4041, Z4043 (s/d 12/6/41), Z4048, Z4058 (crashed 18/6/41), Z4060 (SOC 24/5/42), Z4068, Z4070, Z4087 (s/d 9/6/41), Z4315, Z4354, Z4380, Z4385 (s/d 12/6/41), Z4389, Z4428, Z4502, Z4507, Z4941, Z5140/A, Z5149/C (DBR 25/7/42), Z5326/F (crashed 9/2/42), BD703 (SOC 27/7/42), BD789/G (DBR 8/5/42), BD834 (s/d 29/12/41), BE583 (DBR 2/5/42), BG771 (s/d 24/2/42), BV156/Q (conv from V6790: s/d 22/12/41), BV162/J (conv from N2465: s/d 20/12/41), BV174, DG615 (s/d 21/12/41).

46/126 Squadron (HA³): V7103, V7797, Z2068, Z2256, Z2397 (s/d 12/11/41), Z2418/C, Z2480 (s/d 11/6/41), Z2481, Z2491/D (s/d 24/11/41), Z2526, Z2527, Z2593 (SOC 10/2/42), Z2678, Z2680/XF (s/d 26/12/41), Z2794/G, Z2815 (DBR 7/3/42), Z2824/H, Z2825/XI, Z2827/M, Z2900 (SOC 7/6/41), Z2930, Z2934, Z2941/D (s/d 23/11/41), Z2961/K, Z2981, Z2982, Z3033/XN (collision 8/11/41), Z3055 (crashed 4/7/41), Z3056, Z3158/K, Z3173, Z3418, Z3453, Z3456, Z3462, Z3492, Z3495, Z3498, Z3512, Z3517, Z3521, Z3574, Z3764 (s/d 19/12/41), Z3984 (DBR 27/12/41), Z4005, Z4011, Z4041, Z4315, Z4941/XL, Z5118/S, Z5140/C (s/d 10/3/42), Z5213 (s/d 18/3/42), BD830 (s/d 24/12/41), BG731, BG791, BV156/XA (to 249 Sqn), BV171 (conv from P2674: crashed 19/7/41), BV173 (conv from V7351: s/d 18/9/41),

DG612/H, DG615, DG618.

242 Squadron (LE): Z2402 (s/d 5/3/42), Z2824/H (s/d 1/3/42), Z4002 (s/d 1/3/42), BE343 (s/d 29/12/41), BE344 (s/d 29/12/41), BE346 (s/d 22/1/42), BE351/Y (DBR 6/4/42), BE369 (lost en route 12/11/41), BE402/S, BE555/X, BE561 (lost en route 12/11/41), BG698/U (DBR 6/4/42), BG711/K (DBR 22/3/42), BG712 (lost en route 12/11/41), BG741/O (SOC 24/6/42), BG745, BG746/A, BG752 (s/d 27/1/42), BG755/E, BG756/W, BG765, BG769/W, BG787/H, BV158 (conv from V6785: s/d 25/1/42). (242 Sqn absorbed by 126 Squadron, 18/3/42).

605 Squadron (UP): Z2394, Z2509 (DBR 2/2/42), Z2527 (s/d 12/2/42), Z2815 (SOC 7/3/42), Z2961, Z3517, Z3756 (s/d 1/3/42), Z3757/R, Z3758, Z4014, Z5147, Z5259 (DBR 23/2/42), BE563/F, BG713/O (DBR 6/12/41), BG745, BG753/V, BG754 (DBR 22/2/42), BG755 (s/d 15/2/42), BG784/H, BG792/W (DBR 18/6/42). (605 Squadron absorbed by 185 Squadron, 18/3/42).

MNFU/1435 Flight: Z2098, Z2414, Z2680, Z2794, Z2827, Z2829/G, Z2961/K, Z3033, Z3462/H DBR 6/3/42), Z3505 (DBR 9/4/42), Z3512 (s/d 14/10/41), Z3514, Z3522 (DBR 5/3/42), Z3562/C (crashed 3/3/42), Z3570/D (DBR 3/2/42), Z3571/J (s/d 27/1/42), Z3574/F, Z3580/B, Z3756, Z3762, Z4002/M, Z4004/L, Z4941, Z5325/K, BE347/D (s/d 25/4/42), BE402.

229 Squadron (HB): Z2481/D (DBR 29/4/42), Z2982 (crashed 27/5/42), Z3505/S (s/d 9/4/42), Z4005 (crashed 27/5/42), BD702 (DBR 6/5/42), BE555 (crashed 28/4/42), BE636 (DBR 19/4/42), BE642 (crashed 27/5/42), BE708 (s/d 25/4/42), BM964 (DBR 4/4/42), BN118 DBR 27/7/42), BN120/H, BN122/W (DBR 11/4/42), BN123 (DBR 6/5/42), BN124 (DBR 26/5/42), BN139, BN142 (DBR 11/4/42), BN164 (DBR 25/4/42), BN181/X (s/d 6/5/42), BN182 (s/d 25/4/42), BN184, BN278 (s/d 21/4/42), BN283, BN362 (s/d 18/5/42)

69 Squadron: V7101 (ex-261 Sqn), Z2332 (DBR 26/12/41), Z3053 (s/d 21/11/41), Z3173 (s/d 28/1/42)

Unallocated Hurricanes: Z2479 (SOC 30/8/42), Z3034 (ex-261 Sqn SOC 6/9/41), Z3144 (SOC 30/7/41), Z3515 (SOC 30/7/41), Z3523, Z3575 (SOC 30/7/41), Z3590 (SOC 25/6/42), Z4353 (listed as Missing 23/6/41), Z4356 (SOC 1/7/42), Z4713 (SOC 30/6/41), BE343 (SOC 8/3/44), BE349 (DBR 6/4/42), BE428 (SOC 26/7/42), BE480 (SOC 17/12/42), BE562 (DBR 13/4/42), BE565 (DBR 28/4/42), BE710 (DBR 20/4/42), BE716 (DBR 13/5/42), BG746 (DBR 23/3/42), BG749 (DBR 23/3/42), BG764 (DBR 6/4/42), BG787 (DBR 27/7/42).

Operational Hurricanes mid-1942/3: Z2825/XI (crashed 23/7/42), Z2961 (SOC 13/3/43), Z4941 (to Fleet Rec Unit, SOC 30/6/45), BE110 (SOC 27/10/44), BG766 (to Admiralty 1/7/43), BG770/D (DBR 29/6/43), BN408/E.

AVM Sir Keith Park (1942/3): OK-2 (personal aircraft), possibly Z3574.

APPENDIX IV

418 FLIGHT

Early in 1939 a notice was sent to RAF Volunteer Reserve centres, inviting VR pilots to volunteer for a two week attachment to the Fleet Air Arm, to be spent on an aircraft carrier. Subsequently this was changed to a three week stint, and in consequence most of the volunteers in civilian occupations had to drop out. Upon mobilisation in August of that year, some 40 RAFVR pilots, each of whom had a minimum of 100 hours flying training, and most of whom had previously volunteered for the two week carrier trip, were posted to the Fleet Air Arm airfield at Donibristle on the Firth of Forth. At this stage, the FAA had only recently been transferred from the RAF to the Royal Navy, and many of the pilots who had previously served in the Fleet squadrons had transferred back to the RAF. Sgt Jim Pickering, one of the chosen few, recalled:

> "We were amongst the first RAFVR recruits and were politically aware of the German threat. We had responsible civilian occupations, or were being trained for them. We had no career expectations in the RAF. There was little realisation in 1939 that there would be a long war or any expectation that Germany would win. I think most of the mobilised reserves of all the forces expected to be back in their civilian occupations in a year or possibly two. Most RAFVR pilots hoped and expected to join operational squadrons on award of the RAF Wings."

The new arrivals – 13 RAFVR Sergeant Pilots (Sgts D.K. Ashton, D.H. Ayres, H.W. Ayre, O.R. Bowerman, R.J. Hyde, E.N. Kelsey, J. Marsh, R. O'Donnell, J. Pickering, F.N. Robertson, L.W. Sturges, W.J. Timms and B. Wigginton) and 12 FAA pilots – at Donibristle were allocated either to the TSR Flight to fly Swordfish and Sharks, or to 769(T) Fighter Squadron on Sea Gladiators and Skuas. Operational training was to include deck landings on HMS *Furious*. Indeed, the first VR pilots to arrive were posted to the TSR

Flight, this being considered the better posting by the Navy, since it involved attack, while fighters were only defensive. The later arrivals were admonished for being too late for posting to the TSR unit, but most were in fact pleased to have got on to fighters. Shortly after the outbreak of war, Sgt Pickering and two others found themselves in the front line:

"Jack Marsh, Drac Bowerman and myself were taxiing out for some formation flying in Skuas when a matelot on a bike rode towards us waving his arms (we had no reliable radios). He persuaded Bowerman and myself to stop, but Jack, intent on other things, took off. Our instructions from the matelot were to disperse the Skuas, switch off, and stand by our aircraft, which we duly did. We were then able to hear the air raid sirens, followed shortly afterwards by the crump of bombs in the distance, ack-ack bursts above and the sight of a flight of Spitfires chasing a Ju88. We heard the rasping note of eight machine-guns firing in unison, then the all clear, and we were told to return the aircraft to the tarmac. With no aircraft to formate on him, Jack returned and found that a bullet, obviously fired from the ground, had passed between his left arm and chest. We had seen the first air raid of the war by German aircraft on British soil – and once again, with that genius for doing the wrong thing, the FAA had grounded the only three Naval fighters that could at least have given chase."

After six weeks at Donibristle, 11 of the RAFVR pilots were posted to 770 Squadron at Lee-on-Solent in company with eight FAA pilots; the other two RAFVR pilots – Sgts Robertson and Hyde had 'failed' the course[1] and returned to the RAF, being posted to 66 Squadron on Spitfires. Meanwhile, at Lee-on-Solent, the main group went aboard the old training carrier *Argus* to undertake deck landing training off Toulon, where one Naval pilot was killed, as recounted by Sgt Pickering:

"One Sub Lt pilot spun in and was lost without trace. We – the RN ratings and RAFVR Sergeant Pilots – we lined up and were given a lecture. We were told that if we were so foolish as to follow the example of spinning in, that we would suffer an even worse fate than a watery grave! This materialised next day when we were offered commissions in the FAA so that we could continue to serve under the incompetent who had lectured us!

Most of the RAFVR pilots were now disenchanted with Naval operations of aircraft, and with the obsolescent equipment available, and only two accepted the offer, Sgts Marsh[2] and Wigginton. Sgt Pickering continued:

"It shocked the RN officers that we could be so foolish. Some of them even asked us why. One stuttered: 'You are making a big mistake. We are shortly going to be re-equipped with Fulmars, which will be the best fighter aircraft in any service.' But none of the FAA officers were interested in us. As far as they were concerned, we had failed their course. We were given rail warrants at Toulon Railway station and told to find our own way back to England. This was no hardship. We all spoke some French – it would be three days before we got a train to Cherbourg and a boat to Portsmouth – and a good time was had by all!"

After a few days leave, the nine remaining RAFVR pilots who had been on the FAA course were ordered to report to 3 Bombing and Gunnery School at Aldergrove in Northern Ireland, where they were employed as staff pilots flying Wallaces, Heyfords or Battles. However, on 4 May 1940, all were posted back to the FAA in great haste, joining 759(T) Squadron at Eastleigh. After an intensive two week refresher course they were posted to Hatson in the Orkneys, being intended to fly Gladiators of 263 Squadron and Hurricanes of 46 Squadron onto HMS *Furious* for transfer to Norway, since the pilots of these units had not undertaken carrier landings. Their arrival was too late, however, for the Hurricanes had been hoisted aboard from lighters, while the Gladiators had been flown aboard by FAA pilots. Consequently, the group was posted to 804 Squadron which had just been formed at Hatson, to fly Sea Gladiators on land-based defensive duties. There, Sgt Sturges was killed in a landing accident.

By now the Dunkirk evacuation was underway and, by mid-June, it was the RAF which was short of fighter pilots. The FAA consequently provided about 40 pilots, including the eight remaining RAFVR Sergeant Pilots. After a brief conversion course on Hurricanes and Spitfires at 7 OTU at RAF Hawarden, they were posted to various Fighter Command squadrons[3]. Within a month came the order to report to Uxbridge and the group found themselves together again, joined by Sgts Robertson and Hyde, both of whom had been on the original Donibristle course, and who in the meantime had seen action with 66 Squadron[4]. However, Sgt David Ayres did not rejoin the group but remained with Fighter Command[5]. From Uxbridge the group moved to Northolt, and were flown from there in two Dragon Rapides to Hullavington to collect Hurricanes from 10 MU, and take them up to Abbotsinch near Glasgow. Several more Hurricanes were flown up by ferry pilots, one of which crashed on arrival. At Abbotsinch the RAF pilots were ordered by a Naval officer to remove the wings of their aircraft for loading by barge onto HMS *Argus*, which was then in dry dock. He was surprised and uncomplimentary to find the pilots had neither the tools nor technical knowledge to perform this task, which then had to be undertaken by RN personnel.

Once aboard the carrier, the sergeants were joined by five officers: Flt Lt D.W. Balden (ex-266

Squadron), who now assumed command of 418 Flight, as the group had been labelled; Flt Lt R.N. Lambert, Flt Lt A.J. Trumble (ex-264 Squadron), Flt Lt J. Greenhalgh (ex-1 SD Flight), and Flg Off F.H.R. Bradbury. They were all regulars who had previously served with the FAA, although none had any recent carrier experience and at least two had not previously flown a Hurricane. Flt Lt John Trumble recalled:

"On 18 July I was instructed to report to Abbotsinch from Duxford, where I was flying Defiants with 264 Squadron. On arrival I found that there were a number of RAF officers from other units in Fighter Command. The one common denominator was that we had all served in the Fleet Air Arm; we concluded that the mission concerned carrier operations. The next day 12 Hurricanes were delivered to us; they were painted in desert camouflage and had tropical filters and air cleaners. We surmised our destination was east of Gibraltar. I had not flown a Hurricane before so I had a 20-minute familiarisation flight . . ."[6]

Flt Lt John Greenhalgh was serving with 1 Special Duties Flight at Benson when he received his orders:

"I had just landed from a photo-reconnaissance sortie in a Spitfire that same afternoon, when I was ordered to report to the RTO at Euston [Railway] Station at once. From there I entrained for Greenock, having never previously flown a Hurricane . . ."

Thus, the personnel of 418 Flight were brought together and told that they would be going to Malta, but were ordered not to disclose the destination to their families.

APPENDIX V

THE TAKORADI ROUTE

The trans-Africa air route across Central Africa was officially established in October 1940, with Takoradi on the West African Gold Coast as the unloading terminal, although the first military aircraft to follow it – four Blenheims and five Hurricanes – had set out on 20 September. They safely reached Abu Sueir in Egypt six days later, having flown over the old Imperial Airways route to Cairo. The initial RAF operating party had arrived on 21 August, having first to build considerable workshop and other accommodation: refuelling and rest stations also had to be constructed en route. On 5 September, the first dozen crated Hurricanes and Blenheims arrived at Takoradi by sea. Towards the end of November 1940, HMS *Furious* arrived off the Gold Coast, carrying the Hurricanes of 73 Squadron[1], and these were flown off to Takoradi with just one mishap. However, the first six Hurricanes which set out for Egypt on 1 December in company with a Blenheim as guide, all force-landed in the Sudanese desert; two Hurricanes were written off and the other four all damaged, while one pilot was killed. Nevertheless, by the end of 1940, 107 aircraft had reached Egypt via this route[2]. Late in November, 22 Polish pilots commanded by Wg Cdr M. Izycki arrived, their sole duty to ferry aircraft along this route. A typical trip from Takoradi to Cairo, over 4,000 miles of swamps, jungle or barren desert, if fighters were included in the air convoy and if the trip was uneventful, would be:

Day 1: Takoradi to Lagos, Nigeria (380 miles)
Day 2: Lagos to Kano, Nigeria (525 miles)
Day 3: Kano to El Geneina, Sudan, refuelling at Maiduguri, Nigeria, and Fort Lamy, French Equatorial Africa (960 miles)
Day 4: El Geneina to Khartoum, refuelling at El Fasher and El Obeid (1,060 miles)
Day 5: Khartoum to Wadi Halfa (520 miles)
Day 6: Wadi Halfa to Abu Sueir, Cairo, refuelling at Luxor (500 miles)

One of the pilots to fly the route provided a graphic description:

"On the first day we left Takoradi with its red cliffs and steaming Gold Coast bush for Lagos, the first staging post in Nigeria. The formation coast-crawled to Accra, past steamy swamplands, native fishing villages and the 17th and 18th century Portuguese castles of the old slave traders. From Accra, we flew along about ten miles out to sea to avoid Vichy-French Dahomey and then inland again along the mangrove swamps to put down at Apapa, the airport of Lagos, built on what had once been swampland. The second day the formation flew on to Kano. On leaving the lakes the track turned north-east and inland over threatening dense jungle which began to thin north of the river Niger. At last the red dust of Kano appeared, an antique walled city and a centuries old staging post for land traffic between the Sahara and the Congo. The journey between Kano and El Geneina in the Sudan was made in two stages on the third day. From Kano a heartening patch of advanced cultivation for some 30 miles was quickly succeeded by scrub and arid country until a convenient road from Kano could be followed into Maiduguri where the flight would put down for refuelling.

Leaving Nigeria, course was set across French Equatorial Africa but here the Colonial Troops, unlike their compatriates of the Dahomey, had declared for the Free French and the airfield at Fort Lamy offered a valuable refuelling point and an emergency landing ground. On this stage Lake Fitri was a valuable pinpoint for navigators but could be somewhat disturbing in that, being mainly a mass of swamps, the outline shifted up to 30 miles between the wet and dry seasons. Now in the heart of Africa, the country became progressively more barren, more gruelling, with only outcrops of rock to relieve the monotony. Finally Geneina was reached. Although situated on a large wadi crossing the route, its sandy surface made it somewhat difficult to pick out from the air. On the fourth day aircraft flew from Geneina to Khartoum in two stages, a short one of 190 miles and the other of 560 miles. From Geneina the country retained its desert characteristics with occasional patches of scrub and trees over the short hop to El Fasher where aircraft refuelled. Here in the Sudanese desert aircraft which made forced-landings were extremely difficult to locate and the almost inevitable result for the crews was death from thirst. Accordingly, the direct route was soon diverted for fighter aircraft to El Obeid where a temporary area of cultivation was found. Sandstorms were prevalent over the remaining 250 miles to Khartoum with consequent low visibility so that the aircraft's track was deflected to starboard until the Nile could be located and used as a leading line into Khartoum. From Khartoum the route was comparatively easy. With a convenient refuelling point at Wadi Halfa crews had little to do but follow the magnificent course of the Nile above the Cataracts, Luxor and the Valley of the Kings, until finally the great pyramids and the sprawling mass of Cairo, topped by the Citadel, came into sight."[3]

Furious was back again on 9 January, this time accompanied by HMS *Argus*, with a further consignment of 42 Hurricanes, many of which were stowed below decks in *Furious* with their wings removed. Among the pilots were a sprinkling of Battle of Britain veterans. One of the ferry pilots, Sgt Bert Deacon, a veteran of the fighting in France in May 1940, recalled:

"On arrival off the West Coast of Africa, the two Naval squadrons were flown off to become temporary shore-based at Bathurst [Gambia]. We proceeded south down the coast and, in the meantime, our Hurricanes were having their wings fitted. We were briefed on take-off technique by a Wing Commander who had previous experience of this. On 9 January, we were some three miles off the coast of Takoradi and the poor old *Furious* was just about bursting her boilers to give us a 29-knot wind over the deck. The aircraft were struck up in vics of three and I took off in the first three, with Flg Off Whittingham and the Wing Commander – we landed at Takoradi."

One Hurricane (V7427) crashed in the sea on take-off, the pilot (Plt Off Heath) having taken off in course pitch. He was fortuitously rescued by a destroyer acting as plane guard. A second Hurricane was tipped on to its nose during the take-off run but got airborne nonetheless, only to cartwheel on landing. Its pilot, Plt Off P.A. Mortimer, was unhurt. All the others landed safely. A handful of Skuas of 801 Squadron had been retained aboard *Furious* for the purpose of ferrying pilots and observers of the newly formed 805 Squadron to Takoradi, as recalled by Lt(O) Ron Hinton:

"The crates containing 805 Squadron's Fulmars were transported ashore by barge to the small port of Takoradi. My dislike of Skuas was accentuated further on this occasion as, on landing on the airstrip, the starboard oleo leg collapsed. We spun round on the port wing until finally coming to rest, smothered in dirt and debris. The engine, as is usual in such cases, fell off. Our first thoughts were, of course, one of fire and, as soon as I was able to do so, disengaged my harness and was out of the aircraft like a shot and put at least a hundred yards between myself and the aircraft before collapsing on the runway. The result of all this was that I spent three days in the local hospital, whilst the black doctors and dusky nurses tested every bone in my body. The heat was intense and further time under such conditions was out of the question. We spent a month at Takoradi whilst our Fulmars were put into ferrying shape. The local residents were very hospitable and one evening was spent at the local military base listening to a band of the West African Rifles, resplendent in their red tunics. It was music truly out of this world."

A flight of Sunderlands from 95 Squadron was based at Freetown (Sierra Leone) from February 1941, their task to provide protection for merchant shipping steaming down the west coast of Africa. The squadron had its own Hurricane Fighter Flight for protection against Vichy fighters operating from Dakar (Senegal), and as a deterrent to Vichy Martin 167Fs of Escadrille 5B which attempted to carry out reconnaissance sorties over Freetown. At least three of the Martins were lost over or near Freetown, two being shot down by Hurricanes during 1941 and another seriously damaged the following year.

The first six Hurricanes[4], all whitewashed in case of a forced-landing in the jungle, were led off by Flg Off Whittingham next day, with a Blenheim navigating. On arrival at Khartoum, Sgt Deacon's aircraft was found to have a faulty fuel pump in one auxiliary tank. After a day's delay to get this repaired, he followed on alone. All reached Abu Sueir safely. The others soon followed at regular intervals between the 9th and the 16th. Of this contingent, 38 eventually reached Egypt, where a proportion were earmarked for Malta. One of the Hurricanes, that flown by Sgt Arthur Todd, was delayed at Khartoum due to loss of oil pressure. Eight of the first batch of Hurricanes to arrive at Abu Sueir flew up to Bardia on 19 January, and from there to Malta via Tobruk and Gazala (see Chapter IV). Dozens more Hurricanes would follow this route, but only a few would reach Malta.

Many aircraft were inevitably lost during these long flights including, in early 1942, two Hurricanes which strayed off course; one of which was shot down by AA fire over Konakri on the French Guinea coast and crash-landed on Kalt Island, from where the pilot was rescued by an RAF flying boat. The other force-landed at Cotonou in Vichy-French Dahomey; a few days later another Hurricane attempted to strafe the downed aircraft but without result.

APPENDIX VI

THE RECONSTRUCTION OF HURRICANE IIA Z3055

On 4 July 1941, Sgt Tom Hackston of 126 Squadron took off from Safi in Z3055 at 0345. He failed to return, his aircraft having crashed into the sea shortly after taking off; Sgt Hackston was killed (see Chapter VI).

Fifty years later, in the early 1990s, it was known that a wreck of an aircraft was laying only a short distance from the 40-metre drop-off on Hamrija Bank, a large submerged reef off the Blue Grotto. Fishing nets often got caught in the wreckage. Investigation by scuba diver David Schembri showed it to be the remains of a Hurricane complete with starboard wing and part of the port wing still intact. It was decided to attempt a recovery. Permission to recover underwater historical artifacts was requested from, and granted by, the Director of Museums.

As the aircraft was too large to be raised in one piece, it was decided that the fuselage was to be cut just behind the pilot's seat. This would enable the fuselage and tail to be lifted by use of a 1.5-ton lifting bag, this being achieved on 16 July 1995. The relic was then towed to the shore by means of a dinghy. Whilst the tow was uneventful, the landing was to prove a nightmare. The electric winch used to haul boats out of the water stalled, and it was only the sheer determination of those involved that was to make the operation successful. Plans were made to recover the centre section complete with engine, this being achieved on 19 September 1995 by the use of an A frame barge *Sea Wolf* made available free of charge by Cassar Enterprises Ltd. Cleaning of the engine began in earnest and the reason for its ditching soon became clear as the Merlin engine showed signs of overheating on one of its cylinder banks. This must have resulted in engine seizure.

The reconstruction of the aircraft is currently underway at the Takali Aviation Museum, the main sponsor being Frank Salt of Frank Salt Real Estate Ltd, in memory of his father Flt Lt J.H. Salt, and the groundcrews that served with him during WWII in Malta. From Britain, Hawker Restorations Ltd are providing exchange and missing parts, whilst the reconstruction is in the capable hands of the Malta Historic Preservation Group under the directorship of Ray Polidano, whose young son David is one of the key members of the team, although Vintage Fabrics, also from the UK, supplied and fitted the fuselage fabric. A Merlin engine has been donated to the project by Paul Cardona and this is being reconditioned by Andrew Cilia. The Hurricane will eventually be restored to its wartime configuration and is being prepared to taxiing condition. The Hackston family has been contacted and relatives of the deceased pilot have visited the project.

When completed, Hurricane Z3055 will be displayed together with the Museum's reconstructed Spitfire IX EN199, and possibly restored Gladiator N5520 currently residing at the War Museum at Fort St Elmo in Valetta.

CHAPTER FOOTNOTES

PREAMBLE

1 See *Faith, Hope and Charity* by Kenneth Poolman.
2 Flg Off John Waters had been given some fighter training on the Sea Gladiator by 802 Squadron whilst based at Hal Far.

CHAPTER I

1 Not long before the end of WWI, on 7 April 1918, Zeppelin LZ104 set out from its base at Yambol in Bulgaria to carry out a raid on Malta, but en route was lost at sea.
2 See *Faith, Hope and Charity*.
3 See *When Malta Stood Alone* by Joseph Micaleff.
4 See *Faith, Hope and Charity*.
5 Plt Off McAdam, a Scot, had served briefly with 602 Squadron but after damaging three Spitfires in accidents was posted away for further training.
6 See *When Malta Stood Alone*.
7 A few days before his death, Flt Lt Keeble had learned that his brother had been killed while flying a Blenheim with 82 Squadron in the UK.
8/9 See *The Second World War Volume II: Their Finest Hour* by Winston S. Churchill.

CHAPTER II

1 The Hurricanes were N2484, N2622, N2672 (Balden), N2673 (Trumble), N2700 (Robertson), N2701, N2715 (Pickering), N2716 (O'Donnell), N2717, P3730, P3731 and P3733 (Hyde).
2 See *Victory in the Air*.
3 In April 1941, having been promoted earlier to command 261 Squadron, Sqn Ldr Trumble was posted to Crete, where he was captured when the island fell to German paratroopers.
4 Sqn Ldr Martin was later posted to the Middle East and joined 40 Squadron flying Wellingtons. He failed to return from a raid on 26 August 1941.
5 The SM86W was an unsuccessful attempt by the Italians to produce a dive-bomber by adapting an uprated SM85 in this rôle.
6 There were probably four Hurricanes and two Gladiators airborne; one Hurricane (P3730) was flown by Plt Off Balmforth.
7 See *Times of Malta*.
8 See *The Second World War Volume II: Their Finest Hour*.
9 See *The Second World War Volume II: Their Finest Hour*. Later, Churchill reflected: "When I look back on all these worries I remember the story of the old man who said on his deathbed that he had had a lot of trouble in his life, most of which had never happened. Certainly this is true of my life in September 1940. The Germans were beaten in the air in the Battle of Britain. The overseas invasion of Britain was not attempted . . . We found means to reinforce Malta before any serious attack from the air was made upon it, and no one dared to try a landing upon the island fortress at any time. Thus September passed."
10 Georges Blaize was killed flying an RAF He115 spyplane (BV185) from Kalafrana during a clandestine operation on the night of 22/23 September 1941 (see Chapters VI and VII).
11 See *Senglea During the Second Great War 1940-1944* by Mgr Emmanuel Brincat.
12 See *Faith, Hope and Charity*.

CHAPTER III

1 The six Hurricanes were V7373, V7475, V7487, V7488, V7494 and V7549.
2 Of the missing pilots, Flg Off Horton had been credited with four victories (one shared), Flg Off Walker with two, and Sgt Cunnington with several shares. Of the survivors, Plt Off Eliot had five including two shared, Sgt Norwell seven, of which four were shared, and Sgt Bamberger two. Flt Lt MacLachlan had won his DFC while flying Battle light bombers during the Battle of France, and had only recently transferred to fighters.
3 See *The Second World War Volume II: Their Finest Hour*.
4 See *Churchill's Few* by John Willis.
5 Sgt (later Sqn Ldr AFC) Reg Hyde told New Zealand author Paul Sortehaug that he thought he had 'shot down' about a dozen enemy aircraft (including seven damaged) while at Malta but when an Intelligence Officer (Flt Lt B.T. Anderson) arrived on the island, claims by fighter pilots were re-assessed and Hyde was allowed just two confirmed and two probables. He was, understandably, livid.
6 Part of the diary maintained by Airman X is located in the NWMA archives but, unfortunately, the compiler's identity is unknown.
7 Flg Off William Joseph Woods DFC was soon back in the thick of the fighting, being credited with four more victories (including one shared and two probables) before being shot down and killed over Eleusis

Bay on 20 April 1941.

8 On returning to England, Tommy Balmforth received further treatment for his burned hands. On being posted to Biggin Hill he met a pretty WAAF, Lorraine, who soon became his wife. Later, in 1943, he commanded 124 Squadron, being awarded the DFC, and by the end of the war had received the DSO and Bar for his leadership of the Manston Wing.

9 Almost certainly Sottoten Umberto Curcio of 72^Squadriglia.

CHAPTER IV

1 These were N2484, N2622, N2672, N2673, N2715, N2717, P2629, P2645, P2653, P3730, P3731, P3733, V7346, V7370, V7474, and V7548. The wrecks of N2700 and N2717 were being used for spares.

2 These are believed to have included V7072, V7121, V7545, V7546, V7670, V7671 and V7672; and possibly V7101, V7102, V7114-7117.

3 See *Battle over Malta* by Anthony Rogers. By a strange coincidence, or fate, Bill Timm's French friends René Duvauchelle and Jacques Mehouas were killed at about the same time on this date, when their Maryland was shot down by a Macchi 200 near Catania.

4/5 See *When Malta Stood Alone* by Joseph Micallef.

6 Philip Vella later became a founder member of the Malta National War Museum, and was the author of *Malta: Blitzed But Not Beaten* (with which he was assisted by Frederick Galea); he died in 1987.

7 While operating from Malta the Fulmars did not normally carry a TAG, although on this occasion Lt(A) Henley was accompanied by N/Air A.S. Rush.

8 The Spitfire, P9551, was immediately put to good use, Flt Lt Corbishley making a reconnaissance over Sicily two days later. He was shot down by AA fire on a subsequent sortie on 2 February 1941 and became a POW.

9 Plt Off Worrall had served with 85 and 249 Squadrons during the Battle of Britain and had three victories to his credit (one shared), and Plt Off Wyatt-Smith had flown Gladiators during the ill-fated Norwegian Campaign. The other two were relatively inexperienced, and had ferried Hurricanes from Takoradi across Central Africa to Egypt (see Appendix V). Shortly after his arrival at Malta, Plt Off Ian Currie developed cerebral malaria, which he had probably contracted on arrival in West Africa, and died on 31 January.

10 From Alexandria the *Illustrious* was subsequently to go to the United States for major repairs which were to keep her out of the war for a full year.

11 Flg Off Whittingham, Plt Off Pain, Sgts Deacon and Hodson had all been shot down during the Battle of Britain, both Pain and Hodson having been wounded; Deacon had six victories to his credit including one or two probables from the fighting in France and over Britain, while Pain had five including three probables. Although born in Scotland where his Australian parents were students, Pain was living in Brisbane in 1939 when he applied for a Short Service Commission in the RAF.

12 Although no Do17 unit was based in Sicily, the occasional Do17Z was reported to be operating from the island from time to time, mainly in the reconnaissance rôle. Orr's victim may have been one such aircraft.

13 Pain's diary reference to the Gladiators being dubbed *Faith, Hope and Charity* would seem to suggest that these names were in use this early.

14 See *Faith, Hope and Charity*.

15 See *Hurricanes at War: 2* by Norman Franks.

16 Despite efforts to save Flt Lt MacLachlan's arm, amputation was the only option. However, within two weeks he was in the air, flying a Magister. He eventually returned to England where he was fitted with an artificial arm and before long was back on operations. In 1942 he was given command of a Hurricane night intruder squadron, and the following year was flying daylight sorties, but in July 1943 was shot down over France by ground fire and died due to his injuries.

17 See *Ju87 Stukageschwader of North Africa and the Mediterranean* by John Weal.

18 See *When Malta Stood Alone*.

CHAPTER VI

1 The three pilots involved in the lucky escape joined others for dinner and drinks that evening to celebrate, but the evening went tragically wrong when Lt(A) Bill Barnes was accidentally shot dead by a young Maltese soldier on sentry duty.

2 The three remaining airworthy Fulmars were shortly thereafter flown to Egypt, each aircraft carrying three aircrew, the RN ground party departing for the same destination aboard a destroyer.

3 Within a few days came the announcement of a DFM for Sgt Jock Robertson, whose score now stood at eight confirmed.

4 The five who ferried their Hurricanes to Malta were: Plt Offs C.K. Gray, P.A. Mortimer and D.M. Whitney, a New Zealander, and Sgts A. Livingston and F.J. Jessop, while Sgts H.J. Kelly and J.T. Hitching arrived as passengers on board the Wellingtons. Plt Offs Gray and Mortimer had seen action during the Battle of Britain, and each had two victories to his credit.

5 The eight pilots were Flg Offs E.M. Mason DFC, C.J. Laubscher and J.S. Southwell, Plt Offs D.F. Knight

and Plt Off T.B. Garland, Sgts T.A. Quinn, M.P. Davies and R.J. Goode.

6 See *Malta Magnificent*.

7 The other pilots were Plt Offs J.V. Marshall, P. Kennett and H.F. Auger RCAF (a French- Canadian), Sgts P.H. Waghorn, J.K. Pollard, E.R. Jessop, G. Lockwood, B.J. Vardy, H.H. Jennings and G.A. Walker. None were combat experienced. The Hurricanes are believed to have included Z2837, Z2838, Z2901, Z2902, Z2904, Z3032, Z3036, Z3057, and Z3082.

8/9 See *Imshi* by Alys Myers.

10 See *Battle over Malta*.

11 See *Imshi*. Having spent three weeks in plaster, he managed to hitch a lift in an Egypt-bound Wellington and by June had made a good recovery. By this time 261 Squadron had been posted to Egypt and Mason was promoted to command; he later took command of 94 Squadron only to be shot down and killed in action on 15 February 1942.

12 See *Warburton's War* by Tony Spooner DSO DFC.

13 In addition to Jeffries, Hancock and Doughty, the other pilots, three of whom were conveyed to Malta by other means, were Plt Offs P.D. Thompson, R.A. Innes, P.J.A. Thompson, B.M. Cavan, R.C. Graves, A.J. Reeves, G.G. Bailey, J.H.S. Haig, D. Winton, J.E. Hall, D.C.B. Robertson, A.S. Dredge and R.T. Saunders; Sgts H. Burton, E.L. Lawrence, R.A. Branson, A.W. Jolly, R. Ottey, B.C. Walmsley, D.C. Smith, E.V. Wynne, P.L. Jordan RNZAF and F.G. Sheppard RAAF.

14 It seems probable that there is some confusion in German records and that this action actually relates to the afternoon combat between 7/JG26 and C Flight.

15 The submarine turned out to be HMS *Utmost*; no damage was inflicted.

16 It seems probable that the Maryland chased by Plt Off Hamilton and attacked by Sgt Wynne was AR714 flown by Sqn Ldr George Burges, since the Squadron ORB records his sortie as the only operational flight on this date.

17 The announcement of the DFC was not forthcoming but he did receive a posthumous Mention in Despatches.

18 Sgt Bamberger was later commissioned and returned to operations, gaining the DFC and Bar and increasing his victory tally to six.

19 See *249 at War* by Brian Cull.

20 Plt Off Downie's aircraft was seen to strike the water off Pantelleria while he was looking at his map. He managed to regain control only to ditch further on; he survived to be rescued from his dinghy by the Italians and thereby became a POW.

21 See *Hurricane at War* by Chaz Bowyer.

22 The pilots included Sqn Ldr R.A. Barton DFC (nine victories including one shared), Flt Lt T.F. Neil DFC (13 victories, two shared); Flg Offs H.J.S. Beazley (four victories, two shared), P.H.V. Wells (two shared victories), E. Cassidy, E.F.J. Harrington; Plt Offs A.R.F. Thompson (two victories, one shared), J.T. Crossey, G.C.C. Palliser (four victories, two shared), J.P. Mills, C.C.H. Davis and R.H.McK. Munro; Flt Sgt F.A. Etchells; Sgts D.C.H. Rex, R.W. Lawson, J.G. Parker, R. Rist, C.A. McVean, J.G.K. Hulbert and M. Guest. The other Flight Commander (Flt Lt F.V. Morello) and two other pilots had accompanied the ground party to Takoradi, from where they would ferry P-40s to Egypt, two of the three eventually rejoining the Squadron at Malta.

23 See *Hurricane at War: 2*.

24 261 Squadron was reformed in July 1941 when 127 Squadron at Habbaniya, Iraq, was renumbered. Several of the Squadron's departing pilots were later awarded DFCs including Sqn Ldr Lambert, Flg Off Peacock-Edwards, Flg Off Laubscher, Plt Off Rippon (later killed in action), Plt Off McAdam (also later killed in action), Plt Off Gray, and Sgt Todd, following his commission. Flg Off Barber also received the DFC, but Plt Off Pain, despite his successes, failed the interview with his AOC and was one of those not recognised for their part in the defence of the island. In recognition of his leadership and inspiration on the ground, 261 Squadron's Senior NCO Flt Sgt Harry Allin was awarded the BEM.

25 See *Onward to Malta* by Wg Cdr T.F. Neil DFC.

26 These are believed to have included V6629, V7732 and V7747.

27 Despite their apparent invulnerability while operating against Malta's Hurricanes, few of the pilots of 7/JG26 survived the war. Oblt Müncheberg was killed in Tunisia in March 1943, with his score at an amazing 135 victories; Oblt Klaus Mietusch took his tally to 72 before he was killed in September 1944; Lt Hans Johannsen was lost in March 1942 (eight victories); Uffz Karl-Heinz Ehlen in April 1942 (seven); Obfw Karl Laube in December 1944 (seven); and Uffz Melchior Kestler in June 1943.

CHAPTER VI

1 See *Briefed to Attack* by Air Marshal Sir Hugh Lloyd KBE CB MC DFC.

2 The new pilots were Flt Lts P.W. Lefevre (a Channel Islander, with three shared victories to his credit) and N.W. Burnett (one shared); Flg Offs P.R. McGregor (one victory), J.M.V. Carpenter (four); Plt Offs L.D. Barnes (two, one shared), J.K. Kay (four, one shared), C.A. Blackburn, H.P. Lardner-Burke (South African), D.J. Steadman, P. Rathie, A.G.S. Anderson, J.G.M. Grant (a New Zealander), C.H. Baker; Sgts

N.McD. Walker (two, one shared), A.N.C. MacGregor, T. Hackston, A.S. Mackie, R.R. Carson, J.H. Johnston, F.R. Emery, J.D. McCracken, and Canadians B.W. Main and W.E. Copp.

3 See *Grace under Malta* by Sybil Dobbie.

4/5 See *Onwards to Malta*.

6 Cap Olizio Nioi, Ten Talamini, Sottoten Chellini, Sottoten Ligugnana, Serg Magg Rossi, Serg Magg Romanga, and Serg Buogo each claimed a Hurricane for 17°Gruppo CT in this action. The claimants for 7°Gruppo CT are unknown.

7 See *Briefed to Attack*.

8/9/10 See *Onward to Malta*.

11 The other seven pilots involved were Plt Offs Allardice, Oliver and Veitch, and Sgts Vardy, Hunton, Sheppard and Knight.

12 Flt Lt F.V. Morello and Plt Off Matthews of 249 Squadron had arrived aboard a Sunderland from Cairo on 9 July. They had been engaged in ferrying P-40s from Takoradi to Egypt; together with a third pilot, they had travelled with the Squadron's ground party from the UK and had disembarked at Takoradi. The third member of their small group (Sgt G.A. Stroud) had crashed on take-off en route to Egypt and did not rejoin the Squadron.

13 Sqn Ldr Powell-Sheddon had arrived with orders to form a new squadron, but finding that this had already been done, left a few days later for Egypt. He was soon to return to Malta.

14 New arrival Plt Off David Barnwell was the youngest son of the late Capt Frank Barnwell, former Chief Designer of the Bristol Aeroplane Company, who had been killed in an aircraft crash in 1938. David's two brothers had been killed on service with the RAF, one on fighters and the other on bombers.

15 See *Operation Bograt* by Donald Stones.

16 See *Briefed to Attack*. The 'ditch' referred to was then as wide as a main arterial road and had been cut out of solid rock when Valetta was being built. The walls on each side are 80 feet high. Due to the bombing, a new Operations Room had been constructed within.

17 See *Onward to Malta*.

18 Z2414, 2680, 2794, 2827, 2961, 3033, 3453, 3462, 3505, 3512, 3514, 3571, 3574, 3580, 3756, 3762, 4941, BV156, BV174, BD828, DG615 and DG618 were flown by the MNFU during September alone; although Sqn Ldr Powell-Sheddon stated that the MNFU initially had its own aircraft, some were evidently later borrowed from the day squadrons.

19 See *Operation Bograt*.

20 17 confirmed and three probables are recorded herewith as air-to-air victories; the remaining six refer to the Cant seaplanes claimed destroyed at their moorings in Syracuse harbour on 9 July.

CHAPTER VII

1 See *Onward to Malta*.

2 See *Operation Bograt*.

3/4 See *Onward to Malta*.

5 During August 1941, 126 Squadron marked its Hurricanes with the letter X aft of the fuselage roundel, followed immediately by the aircraft individual letter. It is known that BV156 was coded XA, Z2825/XI, Z3580/XJ, Z4941/XL and Z3033/XN. Apparently the X marking was retained for only a month or so before the code HA was introduced.

6 DG615 was a Hurricane IIA which had been converted from a Mk I and was originally serialled P3068; DG612 (originally P3756) and DG618 (L1596) also reached the island.

7/8 See *Briefed to Attack*.

9 See *Operation Bograt*.

10/11 See *We Band of Brothers* edited by Lloyd Hunt.

12 See *Malta Story* by Howard Coffin.

13 The serial number of Sgt Lee's Hurricane is not known, but Z4360/G of 126 Squadron was eventually written off on 25 November 1941.

14 See *Onward to Malta*.

15 See *Briefed to Attack*.

16 See *Onward to Malta*.

17 The first operational examples of the MC202 arrived at Comiso on 28 September with 4°Stormo CT, under the leadership of Colonello Eugenio Leotta and TenCol Marco Paulello. The MC202 was fitted with the Daimler-Benz 601, the engine used by the new Messerschmitt Bf109F which was also making its first appearance in North Africa. It was far superior to the MC200, and its appearance came as an unpleasant surprise for Malta's Hurricane pilots.

18 Plt Off Lintern had joined 185 Squadron only two weeks earlier.

19 See *Briefed to Attack*.

20 The code letters GN had recently been reintroduced to 249 Squadron Hurricanes.

21 See *Onward to Malta*.

22 Sottoten Ferretti continued to fly photo-reconnaissance sorties over Malta until his death on 5

December 1941, when his aircraft crashed on returning from a flight over Malta. The cause was undetermined but oxygen failure was suspected.

23 See *Briefed to Attack.*

24 See *Onward to Malta.*

25 Flt Lt Jeffries DFC left the island, tour-expired, two days later.

26 See *Briefed to Attack.*

CHAPTER VIII

1 See *Malta Story.*

2/3 See *Onward to Malta.*

4 See *Operation Bograt.*

5 See *Bloody Shambles Volume 1 & 2* by Christopher Shores, Brian Cull and Yasuho Izawa.

6 Those reaching Malta were: 242 Squadron Sqn Ldr W.G. Wells, Flt Lt S.E. Andrews DFM, Flt Lt N.D. Kemp DFC, Plt Offs E.H.C. Kee, C.R. Morrison-Jones, T.B. Macnamara, W.B. Hay, L.A. Hall, C.F. Sluggett RCAF, M.C. Blanchard RCAF (American), J.D. Tew Jr RCAF (American), Sgts G.F.R. Mulloy, D.T. Neale (BE351), R.B. Lawes, W.N. Gardiner, R.V. Harvey RCAF, H. Hale RCAF, and J.L. Boyd RAAF (BG711); 605 Squadron Sqn Ldr R. Reid, Flt Lt S.R. Bird, Plt Offs G. Allen, P. Wigley, R.F. Noble, O.O. Ormrod, P.W. Lowe, J. Beckett, J.I. McKay RCAF, H.C. Lester RAAF, Sgts C.V. Finlay, A.E. Howell, J.W.S. Fletcher RCAF, D.J. Howe RCAF, A.S. Wilson RNZAF, and D.J. Robb RNZAF. Remaining at Gibraltar were Flt Lt E.W. Wright DFM, Plt Off J. Hutton and Plt Off W.M. Lockwood RCAF of 605 Squadron, Plt Off A. Brown RCAF of 242 Squadron, plus the whole of 258 Squadron.

7 Flg Off Joe Hall had only recently returned to operational flying after a spell of duty as a Fighter Controller while recovering from a wound sustained six months earlier.

8/9 See *Hurricane at War.*

10/11 Sqn Ldr Mortimer-Rose had ten victories to his credit including three shared, while Sqn Ldr Norris was credited with eight including one shared; both were former Battle of Britain pilots.

12/13 Both Wg Cdr Rabagliati and Sqn Ldr Barton had recently been awarded a second DFC.

14 See *Onward to Malta.*

15 See *The Memoirs of Field-Marshal Kesselring.*

16 These included Maj von Maltzahn with 49 victories; Oblt Kurt Brändle (StfKpt 5 Staffel, 28); Oblt Karl-Friedrich Müller (StfKpt 1 Staffel, 22); Oblt Gerhard Michalski (StfKpt 4 Staffel, 22); Obfw Rudolf Ehrenberger (6 Staffel, 15); Oblt Helmut Belser (6 Staffel, 14); Lt Franz Schiess (Stab, 14); Lt Walter Zellot (1 Staffel, 12); several others were approaching double figures and, with the arrival of III Gruppe in early 1942, more aces would join battle over Malta.

17 See *Briefed to Attack.*

18 When Lt Brauns was interrogated on recovery he claimed that both his father and brother were pilots with I/NJG2 at Catania, although with a different Staffel. He also claimed to have flown a Spitfire while training at Gatow/Berlin airfield.

19 See *Briefed to Attack.* It is interesting to note that by the end of 1941 British merchant vessels had delivered to the Russians some 676 aircraft (including Hurricanes) in addition to 446 tanks, 867 motor vehicles and 75,512 tons of ammunition and supplies; the Americans had contributed a further 29 aircraft, 35 tanks, 1,506 motor vehicles, 11,460 tons of ammunition and supplies, and almost 25,000 tons of petrol and oil.

20 See *Malta Story.*

21 The official RAF Communique released at the end of the day reported one Ju88 destroyed and two damaged, plus one Bf109 destroyed and damaged. Two Ju88s were reported to have crashed on return from operations, Lt Beiwel's KüFlGr606 aircraft being totally destroyed at Marsala while another from KGr806 crash-landed at Catania; it is not clear, however, if these were the two aircraft damaged over Malta.

22 Plt Off Blanchard had previously served with both the US Army and the US Navy before joining the RCAF to fight with the RAF.

23 Flg Off Rhys Lloyd had arrived at Malta on 15 December, aboard a delivery aircraft, to take command of B Flight of 185 Squadron vice Flt Lt Len Murch who was tour-expired and unfit.

24 Two of the Messerschmitt pilots, Lt Hans Möller and Obfw Rudolf Ehrenberger of 6/JG53, reported they had attacked and sunk two submarines off the Malta coast.

25 Flt Lt Sid Brandt's twin brother Jack was a flight commander with 67 Squadron in Burma flying equally-outclassed Brewster Buffalos against the Japanese.

26 Wg Cdr W.A.J. Satchell had commanded 302 Squadron – the first Polish fighter unit in the RAF – during the Battle of Britain, and had three victories plus three probables to his credit.

CHAPTER IX

1 See *Battle over Malta.*

2 See *The Shiphunters* by Ron Gillman.

3 See *Malta Magnificent.*

4 See *Malta Story*.

5 This was not the first occasion on which Warburton's aircraft had been mistaken for that of the enemy. During his first tour with 69 Squadron his Maryland had been attacked by a Hurricane on more than one occasion (see Chapter V). It was not the first such incident in which Rabagliati had been involved, either; during the Battle of Britain he had erroneously attacked and damaged two Blenheims which he had mistaken for Ju88s.

6 The Albacore was claimed as a Gladiator by Oblt Belser of 6/JG53 (his 16th victory).

7 See *Briefed to Attack*.

8 Wg Cdr H.L. Dawson DFC, a New Zealander, was a former Hornchurch Wing Leader who had recently arrived at Malta.

9 See *Battle over Malta*.

10 Recovered wreck parts of Hurricane Z3571 are with the Takali Aviation Museum. The authors visited the crash site, located in a picturesque valley, in 2001.

11 See *Jagdgeschwader 53 Volume One* by Dr Jochen Prien.

12 The He115, BV187, was the second of the German seaplanes to operate from Malta. It had earlier been captured from the Luftwaffe by Norwegian forces. The remaining two, BV184 and BV186, arrived at Malta shortly after the loss of BV187, although the former soon returned to the UK.

13 See *Malta Story*.

14 These victories raised Wg Cdr Satchell's score to five, three of which he had claimed during the Battle of Britain, while Wg Cdr Rabagliati now had 16 victories to his credit.

15 See *Briefed to Attack*.

16 Sqn Ldr Stan Turner had 14 victories to his credit including one shared. Most of his companions had not been in action.

17/18 See *Five Up* by Laddie Lucas.

19 Another Sunderland arrived a few nights later, also carrying fighter pilots. Those aboard the two flying boats included Battle of Britain veteran Flt Lt K.A. Lawrence, a New Zealander, Flt Lt W.C. Connell RCAF, Flg Off G.A.F. Buchanan (Rhodesian), Flg Off R.W. McNair RCAF, Flg Off Ron West, Plt Off J.G. West DFM RNZAF, ex-Eagle Squadron pilot Plt Off R.E. McHan RCAF, Plt Offs H.A. Milburn, M.W.T. Kidson, R.W. James (another Rhodesian), W.C. Hollis Hallett (from Bermuda), D.W. Kelly, and Sgts C.E. Broad, P.C. Terry and Sgt G.R. Tweedale RAAF.

20 Sqn Ldr Andrews was killed in a flying accident while serving with 10 MU at Ismailia on 9 August 1942.

21 See *Five Up*.

22 249 Squadron was effectively disbanded on 26 February, most of its pilots being transferred to 126 Squadron pending their postings to the Middle East. The Squadron would be resurrected the following month with the arrival of the Spitfires, with which it was to be equipped.

23/24/25 See *Malta Story*.

26 At this time, trials were underway in Britain with both Hurricanes and Spitfires to test the possibility of air-towing from Gibraltar to Malta as an alternative means of reinforcing the island. Wellingtons were employed as tugs. In the hands of skilled test pilots these trials proved relatively straightforward, and both types were successfully towed; however, whether ordinary Service pilots could have coped is a matter of conjecture. In the event, the scheme was never adopted.

27 See *The Memoirs of Field-Marshal Kesselring*.

CHAPTER X

1/2/3 See *Jagdgeschwader 53 Volume One*.

4 See *Battle over Malta*.

6 See *Operation Bograt*.

7 Sgt Tweedale was admitted to hospital where he met some of his new Squadron colleagues for the first time including Flt Sgt Bill Nurse, still nursing his broken leg although now on crutches; Plt Off Len Hall, who had looked up during an air raid and received a piece of bomb shrapnel in his face, splitting his upper lip; newly-commissioned Plt Off Peter Lillywhite, recovering from a severe bout of influenza which had turned into bronchitis, pneumonia and then pleurisy; and Plt Off Oliver who, having survived unhurt after being shot down by Messerschmitts, came off second best when in collision with a motor car.

8 See *Battle over Malta*.

9 See *Malta Story*.

10 Two days later, 185 Squadron reverted to A and B Flights only (commanded by Flt Lts Lawrence and Lloyd, respectively) after several of the time-expired pilots including Flt Lt Stones were stood down ready for posting away from the island.

11 See *Operation Bograt*.

12 See *Spitfires over Malta* by Paul Brennan and Ray Hesselyn.

13 See *Malta Story*.

14 Two days later Sgt Tim Goldsmith was posted to 126 Squadron to fly Spitfires. By the time he left Malta

at the beginning of July he had been credited with 13 victories of which one was shared, and had been commissioned and awarded the DFC and DFM. He believed his actual score whilst at Malta was nearer 20 with one shared.

15 In addition to Sqn Ldr Kain and Flt Lt Farnes the pilots were: Plt Offs D.J. Carter RCAF, E. Andrews and A.S.C. Lumsden, Flt Sgts R.L.K. Carson RCAF and J.K. Fullalove, Sgts R.V. Potts, J.B. Pauley RAAF and N.L. Vidler RAAF; all junior officers and sergeant pilots were inexperienced.

CHAPTER XI

1 See *The Memoirs of Field-Marshal Kesselring*.

2 See *Operation Bograt*.

3 The other pilots were Plt Offs J.H. Nixon, K.L. Lee RNZAF and T.G. Foley RCAF; Flt Sgts D. Roy and L.D. Brooks RCAF, Sgts J.R. Pendlebury and R.J. Lees.

4 See *Jagdgeschwader 53 Volume One*.

5 Cpl Hugh Clawson and LAC Edward Mitchison were each subsequently awarded the George Medal.

6 See *Battle over Malta*.

7 See *Briefed to Attack*.

8 See *Senglea During the Second Great War 1940-1944*.

9 Plt Off Phil Wigley was notified of the award of the DFC shortly thereafter.

10 The other two pilots on this flight were Flt Sgt N.A. Ganes RCAF and Sgt G.H. Wilcox.

11 The six pilots were Flt Lt Bud Connell, Flg Off Norm Lee, Plt Offs Tom Lawrence, Sandy McHan, Doug Booth and Don McLeod, the latter three Americans. Sgt Alan Cairns, formerly of 249 Squadron, was also on board, but he was being posted to Egypt as tour-expired.

12 Just over four months later, on 31 August 1942, Plt Off Ormrod's body was discovered on a rooftop in Cospicua. He now rests in Collective Grave No2 at the Capuccini Naval Cemetery with many of his colleagues.

13 See *Battle over Malta*.

14 See *Battle over Malta*, from which the above account from Dennis Barnham's diary is extracted; this differs slightly from the version in his book *One Man's Window*, which infers that the Hurricane was fired at from the ground.

15 This latest victory brought Wg Cdr Satchell's tally with the twin-Vickers to one confirmed, two probables and a dozen damaged in the previous two weeks.

16 See *Five Up*.

17 See *One Man's Window*.

18 The German pilot, Uffz Erhard Ritterbüsch of II/JG53, was picked up by HSL128.

19 See *The Memoirs of Field-Marshal Kesselring*.

20 Apparently two Italian naval personnel were taken by a German E-boat to a point about five miles off Malta where they transferred to a rubber dinghy and paddled their way close to shore in order to test the vigilance of the defenders from Zonqor Point for a distance of two miles towards Grand Harbour. They did not land, and returned to the E-boat. About half an hour later, at dawn, there was an explosion and the vessel sank. One survivor reached Malta that night and was duly arrested.

21 Plt Off Lee later escaped from the POW camp and reached British lines, for which he was awarded a Mention in Despatches.

22 See *Malta: The Spitfire Year, 1942* and *Spitfires over Sicily*.

CHAPTER XII

1 These included Z3172, Z3453, Z5149, BE428, BE563, BG719 and BG794.

2 BD702, BG787 and BN118.

3 The three Hurricanes were believed to have been Z2961, Z4941 and BE110.

4 Since the beginning of the Mediterranean war, Malta's ASR Unit had rescued in excess of 100 airmen of whom about 40 were German or Italian; in addition, ten bodies had been recovered from the sea.

5 The significance of the code OK-2 is unclear; the serial number of this Hurricane is unknown. When in command of Fighter Command's 11 Group during 1940, Park had flown Hurricane OK-1.

6 See *Spitfire Strikes* by John Houlton DFC.

7 See *A Knave Amongst Knights in their Spitfires* by Jerry Billing.

8 BG766 was transferred to the Admiralty on 1 July 1943, presumably for conversion to Sea Hurricane.

9 See *A Knave Amongst Knights in their Spitfires*.

10 Z3574 was apparently still at Malta at the end of the war, and was finally removed from the RAF's strength on 24/7/45. Whether this was OK-2 is not clear.

APPENDIX III

1 In his report following a court of enquiry into the disastrous operation, Air Chief Marshal Sir Robert Brooke-Popham commented: "Two aeroplanes returned to Tangmere on the 18th, landing at 1200 and re-starting at 1500. The senior of the two pilots informed me that whilst at Tangmere he obtained a verbal

weather report from an individual. The Meteorological Office can find no trace of any such report having been issued by the Met Service, and the individual mentioned has no recollection even of two aeroplanes returning to Tangmere."

2 Following the declaration of war by the Italians on 10 June, a number of raids were carried out by the Regia Aeronautica against French bases and other military targets. During a raid on the Toulon area on 13 June by BR20Ms of 3^Squadriglia from 43°Gruppo CT, defending D520s of GCIII/6 shot down one BR20 and seriously damaged a second. It was upon this scene that a long-range photo-reconnaissance Spitfire of 212 Squadron, flown by Flg Off G.P. Christie from Heston, appeared. Christie spotted the low-flying BR20M, unaware that it had been attacked and was already doomed, on which he carried out feint attacks until it crashed into the sea. The pilot, Ten Catalano, and one other member of the crew were rescued. On his return to Heston, Christie submitted a claim for its destruction, providing photographs of it down in the sea as evidence, and was duly awarded a victory. He later transferred to fighters and raised his score to nine including three probables, for which he was awarded the DFC and Bar, the first DFC in recognition of his PR work.

3 It seems that 126 Squadron marked their Hurricanes with the letter X during August 1941, although this was changed to HA by October 1941.

APPENDIX IV

1 Jim Pickering laconically recalled: "Sgts Robertson and Hyde showed enough lack of enthusiasm for Naval procedures to be returned promptly to the RAF!"

2 Sub Lt(A) Jack Marsh was killed in a flying accident in September 1940, while Sub Lt(A) Wigginton soon found himself in action aboard HMS *Ark Royal* during the Norwegian Campaign. Flying Skuas with 801 Squadron he shared in shooting down a Ju88 and probably destroyed a He111.

3 Sgt Derek Ashton went to 32 Squadron, Sgt David Ayres to 600 Squadron, Sgt Harry Ayre to 266 Squadron, Sgt Oswald Bowerman to 222 Squadron, Sgt Eric Kelsey to 611 Squadron, Sgt Roy O'Donnell to 19 Squadron, Sgt Jim Pickering to 64 Squadron, and Sgt Bill Timms to 43 Squadron.

4 Sgt Fred Robertson had already proved a most promising pilot and had been credited with two victories (one shared), while Sgt Reg Hyde had one shared.

5 Sgt David Ayres was killed in action on 23 September 1940 while flying with 74 Squadron.

6 See *Victory in the Air*.

APPENDIX V

1 See *Hurricanes over Tobruk*.

2 When *Furious* arrived with the next batch of 50 Hurricanes, on 20 March 1941, she carried on board just six RAF pilots whose job it was to ferry the aircraft to Takoradi, which they did successfully, being ferried back to the carrier in a Swordfish of 825 Squadron after each flight. The Hurricanes were then ferried to Egypt by the Polish contingent. By May 1943, when the route was finally closed down, in excess of 5,300 British and American aircraft had been delivered to Egypt from Takoradi.

3 See *New Zealanders with the Royal Air Force* by Wg Cdr H.L. Thompson.

4 The six pilots were Flg Off C.D. Whittingham, Plt Offs P.A. Worrall, P. Wyatt-Smith, J.J. Walsh, a Canadian, I.R. Currie and Sgt A.H. Deacon, all of whom ended up at Malta. It transpired that Ian Currie had contracted cerebral malaria at Takoradi, and died shortly after reaching the island. Wyatt-Smith also fell ill following his arrival in Malta.

BIBLIOGRAPHY

Primary sources
PRO records: Air27 for 69, 126, 185, 229, 242, 249, 261, 605 Squadron ORBs; Hal Far Fighter Flight, MNFU/1435 Flight ORBs.

Diaries/journals, or extracts therefrom: Flg Off (Sqn Ldr DFC AFC) Jock Barber (261 Squadron); Plt Off (Sqn Ldr) Dick Sugden (Fighter Flight); Sqn Ldr Derek Whittingham (261 Squadron); Plt Off (Flt Lt) John Pain; Flt Lt (Sqn Ldr DSO DFC) James MacLachlan (261 Squadron); Flg Off (Wg Cdr DFC) Innes Westmacott; Plt Off (Flt Lt) Douglas Robertson (261, 249 Squadrons, MNFU); Plt Off Oliver Ormrod DFC (605, 185 Squadrons); Plt Off Robert Matthews (249 Squadron); Sgt (Sqn Ldr DFC DFM) Tim Goldsmith RAAF (126 Squadron); Plt Off (Sqn Ldr) Ian McKay RCAF (605, 185 Squadrons); Sgt (Plt Off) Ted Wood (249 Squadron, 1435 Flight); Plt Off Tom Lawrence RNZAF (229 Squadron); Airman X, the unidentified airman of 261 and 185 Squadrons; the unofficial diary/line-book of 185 Squadron.

Published works
249 at War: Brian Cull
A Knave Amongst Knights in their Spitfires: Jerry Billing
Battle over Malta: Anthony Rogers
Briefed to Attack: Air Marshal Sir Hugh Lloyd KBE CB MC DFC
Churchill's Few: John Willis
Faith, Hope and Charity: Kenneth Poolman
Five Up: Laddie Lucas
Flames over Malta: Richard Mifsud
Grace under Malta: Sybil Dobbie
Hurricane at War: Chaz Bowyer
Hurricane at War 2: Norman Franks
Hurricanes over Tobruk: Brian Cull and Don Minterne
Imshi: Alys Myers
JG26 War Diary, The: Donald Caldwell
Jadgeschwader 53 Volume One: Dr Jochen Prien
Malta Besieged: R. Leslie Oliver
Malta: Blitzed But Not Beaten: Philip Vella
Malta, Island Fortress by Air Commodore R. Carter Jonas OBE (unpublished)
Malta Magnificent: Francis Gerard
Malta: The Hurricane Years 1941-42: Christopher Shores and Brian Cull with Nicola Malizia
Malta: The Spitfire Year 1942: Christopher Shores and Brian Cull with Nicola Malizia
Malta Story: Howard Coffin
Memoirs of Field-Marshal Kesselring, The: Feldmarschall Albert Kesselring
New Zealanders with the Royal Air Force: Wg Cdr H.L. Thompson
One Man's Window: Denis Barnham
Onward to Malta: Wg Cdr T.F. Neil DFC AFC
Operation Bograt: Donald Stones DFC
Park: Vincent Orange
Scramble to Victory: Richard Caruana
Second World War Volume II, The: Their Finest Hour: Winston S. Churchill
Senglea during the Second Great War 1940-1944: Mgr Emmanuel Brincat
Shiphunters, The: R.E. Gillman DFC DFM
Spitfires over Malta: Paul Brennan and Ray Hesselyn with Henry Bateson
Spitfires over Sicily: Brian Cull with Nicola Malizia and Frederick Galea
Spitfire Strikes: John Houlton DFC
Warburton's War: Tony Spooner DSO DFC
We Band of Brothers: Lloyd Hunt (Ed)
When Malta Stood Alone: Joseph Micallef
Various issues of *Malta FlyPast* and volumes of *Air-Britain* Serial Registers.

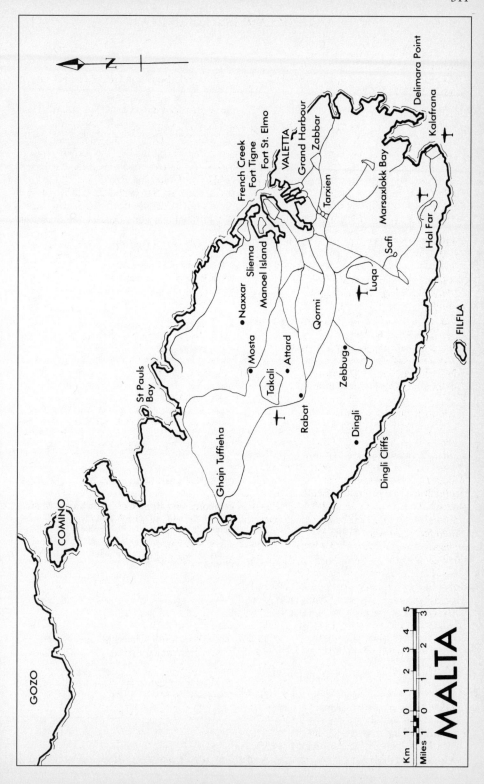

GOZO

COMINO

St Pauls
Bay

Għajn Tuffieħa

Naxxar
Mosta
Sliema
Manoel Island
French Creek
Fort Tigne
Fort St. Elmo
VALETTA
Grand Harbour
Zabbar
Delimara Point
Kalafrana

Tarxien

Marsaxlokk Bay

Takali
Attard
Qormi
Zebbug
Safi
Luqa
Hal Far

Rabat
Dingli
Dingli Cliffs

FILFLA

Km 1 0 1 2 3 4 5
Miles 1 0 1 2 3

MALTA

INDEX OF PERSONNEL